The Greenwood
Encyclopedia of Daily Life

5 19th CENTURY

The Greenwood Encyclopedia of Daily Life

A Tour through History from Ancient Times to the Present

Joyce E. Salisbury
GENERAL EDITOR

Andrew E. Kersten
VOLUME EDITOR

GREENWOOD PRESS
Westport, Connecticut • London

Library of Congress Cataloging-in-Publication Data

The Greenwood encyclopedia of daily life : a tour through history from ancient times to the present / Joyce E. Salisbury, general editor.

    p. cm.

   Includes bibliographical references and index.

   Contents: v. 1. The ancient world / Gregory S. Aldrete, volume editor; v. 2. The medieval world / Joyce E. Salisbury, volume editor; v. 3. 15th and 16th centuries / Lawrence Morris, volume editor; v. 4. 17th and 18th centuries / Peter Seelig, volume editor; v. 5. 19th century / Andrew E. Kersten, volume editor; v. 6. The modern world / Andrew E. Kersten, volume editor.

   ISBN 0–313–32541–3 (set: alk. paper) — ISBN 0–313–32542–1 (v. 1: alk. paper) — ISBN 0–313–32543–X (v. 2: alk. paper) — ISBN 0–313–32544–8 (v. 3: alk. paper) — ISBN 0–313–32545–6 (v. 4: alk. paper) — ISBN 0–313–32546–4 (v. 5: alk. paper) — ISBN 0–313–32547–2 (v. 6: alk. paper)

   1. Manners and customs—History—Encyclopedias. I. Salisbury, Joyce E.
GT31.G74   2004
390—dc21   2003054724

British Library Cataloguing in Publication Data is available.

Copyright © 2004 by Greenwood Publishing Group, Inc.

An online version of *The Greenwood Encyclopedia of Daily Life* is available from Greenwood Press, an imprint of Greenwood Publishing Group, Inc. at: http://dailylife.greenwood.com (ISBN 0–313–01311–X).

Library of Congress Catalog Card Number: 2003054724
ISBN: 0–313–32541–3 (set)
     0–313–32542–1 (vol. 1)
     0–313–32543–X (vol. 2)
     0–313–32544–8 (vol. 3)
     0–313–32545–6 (vol. 4)
     0–313–32546–4 (vol. 5)
     0–313–32547–2 (vol. 6)

First published in 2004

Greenwood Press, 88 Post Road West, Westport, CT 06881
An imprint of Greenwood Publishing Group, Inc.
www.greenwood.com

Printed in the United States of America

The paper used in this book complies with the Permanent Paper Standard issued by the National Information Standards Organization (Z39.48–1984).

10 9 8 7 6 5 4 3 2 1

Everyday life consists of the little things one hardly notices in time and space. . . . Through the details, a society stands revealed. The ways people eat, dress, or lodge at the different levels of that society are never a matter of indifference.

~Fernand Braudel, *The Structures of Everyday Life*
(New York: Harper and Row, 1979), 29.

CONTENTS

Contents

TOUR GUIDE: A PREFACE FOR USERS

What did people, from the most ancient times to the most recent, eat, wear, and use? What did they hope, invent, and sing? What did they love, fear, or hate? These are the kinds of questions that anyone interested in history has to ask. We spend our lives preoccupied with food, shelter, families, neighbors, work, and play. Our activities rarely make the headlines. But it is by looking at people's everyday lives that we can truly understand history and how people lived. *The Greenwood Encyclopedia of Daily Life* brings into focus the vast majority of human beings whose existence is neglected by the standard reference works. Here you will meet the anonymous men and women of the past going about their everyday tasks and in the process creating the world that we know.

Organization and Content

The Greenwood Encyclopedia of Daily Life is designed for general readers without a background in the subject. Articles are accessible, engaging, and filled with information yet short enough to be read at one sitting. Each volume provides a general historical introduction and a chronology to give background to the articles. This is a reference work for the 21st century. Rather than taking a mechanical alphabetical approach, the encyclopedia tries something rather more elegant: it arranges material thematically, cascading from broad surveys down to narrower slices of information. Users are guided through this enormous amount of information not just by running heads on every page but also by "concept compasses" that appear in the margins: these are adapted from "concept mapping," a technique borrowed from online research methods. Readers can focus on a subject in depth, study it comparatively through time or across the globe, or find it synthesized in a way that provides an overarching viewpoint that draws connections among related areas—and they can do so in any order they choose. School curricula have been organizing research materials in this fashion for some time, so this encyclopedia will fit neatly into a modern pedagogical framework. We believe that this approach breaks new ground in the structuring of reference material. Here's how it works.

Level 1. The six volumes of the encyclopedia are, naturally, arranged by time period: the ancient world, the medieval world, 15th and 16th centuries, 17th and 18th centuries, the 19th century, and the modern world.

Level 2. Within each volume, information is arranged in seven broad categories, as shown in this concept compass:

DAILY LIFE

DOMESTIC LIFE

ECONOMIC LIFE

INTELLECTUAL LIFE

MATERIAL LIFE

POLITICAL LIFE

RECREATIONAL LIFE

RELIGIOUS LIFE

Level 3. Each of the introductory essays is followed by shorter articles on components of the subject. For example, "Material Life" includes sections on everything from the food we eat to the clothes we wear to the homes in which we live. Once again, each category is mapped conceptually so that readers can see the full range of items that make up "Material Life" and choose which ones they want to explore at any time. Each volume has slightly different categories at this level to reflect the period under discussion. For example, "eunuchs" appear under "Domestic Life" in volume 2 because they served a central role in many cultures at that time, but they disappear in subsequent volumes as they no longer served an important role in some households. Here is one example of the arrangement of the concepts at this level (drawn from the "Domestic Life" section of volume 1):

DOMESTIC LIFE

FAMILY LIFE

WOMEN

MARRIAGE

CHILDREN

SEXUALITY

Level 4. These conceptual categories are further subdivided into articles focusing on a variety of representative cultures around the world. For example, here users can read about "Children" in Egypt, Greece, medieval Europe, and 16th-century Latin America. Here is an example of a concept compass representing the entry on money in Ancient India:

The articles at each level can stand alone, but they all also offer integrated in-formation. For example, readers interested in food in ancient Rome can focus right in on that information. If curious, they can look at the next conceptual level and learn how Roman food compares with that of other cultures at the same time, or they can see how food fits into material life in general by looking at the highest conceptual level. Readers may also decide to compare ancient Roman food with menus in Italy during the Renaissance; they need only follow the same process in another volume. Readers can begin at any of the levels and follow their interests in all directions: knowledge is linked conceptually in these volumes, as it is in life. The idea is to make it easy and fun to travel through time and across cultures.

This organization offers a number of advantages. Many reference works provide disparate bits of information, leaving it to the reader to make connections among them. More advanced reference tools assume that readers already have the details and include articles only on larger conceptual issues. *The Greenwood Encyclopedia of Daily Life* assumes no previous knowledge but recognizes that readers at all stages benefit from integrated analysis. The concept-mapping organization allows users to see both the details of the trees and the overall shape of the forest. To make finding information even easier, a cumulative subject index to the entire encyclopedia appears at the end of each volume. With the help of detailed running heads, concept compasses, and an index, anyone taking this "Tour through History" will find it almost impossible to get lost.

This encyclopedia is the work of many contributors. With the help of advisory boards, specialists in daily life around the world wrote the detailed articles in the "level 4" concept category. Many of these experts have published books in Green-wood's award-winning "Daily Life through History" series, and their contributions were crafted from those books. Each volume's editor wrote all of the many higher-level conceptual articles that draw connections across the topics, thus providing a consistent voice and analysis throughout the volume.

Coverage

The chronological coverage of this encyclopedia is consistent with the traditional organization of history as it is taught: the six volumes each take on one of the standard periods. But in reality, history is messy, and any strictly chronological organization has flaws. Some societies span centuries with little change, whereas others change rapidly (usually because of cross-cultural interactions). We have addressed these questions of change and continuity in two ways. Sometimes, we introduce cultures in one volume, such as the Australian Aborigines in volume 1, and then we do not mention them again until they were transformed by colonial contact in volume 4. In these entries, readers are led by cross-references to follow the story of the Australian indigenous peoples from one volume to another. At other times, cultures have experienced enough change for us to introduce many new entries. For example, volume 5, devoted to the 19th century, includes many entries on Muslim lands. But some aspects of the 19th-century Muslim world (e.g., education) had long remained largely unchanged, and in these instances readers are led by cross-references to entries in earlier volumes. This network of cross-references highlights connections and introduces users to the complexities of change and continuity that form the pattern of the social fabric.

We also depart from the chronological constraints of each volume when describing cultures that left few written records. Borrowing from anthropological methods, we sometimes (cautiously) use evidence from later periods to fill in our understanding of earlier lives. For example, colonial observers have at times informed our description of earlier indigenous cultures in many parts of the world.

The geographic scope of this encyclopedia reflects the relatively recent recognition that culture has always operated in a global context. In the Stone Age, bloodstone from Rhum, an inaccessible island off the stormy coast of Scotland, was traded throughout Europe. Domesticated plants and animals from Mesopotamia spread to Africa through Nubia in the third millennium B.C.E., and throughout the ancient world the trade between China and the Mediterranean was an essential part of life. Global history is woven throughout these volumes.

We do not attempt to document every one of the thousands of societies that have arisen throughout history and around the world. Our aim—to provide a general reference source on everyday life—has led to a careful focus on the most studied and representative cultures of each period. For example, ancient India is introduced in volume 1 and then reappears in the complexities of a global society in volumes 5 and 6. Nubia, the path from Egypt to sub-Saharan Africa, is introduced in volume 1, but the range of African cultures is addressed in depth in volume 4 and again in volume 6. Muslim cultures are introduced in volume 2 with the birth of the Prophet, reappearing in volume 3 with the invigorated society of the Turks and then again in volumes 5 and 6 with modern Muslim states. This approach draws from archaeological methods: we are taking deep samples of cultures at various points in time. The overall picture derived from these samples offers a global perspective that is rich and comprehensive. We have covered every area of the world from Australia and the South Pacific to Viking Scandinavia, from indigenous cultures to colonial ones, from age-old Chinese civilization to the modern United States.

Another issue is that of diversity within some dizzyingly complex regions. Africa, China, Polynesia, and India, for example, all contain many cultures and peoples whose daily life is strikingly diverse. Rather than attempt exhaustiveness, we indicate the range of diversity within each entry itself. For instance, the many entries on Africa in volume 4 recognize that each society—Yoruba, Swahili, Shona, and all the others—is unique, and each entry focuses on the cultures that best represent trends in the region as a whole.

The United States is yet another complex region. It grew from its inception with a mingling of European, Native American, African, and other cultural groups. Instead of treating each individually, we combine them all within the entries on the United States. For example, as volume 4 discusses Colonial New England, it weaves a description of Native American life within the entries showing the full range of social interaction between native peoples and colonists. This organization recognizes the reality that all these groups grew together to become the United States.

Features

This work has been designed by educators, and pedagogical tools help readers get the most out of the material. In addition to the reader-friendly organization already described, we have added the following special features:

- *Concept compasses*. Each section of each volume contains a concept compass that visually details the contents of that section. Readers are immediately able to see what topics are covered and can decide which ones they want to explore.
- *Illustrations*. The illustrations drawn from primary sources are in themselves historical evidence and are not mere ornament. Each shows some aspect of daily life discussed in the text, and the captions tell what the picture illuminates and what readers can see in it.
- *Maps*. Maps give readers the necessary geographic orientation for the text. They have been chosen to reinforce the global perspective of the encyclopedia, and readers are consistently offered the view of the parts of the world under discussion.
- *Chronologies*. In addition to geography, students can quickly lose track of the chronology of events. Each volume offers a list of the major events of the periods and of the cultures covered in the volumes. These chronologies serve as a quick reference that supplements the historical introduction.
- *Snapshots*. The fascinating details of the past engage our curiosity. Each volume is scattered with boxed features that highlight such evidence of past life as a recipe, a song, a prayer, an anecdote, or a statistic. These bits of information enhance the main entries; readers can begin with the snapshot and move to more in-depth knowledge or end with the details that are often designed to bring a smile or a shocked insight.
- *Cross-references*. Traditional brief references point readers to related entries in other volumes, highlighting the changes in daily life over time. Other "See" references replace entries and show readers where to find the information they seek within the volume.
- *Primary documents*. The encyclopedia entries are written to engage readers, but nothing brings the past to life like a primary source. Each volume offers a selection of documents that illustrate the kinds of information that historians use to re-create daily life. Sources range widely, from the unforgettable description of Vikings blowing their noses in a water basin before they wash their faces in it to a ration book issued by the United States government during World War II.

- *Bibliography.* Most entries are followed by a section called "For More Information." These sections include recommended readings, as one might expect in a bibliographic attachment, but they often provide much more. For this media age, the authors recommend Web sites, films, educational videos, and other resources.
- *Index.* Even in the 21st century, a comprehensive index is essential. Concept compasses lead readers from one topic to the next, but an index draws connections among more disparate entries: for example, the history of the use of wine or cotton can be traced across many volumes and cultures. A cumulative index appears in each volume to allow fast and easy navigation.

The Greenwood Encyclopedia of Daily Life: A Tour through History from Ancient Times to the Present has been a labor of love. At the end of the day, we hope that readers will be informed and entertained. But we also hope that they will come to a renewed appreciation of an often-spoken but seldom-felt reality: at the most basic level all humans, across time and space, share concerns, pleasures, and aspirations, but the ways these are expressed are infinite in their range. The six volumes of this encyclopedia reveal both the deep similarities and the fascinating differences among people all over the world. We can participate in our global village more intelligently the more we understand each other's lives. We have also learned that people are shown at their best (and sometimes their worst) in the day-to-day activities that reveal our humanity. We hope readers enjoy taking this tour of people's lives as much as we have enjoyed presenting it.

~*Joyce E. Salisbury*

1

HISTORICAL OVERVIEW

United States Civil War

At the outbreak of the American Civil War, all but the most astute observers thought that the question of national unity would be settled in a single afternoon of combat. But in the first great battle of the war, the intrinsic drama of Americans locked in mortal combat diverted everyone's attention from the fact that indecisiveness had crept into warfare over the centuries. From 1861 to 1865, Yankees were bushwhacked in western Virginia, and Rebels sniped at near Washington. Federal Red Legs and Confederate Partisans mauled one another across the plains of Kansas and Missouri and were held in contempt by the politicians on both sides. The American Civil War was the bloodiest war ever waged with the bloodiest battles ever fought in North America.

How did the nation come to such an impasse? Historians have long held that part of the answer may lie in the questions about the nature of the American nation that had been left undecided by the Founding Fathers. Of these questions, the continuation of slavery and the political relationship between the state and national governments had resisted resolution. The crux of the slavery issue revolved around the question of whether the United States had been founded as a free republic that allowed slavery, or as a slaveholding republic with pockets of freedom. The question of states' rights held at issue whether the state or the national government was ultimately sovereign. Since both situations had existed simultaneously for decades, which was the aberration? The war itself answered these questions.

Historians have investigated other interpretations, many dealing with economics and society. Southern life was based on cotton production that had originated along the coast and moved into the back country of South Carolina and Georgia by the end of the 18th century, but it quickly spread into all the states that were to become members of the Confederacy. The significance of cotton in the money-conscious 19th century resulted primarily from the fact that it was a cash crop. By mid-century more than five million bales were being produced annually, causing cotton to be termed the king of agricultural exports. The Southern cities, particularly New Orleans, Mobile, Savannah, and Charleston, continued to flourish because of their dedication to the export of cotton. In 1853 New Orleans was described in a child's geography text as "remarkable for the number of ships and steamboats that crowd its levee, or [land] along the river." Yet on the eve of the war, New York was exporting more cotton to Europe than Charleston, much of it transshipped from other Southern ports including New Orleans. Seventy-five percent of all cotton came from plantations, as did almost all of the rice, sugar, and tobacco. The success of the plantation economy, and of the cotton plantations in particular, therefore, was vital to the continuation of the genteel Southern lifestyle. Economic and social changes were sweeping the North in the 1840s and 1850s. Industry and urbanization had moved the North toward a more modern society with an unprecedented set of novel social values, while the South had essentially lagged behind, clinging to the traditions of the 18th century.

Historians have noted that the differences between the folk culture of the South and the modern culture of the North certainly fueled the broad-based reform movements of mid-century and may have ignited the turmoil over state sovereignty and slavery. The debate surrounding these questions, driven by an intensely partisan press, "not only aroused feelings of jealousy, honor, and regional pride, but raised fundamental questions about the future direction of the American society."

The most obvious modern element in the North was the rapid growth of its urban centers as more and more people flocked to the cities to find work in the factories. Although the class structure was still dominated by the old social elite, a new middle class was striving to become socially acceptable; and it was becoming increasingly difficult for the community to distinguish between the two. Unfortunately, the distinctions between these and the urban lower classes continued to be characterized by sharp contrasts in wealth, ethnic origin, and religion.

While many Northerners were still farmers, a growing segment of the population was becoming tied to the cities and factories. Middle-class men who had grown up in the first half of the century could remember a childhood spent living in a family working environment, either on the farm, in a cottage at the mill, or in a room behind the family shop. But as the century progressed men's work increasingly took place in the special atmosphere of business premises such as the factory or office. Fathers commonly left the home to work for 10 to 14 hours, and their children rarely saw them during daylight hours. A father's work and workplace became foreign to his children. This tendency to go to work, rather than to work at home, led to the virtual removal of men from the home environment, leaving it the sole province of the female. The modern 19th-century home increasingly came to focus almost solely on the wife and children. The evolution to a female-dominated household may help to explain the growing formalism and rigid authoritarianism that Victorian fathers demanded when they were present.

With the general availability of the pocket watch, these men increasingly lived their lives by the clock. They valued these timepieces as heirlooms. The last significant act of many Civil War soldiers was to ensure that their pocket watches were passed on to their sons. Factory workers were expected to work in shifts dictated by the public clocks that came to be prominently displayed on towers, in the streets, and on the factory walls. In 1847 John A. Thayer of Stoughton, Massachusetts, published one of the first books of tables for the calculation of wages "at various prices, either by the day, week, or month, for different lengths of time." The idea of being on time represented a significant change in the lifestyle of most city dwellers; and since the North was the most urbanized section of the country, being on time became characteristic of Northern life.

Conversely, Southerners, who had no need to work by the clock, were often viewed as shiftless and lazy. Southern laborers feared the development of the unprecedented work for wage economy of the cities, and they saw Northern wage earners as degraded and enslaved persons. The city worker sold himself into economic bondage for a wage, and the expansion of a similar work for wage system was dreaded by Southerners almost as much as abolitionists dreaded the expansion of slavery. Southern whites were clearly anxious to maintain their status as freemen, even if this required that they be very poor freemen. Many in the laboring class believed that the North was determined to enslave them to the factory system or counting house. The modern egalitarian society of the North was viewed with disdain and seen as degenerate and immoral. Rising crime rates in the cities, flagrant and open prostitution, and the squalid conditions of the urban lower classes were proffered as proof of Northern inferiority.

A privileged planter class whose elite lifestyle was maintained at the expense of the rest of society led the unmodernized South. This planter aristocracy relied on its kinship network and social status as means to personal success. Outsiders saw Southern culture and institutions as backward, inefficient, and harmful to the American nation as a whole. Nonetheless, the Southern elite voluntarily assumed the role of benefactor and knight errant to all other levels of their society. Like cavaliers on a quest, Southern men felt obliged to counsel and defend not only their own families, but also all females and minor children placed under their protection. This obligation was extended to their slaves in an ambiguous, but serious, way. Many Southerners were genuinely concerned for the physical and moral welfare of their slaves, but only in terms of continued racial separation and subjugation. Some historians believe that it was these attitudes and the actions that followed as well as the economic differences between the regions that helped spark the war.

Finally, historians have observed that this widespread political participation almost certainly added to the furor for war. Antagonists on all sides assailed their opponents with arguments taken from the law, the Bible, literature, pamphlets, election speeches, and the press. When unprepared to rebut these arguments on an equal footing, the opponents often resorted to ridiculous remarks and unsupported allegations. A Southern observer wrote of the period: "The hot headed politician and preacher seemed to be molding public opinion without any regard to the country as a whole. Both North and South proving, from their point of view, the righteousness of their positions by resorting to both the Bible and the Constitution."

Intemperate and abusive language, or even fisticuffs, increasingly characterized politics, especially when the subject turned to inflammatory issues such as slavery. When Senator Charles Sumner, a man of "wicked tongue" and "intemperate language" with regard to slavery, was beaten with a cane by Congressman Preston Brooks in the Senate, the blows were struck not only in the halls of Congress, but in the barbershops, parlors, and taverns of every small town and city. The end result of all these aspects was a devastating but perhaps irrepressible war that cost over six hundred thousand lives (Volo and Volo, 1–12).

FOR MORE INFORMATION

McPherson, J. M. *Battle Cry of Freedom: The Civil War Era*. New York: Oxford University Press, 1988.

Paludan, P. S. *"A People's Contest": The Union and Civil War, 1861–1865*. New York: Harper & Row, 1988.

Thomas, E. M. *The Confederate Nation: 1861–1865*. New York: Harper & Row, 1979.

Volo, D. D., and J. M. Volo. *Daily Life in Civil War America*. Westport, Conn.: Greenwood Press, 1998.

United States, Western Frontier

Our popular culture—from Buffalo Bill Cody's Wild West Show and the Beadle dime novels to John Wayne's cinema epics—have bred our image of the frontier into generations of Americans. Although it suggests *some* of the truths of America's westering process, it does not hint at the whole story. The problem is not simply its romanticizing the past. Far more significant is its fundamental imprecision and oversimplification. For this mythic American frontier is fixed in place and time: the Great Plains from roughly 1840 to 1870. In reality, it took almost three hundred years for the frontier to move across a 3,000-mile-wide continent.

To focus only on the Great Plains is to ignore the continent's magnitude and the consequent diversity of relationships between humanity and the land. Today's 50 states incorporate an area of 3,618,770 square miles: 3,539,289 square miles of land and 79,481 square miles of water. In comparison, England has an area of 50,874 square miles inside Great Britain's 89,041 square miles. The highest elevation in the United States is Alaska's Mt. McKinley at 20,320 feet; the lowest elevation is in Death Valley at 282 feet below sea level. Temperatures range from 134 degrees to −86 degrees Fahrenheit.

The midsection of the United States is watered by the Mississippi River, flowing 2,330 miles from northern Minnesota to the Gulf of Mexico, and its two major tributaries—the Missouri, flowing southeast from Montana for 2,465 miles, and the Ohio, flowing southwest from Pittsburgh for 981 miles. This midsection is bracketed by the Appalachian Mountains (a 1,500-mile chain, extending from southern Quebec to northern Alabama; its highest peak is Mt. Mitchell, North Carolina, at 6,711 feet) and the Rocky Mountains (extending from New Mexico to Alaska, its highest point in the lower 48 is Mt. Elbert, Colorado, at 14,431 feet). A cursory glance at a contemporary Burpee seed catalogue reveals 11 U.S. Department of Agriculture

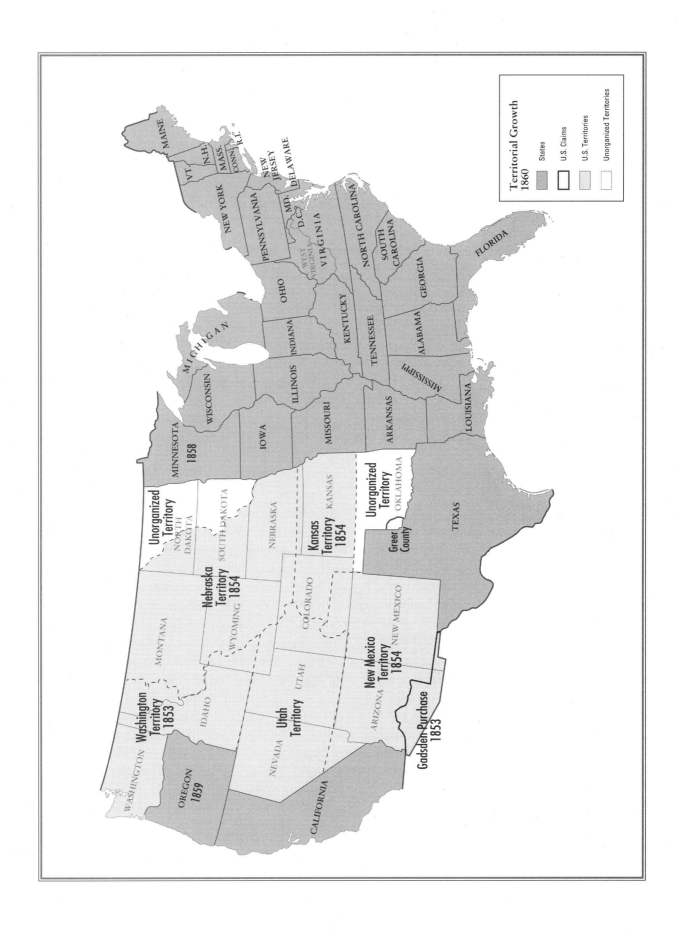

Territorial Growth
1860

States

U.S. Claims

U.S. Territories

Unorganized Territories

MAINE

N.H.

VT.

MASS.

CONN.

R.I.

NEW YORK

NEW JERSEY

DELAWARE

PENNSYLVANIA

MD.

D.C.

WEST VIRGINIA

VIRGINIA

NORTH CAROLINA

SOUTH CAROLINA

OHIO

GEORGIA

FLORIDA

MICHIGAN

INDIANA

KENTUCKY

TENNESSEE

ALABAMA

MISSISSIPPI

WISCONSIN

ILLINOIS

IOWA

MISSOURI

ARKANSAS

LOUISIANA

MINNESOTA
1858

Unorganized
Territory

NORTH DAKOTA

SOUTH DAKOTA

KANSAS

NEBRASKA

Unorganized
Territory

OKLAHOMA

Kansas
Territory
1854

Greer
County

TEXAS

Nebraska
Territory 1854

MONTANA

WYOMING

COLORADO

Washington
Territory
1853

IDAHO

UTAH

Utah
Territory
1854

New Mexico
Territory
1854

NEW MEXICO

ARIZONA

Gadsden Purchase
1853

WASHINGTON

NEVADA

OREGON
1859

CALIFORNIA

hardiness zones for plants based on average annual temperatures, though the editors warn gardeners that "even on a small property . . . many factors such as sun, wind, rainfall, snow cover, and slope (north or south facing) create changes in microclimate." *USA Today* for June 25, 1996, notes temperature ranges from 103 degrees to 72 degrees Fahrenheit in Tucson, Arizona, and 67 degrees to 50 degrees Fahrenheit in Marquette, Michigan, on the same day it snowed near Lake Tahoe, California.

For all the pioneers heading west, such variety in terrain and climate posed a myriad of questions. Where was a good pass through the mountains? How wide were the deserts? How early did grass flourish along a proposed route? Where were salt deposits? When were the last and the first major snowfalls? How wide were rivers—and were there any fords making them passable? More so than for many nations, America's history has been affected by physical reality. Henry Nash Smith made this point quite succinctly: "The character of the American empire was defined not by streams of influence out of the past, not by a cultural tradition, nor by its place in a world community, but by a relation between man and nature."

It is crucial when examining the American frontier to specify what year, what decade, even what century is under consideration. Fixing the mythic American frontier experience in the 30-year period spanning the Civil War also creates misperceptions and inaccuracies. *How* did one go west? Daniel Boone's trek into Kentucky in the early 1770s was by foot and pack horse; those taking the Oregon/ California Trails between 1840 and 1860 mostly used ox-drawn wagons, though some simply walked and others transported their property in wheelbarrows or handcarts; European immigrants to the northern plains in the 1870s and 1880s arrived by train. With the advance of time came advances in technology, which, in turn, speeded the pace of westering. On the Missouri River, for example, during the relatively brief life span of the fur frontier, transportation developed from the bull boat (made of buffalo hides) to the keel boat and then the steamboat. Moreover, as time passed, travelers knew more about their routes and their destinations.

Official policy toward the West also varied tremendously. The Proclamation of 1763 forbade settlement beyond the sources of the rivers flowing into the Atlantic, and even so exuberant an expansionist as Thomas Hart Benton could argue in 1825 that the Rocky Mountains were a convenient natural western boundary for the United States: a location where "the statue of the fabled god, Terminus, should be raised . . . , never to be thrown down." Yet in 1804 Thomas Jefferson had sent Meriwether Lewis and William Clark on their expedition of exploration, following quickly on the dubiously constitutional 1803 Louisiana Purchase. If still frames existed back then to capture images of the constantly moving frontier, they would have shown a vast variety of pictures.

Other variables complicate the picture further. For example, was westering a gradual advance into contiguous territory (as occurred mainly east of the Mississippi), or did migration leap over half a continent, with most of the intervening land to be settled later (as on the Oregon and California Trails—exacerbated by the discovery of gold)? What was the relation to the native inhabitants of the land? Although initial contact was usually benign, even friendly, relationships worsened over time—for a variety of reasons. Even during the same period, major differences occurred. During colonial times most eastern Indians preferred the French to the English because of their land policy. When whites were captured, most longed for repatriation; but others were happily assimilated into their new culture. And responses to atrocities such as the Sand Creek Massacre ranged from celebrations by the citizens of Denver to condemnation by U.S. Army regulars. What means were there in the frontier West of enforcing law and order? Even though the myth portrays the cavalry riding to the rescue, forts were often widely spaced and undermanned; many laws were blithely ignored; and new law was often made up as the situation warranted.

There were those who went west for religious motives: Mormons heading west to practice their religion safe from persecution, and missionaries wanting to convert and, in their minds, civilize Native Americans. Whereas many headed west to establish a permanent new life there, others, like most forty-niners, intended a brief, exploitative sojourn followed by a return to their homes in the East. There were fortune hunters in search of gold or land or railroad subsidies. There were tourists like Prince Maximilian von Wied, who came to hunt game and exotic experiences; and there were immigrants from Europe in search of the American dream. Some brought civilization west. Others, like Simon Kenton, who mistakenly believed the law was after him and fled west to the wilds of Ohio, saw the West as an escape from civilization; they were, literally, outlaws. Washington Irving described them in *Astoria*: "new and mongrel races . . . the amalgamation of the 'debris' . . . of former races, civilized and savage; . . . adventurers and desperadoes of every class and country . . . ejected from the bosom of society into the wilderness." Some Easterners viewed "all emigrants as actually or potentially criminal because of their flight from an orderly municipal life into frontier areas that were remote from centers of control." The Reverend Timothy Dwight, president of Yale, characterized the 18th century West as a vast septic system drawing off the depraved effluvia of New England. Most, though, simply viewed the West as offering hope for a fresh start, for perennial rebirth, and for an opportunity to recover manhood, health, and even virtue.

One can conclude, therefore, that neither while the frontier was still in existence (until 1890) nor since has there been a consensus describing or interpreting its meaning or significance. Like a kaleidoscope, the images are constantly reassembling into new patterns. The individual pieces, sometimes colorful, sometimes dull, are suspended in the fluid medium of the larger American culture. The image can, for an infinitesimal instant, be caught in time and space, but external forces—political, social, or economic—can, like the twist of a wrist, create new patterns. Thus, the daily life on the American frontier that follows is a diverse, often contradictory, always changing composite of the lives of individual Americans who, for whatever reason, sought out an ever-moving, ever-changing American frontier (Jones, 1–10).

FOR MORE INFORMATION

Billington, R. A. *The Far Western Frontier, 1830–1860*. New York: Harper & Row, 1956.
Jeffrey, J. R. *Frontier Women: The Trans-Mississippi West, 1840–1880*. New York: Hill and Wang, 1979.

Jones, M. E. *Daily Life on the Nineteenth Century American Frontier*. Westport, Conn.: Greenwood Press, 1998.

Unruh, J. D. *The Overland Emigrants and the Trans-Mississippi West, 1840–1860*. Urbana: University of Illinois Press, 1979.

Victorian England

Three events before 1837 had a crucial impact on Victorian English life. (1) The Duke of Wellington's victory over Napoleon at Waterloo in 1815 created an atmosphere of national pride. (2) The Industrial Revolution transformed England from an agricultural nation to one based on industry and made it for most of the century the world's greatest economic power. (3) The Reform Bill of 1832, which doubled the number of men eligible to vote, began a gradual progress toward democratic rule and governmental responsibility for the safety and well-being of all citizens.

Victoria became queen on June 20, 1837. The first years of Victoria's reign were marked by social and political turmoil, largely in response to the rapid changes that came with industrialization. In 1801 most people lived in villages or on farms; by 1851 more than half the population was urban. Social problems dominated the urban economic and political scene in the 1840s. The term hungry 40s is sometimes applied to the first part of the decade. Food prices were high and later a potato blight destroyed the economy of Ireland. An economic depression threw many people out of work. In 1842, more than 15 percent of the population received public assistance, many more people were helped by private charities, and the crime rate was higher than at any other time during the century.

Yet even within the economic chaos were the seeds of future change and growth. The new prosperity arose in part from a crucial early Victorian technological revolution: the coming of railways. Rail construction dramatically increased the production of coal and iron. New skills and new techniques were developed in engineering and machine technology; bridges and tunnels and locomotives came into being.

Some other significant innovations in the early Victorian period also influenced daily life. A high point came with the Exhibition of 1851, which celebrated progress, invention, and British supremacy in world markets. Essentially the first world's fair, its official name was The Great Exhibition of the Works of Industry of All Nations, and it was open from May until October. The central building, soon nicknamed the Crystal Palace, was a triumph of engineering and design. The first large structure to be built of metal and glass, its components were prefabricated and interchangeable, with identical girders, columns, and panes of glass throughout the building. (When the Exhibition was over, the Crystal Palace was taken apart and reassembled in a different pattern in South London, where it was in public use, until destroyed by a fire in 1936.) Three times the length of St. Paul's Cathedral, the building displayed over one hundred thousand exhibits: exotic art from China and India; furs from Canada and Russia; furniture and housewares; sculpture and stained glass; the Koh-i-noor diamond; working examples of industrial triumphs such as power printing

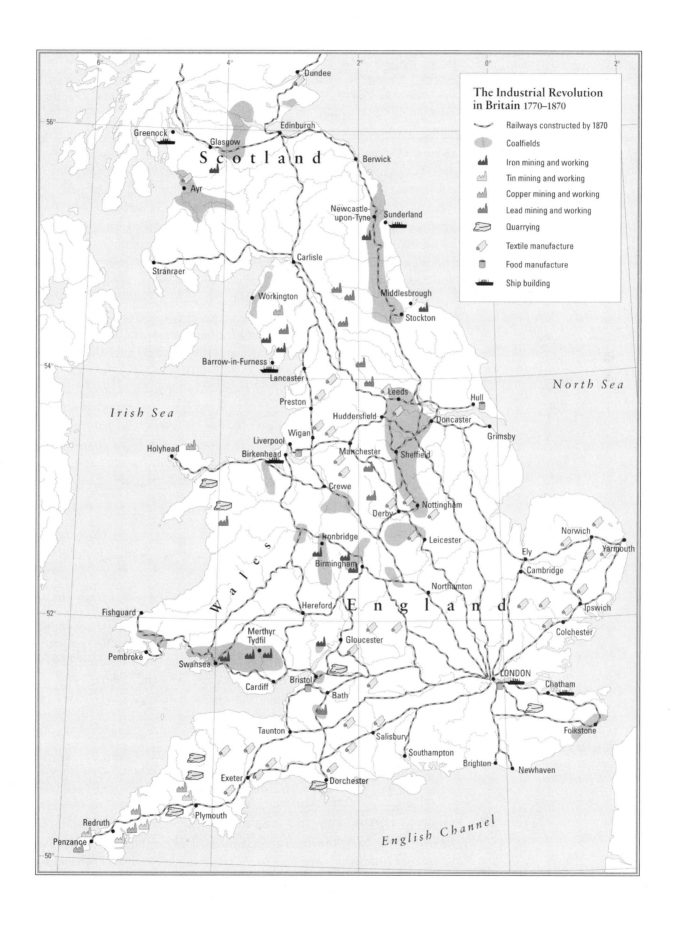

The Industrial Revolution
in Britain 1770–1870

Railways constructed by 1870
Coalfields
Iron mining and working
Tin mining and working
Copper mining and working
Lead mining and working
Quarrying
Textile manufacture
Food manufacture
Ship building

Dundee

Scotland

Greenock
Glasgow
Edinburgh
Berwick
Ayr

Stranraer
Carlisle
Newcastle-
upon-Tyne
Sunderland

Workington
Middlesbrough
Stockton

Barrow-in-Furness
Lancaster

Irish Sea

Preston
Leeds
Hull
North Sea

Holyhead
Huddersfield
Doncaster
Wigan
Grimsby

Liverpool
Manchester
Sheffield
Birkenhead
Crewe

Derby
Nottingham
Norwich
Leicester
Yarmouth

Ironbridge
Ely
Cambridge

Wales
Birmingham
Northampton
Ipswich

Fishguard
Hereford
England
Colchester

Pembroke
Merthyr
Tydfil
Gloucester

Swansea
Bristol
LONDON
Chatham
Cardiff
Bath
Folkstone

Taunton
Salisbury

Southampton
Brighton
Newhaven
Exeter
Dorchester

Redruth
Plymouth
Penzance

English Channel

presses, agricultural machines, locomotives, and an electric telegraph; and newly invented domestic appliances including a gas cooking stove.

In the years after the Exhibition, London became the world's central metropolis, and many of its distinctive features appeared. The new Houses of Parliament (with the Big Ben clock tower) replaced the structure that had burned in 1834. Work on the subway system began in 1854. Sewers and water pipes were laid. New "department" stores came to line Oxford Street, Regent Street, and Piccadilly Circus. Ring after ring of newly built brick housing pushed the city's borders outward. Other cities, especially the thriving manufacturing centers such as Manchester and Birmingham, invested in public buildings (city halls, law courts, concert halls, museums) built in the substantial and dignified Gothic Revival style. America grew far closer; steamships regularly crossed the Atlantic in nine days, and in 1866 the telegraph cable allowed almost instant transmission of news and business messages. The Suez Canal, which opened in 1869, dramatically shortened the sea routes to India and the Far East.

Two overseas military events marred the peace of the 1850s. From 1854 to 1856, England and France were allies in a war against Russia in the Crimea, which lies between the Black Sea and the Sea of Azov and was then a part of the disintegrating Turkish Empire. The causes of the Crimean War have never been entirely clear, but it was part of a struggle between England and Russia to maintain influence in the Middle East and thereby protect trade routes into Asia. The war in the Crimea was noteworthy for the heroic (or suicidal) Charge of the Light Brigade, for Florence Nightingale, and—most significant—for being the first war fought in the glare of daily publicity. The Indian Mutiny of 1857 was also the subject of dramatic newspaper reporting.

By the late 19th century, for the average English person, the standard of living for urban workers improved significantly. Real wages (i.e., the amount of goods that can be bought with a day's earnings) may have doubled, since better transportation lowered the cost of food, and factory production made clothing, shoes, and household goods much less expensive. Working-class families had some money available to spend on things beyond the bare necessities. A final and most significant legislative accomplishment of the mid-Victorian period was the Education Act of 1870, which created government-supported schools and required that elementary education be available to every child in England. The improved opportunities for literacy were soon visible in the increasing number of laborers' children who moved into clerical work, teaching, surveying, nursing, engineering, and other careers on the path of upward mobility.

The later part of the 19th century had a somewhat more difficult and diverse tone than the high Victorian years of mid-century, although not necessarily because times were harder. The balance of domestic political and economic power was shifting, and new groups could make demands of their own. In addition, there seemed to be a cultural transition. George Eliot died in 1880, Thomas Carlyle and Benjamin Disraeli in 1881, and Charles Darwin and Anthony Trollope in 1882. The artists and writers who came to prominence in the *fin de siècle* (Thomas Hardy, Oscar Wilde, George Bernard Shaw, Joseph Conrad, and Aubrey Beardsley) produced work of a less comforting, more modern tone.

Queen Victoria's Golden Jubilee in 1887 was an outpouring of national affection and a celebration of 50 years of domestic progress. The Diamond Jubilee of 1897, by contrast, marked the high tide of empire. It was a massive exhibition of pageantry and power. Subject peoples from around the world sent jewel-bedecked rulers and armies in ethnic dress to pay tribute to the almost mythic empress in London who governed them. The South African war of 1899–1902, in which British and Boer peoples struggled over African territory they both wanted, was a rude anticlimax; but, by the time peace was negotiated, the 20th century had arrived, Queen Victoria was dead, and the Prince of Wales had taken the throne as King Edward VII (Mitchell, *Daily Life*, 1–15).

FOR MORE INFORMATION

Altick, R. D. *Victorian People and Ideas*. New York: W.W. Norton, 1973.
Mitchell, S. *Daily Life in Victorian England*. Westport, Conn.: Greenwood Press, 1996.
Mitchell, S., ed. *Victorian Britain: An Encyclopedia*. New York: Garland Press, 1998.
Morris, J. *Pax Britannica: The Climax of an Empire*. New York: Harcourt Brace, 1968.

China

China's origins extend back over twenty-two thousand years, when, after the last glacial ice age, modern humans appeared near the Ordos desert region (near Mongolia). The subsequent creation of modern Chinese civilization came much later, roughly 2000 B.C.E. Archaeologists have noted that a uniform culture spread during the Hsia dynasty (1994–1523 B.C.E.), which began under the reign of Emperor Yu. From 2000 B.C.E. to the 19th century, the Chinese experienced the rise and fall of 13 other dynasties. All of them followed a similar historical pattern. Ruling families (who claimed a divine political mandate) tended to expand out of the Yangtze and Huang He river basins. They then spread out conquering and unifying the ethnically, linguistically, and socially diverse elements of China. Over time, the dynasties grew too large and succumbed to outside military pressures. Shrinking back to the river basins, the dynasties became weak. After a period of political and economic chaos, a new dynasty appeared, and the process repeated itself. Most certainly, one can see this historical process at work in the 19th century.

The ruling dynasty throughout the century was the Qing or Ching dynasty. Established in 1644 by Manchu invaders from the north, the Qing dynasty expanded China to its greatest territorial extent. But these halcyon years were short-lived. And in fact, because of the Qing emperors' failures, China was reduced to being a subject of European powers by the end of the 19th century.

Key to the downfall of the Qing (and of China as well) in the 19th century was European intervention into the Chinese economic and political life. At the turn of the 1800s, the Qing were opposed to outside trade with Europeans. Soon, however,

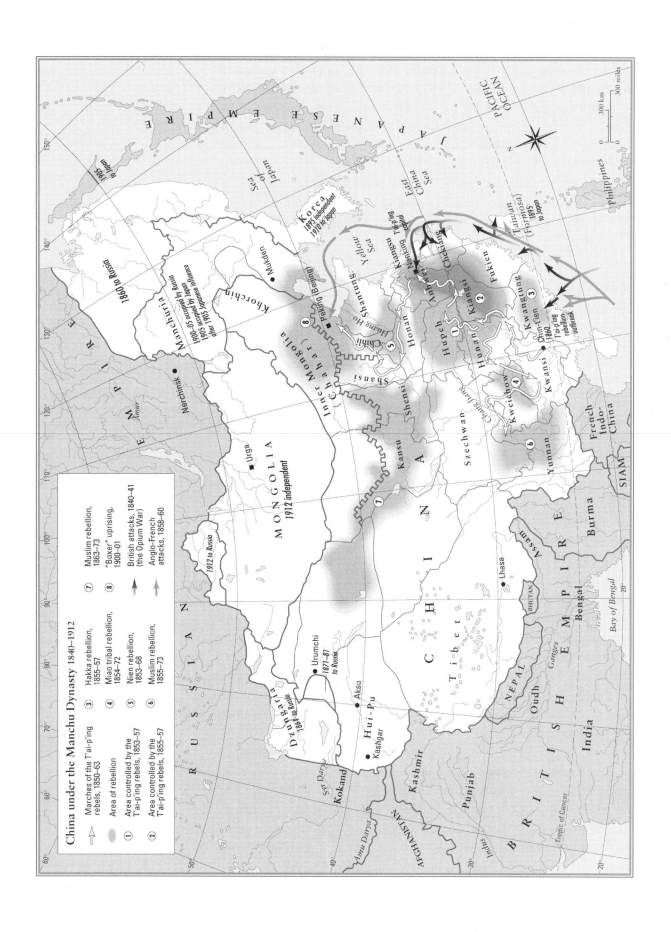

China under the Manchu Dynasty 1840–1912

Marches of the T'ai-p'ing rebels, 1850–63

Area of rebellion

① Area controlled by the T'ai-p'ing rebels, 1853–57

② Area controlled by the T'ai-p'ing rebels, 1855–57

③ Hakka rebellion, 1855–57

④ Miao tribal rebellion, 1854–72

⑤ Nien rebellion, 1853–68

⑥ Muslim rebellion, 1855–73

⑦ Muslim rebellion, 1863–73

⑧ "Boxer" uprising, 1900–01

↑ British attacks, 1840–41 (the Opium War)

↑ Anglo-French attacks, 1858–60

PACIFIC OCEAN

0 300 km
0 300 miles

J A P A N E S E   E M P I R E

Sea of Japan

Japan

Korea
1895 independent
1910 to Japan

East China Sea

Taiwan (Formosa)
1895 to Japan

Philippines

Yellow Sea

T'ai-p'ing capital

Nanking

Mukden

Manchuria
1900–05 occupied by Russia
1905 occupied by Japanese influence after 1905 Japanese influence

Nerchinsk

Amur

Khorchin

Peking (Beijing)

Shantung

Chihli

Huang Ho

Honan

Shansi

Shensi

Kiangsu

Anhwei

Chekiang

Hupeh

Kiangsi

Fukien

② ① Hunan

⑤

Szechwan

Chang Chiang

Kweichow

④

Kwangsi

Kwansi

Kwangtung ③

Chin-Tien
1860
T'ai-p'ing rebellion outbreak

⑥ Yunnan

French Indo-China

SIAM

Burma

Assam

Lhasa

T i b e t

BHUTAN

NEPAL

Oudh

Bengal

Bay of Bengal

India

Punjab

Kashmir

AFGHANISTAN

B R I T I S H   E M P I R E

Tropic of Cancer

Indus

Ganges

M O N G O L I A
1912 independent

Inner Mongolia (Chahar)

Urga

⑦

⑧

Kansu

Urumchi
1871–81 to Russia

Aksu

Hui-Pu

Kashgar

Dzungaria
1864 to Russia

Syr Darya

Amu Darya

Kokand

R U S S I A N   E M P I R E

1912 to Russia

1860 to Russia

1905 to Japan

C H I N A

N

the emperor relaxed trade restrictions. In 1834, the port city of Guangzhou (Canton) was opened for overseas trade. Eventually the British became dissatisfied with the arrangement and waged a war against the Qing. The Opium War (1839–42) was a complete disaster for the Chinese. It was sparked by the British practice of smuggling opium into China and selling it to Chinese merchants and drug users. In 1839, the Chinese government enforced its prohibitions on opium and confiscated a large quantity of the drug at the port of Guangzhou. The British responded by sending in gun ships and defeating the Qing armies. The subsequent Treaty of Nanjing (1842) and the British Supplementary Treaty of the Bogue (1843) established several more trading ports and forced the Chinese to cede Hong Kong to the British. A few years later, the British again attacked China over its attempt to eradicate the illegal importation of British opium. The Second Opium War (1856–60) resulted in another defeat for the Chinese. The treaties that followed opened China to more trade with not only the British but also the French, Russians, and Americans as well. Moreover, the Qing rulers were forced to accept Christian missionaries and legalize the importation of opium.

Enfeebled by the opium wars, by the end of the 19th century, the Qing dynasty could not defend itself from attacks from within and from outside. In 1850, Hung Hsiu-ch'üan, a political and spiritual leader from Guangzhou who developed a Chinese version of Christianity, staged a revolt to establish a new dynasty, the Taiping (great peace). Beginning in the Yangtze river valley, the Taiping rebels captured Nanjing in 1853 and made it their capital. Worried that the Taiping would not honor the unequal treaties that they had forced on the Qing rulers, Western powers fashioned a military counterattack with an army named the Ever-Victorious Army and eventually crushed the Taiping.

A few years later, the Qing faced a serious challenge from the Japanese. In 1894, Japan launched an attack on China to gain control of Korea and to obtain the same economic rights as Western powers in China. In addition to port cities, the Japanese demanded and received the rights to open factories inside China. After the Sino-Japanese War, the Qing dynasty found itself nearly powerless as China itself had been portioned by the Japanese and European nations.

In the last year of the 19th century, the Qing Dowager Empress Tz'u Hsi employed a last ditch effort to rid her country of foreign invaders. She helped an antiforeign secret society called I Ho Ch'uan (righteous harmonious fists or boxers) to become a significant political force. In June 1900, the Boxers began their rebellion against Europeans. For eight weeks, the Boxer rebels occupied Beijing. However, another multinational foreign army composed of American, British, French, German, Japanese, and Russian troops put down the rebellion and forced China to pay a $333 million indemnity and to sign more treaties to the benefit of foreign traders. Although the Qing dynasty lasted another 12 years, by 1900, China was in essence the subject of foreign powers. The Qing dynasty had collapsed.

FOR MORE INFORMATION

Chesneaux, J., M. Bastid, and M.-C. Bergère. *China from the Opium Wars to the 1911 Revolution*. New York: Pantheon Books, 1976.

Fairbank, J. K. *China: A New History*. Cambridge, Mass.: Belknap Press, 1992.

Poneranz, F. *The Great Divergence: China, Europe, and the Making of the Modern World Economy*. Princeton, N.J.: Princeton University Press, 2000.

India

India's historical roots began about 2500 B.C.E. near the Indus River Valley. Over the next 2000 years, the center of Indian culture, which included the Hindu religion, shifted eastward to the Gangetic plain. It was during the reign of Bimbisara (540–490 B.C.E.) that India developed two of its most important cultural belief systems: Jainism and Buddhism. Over the subsequent centuries, India's political and cultural influence grew as did its military might. In 325 B.C.E., Chandragupta, founder of the Mauryan Empire, repelled Greek armies led by Alexander the Great. India's golden age came in the 4th and 5th centuries C.E. when Indian art, literature, and science reached high levels. Five centuries later India was invaded by Muslims who eventually took control. Throughout Muslim rule, Hindus struggled to maintain their culture and political power. Although a powerful cultural influence, Muslims never constituted a majority of the Indian population.

Another significant influence on India's historical development was the arrival of European traders in the late 15th century. In 1498, the Portuguese sailor Vasco da Gama landed at Calicut. Soon the British, Dutch, and French followed the Portuguese. Initially, foreign trade was conducted in a few special stations at Surat, Bombay, and Calcutta. However, by the 18th century, India's ruling elite had become weakened by both invasions from Afghans and internal revolts led by Hindus, and India slowly came under direct control of European powers. By the middle of the 18th century, England and France were fighting each other for the sole right to control India. In 1763, the British defeated the French in India (and in North America) and became the main colonial force on the subcontinent.

Supported by the British colonial administration and backed by a well-armed regular army, the British East India Company helped to exploit India's markets and agricultural resources. The British believed, of course, their rule to be benevolent. They developed India's exports, including cotton and tea, improved transportation routes, and built irrigation systems. When asked, the British also pointed out their cultural impacts such as the spread of Christianity and educational reforms. Yet, not all Indians appreciated British colonial rule. In 1857, British-trained soldiers working for the East India Company staged a mutiny that grew into a widespread revolt against British colonialism, particularly its harsh economic policies, its fostering of Christianity, and its blatant disregard for Indian politics and social customs. For example, the British supplied their Indian soldiers with bullets coated with grease made from cow and pig fat. The use of cows in this way upset the Hindus and the use of pigs upset the Muslims. Although the British later replaced the cartridges, the damage was done. On May 10, 1857, Indian soldiers launched an attack upon the British, capturing Delhi and proclaiming Bahadur Shah II the emperor of all

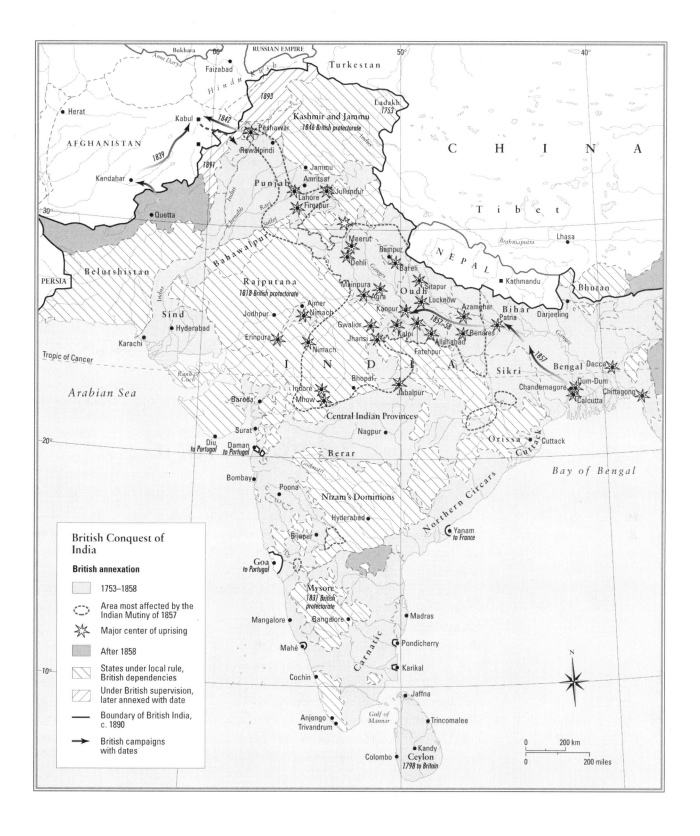

British Conquest of India

British annexation

1753–1858

Area most affected by the Indian Mutiny of 1857

Major center of uprising

After 1858

States under local rule, British dependencies

Under British supervision, later annexed with date

Boundary of British India, c. 1890

British campaigns with dates

India. The revolt was crushed a year later, and the British took steps to reform colonial rule. In fact the East India Company was abolished. Indians themselves were given some voice in colonial government. Nevertheless, the British reinforced their power by making Queen Victoria the empress of India in 1877. The halfhearted nature of these reforms ensured that mistrust remained on both sides. Moreover, although there was no other major Indian revolt in the 19th century, Indians kept the pressure on the colonial government by forming nationalist organizations such as the Indian National Congress (founded in 1885). These groups became critical for the independence movement in the 20th century.

FOR MORE INFORMATION

Bayly, C. A. *Indian Society and the Making of the British Empire*. New York: Cambridge University Press, 1987.

Veer, P. Van Der. *Imperial Encounters: Religion and Modernity in India and Britain*. Princeton, N.J.: Princeton University Press, 2001.

Viswanathan, G. *Masks of Conquest: Literary Study and British Rule in India*. New York: Columbia University Press, 1989.

Islamic World

Literally speaking, Islam is an Arabic word meaning "submission to God." Founded by the Prophet Muhammad in the 7th century, Islam is one of the most influential world religions. A majority of the people in the Middle East and significant groups in Africa, Asia, and Europe practice Islam. During the 19th century, Muslims were largely concentrated in the Middle East and Asia.

The core of the Islamic faith is the Qur'an (Koran), which contains the final revelations from Allah (Arabic for "the God") to Muhammad. Muslims believe in the five pillars of faith: *shahadah* (the affirmation that there is only one God and Muhammad is the messenger); *salah* (the ritual of five daily prayers); *zakat* (giving alms to the poor); *sawm* (the dawn to sunset fast during the lunar month of Ramadan); and the *hajj* (the pilgrimage to Mecca). Another important aspect to Islam is that it acknowledges its relationship to Judaism and Christianity. And it recognizes Old Testament and New Testament figures such as Adam, Noah, Abraham, Moses, and David. Although Muslims disagree with various aspects of Islam, there is enough flexibility within the religion to accommodate various ethnic traditions. This ability helps to account for Islam's success.

For Muslims in the 19th century, their world was dominated by larger geopolitical developments. European powers, particularly Portugal and Great Britain, had been pushing into the Middle East since 1498. In the 18th century, Great Britain managed to make major advances as the old Ottoman Empire began its descent, opening the way for others to take control of Turkey and other Middle Eastern areas. In 1801,

British forces pushed the French out of Egypt. In 1805, Mohammed Ali, an Albanian soldier in the Ottoman army, took control of the Ottoman Empire and began to modernize it along European lines.

As European influences spread through the Middle East and northern Africa, the clash between Islam and Christianity flared up again. But in the 19th century, Muslims infused their religious battle with the Europeans with a sense of nationalism. Islam became a way of reclaiming Muslim identity in the midst of European domination.

FOR MORE INFORMATION

Armstrong, K. *A History of God: The 4000-Year Quest of Judaism, Christianity, and Islam*. New York: Alfred Knopf, 1993.
Armstrong, K. *Islam: A Short History*. New York: Modern Library, 2000.
Esposito, J. L. *The Oxford History of Islam*. New York: Oxford University Press, 1999.

Latin America

In the 19th century, Latin Americans faced a major question: Could they break their bonds with Europe and create successful, independent states? The example of the United States suggested that this was possible, but Latin America might be different. With its strict caste system, could the region generate sufficient political and military support to win a struggle with Spain and Portugal? If Latin Americans gained independence, would they prefer a monarchy, an oligarchy, or a dictatorship? And, would the countries be the size of a continent, a viceroyalty (a royal administrative division), or just a local region? These questions would not find easy or simple answers.

In the early 19th century, Latin America was overwhelmingly rural, with more than 95 percent of its people living in isolated areas. They inhabited vast haciendas, plantations, and Indian territories. Although navigation linked Latin America with Europe and other colonies, within the great interior expanses of the Americas, the horse, mule train, or oxcart served as the main sources of transportation. Although some people lived in large mining centers like Potosí in Bolivia or Guanajuato in Mexico, most mining communities were small. Mexico City was cosmopolitan; with 135,000 residents, it had the largest population in the hemisphere. Lima, Peru, had 87,000 inhabitants, but other colonial capitals, like Santiago, Chile, and Buenos Aires, Argentina, had only 40,000.

At great cost, Spanish America defeated Spain after a 16-year struggle. In Brazil, by contrast, Pedro I, son of the Portuguese king, declared independence. Thus, Portugal and Brazil remained under the control of the same family. After the war with Spain ended, many important Spanish American leaders fled into exile, while in Brazil the monarchy provided continuity and stability. Spanish Americans wrote

Latin America 1892

land over 1000 ft
land over 5000 ft

Caribbean Sea

PANAMA

VENEZUELA
Llanos
Caracas

BRITISH
GUIANA

DUTCH GUIANA
FRENCH GUIANA

UNITED STATES
OF COLOMBIA
Bogatá

Quito
EQUADOR

Negro

Amazon

Manaus

Belém

Fortaleza

Natal

A m a z o n i a

PERU

B R A Z I L

Recife

Lima

A
n
d

La Paz

Salvador

Arica

BOLIVIA

Mato Grosso

San Francisco

Xingu

Araguaia

PACIFIC
OCEAN

PARAGUAY

Gran Chaco

Asunción

Parana

São Paulo

Rio de Janeiro

Tropic of Capricorn

e
s

ARGENTINA

Porto Alegre

CHILE

Pampas

URAGUAY

Juan
Fernandez
(Chile)

Santiago
Valparaiso

Buenos Aires

La Plata

Montevideo

ATLANTIC
OCEAN

P
a
t
a
g
o
n
i
a

Bahia Blaca

Falkland
Islands
(British)

Tierra
de Fuego

constitutions and destroyed them, declared free expression then silenced the press, and opened universities but exiled key faculty members. Meanwhile, conservative Brazil attempted few of these changes. Ironically, Latin America gained its independence from Spain, but most Latin Americans enjoyed few freedoms under their new independent governments. Furthermore, instability threatened the entire independence project. Dictators filled the power vacuum and ran their countries like giant haciendas, ruling with no accountability to legislatures, the courts, or an electorate.

It took a generation to recover from the chaos and tyranny of independence. Nevertheless, legendary heroes, symbols, and a national culture emerged from this process. A desire to end slavery and Indian servitude gained momentum. Native-born persons of Spanish descent, known as criollos, controlled land and labor. Foreign merchants made a beachhead, however, dominating international commerce and national credit. These merchants bought hides, coffee, sugar, tobacco, copper, and silver in exchange for European manufactured goods. They arranged financing for the first steamship lines and railroads. They also loaned money to governments mired in debt and then spent years trying to collect the interest.

In contrast to the weak Latin American governments, the Catholic Church remained strong. Church-state relations were strained while the new governments negotiated a new relationship with Rome, but the church leadership solidified its hierarchy and its financial position, which allowed it to support conservative leaders. The latter opposed freedom of religion and land reforms, which might affect the church's control of its own estates. The rural clergy, however, provided spiritual and material help for those suffering from war and tyrannical leadership. These priests often were more sensitive to local needs than was the government.

Liberals, usually affiliated with Masonic lodges (a secret fraternal society opposed by the Catholic Church), wished to create a new Latin America. They did not believe in democracy but supported creation of institutional governments consisting of an elected executive, a legislature, and an independent judiciary. Liberals were often violently anticlerical (i.e., opposed to the wealth and special position of the clergy), claiming that priests endorsed medieval ideas and institutions. When liberals gained power after 1850, they sought to secularize marriage, birth, and death records. Some liberals, like Benito Juárez in Mexico, even attempted to expropriate church property. Acrimony dominated church-state relations in almost every Latin American nation in the late 19th century, and the rift was not easily closed.

Even after independence, the church still controlled primary, secondary, and university education. As the state's resources increased, it funded parallel, secular schools. Most countries developed state universities with a modern curriculum. In Chile, under the brilliant leadership of Andrés Bello, a Venezuelan, the national university gained such prestige that by the 1880s virtually all presidents, legislators, and judges were graduates. Talented writers and historians, often faculty members of the universities, created a sense of national identity. In Argentina, Domingo S. Sarmiento wrote about the virtues and defects of the gaucho, the cowboy of the Argentine Pampas, while in Chile, Diego Barros Arana lauded the ascendancy of liberal government.

European immigrants streamed into the Pampas, southern Brazil, and urban centers throughout Latin America. A major Japanese immigration transformed agriculture in Brazil. However, most population growth was due to a rise in fertility and improved living conditions. Pressure from Great Britain ended the slave trade, and, in the 1880s, ideas of free labor eventually overturned slavery in Brazil, Puerto Rico, and Cuba. In Brazil, slavery was so closely tied to the monarchy that the disappearance of the former led to the disappearance of the latter. Brazil now began to experience both the change and the instability that had earlier affected its Spanish American neighbors.

With the exception of the French occupation of Mexico from 1863 to 1867, the dominant foreign power in Latin America was Great Britain. The prominence of British merchants largely established this position. Although they avoided direct intervention in politics whenever possible, the British usually sided with conservative leadership. Beginning with the Mexican-American War of 1846–48, and the California Gold Rush of 1849, the United States rivaled the British in Mexico, Central America, and the Caribbean. The U.S. annexation of almost half of Mexico in 1848, the construction of an American-owned railroad across Panama in the 1850s, and the invasion of Cuba and Puerto Rico in 1898 during the Spanish-American War signaled U.S. ascendancy in the hemisphere.

By 1900, all Latin American nations, with the exception of most Caribbean islands, had achieved self-government. Although some still struggled economically and politically, countries such as Mexico, Argentina, Brazil, Chile, and Uruguay were true success stories. The capitals of these nations were cosmopolitan centers with wide boulevards, promenades, theaters, and opera houses. The elite, who often visited Europe, prided themselves on these local symbols of culture. But the rural poor, who now began migrating to the cities, confirmed that such high culture was an island surrounded by impoverished people deprived of education. Latin America's independence had changed world history, but in the 20th century, the unresolved disparities among its social classes would raise tensions and cause revolutions.

~*John L. Rector*

FOR MORE INFORMATION

Bushnell, D. *The Emergence of Latin America in the Nineteenth Century.* New York: Oxford University Press, 1988.

Langley, L. D. *The Americas in the Age of Revolution, 1750–1850.* New Haven, Conn.: Yale University Press, 1996.

Lynch, J. *Caudillos in Spanish America, 1800–1850.* New York: Oxford University Press, 1992.

Chronology of the 19th Century

2000 B.C.E.	Chinese civilization as we now know it begins to develop.
1735–96 C.E.	Emperor Ch'ien-lung expands China's borders to their largest territorial range in history.

1800	Capitol of the United States moves from Philadelphia to Washington, D.C.
1803	President Thomas Jefferson purchases Louisiana Territory from France.
1804–6	Meriwether Lewis and William Clark conduct their expedition of western exploration.
1818	Great Britain takes control of most of India.
1820	Missouri Compromise in the United States limits slavery to areas below 36 degrees 30 minutes north latitude.
1826	Ottoman Empire's fleet is sunk at Navarino.
1831	William Lloyd Garrison begins publishing abolitionist newspaper, *The Liberator*.
1832	First English Reform Bill is passed, beginning a process to increase democracy in Great Britain.
1833	The American Antislavery Society is formed.
1834	China opens its markets to limited overseas trade.
1835	Tz'u Hsi, the Dowager Empress, is born.
1838–42	China loses Opium War to Great Britain.
1839	British government begins to provide money for elementary schools.
1839–41	Africans from the slave ship *Amistad* fight for and receive their freedom in the United States and return to Africa.
1840	Queen Victoria marries her cousin, Prince Albert of Saxe-Coburg-Gotha.
1842	Treaty of Nanjing grants trade concessions to Great Britain.
1844	British Factory Act limits the work day to 12 hours for people less than 18 years of age.
1845	Irish potato famine begins.
1848	Gold discovered in California.
1846–48	United States defeats Mexico; cession of Mexican territory to the U.S. aggravates debate over expansion of slavery.
1848–65	China becomes embroiled in the Taiping Rebellion in which revolutionaries attempt to destroy the Chinese dynasty and its European allies.
1850	Compromise of 1850 in the United States seeks to keep the nation together by offering solutions on new states as well as the Fugitive Slave law.
1851	Harriet Beecher Stowe publishes *Uncle Tom's Cabin*.
1851	Great Exhibition at the Crystal Palace in Great Britain opens.
1853–56	The Crimean War.
1853	Queen Victoria uses chloroform at the birth of her eighth child, thus making medical history and popularizing the use of the medical procedure.
1855	Florence Nightingale introduces hygienic standards into military hospitals.
1857	The Indian Mutiny erupts with thousands of Indian soldiers staging an unsuccessful armed uprising against British rule.

1858	British troops suppress the Indian Mutiny.
1859	John Brown leads raid on Harper's Ferry, Virginia; Brown and his band of men are tried, convicted of treason, and hung.
1859	Charles Darwin publishes *On the Origins of Species through Natural Selection*.
1860	South Carolina becomes first state to secede from Union.
1860	British and French troops loot and burn the Chinese Summer Palace.
1861–65	United States Civil War
1861	Confederate forces bombard Fort Sumter, thus beginning the American Civil War.
1861	Battle of the First Bull Run ends in a victory for the Confederate forces in the American Civil War.
1861	An Indian Council's Act leads to Indian involvement in the legislative process.
1862	Battles of the Second Bull Run and Antietam during the American Civil War; President Abraham Lincoln drafts the Emancipation Proclamation.
1862	Tz'u Hsi, dowager empress, becomes the effective ruler of China and rules through figurehead child emperors until 1908.
1863	President Abraham Lincoln issues the Emancipation Proclamation.
1865	Confederate General Robert E. Lee surrenders to Union forces ending the Civil War.
1865	Abraham Lincoln assassinated.
1867	Second Reform Bill passes in Great Britain, reducing property qualifications for male voters.
1869	Mohandas K. Gandhi born.
1869	Workers and railroad officials drive the golden spike into rails that join the Union Pacific and Central Pacific railroads.
1869	Debtors prisons are abolished in Great Britain.
1876	The Ottoman constitution is proclaimed.
1877	Queen Victoria crowned empress of India.
1880	Elementary education (ages 7 to 10) becomes compulsory in Great Britain.
1883–85	Sino-French War over control of Vietnam is waged.
1885	The Indian National Congress is formed and leads the political movement for Indian independence.
1888	Chiang Kai-shek, future leader of China and Taiwan, is born.
1888	Jack the Ripper kills five women in London.
1889	Oklahoma land rush begins.
1889	Kadambini Ganguly becomes the first Indian woman to address an open session of the Indian Congress.
1890	Battle of Wounded Knee becomes last major confrontation between American Indian tribes and United States military.
1893	Mao Tse-tung, future leader of China, is born.
1894–95	Sino-Japanese War results in China's defeat.

1898–1900	Many Chinese participate in Boxer Rebellion, a last ditch attempt to drive European and other foreign powers from China.
1899–1902	Boer War in South Africa.
1901	Queen Victoria dies.

HISTORICAL OVERVIEW: WEB SITES

http://www.victorianlondon.org/
http://www.lib.byu.edu/~rdh/eurodocs/uk/1918.html
http://www.teacheroz.com/19thcent.htm
http://www.usc.edu/dept/MSA/history/chronology/century19.html
http://www.nationalmuseumindia.org.html
http://www.hoover.archives.gov/exhibits/China/index.html
http://emuseum.mnsu.edu/prehistory/china/later_imperial_china/qing.html
http://www.usc.edu/dept/MSA/introduction/woi_modernera.html

2

DOMESTIC LIFE

The center of daily life is the home and, more importantly, the people who inhabit our domestic space. Domestic life here is defined as the people who share our private spaces, excluding our friends and acquaintances with whom we interact in the public world of work, politics, and sometimes recreation. However, even this definition of domestic life is a little slippery, because we include family members within our private sphere even if they live in separate homes and join us in the holidays and celebrations that mark our domestic life. Over time the definitions of those who are our intimates has changed. Who are the people who might share our domestic life?

The first ties are developed between parents and their children. But even these relationships defy clear definition: throughout history children have often depended upon the kindness of strangers to raise them, whether they were orphaned, fostered, or fed by wet nurses. All these people share the domestic intimacy of home life. Furthermore, households often included others outside the nuclear family, from relatives to servants to slaves. In ancient Rome, the head of the family (paterfamilias) was responsible for family, relatives, slaves, and freed slaves, and he also cared for clients who put themselves in his charge. Families might also include unmarried partners, concubines who shared the private life of rulers, or even roommates who combine living space for convenience or necessity. The relationships that make up domestic life are impossible to define perfectly, but we recognize them when we see them, much like art.

A study of domestic life includes not only the people who create a private sphere, but it also encompasses the roles that they play—including the emotional functions they may fill at times. Fathers of 19th-century families were known to be distant and stern, while mothers were expected to be accessible and nurturing. Mothers in ancient Rome, by contrast, were stern disciplinarians and teachers of values while nursemaids handled the nurturing. Here in domestic life, societies define the roles of men, women, children, and everyone else who shares this space. It is here that we learn early on who we are and how we are to act and feel.

During the 19th century, daily life in the family underwent steady transformation. Some of the changes were geographic. In the United States, families moved from the East to the West. Such treks were hard on families, and to survive all family

DOMESTIC LIFE

|
FAMILY LIFE

MEN

WOMEN

CHILDREN

members had to work, thus changing some cherished traditions. There was not room on the frontier for gender-specific work. Sometimes women had to work in the fields, and sometimes men had to milk the cows. Frontier children also worked at an early age. This, however, shows continuity with the past and similarities across cultures. Child labor was common to nearly all families, whether in England, India, or in the United States. In England, the abuse of child laborers translated into a movement to regulate such work. Notice that no similar reforms took place in India or in the United States.

Daily life in families was also transformed by the century's various political movements. Perhaps other movements were as potent as abolitionism in the United States during the Civil War era. The war freed thousands of families from the oppressive dictates of slave owners. Other political movements foreshadowed changes to come. This is particularly true of the nascent feminist movement, which planted its roots in England, the United States, and India and made some advances. More were to come after 1900. In reading about these movements, be careful to note who was leading them and why.

Given the transformations of familial daily life, it is important to see that one aspect did not change much. In India and in the Middle East, religious and cultural traditions helped maintain traditional family and caste structures. Similarly, no matter what society one studies, it was trifurcated by class. Upper-class lives differed from middle-class lives, which were quite separate from those of the working class. It was not just a matter of relative wealth, although that certainly played a major part. It was also the expectations that families developed for themselves. Upper-class Victorian families, for instance, developed a strict code of behavior, especially for the women. Working-class families did not have the luxury to set such rules; they were too busy laboring for the family's survival to do so.

In comparing families across cultures (and in fact across time), try pulling out major similarities and differences. Keep in the back of your mind certain categories such as class, gender, and life cycle to help guide your analysis. Above all, in making comparisons, be sure to keep your ideas rooted in place and time as well as culture.

FOR MORE INFORMATION

Veyne, P., ed. *A History of Private Life*. Vols. 1 and 2. Cambridge, Mass.: Harvard University Press, 1987.

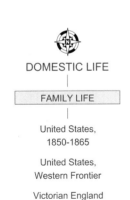

DOMESTIC LIFE
|
FAMILY LIFE
|
United States,
1850-1865

United States,
Western Frontier

Victorian England

Islamic World

India

Family Life

We tend to think of families in terms of their structure. Most families have mothers, fathers, children, grandparents, cousins, and other relatives. To differentiate types of families, particularly across cultural lines, we assign them names such *as nuclear, extended, single parent,* and so forth. But to understand them, particularly in a historical context, we must look at the larger social institutions that influence them. To see how the family changed in the 19th century, we need to examine it in relation to the economy, to class and caste, and to culture.

In the entries that follow, pay particular attention to how the economy shaped family life. In the 19th century, sweeping economic changes propelled transformations in families. For instance, in the United States, about the time of the Civil War, the relatively new, urban, and industrial economy pulled some working fathers from the house thus creating a female-dominated household. Also, different economic situations produced certain types of families. In the American South, family was an extremely important but fragile institution for African Americans. Unlike middle-class families, slave families were subject to harsh and violent conditions as well as to slaveholders' whims. As is mentioned in the section on the United States Civil War, one in three slave marriages that did not last were broken up by slave owners. Economic conditions in the American West were also a main factor in family structure and the power of individual family members. In areas where white women were rare, such as mining districts, the women had unusual power and prestige. Even working-class women of the West, such as prostitutes, were highly valued.

Like economic circumstance, social class played a key role in shaping family life. Compare, for example, the tasteful and quaint marriage practices of middle-class family life in Victorian England with that of the rather raucous working-class marriage on the American frontier—they could not be more different. Nowhere in the literature or history of Victorian England are there stories of a married couple spending their wedding night inside a covered wagon while their friends partied outside, banging cans and shooting guns to disturb the newlyweds. On the frontier, one could not be too choosy in the selection of a mate. In England, however, there were proscriptions about marrying outside one's social circle. In India too, there were similar restrictions. Traditional Indian marriage practices had strict rules about caste and religion.

The same held true for Muslim families where religion was of paramount importance. Teachings from the Qur'an (Koran) set rules not only for marriage but for family roles and duties as well. Men were traditionally the breadwinners while women were the caretakers. Religious doctrines also provided the structure for the ways in which men treated women and how children were raised.

Notice the role of women when reading these entries. When the English ruled India, they were quite critical of Indian customs regarding family practices. The British scoffed at the customs relating to Hindu women. To the colonial rulers, the practice of *sati* (or suttee), or widow immolation, was a sign of the low social position of Indian women. But the attack upon sati was more than an attempt to raise women's social position. It was an attempt to change Indian culture by altering Indian family life. Thus, when reading these entries on family life, pay attention to how specific cultures dictate family life and how cultural dictates become contested. Moreover, compare family life across cultures. Perhaps one can see the differences most clearly in family death rituals; how families care for their dead tells much about their structure, heritage, and belief systems.

DOMESTIC LIFE

|

FAMILY LIFE

|

United States,
1850-1865

United States,
Western Frontier

Victorian England

Islamic World

India

UNITED STATES, 1850–65

During the Civil War era, family life dramatically changed. While many Northerners were still farmers, a growing segment of the population was becoming tied to cities and factories. Middle-class men who had grown up in the first half of the century could remember a childhood spent living in a family working environment, either on a farm, in a cottage at a mill, or in a room behind a family shop. But as the century progressed, men's work increasingly took place outside the home and in the atmosphere of business premises such as the factory or the office. Fathers commonly left the home to work for 10 to 14 hours, and their children rarely saw them during daylight hours. A father's work and workplace became foreign to his children. This tendency to *go* to work rather than work at home led to the virtual removal of men from the home environment, leaving it the sole province of the female. The modern 19th-century home increasingly came to focus almost solely on the wife and children. The evolution to a female-dominated household may help to explain the growing formalism and rigid authoritarianism that Victorian fathers demanded when they were present.

Middle-class family life was quite different from that of the slave family. The slave family, an extremely important institution among African Americans, was an incredibly unstable institution, which was partially due to the influence of whites. A former slave noted, "There were on this plantation about seventy slaves, male and female: some were married, and others lived together as man and wife, without even a mock ceremony. . . . The slaves, however, think much of being married by a clergyman." Since marriage was considered a legal medium by which property was handed down, and slaves had no property, the law saw no reason to recognize the union of slaves as binding. Some morally scrupulous planters encouraged slave marriage as opposed to the immorality of open promiscuity.

Investigators in New Orleans during the federal occupation recorded more than 500 marriages that had taken place among slaves. Of these, fewer than 100 had remained unbroken. While some unions lasted from 20 to 40 years, the average length of a slave marriage was a mere 5.6 years. Records indicate that 70 percent of these marriages ended due to death or personal choice, and only 30 percent of the slave unions were broken up by the planters. Many planters professed an aversion to breaking up slave families because the practice increased unrest among them; but the extravagant lifestyle of the planters, coupled with the regularity of foreclosures on mortgages and demands for the repayment of loans, caused most slaves to see the auction block at least once in their lives. Slaves could be bought or sold, rented out, gambled away, or left in a will as an inheritance to almost anyone; and the law did not provide for the continuity of the slave family as a unit.

Among the frequent rituals that Civil War era families participated in, several related to death. Amid the romanticism and sentimentalism of the 19th century, death was viewed from a different perspective than in earlier times, even than it is today. High infant mortality and the tragic loss of 600,000 soldiers in war made death a part of daily living. Accidents were also common in a society that had few safety regulations for industry and public transportation. Charles Baldwin of Catskill, New York, kept an 1860s diary that contained a special section headed "Accidents, Catastrophes, Etc." Some of his entries involving fatalities included the following:

Explosion of Powder Mills at High Falls; Wesley Sitser severely injured by machinery at Broom Corn Factory; explosion of the boiler on the "Isaac Newton." Honora Barrigan horribly crushed in machinery in Woolen Mills at Leeds; explosion of locomotive at Catskill Station, fireman died; fall at a span of the old bridge; a drowning in a bleach-vat at the paper mill; an explosion of the soda water generator at Smith's Drug Store.

Death rituals were primarily practiced in rural cemeteries, and the number of cemeteries continued to expand into the 1850s. By the time of the Civil War, virtually every sizable city in both the North and the South had its own rural cemetery. The primary focus of the rural cemetery was the family plot. It provided a safe, secure resting place where the remains of loved ones would not be moved, abandoned, or vandalized. Sections in cemeteries were designed to highlight family plots. The winding roads, constructed so that many family plots would have highly desired roadside locations, were built wide enough to accommodate carriages. Gravesite visitations were akin to afternoons in the park. "But the grave of those we loved, what a place for meditation!"

Institutions around death were designed to honor, strengthen, and maintain the family. *Frank Leslie's Illustrated Newspaper* carried a lead story in the April 25, 1863, issue on the increasing volume of mourners at cemeteries. "The cemeteries of New Orleans are very interesting places, for almost every day may be seen parties of mourning relatives and friends decking the grave of some loved one, who, by an early death, has been spared the pangs of regret."

Family monuments were the most obvious man-made structures in the designed landscapes. They were a physical manifestation of the philosophical shift in attitudes toward death from the 18th to the 19th century. Tombstone skeletons and death's heads of previous times, meant to instill fear in the living, were replaced with angels and cherubs who would lead the departed to heaven. Charlotte Selleck's gravestone bears a common 18th-century epitaph, found in several variations into the first third of the following century.

Behold and see as you pass by
As you are now so once was I
As I am now you soon shall be
Prepare for death and follow me.

It was not uncommon for 19th-century tombstones to bear more reassuring epitaphs, such as the following:

Harriet Miles
Fell asleep in Jesus
January 16, 1857
Aged 15 years
Her last word was HAPPY

Rural cemeteries provided separate sections in which young families not yet able to afford a family plot could bury their children. These young or stillborn children would later be reinterred when the family became more established and could afford a family plot. Families that could afford it, however, often created gravestone markers steeped in sentiment and imagery. The most common image was that of the sleeping child. Sleep, as a connection between life and death, was a recurring theme of that period. The image made a connection back to the home where the youth once slept. It brought to mind the comforting picture of a child safely tucked away in bed. A child with a lamb was another recurring image that reinforced the belief in the closeness of children and nature. Empty furniture was also depicted on memorials. An empty chair or bed was commonly used to symbolize a child's unfulfilled life. The song "The Vacant Chair" reinforces this graveyard imagery, as does "Sleep today, O early fallen, In thy green and narrow bed." Judith McGuire reflected, "In all the broad South there will scarcely be a fold without its missing lamb, a fireside without its vacant chair."

Sketch artist Henry Lovie illustrates the conditions for refugee families driven from their homes in the border states during the Civil War. *Leslie's Illustrated Magazine,* ca. 1863–64.

Death rituals among slave families and freed Southern families still retained their African meanings. In dying, one went home. To the slave, this was a reason to celebrate, for it meant freedom. Graves were decorated, as they were in Africa, with the last items that the deceased had used. The most common articles were pottery or glass containers, but medicine bottles, toys, dolls, and quilts were also found. It was essential that the items be broken in order to break the tie to the living. Failure to do so was believed to invite a similar fate for the surviving family. Some slave owners gave a portion of the day off for the funeral of a departed slave and even allotted food for the following celebration. Others required that the funeral be held at night. Mourning clothing were not likely a part of slave mourning traditions; however, some slaves were known to own them. It is very likely that these items were initially purchased for them following the death of a master, which they would later use for their own personal losses (Volo and Volo, 10, 74–77, 283–98).

To read about family life in the United States in the 20th century, see the United States entry in the section "Family Life" in chapter 2 ("Domestic Life") in volume 6 of this series.

FOR MORE INFORMATION

Burns, K. *The Civil War.* PBS Video, 1990. Film.

Paludan, P. S. *A People's Contest: The Union and Civil War, 1861–1865.* New York: Harper & Row, 1988.

Thomas, E. M. *The Confederate Nation: 1861–1865*. New York: Harper & Row, 1979.

Valley of the Shadow Project. <http://jefferson.village.virginia.edu/vshadow2/>.

Volo, D. D., and J. M. Volo. *Daily Life in Civil War America*. Westport, Conn.: Greenwood Press, 1998.

UNITED STATES, WESTERN FRONTIER

DOMESTIC LIFE
|
FAMILY LIFE
|
United States,
1850-1865

United States,
Western Frontier

Victorian England

Islamic World

India

Because they provided extra hands on the farm, in the American West, children were welcome and families were often large. "Our poor man counts each one of his half dozen or half score a blessing . . . stout hands and active heads are the very thing we need," editorialized one newspaper. With infant mortality rates of as high as 25 to 30 percent and epidemics of measles, scarlet fever, or influenza wiping out whole families, a woman had to have been pregnant more than a half dozen times to produce these large families. Some men, like Old Jules in Mari Sandoz's account of her family, believed that "women got to have children to keep healthy." Some women practiced rudimentary birth control—hoping the rhythm method would work, utilizing pessaries for contraception, and nursing their babies as long as possible in the belief they could not then conceive. By word of mouth women passed on contraceptive techniques: the use of petroleum jelly—"a greased egg wouldn't hatch"; rock salt, although most avoided this because "it affected the mind"; and a concoction of cocoa butter and boric acid. Grace Fairchild reflected on her own fecundity: "To have six children in less than eight years is something of a record. You would have thought I was in a race to see how fast we could get that new country settled. I decided to call a halt," and for four years she did not have a child. Once, though, she thought she was pregnant, "took a heaping tablespoon full of quinine" to induce an abortion, and went to bed. So sick she thought she would die, she decided "I'd better stop bucking nature so I could be around to look after the family we already had."

Although family structure was more or less typical, relations between men and women and the creation of families was somewhat unique. Though the homesteaders' frontier had far more European American women than any other, men still outnumbered women. In 1870, when the sex ratio was about even throughout the country, there were 247 men for every 100 women in the West; as the area became more settled, the ratio decreased, but by the turn of the century, the ratio was still 128:100. In 1880, Colorado had 129,131 men to 65,196 women; Montana Territory had 28,177 to 10,792; and Wyoming Ter-

Photographed in 1892, this dugout house, which is typical of many such dwellings built by western settlers on the American plains, was located on the South Loup River in Custer County, Nebraska. Nebraska State Historical Society, Solomon D. Butcher Collection.

ritory had 14,152 to 6,637. It may be hypothesized that this was the reason for two almost antithetical responses to women: respect and domination.

The first was respect, codified if need be. Women—whether they were wives, schoolteachers, immigrant girls fresh off the boat, or prostitutes—were valued. When the bylaws of Yellowstone City, Montana, were written during the winter of 1884–85, there were only 15 women and 300 men in the camp. The penalty of hanging was established for "murder, thieving or insulting a woman." Mollie Dorsey received so many proposals that she sighed, "We do not see a woman at all. All men, single or bachelors, and one gets tired of them."

There was also a surprising sexual frankness between men and women, particularly in the family. In April 1881 Charles Brown, trying to assure his wife, Maggie, back home in Virginia that he was not visiting Colorado prostitutes, wrote:

My virtue is all right and I think that it will remain so for I do not care to meddle with any of the women that I see here, but I look forward to something more soon [when she arrives]. I know that it will be the best in the world, so I am satisfied to think of how nice it will be and go and jack off. Now, don't blame me, for I do get awful hard up at times.

Though there was occasional premarital sex between couples, it was not really condoned. Marriages were opportunities for great celebration. Usually a jolly, rambunctious shivaree or party was held after the wedding:

The newly married couple occupied a wagon for sleeping apartments. The first notice they had of any disturbance was when . . . most of the men and women . . . took hold of the wagon, the men at the tongue pulling, the women at the back pushing, and ran the wagon a half mile out on the prairie. Then the fun began. Such a banging of cans, shooting of guns and every noise conceivable. . . . The disturbance was kept up until midnight, when the crowd dispersed, leaving the happy couple on the prairie to rest undisturbed till morning, when they came [out] amid cheers and congratulation.

Although much research suggests that one effect of the predominantly male society was respect for and joyful pursuit of women, an opposite, darker phenomenon also existed. Some men, like Mari Sandoz's character in *Old Jules*, believed that men had the right to "dominate women and coerce compliance with their wishes." He thought nothing of blacking his wife's eyes, splitting her lip, or "clos[ing] her mouth with the flat of his long muscular hand." After pleading with Jules to castrate two calves before they were too big for her to hold, his wife could not "keep the larger one from kicking." Outraged, Jules dropped the castration knife into manure, stormed into the barn, and fashioned a whip from lengths of baling wire. Shrieking "I learn the goddamn balky woman to obey me when I say 'hold him,' " he slashed her repeatedly. With blood dripping from her face and arm, the abused woman staggered into the house, unstopped "the red bottle with the [skull and] crossbones" with her teeth, and attempted suicide. Though such spousal abuse did occur on the frontier, some women stood up to their men. After receiving a beating from her husband, one woman threw him out of the house and thenceforth supported herself by doing laundry and running a boarding house (Jones, 202–4).

To read about family life on the colonial frontier of North America, see the Colonial Frontier and New England entry in the section "Family Life" in chapter 2 ("Domestic Life") in volume 4 of this series.

FOR MORE INFORMATION

Burns, K. *The West*. PBS Video, 1996. Film.

Demos, J. *Past, Present, and Personal: The Family and the Life Course in American History*. New York: Oxford University Press, 1986.

Dick, E. *The Sod-House Frontier, 1854–1890: A Social History of the Northern Plains from the Creation of Kansas and Nebraska to the Admission of the Dakotas*. New York: D. Appleton-Century, 1937.

Jones, M. E. *Daily Life on the Nineteenth Century American Frontier*. Westport, Conn.: Greenwood Press, 1998.

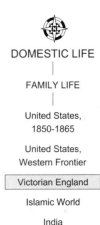

DOMESTIC LIFE

|

FAMILY LIFE

|

United States, 1850-1865

United States, Western Frontier

Victorian England

Islamic World

India

VICTORIAN ENGLAND

The family—made up of a father, a mother, and children—was increasingly idealized during the Victorian period. People developed firm ideas about how family life ought to be, although not everyone could meet these standards. At the same time, real changes in work and income allowed family relationships to develop more fully. In the working class, growing prosperity allowed more space for shared activities and enabled childhood to last longer. Among aristocrats, extended families had formerly promoted economic and political interests rather than encouraging close, affectionate ties. But with Queen Victoria, Prince Albert, and their nine children as models, the upper classes now paid more attention to family celebrations and to establishing a public image of closeness and intimacy.

The middle-class family in its private home was central to the new ideology. Middle-class houses were large enough for family activities yet too small for the separate smoking rooms, morning rooms, and children's wings of aristocratic households. Middle-class women could focus their attention on family and children; they did not need to earn money (as did wives in the working class), nor did they have the social and political obligations of aristocratic women. The model of the mother at home, the father at work, and the family as the center of children's lives (the model taken as natural for much of the 20th century) had its origin in middle-class patterns of life. During the 19th century, English middle-class households were less likely to include unrelated persons (except for servants), and grown children lived at home as long as they were single. An unmarried aunt or widowed grandmother might also live in the house.

Ideologically, the middle-class home and family represented the essence of morality, stability, and comfort. The husband had legal and economic control over his wife, children, and servants. The family depended on his income: the wife did not bring in money through labor (as in the working class) or have a private settlement (as among gentry and aristocrats). The children remained subordinate and obedient. Boys, who needed extended schooling to reproduce their parents' style of life, were under their father's authority until they had enough training and experience to make their own way in the world. Girls were not expected to make their own way—with a very few exceptions, they stayed at home unless or until they married.

The family influenced one's economic prospects as well as one's affections. Many sons took up their father's occupation. As apprenticeship grew less common in skilled trades, fathers and uncles became an important source of boys' training. Kinship connections helped young men find positions in politics, foreign service, business, medicine, and the church. As late as the 1890s, 40 percent of all clergymen were the sons of clergy.

Extended families were still significant. Working-class girls in their early teens might become part of a married sister's household to help with baby care. Middle-class girls were sent to live with cousins in the city as sister governesses. They helped teach the younger children and shared the adults' social life, thereby gaining an opportunity to meet more marriageable men than would be found in the country or in a small town.

Most marriages took place between people of the same occupation or social set. The only commonplace exceptions were women domestic servants, who might marry lower-middle-class tradesmen. Victorians married later than most people imagine. For the country as a whole, the mean age at first marriage was 25 for women and 27 or 28 for men. Members of the working class, on average, married a bit younger; but both men and women of the middle class were often older than 30, because a man wanted to be financially established before he undertook the support of a family. The marriage age grew increasingly later throughout the century. More than 10 percent of the population as a whole never did marry, and among the professional classes one-third of all women may have remained single.

The average number of children per family was six at mid-century. About one-fifth of all families had ten or more children. Because of poor nutrition and other dangers, infant deaths were more common in the working class; many of the really large families were found among the middle and upper classes. The situation changed by the end of the century. Families grew smaller, partly because of later marriage but also because reasonably dependable ways to prevent conception became available. The middle class were the first to limit family size, probably because they recognized the expense of educating children so they could equal their parents' economic status. By 1900, the average manual laborer had twice as many children as the typical professional man.

James Collinson's 1850 painting *Answering the Emigrant's Letter* shows a Victorian English family and the close quarters of a typical cottage. © Manchester Art Gallery.

The death rate among adults in their 20s and 30s was relatively high; workplace accidents, childbirth, infections, epidemics, and tuberculosis killed far more people than nowadays. By some estimates, as many children lived in single-parent families in Victorian times as today, although the cause was the death of either the mother or father rather than divorce or lack of marriage. Whichever parent died, there was hardship. Working women seldom earned enough to support young children; they usually had to go into the workhouse. A father who could not provide child care while working 12 or 14 hours a day might also have to go the Poor Law for help. Children were sent to orphanages or split up among relatives. In the middle class, an aunt or a paid housekeeper would live in a widower's house as a substitute mother; widowed mothers moved in with a relative. Second and third marriages created complicated stepfamilies and half-families. Therefore, the Victorian nuclear family was often large and complex, but the rate of birth outside marriage was—in all classes—extremely low.

Within the family, all legal authority rested with the father. Nevertheless, as middle-class advice books recognized, fathers who worked in business and the professions spent long hours away from home. Mothers were made responsible for moral and spiritual guidance, as well as for supervising all the household's practical affairs. Father was typically distant and reserved.

Middle-class married women with three or four servants did not have a great deal to do each day; nor were they rich enough for the constant visiting, shopping, and entertaining that occupied women who were higher on the social scale. Single women had an even more problematic role. Although the barrier was weakening by the end of the century, most people considered it socially unacceptable for any middle-class woman to do paid work. In some circles, a sort of moral barrier even prevented unpaid charitable work; it might expose an unmarried woman to things she should not know. A middle-aged single woman was expected to stay with her parents as long as they remained alive. After that, she might make herself useful as housekeeper to an unmarried brother or as an unpaid companion and help to a sister or sister-in-law with a large family.

Daily family prayers became a middle-class custom in the 1830s and 1840s. Parents, children, and servants gathered in the dining room just before breakfast. The father read a passage from the Bible and then, while everyone knelt, called the attention of God (and the family) to special concerns about private affairs and ethical behavior.

Family meals, on the other hand, were not the norm. Children ate separately with their nursemaid. The children's hour was their regular daily time with parents—usually after the children's five o'clock supper and before the adults' dinner. In some families, it was a formal event, with children dressed up and on their best behavior. In other cases, the children were already in their nightclothes, and the children's hour was for romping and telling stories. When adults had dinner in the middle of the day, children were brought to the dining room for dessert. This was supposed to be a great treat, but many people remembered hating it because they were expected to show their most polished table manners and practice making polite conversation with grownups.

Sunday was the family day. In the middle class, parents and children went to church and afterward went home to dine together. Sunday tea was also a family event. Tea was taken in the parlor or drawing room, not in the dining room.

Sunday was also a family holiday for most of the working class. Children were sent to Sunday school, although adults probably did not attend church. The father had a late sleep and some time to relax; the mother cooked. Sunday dinner might be the only meal the whole family could have together. Everyone wore better clothes than during the week. Even a man who did rugged manual labor had a Sunday suit if they could afford it. In the afternoon, parents and children went out on a walk or other excursion, perhaps meeting with relatives or close friends for a Sunday evening treat.

During the rest of the week, working-class and middle-class adults were busy and (except for middle-class women) much of their time was spent away from home. Even in classes where work and wages were not a consideration, children's lives were largely separate from those of adults, as the next section explains.

For adults of the leisured class, the day began when a servant brought in hot water for washing and a cup of tea or coffee with something small to eat. Most then spent the next hour or two in their own rooms writing, reading, or attending to private business. Among aristocrats and the substantial gentry, there were usually more than two adults in the house. Houseguests and long visits from relatives were common; single or widowed aunts and sisters were part of the family group. A large midmorning breakfast began the social day.

After breakfast the men engaged in sports, walked out to look over the estate, and conferred with their agent about business. A country squire spent a few hours serving as justice of the peace when the occasion arose. Women occupied their time with calls, visits, reading, music, and needlework. They went out for a walk or ride as exercise and perhaps did some social welfare work. A young woman, for example, might stop at the village school to drop off a book, hear a lesson, and keep her eye out for laborers' daughters who seemed likely to make promising domestic servants. After a late-afternoon rest, everyone changed into dinner clothes for an elaborate meal (Mitchell, *Daily Life,* 141–49).

To read about family life in Chaucer's England, see the Europe entry in the section "Family Life" in chapter 2 ("Domestic Life") in volume 2 of this series; for Elizabethan England, see the England entry in the section "Family Life" in chapter 2 ("Domestic Life") in volume 3 of this series; for 18th-century England, see the England entry in the section "Family Life" in chapter 2 ("Domestic Life") in volume 4 of this series.

FOR MORE INFORMATION

Mitchell, S. *Daily Life in Victorian England.* Westport, Conn.: Greenwood Press, 1996.

Mitchell, S., ed. *Victorian Britain: An Encyclopedia.* New York: Garland Press, 1998.

Wohl, A., ed. *The Victorian Family: Structure and Stressed.* New York: St. Martin's Press, 1978.

ISLAMIC WORLD

Among Muslims, family and religion were generally considered the two most important aspects of life. Respecting one's elders, marrying, and procreating were considered religious duty. It was very rare for an individual to choose anything other than family life. Single adults were very rare in this society and considered to not fit into society.

In most Muslim families of the 19th century, several generations lived together under one roof. When a son married, his new wife would live with him in his parents' house. Sometimes as many as 15 people lived in one home, including grandparents, parents, aunts, uncles, and children. When a daughter married, she left her family and moved into the home of her new husband's family. In most cases each subunit, meaning mother, father, and children, shared their own room in the house, although in smaller homes the entire family lived in only one or two rooms. Cousins grew up together like brothers and sisters, and everyone in the household looked out for all of the children.

Wealthier families who could afford to have the women stay at home rather than work often sectioned off an area of the house called the harem, where the women and children lived. In some wealthy families, men who could afford it had more than one wife, although by the 19th century this was becoming less common. The men would generally visit the women in the harem, or the women would go to other quarters of their home to see the men.

In households where there were enough servants to do the errands and chores, the women sometimes were not permitted to leave the house from the time they were married until their death. In some cases women were expected to wear a chador (or *burka*) whenever leaving the house. A chador is a full-length gown that covers all parts of the body except for the hands, feet, and eyes, although some chadors leave the entire face visible. Certain countries, such as Iran and Saudi Arabia, were more conservative with regards to women's roles, and subsequently, women's clothing. In Turkey most women at this time wore European-styled dresses with long sleeves and a scarf, which covered the head. In families who could not afford servants, women either worked outside of the home as household servants for other families or they were responsible for household chores in their own home, such as food preparation, cleaning, and child care.

Parents and other elders arranged most marriages. There was usually some connection between the two families beforehand, and they were usually from the same social class, or strata. The two sets of parents would then meet and negotiate the match. To determine if the match would work, the future in-laws would assess the quality of the future bride or groom. The young couple often had no say in the matter. Most women married in their mid- to late teens and began having children right away. Men were often at least a few years older than their wives, sometimes much older. In some weddings, a gift was given to the family of the bride in exchange for their daughter. This custom, known as *mair,* is considered sanctioned by the Qur'an.

After marriage, it was generally considered very important to have children. In rural areas couples tended to have many children because the children's labor was useful. In cities most couples had fewer children. Male babies were particularly welcomed as heirs to a family's land and material possessions. Boys were also considered preferable because they stayed in their parents' house while a daughter would leave at the time of marriage. The son was also responsible for the protection and support of his parents when they grew old.

Children, regardless of gender, generally had a lot of freedom. Until a girl was around 12 or 13, she wore comfortable clothing and did not need to cover herself the way adult women did. In most families, girls were trained in the kitchen and around the house from a young age. A young girl was most often permitted to play outside along with her brothers; however, few girls attended school of any sort, including religious school. Only among some liberal families were girls allowed to receive an education comparable to that of their brothers.

At this time most male children learned to read the Qur'an, but only a small percentage received thorough education outside of religion. A system of education based on the European model was available to the middle and upper classes in most countries, and in some cases to the lower class as well. Particularly in Egypt the government focused on modernization through education, and schools of this sort were set up throughout the country. Members of the upper class began attending universities in Europe and sometimes even European boarding schools for high school.

Within the family there was generally a strong sense of hierarchy, determined by gender and by age. The eldest generation was expected to receive the most respect, and women were expected to respect their husbands. In many families, children received harsh disciplining, which included beatings and other punishments when they misbehaved.

Divorce was almost unheard of in this society. In the rare case when divorce was practiced, the stigma on divorce brought shame not only to the couple, but also to the entire family. As a result most couples did not consider divorce as an option.

Religion played an important role in the lives of most families at this time. In addition to learning the Qur'an outside of the home, many children were also coached by their male relatives. The men of the household prayed five times a day. The women had a smaller role in the practice of religion. At certain religious ceremonies, women played an important role in the ritual aspects of the practice.

To read about family life in the medieval Islamic World, see the Islamic World entry in the section "Family Life" in chapter 2 ("Domestic Life") in volume 2 of this series; for the Ottoman Empire in the 15th and 16th centuries, see the Ottoman Empire entry in the section "Family Life" in chapter 2 ("Domestic Life") in volume 3 of this series.

~Dana Lightstone

FOR MORE INFORMATION

Khurshid, A. *Family Life in Islam*. Leicester, U.K.: Islamic Foundation, 1974.

————. *Studies in the Family Law of Islam*. Karachi, Pakistan: Chiragh-e-Rah Publications, 1961.

INDIA

During the 19th century, most family life in India revolved around the joint family structure. In other words, when a son married, he remained in his parents' house, and his new bride came to live there as well. When a daughter married she left her parents' home and moved in with her new in-laws. Generally, among the upper and middle class, the mothers-in-law controlled the women's work inside of the house, and the men often earned a living outside of the house. In poorer families the women often also worked outside of the home.

At this time the majority of marriages in India were arranged, meaning that the families of the prospective bride and groom would meet and decide whether or not their children will make a good match. At the meeting the prospective bride might cook to demonstrate that she was well trained for the role of wife. Arrangements for marriage were usually made between two members of the same religion and the same caste community. Among some communities, it was customary for the match to involve families from different villages. There are some communities in southern India that practiced matrilineal cross-cousin marriage, which is when a man married his father's sister's daughter, his mother's brother's daughter, or his own sister's daughter. Marriage with a father's brother's daughter or a mother's sister's daughter was highly disapproved of. The latter was considered to be too closely related for marriage, like a brother or a sister, despite the fact that biologically the two situations are identical. This is partially due to the structure of a traditional joint family, and the fact that the children of two brothers grew up in the same house, like brothers themselves, while the daughter of one's father's sister lived in a separate household.

There were three main forms of gift exchange at the time of marriage. *Dowry* was probably the most common of these. This is when the family of the bride gave money or gifts to the family of the groom at the time of marriage. During the 19th century, dowries were mostly small, often in the form of jewelry or cooking vessels, which the new bride could control in her new family. At this time dowry was mostly practiced only by the upper castes. Dowry was considered a religious as well as a material gift. *Bride-price*, which at this time was practiced among many lower-caste communities, is when the family of the groom gives money or goods to the family of the bride at the time of marriage. *Mair*, which is typically a Muslim practice, is also when the family of the groom gives money to the family of the bride at the time of marriage. It was considered a religious gift sanctioned by the Qur'an.

Because a daughter left her home upon marriage and a son remained in his, among Hindus it was often considered the role of the son to take care of his parents

> **📷 Snapshot**
>
> **The Case for Arranged Marriages**
>
> On one side, new India is saying: "We should have full freedom in the selection of husband and wife; because, the marriage in which are involved the happiness and misery of all our future life, we must have the right to determine, according to our own free will." On the other, old India is dictating: "Marriage is not for sense enjoyment, but to perpetuate the race. This is the Indian conception of marriage. By the producing of children, you are contributing to, and are responsible for, the future good or evil of the society. Hence, society has the right to dictate whom you shall marry and whom you shall not. That form of marriage obtains in society, which is conducive most to its well-being; do you give up your desire of individual pleasure for the good of the many." (From Swami Vivekananda)

in the parents' old age. A son was also responsible for lighting the funeral pyre at the cremation ceremony after his parents' deaths. Daughters were often considered less desirable than sons because they did not provide this type of security for the parents, and among some communities a dowry was exchanged at the time of marriage, creating an economic burden for the family of the girl.

During the 19th century agricultural families typically had about eight children, in part because more children could provide more labor in the fields. Urban families generally had fewer children, but even in the cities large families were common. Within the family all of the adults usually took an equal part in raising all of the children, regardless of relationship. Cousins growing up in the same house were basically considered brothers and sisters.

Among some communities, a woman returned to her parent's house to deliver her baby, and stayed there for a few weeks to rest. Often the parents catered to their daughter's every need by preparing her favorite foods and insisting that she rest. This was often a welcomed vacation from a more difficult lifestyle in the home of her in-laws.

While it was considered acceptable for male widowers to remarry, many high-caste communities scorned the remarriage of a female widow. During the colonial period, widow remarriage, as called for by Hindu tradition, was looked upon with disfavor. At this time many members of communities that practiced widow remarriage in the past adopted the concept that widows are inauspicious and should not remarry. Often widows were expected to take off all of their jewelry and to wear only a plain white *sari*. Along with the idea of an inauspicious widow is the practice of *sati*, or widow immolation. Some Hindus believe that the husband's death is the responsibility of his wife, and to insure the husband a safe passage into the afterlife, the wife should follow him by killing herself. This has never been common, but over the years has gained a lot of attention, originally by the colonial government, as a sign of women's low position in Hindu society.

Among some conservative Muslim families *purdah* (or *parda*) was practiced. This is when the women of a family remain indoors at all times, and they are not to be seen by anyone outside of their family. During the 19th century many high-caste Hindu families also practiced purdah. This began as a way for the family to prove their high position in society by imitating a custom of wealthy Muslim rulers during the Moghul period.

📷 *Snapshot*

Arguing for and against the Tradition of Widow Self-Sacrifice

Advocate: . . . the real reason for our anxiety to persuade widows to follow their husbands, and for our endeavors to burn them pressed down with ropes: viz., that women are by nature of inferior understanding, without resolution, unworthy of trust, subject to passions, and void of virtuous knowledge; they, according to the precepts of the Sastra, are not allowed to marry again after the demise of their husbands, and consequently despair at once of all worldly pleasure; hence it is evident, that death to these unfortunate widows is preferable to existence. . . . Under these circumstances, we instruct them from their early life in the idea of Concremation, holding out to them heavenly enjoyments in company with their husbands, as well as the beatitude of their relations, both by birth and marriage, and their reputation in this world. From this many of them, on the death of their husbands, become desirous of accompanying them; but to remove every chance of their trying to escape from the blazing fire, in burning them we first tie them down to the pile.

Opponent: The reason you have now assigned for burning widows alive is indeed your true motive, as we are well aware; but the faults which you have imputed to women are not planted in their constitution by nature; it would be, therefore, grossly criminal to condemn that sex to death merely from precaution. By ascribing to them all sorts of improper conduct, you have been subjected to constant miseries. (From Rammohun Roy)

Divorce was almost unheard of in 19th-century India. A woman who was mistreated in the home of her in-laws often, upon returning to her parents' home, was urged to go back to her marriage so as not to bring shame to her family. Even in cases of physical abuse some parents would rather their daughter stay in the marriage then to be the subject of disgrace. The stigma on divorce is related to an idea that single women do not fit into the family structure and therefore have no place in mainstream society. This connection demonstrates the importance of family life in 19th-century India.

To read about family life in India in the 20th century, see the India entry in the section "Family Life" in chapter 2 ("Domestic Life") in volume 6 of this series.

~Dana Lightstone

FOR MORE INFORMATION

Blue, G., M. Bunton, and R. Crozier, eds. *Colonialism and the Modern World: Selected Studies.* New York: M. E. Sharpe, 2002.

Mangudkar, M. P., ed. *Dr. Ambedkar and Family Planning.* Poona, India: S. Mangudkar, 1976.

Roy, R. *The English Works of Rammohun Roy,* ed. K. Nag and D. Burman. Calcutta, India: Sadharan Brahmo Samaj, 1945–58.

Swami Vivekananda. *The Complete Works of the Swami Vivekananda.* 7 vols. Almora, India: Advaita Ashrama, 1924–32.

LATIN AMERICA

Family life was one of the most enduring structures, with deep values, in Latin American society. These ties were essential during the colonial occupation and remained intense after the revolutions that established the Latin American countries.

To read about the changes and continuities of Latin American family life into the 20th century, see the Latin America entry in the section "Family Life" in chapter 2 ("Domestic Life") in volume 6 of this series.

Men

DOMESTIC LIFE
|
MEN
|
United States,
1850-1865

United States,
Western Frontier

Victorian England

India

Given the wealth of scholarship on gender written in the last few decades, it is somewhat surprising that there are not more studies of men in the 19th century. Cynics might say that this is so because all of history generally focuses on men: their achievements, their failures, their thoughts, and their aspirations. Be that as it may, sophisticated gender analysis of men in the United States and elsewhere in the world is still a topic open for research. The entries in this section represent some of the current understanding of the daily lives of men in the 19th century. Clearly, soldiering and war were major influences on men's lives, particularly in the United States. But as much as the Civil War was a male experience, it was also a class experience. In fact, all of these articles deal with class, and one ought to pay special attention to the ways in which class and caste shaped the lives of men.

In India, caste structured men's lives. Being born into a low caste meant laboring as a barber, fisherman, servant, butcher, cook, or a profession that dealt with dead humans or animals. There was no chance for improvement or economic betterment. The good jobs were reserved for the higher castes such as the Brahmins.

Given the more fluid class structure of the United States, one might think that class did not play much of a role. Indeed, there were some aspects of the American Civil War that had little to do with class. As the authors point out, the great conflagration killed rather indiscriminately, regardless of class. Moreover, they argue that Johnny Reb and Billy Yank were in fact quite similar in almost every facet of life. They looked about the same. About one-third of the men in the Union army and about one-third of the men in the Confederate army were married. Most of the men came from rural areas. Moreover, all the men in the war showed an unusual willingness to die. At the battle of Cold Harbor, for example, seven thousand men were killed in just 20 minutes of fighting. Yet, despite these similarities, there were important class differences. The majority of the soldiers on both sides were average farmers. In the South, this meant that the elite planters were disproportionately underrepresented in the fight to perpetuate slavery. At the end of the war, this would cost the South dearly as Confederate soldiers quit their ranks and went back to their farms. Class divisions also affected the North as well. Upper-class men could buy their way out of service by purchasing a substitute, most likely from the working classes, to go in his place. The average American man did not have the money to do that and thus had to go to war.

At first glance, the western frontier and England entries do not seem to have much to do with class. The entry on mountain men is a detailed account of how trappers lived on the frontier. But pay close attention to the critics of the mountain men: What do you think it meant that people considered them "outlandish" and belonging to a "motley crew"? Could it be that they were looked down upon as members of the working class? Similarly, think about class in terms of the changing definition of an English gentleman. At the start of the century, the term only applied to the upper crust of society, but at the end of the Victorian era, anyone with the right upbringing, schooling, and habits could become one. And in that change is another question for cross-cultural comparison, namely: What are the ideals behind manhood? Along with the historical concept of class, the following entries provide some answers to that question as well.

DOMESTIC LIFE
|
MEN
|
United States,
1850-1865

United States,
Western Frontier

Victorian England

India

UNITED STATES, 1850–65

The men who opposed one another on the battlefields of the Civil War were more alike than different. Generally, the soldiers on both sides came from similar backgrounds, spoke the same language (although sometimes with widely divergent regional accents), had the same political history, and suffered the same hardships and dangers offered by soldiering. But the *differences* between Billy Yank and Johnny Reb were nonetheless meaningful enough to sustain four years of bloody conflict and may help to explain the relationship between these two enemies.

The great difference between Billy Yank and Johnny Reb seems to have been in their style of fighting—a characteristic noted by many observers. "Three points I noted with regard to our opponents," observed federal captain John W. De Forest. "They aimed better than our men; they covered themselves (in case of need) more carefully and effectively; they could move in a swarm, without much care for alignment and touching elbows. In short, they fought more like [Indians], or like hunters, than we. The result was that they lost fewer men, though they were far inferior in numbers."

Applying statistical analysis to the Civil War is difficult at best and foolhardy at worst, yet the war generated a noble body of data that begs to be interpreted. Still, hard and fast conclusions based solely on these data should be avoided. Facts and figures on the men who faced one another in 1861–62 are largely unreliable when grouped together with those of 1863–64. The volunteers of the earlier period tended to differ significantly from the troops of the later war, which included draftees, substitutes, and bounty claimers. Moreover, it is difficult to ascertain reliable statistics for Southern troops, as they are simply not available for all theaters or periods of the conflict. Similar inherent inaccuracies in the data notwithstanding, some simple facts stand out about the men who fought in the Civil War.

The average age of the men at enlistment in the federal army was just under 26. The Confederates averaged just over 26 years, a remarkable agreement with the federal figure when the traditional view of the rebels is of an army composed of old men and young boys. The height and weight of federal recruits is well documented; they averaged 5 feet, 8 inches and 145 pounds. As 19th-century men were about this size on average, it can be presumed that Confederates were of a similar height and weight. Of the federal soldiers, 29 percent were married when they enlisted, while more than 36 percent of their Southern counterparts seem to have been married men. This may reflect a greater mobilization of the available population in the manpower-hungry South.

While many men wrote regularly to their families and expressed pitiable longing and loneliness for them, a federal officer testified about receiving a letter from a destitute wife, anxious for news of her husband's health. The wife had received no word of him in months and only nine dollars since he had enlisted. She and her children had therefore been evicted from their home. "Here are four pages of pathos that make me want . . . to kick him for not deserving them," wrote the officer. "Apparently a fairly educated and quite worthy girl has married a good-looking youth of inferior nature and breeding who has not the energy to toil effectively for her, nor the affection to endure privations for her sake."

While only 5 percent of all federal soldiers were killed or mortally wounded in combat, almost 12 percent of the Confederates suffered a similar fate. The death rate from all causes, including accidents and sickness, was much higher. Six hundred thirty thousand Americans died in the conflict. As many as 25 percent of all Southern soldiers may have died. The North actually suffered more war deaths, almost three men for every two lost by the South. The Battle at Gettysburg had

Volunteering for war was thought to be a part of manhood. For the first two years of the Civil War, the Union army was made up of volunteer recruits, many of whom signed up at recruiting offices like this one in New York City. *Leslie's Illustrated Magazine*, ca. 1863–64.

the highest number of casualties in the war, but it was one of the largest battles in terms of the number of men engaged. In terms of the number of wounded and killed as a portion of the forces engaged, the bloodiest battle of the war was Shiloh; the bloodiest single day took place at Antietam; and the greatest losses suffered in the shortest time were at Cold Harbor, where up to seven thousand men fell in just twenty minutes. The single worst one-month period for casualties was May 1864. Almost one hundred thousand Americans lost their lives or were wounded in battle in this period, and General Ulysses S. Grant was called a butcher for continuing his campaign. The willingness of Civil War soldiers to face death in a conflict that offered no chance of personal gain remains one of the most remarkable characteristics of that war.

Billy Yank was generally better educated than Johnny Reb, owing, in part, to the greater number of prestigious colleges and universities located in the North and the greater emphasis placed on basic public education at the lower academic levels. While the South had a number of impressive universities, their number was small in proportion to the total in the country; and Southerners were wary of public education. The rate of illiteracy among Civil War soldiers should not be overemphasized, however. Most of the troops could write their names and read from the

Bible. However, the spelling and grammar found in letters, diaries, and journals frequently fell well below schoolroom standards. A typical white regiment on either side of the contest probably had few illiterates, and many units had none at all. The highest rate of illiteracy was found among black units. This is to be expected, as many of these soldiers had been denied an education. Nonetheless, there were many well-educated black freemen in the ranks. Even the totally unlettered soldier could easily impose himself on a literate comrade to read a newspaper out loud or to write a letter home for him.

Most of the men who served were neither professional soldiers nor draftees. The largest percentage were farmers before the war. The Southern soldier was more likely to be an agricultural worker of some type than the immigrant recruit from the more highly industrialized North. The available data makes no distinction between the plantation owner, the small farm owner or his children, and the paid agricultural worker. The data also ignores all those who were too young to have an occupation when they enlisted, such as teenagers and students, many of whom were listed as unskilled workers.

Skilled laborers made up the second largest group of men to serve in either army. These skilled laborers included carpenters and furniture makers, masons, machinists, wheelwrights and cartwrights, barrel makers and coopers, shoemakers and leather workers, smiths of many kinds, and other skilled tradesmen. The particular trade by which an artisan made his living rarely prepared him for military service. Exceptions to this may have been made for artisans such as butchers, blacksmiths, and farriers, who were organized within the service to practice their trades for the army.

Professional and white-collar occupations made up the largest portion of those who served as officers. Professional men included lawyers, physicians, clergymen, engineers, professors, and army and navy officers. The white-collar category is somewhat obscured, as it is distinguished from the professional class more by degree than by any other characteristic, and many men often crossed the line between the two. These included bankers, merchants, manufacturers, journalists, clerks, bookkeepers, and schoolteachers.

Notwithstanding their civilian occupations, each man came with a set of values that mirrored the home and community he left behind. The majority of the recruits in the first year of the war were volunteers, and they pledged themselves to serve for three months, expecting that the first major battle would decide the issue of secession. Nonetheless, their commitment to serve, their personal and economic sacrifice, and the distress experienced by their families and loved ones should not be minimized because of this limited initial commitment. The motivation of most volunteers seems to have been rooted in the compelling and deeply personal forces of duty and honor. In 1861 both of these were closely linked with concepts of masculinity, morality, conscience, and romance.

Among less popular motivations such as adventure, excitement, patriotism, and ideology, Civil War soldiers were also affected by a need to prove their manhood. Southerners tended to be more boastful in this regard than the Yankees. "They were amiable, gentle, and unselfish in disposition, yet were fearless and daring in spirit, and devoted . . . to those bodily exercises that make the strong and vigorous man," noted one observer. Northerners tended to be more circumspect, worrying whether they would pass the test of manhood posed by battle. The psychological importance of passing this test should not be minimized. Particularly among the young volunteers, the experience of battle, "seeing the elephant" in 19th-century terms, was seen as a rite of passage.

If the recruits' own motivations for volunteering, as set down in their personal letters and diaries, are not accepted at face value, it is difficult to rationalize how so many individuals could have been willing to die for a cause or how such massive volunteer armies could have been raised. Nonetheless, it remains an extraordinary fact that during the first year of the war all those who enlisted and fought on one side or the other chose to do so (Volo and Volo, 97–106).

To read about men's roles in the United States in the 20th century, see the United States entry in the section "Men" in chapter 2 ("Domestic Life") in volume 6 of this series.

FOR MORE INFORMATION

McPherson, J. M. *For Cause and Comrades: Why Men Fought in the Civil War*. New York: Oxford University Press, 1997.

Paludan, P. S. *A People's Contest: The Union and Civil War, 1861–1865*. New York: Harper & Row, 1988.

Thomas, E. M. *The Confederate Nation: 1861–1865*. New York: Harper & Row, 1979.

Volo, D. D., and J. M. Volo. *Daily Life in Civil War America*. Westport, Conn.: Greenwood Press, 1998.

DOMESTIC LIFE

MEN

United States,
1850-1865

United States,
Western Frontier

Victorian England

India

UNITED STATES, WESTERN FRONTIER

On the American Western frontier, men were seemingly defined by their work. Among the most common workers in the West was the mountain trapper. There were three main categories of trappers in the Rocky Mountain system: the *engagés*, supplied and salaried by the companies whose furs were the property of the company; the *skin trappers*, outfitted by the company on credit, who paid off their debt at the end of the season and kept whatever balance there was for themselves; and the *free trappers*, who worked alone or in small groups, owed no allegiance to any particular company, and sold their furs to the highest bidder. Collectively they constitute the mountain man, a unique American type epitomized for many by Kit Carson, Tom Fitzpatrick, and Jim Bridger. The mountain man was "the proudest of all the titles worn by the Americans who lived their lives out beyond the settlements."

Not everyone so thoroughly admired the mountain man. David J. Wishart, an economic historian writing on the fur trade, identifies three stereotypes of the mountain man that, like all stereotypes, have some basis in truth. The trapper is portrayed by some as an "epic hero who confronted and partially tamed the wilderness." This is the type DeVoto calls the Long Hunter, "the man who knew the wilderness and . . . held the admiration of the settlements," the man skilled in "woodcraft, forest craft, and river craft," the man "in flight from the sound of an axe . . . [living] under a doom which he himself created, but westward he went free." This is the man captured by James Fenimore Cooper as Natty Bumppo.

The trapper has also been seen as an outsider, a renegade, a "daring but degraded character who was escaping the strictures of a civilized society." James Clyman describes searching for *engagés* in "grog shops and other sinks of degradation." The fact that some *engagés* were thieves is revealed in a story he tells. One day when their keelboat was drawn up near a settlement, the men went out hunting and came back with "plenty of game Eggs Fowls Turkeys and what not." They built a fire ashore, dressed, cooked and ate their dinner, and then burned the leftovers. The next morning settlers arrived at the keelboat, looking for their poultry. Clyman gave them permission to search the boat, but nothing was found. Later in the day when the wind rose enough to be useful in propelling the boat, the sails were ordered unfurled and "out dropped pigs and poultry in abundance. A man was ordered to Jump in the Skiff and pick up the pigs and poultry."

There is further evidence of the mountain man as socially dysfunctional. One of the later, less well known mountain men was described as "nutty as a pet coon; [he] ate dirt and it killed him." One trader, Edwin Denig, saw trappers as a "desperate set of men more outlandish and more brutal than the traders and more than half-Indian in appearance and habits."

Peter Skene Ogden, a trader for the Hudson's Bay Company, had a low opinion of Americans in the field; his superior, George Simpson, wrote that they were

The mountain man was an icon of the American West. Denver Public Library, Western History Collection, Frederick Remington, call number F-13290.

generally speaking people of the worst character, runaways from Jails, and outcasts from Society, who take all their bad qualities along with them: this "motley crew" acknowledge no master, will conform to no rules or regulations, and are never on their guard so that they are frequently cut off and their camps plundered. When they fall in with friendly Indians, their conduct is so indiscreet that they scarcely ever fail to make enemies of them, and it is a well known fact, that War parties frequently pass our Camps without offering the least annoyance; yet will haunt and watch an American camp, for Days and Weeks, until a favorable opportunity occurs to make an attack.

Even Francis Parkman, who came to consider Henry Chatillon not only the mountain man par excellence but also a friend, called the profession in general "the half savage men who spend their lives in trapping among the Rocky Mountains."

The historian William H. Goetzmann has offered another category for the mountain man: a "Jacksonian man," an "expectant capitalist" like most other Americans of that time. He argues that the primary motive for participating in the fur trade was to accumulate capital rapidly; such capital could then be invested in other ventures. Ashley, Sublette, and Campbell are illustrative of such entrepreneurial behavior, with subsequent ventures into banking, politics, coal mining, and stock breeding.

Finally, Bernard DeVoto could see the mountain man as simultaneous victim and victimizer. He argues as follows:

They were agents of as ruthless a commerce as any in human history; they were its exploited agents. The companies hired them—or traded with the highest order of them, the free trappers . . . on terms of the companies' making, paid them off in the companies' goods, valued at the companies' prices deep in the mountains. They worked in a peonage like the greasers they despised, the freed Negroes of the South, or the sharecroppers of our day. The companies outfitted them and sent them out to lose their traps, their horses, and frequently their scalps—to come back broke and go deeper into debt for next year's outfit. Their trade capitalized starvation, was known to practice land piracy, and at need incited Indians against competitors. It made war on Indians who traded with competitors and debauched the rest with the raw alcohol that was called whiskey in the mountains. . . . The Indians went down before tin tubs curved to fit a packsaddle and filled with alcohol at fifty cents a gallon. . . . And, as they went down, took with them through the hole in the earth the scalps of mountain men.

There is no single description that fits all mountain men. They were of many nations. Aside from Americans (mostly from the Midwest and the upper South), Osborne Russell met Irish, French, Portuguese, and Canadian trappers. Some, like Jim Bridger, were illiterate, though that did not mean barbaric. During the winter of 1863–64 at Fort Laramie, Bridger asked an officer what was the best book ever written. Learning it was Shakespeare, Bridger went to the main emigrant road, stopped a wagon train, and paid for a volume of Shakespeare with a yoke of oxen. He then hired a German boy at $40 per month to read to him. Others, like Charles Larpenteur and Osborne Russell, were literate, leaving their journals as vivid first-hand accounts of the life of the mountain men.

Jim Bridger hired a German boy at $40 per month to read Shakespeare to him.

Most Rocky Mountain trapping parties were small, ranging from six to eight men. By experience, they had learned that a party large enough to defend itself against hostile Indians was too large to trap beaver successfully. Thus, each individual had to learn a wide variety of skills if he was to survive. He had to be a hunter, wrangler, furrier, freighter, tanner, cordwainer, smith, gun maker, dowser, and merchant. The result was a high-level integration of faculties. The mountain man had mastered his conditions—how well was apparent as soon as soldiers, gold seekers, or emigrants came into his country and suffered where he had lived comfortably and died where he had been in no danger.

More specifically, the mountain man had to know the beaver. The beaver is a strict monogamist, the family unit being a colony consisting of a male and a female and their young. Rocky Mountain beaver mate in February and have two to four cubs in late May or early June. The beaver reaches physical maturity—a weight of 30 to 60 pounds—at about two and a half years of age. When the cubs are fully grown, they are driven from their parents' lodge to establish their own colony. Beaver prefer sluggish streams and small lakes but avoid areas that are likely to flood as well as rapid streams that might wash out their homes. Aspen, the preferred food of the beaver, rarely grows more than 100 feet from water; thus, the beaver need not wander far from their home pond. In summer the beaver also eat sedge, cattail roots, and water lilies. Where such conditions prevail, the beaver construct either a lodge of branches plastered with mud or a den hollowed out of the riverbank. One of the best trapping grounds was in Blackfoot country at the three forks of the Missouri. Absaroka, the land of the Crows in the valleys of the Bighorn, Rosebud, Powder, and Tongue rivers, were also prime trapping country.

The very traits of the beaver led to its depletion. Because the pelt demanded by European markets was not the dark brown outer fur but rather the barbed, fibrous under hair, the prime trapping season was spring, although fall was also busy. However, during the summer the beaver pelt was too thin. Thus, some of the heaviest trapping was done during mating and whelping seasons. Moreover, the sedentary nature of the beaver made them relatively easy to catch; they were so plentiful in Absaroka that Indians reportedly could kill them with clubs. To this scene the trapper brought the improved technology of the steel trap.

Because of the beaver's nocturnal habits, traps were usually placed at sunset. Joe Meek describes the process:

[The trapper] has an ordinary trap weighing five pounds, attached to a chain five feet long, with a swivel and ring at the end, which plays round what is called the float, a dry stick of wood, about six feet long. The trapper wades out into the stream, which is shallow, and cuts with his knife a bed for the trap, five or six inches under water. He then takes the float out the whole length of the chain in the direction of the centre of the stream, and drives it into the mud, so fast that the beaver cannot draw it out; at the same time tying the other end by a thong to the bank. A small stick or twig, dipped in musk or castor, serves as bait, and is placed so as to hang directly above the trap, which is now set. The trapper then throws water plentifully over the adjacent bank to conceal any footprints or scent by which the beaver would be alarmed, and going to some distance wades out of the stream.

The beaver would be attracted to the castoreum, and the trap would snap shut on its foot. Unless it chewed off its foot it would drown, weighted down by the trap. Peter Skene Ogden noted in his journal for June 4, 1829, "Our traps have given us but five beaver, and four of this number were with only three feet each, having been already taken in the traps and made their escape."

After its capture, the beaver was skinned immediately and along with the perineal glands, which yield the castoreum, and the tail, which was considered a delicacy, the pelt was carried back to the main camp. There the camp keepers performed the relatively simple task of processing the pelt. First, the flesh side of the skin was scraped clean. Second, the skin was stretched on willow hoops and dried in the sun for a day. And third, the pelts were folded, fur inward, marked with the company's insignia, and compacted into bundles of 60 to 80 skins in preparation for transportation. The rookie had to learn all of this before he earned the title of mountain man (Jones, 27–34).

To read about men's roles on the colonial frontier of North America, see the Colonial Frontier and New England entries in the section "Men and Women" in chapter 2 ("Domestic Life") in volume 4 of this series.

FOR MORE INFORMATION

Hafen, L. R. *The Mountain Men and the Fur Trade of the Far West.* Vols. 2, 5, 6, 8, and 9. Glendale, Calif.: Arthur H. Clark, 1972.

Holliday, J. S. *The World Rushed In: The California Gold Rush Experience*. New York: Simon & Schuster, 1981.

Jones, M. E. *Daily Life on the Nineteenth Century American Frontier*. Westport, Conn.: Greenwood Press, 1998.

Mountain Men and the Fur Trade. <http://www.xmission.com/~drudy/amm.html/>.

Savage, William A. Jr. *Cowboy Life: Reconstructing an American Myth*. Norman: University of Oklahoma Press, 1975.

DOMESTIC LIFE
|
MEN
|
United States,
1850-1865

United States,
Western Frontier

Victorian England

India

VICTORIAN ENGLAND

The typical gentleman was the masculine equivalent of the ideal woman. The term's meaning changed during the period. In earlier times, the gentry was clearly defined as a class: they were landowners, and the feudal origins of landed tenure created a warrior caste governed by manly ideals of chivalry, bravery, and loyalty.

By the 19th century, people generally understood that a man from the landed classes was a gentleman by birth. In addition, Church clergy, barristers, members of Parliament, and military officers were gentlemen owing to their profession. Because patronage and personal contacts were needed to enter the professions, a man's gentlemanly standing was, in part, guaranteed by his sponsors.

However, birth was not the whole story. A man of good family would have a better opportunity to acquire the manners and education that marked his gentlemanly status. Nevertheless, even an aristocrat would no longer be considered a gentleman if his public behavior was outrageously coarse or if he was dishonorable in his dealings with members of his own class. Gentlemanly conduct was an obligation—but not necessarily a natural inheritance—for men of a certain social rank.

The idea that being a gentleman did not depend wholly on birth but also required certain values, standards, and modes of behavior helped to make society in England less rigidly stratified than in some European countries. It combined the aristocracy and upper-middle class into a single ruling elite and, at least to a limited degree, opened the way to class mobility.

By 1862, a writer in *Cornhill Magazine* reported that there was "a constantly increasing disposition to insist more upon the moral and less upon the social element of the word." Birth mattered less and less. People used the word *gentlemanly* to describe a man's ethics and behavior, regardless of his class or profession.

However, polished bearing and carefully correct dress did not make a man a gentleman. "Foppishness" and exaggeratedly genteel manners were despised. The concept of disinterestedness was the core definition of a gentleman, as defined by the high Victorian society. A gentleman was intellectually and morally independent. He cared about something other than money. He did the right thing without thinking about consequences. As a landowner, a member of Parliament, a civil servant, or a rural magistrate, he put the good of the community above any personal self-interest.

Owning a landed estate with a steady income made it possible to live a gentlemanly life of disinterested public service. However, a man could be a gentleman even though he worked for his money. Gentlemanly disinterestedness provided a basis for professional ethics. A clergyman should make no selfish use of information he discovered through his pastoral duties. A doctor should not prescribe useless and expensive drugs made by a company he owned. Teachers should not offer to tutor some students for extra money and then base examinations on material covered only in the private sessions.

It was for ethical reasons that the question of whether a businessman could be a gentleman loomed so large—not because working for a living lowered a man's rank, but because business transactions seemed to be motivated primarily for self-interest. The business of business was to make money; the presumed goal in gentlemanly professions was to earn enough to support one's family while performing an honorable public service.

By the last quarter of the century, the definition shifted once more. In the minds of many people, any boy who had gone to a public school was a gentleman unless his personal behavior was clearly dishonorable. Public-school boys learned to accept hardship without complaining and to take their place in a hierarchical society. Older boys supervised and disciplined the younger boys; they learned to give orders in a way that would not arouse resentment and to

> ### 📷 Snapshot
>
> **The Definition of a Victorian English Gentleman, 1860s**
>
> Hence it is that it is almost a definition of a gentleman to say he is one who never inflicts pain. . . . He has his eyes on all his company; he is tender towards the bashful, gentle towards the distant, and merciful towards the absurd; he can recollect to whom he is speaking, he guards against unseasonable allusions, or topics which may irritate; he is seldom prominent in conversation, and never wearisome. He makes light of favours while he does them, and seems to be receiving when he is conferring. He never speaks of himself except when compelled, never defends himself by a mere retort, he has no ears for slander or gossip. . . . He is never mean or little in his disputes, never takes unfair advantage, never mistakes personalities or sharp sayings for arguments, or insinuates evil which he dare not say out. From a long-sighted prudence, he observes the maxim of the ancient sage, that we should ever conduct ourselves towards our enemy as if he were one day to be our friend. He has too much good sense to be affronted at insults, he is too well employed to remember injuries, and too indolent to bear malice. He is patient, forbearing, and resigned, on philosophical principles; he submits to pain, because it is inevitable, to bereavement, because it is irreparable, and to death, because it is his destiny.
>
> ~[See John Henry Newman, *The Idea of a University,* (1865) as quoted in Mitchell, 270.]

internalize a sense of responsibility. Public schools created English gentlemen to enter Parliament, become military officers, rule the empire—and, by the end of the century, to enter business in a gentlemanly fashion.

Gentlemanly behavior was governed by a strict unwritten code of what was *done* and *not done*. It was clearly *not done* to cheat at cards or question the honesty of another gentleman. A gentleman was courteous, considerate, and socially at ease. He behaved honorably toward all women. He paid his gambling debts and kept his word—a verbal promise was more important than a handshake, and a written contract seemed faintly disreputable, as if it suggested that a gentleman's word could not be trusted.

A gentleman had to accept and exercise leadership. He lived up to his own standards; as a businessman or a professional, he was honorable, dependable, and ethical. He did what was required without supervision—he did not become a clock-watcher, but neither did he work excessively long hours just to make more money. Public-school boys trained one another in the emotional reserve that came to be called the "stiff upper lip." A gentleman exhibited stoic self-control. He did not call attention to his own cleverness, or visibly work harder than others, or show too much enthusiasm. He had been schooled in loyalty, team spirit, courage, and fair play; and he was motivated by an enormous fear of giving way or visibly failing to live up to his standards and responsibilities (Mitchell, *Daily Life*, 269–71).

To read about men's roles in 18th-century England, see the England entry in the section "Men and Women" in chapter 2 ("Domestic Life") in volume 4 of this series.

FOR MORE INFORMATION

Mason, P. *The English Gentleman: The Rise and Fall of an Ideal.* New York: Morrow, 1982.
Mitchell, S. *Daily Life in Victorian England.* Westport, Conn.: Greenwood Press, 1996.
Mitchell, S., ed. *Victorian Britain: An Encyclopedia.* New York: Garland Press, 1998.

DOMESTIC LIFE
|
MEN
|
United States,
1850-1865

United States,
Western Frontier

Victorian England

India

INDIA

In 19th-century India, most men were responsible for contributing to the family's income. Due to the structure of a joint family, in many cases several men contributed to this income. In other families not all of the men worked for one reason or another, and those who did bring home cash had an added responsibility of a large number of family members relying solely on their earnings. Aside from the responsibility of feeding the family, a son had a special responsibility to his parents. It was his role to make sure that his parents were taken care of in their old age. Furthermore, among most Hindus, it is the responsibility of the eldest son to light the funeral pyre of his parents at their cremations.

In terms of labor, most men followed in the profession of their family. According to the Hindu caste system, different castes or families are expected to fulfill their respective role in society. At this time many non-Hindus in India also followed these social conventions.

It was common for many members of a particular caste community to live in a particular area of town. For example, in many towns the area around the river was inhabited mainly by *dobhiwallas,* who were washer men. It was common for people to give their clothes to a dobiwalla, whose job was to wash clothes. The dobiwalla would then return the clean clothes to their owner.

Dobiwallas are regarded as *low caste,* meaning that they are considered lower down on the caste hierarchy. Other low-caste professions include barbers, fishermen, household servants, butchers, cooks, and those professions that deal with dead humans or animals. Higher-caste professions include merchants, militia, and teachers—the latter two were composed entirely of the Brahmin or highest caste.

Brahmin men were responsible for leading religious ceremonies. Therefore, they had to be trained in the rituals and conventions of Hinduism. Brahmin men were expected to wear the sacred thread over their left shoulder to signify their role in society.

During the 19th century an increasing number of Indian men began working in government or other white-collar jobs. The British colonial government recognized the caste hierarchy in India and hired members of the higher castes to fill higher jobs in the government. Not only did these men tend to have more education, but the English also realized that members of the higher castes were more likely to receive the respect of their community. This created a whole new class of Indians who adopted the language, dress, and much of the mindset of the English.

In many professions, young boys began working alongside their fathers at a young age. A boy from a higher caste was more likely to be in school, but the son of a craftsman, farmer, or laborer could provide valuable assistance to his family.

When a young man reached marriageable age, he was expected to take a bride. At this time most marriages in India were prearranged. The parents of the young man and the parents of the prospective bride would meet to discuss the details and try to arrange an appropriate match, largely on the basis of the bride and groom's horoscopes. In some cases, a dowry was exchanged, while in other marriages the groom's family gave gifts to the family of the bride. The young man usually had little say in the decisions regarding to whom and when he married and was often forced to marry against his will. The couple was expected to produce a child soon after the marriage.

Within households, men had little responsibility other than to deliver their earnings. In general, women were responsible for most of the household work, including food preparation, child rearing, and keeping the home environment safe and healthy for the rest of the family, and women often controlled the household budget as well.

> ### 📷 *Snapshot*
>
> **The Hindu Caste System in India**
>
> There can be no denying the fact that the rigidity of the Hindu caste system is the bane of Hindu society. It is a great barrier in the way of the social and national progress of the Hindus. It confronts them at every step and slackens the speed with which, otherwise, the nation would climb up to the heights of national solidarity. The condition of the "low" castes, sometimes described as "untouchables," at other times as the "depressed classes," is nothing short of disgraceful. It is a disgrace to our humanity, our sense of justice, and our feeling of social affinity. It is useless to hope for any solidarity so long as the depressed classes continue to be so low in the social scale as they are. The intellectual and moral status of the community as a whole cannot be appreciably raised without the cooperation of *all* the classes forming the community. So long then, as there are classes amongst us who are untouchable by the so-called superior classes, because of their having been born of certain parents, the moral and intellectual elevation of the community as a whole can only proceed by slow, very slow, degrees. The condition of the depressed classes is a standing blot on our social organization, and we must remove that blot if we are really desirous of securing the efficiency of our social organism. (Lala Lajput Rai)

The men of the household were usually the first ones to eat at mealtime, followed by the children, then the women. It was considered most important that the men get enough to eat because they were the ones who often had important jobs to do outside of the house.

Upon the death of his father, the eldest son would inherit the family's home and assume the role of patriarch. In many ways, this meant that he was the highest respected member of the household, although the eldest woman also held a special position. If there was more than one son, the land or house might be divided among them. Except in the southern state of Kerala, where a matrilineal system was in use, Indian women were generally not entitled to inherit property.

Elderly men, who no longer had the strength to work in the fields, often congregated together at a common meeting place in the village or urban neighborhood and drank tea, smoked tobacco, and socialized. Tobacco was smoked either from a *bidi*, which is a cigarette made from dried leaf, or from a *hukka*, or water pipe.

Paan, made from *betal*, a mildly addictive and intoxicating nut, was common in most parts of India. It was often sold at street stands, and often eaten after a meal.

It is a mild digestive. There are many varieties of paan, some sweet, others not, which vary from region to region. The betal nut and the other ingredients, which include a variety of spices and condiments (opium is sometimes in paan), are wrapped in an edible leaf. Then the entire thing is popped into ones mouth and chewed and swallowed. Paan was consumed mainly by men but rarely by women.

Men were also the main consumers of alcohol. As it is not considered acceptable by most Hindus and Muslims, there was a great social stigma attached to consumption of alcohol. Local brews such as *arak,* which is made from fermented rice, were produced in villages. Those who consumed this forbidden drink were considered by many to be impure. This sort of attitude is thought to have contributed to high levels of alcoholism among those who did drink.

To read about men's roles in India in the 20th century, see the India entry in the section "Men" in chapter 2 ("Domestic Life") in volume 6 of this series.

~*Dana Lightstone*

FOR MORE INFORMATION

Bickman, J. W., ed. *The Changing Division of Labor in South Asia: Women and Men in India's Society, Economy, and Politics.* New Delhi: Manohar Press, 1987.

Lutz, L. *Destined for Royalty: A Brahmin Priest's Search for Truth.* Pasadena, Calif.: William Carey Library, 1985.

Rai, L. L. *Writings and Speeches.* 2 vols. New Delhi, India: University Publishers, 1966.

LATIN AMERICA

Since the time of European colonization of the Americas in the 15th century, the roles of Latin American men had been centered around the idea that they dominated their households, both physically and financially.

To read more about Latin American men's role and their transition in the 20th century, see the Latin America entry in the section "Men" in chapter 2 ("Domestic Life") in volume 6 of this series.

DOMESTIC LIFE
|
WOMEN
|
United States,
1850-1865

United States,
Western Frontier

Victorian England

India

Latin America

Women

Comparing the entries in this section, one quickly realizes that women's lives in the 19th century were a mixture of change and continuity. But which historical force was stronger? Certainly we can find evidence of women playing the traditional roles of housewife and mother. On the American frontier, for example, women were in charge of the homestead, performing the usual, unceasing labors. As frontier songs illustrate, other than sustenance, rewards for daily toils were slim. Similarly, among the upper- and middle-class English, much attention was paid to the proper Victorian woman who also ruled the home. And yet, a close evaluation of these entries shows a dramatic transformation in women's lives.

Decades before the American Civil War, an increasing number of women were becoming active in politics. Although they lacked the right to vote, women nonetheless helped to transform the United States through their activities in the abolition movement and its direct off-shoot—the feminist movement. One interesting theme among several of these entries is the ways in which women attained political and social power. During the Civil War era, women's ability to gain the moral high ground as well as their antislavery rhetoric enabled such radical reformers as Angelina and Sarah Grimké to rise to the top of the abolitionist cause.

In Latin America, the traditions of patriarchy continued to dominate society, and women were largely denied political rights and economic opportunity. However, by the end of the 19th century, small groups of educated, middle-class women in many Latin American countries began to demand political and legal equality by organizing themselves into groups of various kinds. Although they achieved little before 1900, they established a tradition of political activism that won the rights they sought in the 20th century.

On the American frontier, women were able to achieve high social status because of a different reason: there were not many of them. One statistic must stand for many. In 1850, the San Francisco harbormaster counted more than 35,000 men entering the city and only 2,400 women. As a result, women commanded respect, even the so-called "fallen sisters," who incidentally made a good living in the West. In general, a woman could make money in the West by becoming a cook, a washwoman, or a landlord. The experience of women in frontier towns and cities illustrates a general historical truth of that era, which is that it was the suppliers of goods and services that reaped the bonanza of the West. And women were at the center of it.

Women were also at the center of change in India. Under British colonial rule, middle-class Indians with the support of British and American missionaries led movements to change traditional social customs. In particular, there were attempts to end the practice of widow immolation, or *sati*, to remove the ban on widow remarriage, and to foster education among girls and young women. All of these reform campaigns were predicated upon the desire of some Indians to become more like the British.

But note that the British too were changing. Advice manuals from the time presented a strict (if not contradictory) code for proper womanhood. Women were to rule the home and yet be obedient and dependent on their husbands. Assumed in this was the expectation that women were to marry, have children, and please their family while suppressing their own desires. This ideal of the quiet, submissive, prudish Victorian lady was challenged by the *new woman*, who lived alone, enjoyed sports, and even dared to travel without a chaperone. How does this strong, independent woman compare with her American and Indian counterparts? At least one thing is for certain: they all were caught up in social and political movements that would later transform women's social position and daily lives in the 20th century.

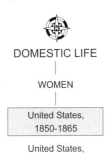

DOMESTIC LIFE

|

WOMEN

|

United States,
1850-1865

United States,
Western Frontier

Victorian England

India

Latin America

UNITED STATES, 1850–65

Women were an integral part of the Civil War era. Before the war, many were active abolitionists who also pursued women's rights. Like many of the female radicals of the period, Abby K. Foster was an abolitionist as well as a women's rights activist. Originally from a Quaker background, she began lecturing for abolition in 1837. She conducted her campaign with Angelina Grimké, reportedly becoming the first woman in the United States to address a mixed audience in public. For this she was denounced by the clergy, who considered her a menace to public morals, and her speeches were periodically broken up by mob violence. Her presence as a delegate to the World Antislavery Conference in London in 1840 caused serious disturbances, as women delegates were refused recognition. As a pioneer feminist and a leader of the radical abolitionists, she was a well-known figure in the North and a target for hatred in the South.

Angelina and Sarah Grimké were sisters born to a slave-owning family in South Carolina. Upon their father's death, the young sisters were able to persuade their mother to apportion the family slaves to them as a share of their family estate, upon which they freed them at once. Originally members of the Episcopal Church, they were attracted to the Quaker sect by friends who lived in Philadelphia, but they found that they lacked the self-restraint to curb their unequivocal hatred of slave owners. In 1836, Angelina wrote *Appeal to the Christian Women of the South*, which urged Southern women to speak and act out against slavery. In South Carolina the 66-page pamphlet was confiscated and burned by postmasters, and the author was threatened with imprisonment if she returned to the state. Angelina followed this work in 1837 with *Appeal to the Women of the Nominally Free States* in which she strongly insisted that the women residing in free states were equally guilty for the national shame of continued slavery.

Sarah and Angelina began their careers by addressing small groups of women on both feminist and antislavery topics and ultimately entered the lecture circuit. So great was the opposition to women speaking in public that the sisters found that they were spending as much time defending their feminism as preaching their antislavery ideals. John Greenleaf Whittier came to their defense, referring to them as "Carolina's high souled daughters" in his writings; but, at the same time, he privately suggested that they limit their efforts to the cause of emancipation.

The efforts of the sisters were important in the development of both the feminist and abolitionist causes, and it is difficult to determine to which cause they were most dedicated. Angelina confirmed her position in the antislavery community when she married abolition activist and author Theodore D. Weld in 1838. As a youth, Sarah Grimké found that it was impossible for her to study law because she was a woman. From this situation flowed her natural devotion to the cause of women's rights. Sarah wrote *Letters on the Equality of the Sexes and the Condition of Women* in the year of her sister's marriage. Her correspondence with her brother-in-law is a source of information about the cause of abolition in this period. As Southern advocates of radical abolition and feminism, the Grimké sisters were particularly detested by traditionally-minded Southern women, who took pains to target them in their journals and letters.

Activists were not the only targets of Southern ire. An outspoken Southern woman listed a number of pro-abolitionists among the day's popular writers and politicians in the following diatribe: "On one side Mrs. Stowe, Greeley, Thoreau, Emerson, Sumner, in nice New England Homes—clean, clear, sweet-smelling—shut up in libraries, writing books which ease their hearts of their bitterness to us, or editing newspapers—all of which pays better than anything else in the world." The same woman called antislavery "the cheapest philanthropy trade in the world" and castigated the abolitionists for "setting John Brown to come down here and cut our throats in Christ's name."

Contrary to the common Southern perceptions of abolitionists—preaching and teaching "hate as a gospel and the sacred duty of murder and insurrection"—the use of violence to attain emancipation never had a great appeal to the mass of people in the North, and the more provocative tactics and strategies of the radicals rarely had any effect outside of New England. Antislavery, as a movement, was far too decentralized and subject to too many local variations to march in lockstep behind the radicals.

During the Civil War, women were active in all efforts to improve the morality of the troops. And for the first time, the female presence within the army was not solely represented by traditional camp followers. While it has been proven that a substantial number of women was able to pass themselves off as men and serve in the armed forces, their number was too small to effect any advantage or disadvantage to the

---

📷 Snapshot

Sojourner Truth Proclaims: "Ain't I a Woman?", 1851

Speech Delivered 1851, Women's Convention, Akron, Ohio:

Well, children, where there is so much racket there must be something out of kilter. I think that 'twixt the negroes of the South and the women at the North, all talking about rights, the white men will be in a fix pretty soon. But what's all this here talking about?

That man over there says that women need to be helped into carriages, and lifted over ditches, and to have the best place everywhere. Nobody ever helps me into carriages, or over mud-puddles, or gives me any best place! And ain't I a woman? Look at me! Look at my arm! I have ploughed and planted, and gathered into barns, and no man could head me! And ain't I a woman? I could work as much and eat as much as a man—when I could get it—and bear the lash as well! And ain't I a woman? I have borne thirteen children, and seen most all sold off to slavery, and when I cried out with my mother's grief, none but Jesus heard me! And ain't I a woman?

~[See Modern History Sourcebook, <http://www.fordham.edu/halsall/mod/sojtruth-woman.html>.]

---

troops. Most women chose to act in less startling ways to support the war effort. A number of war-related jobs was filled by women. Females served as clerks in the clothing branch of the Quartermaster's department and filled the ammunition cartridges and artillery shells with powder at the armories, laboring at this dangerous and exacting task for low wages. Both sides utilized women in these capacities.

A number of wives and female relatives traveled with the army to sew, nurse, and wash clothes. Federal captain John W. De Forest was constantly plagued by his wife's requests to join him on the field, and many of his responses to her were phrased in such a way as to discourage her gently. Confederate general John B. Gordon had his beautiful young wife with him at all times on campaign. Fanny Gordon "turned her two children, aged four and six, over to Gordon's mother, climbed into a buggy, and with one of the family slaves driving she followed her man." Generals John C. Breckinridge and Thomas Rosser brought their wives along as well when things were quiet—much to the chagrin of their superior, General Jubal Early, who was driven to distraction by women on campaign. But Mrs. Gordon was there *all the time*, and Early was overheard to say, "I wish the Yankees would capture Mrs. Gordon and hold her till this war is over."

Major General Benjamin Butler, in charge of the occupied city of New Orleans, may have made the most insulting gesture of the entire war with regard to women. He declared that since federal officers had been "subjected to repeated insults from the women" of that city, any lady would, upon repetition of the offense, "be regarded and held liable to be treated as a woman of the town plying her vocation." The order was severely protested in the South and in Europe. Nonetheless, prostitutes and women of loose morals were much in evidence in the Army of the Potomac under General Joseph Hooker. Historians disagree on the etymology of the term *hooker*, which may or may not proceed from this circumstance as a synonym for prostitute. Nonetheless, a righteous general officer from among the federal forces noted, "The condition of morals among officers who [find] congenial companionship in the society of such women is apparent and needs no coloring from pen or pencil."

Women's fashions from *Godey's Ladies Magazine* from the spring of 1861. Dresses emphasized a narrow waist using tight undergarments and wide shoulders.

On the war's home front, women supported the troops through a variety of activities. Women engaged in needlework crafts including tatting, knitting, crocheting, and netting. Ladies' magazines carried a profusion of patterns for trims, fashion accessories, and small household items that could be made using these handicrafts. Patchwork quilts were another popular activity. Women worked on quilts alone for their families and in group-quilting bees as community activities. Prior to the war, groups of Northern women used their quilting talents to raise money for the cause of abolition. They renamed some traditional patchwork patterns to draw attention to the cause. Job's Tears became known as Slave Chain. Jacob's Ladder became Underground Railway. North Star was so named after the star that guided runaway slaves to freedom. Once the war commenced, Northern women mobilized relief efforts and began to produce quilts to be sent to soldiers in need. U.S. Sanitary Commission records show that an estimated 250,000 quilts were distributed during the war. In Hartford, Connecticut, alone 5,459 quilts were collected during 1864.

Many of the quilts were more utilitarian than those their makers had created in the past, but it is likely that they were made with no less love. One note pinned to a quilt read: "My son is in the army. Whoever is made warm by this quilt, which I have worked on for six days and most of six nights, let him remember his mother's love." Confederate women also made quilts for their soldiers. The Southern blockade, however, severely limited the availability of the requisite materials. Confederate quilts produced during the war were made from whatever makeshift materials were available, including old sheets stuffed with newspaper (Volo and Volo, 86–87, 170, 221–22).

To read about women's roles in the United States in the 20th century, see the United States entries in the section "Women" in chapter 2 ("Domestic Life") in volume 6 of this series.

FOR MORE INFORMATION

Faust, D. G. *Mothers of Invention: Women of the Slaveholding South in the American Civil War.* Charlotte: University of North Carolina Press, 1996.

Murray, J. H. *Strong-Minded Women and Other Lost Voices from Nineteenth-Century England.* New York: Pantheon Books, 1982.

Volo, D. D., and J. M. Volo. *Daily Life in Civil War America.* Westport, Conn.: Greenwood Press, 1998.

Women and Social Movements in the United States, <http://womhist.binghamton.edu/links/resource.htm>.

UNITED STATES, WESTERN FRONTIER

The American West suffered from a sexual imbalance. The harbormaster at San Francisco in 1850 counted 35,333 men arriving as opposed to 1,248 women. For the overland immigrants that year, the count at Fort Laramie was 39,560 men; 2,421 women; and 609 children. Most women arriving by sea stayed in San Francisco or settled in Sacramento; few went to the mines. In September 1849, a miner in Yuba City reported glumly that in the town of 2,000 there were only about a dozen women. Sarah Royce reported that the first time she attended church in San Francisco, there were only six or eight women in the whole congregation. At church—and in the mining camps where she and her husband lived for several months—she was treated with extreme courtesy. On one occasion, men were cutting wood on the mountain above her home when she heard one warn, "Look out not to let any sticks roll that way, there's a woman and child in that tent." On another occasion, a young miner stopped at her tent on his way to work and asked if he could speak to her daughter Mary, "about the size of a little sister I left at home." Many women who were widowed on the overland trip but had continued on had multiple proposals of marriage soon after their arrival. John Banks, reflecting on this scarcity of women, remembered the early myth: "The Amazons got along well enough without men; Californians are trying the opposite experiment. For my part, I pronounce it a complete failure."

Although respectable women were treated with respect, a good living could be made by their fallen sisters. Like so many other commodities in California, their value reflected economic laws of supply and demand. When there were few other women, prostitutes were in demand. Some writers reflected outrage, but their censure in no way affected the business. A shocked John Banks, reflecting on the moral decadence of miners "whose only love is gold," forecast a "far more awful state of society" in the next five years. "Abandoned women seem necessary to make men fiends. These are arriving by thousands and spreading through the mines. In San Francisco $50 to $100 will buy one. Gambling is now mated." Some of these prostitutes donned men's clothes to ride horseback from camp to camp. "One celebrated character of this kind said she had made $50 thousand and regretted that she had not double the capacity for increasing her gains." But William Perkins clucks his tongue at women working in the gambling houses in Sonora, these "forms of angels in the employ of Hell." He muses, "It is terrible! and enough to make a gambler foreswear his unholy trade. And to think that these lost women were once innocent children—once the joy and pride of happy mothers—pure virtuous girls—many of them once happy wives!" Perkins, however, remains pragmatic: "But I am talking flat treason against our only polka partners. It won't do. We must lay aside some strait-laced ideas and accommodate ourselves, as best we may, to this extraordinary scene we find ourselves actors in." Not only did the gold seekers sometimes redefine themselves, but they also allowed social conventions to mutate.

This may be seen in variations on the institution of marriage. In Sonora, Perkins reports, some "adventuresses" attach themselves to men on a semipermanent basis, paying a "nominal tribute to virtue by giving out that they are married." Perkins questions why anyone needs to know the truth. Instead, as in so many other aspects of the gold rush society, "each one strives to cover the nakedness of reality with the

This photograph, titled "Bringing lunch to gold diggers in Auburn Ravine, 1852," illustrates one of the roles that women filled in the West. Although few women actually mined, they did much to supply the needs of the miners—running boarding houses, doing laundry, and cooking meals. Courtesy of the California History Room, California State Library, Sacramento, California.

mantle of illusion." Franklin A. Buck, however, could not ignore reality. He was called in 1859 to serve on a jury in a divorce court that had all the salacious details of a modern soap opera, details so embarrassing that a woman witness asked that the courtroom be closed before she testified. The couple, originally from Tiffin, Ohio, quarreled over her flirting with other men. The husband came to his claim one morning and announced that the "d—d bitch had gone." The wife admitted leaving, commenting on the "*qualifications* of her husband" and his inability to satisfy her; and a best friend of the wife testified that though she had seen her lying on a bed with a young man hugging her, she "didn't think there was 'anything improper' going on or she should have stopped it at once, of course."

Most women, however, maintained moral and social conventions. At the same time, many found ways to profit in California's booming economy. Some took in washing, a tremendous boon to men who had been sending their shirts to Hawai'i. Women could thus earn $50 to $60 a day and at cooking, $30 a day. Others took in boarders. In October 1849, a woman from Maine wrote home that 10 boarders brought in $189 a week, or $75 clear after expenses had been paid. She admitted, "I have to work mighty hard," baking all her bread in a Dutch oven and doing the rest of her cooking at a small fireplace. She also took in ironing, "making seven dollars in as many hours." However, she had absolutely no social life. "I have not been in the street since I began to keep [a boarding] house." She recognized that she had been caught up in the mercenary drive of many forty-niners; "It is nothing but gold, gold . . . and I want to get my part." Another woman seemed almost ebullient despite her hard work:

I have made about $18,000 worth of pies—about one third of this has been clear profit. One year I dragged my own wood off the mountain and chopped it, and I have never had so much as a child to take a step for me in this country. $11,000 I baked in one little iron skillet, a considerable portion by a campfire, without the shelter of a tree from the broiling sun. But now I have a good many "Robinson Crusoe" comforts about me. . . . I bake about 1,200 pies per month and clear $200. . . . I intend to leave off work the coming spring, and give my business to my sister-in-law. Not that I am rich, but I need little, and have none to toil for but myself.

The experiences of these women illustrate a larger truth, that it was not the miners themselves but rather those who supplied goods and services to them who made the expected bonanza. This was especially true during 1849 before competition drove prices down. That first year witnessed enormous inflation: a boiled egg cost 75¢. A steam engine bought for $2 thousand in the East sold for $15 thousand. A farmer cleared $25 thousand selling vegetables. Aside from the saloon keepers, boarding house operators, bakers, entertainers, prostitutes, laundresses, and gamblers, many became merchants and storekeepers; some repaired boots and shoes; some hired themselves out as day laborers to help build banks, stores, and houses in burgeoning cities such as San Francisco. Some river captains and crews transported miners and their supplies from San Francisco to Sacramento; others operated ferries and toll bridges. Some auctioned horses and mules; others packed goods to the mines on these animals. Some delivered scarce milk or fresh meat. Others delivered even scarcer letters and, equally important, established express companies, bonded and guaranteed to carry gold dust safely to the East. As the demand for lumber increased to build flumes and dams, some went into lumbering or became sawmill operators. Some drove stagecoaches. Recognizing miners' hunger for news, some established newspapers. In some localities with a larger-than-usual number of young people, some became teachers, though such men had to face jealous suitors who were upset that the schoolteacher could spend up to six hours per day with much-sought-after young women. As towns and cities grew, some speculated in real estate.

Moreover, as people realized that money could make money, many stopped sending their earnings east but rather invested it in the local economy, garnering interest that was at times as high as 10 percent per month; others loaned money to temporarily out-of-luck miners or, more frequently, for development of commercial enterprises. The economy, driven by gold and the rapid influx of emigrants, was in ferment, establishing California (especially San Francisco) as a prime commercial center to rival even New York. It is worth noting that at least two major U.S. companies—Wells Fargo and Levi Strauss—had their origins in providing goods and services to the forty-niners.

Outside California, women's lives were different. It is clear that on the homesteaders' frontier, everyone worked and work was not gender-specific. Though milking cows was often considered women's work, men did that chore too; conversely, when more help was needed in the fields, women pitched in. Women, however, were generally in charge of the house and the children. They tended the garden, nursed the sick, taught the children before a school was organized, sewed and repaired the family's clothing, and cooked and baked—often without benefit of a stove. Washday was often a nightmare. Before a good well was dug on the claim, women saved a little water every day for the week's washing. Miriam Davis Colt recalls going "to the spring five times today; three times is my usual number," making "five miles travel for me [on foot] to bring sixty quarts of water."

Many women also had to make their own soap. Priscilla Merriman Evans describes her technique: " [I] took an ox and a gunny sack and went out into the field where the dead cattle had been dragged [after the disastrous winter of 1885–86] and I broke up all the bones I could carry home. I boiled them in saleratus and lime, and it made a little jelly-like soap." Miriam Davis Colt wondered what her mother back East would think of her white clothes in this land of little soap or water. All she could say was that they were "clean for brown but . . . awful dirty for white." She and her family stopped wearing nightclothes, she said, once they got to Kansas, "because I could not bear to have them take on the brown color."

When the first labor-saving devices—the sewing machine and the washing machine—became available, women who could afford them were ecstatic. The sewing machine was driven by human power, with the woman working a treadle with her feet. The washing machine was essentially a small tub with a hand-turned paddle for agitating the clothes; its primary advantage was that the children could be assigned the task of operating it, freeing their mother from the drudgery of scrubbing the clothes on a washboard.

Though some women took their unremitting labor in stride—Mollie Sanford said, "I can put my hand to almost anything"—some historians suggest that the hymns they sang may have reflected their hopelessness, their exhaustion, and their yearning for release as much as they did their religiosity:

When at last life's day is ending,
As the ev'ning draweth nigh
And the sun is slowly wending
Down behind the western sky.
'Twill be sweet to think of pleasures
That shall never know decay,
In that home of joy and splendor,
Just beyond life's twilight gray

Chorus:
Rest, sweet rest, and joy and gladness,
Comes when toil, when toil is o'er,
Sweetest resting comes when toil is o'er.
'Twill be joy and rest eternal
On the other shore.

Death, to some, might be preferable to unending labor. Hamlin Garland, remembering his mother, confirmed this: "I doubt if the women—any of them—got out into the fields or meadows long enough to enjoy the birds and the breezes. Even on Sunday as they rode away to church, they were too tired to react to the beauties of the landscape" (Jones, 151–54, 193–94).

To read about women's roles on the colonial frontier of North America, see the Colonial Frontier and New England entries in the section "Men and Women" in chapter 2 ("Domestic Life") in volume 4 of this series.

FOR MORE INFORMATION

Jones, M. E. *Daily Life on the Nineteenth Century American Frontier*. Westport, Conn.: Greenwood Press, 1998.

Myres, S. L. *Westering Women and the Frontier Experience, 1800–1915*. Albuquerque: University of New Mexico Press, 1982.

Women and Social Movements in the United States, <http://womhist.binghamton.edu/links/resource.htm>.

Wyman, W. D. *Frontier Woman: The Life of a Woman Homesteader on the Dakota Frontier*. River Falls: University of Wisconsin-River Falls Press, 1972.

VICTORIAN ENGLAND

DOMESTIC LIFE
|
WOMEN
|
United States,
1850-1865

United States,
Western Frontier

Victorian England

India

Latin America

More nonsense has probably been written about the feminine ideal than any other aspect of Victorian life. Readers should always remember that moralists do not usually waste their time on a topic unless there are alternative viewpoints. When everyone in a society agrees, the subject is simply not mentioned (e.g., advice columnists do not say, "Never serve dog food to human guests"). Many Victorian essays about women's delicacy and fragility, for example, were written by men who wanted to prevent girls from playing sports, studying Latin and mathematics, or planning to practice medicine when they grew up.

In addition, most stereotyped depictions of women's roles are class-bound; they apply only to a narrow segment of society. This is particularly true of the notion that respectable women could not do any paid work. The strongest complaints about women's frivolity and idleness were voiced by people such as Florence Nightingale, who was definitely not idle and was one of the century's most admired women. Economist Harriet Martineau said she was thankful that her father lost his money so she was forced to earn her own living. "A Paris Atelier," an 1886 essay by Dinah Mulock Craik in *Good Words* turned the stereotype on its head. "Working women in all ranks," she wrote, "from our Queen downward, are, and ought to be, objects of respect to the entire community."

The most conventional image of the perfect Victorian woman is found in the title of a long poem written by Coventry Patmore: *The Angel in the House.* The pure woman's life was supposed to be entirely centered on the home. She preserved the higher moral values, guarded her husband's conscience, guided her children's training, and helped regenerate society through her daily display of Christianity in action. If she successfully made the home a place of perfect peace, her husband and sons would not want to leave it for an evening's (morally suspect) entertainment elsewhere.

Yet the stereotype contains irreconcilable contradictions. Although the ideal middle-class woman was legally subordinate, economically dependent, and always obedient to her husband, she was somehow supposed to rule the home. The ideology of separate spheres made her entirely responsible for its comfort, beauty, and morality.

Marriage was an important step in the life of a Victorian Englishwoman. With this painting, James Charles captures the solemn nature of a Victorian wedding. Courtesy of Bradford Art Galleries and Museums.

Marriage was seen as a woman's natural and expected role: it satisfied her instinctual needs, preserved the species, provided appropriate duties, and protected her from the shocks and dangers of the rude, competitive world. In the privacy of the home, her finer instincts—sensitivity, self-sacrifice, innate purity—could have free play. Women had to be kept safe at home; their perfect compliance, obedience, innocence, and refinement would make them too easily victimized in the competitive public world. This conservative ideal was encapsulated (partly for ironic purposes) in Alfred Tennyson's 1847 poem *The Princess:*

Man for the field and woman for the hearth;
Man for the sword, and for the needle she;
Man with the head, and woman with the heart;
Man to command, and woman to obey;
All else confusion.

As long as marriage held so central a place in the conception of ideal womanhood, it was not unnatural that women were trained to please men, help children, and suppress their own wants. But given the state of matrimonial law, the decision to marry defined a woman's entire future. Marriage established her rank, role, duties, social status, place of residence, economic circumstances, and way of life. It determined her comfort, her physical safety, her children's health, and ultimately—perhaps—even her spiritual well-being. And owing to the code of chaperonage, she had to make her decision with very few opportunities to gain firsthand information about her prospective partner.

Advice manuals also insisted that good men were chivalrous even though they made women responsible for defending their own sexual morality. Public standards for male behavior were, however, growing more strict. During the 18th century and throughout the Regency, upper-class men (including those in the royal family) made no secret of their mistresses and illegitimate children. By the 1840s, respectable men kept quiet about their premarital or extramarital affairs. Journalists and clergymen publicized urban vice—not because there was more of it—but because they were beginning to regard prostitution as a problem rather than a natural feature of life.

Stricter moral standards in the middle class influenced both the upper class and the respectable working class. By the end of the period, revelations about extramarital sexuality would cause a man to lose his seat in Parliament. Guides for young women discreetly advised readers to inquire about a prospective husband's personal habits as well as his family's medical history. Alcoholism or tuberculosis among his relatives was a danger because both were thought to be inherited. Careful readers were made aware that gonorrhea blinded infants passing through the birth canal, that syphilis led to congenital malformations—and that even though a man might be free of symptoms, there was no cure for either disease.

Some Victorian discussions of ideal womanhood insisted that a respectable girl should be completely ignorant about sex and sexuality until initiated by her husband on their wedding night. However, unvoiced assumptions about masculine behavior created real dangers for any girl who was that naïve. Because chaperones were essential to protect innocent girls from assault, it seems evident that men assumed any woman walking alone on the streets was sexually available. Prudery—that is, not talking about sexuality or sexual topics—was meant to protect people. Explicit novels, sensuous pictures, and exciting dances were repressed because they might awaken sexual desire in young women and young men who were not yet mature enough to take on its responsibilities.

Although marriage was inevitably presented as woman's natural destiny, the intense and frequent repetition of the message should make us suspect that it was not universally accepted. There were more women in their twenties and thirties than men to marry them (largely because of male emigration and colonial service), but not all single women were unhappy old maids. In the working classes, women in well-paid trades were more apt to remain single than those whose earnings were too low to provide adequate support. Among the middle and upper classes, too, it was quite possible for women to earn decent incomes and live contented, independent lives.

At the end of the century, a counter-ideal of the *new woman* burst into prominence. *Punch* caricatured her as a muscular bicyclist with bloomers and untidy hair who lorded over men. Like *feminist*, the term was claimed with pride even though cartoonists used it for an insult. The idealized new woman was single, well educated, and worked at a white-collar or professional job. She lived alone or shared a flat with friends; enjoyed robust good health; traveled by bicycle or public transport; and went wherever she pleased without a chaperone. She was as firmly based in class-bound perceptions as was the mid-century Angel in the House, but fewer than 40 years separated one from the other (Mitchell, *Daily Life*, 265–69).

To read about women's roles in Chaucer's England, see the Europe entry in the section "Women's Roles" in chapter 2 ("Domestic Life") in volume 2 of this series; for Elizabethan England, see the England entry in the section "Women's Roles" in chapter 2 ("Domestic Life") in volume 3 of this series; for 18th-century England, see the England entry in the section "Men and Women" in chapter 2 ("Domestic

Life") in volume 4 of this series; for 20th-century Europe, see the Europe entry in the section "Women" in chapter 2 ("Domestic Life") in volume 6 of this series.

FOR MORE INFORMATION

Mitchell, S. *Daily Life in Victorian England*. Westport, Conn.: Greenwood Press, 1996.
Mitchell, S., ed. *Victorian Britain: An Encyclopedia*. New York: Garland Press, 1998.
Murray, J. H. *Strong-Minded Women and Other Lost Voices from Nineteenth-Century England.* New York: Pantheon Books, 1982.

ISLAMIC WORLD

By the 19th century, women's roles in the Islamic world had changed little from the centuries that had gone before.

To read about the traditional beginnings of women's roles in the Islamic world, see the Islam entries in the section "Women" in chapter 2 ("Domestic Life") in volume 2 of this series; for the traditional role of women in the Ottoman Empire, see the Ottoman entry in the section "Women" in chapter 2 ("Domestic Life") in volume 3 of this series; for the changing roles of men and women in the 20th-century Muslim world, see the Islam entry in the section "Women" in chapter 2 ("Domestic Life") in volume 6 of this series.

DOMESTIC LIFE

WOMEN

United States,
1850-1865

United States,
Western Frontier

Victorian England

India

Latin America

INDIA

The position of Indian women changed significantly during the 19th century. This was the result of a vast restructuring of Indian society, which sprang from the deterioration of the Mughal Empire and the rise of British colonial rule. By the 19th century, British colonial influence had spread throughout the region. What had begun as a trading relationship expanded into domination. The intimacy this created between the British and the Indians brought their differences—including the social position of women—into sharp focus.

One of the byproducts of the British encounter with India was a host of native reform movements. The colonial economy created a middle class of Indians who sought to transform their own society to be more like the British. This included campaigns against certain practices that came to be viewed as barbaric. Of the various issues and campaigns concerning women that arose in the early 19th century, two of the earliest that we know of were initiated by Ram Mohan Roy. However, the two movements developed in vastly different ways. The Atmiya Sabha, founded by Ram Mohan Roy in 1815 in Bengal, first publicly propagated the importance of educating women. That same year Roy wrote the first text attacking the practice of *sati*, which is when a widow kills herself either willfully or by force, as a way of honoring her late husband.

The movement to abolish sati gained a lot of British support but was short-lived, while the movement for women's education was *Indianized* over the course of the century. The fact that the movement to abolish sati gained so much attention is at least in part due to the spectacular nature of the practice, and various misunderstandings on the part of the British. In most cases of sati the woman throws herself or is pushed onto her husbands funeral pyre. Because of the connection to fire, this very uncommon practice has a long history of international attention, which continues today. It is likely that the 19th-century movement to abolish sati created a myth of the practice where one did not exist before. In actuality sati is neither common nor widespread.

Since the early 18th century, American and British missionaries have cited this practice as an example of Hindu barbarism, and British administrators used it as justification for ruling India (the civilizing mission). However, the campaign launched by Ram Mohan Roy in 1815 marks the beginning of an Indian-led movement against sati. Among the British administration, sati became a subject of major debate. For many years the British Parliament refused to legislate against sati, on the grounds that this would constitute interference in the religious affairs of the Hindus. This led to a series of compromises, including one in the 19th century when they distinguished between forced and voluntary sati. This brought on a new series of attacks, which claimed that this differentiation validates some forms of sati by making it legal. In 1817, a head judge announced that sati was not sanctioned by Hindu belief. One year later William Bentinck, the provincial governor of Bengal, prohibited sati in his province. It took another 11 years for prohibition to be extended to other parts of India, and the Sati Prohibition Act was passed in 1829 after William Bentinck had become governor-general of India. Roy was one of the first to point out that legislation against sati, particularly by foreigners, might lead to protests by the orthodoxy and in turn serve to only exacerbate the practice. While there were some uprisings, the violence attached to this movement was not nearly as serious as Roy and others had feared.

Another major reform movement concerned women's education. Like the campaign against sati, middle-class Indians pushed for this reform in an attempt to conform to Western values. British and American missionaries again provided support, and in the 1810s, they started the first schools for girls. These schools tended to draw students from lower-middle-class and lower-class families. By the middle of the 19th century, upper-class families began to send their daughters to new Hindu schools, demonstrating the limits of the educational campaign.

In the early 1850s, yet another campaign (also influenced by British views) to change women's lives began. Led by I. C. Vidyasagar, reformers sought to remove the ban on widow remarriage. Vidyasagar based his movement on the fact that widow remarriage was not condemned by the Hindu belief system. The press quickly took up the debate, representing both sides of the argument. Those who agreed with Vidyasagar agreed that Hinduism did not condemn widow remarriage, and that it would be beneficial for women to have the option of escaping the position of widowhood. Others argued that widow remarriage was in fact anti-Hindu.

In the same year, J. P. Grant took up the bill in legislative council. Yet Grant focused on only one of Vidyasagar's arguments. This was the fact that many Hindus who would have practiced widow remarriage were now unable to do so because of the declaration of the courts run by the East India company. This is due to the fact that the British government tended to impose Brahmanic ritual on all Hindus, and according to Vidyasagar the ban on widow remarriage was one example of this.

In 1873, Mahatma Jyothirao Phooley (1827–90), who is called the father of social revolution in India, launched the Sathya Shodak Samaj (Truth Seeking Society) to achieve freedom and social justice for the oppressed. With his wife, Savithri, Jyothirao opened the first school in India intended exclusively for the education of untouchable women.

Near the end of the century, tensions between Hindus and Muslims increased. This, combined with an increased awareness of colonial subjugation, created a movement promoting elements of ancient Hindu culture, prior to both Muslim and British influence. The idea of a "golden age of Hinduism" became more and more widespread. Central to this conservative movement was the idea that women had held a better position in precolonial, pre-Muslim society, and there was a movement to reform back to these ideals.

To read about women's roles in ancient India, see the India entry in the section "Women" in chapter 2 ("Domestic Life") in volume 1 of this series; for 20th-century India, see the India entry in the section "Women" in the chapter ("Domestic Life") in volume 6 of this series.

~Dana Lightstone

FOR MORE INFORMATION

Babb, L. "Marriage and Malevolence: The Uses of Sexual Opposition in the Hindu Pantheon." *Ethnology* 9 (1970): 137–48.

Goody, J. "Bridewealth and Dowry in Africa and Eurasia." In *Bridewealth and Dowry*, ed. Jack Goody and Stanley Tambiah. Cambridge, Mass.: Cambridge University Press, 1973.

Rajan, R. S. *Real and Imagined Women: Gender, Culture and Postcolonialism*. New York: Routledge Press, 1995.

DOMESTIC LIFE

WOMEN

United States,
1850-1865

United States,
Western Frontier

Victorian England

India

Latin America

LATIN AMERICA

By the 19th century, patriarchy was a long-standing influence that shaped the lives of Latin American women. The practice of patriarchy, or the assertion of male power or domination over women, was not unique to Latin America nor did it follow any singular pattern across the diverse nations that emerged in the Americas after independence from the European powers. Cultural practices and legal restrictions reinforced the practice of patriarchy, but many women found ways to challenge or otherwise deal with its limits.

Culturally, commonly held understandings of honor and shame continued to affect gender roles into the 19th century. The honor-and-shame complex, with historical antecedents in southern European culture and elsewhere, accorded *honor* to men, especially as they were able to defend and provide for their wives and families. Women, according to the complex, carried *shame* and were expected to behave with public modesty, personal humility, sexual propriety, and docility toward men. All women and men were held to the standards and values of this code, but elite families could better afford to conform closely. Honor and shame tended to strengthen a hierarchy of gender as well as one of social class.

Legally, in both the colonial and postcolonial periods, women were barred from voting, holding public office, testifying in court, and adopting children; married women could sign contracts and work for wages only with express permission from their husbands. Paternal legal authority, a legacy of Hispanic law, meant that married women were expected to be subservient to their husbands in public and at home. Because the civil codes made divorce difficult and did not allow provisions for economically vulnerable women, wives faced significant obstacles to leaving abusive and overbearing husbands

The expected roles and lived experiences of women varied greatly by class, race, and other social factors. Upper-class white women, for example, tended to look down on the majority of women, who were poor, non-white, and expected to labor for and be subservient to the elites.

The institution of slavery, which survived the independence movements of the first quarter of the century, continued to define the roles of millions of black women, especially on the coffee plantations of Brazil and the sugar estates of Cuba and the Caribbean. For centuries, women of African descent had worked under the coercion of white plantation owners, performing a variety of arduous and repetitive tasks. Field slaves tended the crops, picked the harvest, and hauled the goods, while domestic slaves served the master's family by preparing food, cleaning clothes and houses, and even being wet nurses and surrogate mothers for the white children of the plantation.

For many generations, most slave owners employed strategies, such as separate quarters and work regimes for males and females, to discourage biological reproduction among the enslaved population and preferred instead to replenish their labor needs through the transatlantic slave trade. When the British ended this trade in the early 19th century, slave masters gradually began reversing their course and encouraging slave women to reproduce and nurture black children to become working slaves.

Enslaved black women served important roles in plantation life, often clandestinely, as preservers and transmitters of African lore and religion. Among slaves, women were just as active as men in resisting slavery, finding a variety of ways to undermine, rebel against, or run away from their masters.

Most women carried a double burden in 19th-century Latin America. In areas where peasant families were bound to large estates, for example, indigenous women were expected to work in the fields as well as to carry out domestic duties such as feeding the family and sewing clothes. Poor urban women worked long, hard hours outside their households, perhaps laboring in textile sweatshops or preparing and selling food on the street, only to return home to more responsibilities.

Educational opportunities remained limited but began to change for some women by the end of the century. Some men argued that teaching women was pointless and feared that women would forget their place in the patriarchy, but advocates for female schooling often countered that education would enable women to better fulfill their traditional roles as wives, mothers, and homemakers. In Argentina, for example, female students in the 1870s were taught how to shop, raise children, and manage a household budget. In Mexico around mid-century, secular schools sought to imbue female students with the values of patriotism and good parenting. By the end of the century, both nations were preparing females for jobs as nurses, teachers, and clerks, but effectively restricted most women from participating in traditional male professions. Even after women were legally allowed to study for the professions in Mexico in 1888, female students in medical and law schools were rare exceptions. In Argentina, married women needed formal permission from their husbands to work as professionals.

By the final decades of the 19th century, a number of women in different Latin American nations began organizing and mobilizing to improve their status. Although they were a small minority and faced opposition from those who feared that women's equality would break down the family and even society, these activists made significant efforts. Organizing reading circles, social clubs, and outright political movements, these mostly middle-class and educated women challenged patriarchal authority by calling for political enfranchisement, more access to education, and equality before the law. Women teachers were often at the forefront of these struggles. Although these activists did not achieve all their goals, their efforts and open challenges to patriarchy sparked public discussion and left an activist legacy for future generations. Greater challenges to and changes in the patriarchal order would follow in the 20th century.

~*Gregory S. Crider*

FOR MORE INFORMATION

Arrom, S. *The Women of Mexico City, 1790–1857*. Stanford, Calif.: Stanford University Press, 1985.

Bush, B. *Slave Women in Caribbean Society, 1650–1838*. Bloomington: Indiana University Press, 1990.

Navarro, M., and V. Sánchez Korrol. *Women in Latin America and the Caribbean*. Bloomington: Indiana University Press, 1999.

Skidmore, T. E., and P. H. Smith. *Modern Latin America*. 5th ed. New York: Oxford University Press, 2001.

DOMESTIC LIFE

CHILDREN

United States,
1850-1865

United States,
Western Frontier

Victorian England

India

Children

To modern eyes, perhaps the most surprising aspect of children's lives in the 19th century was the fact that most children worked. The entry on the U.S. western frontier shows this most clearly. Boys and girls constituted an extension of the family economy and were expected to work for the family's benefit. By age 10, a child was able to do many farm jobs, including taking care of animals, tending to crops, and handling tools, even sharp ones.

Such laboring on family farms is not that unique in history, especially on Southern plantations where slave children worked at early ages. What is perhaps more startling were the numbers of children that joined the armies during the Civil War. A very few actually bore arms. Rather they were water carriers, barbers, kitchen waiters, couriers, drummers, and buglers. Non-fighting jobs did not mean that children were out of danger. At age nine, John Lincoln Clem joined the Union forces. At the battle of Shiloh, a Confederate shell blew up the drum he was pounding, thus earning him the name "Johnny Shiloh." When he left the Army in 1916, he was the last man to be in active service who had fought in the Civil War.

Child labor was not an American invention. When reading the entries, take note of the ways in which children worked. Indian families also relied on children. During colonial times, the British built factories for Indian boys and girls. If one looks at Victorian England, one sees that in rural as well as urban areas, children also worked in factories, on the streets, and in almost any conceivable job. English children worked as chimneysweepers in chimneys! The English, however, pioneered reform measures first to limit and then to end child labor beginning in 1802.

In the absence of regulation, children were abused, maimed, and killed on the job. Moreover, their wages did not measurably improve their or their family's economic position. Rather, as the entry on India indicates, working children often belonged to poor families who lived in difficult situations. Finally, one might compare the ways in which work kept children from other types of educational and cultural (particularly religious) activities. Although child labor was outlawed in the 20th century in many countries, it still remains prevalent.

UNITED STATES, 1850–65

Children participated directly in the Civil War. The enlistment of minors in the 19th century was based on tradition, and boys had served in armies and aboard vessels for centuries. Minors under 16 were allowed to enlist in the armies and navies of both forces. More than 40 thousand minors may have served in the war, and the majority managed to survive. Many boys considerably younger than 14 served. While figures for the Confederate army are unavailable or incomplete, in the federal army alone there were 300 boys aged 13 or under and two dozen who were 10 or under.

Parental consent was needed in both the federal and Confederate forces for minors to enlist. On this subject Lincoln wrote to the secretary of the navy, "The United States don't need the services of boys who disobey their parents." It is hard to imagine under what circumstances parents would send such young children to war. Yet it was not until March 1864 that the federal Congress prohibited the enlistment of persons under 16 under any circumstances.

Underage youths managed to scheme their way into the ranks of both armies. Hard-pressed enlistment officers often turned a blind eye to the evident youth of willing recruits to fill their recruitment quotas. Many boys entered the Confederate

DOMESTIC LIFE

CHILDREN

United States,
1850-1865

United States,
Western Frontier

Victorian England

India

state militias as railroad and bridge guards or served in the mounted guerrilla units. They often performed necessary but routine duties that freed older soldiers to fight. They functioned as water carriers, barbers, orderlies, kitchen help, mounted couriers, or hospital attendants. Youngsters served at sea as cabin boys, as galley helpers, and as powder-monkeys, bringing shot and powder to the gun decks in battle.

However, most boys served as musicians, drummers, or buglers. These helped to organize the daily routine of the camp by signaling reveille, assembly, officers' call, sick call, and taps; and their music provided a form of entertainment for the troops and a festive flare on formal occasions such as regimental reviews. Yet, the primary purpose of music on the battlefield was to communicate orders over the din of warfare. Precisely blown bugle calls and accurately played drumbeats could carry commands more clearly than the human voice at great distances and more quickly than the fleetest runner or mounted courier. Drummers were generally assigned to infantry regiments behind which they marched into battle. Buglers were allocated to the cavalry or horse artillery, as the bugle is more convenient to carry and play while mounted and riding across the field than the drum.

Looking for a few pennies, street boys in the United States shovel snow for the rich.

However, very young or small boys faced some unique obstacles in these positions. Some cavalry buglers were too short to mount a horse and had to be hoisted into the saddle, and young drummers often had great difficulty in maintaining the regulation 28-inch pace while marching beside the troops carrying a regulation size drum. Moreover, small uniforms needed to be secured and replaced periodically. This was usually done at the expense of the officers, who sometimes provided elaborate and impractical outfits. Properly enlisted boys were paid and drew supplies like the soldier, but frequently needed items such as child-sized shoes, socks, and shirts were often difficult to resupply.

John Lincoln Clem (1852–1937) was nine years old in June 1861 when he stowed away in a regimental baggage car and attached himself to the 22nd Michigan, whose officers appointed him the drummer for Company C. At the battle of Shiloh a shell had shattered his drum, earning him the sobriquet "Johnny Shiloh." At the age of 13, he was discharged, only to return to the army as an officer in 1871. He retired as a major general at age 65 and in 1916 was the last man then active in the service who had served in the Civil War.

The childhood of people like John Lincoln Clem was quite different from that of slave children before and during the war. Young slaves did not belong to their parents but generally were considered the property of the mother's master. The father and the father's master, should he be a different person, were denied any standing in regard to the offspring of slave unions. "Women were generally shown some indulgence for three or four weeks previous to childbirth . . . [and] they are generally allowed four weeks after the birth of a child, before they are compelled to go into the field, they then take the child with them." The offspring of a free man with a slave woman was thereby a slave; yet the offspring of a slave with a free woman was considered to be freeborn even if the woman were black. Even the children of a white master by a slave mother were born slaves. In the case of a dispute in this regard, with very few exceptions, whenever a slave's human rights came into conflict with a master's property rights, the courts invariably decided in favor of the master. The first activity of many refugee slaves during the war was to begin a search for their missing mates or children (Volo and Volo, 75, 106–8).

To read about children in the United States in the 20th century, see the United States entries in the section "Children" in chapter 2 ("Domestic Life") in volume 6 of this series.

FOR MORE INFORMATION

Burns, K. *The Civil War*. PBS Video, 1990. Film.

Genovese, E. D. *Roll, Jordan, Roll: The World the Slaves Made*. New York: Pantheon Books, 1976.

Paludan, P. S. *A People's Contest: The Union and Civil War, 1861–1865*. New York: Harper & Row, 1988.

Volo, D. D., and J. M. Volo. *Daily Life in Civil War America*. Westport, Conn.: Greenwood Press, 1998.

UNITED STATES, WESTERN FRONTIER

DOMESTIC LIFE

CHILDREN

United States,
1850-1865

United States,
Western Frontier

Victorian England

India

On the frontier, children were expected to work. Hamilton Garland, who grew up in the American West, remembered trying to be a "good little soldier" and live up to the expectations of his father, a Civil War veteran. Early on, he and his brother had the responsibilities of grown men. They chopped and stacked wood, hunted cattle that had wandered off, harrowed and cross-harrowed the fields until "tears of rebellious rage" creased the dust on their faces. At age 10 he had been taught to handle bundles of thoroughly dried barley shocks; at age 14 he was one of five men on a crew binding straw after the reaper had passed. Kept out of school during October and November, he first plowed and then husked corn. His father was not unkind, giving him the freedom to do what he wanted and go where he liked on Sunday as long as he was back in time for milking.

His experiences were not unique. Other children, some as young as ages four to six, had chores: to carry in enough fuel—wood or cow chips—each night to last the next day, to bring in water from the barrel outside, and to fill kerosene lamps. For recreation, many had to make do and use their imaginations because toys were not available. Elinore Stewart remembers her daughter calling a block of wood her "dear baby," a spoke from a wagon wheel "little Margaret," and a barrel stave "bad little Johnny."

Sometimes children worked off their homestead. Parents controlled their children's labor, and a father could generally claim his son's wages until he was 21 years old. In 1858, 14-year-old Frank O'Brien was hired out to work on a farm seven miles away; having walked there, he found his quarters to be in the attic, which he shared with seed corn, dried pumpkins, and field mice. His work included washing dishes, helping with the threshing, churning butter, turning the grindstone as his employer sharpened tools, and cleaning the haymow. Farmers, especially widowers, often advertised for hired girls; because of the disproportionate male-female ratio, many girls found themselves married early.

Children's work was not always voluntary. On at least one occasion a farmer, with too many mouths to feed, agreed to indenture two of his children to another man looking for "draft animals." The agreement was that the employer would buy them each a pair of shoes if they worked out. Their mother, who had not originally been consulted, so harassed her husband that a week later they rescued the children, sick, terrified, bewildered, and maltreated. Given the often brutal hardship of work on the frontier and given such treatment of children, it is not surprising that tired animals were also sometimes mistreated. Mollie Sanford told of one man, angered because his horse was balky, who after piling hay around him literally set a fire under the animal, then left him in agony until Mollie's father shot him (Jones, 194–95).

To read about children on the colonial frontier of North America, see the Colonial Frontier and New England entries in the section "Children" in chapter 2 ("Domestic Life") in volume 4 of this series.

FOR MORE INFORMATION

Burns, K. *The West.* PBS Video, 1996. Film.
Demos, J. *Past, Present, and Personal: The Family and the Life Course in American History.* New York: Oxford University Press, 1986.
Jones, M. E. *Daily Life on the Nineteenth Century American Frontier.* Westport, Conn.: Greenwood Press, 1998.
Schlissel, L., B. Gibbons, and E. Hampsten. *Far from Home: Families of the Westward Journey.* New York: Schocken Books, 1989.

DOMESTIC LIFE
|
CHILDREN
|
United States,
1850-1865

United States,
Western Frontier

Victorian England

India

VICTORIAN ENGLAND

Twentieth-century readers are shocked by accounts of the Victorian children—some of them very young—who worked long hours under terrible conditions. However, child labor was not invented by the Victorians. Children in preindustrial societies had always worked. Most took some part in their parents' labor, whether in agriculture or in producing goods at home. Their work was entirely unregulated—English law was extremely reluctant to intervene in family affairs, even to protect children against parental abuse—but it tended not to be seen by outsiders. What the Victorians did invent was concern for working children and ultimately finding the legal means to protect them. Victorian reformers made child labor visible and thereby did a great deal toward bringing it to an end.

In the early years of the Industrial Revolution, the birth rate was high and many people died before middle age. More than half the population was children, and many of them were without parents. Meanwhile, the owners of textile mills had discovered that children (because of their small size) were especially suited to some aspects of the work. There were other factory jobs that children could do as well as adults, because machines supplied the strength and skill that would otherwise have been needed. Mill owners made agreements with the local authorities in impoverished areas to take orphan children as young as age seven off their hands. They were lodged in dormitories and worked in shifts, 12 hours at a time, day and night. Other children went into the factories with a parent or older sister, doing the finicky bits of work that required a small body and small hands. In coalmines, children worked underground in small dark spaces, opening and closing the traps that provided ventilation.

Because it became obvious that protection was needed, Parliament began investigating child labor. In 1802 the first factory act was passed. The government was reluctant to interfere with the freedom of employers and workers to come to their own agreements about wages and working conditions, even when this freedom meant that employees had to accept extraordinarily difficult terms to get a job. But when large numbers of young children without adult guardians were gathered in factories, Parliament had to pay attention. The Factory Act of 1802 applied only to orphans under the age of 12 who worked in factories. It required that they work a maximum of 12 hours a day and that the mill owner provide them with some education. The factory acts were not effectively enforced until 1833, when the first inspectors were appointed. The 1833 act also prohibited the employment of children under age nine in textile mills, and it limited the work of children between ages nine and twelve to 48 hours a week. In 1842, coalmines were added to the list of regulated industries: work underground was prohibited for all women and girls, and for boys under the age of 10.

Victorian girls of the 1890s exercising in gymnasium costumes.

A pattern for increasing intervention was set. Novelists, journalists, or philanthropists would publish terrible stories about exploited children. Then Parliament would conduct an investigation and make new regulations. In 1840, for example, chimney sweeps were forbidden to use climbing boys inside the chimneys. As the years passed, more and more jobs were added to the list of prohibited employments. A minimum age for full-time work at one trade after another was established, and then raised, and then raised again. Hours were shortened, night work was banned, and regular breaks were required. By the last year of Victoria's reign, children under age 12 could not be employed in any factory or workshop. They could still work, but only part-time, in agriculture, retail trades, and domestic service.

Even in 1900, most young people were in full-time employment by the age of 13 or 14. And many younger children throughout the period did the kind of work that was less visible than factory labor. The worst conditions were probably in home industries. Tedious handwork of all sorts (e.g., box making, toy making, painting Christmas cards, coloring fashion plates, assembling artificial flowers, putting matches in boxes, sewing buttons on cards, doing embroidery, knitting, and lace making) was done at home by women and paid for by the piece. Mothers who did this work generally made their children help—both to keep them occupied and because their assistance was useful. If there was no other source of income, a woman and her children might have to work steadily for 14 or 16 hours a day to survive. Children were trained for some of these crafts at dame schools, which also served as "childminding" institutions while mothers earned a living. Girls and boys as young as age three or four would be put to work braiding straw (for hat making) or making baskets and given some instruction in reading. The work they produced paid for their schooling.

A more visible kind of child labor was done on city streets, especially in London. Because streets were crowded with horses and horse droppings, a child with a broom

who cleared a path for a well-dressed man or a woman wearing long skirts could hope to get anywhere between a farthing and a penny as tip. Both girls and boys swept crossings. Flower girls went to Covent Garden in the morning to get the leftovers that were given away or sold at a very cheap price after the regular business was done. Then they made buttonholes, or small bunches of flowers, which they could sell. Girls also sold matches and watercress. Boys earned small tips by holding horses, fetching cabs, and carrying parcels. Before telephones came into service toward the end of the century, boys waited outside business offices hoping someone would have a message to be carried a few streets away. Some of these young workers demonstrated their responsibility and moved into regular employment. Others remained impoverished. The journalist Henry Mayhew wrote many stories about London street workers in 1849–50. Although there is some debate about how accurate Mayhew's reporting was, the narratives provide a fascinating glimpse of marginal working life (Mitchell, 43–47).

In an illustration from Henry Mayhew's *London Labour and the London Poor,* street boys sweep a path across the street for a gentleman in exchange for a tip. Courtesy of Paley Library, Temple University.

To read about children in Chaucer's England, see the Europe entry in the section "Children" in chapter 2 ("Domestic Life") in volume 2 of this series; for Elizabethan England, see the England entry in the section "Children" in chapter 2 ("Domestic Life") in volume 3 of this series; for 18th-century England, see the England entry in the section "Children" in chapter 2 ("Domestic Life") in volume 4 of this series; for 20th-century Europe, see the Europe entry in the section "Children" in chapter 2 ("Domestic Life") in volume 6 of this series.

FOR MORE INFORMATION

Mitchell, S. *Daily Life in Victorian England.* Westport, Conn.: Greenwood Press, 1996.
Roe, F. G. *The Victorian Child.* London: Phoenix House, 1959.
Walvin, J. *A Child's World: A Social History of English Childhood, 1800–1914.* Harmondsworth, England: Penguin Books, 1982.

DOMESTIC LIFE

CHILDREN

United States, 1850-1865

United States, Western Frontier

Victorian England

India

INDIA

In 19th-century India, it was very common for a couple to have as many as 10 or even more children. This was particularly common in the rural areas, because additional children were not expensive to feed, and their labor was useful in the fields or in the household. In an agricultural family, the boys would most often work in the fields while the girls helped in the kitchen and looked after younger children. It was common for girls as young as four or five to be responsible for taking care of younger siblings or cousins. Many urban families also had a large number of children. Nearly all households at this time were home to joint families, meaning that all of the sons stayed in the household even after they were married, and their wives came to live there as well. Households were generally crowded compared to how most people live in the United States today. Each family, meaning mother, father, and children, shared a room in the house. They also either shared a bed or slept together on the floor. Most children had parents, grandparents, and aunts and uncles who looked after them. Cousins grew up together and considered each other as brothers and sisters. In a particularly large family, there might be as many as 20 to 30 children living in one house.

Aside from working in the fields or in the house, some children had other jobs. For example, as the British developed factories, more and more children were sent to work on assembly lines. Other children begged on city streets or sold the family's goods or agricultural products on the streets or at a market. Some children were even sent away to work in another city so that they could send money home to the family.

At this time many children did not make it into adulthood. Lack of medicine, poor nutrition, and sometimes-poor living conditions, such as contaminated water, contributed to a high mortality rate among children. While this must have been very difficult for the family, it was also considered a part of life. The deceased children continued to be considered part of the family. For example, if a woman who had lost three children, and had seven living children, were asked how many children she had, she would most likely answer that she had 10 children.

For several reasons sons were often considered preferable in Indian families. In a Hindu family it was the duty of the oldest son to light the funeral pyre when his parents died. It was also the responsibility of a son to take care of his parents in the parents' old age. The daughter, on the other hand, went off to her marital home and did not provide such security for her parents in their old age. In an agricultural family, the son provided valuable work in the fields. A daughter's household work was sometimes considered less valuable. In the 19th century, there were some cases in which boy children received preferential treatment in the family. If food was short, girls were sometimes given less food then their brothers, even though the nutritional needs of girls are equal to that of boys. In the worst-case scenario, a girl baby was actually killed, for she was considered a liability to the family. As the girl grew up, it was the responsibility of the family to meet her marriage expenses and raise a substantial marriage dowry, a sum that might sometimes be beyond the family's means. However, killing female children was in no way the norm, and in most families, daughters were loved equally to their brothers.

Many children did not go to school, particularly in the rural areas. During the 19th century the British established a few schools in India and helped a number of villages set up schools. It was uncommon for Muslim children to attend regular schools, and many spent a few hours a day at *Ulama*, or religious school. These schools generally only taught religion. In the more urban areas English medium schools were set up, and this type of schooling, based on the British system, and almost entirely in English, became very popular among higher-class members of society. These schools were not free like the majority of schools in India and required a large sum of money in tuition.

Among religious Hindus it was common to hold a ceremony in honor of the beginning of a child's education. This type of ceremony was more commonly held for boys than for girls. At this ceremony writing slates and writing utensils were presented to the child, and a ceremony in honor of Saraswati, the goddess of learning, took place. This was thought to ensure success with the child's schooling.

The British also introduced an examination system, based on their own, which most schools throughout India gradually adopted. At the end of each academic year even the youngest children were required to take a standardized exam to pass into the next class. Different systems of varying prestige developed. Most schools taught in the regional language (presently, India has 14 national languages and hundreds of additional languages are also spoken). Hindi was also mandatory in a large percentage of schools at this time because it was the language spoken by the largest percentage of the Indian population.

With the exception of the most elite schools in the urban areas, schools generally had one or two rooms, and children of different ages were taught together. Children sat on the floor and wrote on a slate. Teachers at this time were generally very strict. It was not uncommon for a child who misbehaved to be punished by the teacher. The teacher, as with all elders, was to receive the utmost respect from his or her students.

After finishing school and chores, a child generally had a lot of freedom to play, either in the fields or in the city, depending on where he or she lived. Without supervision it was pretty safe for children to roam around in groups. Children who lived in a village had a particularly nice playground, which sometimes consisting of mango groves, wooded areas, and other interesting natural places to play. There were many popular games, including cricket and a game similar to hopscotch. On rainy days when children had to play indoors, a game with stones, similar to jacks, was common. Songs and hand-clapping games were also popular indoor activities.

To read about children in India in the 20th century, see the India entry in the section "Children" in chapter 2 ("Domestic Life") in volume 6 of this series.

~*Dana Lightstone*

FOR MORE INFORMATION

Miller, B. *The Endangered Sex: Neglect of Female Children in Rural North India*. Ithaca, N.Y.: Cornell University Press, 1981.

Sud, S. L. *Marital Power Structure, Fertility and Family Planning in India*. New Delhi, India: Radient Publishers, 1991.

LATIN AMERICA

Latin American countries were predominantly Catholic, and thus as a matter of religion most families did not practice birth control. Large families were the norm, and children were highly valued.

To read about child rearing in Latin America, see the Latin America entry in the section "Children" in chapter 2 ("Domestic Life") in volume 6 of this series.

DOMESTIC LIFE: WEB SITES

http://www.history.rochester.edu/godeys/
http://etext.virginia.edu/ladies/ladyhome.html
http://docsouth.unc.edu/ames/menu.html
http://www.lahacal.org/gentleman/
http://frontierindia.scriptmania.com/page39.htm
http://www.lib.lsu.edu/special/exhibits/india/chap1.htm
http://www.metimes.com/issue22/commu/woman'sview.htm

3

ECONOMIC LIFE

People work. The basic principle of economic life is that men and women (and sometimes children) must work to provide for themselves. Of course, throughout history it has always been that some have to work harder than others, but this does not violate the basic importance of work; it only reveals the complexities of economic life that include everything from the production of income to trade to its unequal distribution throughout society. Nevertheless, work has something to do with class status. The elite hold quite different jobs than those of the middle class (which was relatively small in the 19th century) and the masses in the working class. Thus work itself shapes class. In other words, economic class standing has something (but not everything) to do with the kinds of jobs that people did. This is most clearly seen in the entries on work and class in Victorian England. Working-class men and women performed manual labor, for long hours and little pay. In contrast, as one went up the social ladder, less and less physical labor was required. Additionally, class was relative to wealth and birth. Accident of birth often dictated one's working life as well as one's class status. In the essays that follow, it is important to take note of the types of jobs that people held and what relationship those jobs had to their social and political well-being.

Economic activity shaped 19th-century lives in other ways. At the basic level, people work on the land to produce their food and other items they need. However, even at this simplest level, people trade goods among themselves. Thus, economic life moves from the work that we do to the exchange of the products of our labor. This diversification contributes to increasing variety in society, as some people work on the land, living in villages and farms, while others move to urban areas that grow ever larger throughout history. The patterns of farm, village, and urban life exist all over the world and help define the lives of the people who work within them. In the 19th century, people witnessed a dramatic growth in cities. This was particularly true in China, England, and the United States. The expansion of London is probably the best illustration of what was happening on both sides of the Atlantic. The logistical and construction successes and failures in Victorian London typify those faced in many places where economic and geographic growth outstripped people's ability to accommodate rapid change.

ECONOMIC LIFE

WORK

CLASS
& CASTE EXPERIENCE

TRADE

URBAN & RURAL
ENVIRONMENTS

Yet another aspect of economic life is trade. Commerce, or the exchange of goods, is as central to human economic life as the production of goods. From the beginning of town life in Mesopotamia, the excitement generated within shops lining a street is palpable in the sources. Merchants hawking their wares and shoppers looking for the exotic as well as the ordinary form a core of human life. Merchants (and merchandise) have always ranged far beyond local markets as people moved their goods across large areas. Even during the prehistoric late Stone Age, domestic animals native to the Middle East moved down the Nile valley to sub-Saharan Africa, and plants native to the Euphrates valley moved as far east as China. Our global marketplace is only the logical extension of the constant movement of people and things that goes on as people engage in their economic life. Whether one discusses the production of American cotton for British textile mills or the importance of British exports to its colonies, the structure of trade in the 19th century reflected the movement toward a global marketplace. Transoceanic trade was a boon to the nations described in the following entries, and yet, this trade had some negative aspects, such as the Victorian English quest for empire and the American use of slaves to produce exports for the global markets.

All societies have been in part defined by people at work. They have built societies with divisions of labor, of city and country, and of class, as some people grow richer than others. To study daily life through history is in large part to understand people at work. And to understand daily economic life in the 19th century is to understand the roots of contemporary society's economic life.

FOR MORE INFORMATION

Braudel, F. *The Wheels of Commerce*. New York: Harper & Row, 1979.
Wallerstein, I. M. *Historical Capitalism*. London: Verso, 1983.

ECONOMIC LIFE
|
WORK
|
United States,
1850-1865

United States,
Western Frontier

Victorian England

China

Latin America

Work

To 21st century eyes, what might strike some about the 19th century is how hard and long people worked. Of course, this was especially true of the slave who not only toiled all day long on Southern and Latin American plantations but also had to confront daily workplace violence, as we might say. The authors rightly point out that the experience of any individual slave depended on time and place. But they are also correct in that it was evil, brutal, and oppressive. The slave system of labor, however, was so pervasive that at times even black freemen owned slaves. The campaign against slavery was as much of a campaign to eliminate an abomination as it was a campaign to replace unfree labor with free labor. In the United States, the ultimate goal of emancipation was to compensate African American workers in the South for their labor, which often meant working for the master from sunup to sundown and then working late into the night or morning to ensure that family needs were met. In the Caribbean and Brazil, black plantation workers remained enslaved until late in the century while in Mexico, where independence in the 1820s brought a legal end to slavery, many indigenous peasants continued to work for wealthy estate owners of European descent.

Free labor, or paid work, in the 19th century often had some of the same conditions as slavery. The workday and work week were exceedingly long. In England, in China, and in the United States, the work clock for agricultural labor was the sun. But even in the cities, factories and shops stayed open almost all day. Retail shops, for instance, were open for 14 to 16 hours a day with the same employees. A typical day for a domestic worker might be even longer. Factory work had the same hours, was dangerous, and was not very rewarding, materially or spiritually. Only unions (and, in the Chinese experience, guilds) were able to improve shop floor safety, increase pay, shorten hours, and regain some worker authority on the shop floor. Of course, as the entry on England suggests, middle-class workers may have had easier work experiences, but they might not have had more economic security. In fact, as writers like Herman Melville and Charles Dickens illustrated, 19th century white-collar employees faced many of the same challenges as blue-collar ones.

It is interesting to note that despite all the challenges that 19th-century work presented, several working-class icons, if not heroes, were created and still resonate with us today. Two of them come from the United States. One is the cowboy, who is beyond a doubt one of the most recognizable American images. Cowboys were black, white, Asian, and Hispanic. Note in comparing this work to labor in the American South or in Victorian England that the hours were long and the work was hard and dangerous. And yet, somehow the worker with a ten-gallon hat, wearing Angora goat chaps, and armed with a Colt .45 became a symbol of hard work, morality, and sexuality. The American miner, another archetypal icon on the western frontier, did not reflect all of the same values. The dusty miner has more to do with the opportunities and possibilities of the West that came with hard work and sacrifice. Miners toiled with this promise but often without much reward. Most who went to find western gold were bitterly disappointed. Nevertheless, like slaves in the South or factory workers in England, one thing remained constant for miners: their labor in the 19th century was hard and unceasing.

UNITED STATES, 1850–65

Perhaps no other group in the United States was more defined by the conditions of their labors than slaves. A Northern visitor to the South testified, "It is almost impossible to believe that human nature can endure such hardships and sufferings as the slaves have to go through." Though slavery was certainly a great evil and was oppressive everywhere, the burden imposed on the individual slave varied greatly depending on the master and the region of the country in which the slave resided. Profession and practice with regard to slavery were so complex that they were frequently radically different things, and generalizations in this area must be carefully drawn. Unquestionably, the practices that served to underpin the institution of slavery in the South were becoming harsher as the century progressed. This was espe-

ECONOMIC LIFE

WORK

United States,
1850-1865

United States,
Western Frontier

Victorian England

China

Latin America

cially true with respect to questions of black education, manumission, provision of physical care, and the status of blacks, both free and slave.

There seems to have been a striking difference between the treatment of slaves in the small towns and cities of the South and that of blacks held on large plantations. Both the material mistreatment of the whip-driven slave on the plantation and the freedom enjoyed by urban slaves, as well as black freemen, were exaggerated by antislavery advocates at the time and subsequently by some serious historical scholars. Notwithstanding such exaggeration, there was almost certainly a relative disadvantage to being a plantation slave.

> *Incredibly, many free black tradesmen and artisans invested heavily in slaves.*

The systemic abuse of black freemen was generally limited to the rural areas of the South and was much less common before the war than after it. Southern blacks lived hard lives, yet many displayed fortitude, courage, and a sense of dignity throughout. Nonetheless, on the eve of the Civil War there were blacks in the South, themselves free, who owned slaves, used slave labor in their businesses, and condoned slavery. Black slave masters, especially shippers, tradesmen, and artisans, owned many of their fellow African American workers, an arrangement often entered into in lieu of an apprenticeship agreement. Incredibly, many of the free black tradesmen and artisans invested heavily in these slaves. This was especially true of free blacks who owned shipping concerns where slaves served as shipwrights, sail makers, and stevedores. It has been documented that in 1830 more than two thousand black slaves were owned by free African American masters in New Orleans alone.

The campaign to emancipate these slaves raised interesting questions about the sympathies of free blacks who owned slaves. Black masters, who sometimes also owned the members of their families, had their rights recognized in law in most states. They could therefore stabilize their workforce and provide a modicum of legal protection for their loved ones. These men were highly educated, cultured, and sophisticated in their outlook, and they were decidedly against any form of gradual emancipation without indemnification. At the beginning of the war many of them were openly Confederate in their outlook.

The available evidence about the conditions surrounding slavery comes to us from a variety of sources, some of which hardly inspire confidence as to their reliability. Slave biographies and narratives based on oral interviews are one major source of information. Many of these were taken down in the 1920s and 1930s by historians desperate to document the details of slave life before its participants faded away. These narratives were given by people who were, on the average, over eighty years old and had been children when the Civil War began. Additional sources are found in the letters, diaries, and contemporary writings of the slaveholders, and in the collections of plantation records, Freedmen's Bureau documents, and other written material dealing with the slave trade and plantation management that survived the war. Each of these must be subjected to the same type of evaluation by which all sources of historical information are judged.

Slave autobiographies, in particular, have been used by historians extensively, and perhaps too uncritically, because they are few in number. Under close scrutiny they often turn out to be carefully crafted propaganda pieces, rooted in truth but designed by the abolitionists to appeal to all the dissimilar reform groups of the North. In the 1860s there was an explosion of handwritten testimony from slaves recently freed by federal troops. New Orleans fell to federal troops early in the war, and there was an active attempt to document the system of slavery in the area around that city. While historians know more about slaves in New Orleans during the war than in any other Southern city, it was hardly an archetype of Southern slavery. New Orleans boasted the largest black community of any city in the country at the time, composed of numerous free black businessmen and artisans, urbanized former slaves, and recent refugees from the plantations.

Nonetheless, the data that were compiled are useful, particularly since the slaves could not be expected to leave much in the way of other written documentation. Much of the material collected took the form of anecdotal statements by former slaves assembled by well meaning, but not unbiased, investigators. It is not enough to say that all sources are biased. Some sources suffer from other limiting characteristics beyond their obvious intent, such as the author's selective memory or his desire to make himself seem heroic. It is almost impossible to correct the data that we have for the prejudice of "untrained, negligent, or incompetent" 19th-century researchers. Such data have been used by scholars, authors, playwrights, and screenwriters to distort the picture of slavery beyond our ability to know the truth.

The accounts of slave society written by slave owners are used sparingly and with great caution by historians even though they are plentiful and vastly superior sources of detailed information. These sources of information about slavery reside largely in the daily reports of plantation activities and the internal records of slave trading establishments. Considering them along with published tracts on the "Management of Negroes," private letters and papers of slaveholders, and advertisements for fugitives, we can at least surmise an accurate picture of what slaves looked like and did, even if we cannot get a reliable view of how they felt or what they thought. These sources provide firsthand accounts, rather than hearsay evidence, of slavery. They are contemporary with the events and are considered by most open-minded historians to have been written "with the substantial integrity needed for accuracy in business accounts."

If we properly discount the reliability of the self-serving firsthand documents produced by slave owners and their apologists, must we not take into account the subjective influences brought to bear on the autobiographies and narratives of slaves published and recorded by abolitionists? One outstanding slave autobiography, favorable to slavery, is almost totally ignored by historians as "obviously unreliable," yet there is no evidence that the feelings expressed therein are bogus or recorded under duress. The pamphlet, *Slavery and Abolitionism, As Viewed by a Georgia Slave*, by Harrison Berry, a shoemaker and slave, warned against the promises of the abolitionists and pointed to the potential poverty that blacks would experience if let free in an antiblack society. In urging his fellow blacks to be submissive to their owners, Berry was perhaps the only person to address the nation directly on the subject of bondage while still a slave, and he seemingly never disavowed these sentiments.

The narrative of Frederick Douglass is a commonly referenced work in this regard. Douglass was a slave in Baltimore for more than twenty years, and his book, published by the American Antislavery Society, was replete with descriptions of the physical abuses of slavery, including whippings, rape, unwarranted punishments, and cold-blooded murder. The work appealed to a wider audience of reformers than just those who favored emancipation. Proponents of women's rights, temperance, public education, and immigration reform all found something to stir them in Douglass's work.

Southern readers pointed with incredulity to many of Douglass's childhood memories of the whipping and murder of his fellow slaves. As he carefully omitted corroborating details from the incidents, many whites were convinced that the stories were patently false. His accounts of two slaves being murdered in unrelated incidents by individual masters on adjoining plantations within hours of one another rang false to all but the most dedicated of abolitionist ears. Nevertheless, between 1845 and 1850 the book sold more than thirty thousand copies and was regarded by many in the North as a true picture of slavery in Maryland. The *New York Tribune* reviewer, himself an abolitionist, praised the book upon its publication for its simplicity, truth, coherence, and warmth.

Slavery called for long hours of work and trying conditions by modern standards. Most slaves worked from sunup to sundown in the fields, or until the work was finished when working indoors. During harvest or corn husking slaves could be found working into the early hours of the morning. Slaughtering, in late fall, was a bloody and offensive task that allowed no interruption for rest. Nonetheless, the testimony of former slaves suggests that there was time to do extra work "on the side." The workweek ran from Monday to Saturday noon and respected the Sabbath. Attendance at church services in clean clothes was required. Most blacks were restricted to the plantation and lived in the village of shanty huts provided for them. Any slave found off the plantation without a pass ran the danger of being "whipped on the spot" by the slave patrol, and if he resisted capture he could be shot. Slave housing was poor; heat in winter and ventilation in summer were generally haphazard, if not altogether absent. The plantations were therefore a strange combination of labor camp, racial community, and Christian mission (Volo and Volo, 65–69).

To read about work in the United States in the 20th century, see the United States entries in the section "Work" in chapter 3 ("Economic Life") in volume 6 of this series.

FOR MORE INFORMATION

Berry, H. *Slavery and Abolitionism, As Viewed by a Georgia Slave.* Philadelphia: Historic Publications, 1969.

Blassingame, J. W. *The Slave Community: Plantation Life in the Antebellum South.* New York: Oxford University Press, 1972.

Douglass, F. *Narrative of the Life of Frederick Douglass, An American Slave.* New Haven: Yale University Press, 2001.

Jacobs, H. *Incidents in the Life of a Slave Girl, Written by Herself.* Cambridge: Harvard University Press, 2000.

Paludan, P. S. *A People's Contest: The Union and Civil War, 1861–1865.* New York: Harper & Row, 1988.

Volo, D. D., and J. M. Volo. *Daily Life in Civil War America.* Westport, Conn.: Greenwood Press, 1998.

UNITED STATES, WESTERN FRONTIER

ECONOMIC LIFE
|
WORK
|
United States,
1850-1865

United States,
Western Frontier

Victorian England

China

Latin America

There are two main historical icons of work on the western frontier: the cowboy and the miner. The cowboy is, without doubt, the most recognizable of American frontier heroes. Ever since Owen Wister's prototypical cowboy novel, *The Virginian*, the mythic cowboy has been the epitome of valued American traits: physically competent but emotionally reserved; tempered strength that can erupt in action to protect a woman or enforce justice; virtuous, though not prissy; hardworking yet able to enjoy practical jokes; a man among men, yet attractive to women, in part because of his very aloofness. In a postfrontier era, argues William A. Savage Jr., "the cowboy hero is . . . evocative of a significant period in the American past. . . . [H]is myth . . . suggests to Americans what they might have been and what they might yet become. The cowboy speaks directly to the American's need to get through the day." Like heroes of storytellers from time immemorial, the cowboy hero simultaneously serves as an escape from daily tedium and as a role model for what might be. Unlike Cody or Custer or Carson, few are remembered by name; few participated in a single significant event—such as the battle of the Little Big Horn, which was amply documented. Instead, the cowboy's very anonymity may make him a mythic Everyman.

Although in American popular culture the cowboy is central to our imagination, in reality he was, according to some historians, little more than a hardworking, often seasonal employee in a complex, far-reaching web of historical, economic, technological, and industrial forces. Despite Owen Wister's portrayals of the cowboy as a white Anglo-Saxon, the cowboys through the years have been Mexican, Native American, and African American; moreover, immigrants from England, Scotland, and Germany found themselves in the saddle. Though the word *cowboy* was originally applied to pro-British guerrillas of the Revolutionary War, Charlie Siringo, himself a cowboy,

Cowboys, another icon of the West, with a herd of cattle on the open range. © Library of Congress.

said that it first came into popular use during the opening two years of the Civil War when Texas boys not old enough to enlist in the Confederate army "tried to hold the family cattle on the home range and keep the calves branded." Because of their youth they were called *cowboys*.

There was a dichotomy between the cattleman—the investor, the entrepreneur, the businessman—and the cowboy, his employee. Though he was essential to the enterprise, the cowboy usually received from $25 to $40 a month plus room and board. Teddy Blue described receiving 25 cents per head for running a herd of beef in the last open range in Montana during 1878; he noted that he made $125 a month, "big money for a boy in those days when the usual wages ran as low as 10 dollars." A transplanted Englishman, Frank Collinson, recalled earning $14 a month on his first job in Medina County, Texas, in 1872. Charles A. Siringo noted that the greenhorn who wanted to be a cowboy might at first have to work only for his "chuck" (i.e., his board), but this was worth it to "acquire all the knowledge and information possible on the art of running cattle." Starting wages, he remembered, were from $15 to $40 a month, depending on latitude. On northern ranges the wages were higher, but so were expenses; cowboys needed warmer clothing and bedding during the long, severe winters. He continued:

After you have mastered the cow business thoroughly—that is, learned not to dread getting in mud up to your ears, jumping your horse into a swollen stream when the water is freezing, nor running your horse at full speed, trying to stop a stampeded herd, on a dark night, when your course has to be guided by the sound of the frightened steer's hoofs—you command *good* wages, which will be from $25 to $60 per month.

On the debit side, the cowboy's equipment required an initial outlay of funds that could range considerably. A fancy outfit might cost $500: saddle, $100; saddle blanket, $50; quirt and riata, $25; a pearl-handled Colt .45, $50; a Winchester rifle, $75; Angora goat chaps, $25; and a Spanish pony, $25. However, a serviceable outfit could be bought for $82: pony, $25; leggings, $5; saddle, $25; saddle blankets, $5; spurs, bridle, and stake rope, $5; and Colt .45, $12.

In the early Texas cattle industry, it was the custom for cowboys who assisted at branding to receive a portion of the cattle in return. Cowboys could also acquire mavericks (motherless calves whose owners could not be determined). Thus, some cowboys could take the first steps toward becoming cattlemen. However, on the northern plains the mavericks were declared the property of the stock raisers' associations and auctioned off. Thus "mavericking—a way to begin a career of enterprise—became rustling—a way to begin a career of crime."

Often the cowboy was laid off during the winter months, for ranch owners could get by with a skeleton staff and did not want to pay idle hands. During this time, especially on the northern plains, cowboys would take odd jobs around saloons or livery stables, trap or hunt wolves, mine, or simply ride the chuck line—that is, ride from ranch to ranch, staying at each until their welcome wore out. But at roundup, ranches needed a full complement of help.

Roundups, one of the cowboys' principle jobs, were usually held twice a year. At the spring, or general,

Frederic Remington's *Fixing a Break in the Wire Fence,* depicts a common task of western ranch hands. Denver Public Library, Western History Collection, Frederick Remington, call number F-19816.

roundup, the cowboys' main task was to collect the owner's cattle and brand new calves; the fall roundup focused on selecting beeves for market.

On the northern plains, especially in Montana and Wyoming where corporate ranching had produced vast herds, the roundup was a cooperative venture of many ranches, each providing its outfit or crew and its own chuck wagon, which was the center of a moving operation. An old-time rancher recalled roundups in the heyday of the open range:

In the old days on the roundups each outfit had its own mess wagon with from 30 to 50 men. Each man rode from 7 to 11 horses, part circle horses, part cutting horses, and a night horse. We had breakfast at 3:30 A.M., our horses saddled and on the circle at 4 A.M. Some [circles] were 15 M[iles] some 40 M. You would round up from 3,000 to 10,000 on each ride. You had dinner when the last man was in, sometimes 9 A.M. sometimes 4 P.M., then changed horses and worked the herd, cut out the beef and cattle that had drifted from their home range and kept them under herd until you reached their home range where they were turned loose. You also branded all calves in the same brand their mother carried. It made no difference whether the owner had a representative there or not.

Supper was at 6 P.M. Then you saddled your night horse, went to the herd you were holding, and relieved the herders. They were through for the day. You got the herd bedded down at 8 P.M., left two men to guard them, and went to bed. The guard was changed every two hours so sometime during the night your sleep was broken and you smoked cigarettes and sung to the cattle for a couple of hours. This was the procedure followed every day and Sunday too. It was never too hot or too cold, rain or snow, to interfere with the work.

After an early breakfast of sowbelly, hot biscuits, and coffee, the cowboys roped their horses, saddled up, and set off to scour the range for cattle. Few dallied at breakfast; it was considered a disgrace to be the last one ready to go when there was work to be done. They usually rode in a half circle along a diameter marked by the route of the chuck wagon from its morning position to a predetermined afternoon position. There the outfit would have dinner, the main meal of the day. Traditionally a rancher killed one of his beeves for the outfits working on his land. The cook would barbecue this fresh beef, having already prepared a variety of pies and puddings, all of which was washed down with coffee. Then came the afternoon's work.

The cowboys would mount their cutting ponies to separate individual cows and their calves from the main herd. Usually these animals were cut in a strict order, those from the outfit with the most cattle—usually those of that day's home range— selected first. One by one the calves were roped, dragged to the branding fire, and thrown on their side. Roping was considered by many to be the most dangerous job on roundup, for a rope carelessly snubbed around the saddle horn could nip off a cowboy's thumb or finger. The cowboy who threw the calf would sit on its neck while another pushed its top hind leg forward, stretching its hide taut for the branding iron and, if it was a young bull, exposing its scrotum in preparation for castration.

The calf was marked with the same brand its mother wore; the cows usually stayed close to their calves, sometimes attempting to protect them but always identifying them by proximity. The branding iron, heated only to a dull red so it would not burn below the outer layer of skin, marked the calf with one of 4,000 registered brands. Since all brands (except those that represented a unique design, such as

Teddy Roosevelt's elk horn) were made up of combinations of letters, numbers, short dashes or bars, circles or portions of circles, a brand for a cow and a calf could be relatively quickly assembled on the spot. On average, three hundred calves could be branded in an afternoon.

📷 Snapshot

Typical Supplies Needed to Head out West, 1840s

Invoice

Supplies Purchased by C. H. & H. Ellis from Aspinwall & Bro.

1/2 bbl. Pork $18	$18.00
1/2 Sack Flour $8	8.00
1 bbl. Pilot Bread, 100 at 10 cents	10.00
20 lbs. Beans, 5 cents	1.00
1 lb. Pepper	1.00
1 Box Salt	0.38
1 lb. Saleratus	0.62
2 Shovels	2.00
2 Wash Pans	4.50
1 lb. Powder	1.00
6 lbs. Tobacco	2.25
1 Bag	0.50
	$49.25
14 lbs. Sugar, 50 cents	7.00
	$56.25
1 Case Whiskey	7.00
Total	$63.25

~[See John E. Pomfret, *California Gold Rush Voyages, 1848–1849: Three Original Narratives,* (San Marino, Calif.: Huntington Library, 1954), 96; as quoted in Jones, 105.]

While the calf was down it was usually also earmarked—its ears cropped or notched on the end, top or bottom. Generally it was easier on the range to make quick identifications from earmarks than from brands. If the calf was a young bull it was now castrated, both to make it gentler and to encourage more rapid weight gain. For every 100 heifers, eight promising young bulls were left uncastrated as breeding stock. One cowboy kept a tally book as each calf was branded; as an additional check, the bulls' scrota and heifers' ear notches were thrown into separate buckets to be counted at the end of the day's work. Several other processes were completed during roundup. Because the long horns were dangerous, cowboys used special clippers or even axes and saws to remove them.

Another typical type of work in the West was mining. For miners, the promise of their work was gold. Whether they had arrived by ship in San Francisco or by pack train over the mountains, all wanted to get to the gold regions as soon as possible. There the gold seekers, most of whom had no prior knowledge of mining, had to learn how to find and extract the gold. Some had phenomenal success; others barely scraped by; still others quickly realized that fortune lay not in mining but in supplying the miners with goods and services. This varied society, constantly improvising, experimenting, finding ad hoc solutions to conditions as they found them, in the space of a few years brought change—in California and in themselves—that was irrevocable.

Who were these miners? Most were young, under thirty years of age. Over ninety percent were male. "A grey beard was almost as rare as a petticoat," wrote one contemporary. Almost twenty-five percent were foreign born, a fact that Dame Shirley affirmed:

You will hear in the same day, almost at the same time, the lofty melody of the Spanish language, the piquant polish of the French . . . the silver, changing clearness of the Italians, the harsh gangle of the German, the hissing precision of the English, the liquid sweetness of the *Kanaka*, and the sleep-inspiring languor of the East Indian. To complete the catalogue, there is the *native* Indian, with his guttural vocabulary of 20 words! . . . I fancy them a living polyglot of the languages, a perambulatory picture gallery, illustrative of national variety in form and feature.

Although some, like Sarah Royce and her husband, stayed to establish prominent California families, many did not see California as a permanent residence but rather as a place to exploit before returning home. Because of the cost ($750–$1,000 for transportation and equipment when an eastern workman could expect $1 per day), few of the first gold seekers were of the laboring class. Lawyers, teachers, and doctors were represented among them, as were farmers, sailors, merchants, blacksmiths, and tanners; there were, however, few ministers. Dame Shirley wrote of a distinguished-looking man, an "accomplished monte-dealer and horse-jockey" who was rumored to have been a minister in the United States.

Despite their relative scarcity, it was the "poor workman . . . one accustomed to manual labor [who] has a better chance of wealth than one who has hitherto been ashamed to dig," argued "V. J. F." in a letter home. He continued: "The carpet knights and silken striplings, who are perhaps leaving their mothers' sides for the first time, are scarcely capable of sustaining the hardships, privations, and exposure—the digging, delving, and washing, by which the precious metal is obtained. It requires a greater sacrifice not only of the comforts but also of the necessities of life, than is generally imagined."

Daniel Woods recalled with astonishment one of these misfits:

He seemed to have just turned out of Broadway, or to have been turned out of a bandbox. He was exquisite, even to the white kid gloves, eyeglass, and Cologne water, with dancing pumps, and a small gold box suspended about his neck by a gold chain, in which to put his gold. With his dirk knife, elegantly chased, he would go into a hole already dug, and spend an hour in scraping the dirt from the rocks, which he washed with great care, putting the few scales in the gold box around his neck. He had been transplanted from some greenhouse to these rough mountains and soon faded away and died.

Leonard Kip, reminiscing about his 1849 experiences, recalled that less than half those who came to the mines stayed; the majority sought some other livelihood in the cities. Those who stayed did so for a variety of reasons. Kip identified four classes that made up the majority of miners. There were those for whom mining provided the excitement of gambling; they believed, despite the probabilities, that they would strike it rich. There were those who were happy to be working for themselves rather than for an employer; being their own masters compensated for low pay. There were others whose "vicious temperament" attracted them to a life in which, without fear of punishment, they could "drink, fight, and gamble, and indeed, do anything except steal and murder." And there were those who, lured to California by "specious hopes," remained, trapped in the mines by their failure.

Nearly all these men were amateurs who had to learn mining techniques in the field. Under the most favorable conditions, with abundant surface deposits, gold was easily recovered by using spoons, knives, and shovels to scoop pay dirt from river-banks and riverbeds. However, after the first flush, mining techniques grew ever more complicated, initially requiring the collaboration of three to five men; then, as greater mechanization was applied, the investment of significant capital became necessary (Jones, 131–35, 164–75).

To read about work on the colonial frontier of North America, see the entries on Colonial Frontier and New England in the section "Work" in chapter 3 ("Economic Life") in volume 4 of this series.

FOR MORE INFORMATION

Burns, K. *The West*. PBS Video, 1996. Film.

Jones, M. E. *Daily Life on the Nineteenth Century American Frontier*. Westport, Conn.: Greenwood Press, 1998.

White, R. *"It's Your Misfortune and None of My Own": A New History of the American West*. Norman: University of Oklahoma Press, 1991.

ECONOMIC LIFE

WORK

United States,
1850-1865

United States,
Western Frontier

Victorian England

China

Latin America

VICTORIAN ENGLAND

Most Victorians—men, women, and even children—worked long and hard at jobs that required more physical labor than present-day occupations. There were few laws to regulate hours, wages, safety, job security, or working conditions. Workers generally had no contracts, no pensions, and no fringe benefits. Trade unions developed slowly, although by the end of the period the concentration of workers in some fields and the weakening of laws against combination allowed labor to organize and to make some significant improvements, especially in hours and working conditions.

The workday and the workweek were extremely long. In agriculture, labor from sunup to sundown during the busy summer days was not unusual. Other outdoor jobs (building, hauling, dock work) followed the same pattern: long days in summer, when it was light, and short hours (which also meant short wages) in winter. Retail shops stayed open—with the same employees on duty—for 14 or 16 hours a day. Needleworkers stitched almost constantly, day and night, when trade was busy and were laid off (without pay) between seasons. Domestic servants got up before the rest of the household, went to bed last, and were on call at any moment during the day—although there were slack times when they could read or relax in the kitchen.

For most workers except servants, Sunday was a day of rest. Saturday, however, was not; people worked six days a week. Later in the period, short Saturdays became customary: Saturday work ended in midafternoon instead of early evening. Domestic servants usually had a half day off on Sunday, but they were expected to spend part of it attending church services. Servants also had some other regular time off, depending on their employer—perhaps one evening a week or one full day every month.

The regularity of factory work, which required rigorous scheduling and time-keeping, could actually be better for workers than the variable day in other jobs, even though factory hours were long. If the machines ran day and night, there were two 12-hour shifts for workers. Even if there was only one shift, the typical factory day was 6 A.M.–6 P.M. or 7 A.M.–7 P.M. Workers had a half-hour breakfast period in midmorning and an hour for dinner in early afternoon. They brought a snack of bread or cold potatoes for the morning break and went home for their midday meal. Factory workers typically lived only a short walk away; the factory whistle was sounded to get them up and on the job in the morning. In the 1870s, unionized factory workers were able to reduce their week to 54 or 56 hours (10 hours a day for five days, plus a half-day on Saturday); by 1900, miners and some other well-organized workers were getting close to an 8-hour day or 44-hour week. For most occupations, however, 50 or 52 hours was usual. Domestic servants and those in other unorganized and unregulated jobs still had extremely long days and very few holidays.

At the beginning of the Victorian period, the largest single area of employment was agriculture: there were well over a million farm laborers and another 364,000 indoor farm servants (including the dairy

These workers built the London subway system without heavy machinery. This 1862 picture shows the deep trench dug by the navvies for the Metropolitan Line that runs under Baker Street. Courtesy of Guildhall Library Corporation of London.

maids who milked cows and churned butter). More than a million people worked as domestic servants. The other major occupations for women were nondomestic service (in inns, institutions, and so forth), textile manufacturing, and sewing. Men's principal jobs, in addition to farm work, were found in the building trades and in heavy manual labor.

Over the course of the century, the number of agricultural workers shrank and the number in industry and other occupations expanded. The 1851 census reported that 13.3 percent of all employed people were domestic servants and 21 percent were in agriculture. By 1871, with the decline in farming and the growing number of people in middle-class occupations (who, consequently, could afford to employ at least one servant), the proportions had shifted: 15.8 percent of the working population was in domestic service and only 14.2 percent in agriculture. There were also far more workers in industry, mining, building, and transportation. It was partly this concentration of workers in factories and towns that made unionization possible. Isolated workers in small shops—and domestic servants in private homes—remained impossible to organize.

The most significant change in employment during the Victorian period was the great expansion of middle-class and lower-middle-class occupations: teaching, surveying, accounting, drafting, and especially clerical work and retailing. By most

Although Victorian women who worked in factories were not well paid and often labored in dangerous conditions, this drawing from the February 1851 issue of the *Illustrated London News* shows a factory that is clean and well lighted. Courtesy of The Library Company of Philadelphia.

estimates, about 15 percent of all workers were in these occupations at the beginning of the period and about 25 percent at its end. Yet although these jobs were relatively clean and required literacy, they did not necessarily provide more security than manual labor. Indeed, with the growth of unions, manual workers in the 1890s might well have had a shorter workday and greater protection against sickness and unemployment than white-collar employees (Mitchell, *Daily Life*, 41–43).

To read about work in 18th-century England, see the entries on England in the section "Work" in chapter 3 ("Economic Life") in volume 4 of this series; for 20th-century Europe, see the Europe entry in the section "Work" in chapter 3 ("Economic Life") in volume 6 of this series.

FOR MORE INFORMATION

Harrison, J. F. C. *The Early Victorians, 1832–1851*. London: Weidenfeld and Nicolson, 1971.
———. *Late Victorian England, 1875–1901*. London: Fontana Press, 1990.
Mitchell, S. *Daily Life in Victorian England*. Westport, Conn.: Greenwood Press, 1996.
Mitchell, S., ed. *Victorian Britain: An Encyclopedia*. New York: Garland Press, 1998.

ECONOMIC LIFE
|
WORK
|
United States,
1850-1865

United States,
Western Frontier

Victorian England

China

Latin America

CHINA

During the 18th and 19th centuries, a large number of foreign factories established themselves in China. As a result, this period marks a major transition in Chinese labor history. During this time wage labor went from consisting solely of hired hands doing semiskilled and unskilled jobs, including handicraft workers, porters, dockers, boatmen, and farm hands, to a complex system consisting of many different jobs and various labor-related social networks.

Shanghai was the principal commercial and industrial center of China at this time, and it was the location of the majority of China's foreign-owned factories. As a result, members of the rural poor flooded into Shanghai in search of work. This migration occurred in other industrial centers as well, particularly in Beijing and Guangzhou, although the numbers were much smaller.

In the late 19th century it is estimated that over sixty-five percent of the factory workers in Shanghai were women. Women predominated primarily in the silk and cotton industries. They formed the bulk of the labor in spinning, though not in weaving. In the handicraft sector the number of male laborers far exceeded that of females, particularly in construction and manufacturing. However, industries such as box making and ready-made clothing boomed with colonial development, and more and more women worked in these trades. Many women were employed as domestics. Jobs such as waiters, bathhouse attendants, and employees in department stores were filled mainly by men.

Approximately twenty-five percent of factory workers were children, of whom two-thirds were girls. Children rarely did other types of jobs. Many of these children were sent to the cities by their families to find work, and most of their salary was sent home to help the family. It was more common to send a girl child than a boy because girls were seen as more of a financial burden to the family than their brothers, as well as less important to educate.

The majority of laborers in many industries, including silk and cotton as well as others, were illiterate and unskilled. In 1886 only around two percent of workers in these industries were literate, and around the same number were skilled. Only a slightly higher percentage was semiskilled, meaning that their jobs took them about two or three weeks to learn. Female workers and child workers were rarely, if ever, skilled.

As more and more modern technology came to the factories, an increasing number of skilled workers were needed to operate the machinery. Many European factory owners trained men to operate these machines, and in return the men would generally be loyal to the factory owner. This created a new class of factory workers, many of whom were highly instrumental in the nationalist movement.

In the large cities, migrants tended to identify most with their native place. In Shanghai, as in the other industrial centers, many natives of the city looked down upon the migrants as dirty and uncivilized. A hierarchy based on native place developed among the workers. People tended to live in areas with others from their own native place and tended to work in a particular sector along with others from their own home region. Additionally, around 95 percent of these migrants married people from the same region as themselves.

Not only did native-place affiliation provide companionship for migrants to the new city, it also generated connections that served to help workers find jobs and places to live. Job recruitment was generally done by middlemen, who tended to hire workers from the same region as themselves. As a result different enterprises were generally dominated by workers from a particular region. As the number of workers usually greatly exceeded the number of available jobs, workers used native-place connections to find work. In times when work was particularly scarce, native-place relationships were of particular importance.

Another way in which workers from the same native place helped each other when times were difficult was by forming fictive brotherhoods and sisterhoods. These were secret societies in which women or men agreed to help each other out, in any way possible, including financially, should one member of the group come upon hard times. In a society where family was generally considered very important, ties formed through these societies were also treated with great importance.

Guilds were well established in the handcraft, retail, and transportation sectors. They were hierarchical organizations of people working in a particular trade. Because native place was an important part of industry, some of these guilds were organized according to both industry and native-place principles. In terms of economics, guilds sought to regulate the market by regulating the prices of raw and finished materials, as well as wages. In terms of politics they were responsible for several semigovernmental duties, such as the collection of taxes, organization of public works, and keeping order among the people. Guilds provided their members with assistance such as loans, job placement, and coffins and burial plots, among other things. Many of the guilds had their own schools, hospitals, temples, and burial grounds.

Guild leaders were most often high merchants in the particular trade. Often they were elected by the people. Masters of the trade and others with higher earning jobs were always allowed membership, and most guilds also welcomed wage laborers and apprentices. Women were rarely allowed membership in a guild. All members benefited from the security of the guild, and class status does not seem to have been an important element of relations within the guilds.

Over the course of the 19th century, the number of guilds and the number of laborers in the large cities increased. The new social formations that occurred, such as an emphasis on native-place identity, changed the social character of the community. In addition, the demographics of the cities in China changed drastically as more and more migrants from the rural areas came in search of work. Later, in the 20th century, as ideas of nationalism grew, the labor movement played a major role in the nationalist movement. It was the formation of these social structures within the labor movement that paved the way for new ideas of nationalism.

~Dana Lightstone

FOR MORE INFORMATION

Goodman, B. *Native Place, City, and Nation: Regional Networks and Identities in Shanghai, 1853–1937*. Berkeley: University of California Press, 1995.
Lu, X., and E. J. Perry. *Danwei: the Changing Chinese Workplace in Historical Perspective*. New York: M. E. Sharpe, 1997.

ECONOMIC LIFE
|
WORK
|
United States,
1850-1865

United States,
Western Frontier

Victorian England

China

Latin America

LATIN AMERICA

Work in 19th-century Latin America was difficult. Although the terms and relations of work varied significantly across the diverse nations of Latin America and changed dramatically over the century, one constant persisted: almost everyone in society endured physically demanding labor and oppressive conditions.

Political independence from European colonizers in the first quarter of the century did not immediately change the nature of work performed by the great majority of Latin Americans. For instance, indigenous peasants in Mexico, Central America, Peru, and Bolivia continued to toil on large agricultural and ranching enterprises owned by wealthy estate owners of European heritage, while also producing their own subsistence goods. On plantations throughout the Caribbean and northeast Brazil, millions of black slaves still performed the planting, tending, harvesting, processing, transporting, and other arduous tasks involved in producing sugar and other export commodities. Most work remained in the countryside.

In towns and cities, most men and women were poor and tried to sustain themselves and their families by working day jobs in construction and transportation, doing laundry or other services for pay, and selling food and drink on the streets. Some urban poor turned their labors to begging, smuggling, and banditry. Sweatshop workers made textiles and assembled small consumer goods. A small but important number of urban residents were artisans, specializing in carpentry, baking, cobbling, tailoring, or building. Even fewer urban dwellers were privileged bureaucrats, who administered government policies and collected taxes; larger merchants, who brokered trade between town and countryside and between Latin American cities and North Atlantic markets; priests and nuns, who ran the church and its schools; or military and police officials, who served the government and the wealthy.

Patriarchal assumptions and expectations limited women's accessibility to some jobs and occupations. That is, there was an understanding of what women's work meant. Most Latin American women who worked outside of their own homes took positions in other families' homes, where their duties ranged from cooking and cleaning to toting and tending the children. Being a maid was demanding, unrelenting, repetitive work, with girls beginning employment sometimes at age seven or eight, living their lives under the rule of the household patriarch and his wife, laboring around the clock with little time off or even time away from the house, and often enduring sexual and other physical abuse. Considered to be nimble and dexterous, women also found sweatshop jobs spinning thread, weaving textiles, and rolling cigarettes. At the other end of the socioeconomic spectrum, elite women enjoyed significant class privileges but faced legal and cultural obstacles to owning land and businesses and could only pursue an intellectual career by joining a convent.

The character of work did change in important ways by the middle of the 19th century as local Latin American economies were drawn into a grander, growing, and industrializing North Atlantic economy. The liberal dictatorships that consolidated power and built states in the second half of the century sought to exploit new international trade opportunities and also to create domestic conditions attractive to foreign investment. Latin American elites responded to the growing demand from industrializing nations for foods and raw materials. Exports included tin from Bolivia; guano and nitrates (for fertilizer) from Chile and Peru; coffee from Brazil, Colombia, Guatemala, and El Salvador; sugar from Cuba; beef and wheat from Argentina; and bananas from the Caribbean. To service these new large-scale production enterprises, Latin American nations also constructed and expanded railroad and other transportation networks.

Elites adopted a variety of old and new strategies to secure labor for these new enterprises. Cuban sugar planters and Brazilian coffee growers continued to rely heavily on African slavery well into the second half of the 19th century. In situations where chattel slavery proved unprofitable or impractical, owners developed other methods to coerce labor. In Guatemala, for example, estate owners relied on the government to round up indigenous peasants from the highlands to work the coffee groves in the piedmont, especially during the critical picking season. These migrant workers were technically paid wages for their troubles, but they had no choice but to labor under difficult and dangerous conditions, enduring long hours, physical abuse, unsafe food and water, poor housing, and great risk of disease. In rural areas of Mexico, land privatization left many indigenous peasants without the subsistence base they had long counted on, forcing them to seek wages for their labor on large export-producing estates or in cities. Other forms of forced labor in Latin America included debt peonage and indenture.

Immigrants also provided new sources of labor in the second half of the century. For example, immigrants primarily from southern Europe traveled to Argentina for wage work in wheat and beef production. Immigrants cut, bound, and transported wheat and other grains in work gangs on large commercial farms in the pampas, the great plain of Argentina, while others toiled in assembly-line fashion with the dangerous and nasty tasks of slaughtering, butchering, processing, and packing beef in meat plants. In Peru and Cuba, tens of thousands of East Asian indentured immigrants, who had contracted a certain number of years of labor in exchange for their passage and accommodation in their host country, worked in export enterprises.

Even with the support of repressive governments, masters, estate owners, and employers could only go so far in dictating the rules of work and the ways of life of their laborers. Workers found ways to limit the power and orders of their bosses and to bargain the terms and conditions of work. Slaves resisted overtly by rebelling and running away and more subtly by not cooperating, feigning illness and ignorance, and slowing the work pace. Migrant workers manipulated debt and defaulted on loans to gain advantage. Domestic servants paced their work in response to employers' demands and their own needs. Artisans organized guilds. And as capitalist industry became more prominent at the end of the century, factory wage laborers began participating in working-class political parties and organizing trade unions to bargain collectively with owners. Although the balance of power was rarely in their favor and work remained hard, those who labored actively shaped the patterns of work in Latin America throughout the 19th century.

~*Gregory S. Crider*

FOR MORE INFORMATION

Bergquist, C. *Labor in Latin America: Comparative Essays on Chile, Argentina, Venezuela, and Colombia*. Stanford, Calif.: Stanford University Press, 1986.

McCreery, D. J. *The Sweat of Their Brow: A History of Work in Latin America*. Armonk, N.Y.: M. E. Sharpe, 2000.

Skidmore, T. E., and P. H. Smith. *Modern Latin America*. 5th ed. New York: Oxford University Press, 2001.

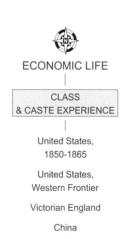

ECONOMIC LIFE

CLASS & CASTE EXPERIENCE

United States, 1850-1865

United States, Western Frontier

Victorian England

China

Latin America

Class and Caste Experience

Class and caste are often difficult concepts to grasp. On one level they deal with money, wealth, and power. The upper classes and higher castes clearly are richer and more influential than the middle and working classes and lower castes. And yet, on the other hand, a rich person like Donald Trump remains among the elite despite at various times declaring bankruptcy. Similarly, in the heady days of the 1990s, many factory workers became paper millionaires as their pension plans went up astronomically in the stock market boom. Still, no one would mistake these line workers for the upper class. Similarly no one would mistake a Brahmin for a fisherman. In other words, class and caste have other and sometimes hard-to-define qualities.

One of them is birthright. In Victorian England, the upper class inherited its economic and political positions. Similarly, if by accident of birth, one was raised in a middle- or working-class family, there were definite limits to one's ability to rise socially. Although it is debatable if the United States ever had a landed gentry along the lines of England, social mobility was also limited as there were always special advantages for the rich. Take, for example, the policy of substitution during the Civil War. The average price for a substitute in war was about $350, which roughly translated to the average yearly earnings of a typical American. Only the rich had the cash on hand to pay for someone else to fight for them. This is not to say that there was no mobility at all. In Victorian England, for example, the middle class grew in size and importance during the 19th century. The same occurred in Latin America, where an increasingly educated middle class centered in growing, industrializing cities gradually acquired more wealth and political power. But, in both places, what class one was born into still continued to matter.

Another aspect of class is work. The upper classes depended on investments and rents for income. The middle class parlayed their education into a professional job that relied more on brainpower than muscles. Of course, working-class men and women had to use their knowledge and skills to perform their sometimes quite dangerous jobs. And yet, what defined their labors was physical work. In the entries that follow, this is most evident in the lives of Chinese factory workers, British miners, and American settlers and cowboys. The terribly difficult work and the hardships that they faced have almost a surreal quality to them. The entry on the West relates stories of cowboys herding as many as 15,000 cows in a single drive! Frontier farmers faced all sorts of dangers from nature including grasshopper invasions, bone-numbing cold, and hail large enough to kill animals. Moreover, there was no choice not to work and live off some store of old wealth like the upper class. As one miner wrote in the 19th century: "it is work, *work*, WORK! *Work or perish!*" No other dictum could better describe working-class life in the 19th century.

UNITED STATES, 1850–65

The biggest class issue during the Civil War was conscription, which both in the South and the North affected the working class more than the upper class. Ultimately, the South was forced to resort to conscription to preserve its forces in the field. The Confederate Conscription Act was the first general draft of soldiers in America. Neither the Confederate Congress nor Jefferson Davis wanted it, but conscription was seen as an absolute necessity. Its purpose was twofold. The 12-month

ECONOMIC LIFE

CLASS
& CASTE EXPERIENCE

United States,
1850-1865

United States,
Western Frontier

Victorian England

China

Latin America

enlistments entered into in the spring of 1861 were about to run out. It was feared that these men, now veterans of war and free from many of the romantic notions they had brought to their first muster, would fail to reenlist. The Conscription Act ensured that the Confederacy would retain the men it had in the army, and, since the war had already lasted longer than anyone had predicted, it provided for the additional men that would be needed.

The Confederate Congress passed the Conscription Act of 1862 by more than a two to one vote. The act made all white males from the ages of 18 to 35 eligible for three years of service. Men who had already served one year were made responsible for two more. The U.S. Congress followed with its own Conscription Act in August of the same year, but Lincoln refused to sign it into law until March 1863. The draft, almost identical in its characteristics to the South's, was universally unpopular, but it was accepted with a certain equanimity, rather than reservation, as in the South. In the North, the first drawing of names in July 1863 set off a violent four-day riot, with a mob of over fifty thousand workingmen swarming through New York. Federal troops, just back from the grim scene at Gettysburg, were called upon to quell the riots, which left more than one thousand rioters dead. Small disturbances also broke out in Boston, Troy, New York, and other towns in the East and in Ohio.

Failure to comply with the draft could end in arrest and imprisonment. Conscripts were generally brought to training camps, given cursory medical exams, vaccinated, and given some basic military instruction. Their time in camp and the extent of their training were dependent in large part on the immediate needs of the army. Now considered soldiers, they were shipped off to join regiments from their own states in the field. It has been estimated that over three hundred thousand men (from 25 to 30 percent of the Union army) were conscripts during the course of the war.

There were a number of ways by which a man could avoid the draft. If he was found to have a physical disability he would be exempt. Disqualifying disabilities included genuine health problems like blindness, missing limbs, lung disease, venereal disease, or an unsound heart. Other genuine problems were less evident. Urine samples were taken; a man's balance and coordination were tested; and even if he could see, his eyesight needed to be normal or at least correctable with the use of glasses. Those who were epileptic or insane were exempt. Chronic conditions such as coughing, shortness of breath, and back pain were more difficult to prove and harder for the authorities to evaluate. Two very simple physical characteristics also freed a man from conscription. First, he could not be less than 5 feet 6 inches tall, which suggests that people were not really shorter in the 19th century than they are today. Second, as a purely practical matter, he needed at least two opposed teeth because the bullet cartridge needed to be torn open with the teeth in firing the musket.

A man could have an exemption from the draft based on a war-related occupation considered more critical to the cause than his service at the front. Among those exempt from the draft were iron founders, machinists, miners, and railroad workers; ferrymen, pilots, and steamboat workers; government officials, clerks, and telegraphers; ministers, professors, teachers of the handicapped, and private teachers with more than 20 pupils. There were protests over the exemptions, but the only outcome of a public outcry was an extension of the exemption to physicians, leather workers, blacksmiths, millers, munitions workers, shipyard workers, salt makers, charcoal burners, some stockmen, some printers, and one editor for each paper. Conscientious objectors who belonged to recognized nonviolent sects did not have to serve if they provided a substitute or paid $500 to the government.

One of the more flagrant exemptions was that one slave owner, or a slave overseer who had more than twenty slaves under his care, would be exempt from each plantation. White overseers were exempt because of a practical consideration—the ever-present fear of slave uprisings. Many felt that this exemption led to "a rich man's war and a poor man's fight." Although this attitude was strongly held in many circles, many slave owners and their sons voluntarily served in the war, very often as well-placed officers and leaders of local partisan groups. As an example, Wade Hampton, a leading slave owner—considered to be the richest man in the South before the war—served with great distinction throughout and was wounded several times. Both his brother and his son lost their lives in battle.

During the Civil War, a man could buy his way out of the draft by finding a substitute.

Finally, and most importantly for our purposes here, a man could buy his way out of the draft by finding a substitute. As much as $400 in gold was offered in 1863 for a draft substitute. The average American worker at this time made less than that yearly. Hence substitution was largely for those who could afford such a luxury. There was a tremendous amount of fraud perpetrated in the hiring of substitutes, and this may have been the greatest weakness of the draft system. Physically unsound men were found to replace sound substitutes before they reached the training camps; underaged boys and overaged men were used in the same manner; and many paid substitutes simply deserted, often repeating the process over and over again under different names.

The Conscription Acts and the exemptions were modified as the war progressed, and more and more men became eligible for the draft. The federal act made all men 20 to 45 eligible. The manpower-starved Confederates accepted boys of 17 years of age and men between 46 and 50 as local defense forces or as railroad guards. These men who were too young or too old to fight on the front lines were able to free thousands of soldiers to do so. The draft had the positive effect of retaining veteran soldiers in the ranks. Without these the Southern armies would soon have collapsed. The conscription system was nonetheless amazingly inefficient and filled with abuses; moreover, it provided a rallying point for antiwar sentiment (Volo and Volo, 108–11).

To read about class and caste in the United States in the 20th century, see the United States entries in the section "Class and Caste Experience & Discrimination" in chapter 3 ("Economic Life") in volume 6 of this series.

FOR MORE INFORMATION

McPherson, J. M. *Battle Cry of Freedom: The Civil War Era.* New York: Oxford University Press, 1990.

Paludan, P. S. *A People's Contest: The Union and Civil War, 1861–1865*. New York: Harper & Row, 1988.

Thomas, E. M. *The Confederate Nation: 1861–1865*. New York: Harper & Row, 1979.

Volo, D. D., and J. M. Volo. *Daily Life in Civil War America*. Westport, Conn.: Greenwood Press, 1998.

ECONOMIC LIFE
|
CLASS
& CASTE EXPERIENCE
|
United States,
1850-1865

United States,
Western Frontier

Victorian England

China

Latin America

UNITED STATES, WESTERN FRONTIER

The class experience on the frontier was quite varied and often depended upon the type of job that one had. In other words, it made a difference whether one was a miner, frontier farmer, or cowboy. Though most did not experience the bonanza they had expected, miners either would not or could not go home immediately. Some simply did not have the cost of transportation. Others could not face having failed in an adventure everyone had expected to be profitable. So they stayed, enduring much hardship. It is worth looking at the conditions of their everyday life.

First and foremost, mining demanded hard physical work in extremely uncomfortable conditions. After the first lucky strikes, finding color required hours of attacking rock with pickaxes, bending and hoisting water (weighing eight pounds per gallon) into the cradle, excavating boulders from riverbeds, and moving them to build dams. Just to get to their claim, miners had to hike up and down precipitous mountainsides. Separating the gold from sand, dirt, or gravel usually meant standing in the river, frigid from melting snows, while the sun beat down. One could be wet from icy streams below the waist and from sweat above. And, after a day of such backbreaking labor, the miner returned to his cabin or tent to cook his dinner, bake bread for the next day, and then fall into his blankets on the ground, still in his clothes that were clammy from the day's work. He did remove his boots, often using them as a pillow. During his sleep he was frequently pestered by fleas or mosquitoes and often so overrun with rats that cats became welcome companions. Indeed, William Perkins was once offered one ounce of gold dust for every pound his cat weighed, so eager were other miners to have a mouser.

In 1851 Dame Shirley tried her hand at mining for a day. Her description of being a "mineress" is unintentionally ironic. To get her sister a souvenir—$3.25 worth of gold dust—"I wet my feet, tore my dress, spoiled a pair of new gloves, nearly froze my fingers, got an awful headache, took cold, and lost a valuable breastpin." Prentice Mulford knew the pain of unexpectedly hitting a boulder with his pick, the vibrations traveling "like a shock along the iron, up the handle, and into one's arm and 'crazy bone.'" He knew firsthand how debilitating such work was—it quickly made a man look 10 years older than he was. "You can't keep up this sort of thing—digging, tugging, lifting, wet to the skin day after day, summer and winter, with no interval of rest, but a steady drag 12 months of the year—without paying for it. There's dissipation of muscle as well as in the use of whiskey." Another miner advised friends at home, "The work here is very hard. $1 a day in New York is better than $10 here." Bayard Taylor likewise tried to disabuse those who thought gold mining was an easy way to gain a fortune. "If anyone expects to dig treasures out of the earth, in California, without severe labor, he is wofully [*sic*] mistaken. Of all classes of men, those who pave streets and quarry limestone are best adapted for gold diggers." Something of the desperation of those "lawyers, doctors, clergymen, farmers, soldiers [and] deserters" who have flocked to the gold fields was captured by Daniel B. Woods:

This morning, notwithstanding the rain, we were again at our work. We *must* work. In sunshine and rain, in warm and cold, in sickness and health, successful or not, early and late, it is work, *work*, WORK! *Work or perish!* [We work] not for *gold*, but for *bread* . . . Cheerful words are seldom heard, more seldom the boisterous shout and laugh, which indicate success, and which, when heard, sink to a lower ebb the spirits of the unsuccessful. We have [today] made 50 cents each.

On sites often named for the first person who worked them (Owesley's Bar, for example) or for notable events (Murderer's, Rattlesnake, Rich, or Condemned Bars, for example), miners' clothing was simple: a pair of heavy pants, often corduroy, tucked into heavy rubber boots; a flannel shirt, usually red or blue; a heavy leather belt into which a Colt revolver was stuck; and a shapeless hat. There was no one to dress for, and the work quickly tore and snagged clothes. This necessitated yet another chore: the miner had to learn how to wield a needle to patch his clothes. Although many wore the same clothing day after day, James L. Tyson, a doctor-miner, recommended a change of "under clothing" and socks for health's sake.

Akin to a miner's daily experience, farmers on the frontier also had a hard life. No matter how potential settlers acquired the land, and no matter how they got there—by steamboats, trains, farm wagons, stagecoaches, or on foot—many were in for a rude awakening. Though establishing a farm in the grasslands initially seemed easier than it had been in the woodland East, where trees had to be girdled, cut, and burned and stumps grubbed out before land could be plowed, the environment of the Great Plains was far from hospitable. This was, after all, a region that George Catlin had pronounced "almost one entire plain of grass, which is and ever must be, useless to cultivating man."

The climate itself was a trial. Howard Ruede remembered that August in Kansas produced temperatures of 108 degrees Fahrenheit in the shade and 128 degrees F in the sun. Hamlin Garland recalled summer in Dakota Territory as "ominous":

The winds were hot and dry and the grass, baked on the stem, had become as inflammable as hay. The birds were silent. The sky, absolutely cloudless, began to scare us with its light. The sun rose through the dusty air, sinister with flare of horizontal heat. The little gardens . . . withered, and many of the women began to complain bitterly of the loneliness, and lack of shade. The tiny cabins were like ovens at midday.

Winter was equally formidable. Garland observed, "No one knows what winter means until he has lived through one in a pine-board shanty on a Dakota plain with only buffalo bones for fuel." Grace Fairchild remembered a cow breaking the ice and stepping into a water hole one winter; one back leg froze and "the next spring her leg dropped off." Her husband fashioned a wooden leg, but after the cow kicked out and the leg hit him in the head, they fattened her and butchered her in the fall.

"We couldn't tell any difference between a three-legged cow and a four-legged one when the steaks were on the table." The winter of 1885–86 was especially hard. According to a South Dakota folk saying, "It was so cold that when he died they just sharpened his feet and drove him into the ground." Elinore Stewart remembered such extremes in Wyoming: "They have just three seasons here, winter and July and August."

Though there were summer droughts, when the rains came they turned the soil to a thick, viscous gumbo. Many settlers recall it clinging to wagon wheels until it was 8 to 10 inches thick before it fell off of its own weight. Later, graded gravel roads made travel easier, but the soil was unchanged. As settlers said, "If you stick to this country when it's dry, it will stick to you when it is wet."

Across the open plains the wind was omnipresent and often nerve-wracking. Mary Clark wrote to her parents from her South Dakota claim:

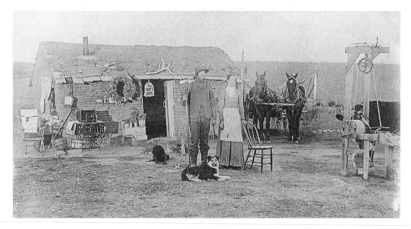

This 1886 photograph of John Curry and his wife in front of their sod house near West Union, Nebraska, shows the few possessions that migrant families had. In heavy rains, sod houses leaked muddy water onto family members. Nebraska State Historical Society, Solomon D. Butcher Collection.

The wind was too fierce. Really it was something awful and it hardly ever goes down. It actually blows the feathers off the chickens' backs. . . . I can't put up many pictures and things for everytime the door opens they all blow off the wall. . . . It's so funny—we noticed how terrible loud everyone talks out here and now we find ourselves just shouting away at the top of our voices. We discovered it must be the wind, and unless you yell you can't be heard at all.

If a windstorm hit on wash day, everyone rushed outside to get the clothes before they blew away. Buckets, pails, and lightweight tools might be blown for miles if they didn't first catch on fences.

The same winds, blowing over sun-baked land, produced dust storms, clouds of soil hundreds of feet high that blotted out the sun, filled the house with dust, almost smothered cattle in the stable, exposed the roots of young wheat, causing it to wither and die, and sent homesteaders into "dull despairing rage."

Bad as summer winds were, winter blizzards were worse. The Ammons sisters, returning from school, saw a blizzard coming "like white smoke," and before they got home they could not see their hands before their faces. With the thermometer at −30 degrees F and the snow blowing at 80 miles per hour, it seemed as if the sun had been "wholly blotted out and that the world would never again be warm." Homesteaders rigged ropes between house and barn so they would not get lost going to feed the animals. Dr. Bessie Rehwinkel, returning from a house call, was caught in a sudden Wyoming snow storm. Driving blindly, her horses becoming more exhausted by the minute, she recalled, "My whole body was becoming numb, and I began to feel an almost irresistible drowsiness creeping upon me." Finally, miraculously, she saw a light through the gloom, and "covered from head to foot with an icy sheet of snow, which had frozen into a crust, so that I had become a human icicle," she was welcomed into that very house she had left three hours earlier. Another winter wanderer was not so lucky. Lost in a storm he killed his horse, ripped him open, and crawled into the body cavity to stay warm. He was found several days later, frozen into his equine tomb.

One of the most terrifying natural disasters was the prairie fire, which might be caused by a lightning strike, a spark from a train, or human carelessness. It was simultaneously horrifying and awesome. "The sky is pierced with tall pyramids of flame, or covered with writhing, leaping, lurid serpents, or transformed into a broad ocean lit up by a blazing sunset. Now a whole valance of fire slides off into the prairie, and then opening its great devouring jaws closes in upon the deadened grass." Such a fire could roar across the plains destroying homes, barns, haystacks, even whole settlements in its path. It was the unwritten law that whenever a fire broke out, every able-bodied person must pitch in to fight it, plowing firebreaks, setting backfires, and slapping tongues of flame with wet rags. To be the cause of such a fire not only was embarrassing but also brought legal penalties. A settler convicted of carelessness with fire could receive six months in jail and a $1,000 fine.

Settlers were also pestered by native critters. Mosquitoes were so bad during summer that some farmers would build a fire at the door and let the wind blow smoke into the house; eyes smarting from the smoke were, to most people, preferable to the welts raised by the voracious insects. Flies mercilessly attacked cows in their stalls—and the women or children milking them. During August and September when men were in the field cutting oats or hay, crickets ate coats or hats left beside the haystack, gnawed pitchfork handles, and devoured any leather straps left lying about. On occasion cinch bugs, small, "evil-smelling" insects, devoured the wheat crops at harvest time, bringing financial disaster to farmers.

Probably the most destructive insects were grasshoppers, which thrived on hot, dry conditions. In 1866 they darkened the sky in a column 150 by 100 miles wide; they were so numerous that they stopped horse races in Fort Scott, Kansas, covering the track up to three inches deep. In 1874 grasshoppers ravaged crops from the Dakotas to Texas. They came in such large numbers that their weight broke tree limbs and mashed corn stalks and potato plants. One settler reported that his chickens and turkeys gorged themselves on hoppers; their meat subsequently had the flavor of grasshoppers. Men had to tie strings around their pants legs to keep the insects from crawling up their legs. Women attempting to protect their gardens by covering them with bedsheets watched in horror as the grasshoppers simply ate through the bedclothes. Creek water was so stained with grasshopper excrement that it was the color of coffee. And near Kearney, Nebraska, grasshoppers were so thick on the Union Pacific lines that trains were stopped. Section hands were called out to shovel the insects off the tracks, which were so oily and greasy that the wheels spun. One intriguing byproduct of the grasshopper invasions was the inventions for dealing with them—among them the grasshopper dozier, a long pan made of tin and sheet iron and filled with kerosene. It was pushed through the fields; grasshoppers fell in and died, their carcasses dumped in the fields in mounds five feet high.

Another hazard, the rattlesnake, was mentioned so often by diarists as to be commonplace. Miriam Davis Colt remembered seeing rattlers crawling or hanging over sills near her front door. At night she would hear "peculiar noises" under the floor, which at first she thought were rats. Instead they were snakes, and her husband kept a stout hickory stick near their bed to drive the snakes away. Mollie Sanford, in her bare feet, heard the telltale sound, killed a snake, and hung its 11 rattles on a tree as a trophy. The snakes did not fear people but slithered into homes, barns, and cellars. Children playing in the yard were their most frequent victims, though adults and livestock also died of snakebite. Nearly everyone carried a hoe to kill any rattlers they might encounter. Sometimes they actually invaded the house. One young boy awoke in the night complaining that his brother, sleeping in the same bed, was pinching him; the parents quieted the boys, and in the morning one was dead—of snakebite.

It was no wonder, with all these natural disasters and herpetological and entomological plagues, that Grace Fairchild "questioned in my own mind how a sane man could [drag] his family into such a . . . country." Indeed, faced with such disasters some homesteaders who could afford it left the country, the sides of their wagons emblazoned with bleakly humorous slogans such as "From Sodom, where it rains grasshoppers, fire, and destruction."

The cowboy on the long drive north from Texas faced additional hardships. The central rationale for the long drive was that the calf survival rate was better in the comparatively warmer Texas climate, whereas cattle fattened better for market on the grasses of the northern plains. Moreover, even before cow towns were established at the junctions between trail and railroad, there were beef markets in the North—army posts, mining communities, and Indian reservations; early on, longhorns were the basis of seed herds on the northern ranches.

When Joseph McCoy established Abilene, Kansas, in 1867, the heyday of the long drive began. Between 1867 and 1887 the number totaled 5.5 million animals. The year 1871 saw the greatest number—600,000—driven north in one year. Over half of these remained unsold; others, driven onto overgrazed land, died during the harsh winter of 1871–72. The ranchers' plight was made worse by the Panic of 1873, during which banks refused to extend credit and many young, thin cattle had to be sent east before they were ready for market, thus further depressing their price. The glorious dreams of men such as Baron von Richthofen had turned to nightmares. By 1875 the long drive sent only 150,000 north from Texas, the end of the first boom in the cattle business.

To the cowboys driving cattle north, weather and working conditions had greater immediacy than did macroeconomics. George Deffield recorded his impressions of one long drive from Texas to Iowa in 1866:

Upset our wagon in River & lost Many of our cooking utencils . . . was on my Horse the whole night & it raining hard . . . Lost my Knife. . . . There was one of our party Drowned to day . . . & several narrow escapes. . . . Horses *all* give out & Men refused to do anything. . . . Awful night . . . not having a bite to eat for 60 hours . . . *Tired*. . . . Indians very troublesome. . . . Oh! what a night—Thunder Lightning & rain—we followed our Beeves *all* night as they wandered about. . . . Hands all Growling & Swearing—every thing is wet

& cold . . . Have *not* got the *Blues* but am in *Hel of a fix*. . . . My back is Blistered badly. . . . Flies was worse than I ever saw them. . . . One man down with Boils & one with Ague. . . . Found a Human skeleton on the Prairie to day.

The long drive continued from early spring to late fall, the herds ranging in size from 300 to 3,000 head, though the largest, in 1859, was 15,000. Generally the cowboy-to-cow ratio was between 1 to 250 and 1 to 400. A day's drive was usually no more than 10 to 15 miles, for if the cattle were to arrive in good condition they had to be allowed to graze along the way. On occasion, in order to reach water, the drive might be as long as 20 miles. For the cowboy this meant a long day in the saddle, keeping the herd together and rounding up the stragglers. Most cattle had been given a temporary trail brand on their flank for identification en route; some outfits also cropped the tails of trail herds. Cowboys took up positions at point (in front of the herd), on the flank, and to the rear; these positions were alternated so that the worst job in the rear, eating dust, was shared by all.

When the herds reached rivers, swimming the cattle across was not easy. Though they might initially plunge into the water to slake their thirst, once in the river (especially when it was swollen from heavy rains) they often panicked, milling around in circles and even climbing atop one another's backs, with the lowest animals being in real danger of drowning. For cowboys, many of whom did not swim themselves, getting these animals out was dangerous work. Other steers drowned in sinkholes or became mired in quicksand. They had to be roped and pulled out. The experience sometimes left them unable to travel. Baylis John Fletcher recalls one instance of a "trail hospital" where crippled and disabled cattle were cut out of the herd and left with a solitary herder until they were able to travel again.

There were other hazards and discomforts on the long drive. Hail was sometimes as large as quail eggs, capable of beating birds and rabbits to death. In May 1874, 78 horses from one outfit froze to death in an unseasonable Texas blizzard. As the herds crossed the Red River, they passed out of Texas law into The Nations—Indian Territory—where Indians might beg or even rustle cattle. In 1881 the Crows of Montana asked $1 a head for a drive to cross their tribal lands; when the figure was refused, they stampeded the herd. The event was captured in a Charles Russell painting. The Indians, however, were generally less of a hazard than homesteaders, who were angry at herds that trampled their fields. By Kansas law, a plowed furrow around a field was the legal equivalent of a fence; any loose stock crossing it was considered to be trespassing, and the owner of the herd was liable for damage. A latter-day trail boss described the drive as "one continual row from start to finish" with homesteaders. By 1882, farmers, angry at crop destruction and fearful of tick fever, were so adamant that virtually all of Kansas was off-limits to trail herds. The cowboys' response was the slogan, "Bend 'em west, boys. Nothing in Kansas anyhow except the three suns— sunflowers, sunshine, and those sons of bitches."

The most common cause of cowboys' deaths was being dragged by a horse; many others, however, also met death from pneumonia, tuberculosis, and being struck by

> *Hail was sometimes as large as quail eggs, capable of beating birds and rabbits to death.*

lightning. Yet cowboys probably feared the stampede most. Almost anything could spook a herd, especially at night: a coyote's howl, a cowboy lighting a cigarette, a sudden rumble of thunder. Fletcher remembers trailing a herd through Victoria, Texas. A woman, fearful that the cattle would trample her roses, waved her bonnet at them, starting a panic; before they were gotten under control, they had smashed most of the yard fences in town.

Usually, though, stampedes happened on the trail at night after the cattle had been bedded down. The single best way to stop them was to ride with the herd until you had caught up with the leaders and then turn them in circles, gradually diminishing in size until the cattle could be gentled into sleep again. For night guard duty cowboys picked their quietest, gentlest, most sure-footed horses. Even so, accidents happened—most likely a hoof plunging into a prairie dog hole. The result could be fatal. Teddy Blue describes such an accident:

[T]hat night it come up an awful storm. It took all four of us to hold the cattle and we didn't hold them, and when morning come there was one man missing. We went back to look for him, and we found him among the prairie dog holes, beside his horse. The horse's ribs was scraped bare of hide, and all the rest of horse and man was mashed into the ground as flat as a pancake. The only thing you could recognize was his six-shooter. We tried to think it was the lightning hit him, and that was what we wrote his folks. . . . But we couldn't really believe it ourselves. . . . I'm afraid his horse stepped into one of them holes and they both went down before the stampede. . . . The awful part . . . was that we had milled them cattle over him all night, not knowing he was there. . . . After that, orders were given to sing when you were running with a stampede, so others would know where you were as long as they heard you singing, and if they didn't hear you, they would figure that something had happened.

Though in this passage the cowboys were told to sing to locate each other, singing was soon seen to be an effective way of soothing the cattle at night and thus preventing stampedes. One cowboy, riding around the herd clockwise, would sing one verse; his partner, riding in the opposite direction, would sing the next from the opposite side of the herd. The worst thing a man could do on night guard was to fall asleep. Singing helped some stay awake too, but a number of cowboys tell of rubbing tobacco juice in their eyes, with the resulting pain preventing sleep.

A string of good horses was essential to the cowboy. Most were relatively small (12 to 14 hands in height and weighing from 700 to 900 pounds) mustangs or mustangs interbred with U.S. cavalry thoroughbreds. Often they roamed grasslands for about four years; breaking them to saddle and bridle took an average of four to six days, though a good cutting horse took longer, and a good horse for night guard required a quiet temperament. One of a cowboy's most expensive purchases was his saddle, often the equivalent of a month's pay. This was not, however, an extravagance, for a good rider in a good saddle could ride for 15 hours and 70 miles and end with a healthy horse, whereas a poor rider in a bad saddle could make a horse sore in an hour. Each cowboy was expected to keep his horse's feet in good condition by trimming the hooves and shoeing when necessary. Their tails were kept thinned out and short by pulling out hair by hand until it reached only to the hock; a "long-tailed horse was the mark of a farmer or a town gambler." How a man treated his horse was a measure of character. Not all were kind or caring, but those who were earned respect. Teddy Blue notes that it was a deadly insult to ride a cowboy's horse without his permission (Jones, 139–41, 171–74, 186–89).

FOR MORE INFORMATION

Burns, K. *The West.* PBS Video, 1996. Film.

Jones, M. E. *Daily Life on the Nineteenth Century American Frontier.* Westport, Conn.: Greenwood Press, 1998.

Limerick, P. N. *The Legacy of Conquest: The Unbroken Past of the American West.* New York: W. W. Norton and Co., 1987.

VICTORIAN ENGLAND

ECONOMIC LIFE

CLASS
& CASTE EXPERIENCE

United States,
1850-1865

United States,
Western Frontier

Victorian England

China

Latin America

The concept of class is sometimes difficult to understand. In Victorian England it did not depend on the amount of money people had—although it did rest partly on the source of their income, as well as on birth and family connections. Most people understood and accepted their place in the class hierarchy. When the railroads designated different cars for first class, second class, and third class, passengers knew where they were expected to ride. Even if a working man had just won a lot of money on the races and could afford an expensive ticket, he would not dream of riding home in the first-class car. Class was revealed in manners, speech, clothing, education, and values. The classes lived in separate areas and observed different social customs in everything from religion to courtship to the names and hours of their meals. In addition, Victorians believed that each class had its own standards; and people were expected to conform to the rules for their class. It was wrong, people thought, to behave like someone from a class above—or below—one's own.

In the strictest legal sense, England had only two classes: aristocrats (who inherited titles and land) and commoners (everyone else). Nevertheless, most Victorians understood that their society was three tiered. In broad terms, the working classes (both men and women) did visible work. Their labor was physical and often dirty; it showed in their clothes and their hands. They were paid a daily or weekly wage. Men of the middle classes did clean work, which usually involved mental rather than physical effort. They earned a monthly or yearly salary. The elite or upper classes did not work for money. They included the aristocracy and the landed gentry. Their income came from inherited land or investments.

Although members of the working class are not much seen in Victorian fiction or in popular conceptions of Victorian life, about three people out of every four did manual work. The largest number was agricultural laborers, domestic servants, and factory hands. In addition there were a great variety of unskilled, semiskilled, and skilled jobs in mining, fishing, transportation, building, the garment industry, and other manual trades.

Most working people earned just enough to stay alive; they could be thrown into poverty by illness, layoffs, or a sudden misfortune (e.g., a factory fire) that caused even short-term unemployment. People in unskilled and semiskilled jobs generally needed additional income from other members of the family. Because manual labor was physically demanding, working men were often most highly paid in their 20s, when they were in peak physical condition. They married then; and for a year or two, while both husband and wife continued to work, there was extra money to buy a few things. Once children came, a woman could not usually continue working a 12- or 14-hour day. She might earn something at home by doing piecework or taking in a lodger, but the family would be quite poor while the children were small. In addition, the man earned less as he grew older. Girls and boys had to start work very young. They had little schooling. Even before they were old enough for regular jobs, they often helped in the work done by older members of the family.

Once the children were all at work, the family's income would again rise above the poverty level. The parents might even accumulate some savings—which they would need after the children married and set up their own households. By that time, hard labor and poor food would have weakened the parents' health. They could not earn nearly as much as when they were younger. If they lived to be old, they would probably be very poor. They might end their days in the workhouse unless some of their children earned enough to take care of them.

Skilled workers, who made up perhaps 15 percent of the working class, were in a more fortunate position. Printers, masons, carpenters, bookbinders, expert dressmakers, shoemakers, and the growing number of highly skilled workers in new trades such as toolmaking had a higher and more dependable income. Because these trades were generally learned through apprenticeship, skilled workers came from families that could afford to do without their children's income while the apprenticeship was served. Many girls who trained as teachers and nurses in the later part of the century were the daughters of skilled workers. In effect, the skilled formed a separate subclass within the working class, with differences in education, training, interests, and ways of life. Artisans such as saddlers, shoemakers, bakers, and builders sometimes became employers and set up their own shops, thereby occupying a borderline territory between working and middle classes.

Poor women did what work they could get. In this 1875 drawing, these women workers from London's East End sew sacks by the light of a streetlamp to save on the cost of candles.

The middle class grew in size and importance during the Victorian period. It made up about 15 percent of the population in 1837 and perhaps 25 percent in 1901. This was a diverse group, including everyone between the working class (who earned their living through physical labor) and the elite (who inherited landed estates). It's important to remember that money was not the defining factor. The middle class included successful industrialists and extremely wealthy bankers such as the Rothschilds; it also included poor clerks such as Bob Cratchit (of Charles Dickens's *The Christmas Carol*). Cratchit earned only half as much as a skilled worker such as a printer or a railway engine driver, but he would nevertheless be considered middle class.

Within the middle class, those with the highest social standing were the professionals (sometimes referred to as the old middle class or upper middle class). They included Church of England clergymen, military and naval officers, men in the high-status branches of law and medicine, those at the upper levels of governmental service, university professors, and the headmasters of prestigious schools. Later in the period, occupations such as architecture and civil engineering might be added. The professional middle classes were largely urban. They educated their sons at boarding school and university; later in the period they often demanded quality education for their daughters as well.

The newer portion of the upper middle class was made up of large-scale merchants, manufacturers, and bankers—men whose success was a direct consequence of the Industrial Revolution. The wealthiest among them achieved some class mobility in the next generation by sending their sons to prestigious schools and preparing them for a profession; their daughters might hope to marry landowners.

Farmers (who employed farm laborers to do the actual physical work on the land) were also part of the middle class. So were men in a number of newer occupations that required a reasonably good education: accountants, local government workers, journalists, surveyors, insurance agents, police inspectors, and so forth.

Small shopkeepers and most clerical workers were generally considered lower middle-class. Such work required literacy but not further education. Children of the lower middle class were probably kept at school until age 12 or 14, after which daughters as well as sons might begin working in the family shop or in some suitable commercial post. As London became a world center of business and finance, the number of people doing what was then called black coated work (we now call it white collar) grew enormously. The group included clerks, middle managers, book-keepers, and lower-level government workers. Women increasingly found clean and respectable work in shops, offices, and telephone exchanges and as schoolteachers.

Despite the range in status and income, the middle class was presumed to share a set of standards and ideals. The concept of a distinctly middle-class way of life developed early in the Victorian period. In addition to maintaining a certain kind of house, the middle class despised aristocratic idleness; the majority valued hard work, sexual morality, and individual responsibility. Education was important; sons who were not sent to the elite boarding schools went to local grammar schools or to private schools with a practical curriculum. The middle classes were churchgoers: generally the professional middle class attended the Church of England, although manufacturers and tradesmen were more likely to be Nonconformists.

Family togetherness and the idealization of family life were typically middle class: many among the working class had to send children out to work when they were very young, and upper-class children were raised by servants and saw little of their parents. Other middle-class virtues included sobriety, thrift, ambition, punctuality, constructive use of leisure, and prudent marriage—indeed, the wish to be financially secure before starting a family meant that middle-class men often did not marry until they were past age 30.

A man's status depended primarily on his occupation and the family into which he was born; a married woman's status derived from her husband. Church of England clergymen in minor parishes might have very small incomes, but they were indisputably gentlemen because of their education, values, and position in the community. It would be inconceivable for such a man's wife or daughters to do paid work.

His sons, of course, would support themselves, but extraordinary sacrifices were made to pay for their education so they could enter professions or government service. There were men in skilled trades who earned enough to live in a comfortable house in a decent neighborhood, keep servants, and send their children to good local schools; but they were nevertheless not considered middle class.

Aristocrats and the gentry made up a hereditary landowning class, whose income came from the rental of their property. A landowner's estate—some owned thousands of acres—was divided into farms that were rented out on very long-term leases. The manor or hall in which the landowner lived was a comfortable country house with a staff of servants. The title (in the case of aristocrats) and the land usually passed intact to the eldest son. With the coming of 19th-century moral reforms, an upper-class life of pure leisure and dissipation lost favor. When the eldest son inherited the estate, he was expected to do something useful—to sit in Parliament, take part in local affairs, use his influence in a charitable cause—although he did not do any paid work. Younger sons might inherit some income, but many were prepared to enter a profession, especially as military officers, clergymen, or colonial administrators.

In 1842 there were 562 titled families in England. The peerage has five grades. The ranks (and the correct mode of addressing titled men and their wives) are shown in the chart "Ranks and Titles." There were very few dukes (the highest rank of the peerage) and several hundred barons. An aristocrat is not promoted up the ranks from lower to higher; he continues to hold the title he inherits. Sometimes, however, a new title is created to reward someone for extraordinary public accomplishments. In late-Victorian times, the banker and philanthropist Angela Burdett-Coutts became the first woman to be made a baroness in recognition of her service to the nation. It may also sometimes appear, in reading novels, that a man has been promoted, because of the custom of using a courtesy title for an eldest son. A duke, viscount, or earl generally holds several additional titles that have passed into his family, over the centuries, through marriage and inheritance. The second most important family title is given to the eldest son, by courtesy, while his father is still alive. Thus the duke of August's son may be known as the earl of June. When the old duke dies, his son will no longer be called the earl of June but will become the duke of August.

This turn of the century photograph of a workhouse lunchroom in London shows not only the vast number of poor but also the fact that many were elderly.

The head of a titled family had certain responsibilities and privileges. He was automatically a member of the House of Lords. He could not be arrested for debt. And if he was charged with a criminal offense, he would be tried by a jury of his peers—a jury made up of other noblemen, in a special court held in Westminster Hall rather than in an ordinary criminal court.

Knights and baronets are technically commoners; they do not have an aristocrat's privileges, although they are addressed as sir. The baronet's title is inherited. A knighthood must be earned; the title is awarded by the monarch for some important public, military, or artistic accomplishment, and it does not pass down to the knight's sons.

In some European countries the aristocracy as a whole formed a separate class under law; the children of a titled man were also aristocrats with special rights. In England, the sons and daughters of peers were commoners. If he wanted to be active in government, a peer's son could run for election to the House of Commons. If he broke the law, he would be tried in ordinary criminal courts. Only after his father died would the eldest son become an aristocrat, inherit the title, and take a seat in the House of Lords.

Peers generally had a residence in London as well as one or more estates in the country. When parliament was in session (during spring and early summer), the family lived in the town house and engaged in a round of balls, dinners, and receptions. It held parties to attend the regatta at Henley, horse racing at Ascot, and cricket at Lord's. Men and younger women rode in Hyde Park; older women took drives in the afternoon, made calls, and shopped. During the autumn and winter they returned to their estates for foxhunting and house parties. Sons were generally educated at the great public schools (which are actually expensive boarding schools, as explained in chapter 8). Daughters were taught at home by a governess.

Baronets occupied an anomalous space between aristocrats and commoners. There were about 850 of them in Victorian times. Although their title is inherited, baronets do not sit in the House of Lords. If they are interested in parliament, they may be elected to the House of Commons. Even in the middle 1860s, about one-third of the men in the House of Commons were either baronets or the sons or grandsons of peers, which helped maintain the political influence of the upper class.

Although aristocrats, who spent half the year in London attending to parliamentary business, were nationally important, the major local influence in the English countryside rested with the landed gentry. *Burke's Landed Gentry*, which lists their names and lineage, was first published in the year that Victoria became queen (1837). A landed estate typically included a hall or manor house, a home farm managed by a bailiff, several farms occupied by tenants, and a village or two in which farm laborers lived.

The landed gentleman usually did not have a house in town. He spent most of the year on his estate and took an active part in local affairs. He was generally called squire, which is not a legal title but rather a customary term for the most influential local landowner. In Victorian times there were about two thousand squires with estates of between one thousand and three thousand acres. Some were knights or baronets, but most had no title. The squire was expected to be a justice of the peace, to take an interest in the countryside, and to promote local charities. His wife and daughters would visit poor people, provide layettes for new babies or soup for the elderly, and probably teach a class in the Sunday school. Theirs was the idealized Victorian life that many people yearn for; there was plenty of time for sports, visiting, hunting, balls, and country festivals.

There were vast differences between the upper levels of the nobility and the smaller squires, yet social contact and intermarriage between the two groups were not impossible. Furthermore, the younger sons of both groups might earn their living in a profession. Education at the great public schools created standards of behavior that were shared by boys from the upper middle class, the landed gentry, and the aristocracy. In the latter part of the century, leading merchants and industrialists also began to send their sons to Eton, Rugby, and other elite boarding schools, where they acquired the values and manners of the landed classes. Class distinctions became more flexible. Society continued to be hierarchical: people saw themselves as occupying a place and offered deference to those above, but some movement was possible. Bankers and businessmen bought country estates and were accepted by the rural gentry. In 1881 the daughter of a manufacturer was, for the first time, presented at court. In the 1890s some industrialists were granted titles (Mitchell, *Daily Life*, 17–25).

FOR MORE INFORMATION

Best, G. *Mid-Victorian Britain, 1851–1875*. London: Weidenfeld and Nicolson, 1971.
Clark, G. K. *The Making of Victorian England*. London: Methuen, 1962.
Mitchell, S. *Daily Life in Victorian England*. Westport, Conn.: Greenwood Press, 1996.
Mitchell, S., ed. *Victorian Britain: An Encyclopedia*. New York: Garland Press, 1998.

ECONOMIC LIFE
|
CLASS
& CASTE EXPERIENCE
|
United States,
1850-1865

United States,
Western Frontier

Victorian England

China

Latin America

CHINA

While class had long been an important aspect of Chinese social relations, in the 19th century the class system underwent a major transition. This was, for the most part, due to the arrival and heavy influence of foreign traders, factory owners, and missionaries in China. While land ownership had previously been the major way in which a family amassed wealth, power, and thus high social standing, trade and involvement in factories brought a whole new element and a major upheaval to the longstanding class system. In addition, while the elite class previously lived in the rural areas, cities took on a new importance as centers of wealth, power, and a new concept of culture, heavily influenced by foreigners. Social connections also became increasingly important among all classes of society.

While the class system in China was never as visible and rigid as in some other parts of Asia, there was a subtle and unspoken, yet understood, class system in China. People were divided into different segments of society based on both economic standing and family background. Since medieval times, in most of China there was a system in which the landholding gentry held a certain amount of power in the society and was considered higher up on the social ladder.

Prior to foreign influence, city dwelling was considered the least appealing lifestyle as it was too far removed from the Confucian ideal that stresses the importance of nature and family life, which are major elements of country life. As money and new modern ideas developed into a new concept of sophistication in the cities, city life became more appealing to many. As more and more people became involved in business and trade and gained wealth in new ways, this system changed. Particularly in the large cities many nonupper-class families gained large amounts of wealth. In addition, many of those who were originally from the cities viewed the new migrants as uncultured and dirty.

The nature of the types of labor needed in the factories also created changes in the class system. During this time wage labor went from consisting solely of hired hands doing semiskilled and unskilled jobs, including handicraft workers, porters, dockers, boatmen, and farm hands, to a complex system consisting of many different jobs and various labor-related social networks. As more and more modern technology came to the factories, an increasing number of skilled workers were needed to operate the machinery. Many European factory owners trained men to operate these machines, and in return the men would generally be loyal to the factory owner. This created a new class of factory workers, many of whom were highly instrumental in the nationalist movement.

Social connections became increasingly important among all sectors of society. As many rural farmers flooded into the cities to work in the factories, they used native-place connections to help them find jobs and places to live. Certain sectors of the workforce came to be dominated by people from particular native areas. As a result a hierarchy developed. Those who dominated the more lucrative and physically easier markets, such as cotton and silk production, came to have a higher place on the social hierarchy. Those working in less desirable types of production, such as metal and coal, came to be lower on the hierarchy.

Among the higher-class members of society, social connections were important as a way to maintain wealth and power within the family. For example, entrance to schools and universities was supposedly based on the Confucian system in which one gains admission through competitive entrance examinations. However, money and political connections also played a large role in determining who gained admission to an elite school.

The legal system was equally corrupt, also favoring those with money and power. Several court records from this period show evidence of this. Torture, such as lashings and beatings, were often used to get a confession out of a witness. Should a judge want to prove someone guilty by gaining a false confession through torture, he would find it fairly easy to twist the evidence. This method was often used to get elite members of society exempt from punishment for a crime they committed. Financial incentives were also used as a way to bribe the judge to make a ruling in one's favor.

While previously the class system in China was fairly rigid, with little room for social mobility, the arrival of foreign traders and foreign-owned factories brought on a redefinition of the class system. This was particularly evident in the large cities, which experienced the most change during this period. Not only did a new class of wealthy merchants come out of this change, but the structure of social relations among laborers also saw major changes, as native-place connections became an important way in which people identified themselves.

~Dana Lightstone

FOR MORE INFORMATION

Goodman, B. *Native Place, City, and Nation: Regional Networks and Identities in Shanghai, 1853–1937*. Berkeley: University of California Press, 1995.

Rowe, W. T. *Hankow: Conflict and Community in a Chinese City, 1796–1895*. Stanford: Stanford University Press, 1989.

ECONOMIC LIFE
|
CLASS
& CASTE EXPERIENCE
|
United States,
1850-1865

United States,
Western Frontier

Victorian England

China

Latin America

LATIN AMERICA

In the last decades of Spanish rule, the American colonies witnessed the growth, in economic power and political sophistication, of a middle class formed by white creoles, people of Spanish blood who had been born in the Americas. Increasingly frustrated by the political dominance of the *peninsulares*, Spaniards from Spain, the creoles allied with the clergy in many parts of the Americas in the early 19th century and became the leaders of local independence movements that overthrew Spanish rule throughout most of the colonies by the 1820s. Thus, the creoles emerged as the dominant political and economic class in the new Latin American republics. However, the creoles formed only a small minority within early 19th-century society.

In the Caribbean, Brazil, and some parts of Central and South America, American-born blacks and black slaves born in Africa were a large percentage of the population. The latter were excluded from virtually all rights and benefits while the rights of the former were generally very limited. Native Indians comprised much of the population in Mexico, Central America, Brazil, and the Andean regions of South America; they too had no political voice and often suffered extreme economic exploitation at the hands of large creole landowners. The largest group in early 19th-century society was the mestizos, people of mixed ancestry, whose position in society varied greatly.

With independence, the social model imposed by the Spaniards in their colonies was repeated; social strata continued to be outlined by race, skin color, and origin of birth, whether in the Iberian peninsula or the new continent. However, unlike what happened between Spaniards and the native population at the beginning of the conquest, when interracial relationships proliferated due to a shortage of European women, 19th-century groups divided along these racial and ethnic lines and tended not to mix. The century was also characterized by a lack of social mobility. It was uncommon to see a black worker or an Indian peasant gain access to social positions generally held by white creoles. The rise of nonwhites up the social scale was implicitly forbidden.

Thus, the first great social divide was between white creoles, who directed and benefited from the region's economic growth in the 19th century, and nonwhites, who comprised the work force that made economic growth possible. Despite their contributions, nonwhite workers, whose concentration in numbers shifted from rural agricultural jobs to urban industrial jobs over the course of the century, lacked the political voice of the creoles and had minimal access to material goods.

Seeking to replace the *peninsulares* as the political aristocracy of the region, the creoles, in the early days of independence, tried various forms of government for the new states. Aspirations of royalty led the creole revolutionary leader Agustín de Iturbide to institute a short-lived monarchy in Mexico in the 1820s. His court contained the most prominent creole families of the time. In Brazil, a prince of the royal house of Portugal established an empire in 1822, which lasted, and protected such colonial institutions as slavery and church-controlled education, until 1889.

The consolidation of independent nations in 19th-century Latin America was achieved mainly by pacts signed by the creole oligarchy, agreements that of course excluded artisans, peasants, workers, natives, and even the lower middle class. By the end of the century, liberalism, a political philosophy that stressed constitutional government and economic progress, transformed Latin American economies, stimulating economic development and foreign investment as well as Latin American politics by giving a greater political voice to the growing middle class. By the end of the century, classes were more broadly defined by occupation and economic status rather than by race or skin color. Nonetheless, the economically advancing middle class still tended to be whiter than the growing working class of the cities, which had a greater concentration of mestizo and Indian members.

The middle class consisted of such traditional mid-level groups as merchants, professional people, army personnel, and the clergy, as well as a growing number of managers in industrial and agricultural concerns and urban entrepreneurs. This group was strengthened by better access to education, an element that defined the substantial difference between this new middle class and the urban working class. The growth of the working class was fed by internal migration from the countryside to the cities, and by waves of immigrants from Europe, who arrived with a strong labor culture that helped them promote new political organizations, as occurred, for instance, in Argentina. These groupings allowed workers to compete with the creoles for political power and resulted in a skyrocketing of political participation by the less favored classes. Among these groups, farmers stood out; in the first decades of the 20th century, farmers became the masses that supported revolutions initiated and led by the middle classes in Mexico, Guatemala, Brazil, Argentina, Cuba, and elsewhere.

In Latin America, the 19th century was characterized by the consolidation of the creole class, by the emergence of the middle and working classes, and by a continuing rift between the social and economic statuses of the highest and lowest classes. At the start of the 21st century, there are still huge gaps in opportunity and lifestyle between the upper classes and the lower or working classes in Latin America, with the middle class much smaller in size due to the economic difficulties experienced in many countries in the late 20th century.

~Ramona Ortiz

FOR MORE INFORMATION

Appelbaum, N. P., A. S. Macpherson, and K. A. Rosemblatt, eds. *Race and Nation in Modern Latin America.* Chapel Hill: University of North Carolina Press, 2003.

Stephens, T. M. *Dictionary of Latin American Racial and Ethnic Terminology.* Gainesville: University Press of Florida, 1999.

Zenteno, R. B., ed. *Las clases sociales en América Latina* (Social Classes in Latin America). Madrid: Siglo XXI Editores, 1973.

INDIA

As early as 1000 B.C.E., the conquerors in India had established a strict caste system through which everyone's place in society was determined by their work. See the section "Class and Caste Experience" in chapter 3 ("Economic Life") in volume 6 of this series for a description of this enduring system, which stood at the heart of India's economic and social structure.

ECONOMIC LIFE

TRADE

United States, 1850–1865

United States, Western Frontier

Victorian England

China

Latin America

Trade

In many ways, systems of trade create the fundamental framework for daily life. This section provides several examples of this. Take, for instance, the trade in the British Empire. It created a cycle of economic booms and busts that dramatically affected not only the daily lives of ordinary people but also the structure of history. As one can see, it was the British imperial trade that sustained the nation through the rigors of the 19th century. The empire also affected people outside the kingdom. In China, for instance, the British came to wield enormous influence through trade. The economic relationship that the British forced on the Chinese brought new influences into China that still have impacts today. British and other European economic influence also grew rapidly in Latin America after the countries of that region gained independence from Spain. Thus to understand the patterns of trade in Victorian England is to also understand (but not necessarily justify) why the crown built an empire on which the sun never set.

For another example of how trade influences daily life, examine the plantation system of the antebellum South. Trade was based upon the products made by slaves such as cotton and tobacco, and the production of these crops had an enormous effect upon daily life in the United States. By the time of the Civil War, there were 10,000 plantations that relied upon slave laborers. In addition to cash crops, slavery, of course, produced other commodities, namely slaves themselves. In 1808, the United States Congress moved to stop the external slave trade, but an internal (and perhaps even more pernicious) trade network developed. In short, the system of trade in the South created many of the parameters of daily life for slaves and for free workers. The continuance of plantation slavery in Brazil and elsewhere also had a profound impact on trade in 19th-century Latin America.

Compare the system of trade set up by the plantation elite in the South and Brazil with that created by those running the fur trade in the American West. In many ways, they are quite distinct. However, both had a deleterious effect upon the lives of workers within the system. Native Americans extracted most of the furs from the North American wilderness to feed the fashion cravings of Europeans and Americans. In return for beaver, bear, mink, raccoon, and wolf hides, the Indians received European and American goods. Many of these trade items wreaked havoc upon the tribes. Rum, or British milk, destroyed countless lives and families as the Indians who had been unfamiliar with the drink succumbed to alcoholism. Other trade goods like copper pots had a different impact. Although a superior pot in every way, such trade items replaced native manufacturing, thus weakening traditional native culture. Finally participation in the fur trade hurt American Indians by exposing them to European and American diseases such as small pox. Such were the tragic rewards of the fur trade system.

UNITED STATES, 1850–65

The system of plantation slavery existed more than a century before the English set foot in any colony of their own. The African slave trade was begun by Arab and Muslim traders in the 15th century, and the Portuguese adapted slavery to their immensely profitable sugar plantations in the islands of the eastern Atlantic before the discovery of the New World. Three-quarters of all the Africans brought to the New World were imported by Spain and Portugal.

Unfortunately, the early history of slavery in North America is poorly documented and inconclusive. It seems certain that none of the founders of the first English colonies anticipated a dependence on black slaves. While the first Africans brought to the English colonies were formerly thought to have been exclusively slaves, recent research suggests that many of them were actually indentured servants or free craftsmen. It is equally clear, however, that there were distinctions made between black and white laborers and servants in even the earliest English colonies; but in a society where whites were often degraded and treated as brutally as slaves, social distinctions often proved more important than racial ones.

The distinction between free blacks, black indentured servants, and black slaves quickly blurred. Free blacks seem to have preferred to live in an urban setting and were twice as likely to live in cities as slaves, who were primarily agricultural workers. In cosmopolitan areas free blacks and slave craftsmen found opportunities for employment, exposure to black culture and religion, and the company of other freemen. However, the majority of free blacks lived on the margins of poverty and were subject to detention and questioning by the authorities without cause. They were continually encouraged to sell themselves back into slavery.

By the beginning of the 18th century, race-based slavery firmly established itself in English North America in place of indentured service. There are a few interpretations for the switch. One theory suggests that whites became unwilling to undergo the physical hardships required of work on another man's plantation, opting instead to hack out a living for themselves on the frontier. The absurd theory that the black race was better suited to the hot climate of the South than the white was put to rest by John Quincy Adams: "Europeans cultivate the land in Greece and in Sicily; why should they not do so in Virginia or the Carolinas? It is not hotter there."

During the 18th century slave labor proved profitable only on large-scale plantations that produced a cash crop. At the time only tobacco and sugar seemed to satisfy this requirement. Growing tobacco had saved the Virginia and Carolina colonies from extinction once the quest for gold and precious metals had been quelled by failure. Tobacco was used as cash, in lieu of cash payments, and as collateral for loans. Tobacco bonds, which encumbered the profits of future crops, were even accepted in lieu of taxes. But intensive tobacco farming was hard on the soil, stripping it of valuable nutrients that could not easily be replaced in an era before synthetic fertilizers. The production of sugar was particularly lucrative, but sugar cultivation was hard on the slaves, who suffered ghastly levels of mortality in the pest-infested humidity of the cane fields. If a large planter of tobacco or sugar were fortunate enough to have three good agricultural years in a row, he could become fabulously wealthy.

Sugar cultivation was hard on the slaves, who suffered ghastly levels of mortality.

Fortunes made in growing sugar and tobacco altered the entire state of colonial society. Whites living in the Southern colonies developed a class structure based on "all the ideals, all the passions, all the prejudices of an aristocracy." Many built manor houses that rivaled the great homes of Europe. So common were these residences that a substantial immigrant population made up of Italian stonemasons, bricklayers, and plasterers came to reside in the South and was supported almost solely by this form of construction.

Rich Southerners maintained their planter aristocracy through the Revolution and into the 19th century. Certainly there were upper and working classes among the whites, but nowhere was the equality between white men so complete as in their ability to force blacks to work without working themselves; and the laws of the new republic lent authority to the white man by divesting the black of two-fifths of his very humanity.

Of the 10,000 plantations that came to rely on slave labor in the antebellum period, fewer than 10 percent had more than 100 slaves. The institution of slavery had been in decline for some time before the war, particularly among the small tobacco planters who had worn out their soil. A South Carolina planter in 1831 reported: "It is an extraordinary thing how far public opinion is becoming enlightened about slavery. The idea that it is a great evil and that one could do without it is gaining ground more and more. . . . We have seen it abolished in the state of New York, then in Pennsylvania; it holds on to a precarious existence in Maryland; there is talk against it in the legislature of Virginia."

The importation of slaves into the United States was outlawed in 1808, but the ownership and selling of slaves within the confines of the country continued. Not until 1848 was slavery abolished in most of New England. This was accomplished by gradual emancipation and not without considerable turmoil over the incorporation of free blacks into New England society. It is an amazing facet of the war that the New England states should so strongly oppose slavery in 1860 when they had tolerated or supported it a mere 12 years earlier.

Cotton saved the plantation system and breathed new life into slavery. By midcentury cotton accounted for two-thirds of the exports of the country and created an unprecedented demand for agricultural laborers. The widespread adoption of the cotton gin, which economically removed the seeds from desirable long staple varieties of cotton, resurrected the plantations of the Deep South in the antebellum period. A slave who could process 100 pounds of cotton per day without the cotton gin, could produce 1,000 pounds of fiber in the same time with it. Estimates show that by 1860 there were more than 3.6 million black slaves in the states that were to form the Confederacy. Profits from cotton in the Carolinas and from sugar in Louisiana provided a financial bulwark for slavery in the Deep South. The archaic plantation system would have faded into obscurity were it not for the ability of slavery to provide the labor needed to produce these crops.

Virginia, noted for its production of tobacco rather than its cotton production, became a major supplier of slaves to other areas of the South. In 1860 the estimated value of all the slave property in the Old Dominion alone was more than $300 million. Virginians found that they could make more profit selling slaves than using them as laborers. In the three decades before the war, more than a quarter million slaves were sold south from Virginia alone. In 1860 young black men aged 19 to 24 could bring between $1,300 and $1,700 in the slave market; and young women between 16 and 20, from $1,200 to $1,500. Slaves with skills brought higher prices. Blacksmiths, wheelwrights, and furniture makers sold at a premium, as did particularly comely young women. Children, the elderly, and unskilled laborers brought less. A healthy four-month-old child was considered worth $100 in North Carolina. The average price for a slave, taking all ages and sexes into account, has been estimated to have been $1,500. The largest number of slaves purchased was young men. Few women, children, or older slaves saw regular trading. This difference helps to explain the high average price of $1,500. It should be noted, to place these values in perspective, that a white overseer on a moderate sized plantation could expect to receive a salary of only $200 to $500 for an entire year's work.

Outside the Deep South, economic and moral attitudes toward the peculiar institution had begun to change before the turn of the century. In the border states, the importance of slavery as an institution continued to erode. Kentucky and Tennessee had few slaves, as they were too mountainous to grow cotton economically. One county in western Virginia was so removed from slavery that there was not a single black person, slave or free, within its bounds in 1860. Nonetheless, as an institution, race-based slavery had a long lifeline. In Maryland and Delaware slaves were found mostly in the cities, serving as tradesmen, artisans, and household help. "I feel that it is degrading the human race to have white men for servants," said a border state congressman. "When one comes to change my plate, I am always tempted to offer him my place at table" (Volo and Volo, 61–65).

FOR MORE INFORMATION

Kirkland, E. C. *Industry Comes of Age: Business, Labor, and Public Policy, 1860–1897.* New York: Holt Rinehart, 1961.

Paludan, P. S. *A People's Contest: The Union and Civil War, 1861–1865.* New York: Harper & Row, 1988.

Volo, D. D., and J. M. Volo. *Daily Life in Civil War America.* Westport, Conn.: Greenwood Press, 1998.

ECONOMIC LIFE

TRADE

United States,
1850-1865

United States,
Western Frontier

Victorian England

China

Latin America

UNITED STATES, WESTERN FRONTIER

Prior to the American Revolution, the North American fur trade was profitable, though the war and its antecedent disruptions caused some decline in exports. Beaver was the glamour fur, the dominant fur in the trade, but in addition the bear, fox, marten, mink, muskrat, otter, raccoon, wildcat, and wolf were trapped for their fur. In 1770, for example, 136,392 beaver worth £23,895 were exported from North America. In that same year, ships carried the furs of 15,136 bears, 20,840 minks, 69,986 raccoons, and 6,581 wolves. In light of the Indian trade, it may be worth noting that in 1770 domestic rum production was 4,807,000 gallons, 30,000 of which went directly into the fur trade to supply the Indians' demand for British milk.

The deerskin trade was also important. In the 1580s Thomas Harriot's list of "Merchantable commodities" from the Roanoke colony included "Furres . . . great store of otters . . . [and] Deer skinnes dressed." Growing steadily through the 18th century, the deerskin trade peaked in the decades before the Revolution. From 1768 to 1772, Great Britain imported an annual average of 721,558 pounds (in weight) of deerskins from its colonies south of Canada. These deerskins accounted for £69,443, or 25 percent of the exports of all 13 colonies—more than the overseas sales of iron, naval stores, and whale oil. Already the peltry trade was part of a broad international trade; from 1790 to 1792 the destinations of American deerskins included England, Scotland, Ireland, France, Spain, Holland, Germany, and Denmark.

Beaver skins and buckskins became units of exchange in backcountry areas of the colonies, influencing not only the economy but also the language. In 1735 a trader complained about a clerk who had that day "sold only eight bucks of goods." And in 1748 the Indian agent Conrad Weiser told Ohio Indians: "Every cask of whiskey shall be sold to you for five bucks in your own town."

Trade—in Weiser's case, deerskins for whiskey—demonstrates an important aspect of initial cross-cultural contact: Europeans and Native Americans did not have the same interpretation of the value of material goods. This basis for misinterpretation dates back to 1492. Columbus's log for October 12 reads, "I want the natives to develop a friendly attitude towards us. . . . I therefore gave red caps to some and glass beads to others. They hung the beads around their necks. . . . And they took great pleasure in this and became so friendly that it was a marvel. They traded and gave everything they had with good will, but it seems they have very little and are poor in everything." Not only does the passage suggest a political motive for trade (to "develop a friendly attitude"), which became important later as France, England, Spain, and the United States competed for the Indians' allegiance, but it also suggests a sharp dichotomy between two societies' definitions of wealth. To Columbus, the natives were "poor in everything"; the Arawaks, however, didn't know they were poor. Indeed, they greeted the strangers with hospitality evidenced by gift giving: parrots, balls of cotton thread, and "a kind of dry leaf." The representatives of one society were acting out of political or economic motives: the others, out of social motives. A mercantile society was meeting one that was not.

Historian Wilcomb Washburn suggests that the Indians had

no particular economic need for the products first offered by the Europeans . . . but received them gratefully for their decorative, aesthetic, magical, curiosity, or amusement "value." When [they] learned what pleased the European[s], the Indian[s] generously offered [their] "products"—such as gold ornaments—in measure that astounded the European[s] who thought in economic terms. This process continued, in some degree, until the Indian[s] adopted white economic values and placed on what [they] "gave" a price appropriate to the system of [their] European trading associate[s].

There was a double failure of communication at first contact, no matter where on the continent it occured, Washburn argues. Europeans failed to comprehend the importance of gift giving in Indian culture—to establish rank or prestige, to mark important occasions in an individual's life, or to symbolize specific messages in intertribal diplomacy. Robert Rogers, as governor at Michilimackinac, argued strongly with his superiors that gifts should be given. However, they opposed giving something for nothing, unable to understand the Indians' psychological and social values. As a corollary, many Indians, who had lived in harmony and balance with nature, could not understand whites' voracious demand for beaver. In 1804 a Mandan observed to Charles Mackenzie of the North West Company: "White people do not know how to live. [To seek beaver] they leave their houses in small parties, they risk their lives on the great waters, among strange nations [tribes], who will take them for enemies. What is the use of beaver? Do they make gunpowder for them? Do they preserve them from sickness? Do they serve them beyond the grave?"

Moreover, the European trade goods initially seemed to have little utilitarian value to the Indian. Washburn cites Thomas McCleish, the chief of the Hudson's Bay Company Fort York. He wrote in 1728 that the Indians turned practical, utilitarian objects into decorative ones: "They always convert [kettles] in making fine [decorative] handcuffs and pouches, which is of greater value with them than twice the price of the kettle."

The Europeans needed to create a demand to get their potential customers hooked. Once a dependency on European goods was established, the fur trade would be more profitable. Once the Indians learned that trade goods could make life easier, those goods would gain value. After all, making a canoe by cutting a tree with a sharpened stone and hollowing out the log with fire was simplified with a metal ax. Sewing was easier with a metal needle and silk or linen thread than with a bone awl and thread made of split animal sinew. An iron or copper kettle made cooking easier. Unlike an earthenware pot, it didn't break; it held water better than the most watertight woven basket; it could be placed directly over the fire. Leather clothing, as David Thompson, mapmaker for the North West Company, noted, "when wet sticks to the skin and is very uncomfortable, requires time to dry, with caution to keep its shape. . . . Every [Indian] is glad . . . to change his leather dress, for one of woolen manufacture of England." Liquor could also make life easier—or seem to—and, despite protests of wise native leaders, missionaries, and governments, it soon became a staple in the fur trade.

Across the entire continent of North America, the fur trade was the "cutting edge of the frontier process." It had high potential for profit. Because furs were "low bulk and high demand," transportation costs over great distances could be offset. Moreover, when the Indian remained the primary "producer of the product" (i.e., did the trapping), there was no need for a line item for salaries, as was required in the system inaugurated by William Ashley (and followed by his successors).

The fur trader in America was, thus, a revolutionary force, creating ever-changing patterns of stability and instability among three major elements: the land itself, the Native Americans, and the Europeans or Euro-Americans. As we shall see, the land itself (its geography, topography, plants, animals, and climate) was at first daunting to the newcomers. At every step the Euro-Americans had to learn how to survive in this land before they could prosper. And although the skills and knowledge learned at Michilimackinac, for example, could be adapted farther west, the diaries, logs, and journals of trappers and traders made constant reference to bitter cold, starvation when meat animals disappeared from a locale, and dangers of frostbite and snow blindness.

The Native American populations—with much broader experience—were well adapted to nature. Not only did they live in harmony with it, but also it was intertwined with their religious beliefs and practices. Unlike Europeans, the Native Americans had no concept of land as private property, though individual tribes did have recognized hunting grounds. To them, although nature provided food, clothing, and shelter, it was not to be despoiled. Thus, in colonial times the eastern Indians in general preferred the French to the English because of policies of land use. Whereas the English cleared the land of trees for farms and settlements, the French tended to leave the forest intact. But corruption also came with trade. In 1804 a Mandan observed to a trader, "In my young days there were no white men, and we knew no wants. . . . The white people came, they brought with them some good, but they brought the small pox, and they brought evil liquors; then Indians since diminish and they are no longer happy."

Despite their superior technology, the Euro-Americans were, at every stage of the advancing frontier, inept, naive greenhorns who had to learn how to survive in the wilderness and among its peoples. The transformation into one who knew enough to survive was often punctuated by formal, though rowdy, initiation ceremonies. A new trapper, for example, was dunked in the Missouri when his keelboat reached the mouth of the Platte. For the trade out of Michilimackinac, the initiation was at Grand Portage, where those who were to winter in the wilderness, the *hivernants*, were recognized as an elite distinct from those who would turn back to the fort. John Macdonnel, a trader, describes his initiation. After water was sprinkled in his face from a "small cedar Bow," he vowed, among other things, "never to kiss a voyageur's wife against her own free will." The ceremony was accompanied by gunshots "fired one after another in an Indian manner" and by sharing a "two gallon keg."

The land was changing the man. And already a reciprocal change had occurred. The Indians were now armed with guns—though they shot them "in an Indian manner." Euro-Americans and Native Americans were heading west together to trap—for business, not merely for subsistence—an activity that would in turn change the land. Not one of the three elements—the land, the Native American, or the Euro-American—would ever be the same again.

As revolutionary as the fur trade was in ecological or cultural terms, it was also inextricably bound up in international politics. France was the pioneer nation in building the American fur trade. As the historian Hiram Chittenden notes, early exploration was linked to trade. Joliet, who with Marquette discovered the upper Mississippi, was a trader, and LaSalle, while exploring new territory, sent back furs. When the English successfully challenged the French for control of the continent during the French and Indian War (1754–60), the border forts were turned over to the English. But treaties alone did not bring peace, and Indians of the border territory remained suspicious of English land-grabbing tendencies. In 1763, Indians of Pontiac's confederacy attacked western forts from Pittsburgh to Michilimackinac. The fall of the latter fort bears recounting. The Indians lured the British commander and many of his troops outside to watch a game of *bagataway*, called *le jeu de la cross* by Canadian voyageurs. As the game continued, squaws entered the fort with guns and tomahawks under their blankets. Seemingly accidentally, the ball sailed into the fort. Players followed it, seizing their weapons—and the fort. None of the fort's French-Canadian traders was harmed, but almost every Englishman died. One of the few survivors, Alexander Henry, described what he saw from his hiding place: "The dead were scalped and mangled; the dying were writhing and shrieking under the unsatiated knife and tomahawk; and from the bodies of some, ripped open, their butchers were drinking the blood, scooped up in the hollow of joined hands and quaffed amid shouts of rage and victory."

Although a similarly detailed examination of other instances of the sweep of frontier history is impossible here, several observations can be made. Although by the Treaty of Paris following the Revolutionary War, English forts south of the border with Canada became American, all geographic boundaries hadn't been determined. (In the Great Lakes area the canoe trade route became the international boundary, but western borders were disputed.) Thus, economic control—through trade—was imperative. The Louisiana Purchase increased exponentially the area in which exploration, trade, and diplomacy were linked. Though Astoria, John Jacob Astor's post on the Columbia river, failed as a step in his developing monopoly of the fur trade, it gave the United States another basis for claiming Oregon. From the Atlantic to the Pacific, the fur trade was at one time or another a factor in international affairs.

Ultimately, however, the fur trade was big business. Unlike others who ventured into unsettled territories—

Keelboats and flatboats were important means for transporting goods in the 19th-century United States. From the Collection of The Public Library of Cincinnati and Hamilton County.

125

missionaries or military officers, for example—the goal of those directing the fur trade was acquisition of money. In contrast to those in more settled regions who trapped for pin money—farmers or storekeepers, for example—the goal was big money, vast profits, and a monopoly if possible. The fact that the fur trade was a complex organization as hierarchical as modern corporations, enmeshed in a pattern of international trade spanning the globe, will become evident in the following discussion. It is also clear that in contrast to those directing the companies, the daily lives of those in the field were often challenging, uncomfortable, and dangerous.

The fur trade centered around the forts and demonstrated the interdependence of the traders and the Indians. Both cultures were changed: most severely and permanently was the Indians'. There were four major social impacts.

The first major cultural dislocation was caused by alcohol, a staple in the fur trade from colonial times onward. In the West almost a decade before the first rendezvous, Major Thomas Biddle warned of the corrupting influences of the fur trade and advocated strict government control to prevent them. Though the U.S. government abandoned Biddle's idea for government factories or posts, laws were passed forbidding the importation of alcohol into Indian territory for the purpose of trade. There were, however, creative circumventions of the law. When in 1831 William Sublette got a two-year trading license from William Clark, he also received a "passport" to carry up to 450 gallons of whiskey "for the special use of his boatmen." However, he was going *overland* to the Rockies. Despite the fact that the Blackfeet preferred West Indies rum, James Kipp at Ft. Piegan concocted "Blackfoot rum" by adding water, ginger, red pepper, and molasses to a barrel of "high wine" (32 or 33 gallons

The railroads were a quick way to ship cattle to the Chicago markets. Montana Historical Society, Helena.

of almost pure alcohol). Along with the dry goods in the hold of the *Yellowstone* when she left St. Louis in 1832 were "1500 gallons of alcohol duly authorized by William Clark intended for the company employees." And when the prohibition against carrying alcohol into upper Missouri became enforced more rigorously, Kenneth MacKenzie set up his own still at Ft. Union to make what he needed from Indian corn.

A second major cultural impact is seen in the third volume of Maximilian's journal. His ethnographic studies during his 1832–34 stay included a compilation of vocabularies—some brief, some extensive—of at least 15 different Indian languages. Most words are basic: parts of the body, names of animals, or counting words. But it is of interest that in almost every language there were, by 1834, words for gunpowder; spirits (alcohol, not divine beings), which in Assiniboine translated "firewater"; gun or rifle; and American, which in Blackfoot, Omaha, Dakota, and Mandan was, literally, "long knife." To the two indigenous words in Mandan for ball (the object and the game women played with it) was added the meaning "bullet," which is the same word as is used for lead. Most tribes apparently did not have a word for money. In Oto, however, it is translated as "white metal" and in Mandan as "that which the white men love very much." Clearly the fur trade had had a strong influence on Native American language, a central element of culture.

Disease, specifically smallpox, had the most disastrous impact. The most catastrophic epidemic swept like wildfire through the Mandan in 1837. The steamboat *St. Peter's* arrived at Ft. Clark late on Sunday, June 18, unloaded merchandise on June 19, and left early on June 20 for Ft. Union. Life went on normally—celebration of the Fourth of July, Indian trade, rainfall, dances, and Indians drying meat—until, on July 14, there is an ominous entry in Chardon's journal: "a young Mandan died to day of the Small Pox—several others has caught it." By July 25 smallpox had broken out in the Mandan camp. On the next day Chardon reports that "the 4 Bears (Mandan) has caught the small pox, and got crazy and disappeared from camp." Each day the death count among the Mandan rose, and the disease began to spread to other tribes. As the disease ravaged them, they began to blame Chardon in particular and whites in general. "They threaten Death and Destruction to us all at this place, saying that I was the cause of the small pox Makeing its appearance in this country—One of our best friends in the Village (The Four Bears) died to day, regretted by all who knew him"—this was Chardon's entry for Sunday, July 30.

Despite his occasional ambivalence toward the Indians, Chardon recorded Four Bears' final speech, delivered on July 30, 1837. With the virtual extinction of the Mandans, the speech marks the end of a comparatively idyllic relationship between the races.

My Friends, one and all, Listen to what I have to say—Ever since I can remember, I have loved the Whites. I have lived With them ever since I was a Boy, and to the best of my Knowledge, I have never Wronged a White Man, on the contrary, I have always Protected them from the insults of Others, Which they cannot deny. The 4 Bears never saw a White Man hungry, but what he gave him to eat, Drink, and a Buffalo skin to sleep on, in time of Need. I was always ready to die for them, Which they cannot deny. I have done every thing that a red Skin could do for them, and how they have repaid it! With ingratitude! I have Never Called a White Man a Dog, but to day, I do Pronounce them to be a set of Black harted Dogs, they have deceived Me, them that I always considered as Brothers, has turned Out to be My Worst enemies. I have been in Many Battles, and often Wounded, but the Wounds of My enemies I exhalt in, but to day I am Wounded, and by Whom, by those same White Dogs that I have always Considered, and treated as Brothers. I do not fear *Death* my friends. You know it, but to *die* with my face rotten, that even the Wolves will shrink with horror at seeing Me, and say to themselves, that is the 4 Bears the Friend of the Whites— Listen well what I have to say, as it will be the last time you will hear Me. think of your Wives, Children, Brothers, Sisters, Friends, and in fact all that you hold dear, are all Dead, or Dying, with their faces all rotten, caused by those dogs the whites, think of all that My friends, and rise all together and Not leave one of them alive. The 4 Bears will act his Part.

The fur frontier had the most powerful effect of all the frontier experiences— perhaps because it was the first, perhaps because it was reexperienced from the Atlantic to the Pacific over several hundred years. The fur trapper as explorer amassed vast knowledge about geography, animals and plants, and about the Native Americans. Personified by John Jacob Astor, the fur industry was the first example of a successful American monopoly. It forever and irrevocably changed both the European and the Native American through experiential, linguistic, mercantile, and epidemiological influences. It was, on occasion, an instrument of national will for France, Spain, Great Britain, and the United States. And it implanted in our national psyche the attitude of exploitation rather than conservation of nature (Jones, 12–22, 51–53).

To read about trade on the colonial frontier of North America, see the entries on Colonial Frontier and New England in the section "Trade" in chapter 3 ("Economic Life") in volume 4 of this series.

FOR MORE INFORMATION

America's West: Development and History. <http://www.americanwest.com/>

Jones, M. E. *Daily Life on the Nineteenth Century American Frontier.* Westport, Conn.: Greenwood Press, 1998.

Wishart, D. J. *The Fur Trade of the American West, 1807–1840.* Lincoln: University of Nebraska Press, 1979.

ECONOMIC LIFE

TRADE

United States, 1850-1865

United States, Western Frontier

Victorian England

China

Latin America

VICTORIAN ENGLAND

From the middle of the 18th century through the 19th century and into the 20th century, the British Empire was in a state of constant flux. The American Revolution had disrupted a very successful trading system. The triangle trade in the Atlantic had made the British arguably the most powerful nation in Europe. It was all predicated upon the production of cash crops, namely tobacco, in the New World. Ships carried the leaves to England, which were exchanged for metal goods, weapons, and rum, which were taken to the west coast of Africa and exchanged for slaves. The slaves were taken back to the colonies and put to work growing more plantation cash crops. American Independence tore one of the legs of that triangle out along with all the auxiliary trade in the colonies that the empire created. The British Empire recovered in the 19th century, but the trading system that was established was not strong and floundered for many decades. More importantly, the rise and fall of the empire's trade affected average Englishmen and Englishwomen with corresponding expansions and contractions in employment.

After the American Revolution, the British recovered quickly with the cotton trade. Industrialization not only created jobs, but British cotton was in high demand in Europe and in the United States. Increasingly, imperial cotton goods were also popular in colonial India and Turkey. However, by the middle of the 18th century, the British cotton trade was hurt by the expansion of industrialization in the United States and Europe. In addition to jobs lost by the competition, the mechanization of the cotton industry to boost productivity (and thus lower prices) reached a plateau. By 1850, virtually no higher productivity was possible, and not many more textile jobs were being created. The situation in other industries was not much better. By the end of the Victorian Age, Germany was poised to sell more manufactured goods in Europe than England.

This drawing of the British Baltic Fleet leaving England for Crimea appeared in the April 14, 1855, edition of the *Illustrated London News*. Note that both sail and steam vessels are depicted. The British navy defended Victorian England's trading empire. Courtesy of The Library Company of Philadelphia.

Despite the trouble with its system of trade, which translated into unsteady job markets, the British did have some advantages. One was the size of its global trading network. It traded with its colonies, of course, but also with a lot of semi-industrialized countries. The list includes Australia, New Zealand, South Africa, India, Brazil, Argentina, Chile, Colombia, Mexico, and Turkey (see Table 1, below). Thus while it eventually lost its European supremacy, it maintained a significant trading empire. In addition, there were some growth industries within England such as coal, which was a major export to the United States and Europe. Finally, the British trade system changed dramatically by the end of the century. Increasingly, the British economy relied upon what is called invisible trade in such things as shipping, insurance, and investment banking. Thus, the service and financial sectors rose in importance as the manufacturing and export trades declined. This was quite a dramatic change since 1800.

To read about trade in Chaucer's England, see the entry on Europe in the section "Trade" in chapter 3 ("Economic Life") in volume 2 of this series; for 18th-century England, see the entry on England in the section "Trade" in chapter 3 ("Economic Life") in volume 4 of this series.

~*Andrew E. Kersten*

Table 3.1

Net Exports of British Manufacturers, 1860–1901, in Millions of Pounds

Year	To Foreign Countries	To Areas Within the British Empire
1860	68.5	34.8
1870	94.4	41.3
1880	72.0	72.1
1890	80.9	70.0
1900	40.5	68.1
1901	25.3	79.4

Table derived from Cain and Hopkins, 156.

FOR MORE INFORMATION

Cain, P. J., and A. G. Hopkins. *British Imperialism, 1688–2000*. New York: Pearson Education, 2002.

ECONOMIC LIFE

|

TRADE

|

United States,
1850-1865

United States,
Western Frontier

Victorian England

China

Latin America

CHINA

By the 19th century European merchants and trading companies had been making their way into Chinese ports for almost three centuries. However, this period saw an increase in trade relations between Europe and China and, as a result, an increase in foreign influence in China. Trade was the main source of contact between the Chinese and foreigners and, thus, a major influence in the development of relations between China and other nations.

The year 1839, which marks the start of the Opium War between China and Britain, is a major turning point in the history of China. Because of this, as well as subsequent British victories, Britain and other foreign nations imposed a series of unequal treaties in China. Over the course of the 19th century, foreign powers came to control certain areas of China, known as leaseholds. Within these spheres of Western influence, missionaries were permitted to proselytize, tariffs on imports and exports were kept low, their own laws judged foreigners, and opium was legalized. The changes that occurred led to a new conception of China's future: a China in which forces from the West joined with traditional Chinese culture.

Beginning with the arrival of the first Portuguese traders in the late 16th century, trade was confined to a few ports where Chinese agents of the court could regulate it and skim some profits from the top. Beginning in 1759, the crown licensed British East India Company, and other Western traders, were limited to trading in the port of Guangzhou. The foreign traders were also bound to a very strict set of Chinese regulations. They had to deal with a guild of Chinese traders, obey Chinese laws, and communication had to go through the Chinese merchant guild. The British free trade philosophy called for governments not to interfere in trade. This caused British traders to be particularly resentful of Chinese trade regulations.

During the 18th century, a trade imbalance had developed between China and Great Britain. By this time tea had become immensely popular among the British. The East India Company purchased massive amounts of Chinese tea to sell both in England and in British colonies such as America. However, as at this time there was no product that the Chinese wanted to purchase from the British in equal amount, the East India Company was forced to pay for the tea in silver bullion. At that time silver bullion was viewed as a main asset of a nation—the cornerstone of a nation's wealth and power. The imbalance of trade led to a serious bullion drain in Britain, which eventually affected the nation's economy. The Chinese economy, on the other hand, flourished from an influx of silver.

Britain sought to find products that the Chinese would buy in equal amounts. In hopes of doing so, a mission was dispatched to China in 1793 under the pretence of wishing the Chinese emperor a happy 80th birthday. However, the actual purpose of the mission, under the command of the experienced diplomat Lord Macarthy, was to attempt to interest the Chinese in British goods and to place a British trade official permanently in Beijing. Although some progress was made, the Chinese court had no intention of establishing equal trade relations with Western powers.

An end to the trade imbalance began when the British discovered opium grown in India was of great interest to the Chinese. The British East India Company had a monopoly on opium in Bengal, India. The company forced farmers to grow poppy, the plant from which opium is derived. The poppy was then processed into opium in factories, also in Bengal. Opium was illegal in China. To keep the East India Company out of direct involvement with the illegal opium trade, private British traders bought the company's opium in Bengal on credit, then sold it to smugglers on the Chinese coast, and finally paid representatives of the East India Company in Guangzhou. The effect of this system was trading opium for tea. Over the next several decades the trade imbalanced shifted. By the 1830s China began to feel the effects of silver draining out of the country, and the Chinese economy became greatly depressed. In addition, a major social problem developed in China, as more and more Chinese people from every social class were becoming addicted to opium.

Many Chinese people benefited financially from the opium trade. Not only did smugglers benefit, but also local officials were often given financial incentives to turn a blind eye to the illegal traffic. For this reason the Chinese government had a difficult time putting an end to the opium trade, despite their repeated efforts to ban the import of the drug. The Chinese government had a two-way battle to fight: both against British importers, and Chinese smugglers and local officials.

Foreigners involved in trade in China were not purely interested in selling only opium. The British crown depended heavily on the tea trade. Thoughtful and intelligent negotiation might have led to a gradual reduction of opium imports to China, while other articles, such as manufactured goods, could have replaced the opium trade.

However, the Chinese government refused to loosen their trade restrictions and, instead of compromising with the British, took a hard-line approach to stamping out the import of opium. Lin Zexu, an experienced official, was dispatched to Guangzhou, where he was to put an end to the opium problem. He acted promptly and swiftly, demanding and eventually seizing around twenty thousand chests of opium that the British stored in Guangzhou. This, along with other minor incidents, was enough for the British government to gain military support for action

---

📷 *Snapshot*

A Celebrated Letter against the Opium Trade from Lin Zexiu to Queen Victoria, 1839

A communication: Magnificently our great emperor soothes and pacifies China and the foreign countries, regarding all with the same kindness. If there is profit then he shares it with the peoples of the world; if there is harm, then he removes it on behalf of the world. This is because he takes the mind of heaven and earth as his mind.

The kings of your honorable country by a tradition handed down from generation to generation have always been noted for their politeness and submissiveness. We have read your successive tributary memorials saying: "In general our countrymen who go to trade in China have always received His Majesty the Emperor's gracious treatment and equal justice," and so on. Privately we are delighted with the way in which the honorable rulers of your country deeply understand the grand principles and are grateful for the Celestial grace. For this reason the Celestial Court, in soothing those from afar, has redoubled its polite and kind treatment. They have enjoyed the profit from trade continuously for 200 years. This is the source from which your country has become known for its wealth. (Tend and Fairbank, 24–26)

against China. In 1839 a British naval force assembled in Macau and the Opium War was on.

To read about trade in China under the Tang dynasty, see the China entry in the section "Trade" in chapter 3 ("Economic Life") in volume 2 of this series.

~*Dana Lightstone*

FOR MORE INFORMATION

Brook, T., and B. T. Wakabayashi, eds. *Opium Regimes: China, Britain, and Japan, 1839–1952*. Berkeley: University of California Press, 2000.

Tend, S., and J. K. Fairbank. *China's Response to the West*. Cambridge, Mass.: Harvard University Press, 1954.

Wyndham, B. *The Land of Green Tea: Letters and Adventures of Colonial C. L. Baker of the Madrass Artillery, 1834–1840*. London: Unicorn Press, 1995.

ECONOMIC LIFE
|
TRADE
|
United States,
1850-1865

United States,
Western Frontier

Victorian England

China

Latin America

LATIN AMERICA

In the first quarter of the 19th century, as most Latin American nations gained independence from European colonial powers, these new states adopted a capitalist economic system that focused on the export of raw materials. Ironically, trade systems strengthened the newly independent nations' connections to European countries, particularly Great Britain. However, throughout the course of the century, Britain lost its monopoly over trade from Latin America, as France, Germany, and the United States also became major buyers and sellers in the region.

The independence wars adversely affected Latin American trade. Overseas sales declined severely, reaching a low point in the 1820s, and recovered very slowly. Between 1829 and 1831, the region's per capita export value remained steady at U.S. $5.10, rising to only $5.20 by 1850 (Bakewell, 407). Beginning in the 1850s, trade increased precipitously, leading to what many referred to as an export boom. In this period, industrial development in Europe, Asia, and the United States generated increased demand for raw materials so that by 1912, Latin American exports had grown more than 10 times (Bakewell, 407).

Throughout the 19th century, as in centuries before, Latin America exported a variety of goods. Some areas established intense mining enterprises, extracting diamonds, gold, and other metals. Colombia and Brazil, the world's principal sources of gold before independence, exported some 30 million ounces (Burns, 29–30). Peru and Mexico dominated the world's silver market, although the independence wars virtually crippled production; not until mid-century did production reach preindependence levels. During the export boom in the latter half of the century, base metals joined precious metals on the export lists. By 1860, Chile was a top exporter of copper, which was in high demand due to the spread of electricity. Much of the tin plating used to prevent rust in steel food cans came from Bolivia.

Latin America was also an agricultural region that exported such consumer products as coffee, sugar, tobacco, and cacao; household commodities like wood, indigo and cotton; and cattle products, including meat and hides. Cuba was the largest and most efficient producer of sugar during much of the century, a position that was in large part due to slave labor and technological advances, including railroads and steam-run mills. Uruguay and Argentina, relying exclusively on their cattle industries, led the entire region in per capita exports at mid-century (U.S. $54.90 and $10.30, respectively) (Bakewell, 407). Chile and Argentina exported hides, tallow, and salted beef to Europe, as well as to Brazil and Cuba. Beef and mutton exports rose quickly with the introduction of refrigeration on ships in the 1880s. Coffee exports were also a major source of income for many countries. In Venezuela, for example, coffee accounted for 40 percent of national exports (Bakewell, 402). Central America was similarly dependent on coffee, particularly Costa Rica, El Salvador, and Guatemala.

Industrial development led to increased exports from Latin America. The demand for electrical insulation and inflatable tires for cars and bikes led to the rubber boom of the late 1800s in the Amazon region of Brazil, Peru, and Bolivia. In the 1870s, invention of the mechanical reaping machine occasioned higher demands from U.S. farmers for twine to bind bales of grain and led to a boom in henequen production on Mexico's Yucatán peninsula.

A unique Latin American export that fell somewhere between mining and agriculture was guano. On the islands off the Peruvian coast, bird droppings had gathered over thousands of years to a depth in some places of 30 meters. Because this manure was rich in nitrogen, it was highly prized as a fertilizer. Production began in the mid-1820s; by the 1850s, guano was Peru's most valued export, with some 500 thousand tons annually going to Europe, and Great Britain in particular (Bakewell, 402).

Latin American nations faced many problems associated with monoculture, or the practice of designating vast tracts of land and labor to the production of only one crop, such as coffee, cotton, or bananas. This practice placed Latin Americans in a particularly vulnerable position on the international market. When the busts came, as with the Great Depression in the 1930s, the region suffered heavily. Moreover, such focus on one product diminished the capital, land, and labor designated to staple crops, such as wheat and corn, for local food consumption. Thus, the region was dependent on foreign markets both to sell their goods and to fulfill their basic dietary needs.

When discussing trade in 19th-century Latin America, it is necessary to note special labor situations, without which most of the region's trade would have not survived. African slavery was one of most salient aspects of the region's history in this period; without slave labor, large-scale capitalist plantations, such as the sugar industries of the Caribbean, would not have existed. While most slaves arrived in the Americas before 1800, numbers continued to rise afterwards. More than a million and a half arrived in Brazil before the end of the trade in the early 1850s, and some three-quarters of a million arrived in Spanish America, including Venezuela, where some 111 thousand slaves had labored by 1800 (Bakewell, 156, 414–15; Keen and Wasserman, 229).

But Africans were not the only forced migrant workers. Chinese indentured servants labored on Peru's guano islands, Cuba's sugar plantations, and Costa Rica's railroad. Chinese and Koreans also labored on Mexican henequen plantations. Workers from the British West Indies toiled on Caribbean banana plantations, as well as railroad projects and the construction of the Panama Canal. And, much like the colonial period, local indigenous peoples continued to be coerced into doing manual labor for landowners and governments. Many countries enforced laws that established labor quotas, as with Guatemala's *mandamiento*.

Along with forced labor, new technology had profound effects on Latin American trade. The Cuban cane industry, for example, would never have reached its heights without the steam-run sugar mill. Steamships appeared for the first time in the 1820s and greatly influenced transport, trade, and communications. These developments further enmeshed Latin Americans with Europeans because Europeans often owned and operated the transport companies.

In conclusion, after recovering from the devastation of the independence wars, Latin American trade increased in both frequency and value. Despite the long struggle for independence, Latin America continued to be highly dependent on foreign nations for goods and technology exchange. Little industry developed in the region during the 19th century, as nations focused on exporting raw materials and agricultural products.

~Molly Todd

FOR MORE INFORMATION

Bakewell, P. *A History of Latin America: Empires and Sequels, 1450–1930.* Oxford: Blackwell Publishers, 1997.

Berlin, I., and P. D. Morgan, eds. *Cultivation and Culture: Labor and the Shaping of Slave Life in the Americas.* Charlottesville: University of Virginia Press, 1993.

Burns, E. B. *Latin America: A Concise Interpretive History.* 5th ed. Englewood Cliffs, N.J.: Prentice Hall, 1990.

Chomsky, A., and A. Lauria-Santiago, eds. *Identity and Struggle at the Margins of the Nation-State: The Laboring Peoples of Central America and the Hispanic Caribbean.* Durham, N.C.: Duke University Press, 1998.

Días, M. Odila Silva. *Power and Everyday Life: The Lives of Working Women in Nineteenth-Century Brazil.* Translated by Ann Frost. New Brunswick, N.J.: Rutgers University Press, 1995.

Gootenberg, P. *Between Silver and Guano: Commercial Policy and the State in Post-independence Peru.* Princeton, N.J.: Princeton University Press, 1989.

Hünefeldt, C. *Paying the Price of Freedom: Family and Labor Among Lima's Slaves, 1800–1854.* Berkeley: University of California Press, 1994.

Keen, B., and M. Wasserman. *A Short History of Latin America.* Boston: Houghton Mifflin, 1984.

Larson, B., O. Harris, and E. Tandeter, eds. *Ethnicity, Markets, and Migration in the Andes at the Crossroads of History and Anthropology.* Durham, N.C.: Duke University Press, 1995.

Tandeter, E. *Coercion and Market: Silver Mining in Colonial Potosí, 1692–1826.* Translated by Richard Warren. Albuquerque: University of New Mexico Press, 1993.

Urban and Rural Environments

ECONOMIC LIFE
|
URBAN & RURAL ENVIRONMENTS
|
United States, 1850-1865

Victorian England

China

The 19th century witnessed a dramatic and sustained growth of cities in the United States, England, and China. Both England and the United States began the century as fundamentally rural nations. Statistics tell the story. In 1800 the United States had roughly five percent of its population in towns with over 2500 people. By 1850 that number had gone up by six times. Similarly England became much more urban, and its major urban center, London, grew by leaps and bounds, becoming the world's largest city. The urbanization was not even. In China, despite the rapid growth of industrialized cities, most Chinese lived in rural areas. Similarly, in the American South, cities were quite small and in many cases inhospitable to travelers. Northern cities by contrast were booming, in part because of the constant movement of immigrants into urban areas like Chicago, New York, and Boston. Yet, the growth of cities was a significant trend whose impact stretched well into the 20th and 21st centuries.

The development of cities was not without some problems. Urban areas require a complex network of overlapping infrastructures. In other words, cities need sewers, power, streets, and transportation. Building these requires a lot of money and manpower. Most cities struggle to put these necessities in place. Take London as an example. The city's streets in the early part of the century were made of dirt, which produced dust storms in dry, windy weather and mud in rain. Fixing that was a major undertaking. So was the construction of the sewer system, as well as the installation of street lights. Victorian Londoners also faced other difficulties such as pollution. In particular, they suffered from air pollution caused by coal fired furnaces and stoves. So deadly was the contamination that it was not uncommon to get a fog of smog in the city that would kill its residents. The switch to natural gas and electricity solved some of London's pollution problems.

Chinese and American cities encountered similar difficulties. In the United States, one of the responses to the challenges to improve the standard of living in urban areas was to attack those living there. Some Americans blamed recent immigrants, who moved to poor sections of cities, for living in squalor. Thus instead of rapidly improving urban infrastructure, Americans often criticized those who inhabited slums. Such anti-immigrant or nativist movements had significant political weight in the years leading up to the Civil War. Eventually, as with the problem of pollution, the solutions to urban crises were found in planning and engineering.

UNITED STATES, 1850–65

In 1800 the United States was essentially a rural country. Less than six percent of its population of 5 million lived in towns with populations larger than 2,500.

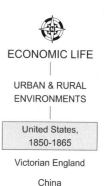

ECONOMIC LIFE
|
URBAN & RURAL ENVIRONMENTS
|
United States, 1850-1865

Victorian England

China

Only Philadelphia and New York had populations greater than 25,000. The settlement of the Mississippi Valley and the Northwest during the first half of the 19th century had contributed to a vast internal migration. By 1850 the country had 23 million inhabitants, and more than 30 percent of the population lived in towns with more than 2,500 persons. Although two-thirds of the population was still involved in agriculture, the expansion of commerce and industry had drawn a large number of people into towns that were both old and new. The urban population became the fastest growing segment of the population. By 1900, cities dominated American life, and a few urban centers such as New York, Chicago, and Philadelphia had become gigantic metropolises housing millions of people.

Even before the Civil War, cities as distinct as Providence, Rhode Island, and Chicago, Illinois, were experiencing similar rates of growth due to their importance in trade. A number of small coastal towns became booming cities by mid-century in response to America's rise to maritime greatness in the clipper ship era. Boston, Salem, Portland, and New Haven, for example, were all active coastal trading cities in 1850. Boston alone was the terminus for no fewer than seven railroads. Westward expansion and the successful navigation of the western rivers by steamboats made a number of inland ports equally important. These included Pittsburgh, Cincinnati,

Entitled *Across the Continent: "Westward the Course of Empire Takes Its Way,"* this 1868 Currier & Ives print illustrates how little transition there often was between urban and rural in the frontier West. Courtesy of the Joslyn Art Museum, Omaha, Nebraska; Gift of Eugene Kingman.

Louisville, Memphis, Natchez, and St. Louis. The number of towns having more than 10,000 people increased from six to more than sixty in less than half a century.

The cities that had been the largest at the turn of the century remained so and experienced the greatest rates of population growth. By 1850 New York City boasted a population of more than half a million. Philadelphia, Boston, Newport, Baltimore, New Orleans, and Charleston had grown to hold hundreds of thousands of persons. Nonetheless, Southern cities had attracted less than 10 percent of the population of the region. The physical size of the American city also increased, from a radius of less than a mile to four or five miles. Northern cities were characterized by a well defined and established business district, socially and ethnically segregated residential areas, and the beginnings of the suburb.

The Southern cities grew along the perimeter of the region's heartland and tended to materialize after the surrounding area was well settled. These cities grew as planters and farmers came in from their outlying and relatively isolated holdings to take advantage of the social and cultural benefits cities offered. Coastal and river cities in the South also had a large itinerant population of traders, bargemen, and clerks, but Southern cities tended to avoid the development of slums and ghettos. Outside of the almost self-sufficient plantations, small towns in the rural South offered a few amenities such as a doctor, a tradesman, or a small store or two, but nothing more. Consequently, Southern towns often appeared shabby and rundown to visitors unfamiliar with rural life.

Immigration from abroad and migration from within the nation outstripped the physical expansion of the cities and stressed their infrastructure to the limit. This remarkable influx of foreigners had an incalculable effect on the nature of Northern culture. Poverty, disease, crime, and social inequality became concentrated in the slum districts of Northern cities as immigrants drew together in the security of their own communities. Antebellum immigration reached its peak between 1845 and 1855. More than 3 million immigrants, 10 times as many as had come to America since the founding of the republic, entered the country. Most congregated in the cities of the North. One had only to walk through an ethnic ghetto to discover the struggles immigrants faced to eke out a basic existence—a condition Southerners quickly pointed to as evidence of the failure of Northern culture. Even the reformers believed that the standard of living among these immigrants had to be improved if the squalor of the cities was not to become a permanent feature of Northern society. Their predictions were borne out by the history of subsequent decades of urban poverty.

Some Americans saw immigrants as the source for the problems in cities. A tone of condescension and disdain even entered the rhetoric of the reform movements. They therefore misguidedly directed their reform campaigns against the foreign born instead of toward the correction of social injustice in the American system. By mid-century a strong ultra-Americanism had coalesced in the form of American only organizations such as the Nativist Party.

There were three major countries of origin for the immigrants that entered America at this time. These were, in descending order of their proportion in the immigrant population, Ireland, Germany, and Great Britain. Together, they provided about 85 percent of all immigrants to the United States up to the beginning of the Civil War. The influx of Italians, Jews, and eastern Europeans would not become significant until late in the century. With the exception of the Germans, the majority of immigrants spoke English. There was therefore little in the way of a language barrier to frustrate economic success or attract prejudice. Immigrants from Great Britain assimilated fairly well into surroundings dominated by an American upper class that had strong English origins.

The Irish, who also spoke English, had an unfortunate history of poor relations with their cousins in Great Britain that followed them to the New World. The Irish were the first truly urban immigrants in American history, banding together in inner-city neighborhoods that quickly took on all of the outward appearances of slums. Many established Americans saw this development only in prejudicial terms and blamed the slum-like conditions on the Irish themselves, ignoring

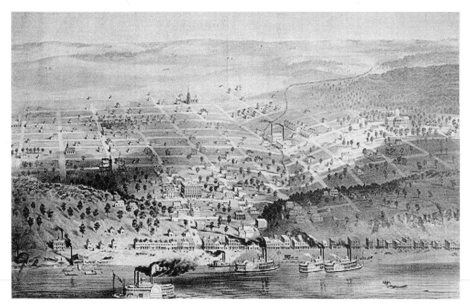

Lithographs such as this one of Sumner, Kansas, were used to draw Americans west. Kansas State Historical Society, Topeka, Kansas.

the anti-Irish bigotry of employers and landlords. In addition to being the victims of social prejudice, the Irish were also accused of voting illegally, of selling their votes to unscrupulous politicians, and of engendering crime and immorality.

The Germans were generally ignored by the social observers of the 19th century. They tended to separate themselves from traditional America by moving away from the cities into more rural agricultural areas in Pennsylvania and the upper Midwest. By this means they avoided becoming targets of overwhelming prejudice and achieved a far greater social solidarity than any other group of immigrants up to that time. Nonetheless, they did not completely escape intolerance. As they generally followed a European Sabbath tradition, Germans hurried home from their religious observances to a convivial afternoon in music halls and beer gardens that violated the more sober American concept of proper conduct on the Lord's Day. This behavior was perfectly acceptable in their homeland, but it was perceived as a blasphemous public exhibition of drunkenness and immorality worthy of censure by the more sober-minded Americans. In this way German immigrants became the particular target of Sabbatarian and temperance crusaders.

By the end of the 19th century, American cities were struggling to accommodate the increasing numbers of urban immigrants. Similarly more and more American migrants were entering cities. Beginning in the late 1880s, for example, tens of thousands of African Americans began to move out of the rural South and into cities in the South, North, Midwest, and West. Physically cities expanded both outward and upward to handle the growing populations. New technologies facilitated this. In the 1870s, elevators and new iron and steel girder construction allowed contractors to erect much taller buildings. By the 1890s, it was apparent that cities, particularly New York City, had developed central business districts with imposing skylines. The tall office buildings were the physical embodiment of a new urban age in America. Not only were cities the centers for American banking and corporations but they also became the centers of American cultural, recreational, and social life. Cities, however, were also at the nexus of social problems. Racial injustice and poverty, which were most notable in American cities, were unresolved and festering issues at the dawn of the 20th century. Moreover, cities were often unhealthy places to live. Smoke, smog, and unsafe water were endemic to urban places. Crime and corruption too became synonymous with urban life. These and a host of other problems were high on the list of progressive reforms at the turn of the 20th century (Volo and Volo, 35–38).

To read about urban and rural environments in the United States in the 20th century, see the United States entries in the section "Urban and Rural Experience" in chapter 3 ("Economic Life") in volume 6 of this series.

~Andrew E. Kersten

FOR MORE INFORMATION

Daniels, R. *Coming to America: A History of Immigration and Ethnicity in America Life*. New York: HarperCollins, 1990.

Miller, Z. L. *The Urbanization of Modern America: A Brief History*. New York: Harcourt Brace, 1973.

Volo, D. D., and J. M. Volo. *Daily Life in Civil War America*. Westport, Conn.: Greenwood Press, 1998.

Ward, D. *Cities and Immigrants: A Geography of Change in Nineteenth-Century America*. New York: Oxford University Press, 1971.

Warner, S. B. *The Urban Wilderness: A History of the American City*. New York: Harper and Row, 1972.

VICTORIAN ENGLAND

ECONOMIC LIFE

URBAN & RURAL
ENVIRONMENTS

United States,
1850-1865

Victorian England

China

In the early Victorian years most cities had no paving, no sewers, and few public buildings. The essential physical features of 20th-century urban life were largely designed and created by 19th-century engineers and civic reformers. London, the world's largest city and most important commercial center, developed in astonishing and complex ways. The name London actually has three meanings. The City of London (usually called The City) is the financial district. It is located where the Romans once settled; it covers about one square mile. Bordered on the south by the Thames, it stretches from the Temple to the Tower of London; its other familiar landmark is St. Paul's Cathedral. Already the location of the Bank of England, The City became increasingly public and commercial during the 19th century. Massive new buildings were constructed for the Royal Exchange, the General Post Office, and the headquarters of other banks, insurance companies, and businesses. Very few people, any longer, lived in The City; four railway stations and the Metropolitan underground brought tens of thousands of black-coated workers daily from all parts of town and from the surrounding suburbs.

The other boroughs, villages, and new developments that had become part of the urban area were consolidated in 1888 under the administration of London County Council. This wider city is what most people mean when they use the word London. It grew enormously during the course of the century—from perhaps one million people in 1800 to five million by 1900. Docks, warehouses, light industry, and vast tracts of working-class housing spread east of the Tower of London (the East End); luxurious shopping precincts, residences for the wealthy, theaters, and cultural institutions filled the West End. The names of villages and boroughs that had been swallowed up remained to label dozens of other neighborhoods, each with a distinctive reputation and character. Much of Victorian London is still visible: Kensington's fine bay-windowed row houses with the railed areaways that give light to the rooms below ground level, the iron and glass technology of stations such as Paddington, the graceful

This view of Fleet Street with St. Paul's Cathedral in the background illustrates the crowded streets that were typical of London in the late 19th century.

engineering of Albert Bridge and the Tower Bridge, and the impressive Gothic Revival architecture of Parliament and the Royal Courts of Justice.

In addition, by the end of the century, suburban rail lines promoted development in an even wider area, covering parts of Middlesex, Essex, Surrey, and Kent, which lie close to London and are known as the home counties. Another two million people lived in this greater London area. The families of men in senior business or public positions (who had a short workday and could afford a longer commute) enjoyed pleasant new neighborhoods with spacious houses, green lawns, and new amenities such as tennis clubs.

Similar expansion took place in Manchester, Birmingham, Leeds, Liverpool, and other industrial cities. There was constant building and rebuilding. Older areas became slums and were then cleared away for new commercial buildings or rail lines. More and more workers were needed not only in factories but also for clerical, administrative, and commercial jobs. Rings of new brick houses spread into the surrounding countryside. Civic officials recognized the need for open spaces and designed the typical layout of walks, shrubberies, play areas, and athletic fields that are still found in most urban parks.

Prosperous cities invested in town halls, law courts, universities, museums, concert halls, libraries, schools, and other substantial building projects. The preferred style for public buildings was Gothic Revival, an architecture consciously intended to express the seriousness, reverence, and majesty inspired by cathedrals in the Middle Ages. (Visualize, for example, Big Ben and the Houses of Parliament, which most people imagine are extremely old, although they were actually constructed in the 1840s and 1850s.) Gothic Revival (also called Victorian Gothic) was used for London's Law Courts and Manchester's Town Hall, for the new parish churches in expanding cities and suburbs, and also for hundreds of schools, workhouses, and administrative offices.

Nineteenth-century civil engineers soon had to tackle the problems that came with densely populated urban areas. Roads were seldom adequately paved; traffic sent up clouds of dust in dry weather and became stuck in the mud when it rained. Streets were jammed with horse-drawn vehicles; sheep and cattle were herded through them to urban slaughterhouses; milk cows were kept in sheds in residential areas. The coal, used for virtually all domestic cooking and heating as well as for the steam engines that drove industry and transportation, polluted the air, stained stonework and brickwork, and left soot and cinders on surfaces inside and out.

Sewerage and water supplies were another serious problem. Piped water inside houses was rare; even Windsor Castle did not have a bath supplied with running water until 1847. Without running water there could be no flush toilets. The Public Health Act of 1848 (largely a response to cholera epidemics in the previous decade) recommended that all dwellings "have a fixed sanitary arrangement of some kind, namely an ash pit, privy, or a water closet." The fact that such a recommendation had to be made reveals that it was still common, in city slums as well as rural areas, for there to be no toilet facilities at all—sometimes not even a shared privy at the end of a street. The very best neighborhoods still dumped household waste into cesspools or sent it untreated into the nearest river.

In 1855, London established a Metropolitan Board of Works under chief engineer Joseph Bazalgette, who was soon nicknamed "the sewer king." Over the next 20 years, hundreds of miles of sewer pipe were put down. All new buildings were required to have drains that fed into the sewer. Bazalgette also constructed the embankment that runs along the Thames from The City west to Chelsea. The embankment not only provides handsome parks, landing stages, and public walks but also protects against flooding at high tide in stormy weather and deepens the channel so the current runs more swiftly.

In the last quarter of the century, virtually all municipalities built reservoirs, provided adequate water supplies, and established sanitary drainage. Indoor toilets became common once water mains and sewers were available. The Public Health Act of 1875 required municipalities to collect trash and garbage on a regular schedule. Streets were paved—although it was difficult to keep them clean as long as horses were the chief means of hauling goods. And coal smoke remained a serious problem in most English cities until the 1960s. (Coal smoke was responsible for the dense and deadly fogs, which could be so thick that people would lose their way while trying to cross a narrow street.)

One early technological improvement in urban safety was the development of gas lighting. Some cities built municipal gasworks (which burned coal to produce the supply of gas) during the first 20 years of the century. In 1842 there were at least 380 London lamplighters to light the streetlamps in the evening, put them out in the morning, and clean the panes of glass. Most cities were well lit by mid-century, which may have had something to do with the diminishing crime rate. In the country, the dim illumination provided by an oil lantern made driving at night quite dangerous: carriage accidents and collisions with farm carts are staple plot events in novels of the period. The gentry planned large evening events for nights when the moon would be full; even so, guests who came from any distance were generally invited to spend the night.

Early gaslights were simple tubes for burning a flame, like a gas stove or a Bunsen burner; they consumed too much oxygen for indoor use except in very large spaces where high ceilings afforded plenty of air. Interior gaslights were used in the new Houses of Parliament built in the 1840s and in other public buildings, factories, and large shops. Later in the century the invention of an incandescent mantle made indoor gas lamps safe and cheap; gas lighting was installed in most homes built after the mid-1880s.

Although Michael Faraday had discovered electromagnetic induction in 1831, electricity was slow to affect everyday life. Not until the late 1870s was an effective light bulb invented (independently but at nearly the same time by Joseph W. Swann in England and Thomas A. Edison in the United States). Electric lights were installed at once in large buildings: the machine rooms of the London *Times* in 1878, the Royal Albert Hall and the British Museum Library in 1879, and Victoria Station in 1880. Public electric generating plants were built in the early 1880s to supply power for trams, streetlights, and some manufacturing operations. Country estates—which were not connected to municipal gas lines—sometimes installed their own electric generating systems. Not very many homes, however, used electricity before the 20th century.

Not very many homes used electricity before the 20th century.

The principle of electromagnetic induction had also been harnessed, earlier, to pass signals along telegraph lines. In England, as in the United States, the telegraph network spread along railway lines for sending signals. During the 1850s, the use of telegraphy for commercial and private messages developed rapidly. In 1851 a cable to France provided links to the Continent; the War Office—as well as the London *Times*— used it extensively during the Crimean War. The Atlantic cable was completed in 1866. A dependable link between London and Bombay, in 1870, greatly enhanced England's ability to govern its distant empire—and also made life less anxious for people with relatives living or working overseas.

The post office took over the domestic telegraph system in 1870, creating an efficient monopoly and ensuring that lines were run to remote rural post offices so that messages could reach (or be sent from) all parts of the country. In cities, telegraph lines served every fire station and linked police precincts to street corner callboxes. Large offices and commercial firms had their own telegraph equipment. Branch post offices in most neighborhoods had messenger boys on duty to rush incoming telegrams to householders as soon as they arrived. Although telephones were invented in the mid-1870s, they were not much used at first, partly because the telegraph links were so good. Even in the 1890s, telephones were installed primarily in larger businesses and in wealthy urban homes. People in the countryside still depended on the post office telegraph.

The postal system was superb. Fast, cheap mail service had been one of the earliest Victorian triumphs of technological expertise combined with governmental intervention. Early in the century letters had been very expensive; even within London they cost two pence or three pence apiece. They were priced by the sheet. Outside London, letters were carried by fast mail coach but charged by weight and distance. To save expense, people would write across the page from side to side and then, turning it 90 degrees, carefully continued the letter by writing across from top to bottom. (A crossed letter can be hard to read, but if the handwriting is small and the letters carefully made, it is not impossible.) To avoid the weight of an envelope, letters were folded and sealed with wax or a sticky wafer. The address was added in some spot that had not been covered with writing. Postage was not prepaid; recipients had to pay before the letter was put in their hands. This could be very troublesome if the charge was high, particularly when the letter was unexpected and the sender and contents were not known.

In 1840, all this changed. Parliament established a uniform mail service that became known as the penny post. All domestic letters—no matter how far they traveled—cost one penny per half ounce. The postage was paid by the sender; adhesive postage stamps were introduced for the purpose. Rail service moved the mail quickly to all parts of the country; clerks in mail cars on the train sorted it according to destination. Rural carriers made deliveries in surprisingly remote places, although in most villages it was customary for people to call in at the post office (generally a counter in one of the village shops) to see if they had letters. Estates and country houses kept a post bag in some central location; mail was locked in the bag and a servant made regular trips to the nearest post office on a rail line. City dwellers had two or three mail deliveries daily, with the first post always arriving before breakfast; mail deposited in London letter boxes before 8 P.M. was delivered anywhere in the city or suburbs by 8 A.M. the next day. In many parts of London it was possible to mail an invitation in the morning, receive an answer in the afternoon post, and still have time to make preparations for dinner the same evening (Mitchell, *Daily Life*, 78–83).

To read about urban and rural environments in Chaucer's England, see the entries on Europe and London in the sections "Urban Economic Life," "The Great Cities," and "Rural Life" in chapter 3 ("Economic Life") in volume 2 of this series; for Elizabethan England, see the entries on England in the sections "Rural Life" and "City Life" in chapter 3 ("Economic Life") in volume 3 of this series.

FOR MORE INFORMATION

Mitchell, S. *Daily Life in Victorian England.* Westport, Conn.: Greenwood Press, 1996.
Mitchell, S., ed. *Victorian Britain: An Encyclopedia.* New York: Garland Press, 1998.

Roebuck, J. *Urban Development in Nineteenth-Century London: Lambeth, Battersea, and Wandsworth, 1838–1888*. London: Philimore, 1979.

ECONOMIC LIFE

URBAN & RURAL
ENVIRONMENTS

United States,
1850-1865

Victorian England

China

CHINA

During the 19th century, the increase of industry, mostly related to foreign-owned factories, greatly influenced the character of many of China's cities. Throughout the century, as migrants from the rural areas flooded into the cities in search of work, the population count and the breakdown of the population of the cities saw major change. By the end of the 19th century the population of some Chinese cities was double what it was at the start of the century. In addition, foreign influence brought a new form of modernization, and an increasing number of European-style structures were erected in urban areas throughout China.

China has always been a mainly rural society. Even today, over 75 percent of the population lives in rural villages. In China it is commonly believed that there are three tiers of the ideal locale of human existence. At the top of this hierarchy is living in nature, such as a poet contemplating life, and writing about it from his cave or cottage in the wilderness. Next is the lifestyle of the rural gentry living in the countryside surrounded by the rural landscape, as well as classical Chinese gardens. According to this belief, urban life is least desirable because it is too removed from both nature and the familial structure that is so much a part of village life.

Prior to European influence, the houses in Chinese cities were not very different in design from rural homes, despite the fact that they were built much closer together and closer to roads. Town houses and country estates were almost identical in design and in size. This might indicate further a lack of identification with the urban lifestyle. However, Chinese cities played an important social role, as centers of both wealth and power. This was only possible in a place with a large population not involved in agriculture. They served administrative and trading functions, which did not take place in rural areas.

The ideals of traditional Chinese architecture and urban planning are linked with the requirements of cosmological representation, as well as Chinese conceptions of social order. Just as China stood at the center of the cosmos, the administrative buildings were where the important officials were located. They were the center of the social hierarchy.

The Chinese system of geomancy, also known as feng shui, played a major role in the early design of Chinese cities. Feng shui includes the determination of auspicious locations for human occupation. At the center of this belief is the idea that the landscape is infused with lines of force, which may be strengthened or blocked whenever a man-made object is introduced. The goal is to arrange objects in a way that will take the most advantage of and cause the least harm to the natural order (*qi*).

Feng shui also incorporates numerological beliefs derived from the proportions of nature. In other words, numbers derived from nature (for example, 5, as in the number of elements, or 12, as in the number of signs in the Chinese zodiac) are used in patterns and measurements of architecture and building location.

Feng shui is most often practiced by a professional. The practitioner analyzes the proposed site for a house, building, or even a city, using an astrological compass that can be read for the determination of auspicious time and place. The practitioner also has a wealth of knowledge regarding the hidden lines of force in the landscape. The ideal landscape, according to the system of feng shui, is one that permits the invisible forces in nature to flow freely and is able to collect good elements for the resident.

The most important elements when choosing the location of a city are hills or mountains and water. Mountains are considered to block lines of force. Rivers carry lines of force. When dragons and tigers are believed to live in a particular mountain, care must be taken so that the city does not rest on the ridge of the mountain and, therefore, on the back of the dragon.

The arrival of the Europeans brought major changes to the Chinese cities. One major change was the population increase and the shift in demographics, as more and more people from the rural surroundings moved to the cities in search of work in foreign-owned factories. The arrival of thousands of rural workers created a new regional diversity in many of the cities. This was particularly evident in Shanghai, which became the industrial capital at this time and saw a particularly large number of new arrivals. This created a new hierarchy based on native place. Locals of the big cities often viewed these new arrivals as dirty and unsophisticated. As a result people tended to associate mostly with those from their same native place. Particular industries came to be dominated by people from a particular place. Neighborhoods were also most often divided this way.

European influence also affected the belief that China was at the center of the cosmos. The increase of foreign influence led some Chinese people to feel that their culture was lagging behind in terms of development. A sort of insecurity arose among many Chinese city dwellers, and as a result the idea of the city following in the larger social order also faded.

In terms of architecture, foreigners brought major changes. In place of the traditional Chinese houses and markets, modern buildings were erected. Modern paved roads and transportation systems were also built. The scale and skyline of many of the cities changed drastically during this period.

The increase of trade in the major cities also effected the social hierarchy. As more and more Chinese worked for and with the foreign traders and amassed more and more wealth, the traditional hierarchy changed. Previously, elite landowning families had been at the top of the social hierarchy, politically as well as economically. As there became more ways to gain wealth, and therefore power, aside from ownership of land, the hierarchy shifted. While certain opportunities were far from egalitarian, more and more Chinese people gained money and power through shrewd business skills, rather than inheritance rights.

To read about urban and rural environments in China under the Tang dynasty, see the China and Changan entries in the sections "Urban Economic Life," "The

Great Cities," and "Rural Life" in chapter 3 ("Economic Life") in volume 2 of this series.

~*Dana Lightstone*

FOR MORE INFORMATION

Chang, C., and W. Blaser. *China: Tao in Architecture*. Basel, Switzerland: Birkhauser Verlag Press, 1984.

Elvin, M., and G. W. Skinner, eds. *The Chinese City Between Two Worlds*. Stanford, Calif.: Stanford University Press, 1874.

Rowe, W. T. *Hankow: Conflict and Community in a Chinese City, 1796–1895*. Stanford, Calif.: Stanford University Press, 1989.

LATIN AMERICA

Although Latin American countries obtained their independence from the old colonial powers in the 19th century, old patterns of rural agriculture remained. Elites continued to hold vast tracts of land and indigenous peoples struggled on subsistence farms or as plantation laborers. See the Latin American entry in the section "Rural Experience" in chapter 3 ("Economic Life") in volume 6 of this series for the ways these old patterns changed in the 20th century.

ISLAMIC WORLD

From its beginnings, the culture of Islam was centered in cities. The Arabian cities of Mecca and Medina formed the heartland of Muhammad's religious life, and Jerusalem, Damascus, and Baghdad soon followed as major sites of religion, culture, and trade. See the Islamic World entry in the section "City Life" in chapter 3 ("Economic Life") in volume 2 of this series for the important beginnings of Islamic city life. Then see the Baghdad entry in the section "Great Cities" in chapter 3 ("Economic Life") in volume 2 of this series for a description of one of the greatest cities in the ancient world. Finally, follow the continuity of Islamic life in the Ottoman Empire entry in the section "City Life" in chapter 3 ("Economic Life") in volume 3 of this series. Muslim cities continued to be hubs of economics, culture, and politics into the modern world.

ECONOMIC LIFE: WEB SITES

http://www.spartacus.schoolnet.co.uk/IRchild.htm
http://www.geocities.com/couple_colour/Worker/

http://pigseye.kennesaw.edu/~ccaldwel/victoria.htm
http://www.gliah.uh.edu/historyonline/housework.cfm
http://memory.loc.gov/ammem/ndlpedu/features/timeline/riseind/rural/rural.html
http://www.sabrizain.demon.co.uk/malaya/straits3.htm
http://www.baliaga.com/english/history/trade.html

4

INTELLECTUAL LIFE

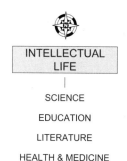

The human mind is an amazing thing that allows people to reflect on ideas so abstract that we can imagine things we could never see or touch. We can think about things as complex as philosophical considerations of ethics, justice, and even thought itself. The study of ideas is called intellectual history and it includes science, philosophy, medicine, technology, literature, and even the languages used to record the ideas.

At the basic level, the capacity for abstraction permits people to impose order (or to see order) in the astonishingly complex universe that surrounds us. As Stone Age people looked at the dark night sky dotted by millions of stars, they organized the view in patterns of constellations that allowed them to map and predict the movement of the heavens. They then echoed the heavenly order in such earthly monuments as Stonehenge in Britain or the Maya pyramids in Mexico. Through time, humans extended this capacity to order and applied it from the heavens to the submicroscopic particles that dominate 21st-century physics, developing mathematics as the language to express these abstractions. An important part of the intellectual life throughout history has been the growing evolution of science, but this is only one aspect of the accomplishments of the mind.

Some people have applied their creative capacity for abstract thought to technology, finding ways to make our lives easier. Technological innovations have spread more rapidly throughout the world than even abstract scientific explanations. Horse collars from China, windmills from Persia, and Muslim medical advances transformed medieval western Europe. In contrast, the Internet dominates world culture in the 21st century.

What makes these escalating advances possible is not an increase in human intelligence. Instead, the ability to record abstract ideas in writing and preserve past accomplishments in education have allowed human knowledge to progress. As a medieval thinker (John of Salisbury) noted, if we can see farther than the ancients, it is only because we build on their knowledge. We are as dwarfs on the shoulders of giants and, through our intellectual life, we can look forward to even greater vision.

In the 19th century, we see a flowering of intellectual life that had significant impacts on daily existence. Take for instance the scientific advances of the day.

Charles Darwin's theory of evolution revolutionized scientific thought. Similarly Louis Pasteur's germ theory sparked new and extremely important avenues of scientific advancement. In literature, some of the greatest works were produced in the 19th century. The fact that Charlotte Brontë, Charles Dickens, George Eliot, Herman Melville, Edgar Allan Poe, Anthony Trollope, Thomas Hardy, and Rudyard Kipling are still read today is testament to their profound influence on literature. Finally, in education, there were also great strides. Even on the desolate American frontier, education was valued. By the end of the Victorian era, many countries, including the United States, England, and India, had made a firm commitment to educate all children. Although the goal in fact was unattainable, the promise of universal education was profound.

Yet, given the intellectual advances of the century, one must also see the shortcomings and cultural differences. While reading the articles in this section, notice how class plays a key role in determining such things as health care and educational opportunities. Frankly, in terms of medicine, money mattered. Compare, if you will, the care that American miners on the frontier received to upper-class people in England. Similarly the impact of intellectual developments often depended upon where one was. Our miners did not have much time or cause to read Dickens or Melville, while in London, New York, or even Montgomery, Alabama these and other authors had a substantial influence. Finally, it is important to note the cross-cultural comparisons. Watch for instances when science and other elements of culture enter into conflict. Colonial India provides several examples of this. From education to medicine, intellectual endeavors produced heated cultural battles over various traditions. But even within cultures, science and other intellectual developments such as Dickens's novels caused quite a stir. Both in the United States and in Europe, new scientific theories challenged some cherished precepts and drove some to vociferously oppose the new views. Moreover, it was not just theories of evolution or of germs that made people upset. Applications of science, in other words technology, caused many to pause and wonder if the machines that were being built were not leading to the end of the human race itself.

FOR MORE INFORMATION

Tarnas, R. *The Passion of the Western Mind: Understanding the Ideas That Have Shaped Our World View.* New York: Ballentine Books, 1991.

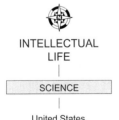

INTELLECTUAL
LIFE
|
SCIENCE
|
United States,
Nineteenth Century

Victorian England

China

Latin America

Science

The idea of science is basically a 19th-century invention. Before 1800, amateur scientists greatly outnumbered their professional counterparts. Moreover, they were the celebrities. People such as Benjamin Franklin and Thomas Jefferson were the renowned investigators of their day. In the Victorian era, however, this shifted. Professional biologists, botanists, geologists, mathematicians, and physicists took center stage. So did universities that fostered and funded scientific research, giving scientists the opportunities to conduct experiments and publish their findings. Throughout the century, scientific journals appeared carrying the latest information to both specialists and the general public (regardless of class). Science was simply popular.

Although neither England nor the United States was the center of the scientific world, they did manage to advance significantly scientific thinking. Arguably, the most important English scientist was Charles Darwin. His theory of evolution revolutionized scientific and theological thought in the Western world. Darwin's theory sought to explain the obvious succession of species on the planet. He argued that, although mutation might play a role, adaptation to environment was the key reason that explained why some species lived and some species died. Darwin's theory made an immediate impact. While some agreed with him, others violently opposed his theory as it appeared to challenge the standard biblical interpretation of history. American scientists also found themselves in the middle of the fight between religious and scientific views of the observable world. In Latin America, the ruling elites found social applications for Darwin's theories, using the idea of survival of the fittest to justify their continued withholding of political and economic rights from poor, nonwhite members of society.

China, a society that in earlier times had been one of the most scientifically advanced in the world, now found itself lagging well behind the West in scientific and technological development. This realization led to both internal reforms and to an increase in anti-Western feeling.

Despite the difficulties that Western scientific advancement caused in other parts of the world and despite the debates that divided the Western scientific community from the general public and within itself, scientists made gigantic leaps during the century that translated into new views of the world and new technologies to control it.

UNITED STATES, 19TH CENTURY

At the beginning of the 19th century, American science was in its infancy. So amateurish were American contributions to all scientific fields that with some seriousness the *New York Times* asked in 1860: "American science: is there such a thing?" Of course, in the 18th century, the new United States had its scientific luminaries such as Thomas Jefferson (botany), Benjamin Banneker (astronomy), and Benjamin Rush (medicine). But their achievements pale in comparison to their European counterparts, particularly those in Germany and France. Although still important, England was largely living off its reputation. The famed Royal Society had lost its governmental support, had come under the control of nonscientific members, and in the opinion of some had turned into a social club for the aristocracy. This is not to say that England did not have its original thinkers. It did (e.g., Michael Faraday), but German and French scientists captivated the world stage in the early to mid-19th century. Americans were well aware of their position in the world of science

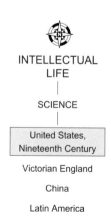

INTELLECTUAL LIFE
|
SCIENCE
|
United States, Nineteenth Century

Victorian England

China

Latin America

Louis Agassiz. © Library of Congress.

and they embraced it by importing en masse European scientific journals and books. American publishers reprinted these works without any consideration of copyright.

In addition to pirating books, the recognition of European scientific intellect caused Americans to do two other significant things. First, in increasing numbers, they began to study abroad at German and French universities to attain the most modern scientific knowledge and methodology. Second, they welcomed with open arms European scientists who immigrated to the United States. From 1846 to 1876, for example, of the 475 leading American scientists, about 50 were born in Europe. These Europeans in America revolutionized the study and practice of science in the United States. Such was definitely the case with Swedish-born naturalist Louis Agassiz.

Born in 1807, the son of a Protestant minister, Agassiz grew up in a religious environment that he eventually rejected in favor of a scientific one. He studied at the University of Munich where he received his M.A. and Ph.D. and continued his studies in Paris with Georges Cuvier, the virtuoso of comparative anatomy. Agassiz became quite famous in Europe and developed a kind of theory of evolution in which God played a central role by choosing a sequence of successive plant and animal species. Despite his successes in Europe, by 1845, Agassiz sought change. His marriage was failing as were his business ventures. Going to America seemed like an opportunity to start over. Thus in 1845, Agassiz boarded a ship bound for Boston. His years in America would be equally productive and profoundly influential.

When Agassiz arrived in Boston, the city's elite were ready to support the establishment of professional sciences in America. Agassiz was a gifted conversationalist and quickly won over the city's patrons. In so doing, Boston (and later Cambridge) became the American center of scientific investigation. A cadre of scientists gathered there, including Agassiz, the naturalist Alexander D. Bache, the naturalist and mathematician Joseph Henry, and the brilliant mathematician Benjamin Pierce. The scientific fervor of the Lazzaroni (as this group of scientists were known) drew serious scholars and researchers such as the entomologist Thaddeus Harris, the physicist Joseph Lovering, the chemist John W. Webster, and the preeminent botanist Asa Gray. Agassiz's contributions cannot be minimized. One historian of the period has written: "on his first American swing, Agassiz managed to touch nearly all the elements in the later development of American science. He visited the major centers and met most of the men who, along with the young pilgrims then in Europe, would dominate American science in his time" (Bruce, 50).

As it developed, American science in the 19th century had some key features that distinguished it among other nations. First was the importance of the natural sciences. Almost all scientists saw the United States as providing enormously rich opportunities to study the land and the creatures that inhabited it. Second, Americans had a nearly unbounded love for science. With that love, however, came an impatience for scientific conclusions, which was the third feature. Agassiz commented on this in 1847 while acknowledging his inability to "learn the American fashion of doing up science *running*" (Bruce, 70).

These general patterns in American science in the 19th century should not be mistaken for a general scientific consensus. There were plenty of rifts between scientists and the public and (not surprisingly) among scientists. One fault line concerned religion. The main contention related to the development of geologic time and geologic chronologies, which seemed to call into question accepted versions of the universe's (and earth's) creation. Simply put, many 19th-century scientists speculated that the creation of the earth lasted much longer than seven days. Aside from theologians, scientists often ran afoul of the general literate public, some of whom questioned the practical implications and applications of new scientific discoveries and theories. Henry Brooks Adams, one of the greatest thinkers and writers of the era, spoke for many Americans when he wrote: "Man has mounted science, and is now run away with [it]. I firmly believe that before many centuries more, science will be the master of man. The engines he will have invented will be beyond his strength to control. Some day science may have the existence of mankind in its power, and the human race [will] commit suicide by blowing up the world" (Bruce, 129). Finally, scientists battled with each other. Part of the contentiousness related to the Civil War, which split the scientific community in half. There were the typical academic internecine squabbles like the one between Benjamin Peirce and William Bond.

Asa Gray. © Library of Congress.

Despite the fights and debates, American scientists not only greatly advanced their fields during the 19th century, but they also made strides in the practical application of science. Indeed, in the next century, the relationship between science and technology grew closer together, intensifying the changes that science brought as well as the controversies surrounding those changes. Finally, there was another aspect of late 19th-century science that carried over significantly into the 20th century: government sponsorship. Beginning in the Civil War, the federal government began to fund scientific investigations. The most important was President Lincoln's Timber Creek project, which paid scientists like Lammot Du Pont to find new methods of creating gunpowder. As historian Robert V. Bruce has written, "the parallels between Lincoln's Timber Creek project and Franklin Roosevelt's Oak Ridge project are striking." Thus in many ways, the 19th century laid the basic groundwork for the 20th century in terms of American science.

To read about science in the United States in the 20th century, see the United States entries in the section "Science" in chapter 4 ("Intellectual Life") in volume 6 of this series.

~*Andrew E. Kersten*

FOR MORE INFORMATION

Bruce, R. V. *The Launching of Modern American Science, 1846–1876.* New York: Knopf, 1987.

Cravens, H., A. I. Marcus, and D. M. Katzman, eds. *Technical Knowledge in American Culture: Science, Technology, and Medicine since the Early 1800s.* Tuscaloosa: University of Alabama Press, 1996.

Reingold, N. *Science, American Style.* New Brunswick, N.J.: Rutgers University Press, 1991.

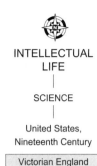

INTELLECTUAL
LIFE
|
SCIENCE
|
United States,
Nineteenth Century

Victorian England

China

Latin America

VICTORIAN ENGLAND

Most of the technological innovations that so dramatically changed the 19th-century world were made by men who worked with their hands—skilled craftsmen or practical inventors—rather than by deliberate research. The word science, however, took on its present meaning during the course of the century. It had previously described wisdom or skill in any field. When the physical world was studied as part of a university curriculum, it came under the heading natural philosophy. By 1900 people generally used the term science to mean a systematic body of knowledge about the natural world, as developed and verified through the research of academics or professionals. Indeed, the term scientist is apparently a Victorian invention.

By the time universities awarded science degrees in the latter part of the century, the generalists who took all of nature as their field had been largely replaced by men (and a few women) who worked on a fairly restricted subject: for instance, botanists, biologists, chemists, geologists, or physicists. Specialized journals published experimental and theoretical papers that could be understood only by those with advanced knowledge of the field. The division between science and technology was greater in England than in the United States; practical subjects such as engineering were not taught in universities but continued to be learned through apprenticeship or in trade schools. (Scientists search for general laws; technologists develop practical applications.) Cambridge began to offer degrees in natural science during the 1850s but did not build its first laboratory until 1871.

The growth of scientific knowledge had a major impact on the way people thought about the world. Information about new discoveries was written up for popular magazines. Many skilled workers and men and women of the middle class had scientific hobbies: collecting shells or fossils, propagating ferns, keeping aquariums, or classifying insects or plants. These self-educated amateurs provided evidence that was useful to professional scientists. Their carefully catalogued and labeled specimens showing variations within a single species can still be seen in local collections and—most impressively—in the vast glass cases of London's Natural History Museum in South Kensington. Amateurs also gained the expertise to conduct sound archaeological work on the Roman and prehistoric finds that were frequently unearthed by local builders or farmers.

By the middle of the century, the general spread of scientific awareness had cast doubt on the biblical account of creation by revealing the great age of the earth and the late appearance of humankind. Geological evidence that the planet was very old could be accommodated by interpreting the seven days of Genesis as seven eras. A greater difficulty lay in what was called the argument from design. As science demonstrated the predictability and regularity of the physical world, many people were confirmed in their belief that the universe had been constructed by an intelligent designer with a rational purpose. However, other explanations were also possible. Intelligent laypeople were sufficiently engaged in this debate to make Charles Darwin's *On the Origin of Species by Means of Natural Selection* an immediate bestseller when it was published in 1859.

Darwin himself was an example of the self-taught amateur; he studied both divinity and medicine but took up neither as a profession. His work in natural science was based not on his education but on close observation and careful thought. The idea of evolution, in general terms, was already in the air; many people who had been collecting fossils or cataloging the regional variations in a living species were grappling to explain what they found. Darwin did not introduce a dramatically new concept (indeed, when he first presented his findings at a scientific meeting in 1858, another paper on evolution, by Alfred Russel Wallace, was also read). What Darwin provided was a theory to explain why species evolved and a great deal of physical evidence from the fossil and living record in many parts of the world to support it. Plants and animals changed, Darwin argued, in adaptation to their environment. The alterations could initially come from chance or mutation, but ultimately those organisms whose physical makeup gave them some advantage would live longer and have more offspring to inherit their traits. Those who were not so adapted would die out. Thus new species evolved, and their physical form was a result of natural selection (survival of the fittest) rather than evidence of God's care in designing each animal for the surroundings in which it was placed.

Charles Darwin. Courtesy of Thoemmes Continuum.

Of course Darwin's work aroused controversy—but the immediate and widespread comprehension of both his theory and his evidence (even by those who vehemently disagreed) indicates the extent to which people's mental outlook was being changed by the habit of scientific thought. Rather than depending on argument or authority, science was now seen to require careful method: hypothesis, observation, measurement, experiment, revision, retesting, and a weight of evidence that could be accepted as proof. By the end of the century, most of the theoretical and experimental sciences had become too complicated for people without training to understand; the division between the amateur hobbyist and the professional scientist was well established. At the same time, however, people in general had great confidence in scientists' abilities to expand knowledge and solve problems (Mitchell, *Daily Life*, 83–86).

To read about science in Chaucer's England, see the entry on Europe in the section "Science" in chapter 4 ("Intellectual Life") in volume 2 of this series; for Elizabethan England, see the entry on England in the section "Health and Science" in chapter 4 ("Intellectual Life") in volume 3 of this series; for 18th-century England, see the entry on England in the section "Science and Technology" in chapter 4 ("Intellectual Life") in volume 4 of this series.

FOR MORE INFORMATION

Altick, R. D. *Victorian People and Ideas*. New York: W. W. Norton, 1973.

Mitchell, S. *Daily Life in Victorian England*. Westport, Conn.: Greenwood Press, 1996.

Morrell, J., and A. Thackray. *Gentlemen of Science: Early Years of the British Association for the Advancement of Science*. New York: Oxford University Press, 1981.

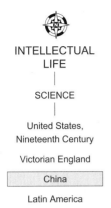

INTELLECTUAL
LIFE
|
SCIENCE
|

CHINA

Prior to the 17th century, China was known for scientific innovation. Several major technological inventions that drastically influenced the history of the world came from China. These included gunpowder, the compass, papermaking, and printing. However, by the end of the 17th century China lost its position as a scientific leader, and little in the way of innovative technology has emerged from China since. In the 19th century China was struggling with this change, and programs to advance China technologically, as well as to transform the education system into one that encouraged the growth of leaders in science and technology, was well underway.

During the 19th century China saw a considerable increase in foreign influence. This was the result of several factors, most notably trade, the opening of foreign-owned factories, and missionary activity. As a result, many Chinese people became greatly aware and self-conscious of the fact that China was lagging behind in terms of science and technology, and this became a terrible embarrassment to the culture that had previously considered itself the world leader in this respect. Not only was China no longer the technological leader, but also in order to be part of the modern economy that was rapidly developing, foreigners needed to be present to run the show.

Some Chinese turned to Western religion, following the calling of the thousands of European and American missionaries who came to China in hopes of attracting the people to the ways of Christianity. To many Chinese, this appeared to be the path to salvation. To others, it was a way of getting closer to the mindset responsible for modern technology and, therefore, wealth and power in the modern world. They hoped that the philosophy behind Christianity would serve to bring them closer to this modern world, which was otherwise beyond reach for many.

Involvement in foreign-owned businesses related to science and technology had large effects on the long-standing class system in China. By the mid-19th century, hundreds of thousands of people from rural areas had flocked to the cities each year in search of work in the factories. As a result, the long-standing class system that generally determined wealth by birthright began to change, as many people from middle- or lower-class families made money by demonstrating good business skills. Further, as many people moved to the large cities in search of work in the factories or in the ports, a new social hierarchy developed, largely related to native-place connections. In other words, in the large cities people came to depend on others from their own native place for help with finding jobs and places to live, as well as for general friendship and support in a new place. As a result certain rifts and bonds developed, and new categories of community formed.

China reformed the education system in an attempt to raise a new generation of Chinese that would be able to rival their Western counterparts in the fields of science and technology. Missionary schools were the leaders in this movement. These schools were based on the European style rather than on the Confucian system that Chinese education had followed for several thousands of years. Soon, schools other than those with religious affiliation began to follow this new system as well. The university system also changed, and many schools began to stress an education based on a combination of Western literature and Western science.

Others felt threatened by these changes and believed that without the traditional system of education, based on the ancient writings of Confucius, Chinese society would become corrupt. The traditional Confucian system emphasizes Confucian morals, which is based on the idea that family is the most important aspect of one's life. The philosophy defines five different social relations and how people should treat one another within these relationships. Many describe these morals as the center of Chinese society and culture.

Another source of contention that evolved at this time was due to the fact that many of the ancient Chinese scientific beliefs were undermined by Western science. Many traditionalists held that by reforming the education system Chinese culture would disappear. One concern was that by ignoring some of the long-standing beliefs that the Chinese had lived by for generations, people would become alienated from their culture and begin to take on some of the characteristics of Westerners, which were viewed as negative.

In some cases, the two systems of science did not completely clash and were actually incorporated into one another. Many held tightly to a strong belief in ancient Chinese scientific traditions such as medicine and geomancy. It was not uncommon to see the Western and Chinese methods combined. For example, many factories and other modern buildings were built only after consulting a practitioner of geomancy. The Chinese system of geomancy, also known as feng shui, is based on the idea that the landscape is infused with lines of force, which may be strengthened or blocked whenever an artificial object is introduced. The object is to arrange objects in a way that will take the most advantage of and cause the least harm to the natural order (*qi*). Feng shui also incorporates numerological beliefs derived from the proportions of nature. In other words, numbers derived from nature (for example, 5, as in the number of elements, or 12, as in the number of signs in the Chinese zodiac) are used in patterns and measurements of architecture and building location. The use of feng shui in the creation of modern structures based on Western architecture is only one example of the combining of the Western and Chinese scientific belief.

Because the Chinese scientific methods differed so drastically from those of the West, at times they caused an uneasy combination. Despite the fact that many traditionalists attacked the use of Western scientific methods in China, monetary incentive was great, and in a very short time foreign influence was evident in all aspects of society, including science and technology, and it was clear that China was quickly entering the world of Western science.

To read about science in China under the Tang dynasty, see the China entry in the section "Science" in chapter 4 ("Intellectual Life") in volume 2 of this series.

FOR FURTHER INFORMATION

Ebrey, P. B. *The Cambridge Illustrated History of China*. New York: Cambridge University Press, 1999.

Shaughnessy, E. L., ed. *China: Empire and Civilization*. Oxford: Oxford University Press, 2000.

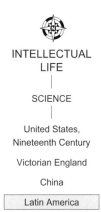

LATIN AMERICA

Although the nations of Latin America gained independence from European co-lonial powers in the early 19th century, they continued to be highly influenced by European currents. Indeed, many Latin Americans spent much of the immediate postindependence era preoccupied with progress and searching for reasons why their region lagged so far behind western Europe in terms of development and moderni-zation. In their quest for answers and for progress, Latin Americans placed much faith in science and technology.

Latin American intellectuals quickly devoured the works of many European En-lightenment thinkers, including Immanuel Kant, Georg Wilhelm Friedrich Hegel, Arthur Schopenhauer, and Friedrich Nietzsche. A particularly strong influence was the positivism of French philosopher Auguste Comte. Positivism sought an orderly explanation for the development of human societies; its followers formulated hy-potheses and laws about social development along the lines of positive sciences (math, physics, chemistry, biology).

Latin Americans added evolutionism and eugenics to the mix. They found social applications for Charles Darwin's theories of natural selection and survival of the fittest and sought better breeding by exploring how new knowledge of heredity could be put to social use. According to these lines of thought, Latin America's poor had innate incapacities; if governments attempted to raise the poor out of their material misery—through literacy and education, for example—they would be acting con-trary to the principles of nature. Such ideas not only rationalized the concentration of wealth in the hands of the few, but they also confirmed the white male bourgeoisie as biologically, morally, and rationally superior, as well as rightfully dominant over all others, including women, workers, and ethnic minorities.

Many of the pseudosciences medicalized important moral issues of the period, such as prostitution and education. At the same time, they medicalized populations, including the working class, minorities, and women. Specialists designated these groups as abnormal and sick, inherently unable to meet prescribed standards. Sci-entists and intellectuals also debated the degeneration of entire nations and national illnesses, a trend illustrated by the titles of contemporary publications: *An Ill People* by Alcides Arguedas, *The Illness of Central America* by Salvador Mendieta, *Social Sicknesses* by Manuel Ugarte, and *The Sick Continent* by César Zumeta.

Because the followers of these and other pseudosciences often occupied govern-ment positions, they were able to institute many policies of discriminatory character. Using the theories of scientific racism, officials revised penal codes; regulated pros-titution; reformed public education, the military, and treatment programs for the mentally unstable; and established sanitary and hygienic standards in private and public spaces.

Positivism and other 19th-century trends glorified science, converting it into a sort of religion of progress. As such, many people lauded outward manifestations of progress. In this sense, they had much to celebrate because, throughout Latin Amer-ica, technological advances were highly visible during the 19th century.

Among the most influential technology transfers of the era was the steam engine. In 1815, a sugar mill in Bahia, Brazil, boasted the region's first steam engine; by 1852, there were 144 steam-powered sugar mills in Brazil alone. Chile had 132 steam engines by 1863, running sawmills, distilleries, blower furnaces, flour mills, and coal mines (Burns, 143).

Steamships first arrived to the region in the 1820s but did not become common until the latter half of the century. These ships not only improved trade and communication, they also quickened the modernization of the port cities where they docked. The port of Guayaquil, Ecuador, for example, had a streetcar, electric lighting, and other amenities well before the nation's capital of Quito, located high in the Andes mountains (Burns, 147).

Steam engines also prompted the rapid spread of railroads. By 1838, Cuba had 30 miles of track. In 1851, both Chile and Peru opened their first operating lines, and by the end of the 1850s, Brazil and Argentina also had short tracks (Burns, 143). Railroads continued to expand in the region well into the 20th century, bringing Latin American nations into contact with European markets and influencing internal political and commercial integration and development (Miller and Finch, 1).

Another advance of the period was the telegraph. Chile and Brazil began cable service in the early 1850s; Argentina, which introduced the telegraph in the 1860s, had 60 stations by 1875 (Burns, 146). Like the railroad, the telegraph not only contributed to national unity, it also influenced international connections. One of the first international cable lines began in 1866, between Buenos Aires, Argentina, and Montevideo, Uruguay. The following year, a cable connected the United States and Cuba, and in 1874, officials sent the first cable transmission between Brazil and Portugal (Burns, 147).

Less visible technology transfers occurred as well, as in industrial procedures, medicines and psychology, and weaponry. By the end of the century, for example, militaries in Latin America used such German innovations as Krupp cannons and Mauser rifles and machine guns (Loveman, 64).

Despite the fact that the new nations of Latin America did not catch up to Europe during the 19th century, their citizens continued to invest great faith in science and technology as a means of bringing progress. The connection between science and progress, as well as government policy, was so strong that Mexican President Porfirio Díaz's cabinet was referred to as *los científicos*, "the scientists." Similarly, the Brazilian flag, designed in 1889, carried the motto of *ordem e progresso*, "order and progress." While many advances were made, particularly in terms of communication and transportation, the effects were often uneven and discriminatory.

~Molly Todd

FOR MORE INFORMATION

Aronna, M. *"Pueblos Enfermos": The Discourse of Illness in the Turn-of-the-Century Spanish and Latin American Essay*. Chapel Hill: University of North Carolina Press, 1999.

Burns, E. B. *Latin America: A Concise Interpretive History*. 5th ed. Englewood Cliffs, N.J.: Prentice Hall, 1990.

Loveman, B. *For La Patria: Politics and the Armed Forces in Latin America.* Wilmington, Del.: Scholarly Resources, 1999.

Miller, R., and H. Finch. *Technology Transfer and Economic Development in Latin America, 1850–1930.* Liverpool: University of Liverpool, 1986.

Stepan, N. L. *The Hour of Eugenics: Race, Gender, and Nation in Latin America.* Ithaca, N.Y.: Cornell University Press, 1991.

Zanetti, O., and A. García, eds. *Sugar and Railroads: A Cuban History, 1837–1959.* Translated by Franklin Knight and Mary Todd. Chapel Hill: University of North Carolina Press, 1998.

INTELLECTUAL
LIFE

EDUCATION

United States,
1850-1865

United States,
Western Frontier

Victorian England

China

Latin America

Education

Investigating the history of education is quite useful in highlighting social divisions as well as the commonalities. For instance, when reading the following entries, pay attention to how educational systems reflect the class structure. In Victorian England, what instruction children received (if any) depended greatly upon the social class to which they belonged. Children of extremely poor parents, of course, worked. Working-class and middle-class kids began at elementary schools of various kinds and qualities. Since schooling was not free, the quality of education often depended upon what one could afford. Poorer schools had fewer teachers and learning materials and they crowded all students into large classrooms.

Victorian England's schools also displayed regional differences. Schools in smaller villages were not as accommodating as those in larger cities. Moreover, there were not as many opportunities for teachers in rural areas. Teaching in the cities was one way that working-class or lower-middle-class men and women could advance economically. This regional difference in schooling was common elsewhere, particularly in the United States. In the 19th century, there was a dramatic increase in the number of American schools, and the growth was prominent in the West. Thousands of teachers went to the frontier to teach not only the academic basics but morality as well. The rural schools were quite different from the urban schools. One Pennsylvania educator despondently wrote in 1861 that the state's rural schools were more fit for cattle than students. Rural districts were also underfunded. They attempted to survive financial ruin by hiring female teachers at salaries much lower than their male counterparts.

In the American setting, education also displayed another kind of regionalism: political regionalism. There was quite a difference between Northern and Southern schools. Education in the South was not only financed differently but aptly reflected a particular Southern ideology. An illustrative example can be drawn from the textbooks that were used. Northern schools used the *McGuffey* readers and Noah Webster's "blue back" *Spellers*. Southerners hated those books, seeing them as pro-Union tracts. Instead, Southern schools had the *Dixie Primer for Little Folks* and the *Dixie Speller* that was based on Webster's but left out any positive reference to the North.

Whether in the North or South, American schools did have some commonalities. One was local control. Communities set school standards and curricula. Rural schools, for example, often had ungraded classrooms and no means of student evaluation. While part of the reasons for this were born out of necessity, it also related to the expectations of the community. Residents in some rural areas did not have grand expectations for their system of schools. Another commonality in the United States was the general mission of the education system in the United States, which was to introduce students to and acculturate children to American values and culture. One can see this especially in the schools for American Indians. These institutions, like Carlisle Indian School, took Indian pupils and made them American by changing their names, cutting their hair, giving them new clothes, and teaching them English, mathematics, and Christianity. The results of this education were jarring. One Chippewa woman recollected from her experience that her cultural past was erased from her mind. Such molding of girls and boys was perhaps most severe on the Indian reservations but was indeed common to schools in the 19th century.

Finally, examining education highlights cultural conflicts as well. Take the example of China. During the 19th century, China developed competing educational systems, one Western and one traditional. The Western system of schools made its first appearance around the time of the Opium War with Great Britain. European and American missionaries sought to teach the Chinese Western values and knowledge by setting up primary and secondary schools as well as universities. Many Chinese resisted this movement to promote foreign ideas and ideals and, in turn, reinvigorated more traditional Confucian education. As in the American West, the clash of cultures through education did not have clear winners. In Latin America, the clash was between the church and the state as independence and the development of liberal republican governments gradually weakened the Catholic Church's traditional control of education. By the end of the century, Latin America contained a wide variety of educational systems with many of them based on French, British, and German models. As one reads these entries, pay close attention to the ways in which education served larger political and economic goals, such as cultural conquest.

UNITED STATES, 1850–65

Americans believed it was essential that children be prepared for the intellectual and cultural life that the 19th century valued so highly. A lesson entitled "The Value of Education" in a school reader states: "The highest objects of a good education are to reverence and obey God and to love and serve mankind. Every thing that helps in attaining these objects is of great value, and every thing that hinders us is comparatively worthless."

The home, of course, was the first place where these foundations were laid. *The Mother's Book* by Lydia Child—the Dr. Spock of her day—advocated the deliberate and early cultivation of a child's intellect. After describing some simple amusements

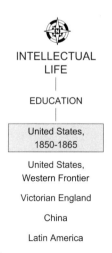

INTELLECTUAL
LIFE
|
EDUCATION
|

United States,
1850-1865

United States,
Western Frontier

Victorian England

China

Latin America

for the small child, Mrs. Child advised, "But something ought to be mixed with these plays to give the child the habits of thought." She then proceeded to describe situations in which basic daily activities could be converted into stimulating intellectual endeavors. She urged that as children grew older they should be told, "The more knowledge you gain, the more useful you can be, when you become a man." Additionally, it was essential that children be fortified with solid moral foundations. Mrs. Child cautioned against selecting readings for children that merely culminated in a moral: "The morality should be in the book, not tacked upon the *end* of it." With such home training, children entered school at age four or five with certain basic moral and cultural understandings upon which would be built a formal education.

In the North and Midwest, schools were community or common schools. These schools would be open to all children from the community. Conditions in common schools varied tremendously not only from the North to the South but from community to community. School revenue was directly tied to the success or failure of local commerce. In an 1861 report, numerous county superintendents in Pennsylvania reported frosts in June and early July. The resulting loss of the wheat crop caused not only "more than ordinary pecuniary embarrassment"; in addition, teaching time was shortened, and in some communities the wages of the teachers were reduced. More than one superintendent lamented a false system of economy that reduced teachers' wages so much that some of the best teachers left the county or became engaged in "other pursuits." Some districts chose to suspend school for the entire year. Nonetheless, remaining teachers were applauded for their self-denial and the manner in which they bore up during a difficult time. In the same year, where lumbering districts were favored by high water, there was increased prosperity.

School buildings were constructed in a number of ways and might be of brick, frame, log, or stone. In the 1861 state report, 58 percent of the Pennsylvania superintendents who responded used negative terms to describe their schools. It was not unusual to see claims that the schools were "less fit for the purpose of schooling, than would be many modern outhouses for sheltering cattle." One schoolhouse was described as "a crumbling, dilapidated, damp, unwholesome stone building with a ceiling 8 feet high, room about 26 by 30 feet into which 117 are crowded and placed at long, old-fashioned desks with permanent seats, without backs." One superintendent reported finding "the teacher and pupils huddled together, shivering with cold, and striving to warm themselves by the little heat generated from a quantity of green wood in the stove." Additional complaints included a lack of "outhouses and other appliances necessary for comfort and convenience." Concern was expressed over the fact that schoolhouses were "placed far off the road and buried in the wildest forest."

Yet a number of new schools were described in more favorable terms. One report described a "tasteful brick building 30 x 45 . . . furnished with first class iron frame furniture for 62 pupils." Other new buildings were of wood, and one was "24 x 36 with four tiers of seats for two pupils each accommodating 64 pupils." Another superintendent boasted, "All the rooms are warmed by coal stoves, most of them have ceilings of proper height, windows adapted to ventilation; plenty of blackboard surface; and they are tolerably well seated." A new schoolhouse was proudly described as having an "anteroom, closets, and platform and in every respect is superior to most of the other houses."

The schools were supervised by a group of designated citizens who oversaw operations. Their duties included "the levying of tax, the location of school houses, the purchase and sale of school property, the appointment and dismissal of teachers, and the selection of studies and textbooks." The dedication and expertise of these directors was, however, often called into question.

Rural districts were often unsuccessful in obtaining a normal school graduate and had to settle for whatever reasonably well-educated person they could find. Although both men and women taught, male teachers were preferred. As the war progressed, many young men left the schoolroom to serve in the army or to fill better-paying jobs. This dearth of males opened the doors for women in education. A county superintendent of schools wrote, "The employment of female teachers caused some dissatisfaction, as they were believed inadequate to the task of controlling a winter school. But superior cleanliness and arrangement of their rooms, the effect of their natural gentleness and goodness on the scholars . . . amply compensated for their want of physical force." These qualities were appreciated even more when it was found that the generally younger women could be paid lower salaries than the male teachers. The average salary reported in 1861 for a male teacher was $24.20 per month. Women were paid $18.11.

Drawing of a typical U.S. schoolroom in the mid-19th century. *Harper's Weekly,* ca. 1863.

"The majority of teachers are between 18 and 25 and are spending a part of the year in attending academies and Normal School," wrote one superintendent. But some of the teachers were little more than children themselves. A superintendent complained:

It is to be regretted, however, that parents will urge their sons and daughters to seek to become teachers at so early an age; and it is a great error in directors, as a general rule, to employ such young persons. Men engage persons of mature age and experience on the farm, in the shop or store, in the kitchen or dairy room; but they hire girls or boys of 15 or 16 to train up and educate their offspring.

School districts established examinations to certify that teachers were competent to assume their duties. Most exams were a combination of written and oral questions. "They were held publicly, and attended by numbers of citizens, who had a desire to see and hear for themselves." Emma Sargent Barbour's sister, Maria, wrote about the examination process in Washington. " [Hattie was] accompanying me as far as City Hall where I was to be examined, when she remarked that she had a good mind to try just for fun. She went in and passed an excellent examination and next Monday will take a position at my school." Not all examinations were quite as simple as Maria implies. Many superintendents in Pennsylvania reported having to turn away applicants who had failed, while others indicated that, considering the rural nature of their district, they were lucky to find teachers at all. "Parents prefer to have there [sic] children work in the mines or learn a trade, and thus but few become qualified to teach school."

Institutes were held periodically to help teachers to improve their skills. Some met only once a year, while others were held semimonthly on alternate Saturdays. Naturally, not all teachers performed to the satisfaction of the districts. A Wayne County, Pennsylvania, superintendent wrote of his teachers, "Two last winter had the reputation of being of intemperate habits, and some few are rough and rowdyish in their manner."

About 50 percent of children outside the South attended school with some regularity. Some areas of the Midwest and New England had enrollments as high as 90 percent. Attendance in rural areas still suffered from the fact that many parents "task their children heavily with farm labor, and [not] until such tasks are finished are they allowed to start school." Not everyone was convinced that public education was beneficial, but public sentiment was gradually becoming more favorable to the system. "People are beginning to see that their children can get a sound practical . . . education in our common schools."

> *Most Southerners were opposed to tax-supported education.*

Most Southerners were opposed to tax-supported education. The school reformers and educational advocates of the 1840s were mostly Northerners. This contributed to a certain skepticism on the part of Southerners, who felt that the school systems were at least partially responsible for Northern attitudes in the decade preceding the war. Most Southerners preferred to send their children to private institutions. By 1860 only four Southern states and a few isolated communities had common school systems.

Popular instructional materials included *McGuffey's Eclectic Reader, Ray's Arithmetic*, and Webster's "blue back" *Speller*. Spelling was just becoming standardized. *Leach's Complete Spelling Book* of 1859 contained a "Collection of Words of Various Orthography," which included words of "common use, which are spelled differently by the three most eminent Lexicographers . . . Webster, Worcester, and Smart." Emma Sargent Barbour's letter from her young cousin Mary gives additional insight into period texts: "I am getting along first rate, at school. I don't always get 10 tough by any means. I always get 9 in writing. I study Robinson's Arithmetic, it is a very hard one. Frost's United States History, Towen's speller, Weld's Grammar, the same almost exactly like the one I studied on east, but the Grammar is not at all like it. I read out of Sargent's Reader." Students were graded by how well they read their readers. Many schools suffered from a lack of uniform class sets of texts, although the adoption of this practice was frequently a goal. "In time, however, as the old books (some of which, carefully preserved, have descended from grand-fathers) are worn out, uniform class-books will be used, much to the advantage of teachers and pupils."

In many schools sufficient blackboards were also wanting. Blackboards were made by taking smooth boards—painted black—and covering them with a chalk dust, which provided the erasable surface. Well-supported schools not only had blackboards but also outline maps, spelling and reading cards, charts, and globes. The average school had only one or two of these instructional materials. Paper was scarce in rural schools. Students commonly wrote on wood frame slates, although these were initially "confined to such as had made advancement in arithmetic; but now we find the smallest scholars engaged with their slates."

Furniture was, at best, sparse in most classrooms. "It is useless to complain of school furniture," lamented one superintendent. "It seems that people would sooner see their children have spinal or pulmonary affliction, than furnish the school room with proper desks and seats." A York County, Pennsylvania, superintendent noted, "I witnessed a great deal of uneasiness, amounting in many instances to intense suffering, among the small children, from . . . being seated too high. In some instances, the desks are still attached to the wall, the scholars with their backs to the teacher."

There were few, if any, educational standards at this time. The length of the school day and year varied as the individual community saw fit. The average length of the school term in 1860 was five months and five and one-half days. A typical school day ran from nine to four with an hour for recess and dinner at noon. The day often commenced with a scripture reading followed by a patriotic song. Emma Sargent Barbour received a letter from her sister, Maria, addressing her teaching duties. "I am a regular schoolmarm. School commences every day at nine o'clock when they write a half hour and the lessons follow." A subsequent letter provides more details of a teacher's day. "School! School!—is the cry, my daily life may almost be embraced in the following programme; rise at seven, breakfast at half past, practice my little singing lesson and ready to start for school at half past eight. Direct the youths how to behave and hear lessons until twelve, then from 20 minutes to a half an hour, hear missed lessons and eat lunch, chat with the boys until one o'clock, then proceed as before until three; prepare for dinner and sometimes attend receptions or receive company in the evening."

Most learning was done via rote memorization and recitation. To motivate the students, less interesting material, such as geographic facts, was sung to popular tunes. Multiplication tables were often taught in verse: for example, "Twice 11 are 22. Mister can you mend my shoe?" or "9 times 12 are 108. See what I've drawn upon my slate." Mental arithmetic was still an innovative technique, and more than one district reveled in the fact that it was taught in their schools. "Mental arithmetic has been extensively introduced during the past two years and will soon be considered an indispensable item even in our primary schools."

In Connecticut, towns with 80 families were required to have a single school for young children that taught English grammar, reading, writing, geography, and arithmetic. Towns with 500 families added a school for older students that offered algebra, American history, geometry, and surveying. Places with larger populations offered study of the physical sciences—sometimes referred to as natural or revealed philosophy—and Greek and Latin. The subjects taught depended on the competency of the teacher and varied greatly from school to school. In the annual report of Armstrong County, Pennsylvania, the superintendent boasted: "The number of schools in which geography and grammar are not taught is steadily diminishing. There is a considerable increase in the number in which mental arithmetic is taught. Algebra was taught in 11 schools; history in 4; natural philosophy in 2; Latin in 1; composition in 5; and in several there were exercises in declamation and vocal music."

In the same report, Beaver County noted, "The Bible is read in 140 schools; not read in 17. I trust that all our teachers may become so deeply impressed with a sense of their duty, in the moral education of their pupils, that we may soon report the Bible read in every school." In addition to the three R's, schools were expected to infuse a strong moral sense, foster polite behavior, and inspire good character. Another instructional objective, presented in a reading text, was "a desire to improve the literary taste of the learner, to impress correct moral principles, and augment his fund of knowledge." An introductory geography book contained the following extraordinary attestation in its preface: "The introduction of moral and religious sentiments into books designed for the instruction of young persons, is calculated to improve the heart, and elevate and expand the youthful mind; accordingly, whenever the subject has admitted of it, such observations have been made as tend to illustrate the excellence of Christian religion, the advantages of correct moral principles, and the superiority of enlightened institutions."

Readers contained lessons entitled "The First Falsehood," "Effects of Evil Company," "Contrast Between Industry and Idleness," and "Dialogue between Mr. Punctual and Mr. Tardy." Stories, poems, and essays used in instruction drilled the message that good triumphed over evil, frugality surpassed extravagance, obedience superseded willfulness, and family always came first. This can be seen even in brief multiplication rhymes—"5 times 10 are 50. My Rose is very thrifty" or "4 times 10 are 40. Those boys are very naughty." The last was inscribed beneath a picture of two boys fighting.

Some texts published in the North during the war contained distinctly pro-Union sentiments. *Hillard's Fifth Reader,* printed in 1863, contained such readings as "Liberty and Union" and "The Religious Character of President Lincoln," as well as "Song of the Union," the poem "Barbara Frietchie," and an essay on the "Duty of American Citizens" among many similar patriotic themes. Caroline Cowles Richards wrote in her 1861 diary, "I recited 'Scott and the Veteran' today at school, and Mary Field recited, 'To Drum Beat and Heart Beat a Soldier Marches By.' Anna recited 'The Virginia Mother.' Everyone learns war poems now-a-days."

Rural schools were often ungraded and had no standard final examinations or report cards. Scholastic success was still given a showcase via exhibition bees and quizzes held for parents. Students demonstrated their expertise in spelling, arithmetic, geography, and history. In addition to praise, winners were given certificates and prizes such as books or prints. Gifted students could pass through the entire local system of schools by age 14 or 15, but only the most affluent could move on to college or university. A foreign visitor to New England found that most men had a basic education that stressed reading and writing, but that few exhibited the fine formal education available in Europe.

Southern teachers were even more challenged by the need for educational materials than their Northern counterparts. The South had depended on the North and Europe for texts prior to the war. Once the war began, Northern publications were held in contempt and the blockade curtailed European imports. A movement commenced in the South to produce its own texts, but shortages of materials and the destruction of printing equipment impeded implementation of the plan. What texts were published tended to be extremely propagandistic and of low quality. Marinda Branson Moore of North Carolina was probably the most audacious of Southern authors in this regard. She published *Dixie Primer for Little Folks* and *Dixie Speller*, which was "revised from Webster and adapted for Southern schools . . . leaving out all Yankee phrases and allusions." Her geography addressed the issues of slavery and secession and laid blame for the war on the North.

Southerners regretted having allowed Northerners to teach their children prior to the war. Teaching was a respectable vocation, but women who taught in the South were often pitied for their obvious dire financial situation. With the outbreak of hostilities, the distaste for Northern teachers spread rapidly. Advertisements for teachers soon came to request that applicants be natives of Dixie or from Europe. Wartime dangers eventually suspended many Southern schools, and the task of educating youngsters fell to the mothers.

While common schools were well established by this time, and enrollments grew throughout the war in Northern cities, the development of high schools, slow before the war, faced even more obstacles. The lure of the military, or opportunities made available by army enlistments, siphoned off many would-be students. High schools were essentially an urban institution, founded with the intention of providing opportunity for boys who wished to become merchants or mechanics. Such an education was seen as terminal. Boston, a leader in educational matters, did not open a high school for girls until 1855. Although some Northern areas required larger cities to establish high schools, most people felt that this was a form of higher education and should not be part of the legal public school system. By 1860 there were 300 high schools in the United States, 100 of which were in Massachusetts.

College enrollments also suffered as idealistic young men rushed to join the forces of their cause. Caroline Cowles Richards listed in her diary a number of young men who "talk of leaving college and going to war." She described a rally at the Canandaigua Academy and detailed how "Capt. Barry drills the Academy boys in military tactics on the campus every day. Men are constantly enlisting." Southern colleges had the additional complications of the loss of funding, physical destruction from battle, and conversion to hospitals, barracks, and headquarters.

> *By 1860, there were 300 high schools in the United States, 100 of them were in Massachusetts.*

College studies were heavily classical. Students read Latin and Greek from Livy, Cicero, Homer, Plato, and others. As in primary school, recitation was the most common form of instruction. Work in the sciences, which covered physics and astronomy, with some chemistry and geology, consisted mostly of lectures along with occasional laboratory demonstrations. Mathematics explored geometry, trigonometry, and calculus and encompassed memorization of rules with some effort to apply them to problems. Rhetoric students studied composition as well as speaking. Other studies included philosophy and logic.

The year 1862 was an important one for education. The Morrill Act passed through the federal Congress, establishing the land grant colleges. It was also the year in which Washington, D.C., made the first provisions for Negro schooling. While the effects of both of these events may have been felt more after the war, they nonetheless show an extremely positive federal attitude toward education, even amid the turmoil of war.

At the outbreak of the war only about 5 percent of slaves could read. As federal troops occupied an area and set the slaves free, many former slaves established schools to help others prepare for freedom. Often Union commanders occupying an area mandated the creation of such schools or allowed their creation by Northern missionaries. These practices led to the creation of the Freedmen's Bureau in 1865, through which the federal government took a formal stance toward the education of former slaves. Northern teachers who traveled to the South during the war suffered tremendous hardships. They were deeply resented by Southerners, who commonly refused them any accommodations, and overworked by the Northern agencies that sent them. What passed for schoolrooms were often worse than the most desolate of Northern facilities.

While the North provided for the education of some free blacks, the idea of racially integrated schools was vehemently opposed. When Prudence Crandall attempted to integrate her fashionable Connecticut school for girls, the white students were quickly withdrawn by outraged parents. Crandall herself was insulted, threatened, and stoned. In the interest of the safety of her students, she was forced to acquiesce. Some common school systems established schools for minority groups such as Amerindians and free blacks. Considering the inadequate support many regular schools were given, one can imagine the facilities that would have been provided when a separate school was established for a minority group. An observer of a "colored school" remarked that although the Black pupils "were not so far advanced . . . if the same facilities be afforded to them, which are given to the children in other schools in the borough, they will soon compare favorably with them, not only in the lower branches, but also in the more advanced departments" (Volo and Volo, 271–80).

To read about education in the United States in the 20th century, see the United States entries in the section "Education" in chapter 3 ("Intellectual Life") in volume 6 of this series.

FOR MORE INFORMATION

Massey, M. E. *Women in the Civil War*. Lincoln: University of Nebraska Press, 1966.
Spring, J. *The American School, 1642–2000*. 5th ed. New York: McGraw Hill, 2000.
Volo, D. D., and J. M. Volo. *Daily Life in Civil War America*. Westport, Conn.: Greenwood Press, 1998.

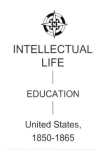

INTELLECTUAL
LIFE
|
EDUCATION
|
United States,
1850-1865

United States,
Western Frontier

Victorian England

China

Latin America

UNITED STATES, WESTERN FRONTIER

Any notion that education was absent or not important to Americans living on the frontier is quite wrong. One purpose of the reservation system was to teach American Indians what was considered to be typically American values and skills. Hence, one of the first priorities on the reservations was to make the Indian a self-sufficient farmer, to teach him to plow and to plant and to harvest. Seemingly innocuous, this process struck at some fundamental Native American beliefs. Smo-halla, a Wanapam dreamer-prophet, commented, "You ask me to plow the ground! Shall I take a knife and tear my mother's bosom? Then when I die she will not take me to her bosom to rest. . . . You ask me to make hay and sell it and be rich like white men! But dare I cut off my mother's hair?"

General Miles reported on one Indian who acquiesced to the idea of planting a garden. He wanted to produce for himself "the best food the white man had" and so wanted to plant a garden of raisins. Sometimes the "assistant farmers," frequently political appointees, knew little more than their Indian pupils about farming. One, apparently assuming all root vegetables were alike, "directed his neophytes to cut turnips in pieces and plant them in hills!"

Education was, according to Francis Paul Prucha, "the ultimate reform. Whether the Indian was granted land in severalty (i.e., land owned by individuals rather than tribes) and whether he received equal treatment under the law were moot issues if he was not educated. At the 1884 Lake Mohonk Conference, reformers summarized the goals of Indian education:

The Indian must have a knowledge of the English language that he may associate with his white neighbors and transact business as they do. He must have practical industrial training to fit him to compete with others in the struggle for life. He must have a Christian education to enable him to perform the duties of the family, the State and the Church.

To achieve these goals, schools—both day schools and boarding schools—were established on the reservations. Elaine Goodale Eastman taught in day schools on the Great Sioux Reservation. At her first school she had about fifty students ranging in age from 6 to 16, none of whom knew any English. Fortunately she, unlike many educators, learned the Dakota language. Although it was official policy that only English could be used in the classrooms (a policy with which she took no public issue), she was able to communicate with her students' parents and thus help to avoid a potentially serious rift between generations and ways of life. Nonetheless, assimilation into the larger American society was a top priority, and so, with the help of philanthropist friends from the East who donated clothing and material, one of her first projects was to teach the older girls how to sew and to convince the boys to have their long hair cut.

Because manual training schools required greater expenditures to equip them with stock, farming implements, tools, and wagons, they had to be boarding schools. Many felt these were preferable to day schools in any case, for, as Indian Commissioner Ezra Hayt observed, "the demoralization and degradation of an Indian home neutralized the efforts of the schoolteacher."

In 1878 there were 137 Indian schools of all kinds provided by the government, with about 3,500 students; by 1887 the numbers had grown to 231 schools and 10,000 students. The need, however, was still greater and was filled in part by contract schools provided by various religious denominations.

Before and after photographs of new students at the Carlisle Indian School. The boys belong to the Sioux nation.

To many, the flagship of the Indian educational system was the Carlisle Indian School in Carlisle, Pennsylvania, established in 1879 by Captain Richard Henry Pratt. (Ironically, it was housed at first in the same barracks where cavalry recruits destined for the Indian wars had received their basic training.) Pratt's educational philosophy was simple: his students were to be prepared for complete integration into white society.

The first days at Carlisle were a tremendous shock for students. Luther Standing Bear described some of his experiences as he battled a sense of isolation and homesickness to learn the white men's ways. A member of the first class, he arrived to sleep the first night on the floor in a room with no furniture other than a stove. Worse, breakfast the next morning was only bread and water, and dinner was some meat, bread, and coffee. "How lonesome [we] were for [our] faraway Dakota homes where there was plenty to eat!"

If the students were to be Americans, they were to have American names; so, one day they arrived in the schoolroom to find the blackboard covered with columns of white marks. One by one the boys were called to the blackboard and told by the interpreter to point at one "word." As they did so, the teacher pinned a piece of cloth with a corresponding set of marks to the boy's shirt. Thus, one boy became

"Luther." If one's personal identity is bound up with his name, each child was thus symbolically stripped of it.

Possibly the most traumatic event of the early weeks—because the boys were acutely conscious of how it redefined them—was their first haircut. Standing Bear writes:

We all looked so funny with short hair. It had been cut with a machine and cropped very close. We still had our Indian clothes [for a few more days] but we were all bald-headed. None of us slept very well that night. . . . After having my hair cut, a new thought came into my head. I felt I was no more Indian, but would be an imitation white man. And we are still imitations of white men.

Forbidden to speak their own languages, stripped of native dress, required to model themselves on white society, many Indian children were confused, lonely, and alienated, caught between two worlds. One young Chippewa woman could scarcely remember what had been. "Gone were the vivid pictures of my parents, sisters, and brothers. Only a blurred picture of what use[d] to be. Desperately I tried to cling to the faded past, which was slowly being erased from my mind."

Despite Pratt's intentions of full integration of his students into American society, the reality was that this was impossible. Many young people thus experienced a second culture shock when they returned to the reservation. Possibly the most extreme example of this was a young Sioux who returned to the Pine Ridge reservation shortly after the battle at Wounded Knee. Plenty Horses killed a cavalryman to prove that his education at Carlisle had not made him a white man (Jones, 247–49).

To read about education on the colonial frontier of North America, see the entries on the Colonial Frontier and New England in the section "Education" in chapter 4 ("Intellectual Life") in volume 4 of this series.

FOR MORE INFORMATION

Jones, M. E. *Daily Life on the Nineteenth Century American Frontier*. Westport, Conn.: Greenwood Press, 1998.

Prucha, F. P. *The Great Father: The United States Government and the American Indians*. Abr. ed. Lincoln: University of Nebraska Press, 1986.

Spring, J. *The American School, 1642–2000*. 5th ed. New York: McGraw Hill, 2000.

VICTORIAN ENGLAND

Children in Victorian England were educated in many different ways—or not at all—depending on their sex and their parents' financial circumstances, social class, religion, and values. In England there was little agreement about what to teach, how to pay for schools, or whom to educate. Disputes about religious instruction and a

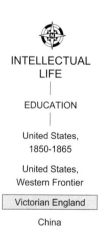

INTELLECTUAL
LIFE

EDUCATION

United States,
1850-1865

United States,
Western Frontier

Victorian England

China

Latin America

conviction that every father had the right to determine how to raise his own children delayed the development of compulsory schooling.

Although there are exceptions to any generalization about 19th-century English education, a few terms were widely used. Elementary schools provided low-cost instruction for working-class and lower-middle-class children. Depending on their type of organization and funding, elementary schools were called by several names: board school, district school, parish school, village school, voluntary school, or national school. Few elementary schools were entirely free until the 1890s; the usual charge was between one and four pence per week.

Children of more prosperous parents received their early teaching and their secondary education (if any) either at home or in schools described as public or private. In either case, the fees were higher than those of elementary schools. Private schools were owned by a single proprietor and provided almost any kind of education. A widow who gave lessons in her dining room during the morning to five or six young children was considered to run a private school. A technical college that taught accounting, surveying, and other vocational skills to youngsters between age 14 and 18 was also considered a private school. Thus the term private school gave little clue about a pupil's age or the curriculum.

Public schools were usually more expensive and exclusive than private schools. They were public because some of their funds came from an endowment or from the sale of shares. A public school therefore did not belong to one person; it was run by a corporation or board of governors who hired the school's headmaster or headmistress. Thus public schools (unlike private schools) had a degree of oversight as well as continuity and tradition.

Education not only varied among classes but also helped determine class. Some historians consider that improved education was the reform on which all other Victorian reforms rested: schooling made democratic elections possible and supplied the training to both develop the economy at home and rule an empire abroad.

At the beginning of the period, education was entirely noncentralized. Elementary schools (where they existed at all) were run by voluntary, charitable, or religious societies. It is hard to evaluate how many people could read and write. Some authorities count the proportion of brides and grooms who signed their name rather than marking an "X" in the marriage register. Some contemporary surveys required people to read and explain a short verse from the Bible. The 1841 census reported that 67 percent of males and 51 percent of females were literate. In any case, few people in the working class had more than two or three years of full-time schooling.

Sunday schools provided some education for children (and adults) who worked all week. Their original mission was to give people the skills to read the Bible for themselves. In morning and afternoon sessions the Scriptures were used as textbooks for teaching basic literacy. Some Nonconformist Sunday schools developed into vigorous working-class institutions, with classes for people of all ages and an extensive range of singing clubs, sports teams, and social activities. In country parishes, teaching a class in the local Church of England Sunday school was a social duty expected from daughters of the clergy and gentry.

Another source of free education for the poor were the ragged schools. Funded through charities and staffed by both paid teachers and middle-class volunteers, ragged schools offered free meals and clothing to lure impoverished children into the classroom. In addition to giving elementary instruction, some ragged schools ran lodgings, nurseries, and employment agencies.

Working-class children who did have full-time education for a few years generally attended the elementary schools built by religious organizations. The National Society for Promoting the Education of the Poor, which drew support primarily from members of the Church of England, operated schools in many country villages. The British and Foreign School Society served other Protestant denominations. (Local elementary schools throughout the century were generally referred to as the British school or the national school, which sometimes misleads readers into thinking they were comparable to the U.S. public school system.)

These schools were inexpensive but not free. Costs were kept down by teaching a great many children in one room with a single teacher. Monitors chosen from the older children helped with the instruction. The first government funding for education, provided in the 1830s, was in the form of grants for these two societies to help them put up buildings and train teachers.

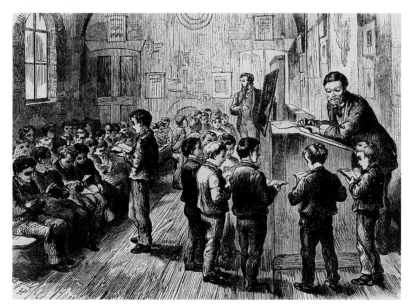

This drawing from the April 2, 1870, edition of the *Illustrated London News*, shows how chaotic the learning environment could be in a London elementary school classroom. Several lessons are proceeding at once, one led by the head teacher and another by his assistant. Courtesy of The Library Company of Philadelphia.

By 1851, according to the census, there were almost five million children between the ages of 3 and 15 in England and Wales. Two million were in school, 600,000 were at work, and the rest were neither working nor attending school. (This does not mean they were idle: many would have been helping with their parents' work, minding children at home, or being taught by their parents.) Recognizing the importance of a literate and numerate workforce—as well as the value of schools to keep children off the streets and promote discipline—Parliament increasingly provided money for existing schools and exerted control over the curriculum.

The government's revised code of education in 1862 established a system known as payment by results. Schools that sought funding were visited by a government inspector every autumn. This was a great ordeal for both children and teachers. Children who passed the inspector's examination moved up to a higher standard— and the size of the school's grant (as well as the teacher's salary) depended on the number of children who passed. Very little was taught except reading, writing, and arithmetic. The church societies required that a clergyman come into school regularly for religious instruction, but teachers had almost no motivation to spend time on history, geography, science, or practical subjects.

In smaller villages, the elementary school had one classroom with a single teacher in charge of girls and boys whose ages ranged from 3 to 12. The teacher might have help from monitors or a pupil teacher. Daughters of the gentry and clergy made it a duty to visit the village school and hear children read or recite a lesson. The revised code also required that girls learn needlework. Because it was hard for them to pay for supplies, lady visitors provided material for girls to make things that could be given to charity. The squire's wife, for example, could give a layette to a poor mother after small girls hemmed diapers, more advanced students made garments, and the star pupil embroidered a dress.

Larger schools had three classrooms: one for boys, one for girls, and one for the youngest children (infants). In very large schools each of the three rooms might have movable partitions. Not until the 1870s was it customary for each standard, or grade level, to have its own room. In one London school, 868 children were taught by one master (for the boys), two mistresses (one for girls, one for infants), and 12 pupil teachers. That worked out to 58 children for each adult—and twelve of the adults were age eighteen or younger.

Discipline had to be strict under these conditions. When possible, small children had gallery-style seats on long benches with shelves (serving as desks) in front that kept them all in place until the whole row moved. All pupils sat still in their seats, stood when an adult entered the room, and lined up to enter or leave. Girls curtsied to the mistress at the end of the day. Knocking a ruler on the knuckles or caning a child on the palms enforced order. For serious infractions, a pupil's name was written in a punishment book. This might lead not only to a more serious caning but also to a poor reference when an employer asked the school for a dependable worker.

> *Knocking a ruler on the knuckles or caning a child on the palms enforced order.*

In 1870, W. E. Forster succeeded in convincing Parliament to pass an elementary education act requiring that schools be available in every part of the country. Local school boards were given the power to collect taxes for elementary schools. Many British and national schools then became board schools. In 1880, education was made compulsory for all children between the ages of 7 and 10; in 1892, the board schools could stop charging fees. The curriculum expanded, the age for compulsory attendance lengthened, and the schooling of working-class and lower-middle-class children throughout the country became more uniform.

Infants were allowed in school from the age of three. (Some schools took babies at 18 months if an older child would otherwise be kept home to look after them.) If the school was large enough, the smallest children would have a room of their own and those between ages five and seven would be put into classes by ability. At age seven, if they had passed the examination for Standard I, they moved on to the boys' school or the girls' school.

As schools grew larger they were divided into classes according to standard; promotion from one class to the next depended on passing the examination, not on age. Additional subjects were added to the curriculum, especially for older children. Most buildings were constructed with separate classrooms, entrances, and play yards for each of the three divisions, which were called schools. That is, the infants' school, the girls' school, and the boys' school were all in the same building, but each had separate space. A head teacher was in charge of each of the three schools; assistant teachers supervised individual classes. The classes were still quite large. Assistant teachers had pupil teachers or monitors to help. Each classroom had a portrait of Queen Victoria and a map of the world (with the countries of the British Empire colored red).

School was typically in session from 9:00 A.M. to 12:30 P.M. and from 2:00 P.M. to 4:30 P.M. With some exceptions, children went home in the middle of the day for dinner. Rural children who had a long walk brought food and stayed at school. In some poor neighborhoods, a local charity provided meals. Because part of the school's funding depended on average attendance, stringent efforts were made to make children come to school every day. There was a two-week holiday at Christmas, one week at Easter, and three or four weeks from mid-July to mid-August. The leaving age was raised to 12 years by the end of the century, but exceptions were made for hardship (if the child's earnings were needed) or if the child passed an examination at the level of Standard IV.

Becoming an elementary teacher was one of the more common routes from the working class into the middle class. Intelligent boys and girls were encouraged to stay at school by being offered positions as monitors. After turning 13 years old they could be hired as pupil teachers, although the pay was barely enough for clothes and spending money; they had to come from families that could afford for them to continue living at home without contributing to the family income.

In addition to helping in the classroom, pupil teachers received evening lessons in secondary-school subjects from the head teacher or attended Saturday classes at a regional pupil-teacher center. When they reached age 18, they could pass an examination (called the queen's scholarship) and attend training college to earn a teaching certificate. The length of the college course varied during the century. At the end of the period, some training colleges were associated with universities.

A certified teacher in a village school in the 1840s earned a salary of £30 to £40 per year. In addition, she received rent-free accommodation in a schoolhouse, fuel was provided, and some of the older girls would do her cooking and housework to practice the skills they needed for domestic service. In London board schools in the 1890s, the starting pay for a woman teacher was £85 per year. For men, pay started at £95. There was an annual raise of £5 for men and £3 for women. Experienced head teachers earned a comfortable income, especially if they had no family to support.

In addition to recruits from the working class, growing numbers of women from middle-class backgrounds entered elementary teaching after it became possible to attend training college directly (by passing the entrance exam) instead of serving an apprenticeship as a pupil teacher. Compulsory schooling and longer attendance vastly increased the demand for teachers. Men with enough education for teaching had access to other jobs with better prospects. Except in one-room village schools, older boys usually had male teachers; but teaching girls and infants became a woman's vocation (Mitchell, 165–73).

To read about education in Chaucer's England, see the entry on Europe in the section "Education" in chapter 4 ("Intellectual Life") in volume 2 of this series; for Elizabethan England, see the entry on England in the section "Education" in chapter 4 ("Intellectual Life") in volume 3 of this series; for 18th-century England, see the entry on England in the section "Education" in chapter 4 ("Intellectual Life") in volume 4 of this series.

FOR MORE INFORMATION

Ball, N. *Educating the People: A Documentary History of Elementary Schooling in England.* London: Maurice Temple Smith, 1983.

Horn, P. *The Victorian and Edwardian Schoolchild.* Gloucester, U.K.: Alan Sutton, 1989.

Mitchell, S. *Daily Life in Victorian England.* Westport, Conn.: Greenwood Press, 1996.

INTELLECTUAL
LIFE
|
EDUCATION
|
United States,
1850-1865

United States,
Western Frontier

Victorian England

China

Latin America

CHINA

In the 19th century, as China opened up to the outside world, a growing number of Chinese people were educated in Western-style schools. At the same time there was a strong movement to keep the old, traditional style of education, which was based heavily on the Confucian ideal. Two political events were crucial in the transition of the Chinese educational system from the old system to a new system that borrowed many elements from other countries. First, the start of the Opium War and the opening of China to the outside world brought in a wave of foreign influence and led to the opening of many Western-style schools. Second, the Boxer Rebellion, which caused an increased desire for foreign ideas, led to a new educational system that borrowed heavily from foreign countries.

In 1839, at the start of the Opium War, Britain, followed by other Western nations, began to control areas of China known as leaseholds. In these areas taxes on imports and exports were kept low, foreigners were tried according to their own laws, and missionaries were allowed to proselytize freely. Proselytization was perhaps the most influential to changes in education, and several missionary schools and universities opened throughout China.

Those favoring the old style of education, based on the Confucian ideal, felt that foreign-influenced ideas corrupted the traditional Chinese concept of morality. Many people felt that while technology such as guns and ships should be learned from the West, other aspects of society, culture, morality, and government, should not. As education is the backbone of all of these aspects in any society, Western-style education was considered by many to be a social evil, which should be avoided at all costs.

Confucius (551–479 B.C.E.) is the father of the Confucian belief system. However, it was not until after his death that his philosophies became an important element of Chinese society. During the 8th century the *Analects,* the major Confucian text, became an important part of the Chinese education system.

The main elements of the philosophy of Confucianism are, in short: one, family is the basic unit of society and two, social hierarchy upholds the structure of society. The way that this social hierarchy is understood is that women must defer to men, youngsters to elders, and everyone should defer to the emperor.

Those who believed that Western-style education was the way of the future for China thought that this type of education enabled Western powers, even while small, to hold so much power. China, on the other hand, due to its non-Western style of education, was large in size, yet lacking in political power. By teaching Western concepts of science, math, and Western languages, Chinese people could learn from the West and grow stronger as a nation.

Along with the movement towards a Western style of education came a movement towards a simpler style of literature based on that of the West. For centuries there were two main styles of Chinese literature: the classical and the vernacular. Classical literature was written in such a way as to be incomprehensible to the majority of the population. Prior to the 19th century, vernacular literature was reserved for the lower classes, and upper-class people most often considered this tradition as not classy enough for them. In the 19th century both Western literature and a new form of Chinese vernacular literature, based on Western works, became popular. The subject of these works most often revolved around reform and modernization and criticized the old ways of China. The looser form and simpler language made these books accessible to a larger percentage of the population and was useful for expressing new ideas and concepts. These works were often read in Western-style schools as part of the curriculum, particularly at the university level.

The new style of literature heavily influenced the formation of certain ideologies behind a new set of antiestablishment movements. The leaders of these movements were mostly educated in the Western style, either in missionary schools in China or in foreign countries. Many of the leaders were professors. Their access to a podium and an audience of young, intellectual, and impressionable minds made it relatively easy for them to gain large followings. Therefore, many social uprisings of the 19th and early 20th centuries came directly out of Western-style universities.

Positivism was the main inspiration in these antitraditionalist movements and, therefore, was commonly incorporated into university curriculums. The works of John Dewey and Bertrand Russell were particularly popular. These men became idols of many people involved in these antiestablishment movements.

As part of this ideology scientific and technological advancement were also considered extremely important to the future of the nation. The universities attempted to give students a strong background in Western mathematics, science, and technology. The hope was that this would give the students the necessary tools to help China advance in these fields.

Education, through the university level, was completely funded by the government. In return, university graduates were required to accept whatever job the state assigned to them.

Western-style schools were usually the most competitive schools into which to gain admission. Entrance to schools and universities was based on the Confucian system in which one gained admission through competitive entrance examinations.

However, money and political connections also played a large role in determining who gained admission into an elite school.

Following the Boxer Rebellion and other political upheavals in 1900, throughout the nation school curriculums for all levels went through drastic transformation. The Boxers emerged in 1898. They saw themselves as the dawn of a new age and believed themselves to be invincible. They were strongly antiforeign and attacked Chinese Christians and foreigners. The empress dowager followed their lead and in 1900 declared war on foreign powers. Complete havoc occurred when a combined effort of Britain, the United States, France, Japan, and Russia defeated the Boxers and caused the empress and her cabinet to flee to Xi'an. As a result a full review of government affairs took place, and a decision was made to blend Chinese culture with foreign culture. Abandonment of the old-style civil service examination based on the classical literary tradition was one major change. This had a major effect on the education system as it meant also doing away with the school curriculum, which was geared towards these exams.

To read about education in China under the Tang dynasty, see the China entry in the section "Education" in chapter 4 ("Intellectual Life") in volume 2 of this series.

~Dana Lightstone

FOR MORE INFORMATION

Postiglione, G. A., ed. *China's National Minority Education: Culture, Schooling, and Development.* New York: Falmer Press, 1999.

World Bank. *China: Higher Education Reform.* Washington, D.C.: World Bank, 1997.

INTELLECTUAL
LIFE
|
EDUCATION
|
United States,
1850-1865

United States,
Western Frontier

Victorian England

China

Latin America

LATIN AMERICA

The Catholic Church, which was the dominant influence on education in colonial Latin America, remained so after the peoples of Latin America achieved independence in the early 19th century. The provision of formal education thus remained largely confined to the region's social and political elites. By the end of the colonial period in the early 1820s, less than one percent of the total Latin American population was literate, although 25 universities had been established throughout the region for education of the governing classes. To protect its economic and social position, the church tended to support the repressive conservative regimes that governed much of Latin America prior to 1850. In return for this support, conservative governments confirmed church control of education. However, this control gradually weakened after 1850 as a growing middle class, anxious for more social, political, and economic opportunities for themselves and their children, demanded an expansion in both the scope and availability of education. Thus, liberal governments, which espoused the principles of constitutionalism, individualism, and, often, anticlericalism, seized increasing control of education in the second half of the century.

However, the development of liberal public education systems did not immediately mean the extension of educational opportunity throughout the population. Although more widely available, especially in urban areas, formal education was still limited to a minority of the population. For the native populations of the countryside, formal education, if available at all, was largely confined to religious instruction, literacy in Spanish, and vocational training, all subjects that allowed continued economic exploitation of the many by the few.

As European investment in the region increased in the 19th century, European educational systems became models for newly created Latin American systems. British professional, technical, and entrepreneurial settlers brought with them the English public school model, which was highly favored by some Latin American elites. The new educational systems of various Latin American republics were also heavily influenced by educational models inherited from Napoleonic France. Under this influence, Latin American education, by the end of the century, was highly secular and placed new emphasis on mathematics, physics, and geography and cosmography. The teaching of theology was modified to include critical church history, and the training of medical doctors was transformed to include modern texts and study in anatomy, chemistry, botany, and clinical practice.

Positivism reinforced this trend in the second half of the century. Arguing that positive knowledge of the world could be obtained through modern scientific research, positivism, by the 1870s, became the dominant educational principle underlying Latin American educational systems. Positivism led to a revision of the curriculum as the teaching and learning of Latin and the scholastic education of the past gave way to practical training in governance and economics for the country's social and political elite. In Mexico under Benito Juárez, president from 1861 to 1863 and from 1867 to 1872, and Porfirio Diaz, president for most of the period from 1877 to 1911, educational reform was influenced by the positivism of French philosopher Auguste Comte, as enunciated by such Mexican educational reformers as Gabino Barreda, Joaquín Barranda, and Justo Sierra. In Argentina, positivism was also influential, and the Colegio Nacional, founded in 1870 on positivist principles, became a training ground for the new leaders of society. Thus, by the start of the 20th century, secularism had largely destroyed church control of education in the entire region. In some countries, such as Argentina in 1884, laws formally removed the provision of education from the control of the church.

Many major educational advances took place, primarily in the southern republics of South America, especially Argentina, Chile, and Uruguay, where a combination of citizen demand for broader education and a growing need for more and better technical training eroded the rigidity of religious doctrine and thus the church's monopoly of education. Under Domingo Faustino Sarmiento, president from 1868 to 1874, Argentina became a regional leader in education. Sarmiento believed an educated citizenry was a key part of a democratic republic and that education was itself civilization, able to banish the barbarism of illiteracy. Teacher training institutions were introduced into Argentina during Sarmiento's presidency. Uruguay, acting under French influence, pioneered universal, free, and compulsory primary education in Latin America. The writings of José Pedro Varela, who was president in 1875–76, convinced the government to enact the Law of Common Education in 1877. In Mexico, where the country's strong liberal movement stood for political modernization and economic growth, liberal educator José María Luis Mora pleaded for a national public school system that would support an enlightened political system and improve the morals of the people.

In the early part of the century, political instability and slow economic growth somewhat hampered the founding of new universities and the development of existing institutions. In Mexico, for instance, the Royal and Pontifical University, founded in 1551, was modified, closed, and reopened several times between 1820 and 1825. Other prominent Latin American universities in the 19th century included the University of Buenos Aires, founded in 1821; the University of the Republic of Uruguay, founded in 1833; the University of Chile, founded in Santiago in 1842; and the private Pontifical Catholic University of Chile, founded in 1888. All these institutions took on increasing importance and exercised increasing influence as the century progressed.

In many ways, Brazil, a former Portuguese colony that became an empire ruled by a branch of the Portuguese royal family, was an exception to the major educational developments in Latin America in the 19th century. A national educational system was created at the founding of the empire in 1822, but the imperial regime was friendly to the church, which retained its control of education until the collapse of the empire in 1889. At the turn of the century, only about three percent of the Brazilian population was receiving formal education, and higher education was confined to technical and vocational institutes. The first Brazilian university was not founded until the early 20th century.

By the end of the 19th century, Latin America contained a variety of educational systems that reflected a diverse array of European influences. Argentina's educational system was influenced by British models; Chile's system by German models; and those of various other countries by French models. Also in the last decades of the century, many national governments established ministries of education to run the schools, and a hierarchical system of school administration developed, which has only recently begun to be challenged and modified.

~*Eduardo Alfonso Caro*

FOR MORE INFORMATION

Brock, C. "Latin America: An Educational Profile." In *Education in Latin America*, ed. Colin Brock and Hugh Lawlor. London: Croom Helm, 1985.

Burns, E. B. *The Poverty of Progress: Latin America in the Nineteenth Century*. Berkeley: University of California Press, 1980.

Smith, H., and H. Little. *Education in Latin America*. New York: American Book Company, 1934.

Super, J. C. "Education." In *Encyclopedia of Latin American History and Culture*, ed. Barbara Tenenbaum. New York: Charles Scribner's Sons, 1996.

ISLAMIC WORLD

Beginning in the 16th century, the Ottoman Turks built upon the strong educational tradition that stretched back to the origins of Islam. The Turks institutionalized the *medreses*—the Muslim theological schools—and from that time into the 19th century, they served as the primary educational institutions throughout the Muslim world. See the entry on Ottoman Turks in the section "Education" in chapter 4 ("Intellectual Life") in volume 3 of this series for a description of these influential institutions.

Literature

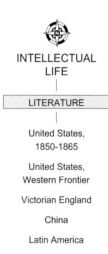

INTELLECTUAL
LIFE
|
LITERATURE
|
United States,
1850-1865

United States,
Western Frontier

Victorian England

China

Latin America

English literature dominated the 19th century. Its influence was vast and reached not only the United States but also non-Western nations such as China and India. (Even today, the works of Charlotte Brontë, Charles Dickens, George Eliot, Elizabeth Gaskell, Thomas Hardy, and Anthony Trollope are widely read.) Moreover, the popularity of English authors gave rise to a profitable and vast publishing industry. The English masterminded the creation of high-speed, cheap presses as well as machines for typesetting and reproducing illustrations. They also devised distribution methods capable of bringing fine literature to everyone. Since books were expensive, authors like Charles Dickens sold their works (even famous, critically acclaimed novels such as *Oliver Twist*) in monthly installments. This lowered the price considerably. Also, given the wide periodical readership, 19th-century writers gained larger audiences than if they were to just publish entire books. This was most true for Victorian authors who wrote for newspapers. There were thousands of different newspapers published in England during the Victorian era. And toward the end of the century, as paper prices dropped further, a flowering of children's literature appeared. Some of these works have also endured. *Alice's Adventures in Wonderland* (1865), *Black Beauty* (1877), and *Treasure Island* (1881–82) remain childhood classics.

Given the literary greats that England produced in the 19th century and their wonderful literature, a fair historical question is: how does the United States, China, or Latin America compare? In America, it depended where one looked. On the western frontier, books were rare, having been left behind in the east because of their weight. Generally speaking, frontier people did not read for pleasure or entertainment. Rather, popular books and magazines had more to do with medicine or geology. Only one book was common to nearly all frontier men and women: the Bible. It was said of the great frontier president Andrew Jackson that this was the only book he ever read. The situation was quite different east of the frontier. Literacy rates were high in the North and the South. Popular works included Charles Dickens and Lord Byron as well as a host of American authors. In 19th-century America, literature was tied to controversial politics, which of course fit well into the debates about good literature. Many authors who wrote about love or the darker sides of human experience, such as Lord Byron or Charles Pelham (who wrote about crime) or Edgar Allan Poe, were considered to have a deleterious influence upon the soul and were banned by many libraries. But the major battle over literature came with the coming of the Civil War. For example, Southerners who read Dickens saw a condemnation of the industrializing North, while some Northerners saw within the tales a moral imperative to reform the urban environment. Similarly, popular works such as Harriet Beecher Stowe's *Uncle Tom's Cabin* (1852) generated sectional controversy. Nevertheless, it sold over 300,000 copies in a single year. Other widely read American novelists like James Fennimore Cooper had a hard time copying that success. Clearly, Stowe's novel was a sign of the times. In an age dominated by sectional politics and a civil war, stories that touched on the nature of that conflict were quite popular.

In China, the 19th century was a critical time of literary change. The two main Chinese literary traditions, classical and vernacular, continued. But new movements, sparked by such things as the New Cultural Movement, produced significant new books that emphasized new ideas. Moreover, some Chinese like Lu Xun and later Lao She were quite receptive to British writers and imitated their style and subject matter.

In Latin America, the traditional genres favored by the social elite continued to predominate until the second half of the century when the tastes of a growing urban-centered middle class led to the writing of novels that reflected their lives and concerns. Many of these works took on political overtones as the middle class strove for political and social equality. Similar to England and the United States, Chinese and Latin American writers and readers in the 19th century discovered new audiences, new literary themes, and new technologies to disseminate their ideas.

UNITED STATES, 1850–65

Literacy was quite high in Civil War America. In the South at least 70 percent of the white male population could read, and in the North the ability to read may have run as high as 90 percent. Prior to 1820, English texts, less expensive and more fashionable, had almost closed the literary market to American authors. The emergence of a new popularity of reading and writing among the middle class underpinned a new national interest in publishing and professional authorship. This circumstance was further fostered by the need to while away long hours of boredom created by the lack of normal social activities brought on by the war. Four types of reading material have been identified as popular with Civil War era readers: religious reading, purposeful (or instructive) reading, newspaper and magazine reading, and reading for escape. These categories, while somewhat arbitrary, can serve to describe the majority of the printed materials sought by 19th-century readers.

Beginning in the second decade of the 19th century, the novel, the most popular form of escapism, was found to have a growing acceptance and appeal among the general reading public. Middle- and upper-class women have long been recognized

INTELLECTUAL
LIFE
|
LITERATURE
|

United States,
1850-1865

United States,
Western Frontier

Victorian England

China

Latin America

as the chief consumers of this literary form. So great was the popularity of the novel that it drew criticism. As late as 1856 the *Code of Public Instruction* for the state of New York recognized the necessity of excluding from all libraries "novels, romances, and other fictitious creations of the imagination, including a large proportion of the lighter literature of the day. The propriety of a peremptory and uncompromising exclusion of those catch-penny, but revolting publications, which cultivate the taste for the marvelous, the tragic, the horrible, and the supernatural . . . [is without] the slightest argument." The code also expressed an "obvious" disgust for works dealing with "pirates, banditti, and desperadoes of every description." A guide to propriety for mothers written by Lydia Child decried "the profligate and strongly exciting works" found in the public libraries. "The necessity of fierce excitement in reading is a sort of intellectual intemperance" producing, in the estimation of the guide's author, "weakness and delirium" in women and young girls. The Pelham novels and the works of Byron, Edward Maturin, Matthew G. Lewis, and Ann Radcliffe were all identified as having "an unhealthy influence upon the soul" that should be avoided.

Of these, the most meaningful name is that of Lord Byron, who, with Shakespeare and Charles Dickens, was among the most famous of British authors known to those outside of Britain. Mrs. Child does not identify her reason for including him in this list, but his collected works along with his letters and journals were available to most American readers in a multivolume edition. Byron typified the romantic movement in literature and politically he was a "genuine and burning liberal." His advanced 19th-century political views may have made him suspect.

The "Pelham novels" referred to by Mrs. Child may be the works of Camden Pelham, who wrote *The Chronicles of Crime*, a series of memoirs and anecdotes about British criminals "from the earliest period to 1841." They were illustrated by H. K. Browne, the famous illustrator of Dickens's works who went by the pseudonym Phiz. The historical novels of Irish American author Edward Maturin were particularly steeped in the romantic. They included *Montezuma, the Last of the Aztecs*, a brilliant, if overly impassioned, history; *Benjamin, the Jew of Granada*, set in 15th-century Muslim Spain; and *Eva, or the Isles of Life and Death*, a romance of 12th-century England. One of his more fiery books was *Bianca*, a story of a passionate love between a woman from Italy and a man from Ireland.

Ann Radcliffe's novels, many written in the late 1790s, were primarily "time-fillers for literarily inclined young women who had no children and did not care for society." Although she died in 1823, Mrs. Radcliffe was the main source of "horror stories with a twist" for 19th-century readers. The significance of her "horror-mongering" on later romantic literature cannot be overestimated. Terror connoisseurs found her heroines melancholy, quick to weep, and endearingly practical. In *The Italian* she created a romantic villain who brought the physical aspects of terror to perfection. This villain, repelled by the enormity of his crime, but fascinated by the looming tragedy of his fate, was the basis for similar characters used by Maturin, Byron, Lewis, and Scott. Her last novel, released in 1826, was *Gaston de Blondeville*. Actually written in 1802, this work preceded Scott's first historical novels and attempted for the first time to paint an authentic historical picture.

Almost totally forgotten today, Matthew G. Lewis was a follower of Mrs. Radcliffe whose writings "ran heavily to the florid romantic." His first novel, *Ambrosio, the Monk,* was universally read and widely condemned in Britain and America. Lewis was charged with being immoral and irreligious when it was discovered that he was recommending that certain passages from the Bible be kept from the young. His work was considered "vicious" and "terrible." Often referred to as the "immoral monk Lewis," he was a man of genuine philanthropy and humane instincts. After inheriting a plantation in Jamaica along with 500 black slaves, Lewis instituted a series of reforms that were "regarded as mad" by his contemporaries. He attested to their effectiveness in *The Journal of a West India Proprietor,* which was published just before his death from yellow fever. Besides several dramas, Lewis produced two romantic novels—*The Bravo of Venice* and *Feudal Tyrants*—as well as *Tales of Terror* and *Romantic Tales,* which were based on German and Spanish legends, and, in collaboration with Scott, a collection of ballads, *Tales of Wonder.* His work is generally neglected today, but he had tremendous influence on the romantic writers of his day.

Like Mrs. Child, the Reverend Doctor Joel Hawes similarly warned young men that in the choice of books there was a "great need of caution." He believed that a person's character could be "ruined by reading a single volume." Yet he confessed that one book, "wisely selected and properly studied," could "do more to improve the mind, and enrich the understanding, than skimming over the surface of an entire library."

Notwithstanding such warnings, novels remained popular, and the potency of this literature to govern the mind of readers proved not to have been underestimated by the good reverend. Fictional characters possessed a remarkable ability to influence 19th-century readers. Uncle Tom, Topsy, Ivanhoe, Hawkeye, Hester Prynne, and Ebenezer Scrooge were deeply familiar characters to a society that read as much as 19th-century Americans did. These characters often seemed to become nearly as real and as influential to the reader as actual friends and relations.

The works of the English novelist and social commentator Charles Dickens were widely read in America. In Dickens's very popular works, both sections of the country found some character, situation, or condition that seemed to bolster the very different views of modern society Americans held. Many social reformers, like Dickens himself, championed the cause of the poor. Nonetheless, Dickens was generally unconcerned with the economic aspects of social reform, choosing rather to deal with an increased appreciation of the value of the human being. Ignorance, for him, was the great cause of human misery. In 1843 he gave a speech in the city of Manchester in which he pleaded for a heightened sense of humanitarianism and an improvement in the system of public education in Britain. In contrast to the ragged schools that had been set up by well-meaning but untrained volunteer teachers to give England's poor children the rudiments of an education, Dickens proposed that the surest improvement in the nation's future was tied to a public investment in education sponsored by the government.

Dickens's stories emphasized the need to change traditional ways of thinking. But many in the South misread Dickens's message and saw the misfortune, destitution, and disease that fills his works as characteristic of all urban life. Modern urban life was the great evil haunting the romantic domains of the Southern imagination. Dickens's novels mirrored the inevitable bleak future of America if Northern concepts of social progress continued to be implemented, as English ones had for decades without noticeably improving society.

Although thoroughly English in its setting and personalities, *A Christmas Carol*, first published in 1843, seemed to embody the very limitations of modern society in mid-century in the interactions of Scrooge with the other characters. The story portrays a secular rather than a traditionally religious attitude toward the holidays. The spirits and ghosts of Christmas are remarkably worldly in their appearance and temporal in their outlook. The awakening of a social conscience in Scrooge is their chief endeavor. Ultimately it is the specter of an unlamented death, a topic of great concern in the 19th century, that brings Scrooge around. Yet even a morally awakened Scrooge refuses to devote his life to social work. Instead, he acts out his reformation on a very personal level.

Southerners despised such ambiguous social remedies as the poorhouses and the workhouses that filled Dickens's pages. The debtors' prison of *Little Dorrit* and the orphanage of *Oliver Twist* were obviously not sufficient to solve the social ills of an urban society. Southerners were left with a portrait of cities, like those of the North, veritably teeming with the exploited masses from which they chose to be separated.

Modern urban life was the great evil haunting the Southern imagination.

Apologists for the Southern way of life proclaimed that Scrooge's treatment of Bob Cratchit emphasized the abuses possible in an age governed by the work for wage system that so lacked a sense of personal involvement and family dedication. The personal responsibility many Southerners felt toward their neighbors, their workers, and even their slaves seemed noble in contrast to the socially anonymous caretaking for the unfortunates found in Dickens's works.

Southern intellectuals of the prewar period were also widely read in the literature of European romanticism, and they used romantic allusions freely in their writing. Confederate General John B. Gordon, who rose to popular prominence when badly wounded at the Battle of Antietam, was described as being "pure as Galahad, knightly as King Arthur . . . [and] as brave as Lancelot . . . a Chevalier Bayard." Southern papers spoke of heroics and crusades. The Richmond *Southern Illustrated News* reported the final minutes of General George Pickett's charge at Gettysburg as "noble and gallant."

The most popular book of the war period was *Les Miserables*. This was closely followed by Tennyson's 1864 narrative poem *Enoch Arden*, in which a shipwrecked sailor returns home to find that his wife, thinking him dead, has remarried. Sir Walter Scott's Waverley novels were immensely popular. Their theme of the Scottish struggle to throw off the dominance and oppression of the English served as an analogy for the position in which the South saw itself with respect to the North. Scott's use of romantic characters, lords and ladies, knights in armor, and grand estates was particularly resonant with the Southern image of itself. So familiar was Scott's work to Southerners that in later years Mark Twain only half-jokingly blamed Scott for causing the Civil War.

Second only to Scott's in popularity were the American adventure novels of James Fenimore Cooper. Although his first novel was poorly accepted by American readers, largely because it imitated the British form, Cooper's second work, *The Spy*, published in 1822, was an outstanding success. Cooper's subsequent novels emphasized American manners and scenes as interesting and important. Still, many Americans considered novels to be "trivial, feminine, and vaguely dishonorable" because they appealed to the emotions and aroused the imagination. Nonetheless, Cooper found that there was a great demand for adventure tales derived from the Revolution, and his writing was sufficiently manly and moral to find acceptance by a wide audience.

Like Scott, Cooper promoted a social vision of a stable and genteel society governed by its natural aristocracy, "perpetuating property, order, and liberty" as represented by a reunited American gentry. That this view resonated with the Southern image of itself would have upset Cooper, with his very Northern attitudes. *The Pioneers*, Cooper's third book, was dedicated to the proposition that the American republic, poised on the verge of "demagoguery, deceit, hypocrisy, and turmoil," could be transformed into a stable, prosperous, and just society. Although the theme of "reconciliation . . . on conservative terms" was almost three decades old, Cooper's novels were very popular with the soldiers, mainly because of their masculine adventure themes, and were often found among their most prized possessions. Dog-eared copies circulated through the camps and were often read aloud around the campfire to eager audiences.

A federal officer, Captain John W. De Forest, found himself "a tolerably instructed man, having read *The Book of the Indians,* all of Cooper's novels, and some of the works of Captain Mayne Reid." Reid was a close friend of Edgar Allan Poe, and his novels were mainly adventure stories. Beginning in 1850, he published *The Rifle Rangers: Adventures of an Officer in Southern Mexico,* which was based on his own service in the 1846 war; *The Scalp Hunters; The War Trail;* and *Forest Exiles.* In 1853 he wrote a novel inspired by his 15-year-old spouse, appropriately titled *The Child Wife,* and in 1856 he wrote a play called *The Quadroon.* De Forest reported that he inexplicably found his thoughts "ranging from the expectation of a [musket] ball through the spine to a recollection of Cooper's most celebrated Indians" while under fire during the siege of Port Hudson.

Nathaniel Hawthorne, convinced that most American literature ran too close to the British style, devoted himself to a uniquely symbolic and allegorical form. *The Scarlet Letter,* published in 1850, was certainly familiar to American readers, and its author was considered a literary giant. But Hawthorne's persistent dark emphasis on guilt and sorrow ran counter to the popular tastes and religious sentiment of Americans at mid-century. In 1851 and 1852, respectively, he published *The House of the Seven Gables* and *The Blithedale Romance.* This last was a study of failed utopian efforts to improve society. He served as the U.S. Consul at Liverpool, England, for four years and was photographed by Mathew Brady before his death in 1864.

When Harriet Beecher Stowe published *Uncle Tom's Cabin* in 1852, the book sold 300,000 copies in America and Britain in one year. Mrs. Stowe's work was one of total fiction; it stressed the evils of slavery and presented a picture of total brutality. Mrs. Stowe had no personal knowledge of slavery. The factual basis for the story was Theodore D. Weld's radical abolitionist tract entitled *Slavery as It Is: The Testimony of a Thousand Witnesses*, which was published in 1839. *Uncle Tom's Cabin* was immensely more effective in preaching the antislavery message in the form of a novel than the earlier tract had ever dreamed of being.

The South considered Mrs. Stowe's work a slander and regarded it as abolitionist propaganda. A Southern woman, familiar with slavery and slaves, wrote that she could not read a book so filled with distortions as it was "too sickening" to think that any man would send "his little son to beat a human being tied to a tree." The same woman goes on to suggest, using other literary references, that Mrs. Stowe's work portrays as much fiction as Squeers beating Smike in Dickens's *Nicholas Nickleby* or the gouging of Gloucester's eyes in Shakespeare's *King Lear*. "How delightfully pharisaic a feeling it must be, to rise up superior and fancy [to] we [who] are so degraded as to defend and like to live with such degraded creatures around us . . . as Legree."

Nonetheless, amicably disposed Northerners found the passages describing the murderous brutality of Simon Legree indicative of the typical behavior of Southern slave owners. The significance of the story, as of many of the attacks on the institution of slavery, lay in its ability to dramatize and emotionalize the issue. Writing and speech making on the subject of slavery in particular—and of the Southern culture in general—were becoming increasingly stereotypical, and the stereotypes, even when presented in novels, were taking on a reality in the minds of the people.

Harriet Beecher Stowe. © Library of Congress.

Although soldiers were quick to write home about finishing *Nicholas Nickelby*, *The Pickwick Papers*, *The Deerslayer*, *Ivanhoe*, or other works of obvious quality, they also read a great deal of low-quality material. Many of these works have been identified. They include such masculine titles as *Con Cregan, Gold Friend, The Quadroon of Louisiana, Son of the Wilderness, Scar Chief the Wild Halfbreed, Wild West Scenes,* and *Our Own Heroes,* but also more popular works such as *Lady Audley's Secret, The Mystery, Macaria,* and *Louisa Elton.*

Soldiers, "burdened by huge blocks of time during which they have nothing to do but wait," were suddenly possessed of an abundant amount of time to read, which "had previously been in short supply to American men." Of the five most common leisure-time camp activities—individual foraging, gambling, sleeping, talking, and reading—only reading was seen to be "a positive force" for the improvement of the troops.

American books were in large supply for the first time during the war. In 1834 fewer than 500 titles were published in the United States. By 1862 this number had grown to almost 4,000. By coincidence the first dime novels were published in June 1860. These were inexpensive paperbound adventure stories. The first title, *Malaeska, the Indian Wife of the White Hunter,* by Ann Stephens, makes it abundantly clear that this was escapist literature of the lowest class. Publisher Irwin P. Beadle's dime novels and their many imitators initiated a whole era of cheap publishing just eight months prior to the war.

At the time there were a number of distinguished American authors of an age to serve in the field and provide a firsthand professional description of the face of war. Theodore Winthrop had written a number of successful books prior to the war and he volunteered to serve. Unfortunately, Winthrop was killed in one of the first engagements of the war at Great Bethel in June 1861.

Another young author distinguished before the outbreak of hostilities was John W. De Forest. From 1851 through 1859 De Forest wrote several books, including the *History of the Indians of Connecticut* and the novels *Witching Times*, *Oriental Acquaintance*, *European Acquaintance*, and *Seacliff*. De Forest went to war as a captain with the 12th Connecticut Volunteers. Many of his battlefield reports were printed by *Harper's Monthly*, and in 1864 he wrote *Miss Ravenel's Conversion from Secession to Loyalty*. In these De Forest shared the simple truth of life in the army and on the battlefield.

The enormous hunger for reading material in the camps was supplied to some extent by social and religious agencies that recognized the need. In part the soldiers and their comrades found their own supply of reading material, but both armies were largely at the mercy of outside sources for their books and newspapers. Much of the work involved in providing books to the troops was done by the U.S. Christian Commission, which supplied both religious and secular reading material. Almost one million Bibles were distributed to the troops, and more than 30,000 other volumes were circulated through a system of almost three hundred portable libraries. Each contained from 70 to 125 volumes, which were transported and stored in wooden, shelved boxes about three feet square. Many of the books were printed in smaller than standard size and included classical titles as well as history, poetry, science, philosophy, and religion. The Confederate Bible Society and the South Carolina Tract Society provided religious works for the Southern troops, but the South had no system of portable libraries (Volo and Volo, 203–11).

To read about literature in the United States in the 20th century, see the United States entries in the section "Literature" in chapter 4 ("Intellectual Life") in volume 6 of this series.

FOR MORE INFORMATION

Kaser, D. *Books and Libraries in Camp and Battle: The Civil War Experience*. Westport, Conn.: Greenwood Press, 1984.

Paludan, P. S. *A People's Contest: The Union and Civil War, 1861–1865*. New York: Harper & Row, 1988.

Volo, D. D., and J. M. Volo. *Daily Life in Civil War America*. Westport, Conn.: Greenwood Press, 1998.

UNITED STATES, WESTERN FRONTIER

For many who came overland, books had been one of the first items jettisoned because of their weight. Many of the novels that frontiersman John Banks saw on the trail or in California "were written by depraved minds." But on the shelves of his cabin he had "quite a number" of good things to read: mostly medical books and magazines, *Knickerbocker's* and *Blackwoods* and the *Edinburgh Review,* an old copy of a biography of great men, Lyell's *Geology,* two books of philosophy, and "an English work entitled *Dialogues of Devils,*" which "comes far short of *Paradise Lost.*" Prentice Mulford remembered that as early as 1854 or 1855 the "boys" at Hawkin's Bar pooled their money and sent down to San Francisco for books to establish a library including geology books and a full set of American encyclopedias: "heavy and nutritious mental food rising into the lighter desserts of poetry and novels." He described one miner who read as he ate; he "devoured beef and lard, bacon and beans and encyclopedias, Humboldt's 'Cosmos' and dried apples, novels and physical nourishment at the same time (Jones, 147–48).

To read about literature on the colonial frontier of North America, see the entries on the Colonial Frontier and New England in the section "Language and Literature" in chapter 4 ("Intellectual Life") in volume 4 of this series.

FOR MORE INFORMATION

Jones, M. E. *Daily Life on the Nineteenth Century American Frontier.* Westport, Conn.: Greenwood Press, 1998.

New Perspectives on the West, <http://www.pbs.org/weta/thewest/intro.htm>.

Scamehorn, H. L., ed. *The Buckeye Rovers in the Gold Rush.* Athens: Ohio University Press, 1965.

VICTORIAN ENGLAND

The Victorians virtually invented mass literature. High-speed presses, cheap wood pulp paper, machines for typesetting, new means of reproducing illustrations, railways to send printed material quickly all over the country, and the steadily growing number of people who were literate enough to read for pleasure encouraged the publication of newspapers, magazines, and novels at every price and for every taste. Hundreds of women and men made a good living as professional writers; some grew very rich. Furthermore, reading for pleasure was not only an individual and private occupation but also a communal activity shared with family and friends.

New novels were expensive. In volume form they were read primarily by people of the middle and upper classes who belonged to private subscription libraries. To increase their profit on rental fees, libraries wanted novels to be published in three volumes. (Imagine, for comparison, that video stores had enough control of the market to insist that films be put onto three separate cassettes so customers had to rent all three to see the entire movie.)

To circumvent the libraries and increase their own share of the profits, novelists and publishers found other ways of putting stories into readers' hands. Serialization proved the most successful. Some novels were sold in monthly parts. To use the work of Charles Dickens as an example, *David Copperfield* was published in 20 parts,

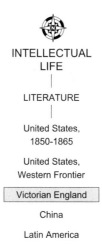

INTELLECTUAL
LIFE

LITERATURE

United States,
1850–1865

United States,
Western Frontier

Victorian England

China

Latin America

issued at a rate of one per month beginning in May 1849. (The last two parts were sold as a double number in November 1850.) Each part was made up of 32 pages, with illustrations, in a paper wrapper, and sold for one shilling. The price for the whole novel was about two-thirds the cost of a three-volume hardback, and the expense was spread out; it would be easier for people to spend a shilling each month than to buy three 10s. 6d. volumes at one time.

Serial publication had another important effect. In many parts of society, reading aloud was customary during an evening at home. While most of the family occupied

Charles Dickens in his study at Gad's Hill Place, ca. 1875. © Library of Congress.

their hands with knitting or jigsaw puzzles and father relaxed in a comfortable chair, one person sat next to the only good lamp and read from a serialized novel or some other publication that would be interesting to both youngsters and adults. Novelists made people eager to buy the next month's installment by introducing surprising new twists or by ending on a note of suspense. When everyone in the family (and most of their friends) was reading the same novel, and when they had to wait almost two years for all the complications to be resolved, people naturally talked about the book and speculated about what would happen next. They knew the characters well and cared about them. Their pleasure in popular novels combined the experience of reading with the public interest, now aroused by a favorite television series.

In addition to serialization in separate monthly parts, novels were divided into installments for publication in magazines. To return to the Dickens examples, *Oliver Twist* came out in the monthly issues of *Bentley's Miscellany* between February 1837 and March 1839. Later, once his name became recognized everywhere, Dickens published his own weekly magazines to print his new novels as well as poetry, stories, and essays by other writers. The issue of *All the Year Round* for Saturday, December 1, 1860, sold for twopence and contained 24 pages of two-column print. In addition to the first two chapters of *Great Expectations*, it included an article about dining in Rome, an essay-editorial about a current social problem (in this case, the need to provide financial assistance for parish clergy who are faced with illness or family disasters), a history of everyday life 500 years earlier, a love poem, a humorous sketch about Cornishmen, and an installment of another novel, Charles Lever's *A Day's Ride*.

Although Charles Dickens was the most successful of the novelists whose reputations have survived into the late 20th century, many other writers were widely popular. Working-class readers bought their fiction in even cheaper form, in magazines or separate serialized parts sold at a penny per week and printed in 16 pages of very small type on paper about the size and quality of a modern big-city telephone directory. G. W. M. Reynolds, like Dickens, edited his own magazines—and may have sold up to 10 times as many copies of serialized titles such as *Wagner, the Wehr-Wolf; The Mysteries of London; The Bronze Statue, or The Virgin's Kiss;* and *The Seamstress, or The White Slaves of England*. Although workers had less time for family reading than did people of the middle and upper classes, there are accounts of public readings in pubs and of mill girls clubbing together to buy a serial paper that one of them would read aloud during the dinner break.

As literature became popular entertainment, novelists found it possible to write for one particular section of the reading public. Charlotte Yonge created family stories with overtones of religious activism; Dinah Mulock Craik wrote about women's tribulations; G. P. R. James wrote historical adventures; Robert Smith Surtees depicted sporting men; Sheridan Le Fanu and Marie Corelli specialized in the occult; G. A. Henty poured out tales of military heroism that were read by men and girls as well as by boys; and Margaret Oliphant (along with many other women writers) crafted romantic and domestic chronicles. In addition, most of the Victorian authors whose books are still read (George Eliot, Elizabeth Gaskell, Charlotte Brontë, W. M. Thackeray, Anthony Trollope, Thomas Hardy, and Rudyard Kipling) were highly successful in their own time in addition to winning lasting critical reputations.

Anthony Trollope. © Library of Congress.

One of the 20th century's most popular forms of light reading had its roots in the 1860s, when a large number of competing shilling monthly magazines were established. Publishers encouraged readers to rush out and buy the next issue by concentrating on what were called sensation novels—stories featuring secrets, surprises, suspense, exaggerated emotions, dramatic chases, and train wrecks, and an overriding mystery whose solution was withheld until the last installment. Writers such as Wilkie Collins, Ellen Price Wood, and Mary Elizabeth Braddon, who specialized in sensation fiction, created many of the conventions that became useful when a young doctor named Arthur Conan Doyle was looking for a way to make some money while he waited for his medical practice to attract patients. The Sherlock Holmes stories began appearing in *The Strand* magazine in 1891.

Magazines of many sorts developed loyal readers. The penny weeklies *Family Herald* and *Bow Bells* published advice, household hints, and romantic novelettes read by workingwomen and workingmen's wives. (*Bow Bells* also had fashion pictures or sheet music on its back cover.) *London Journal* mixed sensational serials about gypsies, vampires, and crime in high places with practical advice on health and emigration. *Eliza Cook's Journal* printed short fiction and serious articles (including reports of American women's rights conventions) for older single women. Comic and satiric magazines such as *Punch* and *Fun* had pictures, satires, parodies, political cartoons, and caricatures. *Ally Sloper's Half-Holiday*, which began in 1884, was an eight-page illustrated joke book that can be seen as the forerunner of the comics. It has been estimated that at least ten thousand different newspapers and magazines were published (at least for a few issues) during the Victorian period.

Women's magazines early in the century had been largely for the upper classes, featuring Paris fashions, intellectual pastimes, and court news. In 1852, Samuel Beeton's *Englishwoman's Domestic Magazine* established a new formula: fiction, recipes, patterns for sewing and needlework, advice about gardening and health, and essays on political issues of interest to women (e.g., new public health measures or laws to improve child welfare). In the 1890s, a new generation of women's magazines added more and more advertising and began to feature articles that helped promote the

Charlotte Brontë. © Library of Congress.

advertisers' products. These more commercial magazines also printed personality news that is useful to modern-day scholars who study the interviews with women musicians, actors, artists, and authors of the era.

At the beginning of the period, few people read a daily newspaper. The London *Times*—which had been published since the 18th century—reported parliamentary and other significant news and was essential reading for influential men. But newspapers were expensive; women often had no chance to see them. Men tended to read the paper at their office or club. The novelist Elizabeth Gaskell shared a subscription with several neighbors; they bought one copy between them and passed it around.

As production costs dropped—and even more dramatically, after the stamp duty was repealed in 1855—newspapers became much cheaper and more widely read. The weekly *Illustrated London News* pioneered pictorial journalism by commissioning artists to cover breaking news (as well as predictable public occasions) and transferring the drawings quickly to woodblocks for mass reproduction. Penny and then halfpenny papers made it possible for members of the working class to become newspaper readers. Reading the tabloid-style coverage in the weekly *News of the World* became a customary recreation for a workingman's Sunday.

Children's literature of all sorts flowered, owing both to changed conceptions of childhood and new production methods for illustrated books. The period of about 50 years following 1860 is often called the golden age of English children's literature. Earlier books for children were chiefly meant for intellectual or moral instruction, although the lesson might be sweetened with entertaining characters and illustrations. Fairy tales had an unsavory reputation. They appeared in crudely printed, cheap books; they were violent; and they didn't teach good lessons.

Beginning in the 1840s, well-designed illustrated fairy tales began to appear, and folklore collectors gave them an aura of respectability. The new fairy tales of Hans Christian Andersen were translated. English writers began to produce entertaining fantasy literature that did not always have a simple or explicit moral. The illustrators whose work is still admired did their best work in the 1860s and 1870s, after colored pictures could be printed at a reasonable price. Walter Crane, Randolph Caldecott, and Kate Greenaway developed the interplay of text with illustrations that has become the hallmark of good books for young children; they also created wonderful art.

After mid-century, writers for older children produced increasingly realistic stories about ordinary children and their doings, as well as adventure tales, school stories, historical novels, and other genres of popular writing. The books usually provided a model for good behavior, or the characters learned an important lesson about growing up—but they had a great deal of fun and excitement along the way, and their admirable behavior could be good, independent heroism instead of good obedience to their elders.

Magazines for little children and for older boys and girls provided a weekly or monthly budget of fiction, illustrations, puzzles, and games for a penny or sixpence. Even cheaper papers for working-class adolescents were published toward the end of the century: for a halfpenny a week boys got jokes and blood and thunder serials and girls got horoscopes, advice columns, and contests in addition to fictional adventure and romance.

Although new books for adults remained expensive, children's publications advertised new and reprinted titles in every price range from one or two pence to six shillings and more. Some of the classic English children's books written during the Victorian period are *Alice's Adventures in Wonderland* (1865), *Black Beauty* (1877), *Treasure Island* (published as a book in 1883 but serialized in the magazine *Young Folks* in 1881–82), *Kim* (1901) and *The Jungle Books* (1894, 1895), *The Water Babies* (1863), *The Little Lame Prince* (1875), *Tom Brown's Schooldays* (1857), and the Andrew Lang editions of fairy tales from around the world collected in the 1890s as *The Blue Fairy Book, The Green Fairy Book,* and so on (Mitchell, *Daily Life,* 233–38).

To read about literature in Chaucer's England, see the entry on Europe in the section "Language and Literature" in chapter 4 ("Intellectual Life") in volume 2 of this series; for Elizabethan England, see the entry on England in the section "Literature" in chapter 4 ("Intellectual Life") in volume 3 of this series; for 18th-century England, see the entry on England in the section "Language and Literature" in chapter 4 ("Intellectual Life") in volume 4 of this series.

FOR MORE INFORMATION

Cruse, A. *The Victorians and Their Reading.* Boston: Houghton Mifflin, 1935.
Mitchell, S. *Daily Life in Victorian England.* Westport, Conn.: Greenwood Press, 1996.
Mitchell, S., ed. *Victorian Britain: An Encyclopedia.* New York: Garland Press, 1998.

CHINA

Prior to the 20th century there were two main Chinese literary traditions: the classical and the vernacular. The classical tradition is the Chinese equivalent of a literary canon. It is highly Confucion in nature and consists of a core of texts written in ancient Chinese. These texts had to be mastered completely by anyone aspiring entrance to the Chinese civil service. It was also the backbone of the Chinese education system. Ironically, it was completely incomprehensible to the majority of the Chinese people.

The vernacular, or folk, dates back to at least a thousand years before the common era. Initially, it was characterized by a vigorous vernacular literature that preceded by several centuries the appearance of modern colloquial literatures in the West. The growth of Chinese fiction and drama during the Yuan (Yan or Mongol) dynasty (1279–1368) may have been the result of the refusal of many scholars to serve the Mongol regime. They instead turned their talents to new fields, such as fiction and drama. Consisting originally of poetry and later of drama and fiction, it grew to include histories and popular stories and tales as well. It was long considered a low-class form of literature. The polished and highly stylized writings of the educated

INTELLECTUAL LIFE

LITERATURE

United States, 1850-1865

United States, Western Frontier

Victorian England

China

Latin America

elite set the standards for the orthodox literary tradition that began about 2,000 years ago. Not until the 20th century did colloquial literature gain the support and respect of the intellectual class. Vernacular literature continued to develop through the modern period, until it finally coalesced with a new and more inclusive literary movement in the late 19th century.

The 19th century was a crucial time when China was torn between traditional culture and modernization. A quest began with the goal of making literature more accessible to a greater number of people. Many resisted this notion and clung tightly to tradition. Many individuals fought to keep the old, traditional school curriculum that emphasized the classical literature. The fact that so much of the new literature and the Western literature in translation emphasized modernization rather than tradition was also a source of contention. This was a time when China was torn between the old and the new. A memory and glorification of the great advanced classical Chinese civilization made it difficult for many people to accept the new and foreign influences.

Around the start of the 19th century, a movement against many elements of Chinese culture began. An attack on the classical literature was one element of this growing ideology. The literary revolution has been viewed as one of six phases in the New Cultural Movement. These phases are: (1) the attack on Confucianism, (2) the literary Revolution, (3) the proclaiming of a new life philosophy, (4) the debate on science and philosophy, (5) the questioning of antiquity, and (6) the debating of Chinese versus Western values.

The classical literature came to be considered aristocratic because only the very educated elite was capable of reading it. This social differentiation came to be viewed as wrong and nonegalitarian—a view influenced by Western ideas. This was one reason that the literature of the past was attacked in favor of a literary language accessible to more of the population.

The attack on classical literature paralleled an attack on Confucianism. This was a time of rising nationalism. A written language that was much simpler and easier to learn facilitated the era of expanding education. It was also a period of strong Westernization in thought and scholarship, and the simpler language provided a more flexible instrument with which to express new concepts. Combined, these factors contributed to the rapid spread of the literary revolution in the final years of the 19th century and into the 20th century.

In the early 19th century, Western novels in Chinese translation became popular. This caused Chinese people to look at their own literature with a more critical eye. They became particularly critical of the classical tradition because it was written in

---

📷 Snapshot

Literary Reform in 19th-Century China

Many people have been discussing literary reform. Who am I, unlearned and unlettered, to offer an opinion? Nevertheless, for some years I have studied the matter and thought it over many times, helped by my deliberations with friends; and the conclusions I have come to are perhaps not unworthy of discussion. Therefore I shall summarize my views under eight points and elaborate on them separately to invite the study and comments of those interested in literary reform.

I believe that literary reform at the present time must begin with these eight items: (1) Write with substance. (2) Do not imitate the ancients. (3) Emphasize grammar. (4) Reject melancholy. (5) Eliminate old clichés. (6) Do not use allusions. (7) Do not use couplets and parallelisms. And (8) Do not avoid popular expressions or popular forms of characters. (Hu, 1–3)

a vastly different language than that which was spoken by modern Chinese people. A desire for national literature based on the vernacular tradition grew stronger.

Lu Xun (1881–1936) was the first major Chinese writer to write in the colloquial Chinese, which the people of China understood. Many consider him to be the father of Chinese literature. Lu Xun is a pen name. His real name was Zhou Shuren. Lu Xun wrote stories, poetry, essays, literary criticism, and literary history. His stories were published in literary journals of the time and were then collected and published as books. He produced three volumes of short stories. His first collection of short stories, *Nahan,* or "Call to Arms," looked critically at China's inability to enter the 20th century with the rest of the world.

Lao She (1899–1966) was another important early novelist. He was born to an impoverished family in Beijing. He studied English in China and later taught Chinese at the School of Oriental and African Studies in London. During this time he was greatly influenced by the works of Charles Dickens and Joseph Conrad and, while in England, began his career of writing Chinese novels. His most famous work, "The Rickshaw Boy," is a critique of the living conditions of rickshaw pullers in Beijing. He died by drowning himself in a lake in Beijing in 1966.

The literary reform movement led to a renewed interest in the great Chinese novels, as well as to social and political criticism responsible for making some changes in the social and political order of the day. However, many argue that the movement produced contemporary literature of little distinction or creative imagination. Many felt that while the new literature made use of rhythm, tone, metaphor, and other literary devices, the ideas put forth in the works were neither interesting nor unique. The new literature was also criticized for lacking feeling and emotion. Because of the troubled and turbulent political background of the times, many writers chose pen names such as "Dead Ash" or "No Birth." Some critics complained that these writers used pure melancholy rather than genuine emotion to make their point. One famous philosopher named Hu Shi (1891–1962) attacked this style of literature by asking, "can salvation be achieved through fears?"

To read about literature in China under the Tang dynasty, see the China entry in the section "Language and Literature" in chapter 4 ("Intellectual Life") in volume 2 of this series.

~Dana Lightstone

FOR MORE INFORMATION

Chinag, C. *The Development of Neo-Confucianism.* 2 vols. New York: Bookman, 1962.

Dolby, W., trans. *Eight Chinese Plays from the Thirteenth Century to the Present.* New York: Columbia University Press, 1978.

Hu Shi. *Hu Shi Wencun.* Taipei, Taiwan: Wenhai, 1977.

INDIA

In 1858, the British government put India under direct rule and, under their colonial administration, the British transformed India. One of their positive reforms was to establish English-style schools for the children of Indian elites. These schools began the process of creating a vibrant new intellectual life that combined the best of East and West. In literature, these efforts would bear wonderful fruit in the 20th century. See the entry on India in the section "Literature" in chapter 4 ("Intellectual Life") in volume 6 of this series.

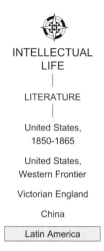

INTELLECTUAL
LIFE
|
LITERATURE
|
United States,
1850-1865

United States,
Western Frontier

Victorian England

China

Latin America

LATIN AMERICA

After most of Latin America broke away from Spain or Portugal in the first decades of the 19th century, some of the newly independent states, such as Brazil, clung to their colonial past. In literature, this tendency was characterized by the continuing popularity of such traditional genres as moralizing tracts, classically inspired theater, and highly academic poetry. Other states, such as Argentina and, somewhat belatedly, Mexico, sought, under European influence, to modernize their societies. This modernization was driven by a growing middle class, the bourgeoisie, and, in literature, was characterized by the rise of the novel, which came to be the chief literary form for interpreting the conflicts and stresses of modern society. As a result, the most interesting and significant 19th-century Latin American novels are associated with countries that most vigorously pursued a process of modernization.

In Argentina, the most important narrative from the period is not a prose novel in the sense of Dickens, Balzac, or James, but rather a pseudoepic poem that many perceptive critics have called a novel in verse. José Hernández's *Martín Fierro* (1872; réprise 1879) is the interpretation by an oligarchic landowner and national senator of the passing of the traditional gaucho nomadic life and its reinterpretation as part of the development of the vast ranching enterprise on which so much of Argentina's legendary wealth is based. Hernández first laments the destruction of the idyll of gaucho life and the disruption of the primitive family unit as the state sought to tame both the Indians and the mestizo nomads. But Hernández, in the 1879 revision of his work, defends the disbanding of the old life and the conversion of the gaucho into the salaried hand of the ranch economy, with the domestic values of the latter a derivative of those of the landowners.

Perhaps the most widely read 19th-century Latin American novel was *María* (1867) by a Colombian writer of Jewish descent named Jorge Isaac (the novel is the first major work by a Latin American with Jewish roots). Since Colombia remained traditionally Hispanic and Catholic, Isaac's novel describes conservative patriarchal family life on a hacienda in the Cauca Valley. The protagonist of the novel is an orphaned relative of the patriarch, who takes her in when she is a child, only to see his son fall in love with her. The son is then sent off to study in Europe. He returns when he learns María is dying, but arrives only after her death. One way of reading Isaac's novel, which has usually been read romantically as the idyll of star-crossed lovers, is to underscore the rigidities of the conservative patriarchy and how it interferes in the happiness of individual lives, a modern concept that one assumes to have been the principal horizon of most readers of the novel.

The most critical interpretations of modernity and the emergence of bourgeois cultures are to be found in the novels of the Brazilian Joachim Maria Machado de Assis. His major works are undoubtedly the finest writing of the century on the Latin American continent and are, therefore, widely available in English. Less important for their details of plot, Machado's narratives are highly wrought ironic perceptions of the conflicts, hypocrisies, inconsistencies, and miscarriages of the middle class that was affirming itself in Rio de Janeiro in the 1880s and 1890s. Machado was himself a mulatto and, although his literary success gave him an entrée into the society he was describing, he had the wit of the privileged outsider who knew there was much to dwell on behind the façade of a genteel and energetically Europeanizing bourgeoisie. His most famous work is *Dom Casmurro* (1900), which follows the constitution of the protagonist's personality and then its disintegration when he is wracked by jealousy over his wife's presumed infidelity.

Alberto Blest Gana's *Martín Rivas* (1862) is perhaps the continent's best example of the triumph of the modern self in the city, in this case, Santiago, the capital of Chile. The hero is a country bumpkin who is taken in by relatives in the city, and the reader follows the stages of his integration into modern urban life. The novel has a distinct sense of progress, which is what legitimates the urbanity and personal success Martín Rivas attains. While Blest Gana criticizes some pretensions of city life, his depiction of Rivas's social triumphs provides a detailed characterization of how the Latin American bourgeoisie, firmly tied to English concepts of urbanity and exhibiting a measure of Frenchified cultural sophistication, succeeds in entrenching itself.

The Peruvian Clorinda Matto de Turner's *Aves sin nido* (1889; *Birds without a Nest*) is an excellent example of the 19th-century use of the novel for political pamphleteering. Although necessarily imbued with certain racist and patronizing views of her day, Matto de Turner nevertheless felt deeply the social and economic injustices suffered by the Indians, both the remnants of the pre-Columbian indigenous populations and their mestizo progeny, who were themselves the result of hundreds of years of sexual domination by Iberian masters and their descendents. The accounts of the plight of the native population that make up the novel are in effect a denunciation of the old Hispanic order of things, especially as it was still lived in the backwaters of the country. In this sense, the novelist had a modernizing agenda in mind, although other novelists would subsequently see the plight of the *indios* in the modernized city to be no better.

An important inventory of novels from this period treats women protagonists as allegorical figures of the nation. *María* is in some way pertinent here, although a paradigmatic example might be José Mármol's *Amalia* (1855), where the heroine is the symbolic anchor of mediating (feminine) civilized values in the face of the bloody Manuel de Rosas (masculine/macho) dictatorship in Argentina in the 1830s and 1840s. The sexualized dichotomy of the novel may also be cast in terms of the dictator's reactionary adherence to Hispanic ways of life and the heroine's embodiment of the civilizing influence of modern Europe.

These works were primarily read by a modernizing urban and bourgeois elite, and many were published in serialized fashion in the exceptionally influential newspapers of the day, as well as by emerging publishing giants. The concerns characterized by these writings unquestionably led to the ongoing efforts at modernizing society that clustered around the turn of the century and to the internationalizing effects of the First World War. At the same time, they look toward the crises of modernity that were so crucial in late 20th-century Latin American writing and help explain why the novel in Latin America has been a vigorous and dominant genre.

~*David William Foster*

FOR MORE INFORMATION

Brushwood, J. S. *Genteel Barbarism; Experiments in Analysis of Nineteenth-Century Spanish-American Novels.* Lincoln: University of Nebraska Press, 1981.

Lindstrom, N. *Nineteenth-Century Spanish American Fiction.* Austin: University of Texas Press, 2004.

Sommer, D. *Foundational Fictions: The National Romances of Latin America.* Berkeley: University of California Press, 1991.

ISLAMIC WORLD

From its origins in its respect for the Arabic language, Islam fostered a vibrant literary life, which continued through most of the long ascendance of the Turks. By the 19th century, however, Turkish literature had become somewhat stagnant. Muslim literature would be reinvigorated in the 20th century with the end of colonialism, which allowed for new voices to emerge in the Islamic literary world. For the beginnings of Muslim literature, see the entry on the Islamic World in the section "Literature" in chapter 4 ("Intellectual Life") in volume 2 of this series. Then, for subsequent literary flowering, see the entry on the Ottoman Empire in the section "Literature" in chapter 4 ("Intellectual Life") in volume 3 of this series. Finally, follow the 20th-century rejuvenation of Islamic literature in the entry on the Islamic World in the section "Literature" in chapter 4 ("Intellectual Life") in volume 6 of this series.

INTELLECTUAL
LIFE
|
HEALTH & MEDICINE
|
United States,
1850-1865

United States,
Western Frontier

Victorian England

India

Latin America

Health and Medicine

From the perspective of the beginning of the 21st century, 19th-century medicine seems almost barbaric or at best backwards. Diseases were a common part of daily life and medical practices struggled to control or cure them. Take the western frontier of the United States. Venereal diseases were the explorers' constant companion. The cure at that time was mercury, whose side effect was temporary madness. Many ailments were the result of poor diets. Miners described a condition that they termed land scurvy, caused by a lack of fresh vegetables. The workers became weak with pain in the joints and had swelling and bleeding in the gums (which eventually turned completely black). Poorly stored foods and unsanitary living conditions led to other problems. Diarrhea, typhoid, and cholera were common on the American frontier. But frontiers were not the only places that one found such diseases. For most of the 19th century, tuberculosis existed in epidemic proportions in England. It accounted for half of all deaths in women between 15 and 35 years of age. Unsanitary conditions in cities made TB and diseases such as cholera common. Other diseases in England had a different source. Factories were extremely unsafe and led to illness. For example, in match factories, workers succumbed to phosphorous poisoning, which caused their teeth and jaws to rot off their faces.

In the 19th century, the quality of medical care depended on where one was and who one was. Workers on the American frontier had a difficult time just finding a doctor. Farmers who settled in the West had virtually no access to doctors. Rather, local priests and ministers tried in vain to care for the sick and dying. Miners were closer to knowledgeable medical practitioners, but it cost them. Doctors in gold mining fields demanded to be paid in gold and often in advance of treatment. Civil War soldiers may have had it even worse. It was not until 1863 that the Union Army created an ambulance service. The Corps of Invalids was made up of hurt and maimed soldiers who assisted nurses and medical aides. Mostly the troops relied on field surgeons, Catholic nuns, and volunteers (who were always in short supply). There were people who made extraordinary contributions. Dorothea Dix organized and ran a tremendously brave, important, and useful corps of nurses. However, she limited the number of her nurses by imposing strict moral requirements upon the women who served. They were to be of high moral character, no less than 30, and plain looking. Given the tragic demand for nurses, it is surprising that such a code remained in place for the duration of the war.

In Latin America, medical care improved greatly during the course of the century. After independence, medical oversight came under the control of national governments, which took steps to improved sanitation, to educate people to better health practices, and to improve the training of doctors and nurses. Nonetheless, access to modern medical care was confined largely to the cities and to the upper and middle classes; the poor of the countryside continued to rely mainly on traditional medical practices.

As much as medicine was a function of place and class, it was also a function of culture. By the end of the Victorian era, in India, there were at least three major competing systems of providing health care. Traditional Indian medicine is based upon the idea that illness relates to an imbalance in one's energies. Pharmacological remedies such as herbs and heavy metals are thus employed to cure the sick. During the medieval period, the Muslims brought another form of medical care based on curing through plants and herbs. Finally, when the English invaded India, they brought their own traditions. Since they were a colonial power, they also established medical schools and hospitals. All these medical practices fought with each other, and by the end of the century (as with other aspects of life in India) there was a native movement to reject Western and Muslim traditions and return to native Indian medical practices. Nonetheless, advancement in health and medical care would wait until the next century, when concerted efforts to improve sanitation and medical practices would raise the health standards of average people.

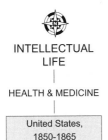

INTELLECTUAL
LIFE
|
HEALTH & MEDICINE
|
United States,
1850-1865

United States,
Western Frontier

Victorian England

India

Latin America

UNITED STATES, 1850–65

The medical services of the armed forces were almost nonexistent. The federal army began the war with fewer than 120 surgeons and assistant surgeons, and some of these were dismissed for suspected disloyalty and served with the Confederate forces. Medical officers and their assistants were commonly assigned to individual regiments, and musicians served as stretcher bearers.

Prior to the Civil War the U.S. Army had not provided ambulances for the wounded and sick. In 1859 experimental carts were tested on the western plains and a less than satisfactory two-wheel version was adopted. Not until 1863 did the federal army organize and outfit a formal ambulance corps for the army of the Potomac. Under General Order No. 85 only four-wheel, two-horse carts would be used as ambulances. Each ambulance had five men assigned as stretcher bearers and drivers. Three ambulances were permanently allocated to each infantry regiment, two to each cavalry regiment, and one to each artillery battery. Moreover, two army wagons were designated to carry only medical supplies for each corps, and two more were placed at the division level. "Obviously, this organization was sorely needed, but it fell far short of the real need," as three ambulances were "hardly adequate" to support a regiment of 1,000 men.

Once off the battlefield the plight of the wounded was complicated by limited medical knowledge, malnutrition, and disease. While American military hospitals were better than those in Europe, they were nonetheless inadequate. Civilian corpsmen, hired by the army at $20.50 per month to staff army hospitals, often proved unreliable. A nursing service, directed by Dorothea Dix and staffed by women, had been established to care for the wounded and sick in the numerous soldiers' rests and regimental hospitals; but the recruitment of nurses was hobbled by the strict moral requirements Dix placed on potential candidates. Women were required to be of high moral character, no less than 30 years of age, plain looking, and unadorned. There was no requirement that they be efficient or capable.

In March 1863, Secretary of War Edwin M. Stanton established a Corps of Invalids from among the "walking wounded" and "convalescent soldiers" of the army to serve as nurses and medical aides. More than 60,000 men ultimately served in the invalid corps "scattered randomly" among the regiments of the army. Although only 42 members of the corps were killed in action, more than 1,600 died of the diseases to which they were exposed in the sick wards. The invalid corps concept received little support from the army hierarchy, and General Grant opposed all plans for retaining it as a part of the postwar army.

Thousands of Catholic nuns served as nurses in the federal military hospitals of Boston, New York, Philadelphia, Baltimore, Washington, and other cities. Sisters of Charity, Sisters of Mercy, and Sisters of Saint Vincent de Paul were all conspicuous in their unique religious habits. The nuns volunteered to serve without pay even though they were often abused by anti-Catholic hospital personnel and patients. Their patience, skill, and persistence won over a good number of bigots. "My mind was filled with prejudice," wrote one soldier. "I did not believe that anything good could come from the Sisters. But now I see my mistake all too clearly."

Catholic sisters were "conspicuously neutral" in their attitude toward the war. Confederate hospitals in Richmond, Charleston, Nashville, and New Orleans were also staffed with at least some Catholic nuns. The sisters consistently failed to leave their work when the vagaries of war changed the nature of the occupying force from South to North, and in Vicksburg they suffered the siege and ensuing bombardment with the beleaguered of the city. The sisters proved to be expert medical and surgical nurses, as they had experienced service in asylums and civilian hospitals during their long novitiates. A Southern woman noted that the

This lithograph illustrates the harsh realities of field medical practice during the American Civil War.

work of the sisters made "all the difference in the world" in the Confederate hospitals of Richmond.

A number of civilian organizations helped to fill the need for additional medical care. The Women's American Association for Relief was closely associated with a number of eminent doctors in New York and furnished medical supplies to the army. Beyond this the U.S. Sanitary Commission made provisions for the relief of the sick, provided ambulances, and cared for the wounded and the dead. Commission representatives, operating in the east and in the west, oversaw the diet and personal cleanliness of the soldiers in camp, provided housing for white refugee families, and raised money to expand their work. A single Sanitary Commission fundraiser in New York City raised over one million dollars. A woman wrote, "The amount realized will no doubt do much toward relieving the poor wounded and suffering soldiers than all the surgeons do. No one can know how much good is done by the Sanitary Commission who is not in the Army."

The South mounted a less formal assault on the medical chaos that plagued the Confederate forces. Less than 30 surgeons and surgeon's assistants from the old army chose to serve with the Confederacy, and wounded or sick men were often left to the tender care of their mates or the local populace. The military hospitals of the South were overwhelmed by the task before them, and wounded men were often shipped home to recuperate under the care of their families. Those who were capable, but still considered invalids, were formed into local militias and railroad guards, rather than hospital orderlies, by the manpower-hungry state governments.

Ambulances were provided by subscription. A newly painted Confederate ambulance, apparently donated by a well-meaning supporter from Fairfax, was among the early acquisitions of federal pickets in northern Virginia. "This capture was an object of much curiosity around the Federal camp near Alexandria. Soldiers stood off and stared at it in awe . . . an omen of what might lie in store for them, this wagon designed for toting the wounded or the dead" (Volo and Volo, 167–69).

To read about health and medicine in the United States in the 20th century, see the United States entries in the section "Health and Medicine" in volume 6 of this series.

FOR MORE INFORMATION

Burns, K. *The Civil War*. PBS Video, 1990. Film.

Denny, R. E. *Civil War Medicine: Care and Comfort for the Wounded*. New York: Sterling, 1995.

Volo D. D., and J. M. Volo. *Daily Life in Civil War America*. Westport, Conn.: Greenwood Press, 1998.

INTELLECTUAL
LIFE

HEALTH & MEDICINE

United States,
1850–1865

United States,
Western Frontier

Victorian England

India

Latin America

UNITED STATES, WESTERN FRONTIER

Disease was a daily factor of life in the United States and particularly on the western frontier. Venereal disease was so common among the western explorers that it was rarely mentioned. At Fort Mandan, William Clark wrote: "Generally helthy except Venerials Complaints which is verry Common amongst the natives and the men Catch it from them." On the return trip Meriwether Lewis notes, "Goodrich and McNeal are both very unwell with the pox which they contracted last winter from the Chinook women." Nearly all the men, at one time or another, suffered from " 'brakings out, or irruptions of the Skin' probably caused by venereal disease."

Medical care varied widely and was often unaffordable or ineffective. The treatment for venereal diseases was standard: ingesting mercury. Lewis routinely administered pills of mercurous chloride to the men. However, there were dangerous side effects of the treatment. Historian Stephen Ambrose notes that the phrase "mad as a hatter" referred to hatmakers who used mercury in their work and became slightly crazy from breathing in the fumes. And Gary Moulton suggests that the mercury treatment may have contributed to the surprisingly high proportion of men of the corps who died young.

Though Lewis may not have been correct when he wrote about curing men of venereal disease "by the uce of mercury," the men remained surprisingly healthy during the two-year trek. Only one, Sergeant Floyd, died, apparently of infection following a burst appendix.

There were, of course, many less serious problems. Mosquitoes and gnats swarmed over the men, compelling "us to brush them off or have our eyes filled with them." While descending the Columbia the men were covered with fleas, apparently from straw at an Indian camp: "every man . . . was obliged to strip naked . . . [to brush] the flees off their legs and bodies." In July 1804 extreme heat, coupled with exertion, affected most of the party; one case of sunstroke was recorded. In October 1804 many men, including Clark, complained of rheumatism; this was not surprising given the cold, damp conditions. The pain and spasms were treated by applying a hot stone wrapped in flannel. Several suffered from toothache; most suffered from boils, which Lewis called "tumors," some of which were enormous. Clark lanced one that discharged half a pint of pus.

There are several references to becoming sick from the food: chokecherries and red haws produced digestive disorders, as did tainted dried salmon. Dysentery—a "lax and heaviness in the stomach," as Clark put it, and which he attributed to the water—was treated by Glauber's salts. Clark describes being "taken verry unwell with a pain in the bowels & Stomach, which is certainly the effects of my diet." The previous night, with nothing to eat but dried fish and roots, he and Lewis were in agony: the meal "Swelled us in Such a manner that we were Scercely able to breath for Several hours." Descending the Columbia, several men suffered from the purgative effects of drinking salt water.

Moreover, many suffered from "feet so mangled and bruised with the stones and rough ground over which they passed barefoot, that they can scarcely walk or stand." Winter brought special hazards—snow blindness from sun reflected off the snow and numerous cases of frostbite; Clark even writes of York's frostbitten penis. Both on the Columbia and on the last stages of the return trip on the Missouri, men complain of sore eyes. Clark describes the problem: "their eyes inflamed and Swelled in Such a manner as to render them extreamly painful, particularly when exposed to the light" and suggests its cause: "I am willing to believe it may be owing to the reflection of the sun on the water." Chuinard, however, suggests that venereal disease may also have been a factor. And, from being frequently wet, the men often suffered from colds and influenza.

Like explorers, miners struggled to stay healthy. Many illnesses were rooted in poor diets. The consequences of such a diet soon became clear. J. D. Stevenson noticed that many men "who came into the town with long purses of the precious metal are broken in health and constitution." He had heard that scurvy had broken out and expected more of it due to lack of fresh vegetables. Miner E. Gould Buffum was among the victims of land scurvy and describes his own symptoms: swelling and severe pain in his legs, which he at first thought was rheumatism; swelling and bleeding of his gums; and increased swelling in his legs, which eventually "turned completely black" and left him unable to work. He treated himself with boiled sprouts from beans apparently spilled from a teamster's pack and a "decoction of the bark of the Spruce tree." Recovering enough to get into Coloma, he lived on a vegetable diet—at $3 per pound for potatoes—and recovered.

Many miners had arrived sick or weakened from their overland journey. Many complained of colds, rheumatism, and arthritis—not surprising, considering the time spent in icy streams. Diarrhea is often mentioned, as is dysentery, typhoid, and, occasionally, cholera. Poison oak grew lushly through most of the mining region, as many were to discover; William Perkins swelled up 24 hours after contact, his hands and feet and face so severely swollen that he was blinded for three days. John Banks fainted one night, the only time in his life; the reason is unclear, though it may have been from exhaustion or possibly from "fantish" (rancid) rice. He narrowly missed smashing his head against his fireplace. One of the more bizarre deaths was recorded by William Perkins—that of a young Canadian who died after eating fresh pork. It turned out that people had set out arsenic to kill rats, and the pig had consumed the dead rats. The meat, nonetheless, was sold by "unprincipled vagabond dealers . . . who richly deserve lynching." And, of course, when miners used quicksilver, they suffered from mercury poisoning. Prentice Mulford describes the results of heating the mercury / gold amalgam to evaporate the mercury:

> The [mercury] covered walls, tables, and chairs with a fine, frost-like coating, and on rubbing one's finger over any surface a little globule of quicksilver would roll up before it. Then we went to Chinese Camp and gave the doctor about half our individual week's dividends to get the mercury out of us. Three weeks of sore mouths and loosened teeth followed this . . . exposure. It was through such experiences as these that we became in California practical mineralogists.

Besides disease, there were accidents aplenty. William Perkins blamed most accidents, including falling into water-filled pits and drowning, on drunkenness. As on the overland journey, guns accidentally discharged. People were swept away by streams suddenly flooded by winter rains or melting snow. Snakes, including rattlesnakes, came into campsites, especially in dry seasons; Banks recalls killing one that "was among our dishes." Grizzly bears still abounded in the mountains. One broke a man's arm so badly that it had to be amputated. Many accidents occurred during construction of dams or diverting of rivers; rocks loosely piled up fell, crushing and bruising men in their way and sometimes breaking bones. Banks tells of a man who died from taking too much opium.

There were far from adequate physicians present to care for those laid low by disease or accident, though Dame Shirley's husband was one of them. Some doctors clearly sought to cash in on the bonanza. "A physician's fee," reports Banks, is "an ounce of gold, no matter how short the distance may be." And most were young and inexperienced. Although one man who broke his leg was amazed at the generosity of his fellow miners, who, in 24 hours, collected $200 for his care, a "Mr. McMeans" opened a hospital in Salmon Falls and required $12 in advance—or securities—before admitting a patient. In Sonora, however, a public subscription raised money for a hospital where "the sick of all nations are tended by nurses and

Some doctors clearly sought to cash in on the bonanza.

a good physician." Banks told of a Dr. Swan, "famed, if not for his skill, certainly for heavy charges." He charged six ounces of gold to ride five miles to a patient; his total bill was nearly $400, of which the young man could pay only $289 because he continued to be sick for months after his treatment and thus could not work. Nonetheless, the doctor sued him for payment. A jury of miners, however, determined that the doctor should return $89 to the patient and pay court costs of nearly $200. William B. Royall had similar complaints: "Physicians are all making fortunes in this country; they will hardly look at a man's tongue for less than an ounce of gold! I have known Doctors, although they are scarcely worthy of the title (for the most of them here are quacks), charge a patient as much as 100 dollars for one visit and prescription."

The doctor, however, could sometimes be the victim. James L. Tyson treated a man who "had been on a drunken frolic, and whooping and yelling as such characters are apt to do . . . had fallen and dislocated his lower jaw." Tyson popped it back in place, much to the man's delight. Though he left with many thanks and promised to return in the afternoon to settle his bill, Tyson "never saw him afterward." Tyson noted that some people, "either from inability or disinclination to pay for medical attention," chose to treat themselves. They frequently died, "or they were walking shadows for months, with impaired intellects, and rarely recovered their accustomed vigor." Though he may not have been entirely objective about those who tried home remedies, Dr. Tyson's assessment of the ravages of mining on general health was clear: "I never saw more broken-down constitutions than I witnessed during my stay in California, and few who work in the mines, ever carry home their usual full health."

In addition to deaths from disease and accidents, there were suicides committed by men disillusioned by poverty after months of hard work. Men who had come to California with high hopes of striking it rich grew despondent as they returned to Stockton or Sacramento or San Francisco with the hope of earning just enough to pay their way back home. Some attempted to work their way home as firemen or stewards on the steamships. Those who found no such escape became truly despondent. One contemporary source, clearly exaggerating, claimed that suicides caused by disappointment were as numerous as deaths resulting from natural causes. Daniel Woods records 12 suicides in October 1849, enough to concern the congregation at the tent chapel in San Francisco. He cites the case of a young man who went to the outskirts of the city, meticulously removed his tie, took his razor from its case, and carefully cut his throat. John Banks described another suicide attempt. A man who had been sick for several weeks and despairing of regaining health gashed his throat three times with a butcher knife. Though he cut deep into his windpipe, he was too weak to cut his jugular and languished for several days before he died.

Settlers were also at the mercy of the frontier's rudimentary medicine. Though there were some frontier doctors (Bessie Rehwinkel's career is one example), they were as scarce as ministers or teachers at first. Despite their absence, neither disease, accidents, nor death took a holiday. Diarists mention almost routinely everything from the common cold, rheumatism, diarrhea, and the mysterious fever and ague to smallpox, scarlet fever, pneumonia, and consumption. Several mention children with worms; one recalls a neighbor hooking a finger into a child's rectum to remove them. For measles Grace Fairchild applied a flaxseed poultice to her daughter's back, an onion poultice to her chest, and a hot-water bottle to her feet "until the measles broke out." Others tried turpentine and sugar to prevent worms and they thickened egg whites in vinegar as a cough syrup. Folk remedies suggested rubbing fresh peach leaves on the head for baldness and eating a handful of sumac leaves twice a week for bed-wetting. Howard Ruede liked to use skunk fat, which was "good for all kinds of sores, rheumatism, etc., and for greasing boots."

People also suffered greatly from toothache. Mollie Dorsey was "piled up in bed with a swollen jaw, my face decorated with a poultice." There are few references to preventive medicine or dentistry, although Miriam Davis Colt remembered one woman who "mopped" her teeth with a little swab, "first dipped into her snuff box."

In areas of contact with Native Americans, some settlers adopted Indian medicine. Mollie Dorsey Sanford tried a version of the sweat lodge to treat herself for chills and fever when quinine failed to work: "I went for three successive mornings and jumped into the creek [it was November and icy], would then wrap myself in a blanket, rush up to the house, pile into bed, and take a sweat."

Some families had copies of popular "medical" books such as Dr. Richard Carter's *Valuable Vegetable Prescriptions for the Cure of All Nervous and Putrid Disorders*. One such book sold over 100,000 copies in its first decade in print. Others resorted to patent medicines. Garland remembers garish almanacs—merely small, badly printed patent medicine pamphlets with a loop of string by which they could be hung by the kitchen stove for reference. Such pamphlets were given for free, but the products they advertised—Harley's Bitters or Allen's Cherry Pectoral—always seemed to cost a dollar a bottle. In a land of hard work and little accessible entertainment, the traveling medicine show (despite its 90 proof quackery) was a hit for farmers that came to town.

Accidents also took their toll. There are frequent references to ax cuts. While one man was cutting wood, the ax slipped and cut his good kneecap. "It was with difficulty that he crawled home," his wife reported. "He was very weak from loss of blood." Howard Ruede seemed almost accident-prone. He narrowly missed cutting off his foot with an ax, which glanced from a log and took a slice out of his shoe. He hit himself in the head with a pick while digging a dugout and "bled like a stuck pig. . . . It made my head ache, and I did no more this afternoon for fear I would bleed again." While hauling sand for the construction of a schoolhouse he was stepped on by his ox but had to walk six miles home—"pretty painful . . . [for] when an ox is pulling hard his tread is pretty heavy, I assure you." Grace Fairchild had an accident with a shotgun and blew her thumb "back over my hand"; she pulled her thumb back in place, tried to tape shut a three-inch gash, and, when that didn't work, got a needle and thread and sewed it up.

The matter-of-fact tone with which people describe accidents is echoed in Elinore Stewart's account of a neighbor woman treating her hired man. He had mashed his fingernail and neglected to take care of it; gangrene set in. She sat him down and told him one could tell whether there was danger of blood poisoning if the patient put his hand on a block of wood and stared at the sun. As he did so, she "chopped off the black, swollen finger," gave the man morphine and whiskey for shock, and, with a razor, laid open the green streak running up his arm, immersed the whole arm in a solution of bichloride of mercury, and then dressed the wounds with absorbent cotton soaked in olive oil and carbolic acid.

The illnesses were not only physical. Repeatedly homesteaders mentioned feeling dwarfed by the immensity of the plains. This sense of insignificance, coupled with brutally hard work, poverty, and loneliness, made many declare, like Maggie Brown, "I would give 5 years of my life if I had never seen this state [Colorado]." Men were not exempt from this depression. Howard Ruede wrote, "If there is anything I hate, it is to have to work alone—without a human being or animal in sight." Occasionally this loneliness blossomed into full-blown insanity, as is described in Ole Rolvaag's novel, *Giants in the Earth*. The character Beret grew "more sober . . . more locked up" within herself, while a "heavy heart lay all the time" in her bosom. Grace Fairchild describes "one of our neighbors [who] lost his mind, and his wife kept him busy carrying . . . coal from one side of the basement to another, day after day" (Jones, 69–70, 143–45, 200–201).

To read about health and medicine on the colonial frontier of North America, see the entries on the Colonial Frontier and New England in the section "Health and Medicine" in chapter 4 ("Intellectual Life") in volume 4 of this series.

FOR MORE INFORMATION

Ambrose, S. E. *Undaunted Courage: Meriwether Lewis, Thomas Jefferson, and the Opening of the American West*. New York: Simon & Schuster, 1996.

Jones, M. E. *Daily Life on the Nineteenth Century American Frontier*. Westport, Conn.: Greenwood Press, 1998.

Wyman, W. D. *Frontier Woman: The Life of a Woman Homesteader on the Dakota Frontier*. River Falls: University of Wisconsin-River Falls Press, 1972.

VICTORIAN ENGLAND

The Victorian era was not a healthy one for the English. The leading disease in the 19th century was tuberculosis. It was responsible for one-sixth of all deaths in 1838; although somewhat less common by 1900, it was still the most frequent single cause of death. Tuberculosis—rather than the dangers of childbirth—was the real reason that so many mothers died young: it accounted for half of all deaths in women between age 15 and 35.

Chronic pulmonary tuberculosis was usually called consumption. Its symptoms are fatigue, weakness, night sweats, loss of appetite, wasting, and coughing. In the 19th century, patients survived anywhere from a few months to several years before they died. Opium was used to control the cough. Rest and a healthy diet helped slow the disease; periods of natural remission sometimes led to false hopes of a cure. People who could afford it extended their lives by taking long sea voyages or moving to warm climates. Italy, Egypt, California, and the South Seas were all popular.

INTELLECTUAL LIFE

HEALTH & MEDICINE

United States, 1850-1865

United States, Western Frontier

Victorian England

India

Latin America

Drawings and prints of Florence Nightingale, like this one printed in the February 24, 1855, edition of the *Illustrated London News,* were popular with the British public during the Crimean War. Courtesy of The Library Company of Philadelphia.

Tuberculosis was not so easily recognized when it infected bones and joints. Scrofula, marked by swollen glands and skin ulcers, was another form of the disease. Fast-moving cases of tuberculosis could be confused with typhus. Other names used for tubercular diseases were asthenia, inflammation of the lungs, hectic fever, gastric fever, and decline.

Until the bacillus that causes tuberculosis was discovered in 1882, the disease was thought to be hereditary. It did often strike several members of a family—especially the ones who did the nursing or spent a lot of time in the invalid's room. (The germs are spread through the air, especially by coughing.) Hospitals generally refused to take tubercular patients. People who could not be cared for at home were sent to the workhouse infirmary.

Tuberculosis was so widespread that almost everyone must have been exposed to it. Those who fell ill were most likely to be overworked, poorly nourished, and confined indoors in badly ventilated spaces. Servants, seamstresses, miners, potters, and married women were especially apt to die of tuberculosis. The disease grew less deadly after the end of the century when improved nutrition and better general health made people less susceptible to germs.

Epidemic diseases seemed worse in the Victorian period than they had for several centuries. Crowded urban conditions allowed them to spread quickly—moreover, better diagnoses and record keeping made people aware of the problem. The first great victory was the conquest of smallpox. The effectiveness of vaccination had already been demonstrated; and after epidemics in 1837–40 and 1848–49, Parliament passed a series of acts making vaccination free and (later) compulsory. Although many people continued to resist the frightening prospect of being injected with a disease to promote immunity, better publicity

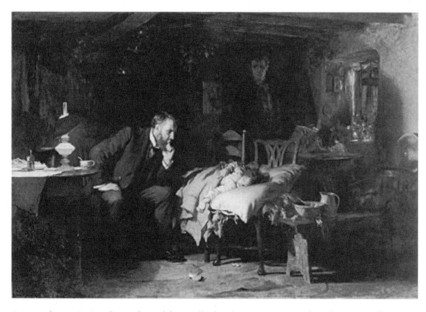

A popular painting by Luke Fildes called "The Doctor" (1891) shows a physician watching over a sick child in an era when doctors made house calls. Tate Gallery, London/Art Resource, N.Y.

and enforcement virtually eliminated the threat of smallpox after a final epidemic in 1870–73.

The term fever applied to many illnesses. Epidemics of typhus and typhoid appeared from time to time. Because it spread in crowded places, typhus was known as Irish fever, goal fever, ship fever, and putrid fever; it is, in actuality, an infection of the blood carried from person to person by body lice. The symptoms of typhus were often confused with those of typhoid, an intestinal disease spread by contaminated food or water. (Typhoid caused the death of Prince Albert in 1861.) Influenza and scarlet fever were often fatal, not only because there were no effective treatments but also because of lowered resistance owing to poor nutrition. Diphtheria (sometimes called inflammation of the throat or putrid sore throat) killed between 15 percent and 25 percent of the children who caught it. An especially widespread epidemic struck in 1855–56.

Cholera aroused terror in 1848–49, in 1853–54, and in 1866. The disease first spread from India across Europe to England in 1831. Its cause was unknown; there was no treatment; and about half the people who caught cholera died of it. Death could occur very quickly (within a few hours) but more often came after several days of stomach pains, vomiting, and diarrhea.

We now know that cholera is spread through food or water contaminated by sewage that contains infected human wastes. Because germs were not yet discovered in early Victorian times, scientifically minded physicians who paid attention to the available evidence thought that cholera and other intestinal problems were caused by miasmas, or bad smells. Opposing that common assumption, William Budd and John Snow argued in 1849 that cholera was "a living organism . . . which multiplied in the intestine." In 1854, Snow traced a large number of cholera cases to a single London pump and argued that water carried the disease.

Despite Snow's prestige (he was the anesthetist who administered chloroform to Queen Victoria during the birth of her eighth child in 1853), most doctors rejected his analysis of cholera. But although the miasma theory was wrong, it led to a number of practical improvements. To prevent bad odors, drainage was improved, sewage was treated, and manure piles and rotting garbage were removed. Cities smelled better—and, coincidentally, the bacteria found in decomposing garbage and untreated sewage were less likely to contaminate the water supply.

Even when Louis Pasteur published the germ theory of disease in

This illustration from the April 27, 1872, edition of the *Illustrated London News* shows the East London Hospital for Children, where poor sick children were nursed back to health. Courtesy of The Library Company of Philadelphia.

1861, many sensible people (including scientists) refused to accept it. Why should disease be blamed on organisms that no one could see, when cleaning up smelly refuse heaps had lessened the incidence of illness? In the effort to eliminate odors, people began paying more attention to bathing and washing their clothes—and thus got rid of the fleas and lice that spread other diseases such as typhus. By 1890, however, research with microscopes had identified the organisms responsible for tuberculosis, cholera, rabies, typhoid, and diphtheria. Although treatments that would safely kill the bacteria without harming the patient were not yet in sight, the miasma theory of disease was abandoned.

Other ailments were related to living conditions and occupational hazards. Rickets (caused by lack of sunlight and insufficient vitamin D in the diet) stunted the growth and twisted the limbs of working-class children. Well-to-do men's overconsumption of meat, wine, and rich sauces led to painful cases of gout (which swells joints, especially in the toes) and to the apoplexy (stroke) that resulted from high blood pressure. Smoky and polluted air caused the chronically inflamed nose, throat, and sinuses known as catarrh. In wintertime, a day or two of dense fog that trapped the smoke always led to a sharp increase in deaths from pneumonia and bronchitis.

Lung diseases were widespread in factories where the air was thick with cotton dust or metal fragments, as well as among coal miners. The phosphorous used to make matches ate away at workers' teeth and jawbones. Mercury and arsenic sickened the workers in many industries. Arsenic, indeed, was used so extensively in color printing, fabrics, carpets, wallpapers, bookbinding, and other everyday products that it may have caused much of the headache and nausea that are mentioned so frequently in Victorian diaries. Lead-based pigments caused painters' colic—and lead in the air near pottery factories must have done a great deal of unrecognized damage to babies and children (Mitchell, *Daily Life*, 193–96).

To read about family life in Chaucer's England, see the entry on Europe in the section "Health and Medicine" in chapter 4 ("Intellectual Life") in volume 2 of this series; for Elizabethan England, see the entry on England in the section "Health and Science" in chapter 4 ("Intellectual Life") in volume 3 of this series; for 18th-century England, see the entry on England in the section "Health and Medicine" in chapter 4 ("Intellectual Life") in volume 4 of this series; for 20th-century Europe, see the Europe entry in the section "Health and Medicine" in chapter 4 ("Intellectual Life") in volume 6 of this series.

INTELLECTUAL
LIFE
|
HEALTH & MEDICINE
|
United States,
1850-1865

United States,
Western Frontier

Victorian England

India

Latin America

FOR MORE INFORMATION

Haley, B. *The Healthy Body and Victorian Culture*. Cambridge: Harvard University Press, 1978.
Mitchell, S. *Daily Life in Victorian England*. Westport, Conn.: Greenwood Press, 1996.
Mitchell, S., ed. *Victorian Britain: An Encyclopedia*. New York: Garland Press, 1998.

INDIA

The two major traditional forms of Indian medicine are Siddha, which is from the South of India, and Ayurveda, which is more frequently practiced in the North.

Both systems date back to Vedic times, around five thousand years ago. They were created by the ancient sages and developed over time. Both systems are based on the medicinal properties in plants. The Vaids, or practitioners of these forms of medicine, are Brahmins who earn their role through birthright and are said to be descended from the sages who first created the philosophy.

There are several aspects of this system of medicine that distinguish it from other approaches to health care. Some of the main elements of traditional Indian medicine include a focus on establishing and maintaining balance of the life energies within us, rather than focusing on individual symptoms. Another major element is recognition of the unique constitutional differences of all individuals, and therefore different regimens are recommended for different types of people. Although two people may appear to have the same outward symptoms, their energetic constitutions may be very different and therefore call for very different remedies. Finally, the ancient Ayurvedic physicians realized the need for preserving the alliance of the mind and body, and ways of nurturing the psyche form an important part of this system. Ayurveda seeks to heal the fragmentation and disorder of the mind-body complex and restore wholeness and harmony to the individual.

Traditional Indian medicine incorporates a large number of drugs and vegetable samples. Indian medical practitioners employed mercury, gold, zinc, iron, and arsenic in their pharmaceutical preparations. Inoculation and hydropathy were applied in various forms. Leprosy, epilepsy, and insanity were some of the illnesses treated with these preparations. The study of poisons, such as snake venom, also formed a major part of these medical systems.

Traditional Indian medicine is based on a perception of the universe as different forms of manifested energy. These same fundamental energies are believed to be in food and herbs. The classification of food and herbs according to their individual actions or energies is how these systems use food and herbs to restore balance to the body.

While these systems have an advanced pharmacology, food is used before medicine to treat illness. For example, yogurt is considered to have a cooling effect, so it is often given to bring down a fever. Yogic exercise and meditation is also considered to contribute to the overall balance of the body. Because it was not always possible to extract the active ingredients of a plant or herb, recipes often combine several plants with specific therapeutic effects. Formulas often have as many as 15 to 20 ingredients to achieve the desired effect.

The spiritual element is also an important part of traditional Indian medicine. It is thought that to achieve balance in the body, religion must play a role. Therefore much of the practices involved in traditional Indian medicine, such as yoga and meditation, are connected to reverence of the gods.

During the medieval period, Muslim invaders introduced a medical system known as Unani Tibb. The practitioners of Unani Tibb are called Hakims and, like the Vaids,

---

📷 *Snapshot*

The First Aim of Yoga

It is not possible to make a foundation in yoga if the mind is restless. The first thing needed is quiet in the mind. Also to merge the personal consciousness is not the first aim of the yoga: the first aim is to open it to a higher spiritual consciousness, and for this also a quiet mind is the first need. (Sri Aurobindo Ghose)

earn their role through birthright. As in the Siddha and Ayurvedic systems, Unani Tibb is based on the medicinal properties in plants. This system had a major effect on Ayurvedic medicine and vice versa, as practitioners of the two systems cooperated and learned from each other. To this day many forms of Ayurvedic medicine incorporate elements of Unani Tibb. However, there is a movement to keep this ancient Indian practice pure, as it was prior to both Muslim and European influence.

During the medieval period veterinary science became an important element of medicine. There are some treatises on diseases common to elephants and their causes and remedies. Horses, cows, and other domesticated animals were also the subject of medical study during this time.

During the early colonial period, there were two classes of medical attendants whose job was to help the British doctors. The first were the apothecaries who were Englishmen by birth, or of European descent. The second were the dressers, who were generally Indians and received no formal medical training. The colonial government realized the benefit of training Indians in Western medicine.

In 1822 the colonial government proposed a medical school with the dual purpose of teaching both the Western and Indian systems of medicine. Some medical classes were also introduced at other types of institutions such as cultural centers in the major cities. In early 1826 Mount Stuart Elphinstone, then governor of Bombay, founded a medical school. The object of the school was to educate Indians in Western medicine and then send them out into the villages to practice. However, as the colonial government began to direct a growing amount of funds towards military endeavors, this project slowly disappeared. The school was abolished in 1832.

The next attempt at a medical school in India proved much more successful. In 1835 the Calcutta Medical College was founded. The school was open to anyone, regardless of caste. The medical profession ceased to be the birthright of a Vaid or a Hakim. Over the next decade, several other medical schools opened in the major cities. As a result, there emerged a population of indigenous doctors practicing Western medicine.

Towards the end of the century there was a growing movement to reject Western and Muslim forms of medical practice and revert to a pure form of Ayurvedic medicine. This was part of a larger movement of Indian nationalism that, in the struggle for independence from colonial rule, sought to weed out later additions to the subcontinent and took pride in the memory of an advanced civilization, which had existed before the arrival of the Muslims.

~Dana Lightstone

FOR MORE INFORMATION

Ayurvedic Foundations. <http://www.ayur.com/>.

Ayurvedic Press, ed. *Textbook of Ayurveda*. Tucson, Ariz.: Ayurvedic Press, 2001.

Sri Aurobindo Ghose. *Birth Centenary Library*. 30 vols. Pondicherry, India: Sri Aurobindo Ashram, 1970–76.

Zysk, K. G. *Religious Medicine: The History and Evolution of Indian Medicine*. Los Angeles: Transaction Publications, 1993.

LATIN AMERICA

INTELLECTUAL
LIFE
|
HEALTH & MEDICINE
|
United States,
1850-1865

United States,
Western Frontier

Victorian England

India

Latin America

During the 19th century, Latin American ideologies and practices regarding health and medicine underwent great change. The rapid growth of urban areas led to changes in sanitary practices, with a growing emphasis placed on hygiene, and to health issues becoming the object of state regulation. Although the region saw many advances in health, many of the benefits were unevenly enjoyed.

Despite advances, the region suffered from generally poor health in comparison to later standards. At mid-century, the average life expectancy of a Mexican was only 24 years. Diseases like smallpox, yellow fever, and dysentery ran rampant throughout the region. During the independence wars of the first quarter century, European royalist forces were five times more likely to succumb to disease than to battle wounds. In the first quarter century, Spanish forces in Venezuela and Nueva Granada (present-day Colombia) suffered a 90–96 percent fatality rate; 67 percent of British soldiers died from disease in Santo Domingo. According to a commanding officer in Riohacha in 1820, "nakedness, hunger, and the fearful spectacle of fever now comprise the sad and melancholy lot of the soldier" (Earle, 123–24).

Many people blamed the climate for such high death tolls. One newspaper cited "the excessive rain, and . . . the excessive heat" (Earle, 124). Furthermore, observers determined, if the harsh climate was to blame for so many deaths, it also explained the region's backwardness and lack of development. Indeed, climatic determinism, along with evolutionism (Darwinism), Lamarckism, and eugenics, were several of the European currents adopted by Latin Americans in their endeavors for national progress during the 19th century.

Many ideas about health and, consequently, medical practices were highly exclusionary, establishing or supporting stereotypes and stigmas about certain populations (women, blacks, Indians, and immigrants) and certain pathologized behaviors (sexuality and manual labor). Specialists classified many infectious diseases alongside criminality, prostitution, and alcoholism, which they labeled social ills that were closely connected to lax morality. For example, many Mexicans attributed the cholera epidemics of 1833 and 1850 to a punishment from God, a response to their general lack of hygiene. Argentines believed tuberculosis to be "a social sickness . . . an accident of the society" caused by social excesses. One magazine article's title read "Alcoholism + Malnutrition + Excesses = Tuberculosis" (Armus, 116).

In extreme cases, health issues served as a rationale for racist policy. During the second half of the century in Argentina, smallpox became a natural ally in the military conquest of indigenous populations. Arguing the need to "whiten the nation" and, concomitantly, eliminate "barbarians" and "savages," government representatives quarantined Indians exposed to smallpox but did not offer them treatment. In Haiti and other countries that imported African slaves, separate clinics and hospitals were established to treat slaves.

Disease also served as a positive stimulus for the modernization of cities, including Rio de Janeiro, Buenos Aires, and Santiago de Chile. Pandemics and epidemics prompted city officials to institutionalize a variety of public health policies: intensified vaccination campaigns; sanitation programs, including street cleaning and waste removal systems; and controls on certain foods and drinks. By the end of the century, many health services and policies had national reach, falling under the jurisdiction of ministries of education, the interior, and justice (Cueto, 14–15, 18).

The 19th century also saw the formation in Latin America of new bacteriology institutes and medical academies. Bahia, Brazil, for example, established its first medical department in 1808 and began offering degrees in the 1830s. Existing programs introduced new disciplines, including anatomy. By the second half of the century, many Latin American nations trained their own doctors, although they continued to follow Western European educational traditions (Peard, 32; Cueto, 14).

A variety of informal associations also existed. Some assumed control of hospitals and asylums, while others launched campaigns against particular illnesses. Still others, such as the *Escuela Tropicalista Bahiana*, conducted research and contributed to debates about parasitology and tropical disease. Interested parties followed the debates of the time in numerous medical journals, such as the *Gazeta Medica da Bahia*.

Although many parts of the region modernized urban hospitals during this period, the continued low quality of care resulted in low demand for services. One observer noted that the Santa Marta hospital in Colombia was "lacking doctors, medicines, in short, everything" (Earle, 128). In 1849, the Mexican Health Board went so far as to list the Hospital de San Miguel as a "sanitary danger," noting in particular that the "shelter [was] so miserable and insignificant" (Oliver, 104).

Doctors were widely distrusted; even the elite often considered doctors "expensive quacks" (Earle, 127). This distrust, combined with doctor shortages throughout the region, and the high fees associated with doctor's visits, prompted many people to seek the services of various kinds of folk healers, such as *curanderos*, who combined Native American, African, and European medicinal traditions. Their procedures often included spiritual and magical ritual as well as herbology.

Governments often persecuted *curanderos*, perhaps because of their popularity. Mexico, for example, prohibited the practice of medicine without a license and obliged all practitioners to register with a national superior health council. In 1842, the Ministry of Justice stepped up the pressure by announcing that *curanderos* caught practicing without a degree would be pressed into military service (Huber and Sandstrom, 65).

In conclusion, the 19th century in Latin America was a time of great progress in health and medicine. General health issues, such as sanitation, became common subjects of discussion and action, and research led to better understanding of diseases and their causes and treatments. Despite these advances, many policies and services continued to discriminate along lines of class, gender, and race.

~Molly Todd

FOR MORE INFORMATION

Armus, D. "Salud y Anarquía: La Tuberculosis en el Discurso Libertario Argentino, 1870–1940." In *Salud, Cultura y Sociedad en América Latina: Nuevas Perspectivas Históricas*, ed. M. Cueto. Lima, Peru: Organización Panamericana de Salud, Instituto de Estudios Peruanos, 1996.

Brodwin, P. *Medicine and Morality in Haiti: The Contest for Healing Power.* Cambridge: Cambridge University Press, 1996.

Burns, E. B. *Latin America: A Concise Interpretive History.* 5th ed. Englewood Cliffs, N.J.: Prentice Hall, 1990.

Cueto, M. "Introducción." In *Salud, Cultura y Sociedad en América Latina: Nuevas Perspectivas Históricas,* ed. M. Cueto, 13–30. Lima, Peru: Organización Panamericana de Salúd, Instituto de Estudios Peruanos, 1996.

Di Liscia, M. S. "Viruela, Vacunación e Indígenas en la Pampa Argentina del Siglo XIX." In *Entre Médicos y Curanderos: Cultura, Historia y Enfermedad en la América Latina Moderna,* ed. D. Armus, 27–70. Buenos Aires, Argentina: Grupo Editorial Norma, 2002.

Earle, R. *Spain and the Independence of Colombia, 1810–1825.* Exeter, U.K.: University of Exeter Press, 2000.

Huber, B. R., and A. Sandstrom, eds. *Mesoamerican Healers.* Austin: University of Texas Press, 2001.

Oliver, L. V. "El Cólera y los Barrios de Guadalajara en 1833 y en 1850." In *Salud, Cultura y Sociedad en América Latina: Nuevas Perspectivas Históricas,* ed. M. Cueto, 87–109. Lima, Peru: Organización Panamericana de Salud, Instituto de Estudios Peruanos, 1996.

Peard, J. G. "Medicina Tropical en el Brasil del Siglo XIX: La 'Escuela Tropicalista Bahiana,' 1860–1890." In *Salud, Cultura y Sociedad en América Latina: Nuevas Perspectivas Históricas,* ed. M. Cueto, 31–52. Lima, Peru: Organización Panamericana de Salud, Instituto de Estudios Peruanos, 1996.

INTELLECTUAL LIFE: WEB SITES

http://www.victorianstation.com/palace.html
http://www.know-britain.com/general/education_in_england_2.html
http://www.bartleby.com/223/index.html
http://www.bartleby.com/227/index.html
http://www.narmad.com/19thcenturyindia.html
http://www.socsci.kun.nl/ped/whp/histeduc/mmiles/
http://www.rand.org/multi/parallels/SM/reed.pdf

5
MATERIAL LIFE

Material life describes all the things we use, from the houses that give us shelter to the food that sustains us, the clothes that protect us, and the items that amuse us. It also includes the luxury items that set us apart from others less fortunate than we. Studying material life is fascinating in its details: We learn that handkerchiefs were a luxury in 16th-century Europe designed to set the wealthy apart from the peasant who used a hat or sleeve, or that underwear was only widely adopted in Europe in the 18th century.

Aside from the delicious details that bring the past to life, the study of material life reveals much about society as a whole. For example, cultures that rely on rice as a major staple have to invest a great deal of labor into its cultivation, while societies that thrive on corn (maize), which is not labor-intensive, have ample spare time. People who had access to raw materials, like iron ore, developed in ways different from those that did not, and groups that had domesticated animals or large plows had different organizing principles from others. If we know what a culture uses, we know a great deal about those people's lives.

As we study material life, it is also important to remember that humans want much more than the bare necessities of life. Indeed, we are creatures of desire rather than need, and this longing has fueled much of the progress in the world. We want spices to flavor our food, not just nourishment; we want gold to adorn us as much as we want clothing to cover us. Cultures (as in the West) that have acquired a taste for change in fashion transform themselves (not necessarily for the better) in all areas much more rapidly than those (as in Asia) that preferred a more conservative approach to clothing. All in all, the details of our daily life matter. From the Stone Age when humans adorned themselves with cowrie shells as they wielded stone tools to the modern world shaped by high technology, humans are defined by the things we use. Our material life reveals and shapes who we are.

And we can tell a lot about Victorian life through an examination of material culture. A few themes stand out. One is class. The materials of daily life such as housing, clothes, food, drink, and technology varied according the group to which one belonged. For instance, working-class people, whether in England, India, or the United States, suffered from terrible disease epidemics. While the rich also got sick,

MATERIAL LIFE
|
FOOD

DRINK

HOUSING

FASHION

TECHNOLOGY

they had access to doctors and hospitals and could freely take off time from work. Similarly, the food people ate varied according to class. The upper classes ate more and better foods. They had access to fresh fruits and vegetables that not only made them healthier but also (as the essay on English food illustrates) taller. Another theme that runs through this section on material life is the importance that race played in material life. African and African American slaves in the American South lived without many of the basic necessities of life. Their housing was poor, as was their diet. Finally, one must pay attention to how culture affects material life. In India, the English colonial government imposed Western material life, with its railroads, factories, and machines. As Indians began to struggle for their independence, one of their goals was the return of native material culture such as clothes and food. Although the materials of our daily lives are essential, they are also contested, which is an important aspect of the 19th century.

FOR MORE INFORMATION

Braudel, F. *The Structures of Everyday Life*. New York: Harper & Row, 1979.
Diamond, J. *Guns, Germs, and Steel*. New York: Norton, 1997.

MATERIAL LIFE
|
FOOD
|
United States,
1850-1865

United States,
Western Frontier

Victorian England

India

Latin America

Food

Food is so central to daily life that it is often overlooked in history: but not here. The entries that follow are among the longest in this encyclopedia and accurately reflect the importance of food. Not only does it give us fuel to go about our business but also it nicely reflects social issues such as class, and political issues such as the Civil War. Also, watch closely for cross-cultural comparisons. For example, how did the American diet compare with the English diet in the Victorian era? Be sure to watch for key variables such as caloric intake and vitamins.

If there was one major theme about 19th-century food, it was that one's class and job mattered. Take for instance the basic diet of the English working class. They regularly consumed bread, potatoes, and tea (tea being cheaper than beer and safer than water that had not been boiled). At most, they had meat once or twice a week. Toward the end of the century as refrigeration methods improved, urban workers added more meats, preserves, and dairy into their diet. Yet the vast majority of the working class ate simply and not that often. Even in the United States, such conditions existed. Gathering and cooking food on the frontier was one of the most important daily jobs. In fact, the cook, or Cookie, was often one of the highest paid laborers on the cattle drive, in the mines, or on the exploring party. Given the nature of the kitchens, food was simple, often cooked all together, and increasingly, by the end of the century, from a can. The results of this diet were clear to anyone. Working-class people were not as healthy as the upper classes. Moreover, they tended to be shorter. To the modern eye, this is a clear indication that working people did not receive the same amount of calories and nutrients as the rich. To the rich, especially in England, this was a sign of the genetic inferiority of those who did manual labor.

The rich tended to have a varied diet of meat, fruit, and vegetables. They also ate in ways that working people could not. For example, breakfast for those living on an English country estate began at 10:00 A.M. and included such things as fresh fruit, bacon, eggs, cold meats, and fresh bread. Lunch was at 2:00 P.M. and was generally hot (as compared to working-class lunches, which were generally cold). Following tea at 4:00 P.M., fashionable dinner was at 7:30 P.M. and again provided meats, fresh vegetables, and dessert. The diet of the rich was also expanded when entertaining. Social dinners were quite unlike anything the working classes ate.

Aside from illustrating class distinctions, food was central to one of the greatest conflagrations of the 19th century. At the beginning of the American Civil War, both sides had ample supplies of food. However, by the end of the war, food was scarce in the Confederacy. Moreover, the South had lost many of its best cooks as African American chefs deserted Confederate lines to join the Union Army. Although Confederate soldiers were not starving, they did not enjoy the same foods as their Union counterparts. To our tastes, Union food probably would not be appealing. The two basic staples were hardtack, an indestructible biscuit, and salted pork, which was stored in barrels and rolled out into strips for eating. And yet, the truism held for the Civil War: armies travel on their stomachs. The South was not able to match the production and supply of food for its soldiers and this contributed to the loss of the war.

What is suggested in the Civil War entry is made clear in the entry on Indian food. Cuisine has always been regional. Just as food in the American South differed from its Northern counterpart, so did food differ among India's regions. The English tended to lump Indian food together. But in fact there is no such thing as curry. Rather there are a myriad of different traditional spices in Indian cooking. Depending on where one ate in India, the actual mix of seasonings varied greatly. What is true generally about Indian food was its transcultural popularity. The British (and later other Westerners) loved Indian cuisine and quickly adopted it into their diet.

In Latin America, the growth of industry drew many peasants to the cities where low wages and high prices made it increasingly difficult for the working poor to feed themselves and their families. As a result, by the end of the century workers' groups began to agitate for government action on their behalf.

As a historical experiment, after reading the entries in this section, go out and try to find the food mentioned. Which ones do you prefer over the others?

UNITED STATES, 1850–65

The federal soldier had the most abundant food allowance of any fighting man in the world at the time, and shortages were commonly short-lived. Most of the food ration was grown in the North and shipped to the theater of operations, by using a diverse network of railways and roads and by taking advantage of an almost un-

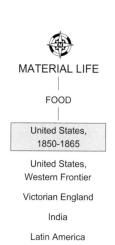

MATERIAL LIFE

FOOD

United States,
1850-1865

United States,
Western Frontier

Victorian England

India

Latin America

challenged ability to ship supplies by water. The soldiers commonly referred to food as grub.

Southern soldiers, serving in the midst of a largely agricultural area, began the war with sufficient foodstuffs. However, living off the land and relying on seasonal harvests led alternately to a superabundance of food or almost none. The Confederacy was hampered in its effort to ship foodstuffs by a lack of adequate railway facilities, by an inability to maintain control of the major water arteries within its own territory, and by the increasingly successful interdiction efforts of federal forces. "Sometimes there was an abundant issue of bread, and no meat; then meat in any quantity, and no flour or meal; sugar in abundance, and no coffee to be had for love or money."

"A soldier in the Army of Northern Virginia was fortunate when he had his flour, meat, sugar, and coffee all at the same time and in proper quantity." Although blessed with widespread fields tended by an army of slaves, most plantations produced cash crops of tobacco or cotton, not food. Foodstuffs were provided predominantly by small farms with few or no slaves. With the increased demand for manpower on the battlefield, white Southern farmers were increasingly becoming fighters, leaving the farm work to less productive old men, boys, and women. The farms of the Shenandoah Valley in Virginia and of middle Tennessee served as breadbaskets for the Rebel army for almost four years. Most farm families in these areas managed to raise a garden crop or fatten a hog specifically for the troops, and they gladly shared their food surplus with them when they had it. Many citizens gave handouts to soldiers from their own tables; and city dwellers reduced the number of their daily meals in an effort to support the cause.

Feeding the troops required a massive supply operation, as illustrated by this drawing of a New York City wharf in 1861.

Standard rations were issued in bulk by the company. The company cooks were generally appointed, and arrangements were made for company cooking with company cooking utensils. In his basic kit each Civil War soldier had a tin cup and plate as well as a spoon, knife, and fork that he kept in his haversack. One federal private recalled his first company meal: "The rice was badly burned and unedible; the hardtack, the first we had ever seen, was of good quality but we had not yet learned to appreciate its value. The pork was very salty, and the coffee had not been made by an expert. . . . It seemed at first that we would starve."

Southern men initially formed messes, each consisting of about 10 men, many employing a black man as a cook. These cooks quickly disappeared from the line of march, and rarely were any soldiers other than officers so served. A Virginia foot soldier provided an insight into early Rebel eating etiquette once the black cook was gone. "We made a fire under the shade of a tree, made up our bread of meal, sliced our fat meat, and commenced to cook. In about two minutes both meat and bread were burned on one side. . . . We were disgusted; but the next day we had better success, and in a few days we got along all right."

Initially the government in Richmond ignored the need for the wide-scale provision of camp equipment, and little beyond firearms, bayonets, and canteens was issued. On the other hand, the federal authorities encumbered their troops with several standard items of camp equipment, including kettles, mess pans, and coffee-pots. A set of metal crutches with a sturdy crossbar served to hang the pots over the fire. The kettles were made of tinned sheet iron in sizes that allowed them to be nested within each other for ease of transportation. Large iron mess pans were used to serve the food. The company mess kettles were provided to make coffee, soups, and stews, but in typical soldierly fashion, they proved excellent for washing clothes. The mess pans were made to fry pork and bacon, yet they also served as washbasins. Such double duty was less than polite society would have tolerated, but for the soldiers any other course was considered impractical.

Each company was initially issued a mule upon which the company cookware was to be carried on the march. Camp cooking equipment was cumbersome and took up much of the limited space assigned to each company in the regimental baggage train. As the mules required careful attention, they quickly disappeared from the line of march; and the company cooking gear, whether through design or by accident, fre-quently deteriorated or was pur-posely abandoned. The concept of company cooking quickly disap-peared under all but the most favor-able of circumstances.

In this manner both Johnny Reb and Billy Yank found themselves in surprisingly similar situations. Each soldier was obliged to use only the limited array of cookware that he could carry. A coffee boiler of some sort was considered a necessity, and any utensil that could serve as a fry-ing pan became indispensable. Small groups of men would pool their money to purchase a coffee boiler or a real frying pan from the sutler, and each would take turns carrying it on the march. The per-son so designated often was entitled

Cut off from supply lines, Union soldiers had to forage for their food. In this drawing from *Frank Leslie's Illustrated Newspaper,* ca. 1863–64, troops celebrate when foragers bring back fresh meat and vegetables.

to the utensil's first use when camp was made. If one of the owners was wounded, killed, or otherwise removed from the companionship of his fellow investors, his share could be sold to an outsider.

A particularly common cookware solution was to unsolder the seam between the two halves of an extra canteen acquired from the battlefield. Each half served as a tolerable lightweight frying pan or plate and could be carried strapped over the canteen. Tin cans with wire handles served as tolerable coffee boilers. As with the soldiers of most wars, Civil War soldiers quickly adopted any serviceable device that proved light to carry and easy to replace.

The standard Civil War ration provided few vitamins or complete proteins.

Hundreds of officers and men were engaged in the day-to-day duty of providing food for the troops. The overall responsibility fell to the Subsistence Department in Washington, headed by a commissary general who contracted for the various types of rations with private manufacturers or packers. The foodstuffs were then apportioned to the respective army commissaries, and by them, in turn, to the corps, brigade, and regimental commissaries. They were then distributed to the troops. Washington continued, from the beginning of the war until its end, to let contracts to private suppliers for all of its rations in this manner.

The Richmond government tried to institute a Confederate Subsistence Department, but found that the independent spirit of the state governments hampered such unified efforts. Although the problem existed in different degrees from state to state, supplies were greedily guarded for consumption by only the troops of the state that provided them. Individual states exacerbated the supply problem by competing for the same scarce resources. As Confederate currency became inflated and prices soared, the Subsistence Department found it necessary to purchase foodstuffs with cotton bonds. The secretary of war made no secret of the fact that it was not possible to provision the troops as Richmond wished, yet the soldiers seem to have taken the shortages in stride.

The government rations distributed to the troops varied slightly with the season and the availability of local supply. Nonetheless, a complete list of all the possibilities is short. These included hardtack, coffee, sugar, soft bread, flour, rice, cornmeal, dried peas, dried beans, desiccated vegetables or dried fruits, fresh or dried potatoes (called chips), salt pork, bacon or ham, pickled beef (called salt horse), fresh meat, and occasionally onions, molasses, salt, pepper, and vinegar.

With only a rudimentary understanding of balanced nutrition, it is a wonder that any soldier survived the war on such a diet. However, the standard ration provided a daily average of over 3,000 calories, heavy in carbohydrates and fats, but providing few vitamins or complete proteins.

The vitamin deficiencies and the lack of protein could have been devastating. An unrelieved diet of cornmeal and salt pork, while sufficient in calories, would ultimately produce such diseases as scurvy and pellagra. Fresh meats will provide protein but cannot afford sufficient protein to make up the deficit alone. Both beans and cornmeal are high protein sources but are individually incomplete in amino acids; yet, in combination they are complementary and provide all the essentials needed to sustain health. Rice and peas are another complementary pair with similar characteristics. In offering these pairs among a small variety of foodstuffs, the government unwittingly supplied a nearly complete diet to its soldiers, yet the unresolved question of a lack of essential vitamins had serious health consequences that cost many lives.

The lack of variety in the soldiers' diet resulted from the need to keep the rations from spoiling while they were being shipped and stored for use. In the absence of refrigeration, meats, if not freshly slaughtered, had to be salted or pickled; and breads, vegetables, and fruits, if not for immediate consumption, had to be dried. Salting and drying retarded the growth of bacteria, as did pickling, smoking, and sugar curing. With the exception of meals aboard naval vessels, there is an amazing absence from the records of cheese being issued as a regular part of the ration.

Some canned foods were utilized by the army. The technology of preserving foods in tinned iron cans had been developed by the French in the first decade of the century and was first patented in America by Ezra Daggett in 1825. The heat used in preparing the contents destroyed the bacteria, and the sealed container prevented new contamination. Although the process was decades old, some enlisted men saw their very first canned foods during the war.

The officers' mess and hospitals seemed to have had a significant variety of canned items, but they were seldom available to the troops unless they were purchased from the sutlers. By 1861 the list of common canned items had expanded to include several types of meat, peas, sardines, peaches, and other fruits; but the most common canned item encountered in the field was condensed milk, much of which was purchased by contract from Gail Borden.

There were two standard rations in the federal army. One was the camp ration, and the other was the campaign or marching ration. The camp ration tended to be more diverse and, for one soldier in the federal army, consisted of meat (1 1/4 lbs. of salted or fresh beef, or 3/4 lb. of pork or bacon) and bread (1 lb., 6 oz. of soft bread or flour, or 1 lb. of hardtack, or 1 1/4 lbs. of cornmeal). He also received approximately 1 1/2 ounces of dried vegetables, rice, dried potatoes, peas, or beans. Fresh potatoes were to be had, but fresh vegetables were rare and allotted in only very small quantities. Salt and pepper were allowed in minuscule quantities. About 1/2 ounce of vinegar was provided for each man daily to help prevent scurvy. About the same amount of molasses was allowed when available.

The marching ration consisted of 1 lb., or 8 crackers, of hard bread; 3/4 lb. of salt pork, or 1 1/4 lbs. of fresh meat; sugar; coffee; and salt. The beans, rice, and so on, were not issued to the soldier when on the march, as he could not carry them. The other parts of the camp ration "were forfeited, and reverted to the government." The revenue from the uncollected rations was supposed to revert to the regiment and be distributed to the rank and file as cash, but few soldiers saw a cent of the money. This was seen by some observers as "an injustice to the rank and file."

The soldier added both quantity and variety to his diet in many ways. Gifts of food from home were always welcome. These included hams, smoked meats and cheeses, pickles, onions, potatoes, chocolate, condensed milk, sugar, salt butter, coffee, tea, cakes, cookies, applesauce, and preserves. Due to delays in delivery, many times the baked goods proved to be stale, the butter rancid, and the preserves, put up in glass jars, too fragile to ship to the front lines without breaking. Intoxicating liquors were frowned upon by the army hierarchy but were often smuggled through hidden in other packages.

When fresh meat was not available, the enlisted men were provided with a basic preserved meat ration of pork—boiled ham, salt pork, or bacon being most common. The South quickly realized that it would experience a meat shortage, and Richmond established an extensive government pork-packing program in close proximity to the rail and river transportation of Tennessee. These plants and their associated salt works were constantly in danger of capture or destruction by federal forces.

Federal forces also relied heavily on preserved pork. Pork's prominence as a foodstuff, when compared to preserved beef, did not lie in any intrinsic nutritional value, although the high fat content provided an excellent source of caloric intake. It was simply easier to preserve than beef and tasted better than pickled beef, which was so poor and unpalatable that the soldiers called it salt horse. No effort was made to comply with dietary restrictions due to individual medical or religious preferences.

In camp boiled ham was often pulled from a barrel into which it had been packed for some months in a thick covering of grease that came from the boiling. The meat came out in long, "unappetizing strips," and "when brought to the surface the sound of the suction was like the noise made when one pulled his feet out of Virginia mud." The grease was scraped off and saved by many soldiers to be used as an ingredient in other recipes. The meat could be fried, roasted, or eaten sliced between two pieces of soft bread or with hardtack.

Salt pork was easy to make and had been used since colonial times as a mainstay of the diet for soldiers and sailors. Salt pork was a favorite among veteran soldiers, who sometimes declined fresh beef for a good piece of salt pork, but recruits had to learn to ignore its overwhelmingly salty flavor and to appreciate its nutritional qualities. The amount of salt used in its processing was staggering, but salt pork could last, unspoiled, for a long time in a sealed barrel. However, once a barrel was opened, the meat had to be used quickly or it would spoil. One reason for the spoiling of salted meats in transit was the lack of good barrels, which sometimes opened between the staves. Southern armies suffered severely from increasing numbers of poorly made barrels as experienced coopers, white and black, were drafted to fill the ranks on the firing lines or streamed north to freedom. So great was the domestic war demand that there developed a worldwide shortage of quality American barrel staves.

Bacon was a common foodstuff reminiscent of home cooking that proved highly acceptable to the tastes of most soldiers. Bacon was made from the sides or flanks of the hog, kept in a slab, soaked in brine, and smoked. This operation cured the meat and so retarded the growth of bacteria that bacon could be kept for long periods of time. Thick slices could be cut from a single slab for several days with no noticeable deterioration of the remainder, and several rations of bacon could be carried in a haversack, wrapped in an oilcloth, without spoiling for some time.

Fresh bread was almost unheard of on campaign in the field. However, several soldiers attest to its presence in established camps. The federal government provided a few portable regimental ovens and built bakeries where they were practical. "Our regiment built a large, double log cabin for a bakery, with brick ovens, and a professional baker from the ranks took charge. We drew flour, and every day had an abundance of as fine fresh bread as was ever laid on a millionaire's table." One soldier wrote home of how he could not live by bread alone: "Of late we have drawn flour and soft bread. The flour we make biscuits and pancakes of. I think I can beat the natives making wheat pancakes. I get them as light and nice as you please and we think they make pretty good eating. But the hardest of it is we have to pay 60 cents per pound for all the butter we get. This makes it pretty high living for a soldier."

The staple ration of the federal army was a square cracker, 3. 1/8 by 2 7/8 inches, with small holes in its top, known as hardtack. Referred to as both army bread and biscuit, it was a very dry, incredibly hard product without leavening and bore little resemblance to either. The army was not being purposely cruel to its soldiers by giving them hardtack to eat. Hardtack was not a new product. It was used as ship's bread for centuries.

The army was not being purposely cruel to its soldiers by giving them hardtack to eat.

The dryness and hardness were functional characteristics. It was dry when packaged to keep the cracker from spoiling and hard so it could be carried in the soldier's haversack without crumbling.

Hardtack provided a good-quality ration when combined with other foods, but it took some time for the soldiers to learn to appreciate its value. Nine to ten crackers comprised a daily ration weighing only about one pound. It was therefore easy for soldiers to carry several days' rations with them in their haversacks. Hardtack was made edible by soaking it in water or coffee or by cracking it—a process that sometimes required a rock and a gun butt. Water-softened crackers were sometimes compared to gutta-percha, a sticky natural material that becomes just soft enough when boiled to be molded into shape. Crumbled hardtack was sometimes mixed with pork grease to form a hot meal called skillygalee. Soldiers with strong teeth were known to nibble at the edges of the dry cracker in camp or on the march. One soldier found this process like "biting into a wooden shingle" with the flavor of "wallpaper paste," but the taste could be improved by adding sugar or salt saved from other parts of the daily ration.

A soldier wrote home to his girlfriend—with some sarcasm—about the unrelenting presence of hardtack in his diet, "Nett, I have become a model cook since entering the Army, and I think you will agree with me when I tell you how many kinds of dishes I can make out of hardtack, 1st make pancakes out of them, 2nd hoecake, 3rd flour gravy, 4th sauce, 5th coffee, 6th, fry them." An officer wrote home sarcastically, "We are living very high nowadays, have pork, hardtack and coffee for breakfast and of course for dinner coffee, hardtack, and pork for a change. Then for supper we have a little coffee, pork, and fried hardtack. . . . I am in danger of getting the gout on account of so high living."

Federal hardtack was made by machine in a factory. Plain white flour was mixed with water and a little salt into a very stiff dough. The dough was rolled thin, about one half inch, and cut into squares by machines, sometimes with the baking company's name pressed into the top, as in "U.S. Marvin's Hardtack" and "Holmes & Coutts, Army Bread, New York." The finished crackers were carefully stacked into wooden boxes in lots weighing 50 pounds. Although most hardtack was made in Baltimore, contractors were located across the North, and hardtack was often months old before it was issued to the troops. When the crackers were poor, they were either too hard, or moldy and wet, or infested with maggots and weevils. It was not unusual for a man to find the surface of his pot of coffee swimming with weevils after breaking up hardtack in it. But the pests were easily skimmed off and left no distinctive flavor behind. If a soldier cared to do so, he could expel the weevils by toasting the bread at the fire. These conditions were mostly due to exposure to the weather, as thousands of boxes marked "Army Bread" piled up at some railway station inadequately sheltered from the weather. Such wanton disregard by federal authorities rankled many Southern sympathizers conscious of their starving forces in the field.

Empty hardtack boxes were common enough in the camps. Although the boxes were sometimes used whole as stools and tables, the wood panels more often became raw material for the building of shelters. They were worked into field fortifications to hold sand and dirt in place or laid on the ground to provide better footing in the all too common mud. The planks were also used as grave markers. Few of the original boxes survived the war, as they provided a good source of firewood.

The supply-starved Confederates appreciated captured federal hardtack in place of the cornbread that was the staple of their daily diet. At times the entire Southern army seemed to run on nothing but cornbread and captured hardtack. The cornbread was usually coarse, dry, and rather tasteless. Baked loaves of cornbread were sometimes available to the troops, but most often dry, ground meal was issued from which the Confederate soldier needed to make his own bread. Without an oven he needed to resort to his ingenuity. A thick corn disk, called hoecake or ashcake, could be made by mixing cornmeal with water and salt into a thick paste in an oilcloth and baking the product in a frying pan or on a hot, flat stone. Such cakes could withstand moderate abuse in a haversack and, like hardtack, were a sight common at mealtime and during breaks along the line of march.

Cornmeal could be mixed with hot water to form a mush and was sometimes eaten with honey, molasses, or milk if they were available. Some soldiers improvised a full dinner stew called Confederate cush, or kush, of cornmeal mush, cooked meat, garlic, and bacon grease, ironically similar to a common preparation of plantation slaves. Cornmeal was also added to soups as a thickener.

Salt was as indispensable to an army as gunpowder. Besides its use in preserving foods, heavy doses of salt were needed to maintain the health of horses and in tanning leather for shoes, saddles, belts, and cartridge boxes. Common salt could be mined or retrieved by evaporating seawater. The Federals east of the Appalachian Mountains relied extensively on the saltworks at Onondaga Lake near Syracuse, New York, for this important substance. Here the brine, which welled up naturally from the floor of the lake, had provided an extensive source of salt for decades. More than nine million barrels of salt, worth in excess of $30 million, were produced in New York in 1862 alone. The captured saltworks of the Kanawha River Valley in Virginia were also important to federal forces. On the eve of the war a new source west of the mountains at the Saginaw River site in Michigan was found. The rapid wartime development of this resource yielded more than 500,000 barrels of salt annually. So successful were the Federals at processing domestic sources that Washington did not need to import foreign salt.

Southern saltworks were a priority target for the invading Federals. Only five months into the war the Southern papers began to fret over a shortage of salt. Besides hundreds of coastal evaporating operations, there were only five principal sources of salt: in Louisiana, Alabama, Virginia, and Kentucky. The major production center in the Kanawha Valley was lost to the South with the defection of western Virginia. The Louisiana saltworks were lost to occupying federal troops about halfway through the war. Saltville, Kentucky, was the largest salt supplier in the upper Confederacy, making 3,000 bushels of salt a day, and it could have supplied the needs of the entire Confederacy alone if enough workers and rail connections had been available. Saltville was continually threatened by no less than two federal armies, yet it was the only Southern provider to remain in operation throughout the conflict.

Although the troops of both armies were at times very hungry, no battle or campaign of the war was lost solely due to a lack of food, and even the Southern forces, who were often at the point of starvation, were provided with at least minimal levels of nutrition to support four years of conflict. Veteran soldiers believed that they had "reached the soldierly perfection" when two or three pieces of hardtack and some coffee could be made to satisfy their hunger for an entire day (Volo and Volo, 115–31).

To read about food in the United States in the 20th century, see the United States entries in the section "Food" in chapter 5 (Material Life) in volume 6 of this series.

FOR MORE INFORMATION

Burns, K. *The Civil War*. PBS Video, 1990. Film.
McPherson, J. M. *Battle Cry of Freedom: The Civil War Era*. New York: Oxford University Press, 1990.
Volo, D. D., and J. M. Volo. *Daily Life in Civil War America*. Westport, Conn.: Greenwood Press, 1998.

UNITED STATES, WESTERN FRONTIER

Given the hardships and difficulties of work on the frontier, people had to eat as much as possible to stay healthy and survive. Such was definitely the case for western explorers. These men consumed an enormous number of calories towing the keelboat, dragging equipment on portages, scouring the countryside for game, climbing mountains, wrestling, dancing—even just staying warm. Their appetites were enormous. A man could eat as much as nine pounds of meat a day along with whatever fruits he could find—raspberries, currants, grapes, watercress, wild onions, and artichokes—and still feel hungry.

Lewis had laid in a supply of rations at Camp Wood during the winter of 1803–4: "4,175 complete rations at $.14 each; 5,555 rations of flour at $.04 each; 100

MATERIAL LIFE
|
FOOD
|
United States,
1850-1865

United States,
Western Frontier

Victorian England

India

Latin America

gallons of whiskey at $1.28 each; 20 gallons of whiskey at $1 each; 4,000 rations of salt pork at $.04 each; plus ground corn." In addition, he had earlier requisitioned a supply of portable soup, a mixture of beans and mixed vegetables that could be reconstituted on the trail. Lewis was so enthusiastic about this soup, which "forms one of the most essential articles in the preparation" for the expedition, that he spent $289.50 on 193 pounds of the stuff, an amount higher than that for any other category of provisions and as much as he had originally estimated for his scientific instruments, arms, and ammunition. The reviews from the men were, at best, mixed.

As the expedition set out up the Missouri, a daily routine was established. Lewis divided the men into three squads, or messes, and each evening Sergeant Ordway distributed the day's provisions. These were to be cooked immediately with a portion to be reserved for the next day, as no cooking was allowed during the day. The basic menu was on a three-day cycle: hominy and lard on the first day, salt pork and flour on the second, and pork and cornmeal on the third. In part to conserve such purchased supplies and in part because the men preferred fresh meat to cold hominy and lard, hunting parties went out every day. Some meat they preserved; Clark records on June 5, 1804, that they "jerked the [deer] meat" killed yesterday.

Jefferson had asked the captains to learn what they could of the indigenous plants and animals along the route. Granted, they collected specimens of new animals, such as the prairie dog, but they also ate their way through a wide variety of species. Clark shot beaver: "the flesh of those animals the party is fond of eating;" they caught catfish: "verry fat, a quart of Oile Came out of the surpolous [surplus] fat of one of those fish." As they approached the Continental Divide, trout were plentiful; once they reached the Columbia, salmon were too, though many men got sick from dried salmon traded by the Indians. (It was probably incompletely dried, thus containing bacteria.) They ate ducks, geese, and brants—even a swan or two. When they killed a grizzly bear, always a formidable opponent, they "divided him among the party" for fresh meat but also boiled "the oil and pout it in a cask for future uce; the oil is as hard as hogs lard when cool." From bear's oil and dried meat they made a kind of pemmican. Occasionally there were treats: Lewis, assigning himself the duty of cook, boiled dried buffalo meat and "made each man large suet dumpling." At the Great Falls of the Missouri, Lewis was almost euphoric: "My fare is really sumptuous this evening; buffalo's humps, tongues, and marrowbones, fine trout, parched meal, pepper and salt, and a good appetite; the last is not . . . the least of the luxuries."

Later Lewis describes in some detail Charbonneau's *boudin (poudingue) blanc* (white gut pudding), which "we esteem one of the greatest delacies [delicacies] of the forest." Charbonneau took about six feet of the lower part of the large intestine of a buffalo, and with his thumb and fingers squeezed out "what . . . is not good to eat," though some of the flavor remained. He then stuffed it with a mixture of the hump meat and kidney suet, to which was added salt, pepper, and flour. When the ends were tied, "it is then baptised in the Missouri with two dips and a flirt, and bobbed into the kettle; from whence after it be well boiled it is taken and fryed with bears oil until it become brown, when it is ready to esswage the pangs of a keen appetite . . . such as travelers in the wilderness are seldom at a loss for."

Food would not always be so ample, however, a fact of which Lewis was acutely aware. Past the Three Forks of the Missouri he noted, on June 31, 1805: "when we have plenty of fresh meat I find it impossible to make the men take any care of it, or use it with the least frugallity, Tho' I expect that necessity will shortly teach them this art." In the mountains game became scarce. On September 6, Clark noted, "nothing to eat but berries, our flour out, and but little corn." They purchased fish and dogs from the Nez Percé, though of the latter Clark wrote, "all the Party have greatly the advantage of me in as much as they relish the flesh of the dogs." They also purchased horses from the Nez Percé, primarily as transportation, but, as Clark added, to "Eate if necessary." It soon was. The journals starting on September 14, 1805, repeatedly have entries saying, "we were compelled to kill a Colt for our men & Selves for want of meat." The first time seemed unique; they named the spot Colt Killed Creek. Descending the Columbia they traded for more dogs, dried fish, camas roots, and acorns.

After a miserable winter at Fort Clatsop—no trading ship was there from which they could requisition supplies—the return trip began, rife with food shortages. Once again they ate horses when necessary, but while crossing the Bitterroot Mountains even the horses went hungry, for the snow was still deep and often crusty from partial thaws. Roots seemed the only food until the salmon should come upstream to spawn. One creek was christened Hungry Creek. Things grew so desperate that on May 21, 1806, the remaining trade goods were divided among the men so they could bargain individually with Indians.

Such privations potentially threatened the mission. The expedition had so little food that despite the services the Nez Percé had rendered during the previous year, in addition to caring for the horses over the winter, the captains were unable to reward them. Clark wrote: "their object I believe is the expectation of being fed by us . . . however *kind as they have been* we must disappoint them at this moment as it is necessary that we should use all frugallaty as well as employ every exertion to provide meat for our journey." Hardly an enviable position for men whose charge was to bring word of the power of the Great Father and to convince the Indians of the advantages accruing from an alliance with the United States!

Lewis ordered the hunters out to "kill some . . . meat for these people whom I was unwilling to leave without giving them a good supply of provision after their having been so obliging as to conduct us through those tremendious mountains." However, this hunt was not successful. By June 29, their bear's oil was exhausted and they were reduced to "roots alone without salt." Fortunately, by July 11, they came upon a huge herd—they estimated ten thousand—of buffalo within a two-mile circle. They killed 11 animals; Lewis notes that the hump and the tongue will feed four men for one day. Nonetheless, pressing hard, almost desperate to get home before another winter set in, by September 18, the party, only 150 miles above St. Louis,

Entitled *On the Plains, Preparing to Feed (Buffalo Chip Fuel)*, this drawing by J. Goldsborough Bruff illustrates how simple dinner was on the plains, where the campfire was often fueled by buffalo chips. This item is reproduced by permission of The Huntington Library, San Marino, California, HM 8044 #16.

was subsisting on papaws (custard apples). Their enthusiastic reception on September 21, by the citizens of St. Charles—who, like most of the rest of the country had given them up for dead—made it worthwhile. Four days later in St. Louis, they enjoyed "in the evening a dinner & Ball."

For the men on the fur frontier, too, the search for food was crucial to survival. Although Ashley's account books with trappers indicate that he brought to rendezvous some products for the trappers' personal use, one could not survive from July to July on them. In his records of an early rendezvous there are repeated references to coffee, sugar, and tobacco; two for pepper; one for flour; and one for soap; such items are clearly in the category of luxuries.

Whereas salt pork, bacon, lye corn, and sea biscuit were available to men on the keelboats, men in the mountains hunted most of their own food: black bear, deer, elk, mountain sheep, raccoons, wild turkeys, and, as bees were plentiful in some locales, honey. Once Ashley noted a "good supper" of a boiled wild goose. Often there were great herds of buffalo, too, which could be shot almost at will. Occasionally this butcher shop on the hoof provided an element of danger, even in camp; General Henry Atkinson described in his journal entry for September 14, 1825, how a buffalo bull ran through camp, almost knocking down the tent of Major Stephen Watts Kearney.

Bread and vegetables were out of the question in the mountains, except for a kind of turnip root; thus, even "poor bull meat" was consumed. Osborne Russell describes a campsite during the winter of 1835–36. At any time of day one could find a fire going atop a bed of coals and ashes, a camp keeper periodically poking the ashes and rolling out "a ponderous mass of Buff beef," which, when hit with a club, "bounds five or six feet from the ground like a huge ball of gum elastic." This beating knocked off the ashes and was preparatory to hacking the meat into huge slices that the trappers would chew while sitting around the fire, looking forward to the fat cows of summer's good grass. At a more felicitous camp, he described "a large fire . . . encircled with Elk's ribs and meat cut in slices supported by sticks down which the grease ran in torrents." Other menus included a stew of bear meat and mutton seasoned with pepper and salt, roasted buffalo tongue, and Indian pemmican (dried meat and "fruit pounded together," mixed with buffalo marrow).

Such celebrations were rare. During inclement weather or when too many hunters had scared away game, mountain men would literally be starving. That—and the sheer number of calories expended in ordinary physical activity—meant well-developed appetites. When a buffalo was shot, the tongue was taken first, then the boss, a small hump on the back of the neck, the hump ribs, then the flesh between the spine and the ribs, and the "lower belly fat"—considered

Snapshot

Christmas Dinner on the American Frontier, 1838

The first dish that came on was a large tin pan 18 inches in diameter rounding full of stewed Elk meat. The next dish was similar to the first heaped up with boiled Deer meat (or as the whites would call it Venison, a term not used in the Mountains) The 3rd and 4th dishes were equal in size to the first containing a boiled flour pudding prepared with dried fruit accompanied by 4 quarts of sauce made of the juice of some sour berries and sugar. Then came the cakes followed by about six gallons of strong Coffee already sweetened with tin cups and pans to drink out of large chips or pieces of Bark Supplying the places of plates.

~[See Osborne Russell, *Journal of A Trapper*, edited by Aubrey L. Haines, (Lincoln: University of Nebraska Press, 1955); as quoted in Jones, 36.]

one of the greatest delicacies. The mountain man would probably take the liver too and such portions of the intestines as his tastes suggested. Then he would "butcher out the thigh bone and use it to crack such other bones as might provide the best marrow." Francis Chardon especially enjoyed "nuts"—the original Rocky Mountain oysters. Many whites would eat the liver raw as soon as it was butchered out, seasoning it with the gall or sometimes with gunpowder. The trapper ate whatever meat was available, from his "own moccasins, parfleche, and lariats, in 'starvin' times,' on through the wide variety of mountain game," including such special tidbits as "boiled beaver tail, 'panther,' and as an acquired taste young Oglala puppy." DeVoto notes that the mountain man boiled some cuts and seared or sautéed others; but most buffalo was slowly roasted, each man to his own fire, unless the trappers were divided into messes with their own cooks. The meat was skewered on a ramrod or a stick.

No man with more tableware than his belt-knife—gravy, juices, and blood running down his face, forearms, and shirt. He wolfed the meat and never reached repletion. Eight pounds a day was standard ration for the Hudson's Bay Company employees, but when meat was plentiful, a man might eat eight pounds for dinner, then wake a few hours later, build up the fire, and eat as much more. . . . Moreover, to the grease that stained the mountaineer's garments were added the marrow scooped from bones and the melted fat that was gulped by the pint. Kidney fat could be drunk without limit; one was more moderate with the tastier but oily belly fat, which might be automatically regurgitated if taken in quantity, although such a rejection interrupted no one's gourmandizing very long.

Nor were table manners carefully observed in the mountains. Frederick Ruxton described one extraordinary feeding. Two mountain men, seated opposite each other on epishemores, or saddle blankets, were enjoying one of the treats, *boudin* (guts), lightly seared above the fire. Squeezing the contents just ahead of their teeth, they began at opposite ends of the intestines, the pile of coiled guts between them. As the pile decreased in size, it became a kind of game between the two to make sure the other did not get more than his fair share.

Every now and then, overcome by the unblushing attempts of his partner to bolt a vigorous mouthful [the mountain man] would suddenly jerk back his head, drawing out at the same moment, by the retreating motion, several yards of *boudin* from his neighbor's stomach (for the greasy viand required no mastication and was bolted whole) and, snapping up the ravished portions, greedily swallowed them.

As with fur traders, miners too put food at the center of much of their day. For them, daily chores included hunting to supplement purchased food supplies and gathering fuel supplies—wood where it was available and buffalo chips where it was not. Those who had cook's duty had chip collecting as first chore each night, providing much amusement to their friends as they "jump[ed] from the wagon, gunny bag in hand, and made a grand rush for the largest and driest chips." It took an average of five bushels of chips to cook supper and breakfast for 12 persons. The fuel contributed to the atmosphere. "The chips burn well when dry but if damp or wet are smoky and almost fireproof," wrote one. Added another, "They emit a delicate perfume."

For a predominantly male population, cooking itself was a chore. The cook often walked ahead to the campsite in order to have supper ready when the rest arrived. Some Wolverine Rangers complained about their cook, a Mr. Bailey, who did not have supper ready even though "he had been . . . here since three o'clock." These hungry campers were perhaps oblivious to the cook's chores. After traveling as far that day as the rest of the company, the cook fetched water for coffee, however far a stream was from camp; collected fuel and made it burn, even in a downpour; and put aside his own exhaustion long enough to feed his companions, who could rest after picketing their animals. To compensate for all this extra work, cooks were excused from night guard duty.

One man, writing to his sister in Kentucky, saw something of the humor of his situation—as well as a new appreciation of women:

You would be amused to see us . . . cooking and washing—but never washing our hands. . . . I feel [I need] advice from you . . . in biscuit-making and . . . brewing coffee. . . . I have always been inclined to deride the vocation of ladies until now. But I must confess it is the most irksome I have ever tried. . . . I wish you could take supper with me, that you might judge the hardness and durability of our biscuits. I must at some time send you a recipe for making this lasting sort.

No matter who did the cooking, food was hardly what it had been at home. William Swain cited a day's menu when they were living "tolerably well." For breakfast: meat fried in batter, boiled beans, pancakes, pilot bread [ship biscuit], and coffee. For dinner: tea, rice, meat, and pilot bread. When the wagons had been lightened to ease up on the oxen and mules, food too was jettisoned; thus, later on the trail, food supplies often ran perilously short. By the time they reached the Humboldt, "many companies subsisted on rancid bacon with the grease fried out by the hot sun, musty flour, a few pinoles, some sacks of pilot bread broken and crushed and well coated with alkali, and a little coffee without sugar." Bayard Taylor notes that it was not unusual for such emigrants "to kill a quantity of rattlesnakes, with which the mountains abounded, and have a dish of them fried, for supper." John Edwin Banks recalled his delight on finding gooseberries and wild peas, which, with venison from the abundant deer in the Sierra Nevada, provided their first fresh food for most of the trip.

Meals necessary to sustain the miner's physical activity were filling but not necessarily nutritious; moreover, food was quite expensive in part because it had to be packed in at a cost of from 50 cents to 60 cents per pound. Staples included flour, salt, jerked meat, bacon, and coffee. For variety there were sometimes dried apples, stewed; boiled potatoes, sliced and fried in lard; mince pie made of "salt beef previously soaked to freshness, dried apples, molasses, and vinegar in lieu of cider." Milk was a luxury costing more than whiskey, though some ambitious miners invested in a cow or two to fill this need. One such entrepreneur, however, returned from mining to discover his cow had eaten his tent and his sweat-soaked change of clothes in its need for salt. Prentice Mulford recalls buying an entire sack of rice for variety—and economy. He did not know, however, that "rice swells amazingly." His first pot "swelled up, forced off the lid, and oozed over. Then I shoveled rice by the spoonful into everything empty which I could find in the cabin. Even the washbasin was full of half-boiled rice. Still it kept on. I saw then that I had put in too much—far too much." After repeated experiments with this astonishing grain, and a "gradually decreased appetite for rice," Mulford calculated that it would take "seven years on that Bar ere I could eat all the rice in that sack." Though told with self-deprecating humor, the incident reveals the difficulties many of the miners found in learning to live without women. Fresh fruits and vegetables, except for potatoes and occasional onions at 90 cents per pound, were virtually unheard of in the mines. In Dry Diggingsville in October 1849, a cabbage cost $1.

Food prices generally were higher in the mines than in the cities. John Banks traveled from his claim to Coloma to buy potatoes at 75 cents per pound; in the mountains they would have cost $1.50. During the winter of 1849–50 when com-munication with Sacramento was cut off by the rains, prices rose in the mines. Flour and pork cost from $1.00 to $1.50 per pound, and other things in proportion. Even in reasonably good weather, freight costs increased prices enormously. J. D. Steven-son wrote to his son-in-law in New York that a barrel of flour costing $12 in San Francisco would cost $12 more in freight to Sutter's Fort and $125 more to the nearest mine, thus costing $152 per barrel in the mountains. E. Gould Buffum cited prices in the mines during the winter of 1849–50:

Fresh fruits and vegetables were virtually unheard of in the mines.

Flour was selling at one dollar per pound, dried beef at two dollars, sugar at a dollar, coffee 75 cents, molasses four dollars per gallon, pork two dollars per pound, miserable New England rum at 50 cents per glass or eight dollars per bottle and tobacco at two dollars per pound. At these prices, the trader and transporter realized a greater profit from the miner's labour than the miner himself.

Akin to miners, the center of the cowboys' world, whether on roundup or on the trail, was the chuck wagon. Though cowboys were not unduly picky as long as their food was clean and reasonably well cooked, no outfit kept a poor cook because bad food eventually made for a grouchy crew. A good cook was prized, and often only the foreman received higher wages. Around his chuck wagon, the cook—often called Miss Sallie or Cookie—was king, though his working hours were long, sometimes leading to extreme crankiness and bizarre idiosyncrasies. A common saying on the range was that "only a fool argues with a skunk, a mule, or a cook." One cook was discovered stirring a pot of navy beans with his Colt .45, then cleaning the barrel of the beans by firing at a nearby rock. Asked why he did this, he replied that he was checking to see if the beans were soft enough to eat.

The cook's day began early, for breakfast was usually over by 3:30 A.M. Before that, he had built his fire and prepared a hearty breakfast of hot bread or biscuits, meat, stewed dry fruit, and coffee for the cowboys whom he sometimes woke by banging lids of Dutch ovens together in a cymbal-like fashion. As they set off to care for the cattle, he washed their tin plates and cups (though cowboys were ex-pected to scrape their own plates clean and deposit them in the communal wreck pan), made bread, packed up the chuck wagon, and now working as a teamster, drove it to the site selected for dinner. Along the way as they reached creeks, cowboys or the cook's helper gathered brush or broken branches for the cooking fire. Elsewhere they picked up prairie coal, that is, dried cow or buffalo manure; this they did wearing gloves, for scorpions often lived under the chips.

The soldiers' health often took second priority to the cook's convenience.

Most of the daily menu was prepared in Dutch ovens: baked beans, roast beef, boiled potatoes, and short ribs with onions; bread was often mixed up in the dishpan. "Son of a bitch stew" was made of marrow from beef bones, sautéed in hot grease, then boiled with peppers and potatoes. Desserts might include more stewed fruit, spice cake made without eggs or butter, pies, or moonshine—rice and raisins simmered until done. More simply, it might mean lick—molasses or Karo syrup dripped over canned tomatoes and leftover biscuits, or straight-from-the-can yellow cling peaches in syrup. Pickles were a real treat in a diet noticeably lacking in fresh vegetables and depending heavily on prairie strawberries, or beans. Charlie Siringo remembered often skipping the noon meal when work was especially pressing. One of his favorite meals was calf ribs broiled by the campfire and a large Dutch oven full of loin, sweetbread, and heart, all smothered in flour gravy. Often forks and knives were not used, being replaced by the cowboys' pocketknives or bowie knives.

Finally, one cannot discuss the frontier without describing the rigors of soldiers' food. It mattered greatly whether a soldier ate in garrison or in the field, and if in garrison, whether they were officers or enlisted men. Paragraph 1367 of Army Regulations in effect during 1868 clearly established "the ration," or the "established daily allowance of food for one person":

twelve ounces of pork or bacon or canned beef (fresh or corned), or one pound and four ounces of fresh beef, or twenty-two ounces of salt beef; eighteen ounces of soft bread or flour, or sixteen ounces of hard bread, or one pound and four ounces of cornmeal; and to have, every one hundred rations, fifteen pounds of pease or beans, or ten pounds of rice or hominy; ten pounds of green coffee, or eight of roasted (or roasted and ground) coffee, or two pounds of tea; fifteen pounds of sugar; four quarts of vinegar; four pounds of soap; four pounds of salt; four ounces of pepper; one pound and eight ounces of adamantine or star candles; and to troops in the field when necessary, four pounds of yeast powder to one hundred rations of flour

Because of their transient status, troops at the induction depots received the worst food in the army. The soldiers' health often took second priority to the cook's convenience. Second Cavalryman James B. Wilkinson reported that "at Jefferson Barracks [1882] pork meat was put around at tables the night before the following morning's breakfast. The meat would be spoiled, turned green, by morning. Some ate it—others did not." Any complaints made to officers resulted in only temporary improvement.

Breakfast at recruit depots was usually salt pork, fried mush, or "stew that had been cooked all night." Dinner was slumgullion stew with dried bread, and supper was "dry bread and coffee, with an occasional treat of three prunes." One soldier hypothesized years later that the awful food may have been "necessary preparation for what was in the offing—field service against the antisocial redskins." Not only was the recruit depot food unpalatable, but it was usually insufficient in quantity. Occasionally newspaper exposés resulted in noncoms being convicted of mismanagement of ration funds.

Even a cursory glance at the army regulations revealed a complete absence of fresh fruits and vegetables from the daily ration; the vinegar (four quarts per hundred rations) was the only attempt to combat scurvy. In part this was due to the difficulty and expense of transport to the western forts—though that was no excuse at recruit depots. For a while the army experimented with a variety of vegetables, "compressed into a large cake, thoroughly dried, requiring but a small quantity for a meal." These, however, were not popular.

Many officers recognized the need for fresh vegetables. Colonel Robert E. Johnson testified in 1876 that "the addition of one pound of potatoes or other vegetables to the daily ration would materially reduce the sick list." At many posts, company gardens were planted. In 1869 at Fort Rice, Dakota, for example, troopers raised lettuce, radishes, spinach, squash, cucumbers, and new potatoes. Other soldiers bought canned fruit and tomatoes at the post commissary with their own funds, traded army issued sowbelly with nearby Indians for fresh meat or vegetables, or purchased treats such as pickles, turkeys, onions, apples, raisins, butter, and spices from the company funds, which were established from the sale of issued rations. (Often surplus flour was sold; the regulations called for 18 ounces of soft bread or flour per day; a pound of flour resulted in more than a pound of bread, and the surplus could thus be sold.)

Because the army wanted its soldiers to be prepared to fend for themselves in the field, food was usually prepared by the men themselves rather than by a cook. Men were detailed to 10-day tours as cooks and bakers. Not only was the food "miserably cooked," but "the man is in the kitchen [just] long enough to ruin his clothing without extra pay to replace it." Soldiers groused that cooks destroyed more men than Indians did.

One officer observed, "nearly as much food is wasted as is used in the Army from ignorance and inexperience of company cooks." Much food was spoiled due to improper handling and storage and poor preservation techniques. Often ancient rations were full of worms and weevils. The bacon loaded at Fort Reno for the 1866 expedition into the Big Horn country was "so old and rotted that the . . . fat had commenced to sluff off from the lean, and it was . . . also full of mice, as was the flour."

Bad as the food was in garrison, it could be worse in the field. In addition, the need to be a lean, mean combat force meant that men took only the essentials. General Crook noted that "in the field one eats only to live" and, on the Yellowstone expedition of 1876, he abandoned his wagon train with supplies and prohibited both officers and men from carrying more baggage than could be carried on the saddle: one blanket, one rubber blanket, coffee, sugar, bacon, and hardtack. This expedition knew real hunger, existing for some days on half rations and then, finally, "for breakfast—water and tightened belts." When they captured American Horse's camp, "there had fallen into our hands 5000 pounds of dried meats and fruits . . . This was a godsend, as we had already had to eat some of our horses. . . . To us who have to depend on them so much it seems like murder to kill horses." Nonetheless, to starving troopers, "fat colts are ever so much better than . . . beef." The infantry made a standing joke that "if we only marched far enough, they would eat all of the cavalry horses."

The hardships of this expedition tried the men in every way, not just by starvation. A young officer wrote of the suffering, particularly to the infantry:

> I have seen men become so exhausted that they were actually insane, but there was no way of carrying them except for some mounted officer or man to give them his own horse, which was done constantly. I saw men who were very plucky sit down and cry like children because they could not hold out. When there came a chance to fight, however, everyone was mad enough to fight well.

This passage also indicates that much time in the field was spent reconnoitering rather than fighting. Such privations captured the essence of many operations of the Indian wars; combat was an almost invigorating interlude in unending boredom and misery.

In extraordinary contrast was Eveline Alexander's recollection of the Fourth of July, 1866, as she accompanied her husband to his new posting. Camped near Fort Cobb in Indian Territory, "we passed a comfortable Fourth and drank to its many returns in a large tin cup of lemonade. We dined about seven: had tomato soup, wild turkey, beefsteak, green peas, and canned peaches for desert [sic]." In October of that year the Alexanders entertained General Sherman at Fort Stevens, Colorado. Though their quarters was a tent, and though the day before the wind blew so hard that it broke some of her plates, overturned the soup, and blew dust into the blancmange she was preparing, the dinner was a success. In her rather self-mocking style, Eveline wrote: "It is the fashion after entertaining great men to publish the bill of fare, so I will note mine here. First course, beef vegetable soup; second, saddle of mutton with jelly, green peas, kirshaw squash, cabbage, and beets; third, soft custard blanc mange with cream and sugar, and coffee." One must remember that her husband was a very junior officer entertaining the commander of the Division of the Missouri and that such a meal was far from typical (Jones, 35–38, 62–65, 127–28, 141–43, 175–76, 225–28).

To read about food on the colonial frontier of North America, see the entries on the Colonial Frontier and New England in the section "Food" in chapter 5 ("Material Life") in volume 4 of this series.

FOR MORE INFORMATION

Ambrose, S. E. *Undaunted Courage: Meriwether Lewis, Thomas Jefferson, and the Opening of the American West.* New York: Simon & Schuster, 1996.

Jones, M. E. *Daily Life on the Nineteenth Century American Frontier.* Westport, Conn.: Greenwood Press, 1998.

Luchetti, C. *Home on the Range: A Culinary History of the American West.* New York: Villard Books, 1993.

Utley, R. M. *Frontier Regulars: The United States Army and the Indian: 1866–1891.* Bloomington: Indiana University Press, 1973.

VICTORIAN ENGLAND

Information about food and eating during the Victorian period can be found in parliamentary and public health investigations that looked at household budgets. In addition, cookbooks were published for people of all classes. Charitable organizations put out recipes to help workers get the best value for their money; commercial publishers found a ready market among middle-class and upper-class women for books to be used by themselves or their cooks.

It is always necessary to look critically at cookbooks—practically any guide on the kitchen shelf contains some recipes that hardly anyone uses. Nevertheless, the successive editions of bestsellers such as Eliza Acton's *Modern Cookery for Private Families* (first published in 1845) and Isabella Beeton's *Book of Household Management* (first published in 1861) provide a good deal of information about the foods that were available. The 1861 edition of Beeton's book, for example, has many pages of soup recipes for winter vegetables such as turnips, carrots, parsnips, potatoes, beets, dried peas, and onions, but even the summer soups never call for tomatoes as an ingredient. Twenty years later, with improved transportation and greenhouses as well as canned foods, tomatoes were easily obtained and routinely appear in recipes.

People in the working class got most of their nutrition from bread. The budgets collected by factory commissioners in the 1840s show purchases limited to bread, cheese, butter, sugar, tea, salt, and potatoes. A tiny amount of bacon or other meat might be used for flavoring. Workers' diets were short on both protein and fat. Men from the urban working class were noticeably shorter than upper-class men—although most people believed this was an inherited (racial) difference rather than a consequence of nutrition.

The staple diet of rural laborers was bread, potatoes, and tea. (Tea was cheaper than beer and safer than water that had not been boiled.) Bacon—usually very fat, and more like salt pork than the crisply fried bacon eaten today in the United States—was used in small quantities for flavoring once or twice a week. In prosperous times, farm laborers also had milk and cheese. A medical man in 1863 found that 30 percent of the rural laborers he talked to had never tasted any meat except for bits of bacon. (The people who occasionally poached a hare or grouse from the local woods presumably did not mention it.) Nearly 20 percent of factory workers in some districts also claimed they had not eaten any meat other than bacon.

Poor people's eating habits reflected their living conditions as well as the expense of food. When everything had to be cooked over an open fire, and when women worked either away from home or at home to bring in some income, elaborate meals were impossible. Bread was always ready to eat; potatoes were easily boiled. In cities, a common meal was bread and dripping. Dripping was the fat from roasted meat; household and institutional cooks sold it to dealers. Used instead of butter, dripping gave bread a tasty meat flavor and supplied some needed fat.

Because it was hard to store food (and wages might have been paid daily), poor people shopped in extremely small quantities. Young children were sent to do errands, because the shopkeeper might be generous when a child asked for a half-penny's worth of butter. Adults were sometimes told that the shop did not sell such small amounts.

In cities, street food could be bought by workers who had no time or place to cook. Stalls and hawkers sold coffee, lemonade, ginger beer, roasted potatoes, pea soup (pease porridge hot), sandwiches, meat pies, pickled eels, smoked herring, fruit tarts, gingerbread, and luxury treats such as oranges, lemons, and pineapples. After railways and ice brought fresh fish to inland towns, fish and chips became popular. Chips, in England, are the same as French fries in the United States. A heap of greasy potatoes and a fillet of batter-fried cod or plaice, served in a twist of newspaper and sprinkled with vinegar, made a cheap and substantial meal.

The diet of working people improved later in the century. With cheap wheat imported from North America and the development of technology to ship chilled meat from the Americas and Australia, a typical working-class food budget fell by 30 percent between 1877 and 1889 and could include more meat. Investigators in the 1880s noted that working families had added jam, margarine, eggs, milk, coffee, and cocoa to their regular diet and also consumed tinned salmon, sardines, and larger quantities of butter and cheese.

As long as there was no oven in the kitchen, a roast of meat remained a rare Sunday treat; it was carried to the neighborhood baker for cooking. Stews and fried meats such as sausages and kidneys could be managed on a fireplace grate or on a small iron stove without an oven. When there was meat, the largest portion went to the man of the family. Sunday's leftovers were added to the bread or potatoes he took for his meal at work. It was almost universal among the working class to give the best food to men and boys who did physical labor. This made practical sense when the primary income depended on a male wage earner's strength. Women who moved into the middle class (through marriage or by training as a teacher) found it odd that

---

📷 Snapshot

Plain Family Dinners for a Victorian England Family, 1860s

Sunday—

1. Vegetable-marrow soup.
2. Roast quarter of lamb, mint sauce, French beans, and potatoes.
3. Raspberry-and-currant tart, custard pudding.

Monday—

1. Cold lamb and salad, small meat pie, vegetable marrow, and white sauce.
2. Lemon dumplings.

Tuesday—

1. Boiled mackerel.
2. Stewed loin of veal, French beans, and potatoes.
3. Baked raspberry pudding.

Wednesday—

1. Vegetable soup.
2. Lamb cutlets and French beans; the remains of stewed shoulder of veal, mashed vegetable marrow.
3. Black-currant pudding.

Thursday—

1. Roast ribs of beef, Yorkshire pudding, French beans, and potatoes.
2. Bread-and-butter pudding.

Friday—

1. Fried soles and melted butter.
2. Cold beef and salad, lamb cutlets, and mashed potatoes.
3. Cauliflowers and white sauce instead of pudding.

Saturday—

1. Stewed beef and vegetables, with remains of cold beef; mutton pudding.
2. Macaroni and cheese.

~[See Isabella Beeton, *Book of Household Management*, (1861); as quoted in Mitchell, 124.]

women were chivalrously served first. In the homes where they grew up, the mother served the meal and stinted herself if the supply was short.

The middle and upper classes could afford a wider variety of food. Not much was accurately known, however, about diet and nutrition; vitamins had not yet been discovered. Moreover, the lack of refrigeration meant that even the meals of fairly well-to-do families were limited by the available local food supply. Typical items on English menus included vegetable marrow, which is a summer squash similar to zucchini. Pudding, in England, is any boiled, steamed, or sweet dish that is served as dessert. One can have almost anything for pudding, including layer cake or fresh fruit. A boiled pudding is an English staple not much known in the United States. A thick batter made of flour, eggs, suet (animal fat), milk, dried fruit, and spices is tied in a cloth, boiled for several hours, and served with a sweet sauce. Puddings come in many varieties, depending on proportions and seasoning; stale bread, rice, and other grains can be substituted for the flour. Among its other advantages, a boiled pudding does not need an oven or require much attention after the batter is mixed, and leftovers put into a covered tin will keep for several days without drying out. The suet makes the pudding a heavy and filling dish as well as a sweet ending to a meal.

The family menus in Beeton's cookbook call for a surprising amount of meat. In fact, the English middle and upper classes ate more roasted and cooked meat (and fewer stews or casseroles) than did Europeans of a similar class. In addition, cooking two or three different kinds of meat in the same oven at the same time saved fuel and labor. Portions eaten at the table could be small; the cold or reheated leftovers would be used for breakfast and luncheon, for children's nursery meals, and for servants' dinners.

With their ordinary meals, people generally drank beer or ale; working people who could not afford the expense drank tea instead. Both beer and tea were safer than water that had not been boiled. Milk was also problematic, even in rural areas, until very late in the century. Before pasteurization was discovered, milk could spread tuberculosis. There were other dangers in the food supply as well. Bakers added alum and chalk to make bread look whiter; copper salts gave color to pickles; arsenic added tanginess and emphasized the flavor of some prepared foods. Many of these practices were brought under control in 1872 when Parliament passed the Adulteration of Food, Drink, and Drugs Act.

By the last quarter of the century, the diet of the middle and upper classes (as well as the working class) had improved. Fruits and vegetables from parts of Europe with longer growing seasons were available during much of the year. Packaged foods and trademarked brands—as well as laws preventing adulteration—increased the range and quality of foods available. Thomas Lipton built a chain of grocery stores that became famous for many products besides tea. Imported bananas and chocolate bars became popular new delicacies.

It also became possible to safely feed infants whose mothers could not breastfeed them. Although sending a baby out to nurse with a countrywoman was still common in some parts of Europe, wet nurses had seldom been used in England except by people of extremely high social position. It was not uncommon, however, for mothers to die in childbirth or get infections that prevented nursing. Cow's milk was apt to be contaminated and needed diluting so babies could digest it; the water was even more likely to be dangerous. For centuries, milk had been put into an animal horn or a stoneware bottle with a rag stuffed in the end so the infant could suck. This, we now realize, made an ideal environment for germs; no wonder that in some foundling homes 90 percent of the newborns died. Glass bottles and rubber nipples became available in the middle of the century; and the importance of sterilizing the milk, water, and bottle was understood in the 1890s. For the first time, conscientious mothers could consider bottle-feeding when it was difficult to nurse.

Eating habits changed during the 19th century. In addition, there were class differences in the hours and names for meals. During the 18th century, prosperous people ate a late and very large breakfast, probably a holdover from the medieval practice of having dinner in the morning. An 18th-century breakfast could include cold roast meat, cheese, fish, eggs, steaks, and ale. Lunch—if eaten at all—was a small, cold meal. Dinner was at 5 or 6 P.M.

Afternoon tea was thought of as a lady's meal, although men were sometimes present.

By the Victorian period, breakfast on a country estate when there were many guests might still be an elaborate meal at 10 A.M. Usually, however, it was less formal. People served themselves from foods set on a sideboard: eggs, hot rolls, toast, and perhaps some cold meat. Other breakfast foods might have included fish, tongue, meat pies, ham, mushrooms, bacon, and muffins. A small family ate together; but in larger households and when there were guests, breakfast was available from 8 A.M. on, and people ate when they were ready. (The servant who knocked on the door with hot water early in the morning would have brought up a cup of tea or coffee and a sweet biscuit to have while dressing.)

Among the middle classes, because breakfast was early and fairly small, the husband generally ate a substantial hot lunch at his club or at work. Many businesses, including banks and law offices, had meals brought in for the upper-level employees. A middle-class married woman ate a light cooked meal at home. The children ate with her unless she had guests. The children's cooked lunch served as their main meal; they had a supper of bread and milk or something similar before bedtime. In upper-class households, a hot luncheon or an assortment of cold dishes from which everyone helped themselves was served between 1 and 2 P.M.

The earlier practice among ladies of having cakes and wine when friends came to call evolved into afternoon tea as women began to consume less alcohol. Afternoon tea (between 4 and 5 P.M.) became popular during the 1840s. It was thought of as a lady's meal, although men were sometimes present. An urn of boiling water was carried into the parlor or drawing room along with teapots and a caddy, which held the loose tea. The lady of the house made the tea and poured it out; servants handed the cups to guests. Small cakes, rolled bread and butter, and other dainty finger foods were offered around. Afternoon tea, in other words, was an occasion for visiting rather than a meal.

As luncheon grew more substantial and afternoon tea became more general, the dinner hour grew later. The urban middle classes generally had dinner at home between 6 and 7 P.M. (or later for suburbanites who had a long trip). Fashionable people dined at 7:30 or 8 P.M. In lower-middle-class and working-class families, however, dinner was a hot meal served between noon and 2 P.M. It was the main meal of the day, especially when the man of the family was a farmer, artisan, shopkeeper, or other worker who could be at home in the middle of the day. Otherwise, a hot supper was provided for the man when he arrived home in the evening. On Sundays, everyone except the upper class had dinner at 2 P.M. It was the week's most substantial meal, eaten after church, with the entire family sitting down together. The rich dined in the evening, even on Sundays.

It may seem confusing that the working-class evening meal was increasingly called tea, even when it consisted of bread, beer, and something tasty such as kippers or sausage. While father had his tea, the children had bread and water (or weak tea) and some tidbits from his plate. When times grew more prosperous, the worker's evening meal became indistinguishable from what in the United States would be called dinner—but it was still generally called tea.

High tea, in good society, was a meal found only in the country or in the suburbs on a Sunday evening, when servants had been given a half day off after clearing away the Sunday dinner. Originally it was a way to entertain on the spur of the moment when unexpected guests came from a distance. One foreign visitor described a Sunday high tea in the country as a sort of indoor picnic, with an odd assortment of hot and cold food, tea, and wine; guests helped themselves because most of the servants were out. Fashionable late dinners were somewhat unsuited to country life; visitors would have to travel home in the dark or rise early for hunting or shooting. High tea became a late-afternoon or early-evening meal eaten instead of dinner. Fruits, cakes, and hot muffins were placed on the table with a tea tray at one end and coffee at the other. As at breakfast, more substantial dishes such as cold salmon, meat pies, and roast game birds were available on the sideboard.

Supper, like tea, had several meanings. The name might be used for the evening meal in suburban families where the man ate dinner in town at midday. (The middle-class supper, in other words, was often the same meal as the working-class tea.) Nursery children had supper in the late afternoon and went to bed before their parents dined. A supper was also the very late meal at a ball or an evening party. In that case, it could be almost as elaborate as a society dinner; guests were seated at tables set with a full range of silverware and served by footmen.

The formal dinner party had become a ritualized event. The appropriate hour at the end of the century was 7:30 or 8:30 P.M. Guests arrived punctually; etiquette books said they must be no more than 15 minutes late—except in the country, where a little more leeway was allowed for difficult transportation. Everyone assembled in the drawing room, and the host told each gentleman which lady to escort down to dinner. This would not be his wife—married couples were not seated together but made conversation with others. As soon as all the guests had arrived, they went down to eat; there were no before-dinner drinks.

Although formal dinners involved vast amounts of food, no one was expected to eat everything. Servants carried the bowls and platters around; guests had a written menu, knew what was coming, and said yes or no to each dish. The butler offered appropriate wines for every course. Etiquette books told the host and hostess not to insist that guests take wine or urge them to have more food. Properly, no one even mentioned what was served; the conversation was to focus on other topics.

At the end of a dinner, servants cleared everything except the flowers and (using a silver knife) removed crumbs from the tablecloth. Then finger bowls, dessert plates, and fresh wine glasses were put at each place. After offering desserts, the servants left. (During dinner they remained in the dining room, although they had to act as if they could not hear any of the conversation.) After a short time the hostess caught the eye of the lady on her husband's right (the wife of the most important male guest) and stood up. The gentlemen rose while the ladies left the room, and then sat down again for brandy or port and masculine conversation. (After cigarettes became popular the men might also smoke, but it would not be acceptable to rejoin the ladies with clothes reeking of cigars; a man who smoked a cigar in his study or billiard room would put on a smoking jacket.) The ladies were served coffee in the drawing room. The gentlemen were to remain (all etiquette books insisted) only a *short* time over their wine. Then they joined the ladies in the drawing room, and tea was brought in. The guests left at 10:30 or 11:00 P.M.

Dining out socially in hotels and restaurants began only in the last years of the century. Before then, middle-class and upper-class women simply did not eat in public, even with their husbands, unless they were traveling. In addition to the new restaurants (many of them run by immigrants from Europe) that welcomed respectable couples, department store tea shops and lunchroom chains such as the ABC began serving modest noontime and late-afternoon meals to women alone or in groups (Mitchell, *Daily Life*, 122–29).

To read about food in Chaucer's England, see the entry on Europe in the section "Food" in chapter 5 ("Material Life") in volume 2 of this series; for Elizabethan England, see the entry on England in the section "Food and Drink" in chapter 5 ("Material Life") in volume 3 of this series; for 18th-century England, see the entry on England in the section "Food" in chapter 5 ("Material Life") in volume 4 of this series; for 20th-century Europe, see the Europe entry in the section "Food" in chapter 5 ("Material Life") in volume 6 of this series.

FOR MORE INFORMATION

Burnet, J. *Plenty and Want: A Social History of Diet in England from 1815 to the Present Day.* 2nd ed. London: Scholar Press, 1979.

Mitchell, S. *Daily Life in Victorian England.* Westport, Conn.: Greenwood Press, 1996.

Mitchell, S., ed. *Victorian Britain: An Encyclopedia.* New York: Garland Press, 1998.

MATERIAL LIFE
|
FOOD
|
United States,
1850-1865

United States,
Western Frontier

Victorian England

India

Latin America

INDIA

Each region of India has a distinctly unique cuisine. This was particularly evident in the 19th century, when there was less borrowing of food styles between regions. The cuisine of the North was heavily influenced by the Muslim invaders. Many

British in India during the colonial period embraced Indian cuisine, and exchanges occurred in both directions. In other words, the British influenced Indian cuisine, and the Indians influenced some aspects of British cuisine. British cookbooks from the Victorian period often include Indian recipes under the heading of "British recipes."

Many people are surprised to learn that there is no such thing as curry in Indian food. Curry is an English word used to describe the entire diverse range of Indian spicing. This term is derived from the Tamil word *kari*, which is the name for a specific type of vegetable dish that is popular in the Southeast of India. There are over 30 different spices used in different combinations, in various parts of India, to create different tastes. Some of these dishes are spicy, while others are not. Some common spices in Indian cooking include turmeric, saffron, cumin, chilies, ginger, garlic, fenugreek, cardamom, coriander, pepper, and bay leaves. Spices played a major role in early colonial adventures and were a major source of motivation in the search for sea routes to India and, later, for economic interest in India, which was the root of colonialism.

Indian dishes can be vegetable, meat (usually chicken or lamb), or fish. The spices are fried in ghee (clarified butter), or oil. This releases their flavors. The most basic and common Indian dish is dahl, or lentils cooked with spices. A variety of different types of lentils and spices are used, and at most meals dahl is present in some form.

Two types of Moghul-influenced dishes are popular in the Northwest. Tandoori refers to the clay oven in which the food is cooked after first being marinated in a mixture of herbs and yogurt. *Biryani* is a rice dish consisting of meat and sometimes dried fruit.

Rice is the basic staple of South Indian food. However, throughout most of North India, wheat is the main staple. There are many different types of rice grown in India. The one that is considered premium and is often expensive is basmati rice, which is primarily grown in the Dehra Dun Valley in Northwest India. Its long, yellowish grains have a slightly sweet smell. In the North, rice is often eaten along with a variety of breads known as rotis. In the Northwest, nan (bread baked in a tandoori oven) is common. In other parts of North India chapati, a round flat bread cooked on a hot plate known as *tawa*, and the deep fried puri are both common. Both are made from a mixture of flour and water. *Paratha*, which is also cooked on a *tawa*, is similar to the chapati, although ghee is used.

One of the most common foods found in South India is the *dosa*, which is basically a thin pancake made from ground up lentil and rice flour. The *idli* is also made from ground up rice and lentil flour, but it is steamed in the shape of a small ball. Both *dosas* and *idlis* are most often eaten with a coconut chutney and a sambar, or lentil broth.

There are generally a number of side dishes to go with the main meal. One of the most popular is *dahin*, or yogurt. Sometimes the yogurt is mixed with cooked or raw vegetables. This is called *raita*. Chutney is pickled fruit or vegetables and is also a standard side dish.

Street food is also very popular in India, and each region has its own specialties. These include *samosas* (pastry triangles filled with spiced meat or vegetables), *pakoras* (battered and deep fried vegetables), and a variety of other types of snack foods. During the 19th century vendors generally made these snacks while hunched over a flame on the street or on a railway station platform.

Sweets are very common throughout India, but Bengal, the area in the Northeast, which includes Calcutta and Dhaka and is now in Bangladesh, is particularly famous for its sweets. The sweets are rice or milk based and often contain ground nuts. Many Indian sweets are covered in a thin layer of silver that is edible. Some common sweets include *gulab jamun*, which is made from thickened, boiled-down milk and flavored with cardamom and rose water, and *ladu*, which are yellow-colored balls made from chickpea flower. There is also a wide variety of fruits and nuts grown in India, including coconuts, mangos, pineapples, litchis, oranges, watermelon, and several varieties of bananas, including a red banana found in South India.

Paan, made from *betal*, a mildly addictive and intoxicating nut, is common in most parts of India. It is often sold at street stands and often eaten after a meal. It is a mild digestive. There are many varieties of *paan*, some sweet, others not, which vary from region to region. The *betal* nut and the other ingredients, which include a variety of spices and condiments (opium is sometimes in *paan*), are wrapped in an edible leaf. Then the entire thing is popped into one's mouth and chewed and swallowed.

Utensils were not commonly used in India, although at this time many elite Indians were beginning to use them. Typically one sits on the floor or on a mat and eats with one's right hand (the left hand is considered dirty). At this time banana leaves were commonly used as plates.

In the 19th century women most often prepared the family's meals. It was common for the women of the house to serve the men and children before they themselves ate. Then, once the men finished eating, the women ate what was left. This was not necessarily because the men were more important, but rather because it was the role of the women to take care of their husbands and children and preparing the food and insuring that they had enough to eat was one way of doing this.

To read about food in ancient India, see the India entry in the section "Food" in chapter 5 ("Material Life") in volume 1 of this series; for India in the 20th century, see the India entry in the section "Food" in chapter 5 ("Material Life') in volume 6 of this series.

~*Dana Lightstone*

MATERIAL LIFE
|
FOOD
|
United States,
1850-1865

United States,
Western Frontier

Victorian England

India

Latin America

FOR MORE INFORMATION

Basu, S. *Curry in the Crown*. New York: South Asia Books, 1999.
Wickramasinghe, P. *The Food of India*. Los Angeles: Whitecap Books, 2002.

LATIN AMERICA

Issues of food supply and consumption became increasingly politicized in Latin America during the 19th century. As rich/poor and urban/rural disparities grew, those people that held a subordinate position in society began actively demanding government intervention. While officials did, indeed, institute food-related regulations, a combination of factors—including population growth, food shortages, and rising prices—meant that more people were unable to satisfy their dietary needs.

The independence wars of the first quarter century had little long-term effect on agriculture and food consumption in most regions of Latin America. Where cultivation had been interrupted during wartime, it quickly picked up again once the fighting ended. Cities continued to offer open spaces for garden use, helping to supplement diets, particularly for the urban poor.

However, independence did bring some changes. For example, new *juntas de benficiencia,* or charity boards, supported or replaced church organizations as dispensers of food aid in urban areas. Patterns of water use also changed over the course of the century. In the early days, most people hauled their own water from nearby streams and reservoirs. Later, people bought water from the *aguadores,* or roving vendors who ladled out portions from barrels filled at local sources. Eventually, most city centers boasted in-home water systems that were principally enjoyed by the upper classes.

Cuisine and product availability varied according to region, geography, and rural or urban location. The food of some areas of Mexico, for example, used a variety of hot chiles, whereas the *guisados,* or dishes, of other areas were much blander. The cuisine of Lima, Peru, was known for its "extraordinary inventiveness." One visitor to the city in the late 1870s noted that Lima's diet was an "incongruous mixture of foreign and native style, the latter predominating in private meals, the former in all formal or public banquets."

Main dishes incorporated beef, pork, fowl, peppers, tubers, rice, and noodles. Seafood was also popular, especially the prized ceviche, a lime-marinated fish salad, and *parihuela,* a spicy seafood stew. Chinese-influenced cuisine gained popularity after the 1850s. Drinks in urban Peru were also varied. Coffees, teas, chocolates, wines, and different rums and *piscos* (grape brandies) were available. A corn beer, known as *chicha,* was popular in both urban and rural areas.

Hosts and hostesses in Lima also served desserts of corn, wheat, honey, and quince, as well as *mazamorra morada,* a mixed fruit pudding. The ice trade introduced a new delicacy for the sweet tooth: *helados,* or ice creams. Traders first carved and shaved blocks of ice from glaciers high in the Andes mountains; they then loaded the blocks on the backs of mules that hoofed it back down the mountain (Peloso, 51). In the latter part of the century, ice trains were used to quickly transport this perishable commodity.

Although visitors often assumed that all Peruvians enjoyed the same variety, top-quality goods were not accessible to all. Indeed, many products were virtually unknown in the highland interior of the country. Although rural diets lacked the variety of the coastal capital region, highland locations such as Cuzco and Arequipa boasted their own regional specialties, many of which used potatoes as a main ingredient. For example, highlanders enjoyed *carapulcra,* a potato-thickened chicken and pork soup; *ocopa,* a crayfish-potato-peanut salad; and *paua a la huancaína,* a sweet and sour potato salad. Aside from these dishes, highlanders ate potatoes in many different forms: boiled, roasted, and *chuño,* or freeze-dried.

Other cold-crop foods were common throughout highland Peru, including apricots, goat, maize, beans, and *quinua*, a highland cereal. Indigenous communities of the highlands also ate *olluca*, a nut-flavored tuber; goat's milk; lamb; and *cuy*, or guinea pig. Feast-day specialties included *pachamanca*: corn, potatoes, and a whole goat roasted underground on heated stones.

As the 19th century progressed, and nations became increasingly enmeshed in the international market, food disparities between various groups became more apparent, especially after the 1850s. Coastal populations profited, while outlying regions were at an extreme disadvantage. Andean highland producers, for example, frequently exported to Europe but rarely received products in return. Moreover, both merchants and consumers of the highlands were more dispersed than their coastal counterparts, making sales and shipments much more difficult.

Also, at mid-century, urban elites began to distinguish themselves from the popular sectors through their haute cuisine. New luxury food markets appeared, catering to these aristocrats. The upper classes stopped frequenting local street vendors and the once-popular *comedores* and *picanterías*.

Changes also occurred in the typically Indian markets. In the early century, bartering was common at Indian markets. As the century moved forward, however, cash exchanges became more common so that, by the end of the century, many people from indigenous communities found it necessary to work in the mines or as seasonal laborers on plantations to subsist.

Similarly, slaves and indentured servants suffered extreme deprivation. Until abolition in 1854, the plantation slaves of Peru often struggled to survive on a total diet of *menestras* (vegetables), occasionally supplemented with *chicha* and *guarapo*, or cane whisky. These conditions persisted despite the fact that Peruvian law required coastal plantation owners to provide field hands with adequate rations. Indentured Chinese servants also received inadequate nutrition; often they survived on rice alone, supplemented by evening doses of opium, coca leaves, and *guarapo* (Peloso, 53).

The growth of the urban population, coupled with the export-oriented economies of Latin America, led to increased demands for foodstuffs. Moreover, large landowners dedicated vast tracts of land to crops that fared well on the international market. For example, as the Civil War raged in the United States in the 1860s, international cotton prices soared, prompting many Latin American growers to turn their soils over to cotton production. This trend, in turn, further threatened the production of goods for domestic consumption. Similar processes occurred with sugar and coffee. Eventually, many countries began importing staple grains that they had previously produced for themselves. Importing such goods was not only more expensive, it placed the region's population at high risk in case of market crashes and shortage-based price hikes.

Food prices rose steadily throughout the latter half of the century. In Peru, in just one decade (1854–64), rice and garbanzo prices climbed by 110 percent, butter prices by 54 percent, and bean prices by 163 percent (Peloso, 56). Wages did not rise at the same rate. The working classes routinely dedicated at least one-half of their total income to food purchases; it was not uncommon to spend 70–80 percent of one's income and still fail to achieve adequate nutrition (Wright, 32).

Therefore, by the 1870s, the poor began to actively agitate for relief. Demonstrations in Lima and elsewhere drew attention to the working class's inability to keep up with high prices. During the 1878 corn riots in Durango, Mexico, strikers demanded wage adjustments to compensate for inflation. Food issues contributed to the creation of working class solidarity in Latin America, as workers formed mutual aid societies and joined forces with other labor organizations in marches and protests.

Although local governments regulated sanitation and the accuracy of market weights and measures, they refrained from the more interventionist practices of the former colonial governments, such as fixing prices and purchasing grains directly from local farmers. However, increasing unrest forced many governments to become more involved by regulating prices and establishing other controls. The Mexican government, for example, suspended import duties and lowered rail travel rates to offset high food costs. The Chilean government also cut rail rates. The Peruvian government adopted different strategies: a commission of inquiry conducted a survey in 1869, and officials sponsored contests in 1870 and 1873, offering prizes for the best essays addressing the high cost of food (Peloso, 56; Wright, 31). Ultimately, candidates for public office even included food themes in their election campaigns.

Although Latin American agriculture did not suffer long-term damage as a result of the independence wars, the 19th century introduced many changes, not all of which were positive. Group divisions and distinctions became more obvious and, as it became increasingly difficult for poorer populations to satisfy their basic dietary needs, they often took to the streets to voice their concerns and force an immediate government response.

~*Molly Todd*

FOR MORE INFORMATION

Peloso, V. "Succulence and Sustenance: Region, Class and Diet in Nineteenth Century Peru." In *Food, Politics, and Society in Latin America*, ed. John C. Super and Thomas C. Wright, 46–64. Lincoln: University of Nebraska Press, 1985.

Wright, T. C. "The Politics of Urban Provisioning in Latin American History." In *Food, Politics, and Society in Latin America*, eds. John C. Super and Thomas C. Wright, 24–45. Lincoln: University of Nebraska Press, 1985.

ISLAMIC WORLD

The Ottoman Empire dominated the Muslim world throughout the 19th century, and its rich culinary tradition represented a cultural continuation from an earlier period. See the Ottoman Turks entry in the section "Food" in chapter 5 ("Material

Life") in volume 3 of this series for a description of this cuisine, which remains a highlight for travelers to Turkey.

CHINA

From their earliest history, the Chinese took advantage of the most varied foods to provide for their large population and were widely known for careful and creative preparation of their foods. Both these characteristics continued into the 19th century. See the China entry in the section "Food" in chapter 5 ("Material Life") in volume 2 of this series for the remarkable variety of the Chinese diet.

MATERIAL LIFE
|
DRINK
|
United States,
1850-1865

United States,
Western Frontier

India

Drink

Consider for a moment this wild historical argument: plants have determined human history. Let me restate this differently. People are not now nor have they ever been in control of themselves or their environment. Rather, for thousands of years, plants—albeit certain plants—have made humans do their work for them. Addicted to the chemicals found in plants or believing that we must grow certain plants to survive, humans have created extremely complex social and political structures, conquered foreign lands, enslaved millions, and even engaged in revolution all in the name of growing, cultivating, and trading plants. Why did Columbus sail West? Answer: to get into the spice trade. Why did the Portuguese invent plantation slavery? Answer: to cultivate sugar. Why were the British in Virginia? Answer: to grow tobacco. Why did the Americans revolt again British colonial rule? Answer: they opposed a tax on their tea. Plants, not humans, have ruled the earth.

Certainly this interpretation of history (which one can call botanical determinism) is farcical. But nevertheless, consider the important place that coffee held in American history. No cowboy was ever without his coffee. Of course, they enjoyed the drink, but it also kept them awake and alert. Cattle drives were dangerous and required the cowboys to be sharp. In fact, cowboys tended not to drink alcohol except between cattle drives. It was just too risky. During the American Civil War, coffee was the basic staple of the soldier's diet. Whether Union or Confederate, the armies did not move without their daily dose of coffee. The Army of the Potomac used 80 tons of coffee each week! Confederate soldiers crossed Union lines just to trade their scarce tobacco for it. Making coffee was the first and last activity of the day. It was brewed between meals. Each soldier carried coffee boilers and tin cups. In fact, as the Civil War entry mentions, soldiers so noisily made their coffee that their commanders had to order their troops to stow their coffee gear so that the troops could travel in stealth.

Coffee as well as tea was central to the history of India in the 19th century. In fact, the Indian Darjeeling and Assam teas are world famous and have a lot to do with not only people's material lives in terms of drink but also in terms of economics.

By comparison, it's interesting to note that in India drinking has a regional flavor. Whereas nearly all Americans drank the same coffee, tea is more poplar in southern India while coffee is more popular in the North. Regardless, it is what both coffee and tea have in common that makes them so popular. Caffeine, more than coffee or tea, is what humans crave.

UNITED STATES, 1850–65

The importance of coffee to the Civil War soldier cannot be underestimated. Their diaries and letters are full of reverent references to the hot brown liquid. Coffee was included in the official federal ration, as was sugar to sweeten it. Condensed milk of two brands, Lewis's and Borden's, and a dry powder called the Essence of Coffee were available through the sutlers.

Federal soldiers rarely had trouble getting their regular daily ration of 1 1/2 ounces of coffee beans. Confederate soldiers showed an equally intense liking for coffee, but due to the effectiveness of the blockade, they often had to do without coffee or find a coffee bean substitute. Several substitute materials were commonly used either to make coffee or to stretch a limited supply. Acorn coffee was made from the parched meat of the shelled nut roasted in a little bacon fat. Kernel corn, dried apples, wheat, seeds, and dried yams were tried, but wild chicory root seems to have served best. The quality of this substitute coffee was questionable, and Confederates would take great risks to trade scarce Southern tobacco for good Union coffee by trading with the enemy pickets across the lines.

The Army of the Potomac used 80 tons of coffee and sugar every week. Nonetheless, federal soldiers were very concerned lest they somehow be deprived of even the smallest part of this coffee and sugar allowance, and steps were taken to ensure that favoritism in apportioning the ration was thwarted. The appropriate amount having been issued on a company level, the orderly sergeant would place a gum blanket on the ground and make as many piles of coffee beans and sugar as there were men to receive the ration. Great care was taken to ensure that the piles were uniform. To prevent any charge of unfairness, the sergeant would turn his back, and an assistant would point to a pile randomly. The sergeant would call out the company roll by name, and the named man would retrieve his allowance. The veteran soon learned to place both the sugar and the coffee together in a cloth bag and scoop out the two together without ceremony, but some men preferred to keep them separate and use each in proportion to their taste.

Coffee was furnished to the soldier as green beans from the sack. Roasting was done in a camp kettle, which often meant the beans were burned rather than roasted. To grind the beans the soldier seized his musket by the barrel and used the butt as a tamper. The ground coffee more properly should have been called cracked coffee, as many of the grains were halved, more quartered, and the rest of a very coarse texture. Yet an army surgeon believed that army coffee had "no equal as a preparation for a hard day's march, nor any rival as a restorative after one."

MATERIAL LIFE

DRINK

United States, 1850-1865

United States, Western Frontier

India

The army recognized this value, and each soldier was issued a tin dipper in which to boil his coffee. This was a large metal cup holding between a pint and a quart of liquid. The ground coffee was placed directly into the water without a filter of any sort. With little enthusiasm, Pvt. John D. Billings recalled making coffee with the tin dipper, which proved "an unfortunate dish for that purpose, forever tipping over and spilling the coffee into the fire." Such utensils soon disappeared, to be replaced by a tin can with an improvised wire handle. Astonished recruits were amazed to see veteran soldiers holding this improvisation on the end of a stick, boiling their coffee at the campfire in happy security. For those who recoiled at resorting to cast-off tin cans, sutlers offered an improved device for boiling coffee with a hinged lid and a stout wire handle by which it might be hung over the fire. The price of such an article could strain the financial resources of a single soldier, but several men might pool their money to purchase one and take turns carrying it.

The Civil War soldier would not be denied his coffee. If an early morning march was intended, and fires were permitted, the march was preceded by a pot of coffee. If a halt was ordered in mid-afternoon, coffee was made. Coffee-making equipment was generally carried strapped to the outside of the kit where it was easily accessible. The movement of an army could be heard from far off by the resulting unmuffled rattling of countless coffee boilers and tin cups. So significant was this noise that special orders were frequently issued prior to stealthy movements of the army to place these items inside the haversack. At the end of each day's march, as soon as the army began to bivouac, small groups of men would invariably make the preparation of coffee their first task. A supper of hardtack and coffee followed, and then each man would roll up in his blankets for the night.

In camp, company cooks were issued large coffeepots holding several gallons. John Billings recalled, "It was coffee at meals and between meals; and men going on guard and coming off guard drank it at all hours of the night." The U.S. Christian Commission made the rounds of the camps with coffee wagons made from old artillery limbers nicknamed by the troops "the Christian Light Artillery." The coffee wagon was provided with compartments for ingredients and three large coffee boilers that could produce 90 gallons of coffee every hour. Whatever grumbling there may have been about the quality of the other rations, "there was but one opinion of the coffee which was served out, and that was of unqualified approval" (Volo and Volo, 129–30).

To read about drink in the United States in the 20th century, see the United States entries in the section "Drink" in chapter 5 ("Material Life") in volume 6 of this series.

FOR MORE INFORMATION

McPherson, J. M. *Battle Cry of Freedom: The Civil War Era*. New York: Oxford University Press, 1990.

Swartwelder, A. C. "This Invaluable Beverage: The Recollections of Dr. A. C. Swartwelder." *Civil War Times Illustrated*, October 1975.

Volo, D. D., and J. M. Volo. *Daily Life in Civil War America*. Westport, Conn.: Greenwood Press, 1998.

UNITED STATES, WESTERN FRONTIER

MATERIAL LIFE

DRINK

United States,
1850-1865

United States,
Western Frontier

India

Coffee was a staple for the cowboy. Green coffee beans bought in 100-pound sacks from the Arbuckle Company were parched in Dutch ovens; preferred were roasted beans (more expensive) bought in 30-pound cans from the Oriental Tea Company of Boston. The coffee grinder was usually side mounted to the chuck wagon. Most cowboys did not drink their coffee straight. Because white sugar was rarely available, granulated brown sugar was used, unless Cookie was angry and the coffee was sweetened with molasses. The granulated brown sugar often became so hard in its barrel that it had to be chipped free and then run through a meat grinder before it could be used. On the range the coffee was often brewed with water collected from bogs, where streams had been dammed up for cattle to drink. When, on occasion, an animal had become stuck and died in the bog, the cook's helper would "pull bog"—that is, wade into the muck and pull out the animal. Nonetheless, they "without flinching, drank . . . and enjoyed it."

On most outfits, liquor was forbidden in camp. However, camp was defined as 100 feet from the fire. On only one occasion in his whole career did Teddy Blue see this rule broken—and then the cowboys went out into the sagebrush to consume a bottle of whiskey. The fact that it happened even once was surprising, for "drinking and cattle didn't mix"; it was far too dangerous (Jones, 176).

To read about drink on the colonial frontier of North America, see the entries on the Colonial Frontier and New England in the section "Drink" in chapter 5 ("Material Life") in volume 4 of this series.

FOR MORE INFORMATION

Abbott, E. C., and H. H. Smith. *We Pointed Them North: Recollections of a Cowpuncher*. New York: Farrar & Rinehart, 1939.
Jones, M. E. *Daily Life on the Nineteenth Century American Frontier*. Westport, Conn.: Greenwood Press, 1998.

INDIA

MATERIAL LIFE

DRINK

United States,
1850-1865

United States,
Western Frontier

India

The most common beverages in 19th century India, with the exception of water, were tea and coffee. The foothills of the Himalayas are the ideal tea-growing climate, which is one of the main reasons that the British first became interested in India as a colony. Europeans first discovered and began exporting tea from China in the early 17th century. Prior to this coffee was the main caffeinated drink consumed in England. During the industrial revolution the English became interested in India as a means of economic gain, and the export of tea was one of the first economic endeavors they took on. Not only was tea produced by cheap Indian labor to be sent home to England, but tea from India also found its way to much of the world. The tea that was dumped into the Boston harbor during the Boston Tea Party of 1773 was grown in Darjeeling and shipped to America by the East India Company. The East India Company profited from highly inflating the price of tea, and England profited from the fact that imported tea in America was heavily taxed.

In India tea is most often prepared with a lot of milk and a lot of sugar. Sometimes other spices such as cardamom, ginger, or black pepper are also added. All of the ingredients and the tea leaves are thrown together in a pot and then brought to a boil. The tea leaves are then strained out and the mixture is ready for drinking.

Two of India's most famed teas are Darjeeling and Assam. They are considered, arguably, the best teas in the world. Darjeeling tea is named after the summer capital of the colonial government of the state of Bengal. In Darjeeling, tea is cultivated at altitudes of 4,000 to 10,000 feet. Because the territory is extremely mountainous, the tea is grown on terraces, on several different levels. India's other major tea, Assam, is named after the state in which it is grown, which is on the border of India and Myanmar.

In South India, coffee is more commonly consumed than tea. This region is more ideal for coffee growing because of its warmer temperatures. Coffee in South India is made in much the same way as tea in the North, using a lot of milk and sugar. Children also drink tea and coffee, or sometimes hot milk with sugar. Milk is rarely drunk cold.

The cows in India generally roam free, whether in the village or in the city. They naturally come home at a certain time each day, and their owners milk them. Because both cows and the milk that they give are considered sacred in Hinduism, there is little problem of cow or milk theft. Cows represent the Hindu god Krishna, who was a cowherd.

Another common beverage is the milk from a tender coconut. This is believed to be healthy because it replaces electrolytes in the body, which are lost through perspiration. To retrieve the coconut from the tall palm tree someone must scale the tree and throw down the coconuts. Upon returning to the ground he takes a semi-circular shaped axe and removes a small circle at the top of the coconut. Certain families do this as a profession. The sweet juice can then be consumed. After the liquid is gone the fruit can then be cut open and the soft tender coconut meat can be eaten.

Both Hindus and Muslims generally look down upon consumption of alcohol. However, throughout India local brews were fairly common. Some of these include arak, a clear, distilled rice liquor, and toddy, which is made from fermented coconut and palmyra palm juice, and was found mainly in the South. Sometimes arak was laced with methyl alcohol, which made it cheaper to produce but also highly toxic. Many people were blinded as a result of drinking arak that was not properly made. There are also several other types of locally made liquors in India.

The British also introduced whiskey and other types of imported liquor. Very few Indians consumed these foreign liquors. Women rarely or never consumed alcohol. Because of the social stigma of drinking, those who did partake in drinking sometimes had a tendency to drink too much and too often. Among those who consumed alcohol in 19th-century India, there is evidence of a high rate of alcoholism.

Drinks made from *bang*, or the dried leaves from the cannabis plant, were commonly used during religious ceremonies. The ground up *bang* is mixed with ground up milk sweets and milk or yogurt, as well as various other types of seeds and spices. *Bang* is generally considered more socially acceptable than alcohol because it can help one to reach spiritual enlightenment.

Many English people living in India at this time consumed tonic water, which was produced in India. Quinine, a major ingredient in tonic water, is believed to help prevent malaria, which is transmitted through mosquitoes, and a major concern for many English people living in India. Gin and tonics were first popularized at this time.

Another drink, which was popular among the English in India, was fresh lime soda, which consists of water or club soda, lime juice, and sugar. This was also adopted by many Indians and remains very popular in India.

Lassies, which are made from yogurt sweetened, salted, or plain, were also popular. The yogurt is made thin and consumed like a shake. Yogurt is considered to have a cooling quality and is good to counter a fever or hot weather.

FOR MORE INFORMATION

Chaudhuri, M. *The Tea Industry in India: a Diagnostic Analysis.* New Delhi, India: Oxford University Press, 1978.

Wickramasinghe, P. *The Food of India.* Los Angeles: Whitecap Books, 2002.

CHINA

From ancient times, the Chinese had discovered the remarkable benefits of tea as a drink. They cultivated it carefully, and the taste for tea slowly spread all over the world creating millions of adherents by the 19th century. See the China entry in the section "Drink" in chapter 5 ("Material Life") in volume 2 of this series for the beginnings of tea cultivation.

Housing

MATERIAL LIFE
|
HOUSING
|
United States,
1850-1865

United States,
Western Frontier

Victorian England

India

Latin America

As is the case even today, the housing that people used depended heavily upon class, geography, and historical accident. The best housing was found in cities among the upper classes. It was also the most expensive. Only the very rich owned their own houses. Most, including the middle class, rented. City houses tended to be narrow and tall since land was expensive. The basement and attics (or garrets) were for servants. The family entertained and conducted daily business on the main floor while bedrooms were above the drawing and dining rooms. In England, the higher the class standing the more rooms one had. For instance, for an upper-middle-class family with children, the smallest house had 10 rooms all of healthy size. It goes almost without saying that the rich also had the most decorated homes.

Compare England's urban dwellings with those on the American western frontier. Housing was shockingly rudimentary. A 19th-century missionary teacher in the West, Arizona Perkins, found herself "lost in surprise again in spite of my previous resolution *not* to be astonished at anything I might meet out here. I lifted up my eyes, and behold! Before me were *houses*, but not of no material I ever dreamed it possible for them to be constructed. They were, literally *earthly habitations*, being built thro' out of *sods*, and thatched with straw or grass" (Kaufmann, 124). Wood was too valuable to be used as a building material. Hence, houses were made of dirt, cut sod from the ground. Most of the structures were roughly 10 feet square. Although safe from the rougher elements, these houses were not comfortable. Insects and mice found the dwellings irresistible. Only the added expense of plastering walls minimized the problems of bugs and vermin. A similar housing situation existed in India at the time. In fact, note how both Indian and western frontier houses were built from the same materials. Indian houses, like American and English ones, also demonstrated the difference that class or caste standing made. The higher one was on the social ladder the better housing one had. Thus, as in the United States, in India, the poor suffered from problems caused by exposure to the elements.

Civil War soldiers faced similar hardships. Though there were a thousand variations on the standard army tent, nearly all Union and Confederate soldiers used some sort of canvas shelter. The basic tent was called the Sibley after its inventor Henry Sibley. Although Sibley himself joined the Confederates, his tent was used by both sides. It was large and spacious enough for 12 men. Another common tent was the "A" or wedge tent. It was smaller and fit only about six men. Yet another tent, the dog tent, was frequently used by the Union soldiers and housed two men who slept quite close to keep warm in the night. Mirroring society at large, in the army, the higher the rank meant the better the housing conditions. Officers had large tents or huts with several rooms and doors. They were even allowed to furnish the dwellings with a small amount of utilitarian furniture such as desks, dressers, beds, and chairs. When weather became inclement, officers often left the field and found shelter in private houses. Of course, the regular soldier did not have such luxurious accommodations. Rather, when it began to rain or get cold, soldiers got out their rubber blankets. Such was the only comfort in their otherwise miserable housing conditions.

Housing changes in 19th-century Latin America occurred mainly in the cities, where increasing industrialization attracted great numbers of rural peasants. As the middle and upper classes moved to the suburbs and outlying districts, where they built more elaborate homes of more durable materials, city centers were soon crowded with more shabbily constructed tenements and apartments that were built to accommodate workers. Thus, in many ways trends in urban housing in Latin America mirrored contemporary developments in the United States and Europe.

FOR MORE INFORMATION

Kaufman, P. W. *Women Teachers on the Frontier.* New Haven, Conn.: Yale University Press, 1984.

UNITED STATES, 1850–65

Civil War soldiers found shelter from the elements in many ways. Which of these was used depended largely on the season of the year and the accident of location. Permanent and semipermanent shelters, barracks or huts made largely of wooden planks or logs, were considered to be winter or permanent quarters. When on campaign the army was constantly on the move, and permanent structures were obviously impractical. Shelter was then provided almost exclusively by canvas tents. As the campaigning season truly began in late spring or early summer and ran on into early winter, the soldiers were under some sort of canvas shelter for most of the year, under a wide variety of weather conditions ranging from dry heat to wet, snowy cold.

The science of encamping an army is called castramentation, derived from *castra* (the Latin word for camp). The armies of ancient Rome were highly regarded for the regularity of their legionary camps, which served as a model of proper Civil War castramentation. A castramentation officer was usually appointed from among the subalterns to arrange the regimental quarters. A standard plan was followed as well as the vagaries of the campground allowed; yet in an establishment as big as an army, so many regiments needed to be accommodated that even on the best of sites some regiments were allotted poor ground. This led to some unfortunate consequences for the newly raised units and inexperienced officers of the volunteer regiments when the precincts of the camp reached into uneven, wet, or swampy ground.

The regimental site would be broken down by the castramentation officer according to battalions and companies. An effort was made to keep the company organization together, and a single company usually occupied a whole lane, called a company street. These streets often ended on a main road through the encampment. One of the more difficult tasks of the castramentation officer was to locate the latrines, which were usually no more than simple slit trenches. These needed to be within a convenient distance of the company but placed far enough away from both his regiment and all others to mask the odors that would unfortunately be present.

The textbook scheme dictated exactly the relative position of each billet, whether that of an officer, an NCO, or an enlisted man, in a double row along the company street. NCOs and officers were expected to maintain a certain level of social distinction and separate themselves from the private soldiers. Regimental areas such as headquarters, the hospital, and the commissary were also carefully dictated so that those new to a particular encampment, who were nonetheless familiar with the system, could comfortably make their way around without the least perplexity. Civilian commissions, Bible societies, missions, and sutlers usually occupied an area separate from the soldiers. Nonetheless, an "astonished" federal officer found one brigade encamped "with no boundary lines between the different regiments, all being tumbled together higgledy-piddledy, officers mixed up anyhow with the men, and the brigade commander in the middle."

Winter quarters for 16 men were to be made of wooden planks or logs with a one-room layout, 16 by 20 feet. A single entrance was made at the narrow end along a company street and was opposed at the rear by a fireplace with a chimney of crossed, notched sticks coated with mud. A cord or more of firewood would be stacked outside each hut. The roof was made with riven boards split from short logs or the sides of hardtack boxes used as shingles. Inside, the hut was designed to have wooden bunk beds paralleling the long walls and was supposed to accommodate 16 men. The bunks were "simply broad shelves one above the other, wide enough to accommodate two men spoon fashion." Straw-filled canvas sacks, called ticking, served as mattresses. No provision was made for any flooring other than the packed earth.

The soldiers were expected to build their own winter shelters with the tools given to them. No provision was made for furnishings beyond the creativity of the occupants. "We built bunks clear of the ground, to sleep on; made rustic arbors about our streets . . . every rude improvement was encouraged by the company officers." The hut could be furnished with tables and chairs in the form of discarded barrels and hardtack crates; a shelf was usually made for the all-important fresh water bucket of tinned iron. Canvas flies and shelter halves were sometimes stretched over the rafters to improve the roofs. The ingenuity of the occupants usually provided for a small section of wall or a part of a log to be removed to provide light and ventilation if a window could not be found for the purpose. The soldiers sometimes crowned the chimney with a nail keg or flour barrel to improve the draw of the fireplace; but, as these caught fire with frustrating regularity, only constant attention kept the entire structure from burning.

A sergeant described the NCO hut that he built in a letter to his friend: "We have been at work for about a week past building log huts to make us comfortable. We have about half of them finished. I have succeeded in getting one built for myself and a very comfortable one too. It is about as large as Molly Walker's front room, with a good fireplace in it. Two nice bunks and a stationary table built up on one side, and stools around it, these with other little conveniences make it quite comfortable."

Officers' huts were constructed by details of soldiers in a similar fashion and were of the same dimensions, with the exception that the layout called for two rooms with separate doors. Company captains and adjutants rated separate rooms, while junior officers were normally expected to double up. A federal officer wrote in 1864, "I am not as nicely furnished as regards furniture as I was at Atlanta, but I still have enough to be quite comfortably situated. My furniture consists of a bedstead, bedding, etc. three chairs, one camp stool, one table and my office desk and table, also a wash bowl and pitcher. My room has a good fireplace in it." Not infrequently officers absented themselves from the army during the winter to sleep in private residences. "Since I wrote you last our regiment and brigade have moved camp about a mile and a half. . . . My office is [now] located in a dwelling house and I again have a parlor of the house for my office room and a room just across the hall for storing my things in."

During most of the year, and in the South even during the winter, the troops found shelter under canvas. Tents came in various standard patterns, but the ingenuity of the individual soldier provided infinite variations. An officer noted the vagaries of living under canvas for long periods. "Rain streams at will through numerous rents and holes in the moldy, rotten canvas. Nearly every night half the men are wet through while asleep unless they wake up, stack their clothing in the darkness, and sit on it with their rubber blankets over their heads."

The Sibley tent was invented by Henry Sibley in 1857 while he was an active duty officer with the U.S. Army. When the war arrived Sibley joined the South, ultimately attaining the rank of Brigadier. Nonetheless, the Sibley, or Bell Tent, went to war on the side of the Federals. The pattern resembled a Native American tepee with a large canvas cone 18 feet in diameter and 12 high with a single entrance and a smoke hole

Sibley tents were comfortable for a dozen men under moderate weather conditions.

at the top 1 foot in diameter. This served the dual purposes of providing ventilation and emitting smoke in cold weather. A canvas cap was provided to close the hole in foul weather. Unlike the tepee with its numerous long poles, the Sibley tent sported a unique design innovation that provided for a single nine-foot center pole resting on an iron tripod. The tripod could be adjusted to tighten or relieve the tension in the canvas. The area under the tripod provided a place for a conical sheet iron stove. With its several short lengths of stovepipe protruding through the opening at the top, the Sibley stove provided a good deal of smoke-free heat.

Sibley tents were comfortable and capacious for a dozen men under moderate weather conditions, but they quickly disappeared from the line of march principally because their large canvas sheathing proved cumbersome to transport. Even in moderate weather, the tents could become foul and unwholesome if closed up for long periods. In some cases only the tripods were retained to be used over the company fireplace. Though the federal government withdrew the tent from active campaigning, it continued to be popular with the state militias camped outside the war zone.

The "A" or wedge tent was quite common during the Civil War. The one-piece canvas tent was stretched over a horizontal bar six to seven feet long supported at each end by an upright pole of about the same length. One end of the wedge was split up the center into flaps, which could be opened and fixed back to provide ventilation or tied closed in foul weather. The rectangular floor was about seven feet square. The shape permitted standing only in the very center, but six men could comfortably occupy the floor space with their equipment by spooning together to fit. The tent was widely used during the war, but took up too much room on the march and was most often seen in camps of instruction and used by troops permanently located near important military centers.

Wall tents were often used by officers for their quarters or as headquarters tents. An extra piece of canvas fly, of the same size as the roof of the tent, could be stretched over it to provide extra protection from the sun and rain. The air space between the fly and the actual roof of the tent also served tolerably well as insulation. The fly was sometimes placed in front of the entrance, creating a porch-like area, or set alone as an airy canopy or sunscreen. The wall tent used poles much like those of the wedge tent, but it required more than two dozen tent stakes and a dozen supporting ropes to erect properly. The all-around canvas wall served well, "as one could stand erect and move about in them with tolerable freedom." In long-term camps wall tents were often provided with platform floors made of wooden planking.

The dog tent, or shelter tent, was used almost exclusively by the Federals, and its squat shape became symbolic of the rank and file federal soldier on campaign. Open at both ends, the dog tent was composed of two shelter halves joined by an overlapping seam fastened with a series of brass buttons and buttonholes provided for the purpose. Each half was approximately 5 1/2 by 4 1/2 feet and fitted with loops for tent stakes on the long side. In an open field two muskets with bayonets fixed could be stuck into the ground and a stout guy rope tied between the trigger guards to support the ridge of the tent. "As you make by leaning two cards against each other," the buttoned pair of shelter halves was quickly draped over the rope and fixed to the ground by stakes. This was not the use the military had visualized for muskets and bayonets, but it was more practical than carrying tent poles or having thousands of men trying to find new ones each night. In wooded areas the guy rope might be tied between two trees, and artillerymen commonly draped the shelter halves over the wagon tongue of their limber. The dog tent provided a space about six feet square on the ground and nearly four feet high at the apex and could be erected in a matter of minutes by veteran troops.

If time and material permitted, the soldiers used tree limbs and green boughs to build canopies over their little structures to keep off the sun, or they raised the entire enterprise off the ground several feet and built a platform on which to rest away from the ground. It was not uncommon to see the bottom of dog tents raised several feet on a stockade of logs or planks, which made them very spacious and comfortable for winter quarters. "In stockading a tent the posts were split in halves, and the cleft sides all turned inward so as to make a clean and comely inside." By far the most common way of "logging up a tent" was by notching the logs together at the corners like a cabin. This took much less time and material than splitting out planks.

A favorite alternative was to place a large bed of straw, hay, or leaves a foot or more thick between two large logs. Over this snug nest the tent could be pitched. Covered with a rubber blanket in case of rain, such straw pens could provide a comfortable shelter for a season. In cold, dry weather some men burrowed into the ground, digging a trench under the shelter. This "lowering the floor instead of raising the ceiling" concept had several drawbacks, as digging was hard work and rain quickly filled the trenches with water in all but the best locations. Since the army might move at any moment, most men chose not to invest the physical effort needed to make these modifications until they had gone into winter quarters.

Although the dog tent was designed for two men, ice in the washbasin, numb fingers, and frosty breath often brought three men to bunk together. This allowed a third shelter half to be draped over the open end of the tent or over the seam at the top or placed on the ground with the gum blanket as an additional barrier against dampness. Three blankets were now available. One was spread beneath and the other two on top of the men, who spooned together to conserve body heat. Shelter tents were otherwise free of all creature comforts. As one soldier noted: "These tents were to be used chiefly for sleeping, as one could barely sit erect at the highest place in the center. They were far from comfortable living quarters. Yet they were the only kind of shelter we would have in the field during our term of service . . . and we soon became used to the little tents and were thankful to have them."

The success of the shelter tent lay in the ease with which it could be erected and carried. Recruits rolled it with the blanket on top of the knapsack. Besides the convenience of always having the tent in their possession, soldiers understood that the elimination of baggage allowed more wagons to be used to bring food to the front. Veterans, having dispensed with their knapsacks as useless impedimenta, commonly rolled their blanket, shelter half, and rubber blanket lengthwise and wore them as a tube over their left shoulder in bandolier fashion with the ends tied at the right hip. Some men of macabre disposition abandoned their shelter halves on the morning of battle in the knowledge that they could resupply themselves at day's end from the unclaimed baggage of those killed in the engagement.

In the early days of the war several Confederate units provided themselves with tents, but these quickly disappeared. Shelters of any kind were rarely seen in the field. Rather, two men generally slept together, each having a blanket and an oilcloth. The oilcloth served as an inferior alternative to the gum rubber blankets carried by the Federals. One oilcloth went on the ground. The two bunkmates covered themselves with one or both blankets, with the second oilcloth on top to protect them from the elements. Their haversacks served as pillows. Confederate encampments came to be characterized by numerous small mounds of sleeping men rather than neatly arranged tent lines. One Southerner noted in a letter, "Bivouacked for the night in an open field. The night was very cold and the only way we could keep warm was to build up a good fire and sit or wrap ourselves up in our blankets and lay down beside it" (Volo and Volo, 133–39).

To read about housing in the United States in the 20th century, see the United States entries in the section "Housing" in chapter 5 ("Material Life") in volume 6 of this series.

FOR MORE INFORMATION

McCarthy, C. *Detailed Minutiae of Soldier Life in the Army of Northern Virginia, 1861–1865.* 1882. Reprint, Lincoln: University of Nebraska Press, 1993.

McPherson, J. M. *Battle Cry of Freedom: The Civil War Era.* New York: Oxford University Press, 1990.

Volo, D. D., and J. M. Volo. *Daily Life in Civil War America.* Westport, Conn.: Greenwood Press, 1998.

UNITED STATES, WESTERN FRONTIER

Although breaking the sod and getting the first crop in were the first order of priority, making a homestead habitable required finding water, building a home, and

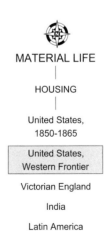

MATERIAL LIFE
|
HOUSING
|
United States, 1850-1865

United States, Western Frontier

Victorian England

India

Latin America

fencing the property. Good water close to the house was not only a convenience to eliminate the labor of carrying buckets great distances for washing, cooking, and watering the garden, it was also a matter of health, as there were numerous instances of people getting diarrhea or worms from questionable water sources. Finding a good water source was the first problem. Folk wisdom advised that one should observe the surface of the land just before sunrise; green spots in the grass suggested water below. If spiders were present in such locations, the odds were even more favorable. Many homesteaders engaged professional water witchers who ranged over the land with a forked stick (preferably of witch hazel, peach, or willow); the stick dipped from its horizontal position to point to an underground water source. After the well was dug in such a location, farmers' wives brought up the water with a bucket and windlass. As time went on, hand pumps or windmills made the chore easier.

On most of the Plains, wood was too valuable to be used for fencing. Consequently hedges were planted, the most successful of which was the Osage orange. Only gradually, as farmers became more successful, did barbed wire make its appearance.

Vaguely worded land ordinances led to fraud houses that were used to claim land. The standard requirement for a house was that it be "twelve by fourteen." This illustration from Albert D. Richardson's *Beyond the Mississippi* (1867) shows a 12-inch by 14-inch house.

The first home for most farmers was either a tar paper shack or a dugout. Most were small, only large enough to meet government requirements of a 10-foot by 12-foot structure. The Ammons sisters, who had purchased a relinquished claim and were happy there was already a house on it, were horrified to discover it was a shack resembling a "none too substantial packing-box tossed haphazardly on the prairie." Such shacks were easy to build, requiring minimal materials: some cheap lumber for framing, a couple of rolls of tar paper, and some nails. They were flimsy, however, and if not anchored down might fly away in a high wind. To keep them warmer in winter, settlers often lined them with red or blue building paper, the color indicating the quality. The inferior red paper was thinner, costing $3 a roll, whereas the blue was twice as expensive. Said one settler, "Blue paper on the walls was as much a sign of class on the frontier as blue blood in Boston." As further winter insulation, farmers often banked these structures with manure from the barn. Grace Fairchild noted that "when the smell got too bad in the spring, we knew it was time to take the insulation away." During the summer the tar paper shacks were unbearably hot, as the black exterior absorbed the sun's rays.

The dugout was generally more comfortable. The homesteader excavated an embankment to create a space approximately fourteen feet square and then added a front wall of sod bricks. The cost was minimal. Although there were some disadvantages, as when a cow or horse crashed through the roof, the dugouts were usually warm in winter and cool in summer. Cattlemen often scornfully referred to homesteaders living in such dugouts as nesters or scissorbills.

Some people built an above-ground addition to the dugout, using its walls as a foundation for a sod house, or soddy. Most started from scratch. Often neighbors would gather for a house-raising bee and erect a house in a day. First the sod was cut—2 1/2 inches was an ideal thickness—in strips 12 inches wide; these were then cut into 18-inch lengths with a spade. The best time for breaking sod for a house was when the ground was soaked from rain or snow. Like large, flat bricks, the sod was laid layer after layer in the desired dimensions, though " 'seven feet to the square' is the rule, as the wall is likely to settle a good deal, especially if the sod is very wet when laid." Generally the door and windows were set in place first, and the sod walls built around them. Forks of a tree were then placed at each end of the house, and a ridgepole laid between them. Rails of any available material—sorghum stalks, willow switches—were then laid from the ridgepole to the walls. Atop them, more sod was placed for the roof. Howard Ruede spent $10.05 for such a soddy and a year's supply of firewood in Kansas in 1877. Sometimes an especially heavy rainfall would leak through the roof, muddying clothes hung from the wall or even dripping onto the beds, thus adding to the housewife's chores. Many diarists remember various sorts of vermin (especially fleas, mice, and bedbugs) that infested these houses. One woman recalled helping her grandmother take down the canvas tacked over their ceiling each spring and fall to get rid of dirt and vermin that had fallen from the roof. The problem with bugs was minimized when settlers plastered interior walls with a mixture of clay, water, and ashes.

In most areas of the Plains frontier, a frame or brick house was seen as a status symbol, indicating that the farmer had achieved a degree of success. The social stratification was even more apparent in town. However, in part because the margin between success and failure was so narrow for farmers in this region, depending largely on vagaries of climate, there was in the country a kind of pure democracy. Though a family might live in a shack, no one looked down on them. As Howard Ruede notes, "A man in rags is as much respected as if he was dressed in broadcloth, provided he shows himself a man" (Jones, 195–97).

A floor plan of a typical antebellum home. *Arthur's Home Magazine* (1855).

To read about housing on the colonial frontier of North America, see the entries on the Colonial Frontier and New England in the section "Housing and Furnishings" in chapter 5 ("Material Life") in volume 4 of this series.

FOR MORE INFORMATION

Bartlett, R. A. *The New Country: A Social History of the American Frontier, 1776–1890.* New York: Oxford University Press, 1974.

Jones, M. E. *Daily Life on the Nineteenth Century American Frontier.* Westport, Conn.: Greenwood Press, 1998.

VICTORIAN ENGLAND

Except for aristocrats and the gentry, who inherited their country estates, people did not usually own houses. Most middle-class town dwellings were leased for a term of three, five, or seven years. The tenant took care of the furnishing and decoration; the landlord was responsible for major renovations.

MATERIAL LIFE

HOUSING

United States, 1850-1865

United States, Western Frontier

Victorian England

India

Latin America

City houses were narrow (because land was expensive) but several stories tall. The most desirable homes were on a square rather than a street. One row of houses faced each side of a parklike garden. The square was enclosed by a railed iron fence; each householder had a key to the gates. Other rows of new houses were built along streets in towns and suburbs.

The bottom story of the house was about halfway below ground level. In the front, a space was dug out and paved so the basement could have full-sized windows. This space, known as the area, was protected at street level by railings with a locked gate. Steps leading down to the area provided a service and delivery entrance. The basement was servants' territory: it contained the kitchen, pantry, scullery, and (if the house was large) a sitting-dining room for the servants. The scullery was supplied with water from mains or a pump; washing and other wet chores were done there.

The front entrance to the ground floor of the house was several steps above street level. On the ground floor were an entrance hall, a dining room, and a room set aside for the man of the house. This room was known as the library, study, or office. Some professional men, including physicians, saw most of their clients or patients in the office on the ground floor of their residence.

From the entrance hall, a broad stairway led up to the floor above. (In England it is called the first floor; in the United States it is called the second floor.) The most elegant rooms of the house were on the first floor, well above any noise that might come from the street or kitchen. Most of the floor was taken up by the drawing room,

As illustrated by this drawing from the March 13, 1875, edition of the *Illustrated London News,* a working-class home in Victorian England typically had one room for washing, cooking, eating, sitting, and sleeping. Courtesy of The Library Company of Philadelphia.

although (depending on the space and the architecture) it might be divided into two or three rooms with archways or folding doors between them. These rooms could be given names such as music room, gallery, or conservatory. When guests came to the house, a servant let them in, took their coats, and showed them up the stairs to the drawing room. The hostess welcomed them at the top of the stairs. Later, the guests went down to dinner—to the ground floor, where the dining room was located.

The floor or two above the drawing room had family bedrooms. Depending on the size and design of the house, the master bedroom might be flanked by separate dressing rooms for both wife and husband, which allowed them private space for their clothing and personal possessions. For children, there was a day nursery (where they ate and played) and a night nursery with beds for all the younger children and their nursemaid. Children over age eight or so shared a room with siblings of the same sex; youngsters did not generally have private bedrooms until they were grown. In larger houses there was a schoolroom where a governess gave lessons to the girls and the younger boys. Later in the period, when both girls and boys were more likely to go to school, the schoolroom was the children's living room, where they worked on projects, entertained their friends, and had meals separate from their parents.

The top floor (called the garret or attics) had storage space and servants' bedrooms. Besides the formal front stairs, which reached the first and second floors, back stairs ran from the cellar to the attic. Servants used the back stairs to go up and down with water, food, and coal, as well as to reach their own bedrooms.

For an upper-middle-class family with children, the smallest appropriate house had 10 rooms: kitchen, dining room, drawing room, library; three family bedrooms; a nursery (which would become the schoolroom when children grew older); and two servants' rooms. A household guide published in 1881 suggests the ideal furniture and decoration. The entrance hall should have a stone floor, Oriental rugs, an umbrella stand, and one or two plain high-backed chairs. In the dining room, a round or oval table with a center leg would allow everyone to be comfortably seated. Leather chairs were best, because velvet attracted dust and pulled at the delicate fabrics of women's dinner dresses. A sideboard should display silver serving dishes and good china; it should have locked cupboards for liquor. A dumbwaiter connecting a serving pantry outside the dining room to the kitchen on the floor below would make servants' work easier.

Unless the house was grand enough to have a separate morning room, the drawing room was essentially a ladies' room. It was furnished with comfortable couches and chairs, a piano, and a substantial center table (often round) covered with a tablecloth. (It is partly this table that gives pictures of Victorian rooms such an overcrowded appearance.) At tea time, servants put the urn on this table; people pulled up chairs or had cups handed to them by the parlor maid. The table was used for doing needlework and crafts, for looking at photograph albums and heavy books, for working puzzles, and for playing cards or games. Women generally had a desk, which was not a piece of furniture but rather a portable wooden box with a slanted lid where writing materials were kept. A woman would fetch her desk and put it on the drawing-room table to write. (Men worked in their office or study, where they used a library table or a partners' desk with drawers.)

The drawing room generally had light walls or patterned wallpaper. The floor might be painted dark brown, with a flowered or Indian rug in the center. Ideas about furnishing and decoration abounded in books and magazines. Middle-class people had more money to spend, and keeping the house up-to-date was an appropriate interest for women. Japanese decoration was all the rage for a while; so were styles influenced by the Middle East and by classical Greece. The most long-lived furnishing style was Gothic, or antique: heavy, dark wood with carved decoration. New ways of making springs allowed chairs and sofas to be more rounded. Mahogany, walnut, oak, and elm were the popular woods. Interior decorators (known as upholsterers) and furniture dealers brought pattern books to help customers make their choices.

Rooms were crowded with plants, fire screens, embroidery frames, bird cages, decorative china and glass, paintings, family pictures, collections of seashells, or souvenirs. The cluttered and crowded appearance arose partly from the casual arrangement (romantic disorder), a distinct contrast to the formality of 18th-century rooms, where delicate furniture was symmetrically lined up along the walls.

Bedrooms were more sparsely furnished, even in prosperous homes. After the middle of the century, people began to understand the need for ventilation. Four-poster beds with curtains and piles of dust-catching pillows were replaced with brass or iron bedsteads. (Victorians made a distinction between the bedstead—that is, the frame—and the bed, which lay on top. The bedstead generally held a straw or horsehair mattress, topped by a bed stuffed with feathers.)

A healthy modern bedroom, according to Victorian decorating manuals, should have rugs that could be shaken every day, a wardrobe to hold clothing, a dressing table with mirror, and a washstand. On the dressing table should be a set consisting of a tray, a ring stand, and some cut-glass bottles and china containers for homemade toilet water and hand cream. There was also usually a tidy—an embroidered bag for disposing of hair combings. (Tidies, like pen wipers, needle books, and pincushions, were gifts that girls made for their mothers and aunts.) A chamber pot or slop pot was kept in a closed bedside cabinet or under the washstand. Although most bedrooms had a fireplace with a grate, the fire was seldom lit except in cases of illness—bedrooms were for sleeping and dressing, not for spending private time during waking hours (Mitchell, *Daily Life*, 109–12).

To read about housing in Chaucer's England, see the entry on Europe in the section "Housing" in chapter 5 ("Material Life") in volume 2 of this series; for Elizabethan England, see the entry on England in the section "Houses and Furniture" in chapter 5 ("Material Life") in volume 3 of this series; for 18th-century England, see the entry on England in the section "Housing and Furnishings" in chapter 5 ("Material Life") in volume 4 of this series.

FOR MORE INFORMATION

Mitchell, S. *Daily Life in Victorian England*. Westport, Conn.: Greenwood Press, 1996.
Mitchell, S., ed. *Victorian Britain: An Encyclopedia*. New York: Garland Press, 1998.
Quiney, A. *House and Home: A History of the Small English House*. London: British Broadcasting Corp., 1986.

MATERIAL LIFE
|
HOUSING
|
United States,
1850-1865

United States,
Western Frontier

Victorian England

India

Latin America

INDIA

Various types of houses were found in different regions of India during the 19th century. The most common type of house, found primarily in the villages and in the urban slums, was the clay hut. Clay huts were made from earth and water, sculpted and baked in the sun to form a relatively secure structure. The roofs were generally made of straw and wood. These houses were usually only one small room, which might house several people. In the hot climate of most of India, the clay huts remained relatively cool. Cakes of cow dung were routinely placed on the outer walls of the clay huts to supply more support.

Larger village houses were often made of wood and also often had the same straw thatched roofs. Most of these houses incorporated both indoors and outdoors into the everyday living space. One common style of this type of house had a large courtyard in the center surrounded by several rooms and the main door. There was always a kitchen, and the other rooms were most often bedrooms: one for the father and mother and one for each son, his wife, and their children.

In larger village homes farm animals, particularly cows, often lived inside the house with the family. While it might seem that this would bring a lot of germs, mites, and disease to the family, the cows were considered sacred, and not dirty, so people often saw no reason why they should not live in the house.

There was no modern plumbing, and few of the houses had bathrooms; the fields and sometimes the city streets were used for this purpose. Beginning in the 19th century the British undertook several projects to have communal latrines put in the slums in attempts to make the cities more sanitary. Water for drinking, cooking, and bathing came from the well or river. The women were generally responsible for carrying water in pots from the water source. Bathing was usually done in the village well or river.

Food was usually cooked over firewood. Sometimes there was a hole in the wall for the stove, but more often the wood was simply placed in a pile in the middle of the room. If the house was larger, there was usually a separate room for the kitchen.

At this time most people slept on the floor or on mats, although bed rolls and cots (originally a Hindi word) that were made from wood and cloth were common among wealthier people, particularly in North India. It was uncommon for members of the same family not to sleep in the same room, and very large beds for the entire family were also common among members of the middle and upper classes. In a joint family often each brother and his wife and children would have their own room of the house and sleep together on the floor or on a large bed.

During the latter half of the 19th century in the urban areas, a new type of house became increasingly popular. These houses were usually made of wood and/or cement, with ceilings up to 15 feet high, very large rooms, and many open doorways and windows to maximize cross ventilation throughout the entire house. The walls were often painted bright colors such as pink or bright blue, and colorful fabrics were often hung in doorways between rooms. There was usually not much furniture, which avoided clutter and gave an appearance of a large, open space. These homes often had servants living in the house, who usually slept on the floor by the main door, in part to guard the home from burglars.

Larger, urban homes usually had a bathroom within the house. A typical bathroom in an urban Indian home had no running water and a hole in the ground for a toilet. A bucket of water from the neighborhood well was kept in the bathroom. After using the toilet one would dump a few cupfuls of water into the hole to flush out the ditch. Bathing was done by taking a dipper, which was a small metal or clay cup, and pouring cupfuls of water over ones head, soaping up, and then rinsing off. In the corner of the room was a hole through which all of the water could drain out to the outdoors. These holes were common in other rooms of the house as well.

The British built large houses, called bungalows (originally a Hindi word), usually with a large veranda (also a Hindi word), or circular porch. These and modern apartment buildings in the big cities became popular living choices for wealthy

Indians as well. Sometimes these structures were next to and towering over urban slums filled with small clay huts.

In the hills where it is colder, most houses were constructed entirely of wood. This kept the homes warmer, although a fire in the middle of the room was often needed for heat. Rugs were also popular in these homes and helped to contain the heat. These homes were usually small, often only one room. They sometimes had outhouses, which were basically just a fenced in hole in the ground.

In many of the hill stations members of the British government built large vacation homes for themselves. These homes were usually also constructed of wood but were much larger and sturdier than the majority of local homes. During the summer many of the English families stationed in India retreated to the cooler hills. Some of the colonial state governments, such as that of Bengal, had official quarters in the hills to make the summer more pleasant for their staff. Many wealthy Indians adopted this practice as well and built large vacation homes in the hills.

The 19th century was a time when British colonial ideas influenced all aspects of Indian society. Housing, particularly among the elite, changed drastically during this time period. A class of Indians who imitated the style of the British emerged and this is reflected in the homes that they built.

To read about housing in India in the 20th century, see the India entry in the section "Housing" in chapter 5 ("Material Life") in volume 6 of this series.

~*Dana Lightstone*

FOR MORE INFORMATION

Pawar, R. S. *Cultural Geography of Folk Houses*. Jaipur, India: Pointer Publisher, 1992.

Pramar, V. S. *Haveli: Wooden Houses and Mansions of Gujarat*. Ahmedabad, India: Mapin Publishers, 1989.

MATERIAL LIFE
|
HOUSING
|
United States,
1850-1865

United States,
Western Frontier

Victorian England

India

Latin America

LATIN AMERICA

The achievement of political independence in the early 19th century opened the new republics of Latin America to increased foreign investment. This influx of capital helped transform the major cities of the region from colonial establishments to bourgeois urban centers as traditional Spanish forms gave way to an avalanche of new architectural styles, especially those derived from Europe.

During the first decades of the 19th century, new housing in the cities was increasingly built with such materials as brick and tile, while rural housing continued to be built of more traditional materials, such as adobe and straw, which could be obtained locally. Most peasant dwellings in the countryside also continued to be built in small village settlements surrounded by the cultivated fields that belonged to the large landowners for whom most peasants worked.

In the cities, changes also occurred in housing dimensions and in the selection of building sites. Many of these changes were driven by the growing affluence of the middle classes and by the need for more housing as peasants left the countryside to find industrial jobs in the growing cities. The second half of the century also saw increasing European immigration into the region, a trend that increased foreign, particularly French, influence on urban architectural styles, and that also led, mainly in South America, to the establishment of European agricultural colonies in rural areas (called cattle stations in South America, *haciendas* in North America, *fazendas* in Brazil, and plantations in Central America and the Caribbean). Following trends derived from France and Spain, many Latin American cities of the period also entered into their first experiments with modern urban planning, as urban economic elites sought to give their hometowns the look and feel of contemporary European cities.

Toward the end of the century, as increasing wealth and industrialization drew more people to urban areas from the countryside, most Latin American cities were unable to effectively support the explosive growth in their populations. Peripheral suburbs developed around city centers; these suburbs were often promoted by major landed proprietors who sought to take financial advantage of their extensive landholdings outside growing towns. Other settlements arose more haphazardly, as rural immigrants to the city sought homes wherever they could, usually on marginal lands or in unhealthy locations. This phenomenal and increasingly unplanned growth of urban suburbs led to the development of extensive slums and shanty towns around many large Latin American cities in the 20th century.

As urban developments grew, their problems increased. Downtowns, which until the mid-19th century had been occupied by families with higher economic resources, suffered substantial changes. Upper- and middle-class families moved to new and exclusive districts and suburbs, distant from the daily urban movement. This phenomenon was also accompanied by changes in dwelling style and construction. The tradition of large houses for one family and of small colonial palaces for the wealthy gave way to multiple and smaller housing units. The larger traditional structures had a great number of rooms and spaces that were dedicated to the various personal and social activities of the family; in the smaller, multiple dwellings of the later 19th century, rooms were fewer, and personal space for family members was more limited. This breakup of larger traditional housing units into smaller ones occurred throughout the region, and the resulting tenements had different names in different countries, including *vecindades* (México), *conventillos* (Argentina), *mesones* (Peru), *favelas* (Brazil), and *ciudadelas* (Venezuela).

City centers became more industrial and commercial, and new constructions tended to use less of the marble and other types of stone and rock that had characterized earlier urban construction. As the elite moved to the suburbs and to semi-rural districts increasingly removed from the city center, peasants seeking industrial jobs moved into the city. The establishment of liberal governments after 1850 accelerated this trend, as the new regimes, which were interested in constitutional government and economic growth, broke up large landed estates. Peasant cultivators displaced by such land policies found work in the factories built by foreign investment and liberal economic reform, or as providers of the increasing array of services demanded by the urban upper and middle classes. Liberalism, which also tended to be anticlerical, promoted the sale of church lands and further increased the number of peasants seeking new opportunities in the cities.

The emigration of farmers to the city to become industrial workers is a major reason for disorderly urban growth in 19th-century Latin America. Once they were located in urban areas, peasants were gradually forced into overcrowded and poorly constructed tenements. A shortage of good housing was one of the chief urban problems of Latin America at the start of the 20th century. The problem was aggravated by the concentration of property in the hands of a few landowners. These property holders became lenders and landlords to workers who did not possess enough capital to buy their own housing. The landlord-tenant relationships that developed in most Latin American cities by the end of the century mainly benefited the former and kept the latter poor and in debt.

Worker housing occupied increasingly smaller spaces, contained few or no basic services, and was built with flimsier materials to economize on construction costs. The increase in city populations resulted in urban segregation, which was evidenced by the excellent quality and appearance of housing located at the outskirts of town, by the districts where wealthy upper-class families lived, and by the scant space and bad quality of working-class tenements in central cities and suburban slums.

~*Ramona Ortiz*

FOR MORE INFORMATION

Bähr, J. *Housing in Latin American Cities*. Kiel, Germany: Im Selbstverlag des Geographischen Instituts der Universität Kiel, 1988.

Koth, M. N., J. G. Silva, and A. G. H. Dietz. *Housing in Latin America*. Cambridge, Mass.: M.I.T. Press, 1965.

Sociedad Interamericana de Planificación (SIAP), Centro Internacional de Investigaciones para el Desarrollo. Oficina Regional para América Latina y el Caribe y Sociedad Colombiana de Planificación. *En América Latina* (In Latin America). Bogotá, Colombia: Industrias Gráficas Gaviota, 1977.

MATERIAL LIFE

| FASHION |

United States,
1850–1865

United States,
Western Frontier

Victorian England

India

Latin America

Fashion

Fashion tastes are one of those inexplicable aspects of daily life. Why one person would favor, for example, a dress that is in the shape of an "O" while another would prefer a "V" shape is hard to put into words. Nevertheless, personal tastes differ and fashions change. Historians of the 19th century are fortunate because fashion and fashion sensibility was recorded in print and on film for future generations. Thus, we know a great deal about Victorian fashion. And as with other aspects of daily life such as education or housing, class and in some cases racial distinctions made all the difference.

In nearly all countries, fashion, particularly women's clothing, connoted class and caste status. Examining the popular American magazine *Godey's Lady's Book* (or similar publications that are all readily available on microfilm) yields a wealth of information on the genteel tastes. Favorite fabrics were silks, linens, and soft cottons (generally not found among the lower classes). And the great fashion debate of the day concerned the bodice. Three styles competed: the "V" bodice, the "O," and the "Y." There were similar style changes with collars and sleeves. As with the present day, no aspect of clothing went unexamined. In England, fashions also indicated social rank. Victorian gentlemen, whose clothes were not homemade but tailor-made, had strict rules about fashion. Work clothes consisted of black suits with white shirts. Only troublemakers and slackers wore colored suits or ones with stripes or checks. The upper class also had clothes for occasions. For instance, when not at the office, English men would wear tweeds to their sporting events. In India too, fashion was a clear sign of caste as well as religious and regional affiliation. As is common nearly everywhere, the higher the social standing the finer the garments and jewelry. In this, India was much like the West.

The working classes in India, Latin America, England, and the United States rarely had many changes of clothes, and most did not own fine clothes. If they did have a silk dress or a black suit, they were cherished and seldom worn. Rather, those who used their hands to earn their bread tended to own coarse clothes that would ideally last a long time. This was true in England and the United States. In other words, utilitarian concerns rather than an overriding concern about taste guided the working-classes' fashion sense. American explorers worried about boots that did not get holes. Frontier settlers needed clothes to keep them warm in the harsh winters. English factory workers wanted clothes that would not get caught in machines and would protect them from any hazards. In 19th-century Latin America, clothing styles were also heavily influenced by climate and practical necessities as well as by social norms and foreign influences. In India, British rule introduced Western fashions to the upper and middle classes although tradition, especially religious tradition, continued to dictate the clothing of most 19th-century Indians.

Thus, clothes and fashion had a lot to do with social class. But in the United States and the slave-owning areas of Latin America, fashion also took on a racial dimension. Slave clothing was simple and utilitarian. Although slaves who worked in people's homes had finer clothing than those who worked in the fields, it was all at root serviceable. At best slaves received a new suit of clothes each year. At worse, they received worn hand-me-downs from other slaves. To southern whites and white Brazilians, the coarse and unattractive nature of slave clothing was important because it was a reminder of social place. Beautiful fashions, in the mind of white southerners, were for whites only.

UNITED STATES, 1850–65

Students of historic fashion find 19th-century attire particularly exciting because this is the first period for which widespread photographic documentation of what people actually wore is available. No longer is the study merely subject to interpre-

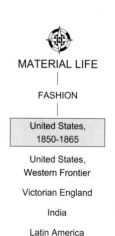

MATERIAL LIFE
|
FASHION
|
United States,
1850-1865

United States,
Western Frontier

Victorian England

India

Latin America

tations of the hand drawn or engraved fashion plates to which period women may have aspired.

One of the greatest influences on American women's fashion during the 1860s was *Godey's Lady's Book*, a magazine founded by Louis B. Godey in July 1830. In addition to serials, essays, poems, and craft projects, it featured engraved fashion plates. Each month the magazine depicted morning dresses, walking dresses, seaside costumes, riding habits, dinner dresses, and ball gowns. Such wardrobe depth was seldom needed for the vast majority of the magazine's readers, whose clothes could generally be divided into public or social and domestic or work, with a few seasonal additions for summer and winter. As time passed, *Godey's* began to show fashions better suited to the lifestyle of the American woman. By the 1860s *Godey's* had become a fashion institution, setting the standard for fashion savvy. Other magazines such as *Peterson's*, *Arthur's*, *Graham's*, *Leslie's*, and *Harper's* began to follow suit or grew in popularity. Parthenia Hague, a woman living in the blockaded South, observed, "Of course we used the same style the whole four years of the war, in our secluded settlement; not a fashion plate or 'ladies' magazine did we see during that entire period, so we were little troubled by the 'latest styles.'"

Whether a woman could afford the extravagances touted by the fashion plates of the day or not, the look she was hoping to attain was the same. Women of the Civil War period wanted to create the appearance of a narrow waist. Virtually all lines of garments emphasized the smallness of the waist by creating the illusion of width at the shoulders and hips. This was further accentuated by foundation garments that altered the body's physical appearance.

The dress bodices during this period can be classified by three basic styles. There was the "O" bodice, distinguished by the fullness of the fabric as it cascaded over the bust and gathered in around the waist. "O" bodices were especially popular prior to the war but continued to be worn throughout the conflict. Period photographs

This photograph shows the pagoda and fitted sleeves of Civil War era dresses.

indicate that it was the most common style during the early war. The bodice that was becoming fashionable at this time was the "V" bodice. This very fitted style was characterized by double or triple vertical darts extending from the waist. The darts, as well as the side and back seams, were usually boned. Stays could be made from whalebone, metal, or even wood. By the end of the war this style was most popular. The third bodice style was the "Y." This style has a fanlike appearance. It had been in vogue since the early 1840s and had begun to fall out of favor. Like the "O" bodice, "Y" bodices were relatively loose fitting.

Often sleeves had sleeve caps. These were ornamental pieces of fabric that covered the top few inches of the sleeve, supporting the image of the wide, sloping shoulder. Sometimes the impression of a sleeve cap would be created through the use of trim. Short cap sleeves that revealed a woman's arm could only be found on ball gowns.

The necklines of day dresses usually came to the base of the neck. Many were trimmed by small, white collars that were sewn flat and met in the front. Some had very short stand-up collars. Collars were basted inside to protect the garment from wear and soiling. They could easily be removed for frequent launderings from which the entire garment could be saved. The collars would be constructed of sturdy white or very light-colored fabric that could stand up to the repeated washings this portion of the garment required. Sometimes these collars had matching sets of cuffs that were similarly attached and served the same purpose. Collars were frequently decorated with a brooch at the center of the neck. If a bow was used, the tails of the bow would extend diagonally away from the center, continuing to proffer the illusion of the broad upper torso. Ball gowns often had wide bateau necklines.

Many of the fabrics and dyes used at this time did not hold up to frequent laundering. Garments were often taken apart and resewn when cleaned. *The Housekeeper's Encyclopedia* provided nine pages of instructions for washing various fabrics, for example, "Take rice-water, and wash them quickly, without soap." Other methods included the use of bran, ox-gall, salt, elixir of vitriol, and egg yolk. Most women's dresses were never totally laundered but rather spot cleaned as needed.

Skirts were long but seldom touched the ground. An exception was the elliptical skirt popular during the late war. These skirts were shorter in the front but lengthened in the back to a point where some actually dragged on the ground. Hem tapes were common on skirts. The tapes or trims were wrapped around the finished hem and could be removed for cleaning or replacement. Skirts were very full and were either fully gathered or pleated at the waistline. No effort was made to make the stomach area appear flatter because, once again, the fuller an area away from the waist seemed, the narrower the waist appeared.

Fabrics used for dresses and skirts included silk, linen, wool, and cotton. These were available in an almost infinite variety of weights and weaves, some of which are no longer available today. By far cotton and linen were the most common choices for everyday wear. Silk was expensive. If the average woman owned a silk dress, it would be saved for very special occasions. Linen, because of its extreme durability and ability to be produced at home, was considered frontier or laborer clothing. This was particularly true in the South, where it was in common use among the slave population. Wool continued to have its place because of its warmth and especially because of its fire-retardant qualities. Cotton, a status symbol earlier in the century, had become readily available and affordable for even modest households by the 1830s, thanks to the tremendous development of the textile industry after the invention of the cotton gin. From time to time, there were movements in the North among abolitionist women to avoid the use of cotton due to their belief that it was produced largely as a result of slave activity, but this tended to be confined to relatively small groups.

The blockade and the resulting interruptions in trade caused great hardships for Southern women who had once been the most fashionable element of the population. Parthenia Hague observed, "Every household now became a miniature factory in itself, with its cotton, cards, spinning-wheels, warping-frames, looms, and so on." Mary Chesnut recounted the following exchange after being asked for a bottle of brandy by a visitor. "I replied, 'Whenever you bring me that roll of linen cambric you said you had from a blockade-runner for me.' J. C. said gravely, after Brewster left with the brandy bottle, 'Surely you did not ask that man for a bolt of linen cambric?' Surely I had."

Some Southern ladies continued to dress and to dance in whatever prewar style they could manage as a means of keeping up their courage. With Yankee gunboats anchored off Baton Rouge and Union troops occupying the city, Sarah Morgan made the following entry in her diary:

Suppose we each took a fancy to consider ourselves the most miserable of mortals, and acted accordingly, going about with our eyes streaming, groaning over our troubles, and never cease to mourn. What a jolly world this would be!—And wouldn't my white dress that Tische is ironing for me to wear to church tomorrow get woefully damp!—Ah no! let us all learn to laugh and be happy, and sing "Better days are coming," even if we don't believe it, it will make those around us happy.

Drawing upon their resourcefulness and creativity, Southern women managed to rework prewar finery and to use natural materials. Mary Chesnut wrote: "Went to sell some of my colored dresses. What a scene—such piles of rubbish—and mixed up with it all, such splendid Parisian silks and satins. A mulatto woman kept the shop under the roof of an out of the way old house. The ci-devant rich, the white ladies, sell to, and the Negroes buy of, this woman."

Prices soared. By 1864 Judith McGuire recorded prices that would give a purchaser pause today. "I gave $110 for ladies' Morocco boots; $22 per yard for linen; $5 apiece for spools of cotton; $5 for a paper of pins." Women needing funds to keep their households together often reworked old finery to create collars, under sleeves, neckties, and other items that brought handsome prices in the inflated Confederate currency. In the face of such adversity, Mary Chesnut described the ingenuity she and her friends displayed in preparation for a wedding. "Julia Rutledge was one of the bridesmaids, and we could not for a while imagine what she would do for a dress. Kate remembers some [material] she had in the house for curtains bought before the war and laid aside as not needed now. The stuff was white and sheer, if a little coarse, but we covered it with no end of beautiful lace. It made a beautiful dress." Parthenia Hague remarked, "It was really ridiculous, our way of making raids upon what remained of our fine bed-linen, pillow shams, and slips, for garments of finer texture than our own homewoven cloth."

The color palette available at this time was basically that which could be achieved by natural dyes. While Southern women tended to wear lighter hues, popular colors included browns, soft blues, greens, lavenders, and grays. Yellows and deep berry-toned reds were also in use. Black was a common color for trim and detailing. Even though chemical dyes had been introduced by the end of the 1850s, these colors were mostly found in decorative fabrics for the home. Although some showy young women in the North did wear them, proper ladies did not. *Peterson's* counseled against the use of bright colors: "Though they may gratify the savage, [they] will not please the educated eye." Readers were warned about wearing yellow and yellow-greens. "It is scarcely necessary to observe that, of all complexions, those which turn upon the yellow are the most unpleasant in their effect—and probably for this reason, that in this climate it is always a sign of bad health."

Readers were warned about wearing yellow and yellow-greens.

Popular patterns included geometrics such as dots, checks, and stripes. Sometimes these were combined with small floral motifs or grouped into small clusters. Large florals were not in style, nor were very small floral calicoes, which were not popular until later in the century. Patterns were also created by variations in the weave or with the use of shiny and dull threads.

Trim for dresses was generally placed in horizontal or diagonal lines continuing the illusion of the narrow waist. Day dresses had little trim except on the sleeves or bodice. Skirts, if trimmed, were done so near the hemline. The trims used included braid, piping, binding, and ribbon. Ribbons were commonly gathered, pleated, or ruched. Some skirts appeared to be trimmed at the hem but had actually been fitted with a tape wrapped around the hem to protect it from wear. It was much less expensive to replace a worn hem tape than to replace the garment, and the process was less labor-intensive than turning the skirt. Some ball gowns had flounces or even a series of ruffles along the skirt. Trims on gowns tended to be more expensive and elaborate than those on everyday dresses.

Dresses were updated or embellished by the use of accessories. A dress might be given a different look by the addition of a fichu. Fichus were often made of sheer, gauze-like fabrics. They were decorated with ruffles, ribbons, lace, and bows. Fichus were particularly popular in warmer climates at a time when propriety dictated that a lady's shoulders be fully covered until evening. A cooler dress with a scooped neckline could be worn and covered by the lightweight fichu. They were also worn over ball gowns by older women. Once again, practicality dictated that the fichu be a separate piece that could be cleaned more easily than the entire dress. This also allowed dresses to be easily changed to reflect new trends in fashion. There were several styles of fichu, but basically they covered the upper back much like a shawl collar and extended over the front in long tails that either met at the waist or crossed over each other. Some extended down the skirt a foot or so. *Berthes* served a similar purpose, but were like oversized collars rather than wraparounds.

Sashes and waistbands were made of rich fabrics often embroidered or trimmed. They extended well down the length of the dress. Belts of many different styles were worn. Some were quite elaborate. The Medici belt stands out as perhaps the most notable style. It was several inches wide at the sides and back, but the front flared out into two exaggerated points that extended up to the area between the breasts and down to the mid-stomach. The *bretelle* corset was similarly shaped, with shoulder straps almost like braces.

Ball gowns, naturally, would not have been found in the majority of women's wardrobes, but their splendor and overstated nature demand some comment. Ball gowns had scooped necklines, short sleeves, and extremely full skirts. Silk was the fabric of choice. Ball gowns were elaborately decorated with long sashes, tiers of laced ruffles, flower garlands, or whatever extravagance might have struck the wearer.

Skirts worn with shirts and jackets, or with vests and jackets, were popular among young women in their teens and 20s. It was not until the very end of the war that the skirt and blouse were seen unaccompanied by the jacket. The jackets were similar to what is called the bolero today. Jackets frequently matched the skirt fabric. One of the most popular styles was the Zouave jacket, which was copied from the French military uniform of the same name. As the fashion grew more popular, the jackets became decorated with more and more black braid in increasingly ornate patterns. Vests were generally of a solid fabric.

Blouses were white and generally closed by buttons rather than hooks and eyes. The end of the blouse was sewn into a waistband as opposed to hanging loose. The Garibaldi shirt—based on the unique garment of the freedom fighters who succeeded in uniting Italy in 1860—was a very distinctive style of shirt worn during the Civil War. It was characterized by trim at the center front, the waistband, the shoulders, and the cuffs. As a rule, they were made of colored fabric.

Riding habits consisted of a skirt, jacket, blouse, and occasionally a vest. Hats were small and frequently had a veil. Jackets were decidedly plainer and more masculine during this time than they had been during the previous decade. The fabric was closely woven to withstand snags on branches, and dark colors were preferred for practicality. Of course, not all women rode for exercise. Some rode in parks to be seen, and these ladies often preferred more elaborately decorated outfits. *Godey's Lady's Book* gives us this description of an illustration: "Riding habit of black cloth with fluted worsted braid and large gilt buttons; white cashmere vest; scarlet cravat; black felt hat with black feather and scarlet bow."

By the 1860s white wedding dresses had come into fashion. However, many women still followed older traditions and were married in their "best" dress. Mary Chesnut wrote: "The bridesmaids were dressed in black and the bride in Confederate gray homespun. She had worn the dress all winter, but it had been washed and turned for the wedding. . . . [S]he wore a cameo breastpin. Her bonnet was self-made." Those fortunate enough to be able to afford such a specialized garment tended to choose dresses that might be considered plain by ballroom standards. Expense was more likely to be put into the fabric rather than trim. Generally, weddings were held during the day. Wedding dresses were therefore day dresses with jewel necklines and long sleeves. In keeping with the look of the day, headdresses and veils tended to lie flat on the head to avoid adding height. Coronets of real or artificial flowers were arranged so that they framed the face and added width. Mary Chesnut described another bride. "Maggie dressed the bride's hair beautifully, they said, but it was all covered by her veil. Which was blonde lace—and the dress tulle and blond lace." She also recorded the details of a "Negro wedding." "The bride and her bridesmaids in white Swiss muslin, the gayest of sashes—and bonnets too wonderful to be described. They had on red blanket shawls which they removed as they entered the aisle. . . . The bride's gloves were white."

Just as the average woman did not have a specialized outfit for every task of the day, most men did not enjoy wardrobe depth. In his handbook of etiquette, Arthur Martine remarks, "There are four kinds of coats which a man must have: a business coat, a frock-coat, a dress-coat, and an over-coat. A well dressed man may do well with four of the first, and one each of the others per annum. An economical man can get along with less." Nonetheless, Martine's idea of getting along was nowhere near reality. Like women's clothing, men's clothing in practical application tended to fall into formal and informal, summer and winter. New clothes would be considered best dress until they became worn, and they would then be relegated to work status. A shirt, vest, and trousers would be the very least in which a man would allow himself to be seen. A man appearing with anything less was considered to be in a state of undress. Even laborers and farmers would not allow themselves to go with less. It was the basest menial or workman who would not be so attired, such as the blacksmith, who would wear a heavy leather apron that covered him above the waist.

Dress shirts were made of white cotton. Longer than the modern shirt, they were pullovers that buttoned from the mid-chest to the neck. Small vertical tucks commonly decorated either side of the buttons, but this became less favored as the 1860s progressed. Shirts had neck bands and detachable collars. For formal day wear, the collar was upright with a gap between the points, which just touched the jaw, allowing for freer movement of the head and neck than had been the style earlier in the century. For informal occasions, men wore either a shallow single collar with sloping points meeting at the center and forming a small inverted "V" opening, or a shallow double collar similar to the modern collar. Work shirts were made in a variety of colors and checks and could be made from cotton or linen.

Cravats, which more closely resemble the earlier neck stock than the modern tie, were worn around the neck. The term necktie was just coming into use. The cravat might have been tied in a flat, broad bow with the ends extending across the top of the waistcoat or secured with a pin. Basically, however, it was a band of fabric passed around the neck and tied in either a bow or a knot with hanging ends. Silk was the fabric of

> *A shirt, vest, and trousers would be the very least in which a man would allow himself to be seen.*

choice, and it was one area where a man might be able to display his good taste even if his purse prohibited further extravagances. The decade began with a preference for light-colored cravats, occasionally decorated with embroidery or other fancy work. As the war progressed, however, darker colors became more prominent. Striped, plaid, and dotted cravats were also worn, but with less regularity. Even laborers would simulate the look, although they may only have been able to knot a cotton kerchief around their neck. Ladies' magazines of the period offered patterns for woolen and cotton knitted cravats. A pattern for a striped tie done in brioche knitting in *Peterson's* ended with, "We recommend this for a present for the holidays."

Vests or waistcoats could be made of the same fabric as the suit, or they could be of much finer, dressier fabrics such as silk taffetas, embossed silks, or brocades. Patterns ranged from tone on tone to stripes, checks, and paisleys. The neckline cut was moving lower than in the previous decade. Watch pockets became common. Suits were either loose fitting, almost baggy, or very formal with knee-length frock coats. The fuller suit seems to have been favored by the average man, perhaps because it was more comfortable or needed less skilled tailoring. The formal suit appears to have been the look to which men of power aspired. Lapels sported a more modern single notch than earlier in the century. Frock coats sometimes had velvet collars and cuff link-style buttoning. Work trousers had buttoned, full fall fronts, while dress trousers had French flies, which concealed the buttons.

Wool was the fabric of choice for these items, with linen being popular during the summer, especially in the South. Farmers seemed to favor tweeds and more sturdy woolens. Generally, solids dominated, with browns and grays most common. Black was the choice of professionals, who also preferred fine woolen broadcloth, serge, and twill. These fabrics often had a certain amount of silk woven in to give them a finer finish and lighter weight.

When it came to lounging in the privacy of one's home, gentlemen had several specialized items of attire. Lounging or smoking caps were elaborate items made of rich fabrics and adorned with embroidery, beadwork, or braid. They generally came in three basic styles: the round pillbox style, the fitted six-panel cap, and the tear-drop-shaped Scotch style. The first two styles ended with a tassel on top. The last was finished with a narrow ribbon at the back of the cap at the point. Ladies' magazines also carried patterns for making and decorating these caps. *Peterson's* suggests that a handmade lounging cap "would make a very pretty Christmas, New Year's, or birthday gift for a gentleman." In addition to slippers, which greatly resembled the woman's slipper for relaxed footwear at home, a man might have preferred the dressing, or lounging, boot. *Peterson's* advises: "The Lounging Boot, will almost supersede the slipper, as many gentlemen catch cold by changing from a boot to a slipper, even in the house." These boots were made of fabric and were decorated with elaborate embroidery.

Nightshirts were made of white cotton and extended to the ankle. They had long sleeves and small turned-down collars. The nightcap was a bag-shaped item with a tassel on top. Some were knit or crocheted, but these were going out of style. Over his nightshirt a gentleman may have worn a wrapper. This was a long, sack-style robe with plain sleeves, confined by a cord at the waist.

The clothing of slaves varied with the economic status of the slaveholder and with the tasks the slave was required to do. Slaves who worked in the household, often well dressed in suits, dresses, or colonial outfits, were seen by visitors to the home, and therefore their appearance would have been a reflection on the slaveholder. Slaves who worked in the fields needed serviceable clothing that would survive the rigors of the work being done. Any benefit that the slave gained in the way of clothing was an accidental advantage of the owner's desire to run an efficient plantation and a model household.

Sarah Stone was the daughter of a Mississippi plantation owner who held 150 slaves. In her diary she described the semiannual process of getting clothes ready for the slaves, which she admits "was no light work."

Male slaves were furnished with only two or three suits a year. Women were supplied with a calico or linsey dress, head handkerchiefs, and gingham aprons for Christmas. The fabric was sturdy and became as soft as flannel as it was washed. The slaves often dyed the white suits tan or gray with willow bark or sweet gum.

The quality and quantity of clothing for slaves during the war varied greatly, and generally both suffered as the war continued. These garments often represented white folks' hand-me-downs, remnants, and discards. Slaves, especially those in urban areas, could often be seen in slightly unfashionable, but serviceable, suits of clothing and dresses of cotton and wool. As whites felt the pinch of the blockade, hand-me-downs and discards took on a new value in their eyes and were rarely passed on to slaves. In this manner the slaves were made to bear the worst effects of the shortages.

Plantation slaves were often clothed in coarse but durable "Negro cloth," which was produced from linen in the mills of New England or in coarse woolen broadcloth. Prior to the opening of hostilities, plantation owners commonly purchased cloth by the yard and allowed the slaves to fashion the clothing on the plantation. This cloth took the form of trousers and shirts for the men and boys, while slave women wore woolen dresses with cotton aprons. The wool helped to prevent the skirts from catching fire and was favored by women, both black and white, who worked near open hearths. Both sexes used straw hats and handkerchiefs in a variety of ways, but generally they were tied to form head coverings or neck cloths.

Shoes were a difficult item to provide for the slave at a reasonable cost, and most ex-slaves complained of rarely having owned shoes that fit well. Unless they owned a slave that was trained in shoemaking from raw leather, plantation owners resorted to buying shoes in bulk. There existed an entire trade in New England dedicated to the manufacture of cheap shoes for slaves. These shoes rarely gave long use without the services of a cobbler. Wooden clogs, a type of sandal with a large wooden sole, often served in place of shoes. Slaves generally preferred to go barefoot in the fields, as did their white farmer counterparts, because shoes did not hold up well in plowed fields. Contemporary illustrations from *Harper's* and *Leslie's* almost always show slaves to be shod. Slaves who were forced to go barefoot in winter greased their feet with tallow to protect the skin, but this circumstance seems to have been rare except in the Deep South. Slaves rarely went unshod in town or in the Northern border states, as such a thing would have embarrassed their owners (Volo and Volo, 237–54, 257–69).

FOR MORE INFORMATION

McPherson, J. M. *Battle Cry of Freedom: The Civil War Era*. New York: Oxford University Press, 1990.

Volo, D. D., and J. M. Volo. *Daily Life in Civil War America*. Westport, Conn.: Greenwood Press, 1998.

Woodward, C. V. *Mary Chesnutt's Civil War*. New Haven, Conn.: Yale University Press, 1981.

Zwick, E. *Glory*. 1989. Film.

UNITED STATES, WESTERN FRONTIER

On the 19th century western frontier, fashion was a luxury, often an unnecessary one. Explorers' clothes were designed for protection and warmth and quickly wore out. Hunters sent out for game below the Teton River on the Lewis and Clark expedition complained that the alkali and other "mineral substances" ate through their moccasins. As early as June 1805, uniforms were in tatters and everyone was wearing elk skin shirts and breeches. By the time they were in view of the Pacific, Clark purchased two beaver skins from which to make a robe "as the robe I have is

rotten and good for nothing." Life during the rainy season at Fort Clatsop was even more miserable because nearly half the men's leather clothes had rotted. Wrote Clark: "if we have cold weather before we can kill & Dress skins for clothing, the bulk of the party will Suffer verry much." On August 8, 1806, as they arrived back at the mouth of the Yellowstone River, Lewis wrote that since they left the west side of the Rockies, they had not had time to dress skins and make clothes; thus, most of the men were "extreemly bare." It is thus no surprise that as they approached St. Louis in September 1806 and met up with the trader Auguste Choteau, "several of the party exchanged leather for linen shirts and beaver for corse hats."

On the homesteaders' frontier, most clothing was more utilitarian than fashionable, though new clothes brought a lift to the spirits. Keturah Penton Belknap remembered spinning flax all winter in her spare time and weaving a piece of linen to sell. With the money she got a "new calico dress for Sunday," a pair of new shoes, and material for an everyday dress. "It was cotton warp colored blue and copper and filled with paler blue filling, so it was striped one way and almost as nice as gingham." Her plan was to make one new dress each year so she always had one "for nice"; with a "clean check apron I would be alright." Priscilla Merriman Evans learned to weave different shades of gray by varying the proportions of black and white wool, though when making skirts she always added a row of bright colors—red, blue, green—halfway up the skirt. She learned to use madder, indigo, logwood, copperas, and other roots to provide color. And, with their simple patterns, "when our dresses wore thin in front, they would be turned back to front and upside down and have a new lease on life." Elinore Stewart remembers sewing underwear out of sugar and flour sacks, petticoats from the larger ones and "drawers" from the smaller. Howard Ruede bought overalls for $1.25; when they sprouted holes, he patched them himself with whatever was at hand, often using a variety of colors and fabrics, even feed sacks, so that sometimes his backside was adorned with a feed mill slogan. He took to wearing no socks or underwear, and on one occasion mentions that he is writing a letter clad only in his shirt and cap. Despite all his mending, his favorite coat is "ripping fast . . . one pocket entirely out." Morever, "my shoes are well ventilated at the toes." He notes that prairie grass is awfully hard on shoe leather. He later bought two pairs for $2.25, a 25-cent discount for buying several. Despite the danger from rattlesnakes and the toughness of the grass, many took to going barefoot. Hamlin Garland mentions burning his bare feet while trying to put out a prairie fire.

Boys wore long pants, not celebrating the transition from boyhood to adulthood, as did their eastern cousins, by changing from short pants to long. Perhaps because children did adult work, "even my eight year old brother looked like a miniature man with his full-length overalls, high-topped boots, and real suspenders." In summer, work clothes generally consisted of a "straw hat, a hickory shirt, and a pair of brown denim overalls." But since their best suit (they only had one) was made of "blizzard weight" wool, they endured "tortures" in their Sunday best, replete with starched shirts and paper collars. On the farm they wore cavalry boots; only when they moved to town did shoes become an option. One of Garland's fondest boyhood

> *On the homesteaders' frontier, most clothing was more utilitarian than fashionable.*

memories was getting new boots—his had red tops with a golden moon in the center—even though his father insisted they be a size too large so they would last longer.

Although some young women attempted to keep up with fashion, replacing their worn-out hoops with grapevines, many also adopted more practical expedients. Mollie Sanford found her skirts an impediment when searching for a strayed cow and thus went out in an "old suit of Father's clothes." And Miriam Davis Colt, tired of having the hems of her dresses burned by cooking fires and frayed by grass, adopted bloomers; in them, she also rode a horse astride instead of sidesaddle.

For frontier soldiers, clothing was also a point of daily frustration. The soldier of the Indian wars might at first look like the little brother of the Civil War soldier wearing hand-me-downs, for from 1865 to about 1872 uniforms were Civil War surplus. Consequently the frontier regular suffered, as had his predecessor, from shoddy materials and poor workmanship that unscrupulous, profiteering suppliers had foisted on the War Department. The standard clothing issue provided at the recruit depot was a "navy-blue wool sack coat, two pairs of light-blue kersey trousers, two gray or dark blue flannel shirts, a couple of suits of wrist and ankle-length, two-piece underwear, a caped overcoat of light-blue wool, a pair of rough boots or ankle-high brogans, a forage cap (or kepi), and a leather waist belt."

Rarely did the uniforms fit, so the soldiers had them altered by the company tailor—at the soldier's expense, with the cost deducted from his pay. In 1872 the army introduced a new uniform with revised sizes and patterns, presumably more compatible with the human body. H. H. McConnell was none too sure: "None of the clothing issued was fit to wear until it had been altered from top to bottom. The clothing furnished was of four sizes—from number one to number four—and the [limited] . . . stock on hand often necessitated the issuing of a number four garment to a number one man." The tailor could usually alter these into "respectably fitting uniforms"; however, McConnell found little else good to say about the tailor, "a non-combatant, usually of the same kind as the dog-robber or the company clerk." (Some of the combat soldier's resentment of the noncombatant is evident here. Later McConnell observed that most "real" soldiers regard band members, clerks, tailors, and "extra-duty men of all kinds as . . . shirking or getting out of legitimate duties.")

The uniform, even altered by the tailor, had many shortcomings. The material tended to wear out quickly in the field or in garrison fatigue duty. It was far too hot for summer or for southern posts, and not nearly warm enough for winter on the northern plains. The long underwear and woolen socks itched, despite orders to change socks frequently and underwear once a week. The shoes were especially uncomfortable, made of stiff leather with the soles fastened by brass screws that conducted heat and cold and, worse, raised blisters and gouged holes in the wearer's feet. Shoes and boots, manufactured at the military prison at Fort Leavenworth, were so inexpertly crafted that rights and lefts were almost indistinguishable. One soldier solved the matter of fit by walking through a creek until the uppers were thoroughly soaked and then wearing the wet shoes for the entire day, thereby getting a "foot form and comfort." Soldiers usually rubbed soap on their feet and socks to avoid blisters from new shoes. There were no overshoes or rubbers; to protect their feet from the northern Wyoming winter, soldiers of the Eighteenth Infantry competed for burlap sacks with which they wrapped their feet to keep from freezing. Colonel Richard I. Dodge of the Eleventh Infantry wrote in 1887, "The shoe furnished the enlisted soldier is a disgrace to the civilization of the age. . . . Many a man is discharged from the service a cripple for life, from having been forced to wear the things called shoes now furnished by the Government."

Eventually changes—some official, some not—were achieved to make the uniform more serviceable. In the Southwest, clothing of lighter materials and colors was issued—white shirts, white canvas trousers, and even the white cork helmets used by British troops in India. In the North, the Clothing Bureau experimented with all manner of furs and even canvas lined with sheepskin or blanket materials. One officer's wife described her husband "clad in buffalo skins, trousers and overcoat with the fur inside, mufflers over his ears, his hands encased in fur mittens, his face in a mask, leaving space sufficient only to see his way, he presents an appearance rivaling his Eskimo brother."

From individualism or necessity, frontier soldiers often created variant uniforms never thought of by Uncle Sam. Some cavalrymen adopted the more comfortable Indian moccasins, lined their pants with canvas, and wore shirts of many nonregulation colors, including checks, often made by their wives; some were even seen in fringed buckskin. Charles King, campaigning with Crook, talks about troops making "rude leggins, moccasins, etc." from the skins captured from the Indians on the previous day, when they defeated American Horse's band at Slim Buttes. To the outside observer, frontier soldiers might look more like banditti than military men. A *New York Times* reporter described the arrival of the Fifth Cavalry at Fort Fetterman in July 1876:

To a fastidious eye . . . there was something shocking in the disregard of regulation uniform, and the mud-bespattered appearance of the men; but it was a pleasure to see how full of vim, of spirit, and emphatically of fight, the fellows looked. . . . About the only things in their dress which marked them as soldiers were their striped pants and knee boots, both well bespattered with mud. Their blue Navy shirts, broad brimmed hats, belts stuffed with cartridges, and loose handkerchiefs knotted about the neck, gave them a wild, bushwhacker appearance. (Jones, 62, 198–99, 223–25)

To read about fashion on the colonial frontier of North America, see the entries on the Colonial Frontier and New England in the section "Male Clothing and Female Clothing" in chapter 5 ("Material Life") in volume 4 of this series.

FOR MORE INFORMATION

Jones, M. E. *Daily Life on the Nineteenth Century American Frontier*. Westport, Conn.: Greenwood Press, 1998.

Luchetti, C., and C. Olwell (contributor). *Women of the West*. St. George, Utah: Antelope Valley Press, 1982.

Utley, R. M. *Frontier Regulars: The United States Army and the Indian: 1866–1891*. Bloomington: Indiana University Press, 1973.

VICTORIAN ENGLAND

Many good books about historical costuming are available in libraries; in large cities and university towns it is fairly easy to find collections of 19th-century fashion magazines. It is important to remember, however, that only a very few people (as now) wore the elaborate clothes typically featured in magazines. Museum costume collections tend to display wedding dresses and other garments that survived in good condition because they were seldom worn; even the outfits that people put on to have their photograph taken are unlikely to have been ordinary everyday wear.

During the Victorian period, men's clothing became less colorful and more businesslike. The basic woman's dress had a fitted bodice and a long full skirt, although there were frequent changes in shape, detail, and trimming. Colored plates in women's magazines and popular prints of people in high society publicized the newest designs; the constant small changes promoted (for the first time) a sense that fashionable women should have new clothes in the latest style for every season. Most people, however, even among the middle class, had only two or three changes of everyday clothing at any one time.

From the 1840s onward, the clothes men wore in the city (either for work or for evening) were generally dark and plain. The bright colors, ruffles, and delicate fabrics of the Regency vanished. By 1820, trousers had replaced knee breeches except for a few ritualized costumes (and footmen's livery). Changes in men's clothing involved relatively minor matters such as the way coats were cut, the tightness of trousers, and the details of collars and lapels. Men working in offices or professions almost always wore a black coat and trousers with a white shirt. Checks and stripes were unserious—and regarded as the mark of a loafer or swindler. Other colors and fabrics were permissible on social occasions. Special clothing for certain sports became common toward the end of the century. Travelers and outdoorsmen wanted practical boots and overcoats; Charles Macintosh and Thomas Burberry began producing the outerwear that turned their names into household words.

According to an etiquette guide published in the 1890s, in the summer a gentleman going to a big London function, to the Ascot races, or to a wedding must wear a suit with frock coat, a light waistcoat, a high silk hat, gray gloves, and a dark gray tie. In winter, the coat and waistcoat were to be black and the trousers striped gray. On the river or at the seashore he could wear plain gray flannel trousers with a shorter gray coat, or white ducks. A suit with knickerbockers that fastened below the knee was appropriate for cycling, golfing, or shooting. Tweeds were worn only in the country, on an estate, or in the nearby village. A gentleman's clothing was made for him by a tailor.

Working-class men wore clothing of plain cut and heavier fabric. Ready-made canvas trousers were available, although many working men bought both coats and trousers from used clothing stalls. Some trades still required traditional garments, especially those that had a practical function (e.g., the smith's leather apron or the sailor's bell-bottom trousers). The farm laborer's linen smock gradually went out of use during the period. Working men generally wore short jackets rather than the longer coats of the middle class. At the end of the period, standard sizing for factory-made garments and shoes improved the look and comfort of the clothes available to people with limited budgets.

Poor people slept in their clothing or underwear. Among other classes, men wore nightshirts. Both men and women usually slept in a nightcap. Remember, bedrooms were unheated; caps helped the body retain its warmth.

From sleepwear to day wear, in the first half of the period, children in middle-class and upper-class families wore clothes that were very similar to adult garments. Separate styles for children first appeared in the 1860s and 1870s. Books were responsible for some of the fads: *Little Lord Fauntleroy* inspired black velvet suits for boys; many styles of girls' dresses were based on the illustrations from *Alice's Adventures in Wonderland* or the loose mock-Regency gowns depicted in Kate Greenaway's drawings. Also popular (in imitation of the queen's children and grandchildren) were Scottish tartans made up into kilts for boys and dresses for girls. As with elaborate adult garments, outfits of this sort were probably worn more often for family photographs—which were a rare and special event—than in actuality.

However, there were also new and practical children's clothes starting in the 1870s. Instead of trousers, boys wore knickerbockers fastened below the knee; although the socks slipped and drooped, the full upper leg and loose knee were good for running and climbing. Boys' sailor suits (usually with shorts rather than long trousers) were also easy to put on and less constraining than a fitted coat. Schoolgirls often wore a dark skirt and middy blouse or a comfortable, loose, pleated dress.

Younger children had long, full pinafores to cover their clothes. These were often made of a sturdy brown or dark blue fabric instead of the impractical white, which one usually sees in pictures. Children, like adults, wore hats or caps outside. Boys were breeched—given their first trousers—when they started learning lessons, usually between ages three and five. Until that time their clothes were like loose dresses—actually, rather practical for a child in diapers. Young children in poorer families wore the same style of garment, but among the well-to-do a boy's skirts were less frilly and delicate than his sister's.

A little girl wore her skirts just below the knee, with dark socks or stockings for most of the year and white stockings when she dressed up or in the summertime. Her skirts were lengthened somewhat as she grew older. Girls' hair was worn loose while they were younger and pulled into a ribbon at the back of the neck when they approached their teens. Putting her hair up and letting her skirts down to her shoe tops signaled a girl's transition to womanhood. A working-class girl generally made the change when she started her first full-time job, even though she might be only 12 or 13 years old and still physically preadolescent. For girls in higher circumstances the change could be made any time between ages 15 and 18, depending on her family and its social customs.

Poor and working-class children did not generally have clothes that were bought or made for them. Their garments were hand-me-downs or secondhand; they might be cut down from adult cast-offs. Shoes were a particular problem. Autobiographies and memoirs offer recollections of going through a winter with shoes two sizes too large and handing them on to a brother just as they began to fit. Photographs from the period show that the poorest children, in both city and country, played outside and even went to school with bare feet.

Despite the annual excitement over new fads and fashionable designs, the general look of women's dresses did not change a great deal over the Victorian period. The loose, high-waisted dresses of the Regency disappeared before 1830. Low-necked daytime clothing, which had been worn for three centuries, was seldom seen after 1840. The basic style for the rest of the century involved a fitted bodice that came at least to the base of the neck, long sleeves, and a small waist. The skirt, made of the same material as the bodice, was at least moderately full and came down to the shoes.

Within that framework, the general look of women's clothing varied roughly by decade. At the beginning of the 1840s, skirts had no special padding to hold them away from the body; they were full but more or less natural in shape. Petticoats then grew increasingly heavy and stiff. By the mid-1850s, the fashionable skirt was enormously full and supported by crinolines or steel hoops—which provided a good deal of fun for the popular humor magazine *Punch*.

The crinoline was not popular for long, and many women did not adopt it. (Queen Victoria never wore one.) It was impractical, inconvenient, and immodest (because the swaying hoop revealed a woman's underclothes when she bent over). Hoop skirts also increased the danger that a woman's clothes would brush into the fireplace. Accidental deaths caused by delicate fabrics suddenly bursting into flames were fairly common; one household guide recommended that a large table cover or piano shawl of firmly woven wool gabardine always be kept at hand for quickly enveloping a victim and smothering the fire.

A WHOLESOME CONCLUSION.

Lady Crinoline. "Yes, Love—a very Pretty Church, but the Door is certainly very Narrow!"

This cartoon by John Leech, which appeared in the February 6, 1858, edition of *Punch,* shows the contemporary fad for enormous crinolines.

By the late 1860s the crinoline was passé. Women's dresses over the next two decades experienced a series of changes created by pulling fullness to the back, sometimes with the support of a bustle or some other kind of padding. At the end of the century, skirts were long and flowing but not padded; the popular outline had a puff-sleeved bodice and gored skirt.

Fashionable clothing required a great deal of expense and care. Women's dresses were not bought ready-made until the very end of the period, because the closely fitting tops required that bodice, shoulders, and sleeves be individually measured and cut. A woman who was clearly middle-class but not very well-to-do (including, for example, the novelist Elizabeth Gaskell, who was married to a clergyman and had four daughters) might have a dressmaker to do the cutting and fitting but then take over the time-consuming hand stitching of all the seams and hems herself. Poor women generally wore secondhand garments that fitted badly, or they ignored styles and made themselves looser bodices in which they could comfortably do physical labor.

Most middle-class women wore two or three woolen dresses in rotation, perhaps replacing the oldest each year and having the others remade. Most dresses were not washable—and there was as yet no satisfactory dry cleaning. Clothes were sponged, brushed, and protected by layers of underwear. To remake a dress for another season, a woman undid the seams and gently hand washed the garments. She could make a few changes in style and trimming when she sewed it up again. A middle-class woman had a plainer garment to wear while doing chores at home. When a woman dressed in the afternoon, it did not mean that she had been wearing her nightclothes all morning, but rather that she changed from her working dress into something better. Servants' clothing was made of cotton fabric with very little in the way of ruffles or trim; it could be washed easily and frequently.

Dressmaking became less time consuming once sewing machines were available. Women's magazines began selling paper patterns in the 1850s, although adult garments were so complicated that cutting and assembling them took more skill than most untrained women had. Later in the century, some shops sold partly made clothing. The skirt and sleeves were already put together; the garment would be fitted before sewing the final seams of the bodice and waist.

In the 1870s, women of the intellectual and artistic middle class took up a style known as aesthetic. Their dresses were softly draped and made of the printed art fabrics sold by Liberty and Company of 218 Regent Street. Most well-to-do women continued to wear stiff and tightly fitted clothing, but there were acceptable alternatives. Women professionals and office workers in the 1890s happily adopted a new costume: the skirt and blouse. Attractive garments could at last be bought ready-made; with a loosely cut blouse and no waistline seam, fitting was no longer a problem. One dark skirt, carefully brushed, could be worn every day with a change of blouse; the lightweight linen or cotton blouses were easily washed.

This cartoon of the Epsom Races from the May 22, 1847, edition of the *Illustrated London News* provides a view of the class differences in Victorian dress and fashion. Courtesy of the Bodleian Library, University of Oxford, Reference N. 2288 b.6.

Elaborate clothing made of fragile fabrics, which made moving difficult and required a servant's help to dress, was a declaration of higher social status. Etiquette books suggested that when women paid calls or visited friends on foot, they should dress plainly so as not to attract attention. The style was called morning dress, but really meant daytime wear, with arms and shoulders fully covered.

Truly fashionable women changed clothes several times a day. Women wealthy enough to pay calls in their private carriage could wear carriage dress, which was cut according to daytime fashion but made of brightly colored silk with feathers or lace for trimming. Tea gowns, worn on a country estate when the ladies had afternoon refreshments while the men were occupied with outdoor sports (or the drinking that followed), were loose and comfortable but made of delicate fabrics. Dinner dress was somewhat low cut and usually made of silk or velvet. Ball gowns had short sleeves and were cut even lower.

Other social events required appropriate costumes. For garden parties, flower shows, and similar summer affairs, young women wore bright or flowered dresses made of thin cotton. Older women wore light silks. All wore large hats. Tailor-made serge or tweeds were worn in the country. Lawn tennis called for a flannel dress with a full bodice and a skirt of about ankle length.

Respectable women did not use visible makeup. Fictional works written during the period mention that girls would bite their lips and rub their cheeks to bring out the color. Some women used dangerous chemicals to promote beauty: arsenic in small quantities was said to be good for the complexion, and belladonna drops were said to make the eyes sparkle. Women's magazines advertised invisible (uncolored) face powders for red or shiny skin. There were also preparations of "healing lip balm," which included a mild pink coloring.

Women and girls wore some sort of hat outdoors on every occasion. Fashions in millinery changed often, from high to low, wide-brimmed to narrow, with great variety in color, decoration, and trim. Photographs of theatrical audiences in the 1890s show large hats that would have been annoying to people in the seats behind. Although buying a dress was a major purchase, getting a new hat was a relatively inexpensive way to keep up with the season's latest style. Basic hat shapes were sold untrimmed; older girls brought their collections of ribbon and braid and artificial flowers to trimming parties, where they traded advice and finished their own hats.

Customs about indoor head covering changed during the period. In the 1840s, almost all women wore a cap in the daytime. Young women in social classes that dressed up in the evening put flowers or ribbons in their hair. Ten years later, young women had stopped wearing caps in the daytime, and their mothers soon followed. Widows wore a distinctive mourning cap for the first year or two after losing their husbands; some continued to wear a smaller head covering for the rest of their lives. By the 1880s, however, it was usually only elderly women who wore caps in their own homes. Women's caps had largely become occupational badges, seen on people such as servants, waitresses, shop workers, and nurses (Mitchell, *Daily Life*, 133–40).

To read about fashion in Chaucer's England, see the entry on Europe in the section "Clothing" in chapter 5 ("Material Life") in volume 2 of this series; for Elizabethan England, see the entry on England in the section "Clothing and Personal Appearance" in chapter 5 ("Material Life") in volume 3 of this series; for 18th-century England, see the entries on England in the section "Male Clothing & Female Clothing" in chapter 5 ("Material Life") in volume 4 of this series.

FOR MORE INFORMATION

Cunnington, C. W., and P. Cunnington. *Handbook of English Costume in the Nineteenth Century*. Philadelphia: Dufour Editions, 1959.

Mitchell, S. *Daily Life in Victorian England*. Westport, Conn.: Greenwood Press, 1996.

Mitchell, S., ed. *Victorian Britain: An Encyclopedia*. New York: Garland Press, 1998.

INDIA

Indian fashions in the 19th century varied among different regions and communities. In India, clothing is often representative of a person's place in society. Most

MATERIAL LIFE

|

FASHION

|

United States,
1850-1865

United States,
Western Frontier

Victorian England

India

Latin America

people wear clothing that is considered appropriate for their particular caste or community.

The most common dress for a Hindu woman is the sari. This is a piece of fabric, which is about 3 1/2 feet wide, and between 18 and 24 feet long. A tight fitting blouse and a long, often translucent skirt are worn under a sari. The sari is wrapped around the woman's waist, tucked into the skirt, and then stashed over her right shoulder.

Saris come in many different varieties. There are formal saris for weddings and other dressy events. They are often made of silk. In the 19th century most saris were made of cotton, but the quality of the material varied greatly. Higher-class women sometimes had saris with real gold threads woven through part of the material. An old sari demonstrated poor social status, as did a generally dirty or messy appearance.

Once a higher caste woman was married she wore many bangles on her arms, toe rings, ankle bracelets, and other jewelry. This symbolized the fact that because she belonged to a higher caste and was a woman, she did not need to work, so she could be decorated in jewelry that sometimes inhibited physical activity. A *bindi*, which is a dot on the forehead, was worn to match her outfit. At this time *bindis* were generally painted on temporarily and washed off at the end of the day. Once married, a woman often applied a crimson powder to the front of her hair part, demonstrating her marital status.

Certain regions had variations of the typical sari. For example, in the Western state of Rajesthan, women generally wore backless sari blouses. In the Southern state of Kerela many women wore a decorative skirt and blouse instead of a sari. In the Southern State of Tamil Nadu, most women did not wear blouses but threw the small part of their saris over their left shoulders to cover their breasts.

Hindu widows were expected to get rid of all of their fancy clothes and jewelry to demonstrate devotion and respect for their deceased husbands. Following the death of one's husband, a woman wore only a plain white sari and did away with the *bindi*, bangles, and jewelry of any sort.

At this time Hindu men usually wore either a *dhoti* or a *lungi*. A *dhoti* is a piece of white fabric that covers the body below the waist. It covers only above the knees. A *lungi* is wrapped more like a sarong and, when on, resembles a long skirt. The *lungi* is a Muslim cultural import. Generally poor laborers and lower caste men wore *lungis*, while higher caste men wore dhotis. Most men in the South did not cover their chests with any clothing. However, during the 19th century some men began to imitate the dress of the British, and shirts, pants, and dress suits all became popular among elite Indians.

Children often wore very few clothes. Most young girls wore long skirts. Lower caste girls in the villages most often wore only a long skirt, or sometimes nothing at all, particularly if they were under the age of around five. Young boys in the village often wore nothing at all for the first few years of their lives. During the 19th century, English styles became more and more common among urban children. School attending children often had school uniforms, which were modeled on the English school uniforms, and frocks, skirts, blouses, and shorts became popular clothing for children even when not at school.

Most Muslim women wore the *salwar kameez*, which originated in the region in and around Afghanistan. It is a three-piece outfit including a long dress, pants, and a *dupatta*, or scarf, all made of one fabric. Muslim women generally used the scarf to cover their heads. In the 19th century some Hindu women and girls also wore this style of clothing; however very few Muslim women adopted the style of the sari, probably because it is difficult to get accustomed to the sari.

When in public very religious Muslim women usually wore a *burka*. This is a black cloth that covers nearly every inch of skin on the woman. Depending on the type of burka, sometimes as little as only her eyes are exposed.

The typical Muslim man's clothing was in a similar style to the *salwar kameez*. It consisted of a white *kurta*, which is a long shirt with slits in the sides from the waist to the bottom, worn over pyjamas, or pants. This is the origin of the English word pajama. The outfit was usually beige or white. Muslim men usually wore a small white hat with this outfit to cover their heads. Many Hindu men also wore this type of outfit, minus the hat.

Most of the Indian population walked around barefoot at this time, although wealthier people usually had some sort of sandal. These sandals were often in a style with a leather loop that goes around the big toe and a strap across the instep of the foot to hold the shoe in place. In Rajasthan, pointy, enclosed shoes were popular.

During the 19th century, the British-made cloth became more and more popular among Indians, as the English exported cotton from India, wove it into cloth, and then sold it back to Indians at an inflated cost. Eventually, in the early 20th century, there was a movement to boycott this economically exploitive practice. However, during the 19th century, many Indians bought foreign-made cloth for both its quality and a lack of alternative options.

~Dana Lightstone

FOR MORE INFORMATION

Bharati, R., ed. *From the Seams of History: Essays on Indian Women*. Delhi, India: Oxford University Press, 1997.

Phillips, R. B., and C. B. Steiner. *Unpacking Culture: Art and Commodity in Colonial and Postcolonial Worlds*. Berkeley: University of California Press, 1999.

Tarlo, E. *Clothing Matters: Dress and Identity in India*. Chicago: University of Chicago Press, 1996.

LATIN AMERICA

Fashion in 19th-century Latin America was extremely varied. Each country, each region, and, sometimes, each town had distinctive dress. There were notable differences between the styles of city and country dwellers, between rich and poor, and between different ethnic groups.

As in the world over, climate, available resources, and utilitarian needs often dictated fashion in Latin America. Inhabitants of the Andes region, for example,

MATERIAL LIFE
|
FASHION
|
United States,
1850-1865

United States,
Western Frontier

Victorian England

India

Latin America

used wool from two local animals, alpaca and llama, to weave clothing and hats that fended off the winter cold. People in other regions used skins and hides of other animals, including vicunas and cows. In contrast, the oppressive heat in the Amazon jungle meant that many indigenous groups required very little clothing.

In large cities, many inhabitants emulated popular European styles. One visitor to Mexico observed, for example, that the locals "conform[ed] in general to European civilization, and particularly to the fashions of the French, with reminiscences of the Spaniards" (Sayer, 99). Flora Tristan, a famed travel writer of the time, observed of 1830s Peru that "[t]he clothes of the upper classes do not differ at all from those of Europe; women and men dress exactly as in Paris; women scrupulously follow the dictates of new styles, save that they do not cover their heads and that custom requires that they attend church dressed in black. . . . The men ruin themselves at play, the women at buying clothes" (Keen and Wasserman, 231–32).

This European style was not static, however. At the start of the century, the wealthy dressed as extravagantly as possible, with many items embroidered in gold thread, and people regularly displaying diamonds, pearls, and other jewelry. Upon independence, however, such finery became rare and, due to poverty and mourning, most people donned uniforms of simple black. As people recovered their fortunes, more lavish fashions returned.

Because trade with Europe rapidly increased after independence, Latin American shoppers could find imported French silk stockings, Chinese crepe shawls, German and Irish linens, French and Indian muslins, and English calicoes. Such imports were always in demand; Latin Americans contracted with local tailors and dressmakers to recreate the latest foreign fashions depicted in popular fashion magazines.

Although European styles were common throughout Latin America, many populations continued using costumes with distinctly indigenous characteristics. For example, a common women's item in Mexico and Central America was the *huipil*, a long and wide cotton shirt embroidered in bright colors and rich designs that often depicted scenes from nature. Women also wore long, wraparound skirts, secured at the waist with a cloth belt. The woven fabric of these skirts, or *refajos*, often displayed intricate striped designs.

Women in these regions also used a rebozo, which became, according to one observer, the most important garment in both city and country. A long, rectangular piece of cloth, the rebozo had many uses; it could be a shawl, a shield from sun and rain, or a carry cloth. As one 19th-century visitor to Mexico noted, "They use it like a mantilla, like a cape, in public buildings, during promenades, and even in the home; they wrap it diagonally about themselves, they put it on their heads, they muffle themselves up in it, and tie and knot it around their bodies" (Sayer, 106). Indigenous women regularly used rebozos to tie small children to their backs, thus freeing their hands. While indigenous women weaved their own rebozos out of cotton or wool, upper-class city women bought rebozos of silk and other expensive fabrics.

Indigenous men in Mexico and Central America wore cotton *calzones*, or drawers, sometimes with leather *calzoneras*, or over trousers. Their long-sleeved shirts, also made of cotton, were known as *cotones*. Many men in Mexico also carried a sarape, a woven cotton or wool blanket. Like the women's rebozo, the sarape was a multi-purpose garment, used by Indians and whites, rich and poor. In Mexico, the sarape was, according to one observer, "a national institution" (Sayer, 102). Men usually wore it as a cloak, with their heads protruding through a slit in the middle, the end flung over a shoulder. But it also served as a saddle blanket, a sleeping blanket, and rain gear.

Decoration was also an important part of indigenous costume. Many groups used tattoos and body paint; the intricate designs and symbols often identified them as belonging to particular tribes or families, with distinct designs used on special occasions. Body piercings and jewelry served similar functions. Some native Ecuadorans used feathers, buttons of vegetable ivory (the insides of large nuts), and necklaces of beads or animal teeth. In Guyana, necklaces of bush hog teeth marked a man's hunting successes, and Guambiano Indian women of Colombia denoted their wealth by the number of beaded glass necklaces that they wore. Some native groups of Guyana and Brazil adopted a particularly unique method of decoration by tightly binding their legs just below and above the calf; this practice produced a swelling in the calf, considered a sign of beauty. Another unusual decoration style was the carefully patterned facial scars of the Paraguayan Toba Indians.

Many populations of Latin America were also highly influenced by African traditions. In Bahia, Brazil, for example, the layering of brightly patterned skirts was reminiscent of a Sudanese style. Other African traditions were preserved as well, including elaborate headgear and turbans, bodice and skirt styles, and particular clothing colors and patterns.

> *Many populations of Latin America were also highly influenced by African traditions.*

The cattle ranchers and cowboys of Latin America also shared similar styles that distinguished them from men of other professions. The gaucho of Argentina wore baggy trousers, known as *bombachas*, tucked into soft leather boots. A silver belt, sometimes decorated with coins, supported a *chirpá*, a square of material forming a sort of apron. The gaucho often used silver spurs and a felt or straw hat, tied under the chin. An indispensable item of the gaucho's wardrobe was the poncho, similar to the Mexican sarape. The gaucho's counterpart in Chile, the *huaso*, also wore a poncho, woven of llama or guanaco wool and often dyed in shades of red or yellow. *Huasos* also used gaiters over their boots, which fastened with buckles at the side. Around their knees, they tied bands of leather with long tassels that dangled down to their ankles. The vaqueros of northeastern Brazil dressed head to foot in leather as protection against thorn bush and scrub, whereas vaqueros from the southern regions of Brazil wore lighter clothes and broad brimmed straw hats.

In conclusion, costume in 19th-century Latin America was extremely varied. Clothing styles were heavily influenced by climate and practical necessities, as well as by the pressures of colonialism, social standing, and foreign fashions.

~Molly Todd

FOR MORE INFORMATION

Cubas, A. G. *The Republic of Mexico in 1876.* Translated by G. F. Henderson. Mexico City, D.F.: La Enseñanza Printing Office, 1876.

Keen, B., and M. Wasserman. "A History of Latin America." In *A History of Latin America*. 3rd ed. Boston: Houghton Mifflin, 1988.

Sayer, C. *Costumes of Mexico*. Austin: University of Texas Press, 1985.

Sichel, M. *South America*. London: B. T. Batsford Ltd., 1986.

CHINA

One of the things that most sets traditional Asian societies apart from those of the West is the matter of fashion. While people in the West vied with each other to create new fashions, Asian elites proudly preserved their old styles of formal attire to demonstrate the endurance of their culture. See the China entry in the section "Clothing" in chapter 5 ("Material Life") in volume 2 of this series for traditional court fashions that continued into the 19th century.

MATERIAL LIFE
|
TECHNOLOGY
|
United States,
1850-1865

United States,
Western Frontier

Victorian England

India

Technology

In terms of technological advances, the 19th century was England's century. From the steam engine to the development of iron as a modern construction medium, England pioneered, developed, and perfected much of the technology that shaped the Victorian era. That said, one must note that technological developments in other nations were profoundly influential. In some instances, the application of modern scientific methods and ideas to daily life made all the difference. Take, for example, the American Civil War. It has been a historical truism that the North's use of modern technology was a crucial factor in the defeat of the Confederacy. The North had better uniforms, which kept its soldiers dry and warm. Northern soldiers had better rifles, better blankets (which had a rubber backing), and boots. The North also employed railroads in the conflict. By building and using high-speed transportation networks, Union soldiers were able to outpace their opponents and thus chase them down. The Confederacy had access to similar technology but was unable to master it. Southern railroads, for instance, carried Confederate soldiers into many battles. However, the South failed to maintain its lines, which by the end of the war were in desperate need of repair.

Technology was crucial in other areas of Victorian life. Miners on the American frontier were attuned to all developments in their line of work. At first, mining for gold was a relatively simple affair and miners used only basic tools such as shovels and pans. But by the 1850s, most of the gold that could be extracted from streams was gone and new methods other than panning were developed. Sophisticated machines and methods were developed to find gold deeper and deeper in the ground. The key to these methods was hydraulics, which made use of water to dig and rinse stones. The pinnacle of this technology came with the water cannon invented by Edward E. Matteson that drilled into sides of canyons in search of gold.

There was not much questioning of the technological developments in the United States. However, compare that with the Indian experience. In India, western technologies such as railroads, steamboats, and factories dramatically changed daily life. In some cases, of course, these transformations brought better things. British agricultural methods increased local production of staples that in turn helped to feed the growing Indian population. However, the reduction of indigenous technologies and manufacturing created resentment against the British colonial governments. Indeed, central to Mahatma Gandhi's independence movement was a call for the return of native cloth, known as khadi. Thus technology itself was an important part of the political and cultural wars of the 19th century.

📷 *Snapshot*

Major 19th-Century Inventions

1800	Clothes Dryer
1803	Steam Engine
1813	Can Opener
1827	Camera
1830	First Mass-Produced Sewing Machine
1843	Fax Machine
1850	Dishwasher
1860s	Hot Dogs
1868	Traffic Light
1876	Telephone
1877	Recorded Sound
1879	Lightbulb
1890	Zipper
1898	Typewriter
1898	Flashlight

~[See Canadian Broadcasting Corporation, <http://www.cbc4kids.cbc.ca/general/the-lab/history-of-invention/default.html>. Accessed: 15 March 2003.]

UNITED STATES, 1850–65

The ability of the North to win the Civil War was partially based on their access and production of technologically advanced tools of war. While Confederates were characteristically destitute of equipment, federal recruits came to the war zone overloaded with useless articles of convenience. However, the equipment retained and valued by veteran soldiers of both armies was remarkably similar. Woolen uniforms—jackets and trousers—were almost universal, as wool retains its insulating qualities even when wet. Armies on the march in warm weather "could be smelled before they were seen." Soldiers were issued unbleached cotton or linen shirts but wore a variety of civilian colors and patterns. The most characteristic hat of the period was the cloth kepi, which was a cap fashioned after a style made popular in European armies. Slouch hats, with a wide brim all around, were issued to some regiments and were particularly popular with troops in the western theater.

Uniforms came in a variety of colors, and the lack of a standard color scheme quickly proved the cause of serious confusion. In the Battle of Bull Run, Southern troops were fired upon by their own side after being identified as Federals because of their blue jackets and vice versa. As the war continued the Confederates generally limited their colors to gray and butternut. The Federals commonly resorted to dark blue jackets, but in some cases, as with Zouaves and Berdan's Sharpshooters, vivid red or forest green might predominate. Federal trousers, of heavy kersey wool held up by tape suspenders, were sky blue in color. Confederate trousers were black, blue, gray, or butternut. As the war progressed, the South relied increasingly on captured federal clothing supplies or cloth that had not been dyed. By 1863 many Southerners

MATERIAL LIFE
|
TECHNOLOGY
|

United States,
1850–1865

United States,
Western Frontier

Victorian England

India

were wearing sky blue trousers or trousers made of linen canvas, cotton, or tent cloth.

Shoes were issued to the infantry and were made of leather uppers, soles, and heels. Leather laces were worked through as few as two sets of unreinforced eyelets. The most common shoe was the brogan, or workman's shoe of European design. The brogan covered the entire foot, coming up to the anklebone. The brogan was often fitted with metal plates on the heels to protect against wear. Leather or cloth leggings were often buckled on over brogans to protect the lower leg. Federal shoes were dyed black, as were Confederate ones at first. Later in the war, when black dye became unavailable, Southern leather goods were done in russet brown. A severe leather shortage caused some Rebel shoes to be made with wooden soles.

Both shoes and boots were issued to the cavalry, the horse artillery, and mounted officers to protect the leg from the chafing of the stirrup leathers. Very stylish boots, hearkening back to the days of the English cavaliers, were popular among the gallants of the Confederate and federal cavalry, but by the end of the war many riders found that shoes were more comfortable and serviceable. Federal riders were issued pants with a double layer of fabric on the inseam to be worn with shoes when astride.

Southern troops often equipped themselves with captured federal equipment.

The prescribed uniform allowance for a one-year enlistment in 1861 was identical in both armies and included the following items: hat (1); kepi or cap (2); havelock, or cap cover (1); coat (2); trousers (3); shirt (3); blouse (1); drawers (3); shoes, pair (2); stockings, pair (2); stock, or tie (1); greatcoat (1); wool blanket (1); and ground sheet, gum rubber blanket or oilcloth (1). Theoretically the year's allotment was divided into two batches: one for issue in the spring and one in the fall. The Confederacy quickly found that it was unable to provide many of these items, and Southern troops often equipped themselves with captured federal equipment.

With the exception of the cavalry, who were provided with a wide assortment of firearms including pistols and rapid-fire repeaters, both armies issued muzzle-loading, rifled muskets with percussion cap ignition to the infantry. Most commonly they were American made .58 caliber Springfields or British .577 caliber Enfields. The soldiers found Enfields more accurate than Springfields. "At long range we are rather afraid of them," admitted a federal officer in 1864. Troops would trade their weapons for Enfields on the battlefield if the opportunity presented itself, and whole companies were sometimes rearmed in such a manner after a major engagement.

The similarity in musket calibers proved a great advantage in distributing supplies and was a godsend to the Confederacy, which could use captured federal ammunition. The ammunition for Springfields and Enfields was interchangeable for all practical purposes, but cavalry ammunition was generally made in a smaller caliber, .52 caliber being a popular size, to relieve some of the recoil experienced with lighter weapons. The most common pistol calibers were .36, .44, and .45, but almost any size bullet might be fired in anger from the hundreds of private weapons carried to the battlefield by recruits. Thousands of pistols, sometimes advertised as lifesavers, were returned to families in the North by Federals who found them useless encumbrances once they had become veterans.

With the minié ball, a conical bullet with a hollowed base, the rifled musket was capable of hitting a man-sized target at 800 yards and had plain sights that were adjustable to that range. Effectively, a target the size of a man could barely be seen at 800 yards. However, used in a volley—hundreds of muskets firing simultaneously—the musket could be deadly over open ground. The need to ram down the charge before firing slowed the sustained rate of fire of most troops to about three aimed shots per minute.

Sharpshooting, the use of carefully aimed shots by individuals designated to pick off officers, artillerymen, or other conspicuous persons, was a peculiar characteristic of the Civil War battlefield that hearkened back to the activities of the fringe-shirted riflemen of the Revolution. Generally, no special weapon was used for this purpose, though many sharpshooters were equipped with telescopic sights.

Breechloaders, like the Sharps or Smith carbines, could fire 9 rounds a minute, and the fully self-contained brass cartridge of the Spencer repeating rifle allowed for 20. There was a genuine concern among military experts, lasting through World War I and diminishing only after World War II, that the soldiers would quickly expend all of their available ammunition with repeating weapons. Nonetheless, breech-loading designs and revolvers were widely issued to the cavalry and other specialty troops.

The majority of muskets were fitted with a socket bayonet about 18 inches long. Some regiments were issued short swords, instead of bayonets, that could be fitted to the barrel of the musket. Although great reliance was placed by military tacticians on the ability of cold steel to drive the enemy from the field, in practice very few combatants came to such close quarters before the psychological effect of the bayonet caused one side or the other to flee. Captain J. W. De Forest noted that "bayonet fighting occurs mainly in newspaper and other works of fiction." Bayonets, however, proved to be excellent digging tools, skewers for roasting meat and potatoes, and good candleholders.

The deadly accuracy of the rifled musket at a distance, combined with the use of entrenchments and fortified positions, caused bayonet wounds to account for a very small percentage of injuries. As the war progressed and troops settled into trenches and fortifications for prolonged sieges, head wounds "between the brim of the hat and the top of the head" predominated, and most of these occurred in the first day after entrenching as the enemy sharpshooters probed for defensive weaknesses and the occupants had not yet identified the "dangerous locations." The soldiers learned to cut "loopholes" in the works or erect "head logs" to defend against these wounds. Placed on the top of the parapet with widely separated supports, the head log provided a small space beneath which the men could fire without exposing the top of their heads.

Woolen blankets were issued in warm weather, and lined woolen greatcoats, weighing several pounds, were provided for winter. The greatcoats were particularly effective in retaining body heat, but having both blanket and greatcoat simultaneously was thought to be too cumbersome. While most men cherished their blankets, some threw them away on a hot march and regretted their actions when the weather changed. Green troops marched poorly, "straggling about the roads . . . and the fields." Their columns, flanked by discarded equipment, were described as "a spectacle of disorder."

All federal troops were issued a thin canvas ground sheet coated with gum rubber, called a rubber blanket by most men. Some soldiers carried two, as they could be rolled very tightly. There is some disagreement among historians as to whether rubber blankets were designed to be worn as ponchos in case of rain or if the soldiers altered them to be used in this manner. About 6 1/2 feet long and 3 1/2 feet wide, rubber blankets were provided with eyelets in the sides and ends, which allowed them to be used in the same manner as the shelter half. Confederates were issued oilcloths to ward off rain and damp, but they highly prized gum rubber blankets.

Soldiers were expected to carry their field equipment, extra clothing, and personal items in a knapsack. Blankets and dog tents were rolled and fastened to the top of the knapsack. Numerous knapsack designs were patented during the war, but most proved uncomfortable on long marches. On going into battle it was common for the troops to pile their marching gear and knapsacks in a remote spot to which they would return if they were victorious. Should the encounter go against them, the baggage would almost certainly pass into the hands of the enemy.

Private Jay Butler recalled his headlong retreat at the Battle of Stones River: "When we got back as far as my knapsack, I picked it up and attempted to carry it and did so for a quarter of a mile when I found that I was getting behind and that the bullets came nearer and thicker, so I dropped it, took out my rubber blanket and went on my way feeling very down hearted at leaving so many good and useful articles to the enemy."

The string of Confederate victories in the first two years of the war helped supply the Rebel army with captured equipment and conveniences otherwise unavailable to Southern soldiers. Breech-loading weapons, shoes, blankets, and gum rubber blankets were particularly valued prizes. Captured brass-cartridge weapons proved less valuable to Confederates than one would suppose, as the South was incapable of producing replacement ammunition.

Equally important to the equipment that Civil War soldiers carried was the technologically advanced way that many of them were transported to the battlefields. The abominable condition of Southern roads during the rainy season and in the winter added to the importance of its railways. Although the South controlled only one-third the railway mileage of the North, the Southern railways were strategically located within the theater of operations and were used with great tactical skill by Confederate commanders. Virginia was crossed by several important railways that could be used with great effect to move supplies and manpower throughout the eastern theater. At First Bull Run, Confederate reinforcements were brought to the field by rail in time to turn the tide of battle and rout the Federals.

Much of the Northern rail mileage was used for the distribution of manufactures in the Northeast. The most prominent railways—the Pennsylvania, the Erie, and the New York Central—were outside the war zone. Those in New England were almost entirely shut off from army transport. However, the north-south lines—the Illinois Central and the Cleveland, Columbus, and Cincinnati—prospered on army business.

The Baltimore and Ohio, with a right of way in the war zone, was strategically important as a line of communications between Washington and Ohio. In May 1861, General Jackson was able to steal 300 railroad cars and 56 locomotives from the B. & O. in a single operation. Much of this rolling stock was horse-drawn down the Shenandoah Valley Pike from Winchester to Strasburg to be used on the Southern railways. At a later date, when loss of the line to Federal forces seemed imminent, Jackson was given the task of destroying the 400-mile railway. He burned the bridges, derailed the freight cars, and burned more than 40 engines. The Federals learned to repair the damage quickly, but raids along the B. & O. were a constant source of trouble to Federal commanders.

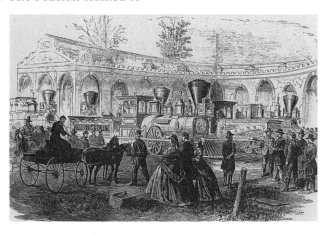

Steam locomotives were critically important for the movement of troops and supplies during the American Civil War. *Leslie's Illustrated,* 1864; sketch by F. B. Schell.

The railways of the western theater, which had been built in the 1850s, far in advance of any immediate war need, proved very important. The line between Louisville, Kentucky, and Nashville, Tennessee, provided a vital link for the invading Federals. Yet no strategic railways were built, and no thought was given to the development of the principles of military operations and maintenance of railways. "In no direction could cars run long distances without changes and delays." Freight, as well as passengers and their luggage, often had to detrain and cross town from one line to another either by wagon or on foot. The construction of five short connections between competing lines, for a total of 140 miles, would have provided the Federals with an uninterrupted railway from Washington to the entire North.

An obstacle to rail transport in all parts of the country was the different gauges, or track widths, used on different lines. In New York and New England a gauge of 4 feet 8 1/2 inches was used. In Ohio, and to the west and south of Philadelphia, the gauge was 4 feet 10 inches. Some rails were placed as much as 6 feet apart in special cases. Many ingenious expedients were used to overcome this problem. These included third rails, wide wheels that would accommodate both narrow and wide track, and adjustable train axles. The longest single gauge track of the war belonged to the Atlantic and Great Western line, which connected New York with St. Louis more than 1,000 miles away.

There was an attempt by Richmond to adopt a standard gauge of 5 feet throughout the nation, but a national dedication to the ideal of states' rights generally got in the way of any standardization. The length of Southern railway mileage, the tonnage of rolling stock and engines, and the number of interconnecting systems were severely limited throughout the war. Nonetheless, there were more than 1,000 miles of strategically important track in Tennessee alone with connections passing to the southeast. The heart of this rail network lay in Corinth, Mississippi. The line connecting Cairo, Illinois, with Corinth drove directly south and continued on to New Orleans, creating a network that pumped vital supplies from the Gulf, north to Tennessee, and east to Virginia. The Confederates were therefore theoretically able to use their railways to bring troops from the Deep South into Virginia or the western theater. In 1862 more than 2,500 men and their equipment were brought to Nashville from Louisiana in just two weeks—a remarkable feat given the dilapidated state of the railways and the fact that the troops had to wait for available cars or march between unconnected lines.

A major limitation on the use of Southern railways for military purposes remained a lack of maintenance. In April 1863 Lee wrote to the War Office that "unless the railroads be repaired, so as to admit of speedier transportation of supplies," he could not maintain his position. Damaged cars and worn-out engines became the victims of the South's limited industrial technology. A damaged locomotive boiler might take more than a thousand man-hours to repair if the boiler plate were found to do the job. Tracks and especially wooden ties were simply unable to withstand the wear and tear of wartime demand. "There were no means at hand for their repair. The wooden ties rotted, the machinery was almost exhausted, the rails were worn out, and thus the speed and capacity of the trains were greatly reduced." An engine could be required to lug a supply train weighing up to 120 tons (Volo and Volo, 139–44, 155–58).

To read about technology in the United States in the 20th century, see the United States entries in the section "Technology" in chapter 5 ("Material Life") in volume 6 of this series.

FOR MORE INFORMATION

McPherson, J. M. *Battle Cry of Freedom: The Civil War Era.* New York: Oxford University Press, 1990.

Paludan, P. S. *A People's Contest: The Union and Civil War, 1861–1865.* New York: Harper & Row, 1988.

Thomas, E. M. *The Confederate Nation: 1861–1865.* New York: Harper & Row, 1979.

Volo, D. D., and J. M. Volo. *Daily Life in Civil War America.* Westport, Conn.: Greenwood Press, 1998.

MATERIAL LIFE
|
TECHNOLOGY
|
United States,
1850-1865

United States,
Western Frontier

Victorian England

India

UNITED STATES, WESTERN FRONTIER

Advanced mining technology, of course, was essential on the frontier. Nearly all these men were amateurs who had to learn mining techniques in the field. Under the most favorable conditions, with abundant surface deposits, gold was easily recovered by using spoons, knives, and shovels to scoop paydirt from riverbanks and riverbeds. However, after the first flush, mining techniques grew ever more complicated, initially requiring the collaboration of three to five men; then, as greater mechanization was applied, the investment of significant capital became necessary.

The most common form of mining during the gold rush was placer mining, in which the gold, found mixed with gravel and dirt, was shaken free. The simplest implement for this method of extrication was a pan (or *batea*, as the Mexicans called it); thus, the method is known as panning. E. Gould Buffum, who spent six months in the gold fields in 1849–50, described this process:

The process of pan-washing is the simplest mode of separating the golden particles from the earth with which it is amalgamated. A common-sized tin pan is filled with the soil containing the gold. This is taken to the nearest water and sunk until the water overspreads the surface of the pan. The earth is then thoroughly mixed with water and the stones taken out with the hand. A half rotary motion is given to the pan with both hands; and, as it is filled, it is lifted from the water, and the loose light dirt which rises to the surface washed out, until the bottom of the pan is nearly reached. The gold being heavier than the earth, sinks by its own weight to the bottom, and is there found at the close of the washing, mixed with a heavy black sand. This is placed in a cup or another pan till the day's labor is finished, when the whole is dried before the fire and the sand carefully blown away.

A slightly more sophisticated mechanism for separating gold was the cradle. John Edwin Banks described its use:

The cradle is shaped much as its name would indicate; usual length four to five feet, breadth at the bottom twelve inches, the top eighteen, a box placed on top and in the back occupying one third its length. The box contains a screen to prevent large stones or lumps of earth from passing through. Just below this is an apron, or cloth, sloping towards the back of the cradle is that the earth and water must pass through its whole length. The bottom of the cradle is divided by two or three bars to prevent the gold from washing out, which, being much heavier than any of its neighbors, is caught here. The cradle is placed on legs over the stream; the operator seats himself on the left, using his right hand to dash in water while he rocks with the other. The screen is made of zinc, sheet iron, tin, or sticks, the meshes one-fourth to one-half an inch in diameter. With one of these a man will wash from twelve to twenty bushels of earth per day, having one or two men in the meantime to dig and carry it to him. The last washing must be carefully performed in a pan.

Most diarists note that the cradle allowed three to five men to work cooperatively. Usually one shoveled dirt into the cradle, a second poured in water, a third rocked, while two others brought dirt to the river's edge. Prentice Mulford, describing his first efforts of trial and error at using a borrowed cradle by himself, wryly demonstrated the need for partners:

I had no teacher [in the use of the cradle], and was obliged to become acquainted with all its peculiarities by myself. First I set it on a dead level. As it had no "fall" the sand would not run out. But the hardest work of all was to dip and pour the water from the dipper [onto] the gravel in the sieve with one hand and rock the cradle with the other. There was a constant tendency on the part of the hand and arm employed in pouring to go through the motion of rocking and vice versa. . . . I seemed cut up into two individuals, between whom existed a troublesome and perplexing difference of opinion as to their respective duties and functions. Such a conflict, to all intents and purposes, of two different minds inside of and acting on one body, shook it up fearfully and tore it all to pieces. I was as a house divided against itself and could not stand. However, at last the physical and mental elements thus warring with each other inside of me made up their differences, and the left hand rocked the cradle peacefully while the right hand poured harmoniously, and the result was about $1.50 a day. Soon after I found my first mining partner.

As more miners swarmed into the fields (it is estimated that in 1852, one hundred thousand were actively engaged in mining), it became increasingly harder to find gold along the riverbanks. Thus, the rivers themselves were turned out of their courses. Knowing that gold lay in alluvial deposits, miners constructed dams and dug new channels into which the rivers were turned.

E. Gould Buffum noted that in one spring and summer 15 different points on the North Fork of the American River had been so diverted. To dam a space of approximately 30 feet took two weeks of backbreaking labor in digging, moving dirt, and wrestling rocks. Such labor was not always rewarded, for in some locations little or no gold was found. He estimates, however, that an average for productive locations was $50 per day per man. Banks, however, told of his group laboring for three months with nothing to show for it.

To provide water for the washing process, some companies built intricate aqueduct-like sluices. But water—or lack thereof, because rivers had been diverted—sometimes caused trouble. Those working downstream no longer had necessary water. Banks told of one instance in which downstream miners came up to a place where a dam had been constructed, threatening to destroy it. Those who had worked so long on it replied they would defend the dam with their lives. They did so, shooting 13 men caught in the act of tearing down the dam. He told of another location where two "gentlemen" agreed to settle the dispute over water by a duel. Their hands shook so badly that no one was hurt. And that, wrote Banks, "is one of the last evidences of civilization being in these parts." Despite several meetings held among the miners in his location, the "end result is to get water *if you can*."

Though offering no legal solution to such squabbles, Buffum foresaw the necessity of combining capital and labor. "As yet no scientific apparatus has been introduced, and severe manual labor has produced . . . golden results. When steam and money are united for the purpose, I doubt not that the whole waters of the North and

John Gast's 1872 print entitled *American Progress* shows railroads and telegraph lines leading the march of progress across the American frontier, the conquest of which was seen as the country's manifest destiny. © Library of Congress.

Middle Forks will be turned from their channels, and immense canals dug through the mountains to bear them off." The time of the individual miner working with primitive tools was drawing to a close.

One successful combination of capital and science was hydraulic mining, by which a powerful stream of water from a large hose was directed against hillsides to reach the gold buried there. Devised in 1853 by Edward E. Matteson of Connecticut, this method opened new sources after placer mining had exhausted the gold from river-beds. An article from the Sacramento *Weekly Union* in 1854 described the process by which 120 feet of hillside were washed away to reveal bedrock:

With a perpendicular column of water 120 feet high, in a strong hose . . . , ten men who own the claim are enabled to run off hundreds of tons of dirt daily. So great is the force employed, that two men with the pipes, by directing streams of water against the base of a high bank, will . . . cause immense slides of earth, which often bring with them large trees and heavy boulders. To carry off these immense masses of dirt, they have constructed two sluices. . . . After these immense masses of earth are undermined and brought down by streams forced from the pipes, those same streams are turned upon the tons of fallen earth, and it melts away before them, and is carried away through the sluices with almost as much rapidity as if it were a bank of snow. No such labor-saving power has ever [before] been introduced to assist the miner in his operations. However efficient this technique, it ravaged the terrain and was prohibited in 1884 because of the pollution it caused.

Yet another method of mining that combined science and capital—quartz, hard rock, or lode mining—involved sinking shafts and bringing ore to the surface. Early on, such ore was crushed by the *arrastra* introduced by Mexican miners. A mule dragged grinding stones through a circular rock-lined trough to pulverize gold-bearing quartz. (Later, steam power and stamping machines accomplished the task.) Next, mercury or quicksilver was used to separate the gold from the pulverized rock. Bayard Taylor observed that quicksilver might well be used by individual miners. Mixing quicksilver with some of the sand left after panning or rocking would create an amalgam. The quicksilver could be evaporated by heating the amalgam in a retort. The result: gold that had previously been unobtainable. The human consequences were less golden (Jones, 133–37).

FOR MORE INFORMATION

Buffum, E. G. *Six Months in the Gold Mines*. 1850. Reprint, Ann Arbor, Mich.: University Microfilms, 1966.

Jones, M. E. *Daily Life on the Nineteenth Century American Frontier*. Westport, Conn.: Greenwood Press, 1998.

VICTORIAN ENGLAND

England was at the center of all major technological changes of the 19th century. The list of inventions is truly staggering. The English developed and perfected

MATERIAL LIFE
|
TECHNOLOGY
|
United States,
1850-1865

United States,
Western Frontier

Victorian England

India

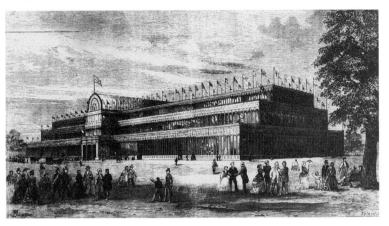

The Crystal Palace Exhibition of 1851 demonstrated England's technological might.

the steam engine, roads, railroads, construction techniques with iron, and factory machines including textile looms. These English technological advances sparked an industrial revolution. This technological supremacy also rearranged social relations in England, and it became part of the nation's identity. Nothing demonstrated this more than the 1851 Great Exhibition that touted British ingenuity in science, industry, and business.

The Exhibition was the brainchild of Queen Victoria's German husband, Albert (né Francis Xavier Winterhalter). The idea behind the event was to demonstrate English technological prowess by showing their achievements alongside those of other countries. Hosting the exhibition in London only added to the feeling that the 19th century was the "Victorian" era of achievement. Prince Albert and his team of planners also thought that the exhibition should be housed in a special hall. Thus in 1849 plans were made for a Crystal Palace to display the event's exhibits. Sir Joseph Paxton drew up the original design in less than two weeks. Large enough to display the 100,000 demonstrations, the huge structure was built in about a year. The palace was unlike any other building known. It had an internal iron skeleton over which a million feet of glass were laid.

The Great Exhibition at the Crystal Palace opened on May Day, 1851. 25,000 people went through during the first day alone. By the end of the exhibition, over 6 million had visited the palace as well as its grounds which had a magnificent series of fountains. There were over 12,000 individual water jets in all. 120,000 gallons of water flowed through the system daily. The park also contained statues and life-size restorations of extinct animals including dinosaurs. However beautiful the palace and its environs were, the real treasures were on the inside. There were about 100,000 formal exhibits sent in by 14,000 individuals.

Prince Albert and his planners devised a complicated classification system to organize the exhibits. The British exhibits alone were divided into four sections (raw materials, machinery, manufactures, and fine arts), each of them containing thirty classes. For instance, under manufactures were cotton and silk goods and under machinery were philosophical instruments, agricultural machinery, and railroad engines. The exhibitions and demonstra-

This illustration from the December 12, 1874, edition of the *Illustrated London News* shows men and women working together at the same jobs in the central telegraph office. Courtesy of The Library Company of Philadelphia.

tions reinforced the notion that England led its colonies and the world in the extraction of raw materials like iron and wood and their fabrication into useful items that enhanced human existence. True, other nations such as the United States displayed some of their great technological products like the Colt handgun. But this paled in comparison to the British, whose machines, like the newly fashioned cigarette machine, produced 90 high-quality cigarettes per minute. These exhibits drew the attention of the onlookers.

After the 1851 Great Exhibition closed, the Crystal Palace was moved to South London. Although the palace remained closely tied to technological advances (one of England's first television stations began its broadcasts there in 1934), it deteriorated rather quickly. In 1936, the palace was completely destroyed by fire. For 85 years it had stood for England's Victorian-era technological advances and power. However, by the 1930s, other nations such as the United States had supplanted England's position. And in fact, the 20th century was America's century in terms of science and technology

To read about technology in Chaucer's England, see the entry on Europe in the section "Technology" in chapter 5 ("Material Life") in volume 2 of this series; for 20th-century Europe, see the entry on Europe in the section "Technology" in chapter 5 ("Material Life") in volume 6 of this series.

~Andrew E. Kersten

FOR MORE INFORMATION

Auerbach, J. A. *The Great Exhibition of 1851: A Nation on Display.* New Haven, Conn.: Yale University Press, 1999.

Bird, A. *Paxton's Palace.* London: Cassell, 1976.

INDIA

During the colonial period the British introduced many new forms of technology. This included the telegraph, railroads, automobiles, steamboats and factories. These were motivated by separate considerations. Steamboats and railways were largely initiated and financed by private merchants for the expansion of trade. The electric telegraph system was entirely managed by the colonial government.

In 1849 a plan to build an electric telegraph system in India was officially proposed. On August 17 of this same year the railway contracts were signed. At this time the colonial government was expanding quickly, and a more efficient means of communication was urgent. As a result, the court decided not to wait for the construction of telegraph lines along with the railways. The next year an experimental line was set up between Calcutta and Chinsura, and other lines throughout the territory soon followed.

The introduction of steam vessels during the 1820s was a decisive development in Indian maritime activities. Indian rivers were an important line of transport prior to the involvement of the English East India Company. However, as the East India

MATERIAL LIFE

TECHNOLOGY

United States,
1850-1865

United States,
Western Frontier

Victorian England

India

Company established a post in Calcutta and thus needed resources to be shipped domestically to Calcutta, the local boats proved insufficient. Steamboats first appeared in Europe in 1815. However, at that time the Company feared change in India that might speed up the activities of British merchants and other private citizens in India. Hence, it was only after three or four years of speculations that the Company finally brought steam vessels to India in 1822.

As with the steam engine, at first authorities were skeptical about railways.

When war with Burma broke out in December 1824, steamboats were used to mobilize British troops on the Irrawaddy river. As a result all apprehensions of the practicality of steamboats was erased. Steamboats became commonly used by the British East India Company to move goods both up and down the rivers of India to and from the ports. Steam engines were a major factor in strengthening British power in India.

The introduction of the railways was another technological innovation that helped in trade. As with the steam engine, at first authorities were skeptical about railways. In 1852, after much debate, construction began on a line connecting Delhi and Calcutta. The line proved to be a great success both as a form of public transportation and as a shipping enterprise.

The development of railways in India during British rule was more or less an exercise of technology transfer under colonial relations. But in maneuvering the operation, the British faced great technical challenges. For example, the subcontinent is a large territory with numerous rivers and mountain ranges (including some of the world's tallest peaks). The poor quality of iron found in India also created a major challenge. Iron for rails and bridges had to be imported from England. Over the next decade the British government funded the construction of a major railway system throughout the colony.

The British brought new agricultural technology to India. They attempted to replace the wooden plough and the frill with iron ploughs imported from America and Europe. After initial introduction these ploughs were sold to local farmers at a low price. The iron plough proved unsuccessful in Indian conditions. The British also introduced a threshing machine and water pump irrigation, both of which were very successful in India. The British replaced the mortar-and-pestle sugar mill with the roller mill. The most successful imports were those that were most simple, such as the water mills, which consisted of a small vertical wheel with oblique, horizontal spokes that were slightly hollowed, on which the water impinged. The British also brought other mechanical devices, such as brick-making machines, air-cooling fans, and the American cooking stove.

Inventions in textile technology marked the beginning of industrialization in England during the end of the 18th century. British cotton mills crushed the competition, particularly the Indian weavers. The success of the British mills depended on the supply of raw cotton from the colonies. Prior to the invention of the cotton gin by Eli Whitney in America, Indian cotton competed with American cotton. Once the cotton gin was used in America, India could no longer keep up. Although the British introduced the cotton gin in India, it did not work properly with the short staple cotton of India.

After the United States gained independence, the British turned to India for a major part of their cotton supply. The British soon discovered that Indian cotton had more impurities than American cotton. In attempts to weed out these impurities, the British introduced packing screws and newer cotton-cleaning machines in India. However, these tools did not improve the amount of labor required for cotton cleaning. In 1818 a new type of cotton screw was introduced that greatly cut down on the amount of manual labor involved.

The one mechanism still missing was a version of the cotton gin suitable for Indian cotton. In September of 1849, the Indian government offered a generous reward to anyone who invented such a device. The Glasgow East India Company also offered a similar reward. Many enterprising mechanics began to work on different models of the cotton gin. The one that was ultimately settled on was based on the model of the Indian *charka*, or spinning wheel, which weavers had been using for centuries.

This created a backlash for the British. Their goal of introducing a cotton gin that would work well with Indian cotton was to increase production for export to England, where the cotton would then be made into material. Once the gin became widespread in India, the Indians began making their own material, similar to the British cotton material, at the local level.

Eventually a ban was placed on Indian cotton. Many Indians saw this as exploitation, and as part of Mahatma Gandhi's philosophy for achieving independence for India, foreign-made cloth was boycotted by many. Instead, Indians were urged to spin their own cloth, known as *khadi*. Throughout the colony nationalists symbolically burned foreign cloth.

~Dana Lightstone

FOR MORE INFORMATION

Baber, Z. *Science of Empire: Scientific Knowledge, Civilization, and Colonial Rule in India.* Albany: State University of New York Press, 1996.

MacLeod, R., ed. *Nature and Empire: Science and the Colonial Enterprise.* Chicago: University of Chicago Press, 2000.

MATERIAL LIFE: WEB SITES

http://www.ivu.org/history/england19a/
http://www.angelfire.com/ar3/townevictorian/victorianfashion.html
http://www.victorianstation.com/vicarch.html
http://www.pbs.org/hiddenindia/food/
http://www.sfusd.k12.ca.us/schwww/sch618/islam/nbLinks/Islam_Clothing_Jewelry.html

6

POLITICAL LIFE

The ancient Greek philosopher Aristotle (384–322 B.C.E.) claimed that humans are by definition political animals, and by this he meant that an essential part of human life involves interacting in the public sphere with people who are not our intimate families. It is these relationships—along with their complex negotiations—that permit the development of cities, kingdoms, nations, and civilization itself. Throughout history different cultures have developed different political systems to organize their lives, and all political systems are in constant states of change as they accommodate to the changing needs and interests of the populace. In the 19th century, political systems clearly illustrated these two points. All governmental systems discussed in this section, particularly Chinese, English, and American, were quite distinct. And yet, all three underwent considerable change during the century. Political reform movements were perhaps most transformative in the United States, where abolitionism not only radically changed society but politics as well. Nevertheless, all these nations created styles of politics that in some fashion met the needs of the people.

Political life involves two different spheres of influence: organizing the relationship among those within a political unit and negotiating the relations between different political entities (countries, tribes, or kingdoms). However, at its basic level, all politics is about power—finding out who has it and who does not. For those who did not have power, life was harsh in the 19th century. For instance, the English poor were subjected to political reform known as the New Poor Law, which broke up families and forced people to work and live in workhouses. Clearly the poor did not have the political power to fashion their own welfare reforms.

People create a political system first of all to assure themselves of internal peace and security. As the political theorist Thomas Hobbes (1588–1679) noted, without a strong authority, people's incessant struggle for power would result in a life that is "nasty, brutish, and short." This is why we want our power structures clear. Our political systems also clarify and solidify our loyalties and allegiances—nationalism has served as a sentiment that can unify people with diverse interests and backgrounds. Definitive structures of law also establish domestic tranquility. In other words, a strong political system often leads to a strong legal system in which crime is punished. In 19th-century China, England, and the United States, justice was

POLITICAL LIFE

GOVERNMENT
& POLITICS

LAW & CRIME

EMPIRE

WAR & MILITARY

REFORM MOVEMENTS

swift, deadly, and often preyed unfairly on the poor. Again, laws to fight crime are an important social good, but in politics those who do not have much power are often at the mercy of those who enforce and create the laws. This was the case in the United States where justice was not blind and in fact was quite racist. Blacks were persecuted, not just prosecuted, by the American laws. In England, in 1800, there were over 200 crimes for which death was the punishment. By 1838, that number had been reduced so that, for example, shoplifters were no longer sentenced to hanging.

Political life influenced people in yet one other way. As people interact in ever-widening circles, our political life must negotiate the often difficult relations with other kingdoms, countries, or empires. Diplomacy is the tool of our political life that smooths these interactions, and war is the breakdown of these negotiations. This of course assumes that diplomacy is always conducted in an honest fashion. In the American West, native peoples learned the hard way that American diplomats spoke with forked tongues. Cynics will maintain that in this case diplomacy was just a pretext to war. In any event, wars have unfortunately dominated much of human history and, indeed, much of the 19th century. In them, we can often see the noblest and worst expressions of our human spirit. In war we can also definitively see the struggle for power that marks our political life. The bloodiest war of the 19th century was the American Civil War in which 600,000 people died. At its root, this was about politics, the failure of compromise, and the integration of a significant reform movement into American life. Thus, to understand politics is to understand the causes of war.

FOR MORE INFORMATION

Van Evera, S. *Causes of War: Power and the Roots of Conflict.* Ithaca, N.Y.: Cornell University Press, 1999.

POLITICAL LIFE
|
GOVERNMENT
& POLITICS
|
United States,
1850-1865

Victorian England

China

Latin America

Government and Politics

Politics and government provide basic structures of daily life. Take the case of China, where dynasties ruled for centuries bringing political order to millions of lives. There is just no underestimating the ways in which politicians, political ideologies, and governance systems influence ordinary people. Depending on where one lived, politics in the 19th century either represented continuity in life or chaotic change. Compare, for example, the politics of China, England, and the United States. British political life displayed continuity throughout the century. Much of this was embodied in the queen of the United Kingdom, Victoria. She ascended to the crown in 1837 at 18 years of age and ruled until 1901. Moreover, the English structure of government went virtually unchanged with the two houses of Parliament, an unwritten constitution, and a prime minister. Change was on the horizon, however. The women's suffrage movement led by women such as Millicent Garrett

Fawcett and later Emmeline Pankhurst would radically restructure politics. Moreover, the old system of local government was quickly becoming outmoded as larger economic issues required responses by larger governmental units. In any case, the fruition of those movements was realized in the 20th century. In the 19th century, tradition and not change defined British political life.

Quite the opposite was true in the United States. The 19th century saw the most fundamental and profound transformation of American politics. The system of government as well as political ideologies were completely disassembled and rebuilt from the 1850s to the 1870s. The struggle over slavery transformed every political party and every politician. Eventually the conflict reshaped the structure of government, eliminating unfree labor from the United States and making slaves into citizens. Although there were indicators of the deep political divisions between the North and South as far back as 1776, it was in the 1850s that the system of politics began to unravel. In that decade both the Democrats and the Whigs, the two largest political parties, began dividing internally on the issue of slavery. This led in turn to the formation of new parties such as the Republicans and the disappearance of the Democratic Party in the North. Quite quickly, politics became sharply polarized. The issue was slavery. The Democrats supported it and the Republicans wanted its abolition. Few politicians felt there was room to compromise. More agreed with Abraham Lincoln who said in 1858, "a house divided against itself cannot stand." In other words, the United States was to be either slave or free. The 1860 election was a referendum on slavery. When the Republicans won the White House, many southerners felt that they had no recourse but to leave the Union and form a government of their own. Central to the Confederacy was perpetuating slavery. Thus the politics of the 1850s and 1860s and the war that it brought answered the question that had nagged America since its creation: did the Declaration of Independence apply to everyone? By answering that question in the affirmative, Americans redrew politics and transformed their government.

In China, the system of dynastic rule became weak and moribund. Chinese rulers faced pressure both internally and externally. Several rebellions undermined the Qing dynasty's hold on power. Foreign trade, missionaries, and war with Europe crippled the government's ability to govern. In this chaos, new ideas about changing the system of politics and government in China were forged. Although the fruits of these new political movements would develop in the 20th century, it is important to see that like the United States, China underwent tremendous political change during the 19th century, and these transformations had impacts well into the 20th century.

In the 19th century, the newly independent Latin American republics came increasingly under the control of the liberal middle class, which used the national government to regulate the economy and control education and internal development. By the end of the century, more radical working-class parties and organizations advocated greater government intervention on behalf of workers and other disenfranchised groups. Thus, at the start of the 20th century, Latin America was also poised to undergo greater political change.

UNITED STATES, 1850–65

During the 1840s, the Whigs and Democrats, the two oldest political parties in the United States, had reached agreement on several issues that had plagued the early republic. The tariff, the National Bank, and the regulation of internal commerce ranked high among these divisive issues. Americans celebrated their limited form of federal government and considered any of its remaining weakness essential to the safeguarding of personal and political freedom.

The next decade was one of rapid economic and social change in America, and politics was gaining a more general audience than at any time since the Revolution. The Whigs and Democrats were searching for new issues that would mobilize the voters behind the old party structure. This attempt to underscore the meaning of the old parties was to have far-reaching consequences as political and social agendas began driving forward proposals that required strong federal action. One unforeseen consequence of trying to bolster the parties was that, ironically, it eventually led to the virtual dissolution of both.

In the 1850s the Democratic Party became divided over the issue of the extension of slavery. The Northern branch of the party favored popular sovereignty, wherein the voters decided for or against the extension of slavery to new states or territories; the Southern branch preferred an unequivocal assertion that the Constitution absolutely protected the practice of slavery. Stephen A. Douglas became the leader of the Northern group, while Jefferson Davis led the Southern position. When Congress voted to ease the tensions over slavery with the passage of the Compromise of 1850, Davis voted against every provision of the bill except that which strengthened the Fugitive Slave Law. When Davis introduced legislation that would have condemned Northern interference in Southern domestic institutions, the Douglas faction refused to support their own party.

An example of this political realignment can be seen in the reaction to the passage of the Kansas-Nebraska Act in 1854. A product of the optimism of the Northern Democrats and Stephen Douglas, the Kansas-Nebraska Act seemingly sabotaged the political compromises that had characterized the previous decades of American politics. The measure was popular among Northern Democrats, and the Southern Democrats gave it support, but its passage ultimately caused a split in the party. Moderates in the North felt betrayed. Outraged by the act, Northern voters began to speak of the existence of a slave power conspiracy. In response, moderates in the South began to harden their position and seriously consider disunion.

While the Northern Democrats were hurt by the response to the act, the Whigs were devastated by it. The Southern wing of the Whig Party, sympathetic to compromise on the slavery issue, bolted, thereafter aligning themselves with the Southern Democrats; and the Whig Party, already weak after years of deterioration, was left in disarray and all but destroyed. A serious misreading of the temper of the voters had taken place, and they were left simmering in anger at the old parties. Significantly, this political upheaval came at a time when the old party system was already suffering from weakening voter support and poor party discipline. Yet in the wake of the disaster that followed the Kansas-Nebraska Act, interest in politics and political discussions increased, and several new parties moved in to fill the void.

Among these, two major new parties stood out, the Nativists and the Republicans. The Nativist, or American, Party rose very rapidly in popularity but failed in carrying its agenda to the national scene. The Republicans, after a false start in 1856, managed to win the White House in 1860, a victory that brought the country to civil war.

Nativist propaganda was widely promulgated throughout the nation, and even those who disagreed with Nativist positions were well aware of them. Nativists were solidly Protestant and radically anti-Catholic in their rhetoric. For support they tapped into the growing fear and resentment that paralleled the rapid changes taking place in American society. Nativist rhetoric portrayed Catholics, and especially the Catholic immigrants, as crime-ridden and intemperate, a drag on the economy, and a danger to the fabric of society. They viewed the acceptance of Catholics by the Northern wing of the Democratic Party as proof that the old political system would fail to support traditional American values. By tapping into a growing sense of resentment of politics as usual, out of touch with the pulse of the people and dedicated only to entrenched interests, the Nativists found an agenda designed to ensure the defeat of the old parties.

The Nativists were deeply immersed in the Evangelical movement and were strongly supported by some of the finest established families in the North. Politically, they made some gains at the state level, especially in Massachusetts, only to have the party collapse after a few years because it failed to generate enough voter support nationally. Nativists were particularly embarrassed by their inability to bring about the passage of more stringent immigration laws. They did poorly with Southerners, who were more accepting of immigrants and more tolerant of Catholicism than many in the North. More generally, the Nativists failed because of their lack of political experience, their association with several prominent old-party Whigs, and their violent anti-Catholic rhetoric, which bothered many politically active Protestants.

The Republican Party benefited from the collapse of the Nativists; developing more slowly, it avoided a similar meteoric rise and fall. While Nativists generally identified with social and cultural ideals, the motivations of the Republicans were purely those of political ambition. Even early Republicans were astute politicians. The party agenda called for a restructuring and expansion of government on all levels. The positions taken on abolition, urbanization, extension of the vote, and free labor were all carefully crafted to foster a positive public impression of the party and to increase its power and prestige.

Free labor seems to have been the most fundamental element of the Republican belief system and identity. It embodied the ideals of a classless, socially mobile society within the framework of a harmonic and expansive economic system, all deeply rooted in personal prosperity and capitalism. While Northern Democrats espoused many of these same principles, Republicans were more optimistic about the future of a highly industrialized America and were certain that the new society and culture of the North would ultimately supplant that of the South to the betterment of the nation as a whole.

The Republican Party benefited greatly from the rising tide of sectional resentment. The Kansas-Nebraska Act was a godsend for the Republican Party. They used the passage of the act and the subsequent decision of the courts in the Dred Scott case as symbols verifying the existence of a slave power conspiracy. Not only was such a conspiracy dangerous in itself, but also it was clear evidence that the old powers wished to spread slavery to every corner of the land. The Republicans were in the unique position of being able to stand as the defenders of an idealized Northern culture, untainted, as were the Democrats, by former associations with the South.

Many viewed the Democratic toleration of Catholics as self-serving and insincere.

An important part of the Republican arsenal of ideals was its characterization of the Southern planter class as the slave aristocracy, viciously suppressing a large Southern white population and all Southern blacks, denying them the benefits of true political democracy. The Republicans were able to transform the fears of papistry, slave power, and the unrestrained expansion of slavery into issues that could be blamed on the Democrats, North and South.

The Northern Democrats also used the symbols of progress, opportunity, and mobility to considerable effect. However, they had to defend their party's historic position on slavery. Southern planters were portrayed by the Democrats as favoring progress and opportunity, but only for whites; and some movement was made in the Southern states toward the expansion of the vote for white males. But the Democratic Party was often viewed as part of the problem, deeply involved in the political corruption of the day and supporting a widespread system of patronage. Voters were generally disenchanted with the party's politics-as-usual agenda, and many viewed the Democratic toleration of Catholics as self-serving and insincere. The Northern Democrats, although considerably weakened, were able to remain a political force until the outbreak of the war. The Southern branch maintained itself by championing the resistance to outside intervention in Southern lifestyle and culture, which were inexorably linked to slavery.

The 1856 election proved to be the death knell of the old two-party system. In the presidential race, the Republicans championed the slogan "Free Speech, Free Press, Free Soil, Free Men, Fremont, and Victory." John C. Fremont may have been made a national hero for his role in mapping and exploring the West, but he was an unacceptable presidential candidate in the South. Governor John Wise warned that if Fremont won the 1856 election, Virginia would secede. Consequently, the Democrats, fearing to incur the wrath of the Northern voter by nominating Stephen A. Douglas, the author of the Kansas-Nebraska Act, decided to run James Buchanan of Pennsylvania. Buchanan won the election against Fremont due to the entry into the race of a weak candidate from the American Party, a coalition of Nativists and Know-Nothings. This third party candidate was former President Millard Fillmore. Buchanan received only a minority of the popular votes for president, yet he handily won the electoral college.

As a new party, the Republicans had not had time to organize an electoral victory behind Fremont. Nonetheless, by the end of the decade the Republican Party had become the foremost instrument of antislavery sentiment in the country. Its condemnation of the slave power forces, coupled with the Kansas-Nebraska Act and the Dred Scott decision, brought it adherents. The events, both real and fabricated, taking place in Bleeding Kansas and the schemes of fanatical abolitionists like John Brown to forcibly liberate slaves and promote slave insurrections, tended to radicalize even the most moderate politicians.

Northern office seekers, with their sights set on 1860, began calling for an assault on the traditions and honor of the South with all the enthusiasm that their rhetoric could convey. Such attacks fueled Southern indignation, created a desire for vindictive satisfaction, and led Southern moderates to retrench their positions. Southern radicals began to call for disunion as the best means of protecting sectional interests. "Both North and South seemed to be swayed by the demagogue," observed William Fletcher, who would go on to fight as a Rebel private. Under the perceived weight of "accumulated wrongs and indignities," the South was swept up in a reckless euphoria for secession and the establishment of the Confederacy.

James Buchanan's legacy as the 15th president of the United States was to follow, rather than to lead, the country to the brink of civil war. Buchanan entered office knowing that he was unpopular with most of America. He was seemingly unwilling or powerless to control the radicals of either the North or the South. He had an honest desire for peace; but he was a pro-Southern unionist and as such was willing to make concessions to the South to maintain at least the semblance of national unity. Nevertheless, pro-Southern forces thought his concessions too harsh, while Northerners found him weak and pusillanimous. Buchanan was saddled with a cabinet divided by controversy over the same issues that split the country, and his vacillating policies did little but engender both social and political turmoil.

The rising star of national politics in the 1850s was a young former Whig politician from Illinois. Abraham Lincoln had not rushed to join the first groups that formed the Republican Party; but in 1854, in a speech in Peoria, Illinois, he began to speak out against the Kansas-Nebraska Act. The deep crusading tenor of this speech was closely linked to Lincoln's ambition for office. Instead of casting his fortunes with the Republicans, who were expounding on the issue of expanding slavery into the territories, he mistakenly continued to identify himself with the nearly defunct Whig Party. Viewed as an old-party candidate, he lost the 1854 Senate election in a close race.

Immediately thereafter, he transferred his allegiance to the Republicans and helped to organize the party in Illinois. It was no surprise when Lincoln was chosen by the Republicans to face Stephen A. Douglas in the 1858 race for the Senate. Lincoln began his campaign with his famous "House Divided Against Itself" speech. In this address Lincoln gave the most radical speech of his entire life, calling for the country to become all free or all slave. Never again did he express such radical views. His words were widely interpreted as a declaration of war on Southern institutions. In a highly publicized series of debates, Douglas carefully pointed out that the country had been split for quite some time on the issue of slavery and could continue to be so indefinitely if the hotheads on both sides would leave well enough alone. By espousing moderation Douglas narrowly won the race, but Lincoln's stance had catapulted the young lawyer into a position of leadership in the Republican Party. By aligning himself with the influential radical wing of the party, he went on to engineer the Republican national convention in 1860 and received the party's presidential nomination instead of William H. Seward, a moderate on the slavery issue.

The radicals who joined the Republican Party did so largely because of the slavery issue. They generally came from the agricultural areas of the North or the cosmopolitan urban centers of the Northeast. The latter seemed especially absorbed by the concept of the immediate abolition of slavery and the granting of full civil rights to blacks. They saw no room for compromise in these matters and were willing to destroy the party if necessary to attain their goals. If the Union did not stand for liberty, it too was expendable.

While Lincoln had used the radicals to gain the nomination, he immediately began to modify his radical image to make himself more acceptable to other factions of the party. The moderates made up the majority, but there was a wider variety in their beliefs than among the radicals. The moderates tried to control the party by holding a balance of power. They emphasized that slavery was a territorial issue and were willing to leave slavery alone in areas of the South where it had long been established. Many believed in gradual emancipation and foreign colonization efforts by black freemen. By failing to center himself within the party spectrum, Lincoln essentially drove moderate Republicans toward the radical position. Certainly this is the light in which the South viewed the Republicans and Lincoln during the election. Southerners began to preach of Black Republicanism as a counterpoint to the charges of a slave power conspiracy.

Lincoln probably would not have won the presidency in 1860 had the election not become a four-way race. The Democratic Party split between two candidates: proslavery John C. Breckinridge, a former vice president of the United States, and Stephen A. Douglas, a moderate, who attempted to reprise his defeat of Lincoln in 1858. The fourth candidate, on the ticket of the new Constitutional Union Party, composed of former Whigs and Nativists, was John Bell of Tennessee. Tariffs, homesteads, railroads, immigrants, and political corruption all figured in the campaign, but slavery and the fear of disunion remained the pivotal questions. When it became obvious to the candidates, based on the results of gubernatorial elections in Pennsylvania and Indiana, that Lincoln was going to win, Bell and Breckinridge proclaimed dedication to immediate disunion; but Douglas, to his credit, disavowed any ideas of secession, saying, "If Lincoln is elected, he must be inaugurated."

Lincoln won the election with just under 40 percent of the popular vote and 59 percent of the electoral votes. He carried 18 states; yet, with the exception of coastal California, not one of them was below the Mason-Dixon line. This result reinforced his position as a sectional leader rather than a national one. Significantly, Douglas, who beat both Breckinridge and Bell with 30 percent of the popular vote, represented the views of at least some of the electorate in all parts of the country, but he received a mere 4 percent of the electoral votes. Besides Mississippi, the only other state won by Douglas was New Jersey. This seemingly strange pairing effectively ended the influence of Douglas and the Northern Democrats. Breckinridge, with 18 percent of the popular vote, carried every state that would come to be in the Confederacy except Mississippi and Virginia. The former vice president also carried

Maryland and Delaware. Bell captured the states of Kentucky, Tennessee, and Virginia and received 13 percent of the popular vote. Notwithstanding this result, 70 percent of the voters had shown support for at least a moderate stand against slavery, but they almost all resided in the North.

A group of moderate Virginia residents declared that "the election of a sectional president even with odious and dangerous sentiment" would not of itself be sufficient cause for secession. Yet they saw the election result as "an alarming indication" of the ripening schemes of abolitionists to "plunder" and "outrage" the Southern way of life with their growing fanaticism. The abolitionists exacerbated the seriousness of the situation by taunting Virginia as a "Plunderer of Cradles—she who has grown fat by selling her own children in the slave shambles: Virginia! Butcher-Pirate-Kidnapper-Slavocrat—the murderer of John Brown and his gallant band—at last, will meet her just doom." Secessionists warned that Virginia could soon expect an invasion of armed abolitionists and would become, as it subsequently did, the primary theater of the military campaign to eradicate slavery.

In light of subsequent events, it seems certain that the election of Lincoln in 1860 was the precipitating event that led to secession and ultimately to the Civil War. Lincoln, following the generally unpopular Buchanan, was the second minority president elected in succession, which suggests a growing lack of faith in the national government. But the question of secession had appeared much earlier than 1860 and from many quarters. The most serious confrontation between the federal government and the states had come in the nullification crisis of the 1830s. The question had been a political issue in the national elections in both 1852 and 1856. Virginia had threatened secession in 1856, and South Carolina had threatened to secede in both these years.

From the 1830s, the threat of secession dominated the rhetoric of Southern politicians.

While the concept of state nullification was a moderate position compared to secession, its logical conclusion would have rendered the federal government impotent. John C. Calhoun, a brilliant legal mind, realized that, even in a democracy, 49 percent of the people could be tyrannized by the other 51 percent if the majority were well organized behind a single issue. Therefore, if the majority was to rule, the minority must be willing to assert its rights. In this case the right was that of state nullification. The administration of Andrew Jackson had reacted to nullification with the passage of a Force Bill, authorizing the president to send troops to South Carolina if the state persisted in its refusal to allow the collection of the tariff and persisted in its marshalling of an armed force in the form of a state militia. The crisis was averted by the passage of a compromise federal tariff acceptable to South Carolina and by the nullification of the Force Bill by the state. While disunion was averted by this face-saving device, the entire scenario would be played out again in 1860 with very different results.

In the nullification crisis the South found a new weapon with which to enforce its will on the national government. The threat of secession thereafter dominated the rhetoric of Southern politicians. The radical politicians of the South raised the concept of states' rights to the level of political gospel during the decade of the

1850s. Many Southern leaders espoused secession only sporadically, and usually only during an election campaign. Those who did otherwise did not achieve lasting prominence. However, with the help of the Southern radicals called fire-eaters, what had started as an intriguing political device soon got out of hand.

Although there were numerous radicals actively pursuing disunion in all the Southern states, some fire-eaters are worthy of separate consideration, as they were conspicuously in the forefront of the clamor for secession and served as consistent and effective proponents of disunion.

Edmund Ruffin was an aged Virginian who had taken up the torch of secession in midlife and allowed his quest to become an obsession. Ruffin devoted 20 years to the espousal of secessionist doctrine. He became a professional fire-eater, traveling widely, speaking to public gatherings, and writing prolifically on this sole theme. Ruffin was in his mid-60s by the time secession became a reality; but he was still active in the cause and had the honor of firing the first shot on Fort Sumter.

Robert B. Rhett was from South Carolina and, as early as 1828, he was urging resistance to the rule of the federal government. Rhett was one of the earliest and most outspoken of the fire-eaters. He introduced amendments to the Constitution to protect Southern rights and, in 1844, he led an abortive tariff nullification movement. Rhett used his Charleston-based newspaper, the *Mercury*, to plead with the Southern states to secede en masse in defense of states' rights and Southern culture.

On December 20, 1860, South Carolina voted to secede from the Union. Depicted here is a session of the South Carolina Secession Convention.

When these supplications fell on deaf ears, he urged South Carolina to set an example and secede alone, believing that the rest of the South would follow. His long dedication to the cause earned him the appellation Father of Secession.

William L. Yancey of Alabama was one of the best spoken of the disunion apologists. Yancey had lived as a youth in the North and never tired of using his personal experiences to reinforce the perception of its moral and cultural degradation. In the 1830s he became convinced that the South could no longer protect itself from the degrading Northern influences that seemed to be gaining control of Congress. When the Democrats refused to include a proslavery plank in their 1848 election platform, he became an ardent and unapologetic secessionist, urging immediate disunion. He hammered relentlessly on the themes of Southern unity of action and immediate disunion. The Southern states, he said, "all united may yet produce spirit enough to lead us forward, to call forth a Lexington, to fight a Bunker's Hill, to drive the foe from the city of our rights." It was Yancey, in the spring of 1860, who engineered the split in the Democratic convention that all but ensured the election of an antislavery Republican.

Of the prominent fire-eaters, few went on to serve in battle, choosing rather to remain in politics. William Barkesdale of Mississippi, however, was a notable exception. Barkesdale, a true fire-eater, had been a vociferous and effective proponent of secession. The Southern war office made him a brigadier general, and he proved one of the most effective political commanders in the war. The tenacity with which his Mississippi regiments opposed the river crossing of federal troops during the Battle of Fredericksburg won him great renown. During the Battle of Gettysburg, Barkesdale was killed as he fought in the peach orchard.

In calling for secession, the fire-eaters were aided by a highly partisan and radical press. Public orations, debates, and harangues were a popular instrument of the fire-eaters and were well attended. Yet these forums addressed only those who could be present, producing a somewhat transient enthusiasm for the particular topic of discussion. Therefore, the 19th-century citizen favored the newspaper as a more individualized form of communication. Newspapers gained influence steadily during the first half of the century. An amazingly large number of local publications appeared. Speeches were printed in their entirety within a few days of being given. Printed political arguments, essays, letters to the editor, and discussions among dedicated readers—both genuine and planted for effect—flowed in the wake of every issue.

People read alone or in small groups, with the leisure to reread and analyze what was printed. The power of the press to influence a wider audience than could be assembled at any one place and time was not to be underestimated. Some papers tried to remain neutral, but others sought out political alliances either because of the agenda of the editors, or, more commonly, to attract a lucrative trade in political advertising and public printing. Neutrality on any topic of public interest often doomed a newspaper to failure. "We have perfect unanimity in the press," wrote one Southern observer. Local newspapers commonly filled their pages with reprinted articles and speeches reported in other journals from around the country, often with biting editorial preambles.

Besides Rhett's Charleston *Mercury*, several newspapers were actively stressing Southern independence. *DeBow's Review*, a monthly commercial publication located in New Orleans, urged the South to diversify its economy and to build railroads, factories, and canals, thereby freeing itself from dependence on the North. By mid-century *DeBow's* was increasingly seen as a vehicle for secessionist propaganda. The Richmond *South*, edited by Roger A. Pryor, and its sister paper, the *Enquirer*, edited by Henry A. Wise, both stressed secessionist themes. The Richmond *Examiner* was described as firing "shot and shell" at those moderates on secession. The *Whig* went "into the secession movement with all its might." The *Dispatch*, once neutral and conservative, threw "all its powers, with its large circulation, into the cause" by 1860. Southern nationalism was hawked by the respected *Southern Literary Messenger*, once edited by Edgar Allan Poe, and even the *Southern Quarterly Review* was pleading the cause of disunion.

Secessionist sentiment pervaded the churches, the shops, and even the schools. Prosecession radicals smashed unfriendly presses, banned books, and fought duels with Unionists. The fire-eaters turned every news article, pamphlet, sermon, and play into a propaganda piece for secession. Even minor confrontations with the Unionists, or with the abolitionists, were declared a crisis upon whose immediate resolution rested the very survival of the South. Warfare in Kansas, the publication of *Uncle Tom's Cabin,* and the antislavery raid of John Brown at Harper's Ferry gave credence to the tales of the fire-eaters. When there was no crisis, the radicals were fully capable of fabricating one. Southern leaders in Congress proposed the re-opening of the transatlantic slave trade in 1859 without hope of the question being resolved in their favor so that the radicals might use the issue to good effect as propaganda.

Secessionists proclaimed South Carolina the leader of disunion, and it remained the natural home of secession throughout the period. This view was held by both the North and the South and was one of the few things that evoked widespread unanimity. The nullification crisis had all but eliminated any pro-Union feeling in the state. Radicals claimed that if South Carolina were to act for itself, the secession of the entire South would be "three-fourths finished." Many in the Deep South thought that the border states—Virginia, Maryland, Kentucky, and Tennessee among them—would ultimately join a new confederacy in their own time.

It is not clear what a Lincoln defeat in 1860 would have meant to the secession movement.

The Palmetto State had renewed its threat to secede in 1859 by inviting its sister slaveholding states to consider a course of concerted action. Nonetheless, a positive decision was deferred pending the outcome of the 1860 election. It is not clear what result a Lincoln defeat or a Breckinridge, Douglas, or Bell victory would have meant to the secession movement. But in its declaration the Secession Convention listed as one of the reasons for its secession "the election of a man to the high office of President of the United States whose opinions and purposes are hostile to slavery." Certainly, a Republican victory had been a signal for action.

Some secessionists, including William Yancey, began the movement toward disunion on the eve of the presidential election by calling for part, if not all, of the South to make an immediate break with the North. These men were willing to leave Virginia and the other border states, thought to be soft on the question of slavery, in the Union to save the rest of the South from further Northern degradation. A border composed of states in the Union, yet amicable to slavery, might prove more effective to a new confederacy than confederated states that were lukewarm to disunion. The new nation would thereby have a border free of hostile abolitionists; and it was thought that neutral border states might be unwilling to allow the predicted Northern invasion to be marshaled in their territory.

On the afternoon of December 20, 1860, the South Carolina Convention passed an Ordinance of Secession. Five additional Southern states quickly followed its example: Mississippi, Florida, Alabama, Georgia, and Louisiana. In February, Texas came on board. At first it appeared that only these seven states would secede, and early Confederate flags sported only seven stars. However, in April, after the bombardment of Fort Sumter and Lincoln's call for 75,000 volunteers to defend the Union, Virginia joined its sisters. A Confederate officer's teenage wife wrote in her journal, "Dear Old Virginia, long did she strive to keep her place in the Union, but trampled rights, a broken Constitution, and a dishonorable Government compelled her to join her sister states in a new Confederacy." This news was followed in May and June by the secession of Arkansas, North Carolina, and Tennessee.

Secessionist sentiment in Missouri and Kentucky was somewhat split. As large areas of these states were quickly brought under federal control, actual secession was impractical. Eleven states had actually seceded; nonetheless, when the new Confederate battle flag was designed, it sported 13 stars, the last two representing the fiction that Missouri and Kentucky were willing but unable to join their sisters. The use of 13 stars was thought to reinforce the symbolic connections between the infant Confederacy and the American Revolution.

Although the radicals and fire-eaters had set secession in motion, they soon lost control of the new Southern nation. Few fire-eaters served successfully for any time in the new government. More moderate heads prevailed. Jefferson Davis, the first president of the Confederacy, had been a strong advocate of states' rights, but he was far from being considered a radical. Alexander Stephens, a recent convert to disunion, was chosen to serve as the Confederate vice president. Other moderates like Judah P. Benjamin and Robert E. Lee would lead the prosecution of the war.

Nonetheless, disunion was very popular in the South, not only among the social and political elite, but also with the average white Southerner. "The unanimity of the people was simply marvelous. So long as the question of secession was under discussion, opinions were both various and violent. The moment secession was finally determined upon, a revolution was wrought. There was no longer anything to discuss, and so discussion ceased. Men got ready for war, and delicate women with equal spirit sent them off with smiling faces." In 1861, after Lincoln's call for a Northern mobilization of 75,000 men, a clerk from the Confederate War Department noted, "From the ardor of the [Southern] volunteers . . . they might sweep the whole Abolition concern beyond the Susquehanna, and afterwards keep them there." All seemed to understand the consequences if the cause of secession did not succeed. Southerners could not, without a complete sacrifice of their honor, do anything else but fight on to victory or utter defeat. "This is the irrevocable blow! Every reflecting mind here should know that the only alternatives now are successful revolution or abject subjugation."

The function of honor, as an important component in the Southern rationale that led to secession and war, should not be minimized. While no one can exactly define the reason for which each Confederate soldier fought, their diaries and letters suggest that the defense of Southern honor, which had been disparaged by Northern fanatics, was high on the list. Rebel private Carlton McCarthy noted, "When one section of the country oppresses and insults another, the result is . . . war!" With respect to the secession of Virginia, General Robert E. Lee wrote, "We could have pursued no other course without dishonor. And sad as the results have been, if it had to be done over again, we should be compelled to act in precisely the same manner."

Northerners responded to the act of disunion in a variety of ways. A young woman wrote, "The storm has broken over us. . . . How strange and awful it seems." In the North the stock markets fell and banks began to call in their loans. Many businessmen, forgetful of their recent enthusiasm for abolition, panicked at the specter of near bankruptcy. Yet initially the majority of the people celebrated the coming of the storm with fervor and enthusiasm. "We have flags on our papers and envelopes and have all our stationery bordered with red, white, and blue. We wear little flag pins for badges and tie our hair with red, white, and blue ribbons and have pins and earrings made of the buttons the soldiers gave us." Women gathered to sew uniforms and made up "scrap lint and roll up bandages" in the churches and the local courthouses.

Troops paraded through the streets of large cities and small towns. "It seemed," wrote Theodore Winthrop, "as if all the able-bodied men in the country were moving, on the first of May, with all their property on their backs, to agreeable, but dusty lodgings on the Potomac." Soldiers in gray and blue, and in the garish uniforms of Zouaves, Chasseurs, and Dragoons, carried their regimental flags past the White House. Six regiments from three different states arrived in Washington in such close succession that their separate parades formed "a continuous procession." The War Department could not provide for all the volunteers arriving in the capital and placed them in warehouses and markets to sleep until proper camps could be arranged on the ring of hills around the city. Like irresponsible children, some soldiers joined the gaily dressed and carefree crowds that roamed the city, even to the grounds of the Executive Mansion, waving flags to the strains of patriotic songs such as "Yankee Doodle," "The Girl I Left Behind Me," and "Columbia, the Gem of the Ocean." Lincoln's call for volunteers had been answered with a vengeance (Volo and Volo, 15–29).

To read about government and politics in the United States in the 20th century, see the United States entries in the section "Government" in chapter 6 ("Political Life") in volume 6 of this series.

FOR MORE INFORMATION

American Memory. <http://memory.loc.gov>.

Paludan, P. S. *A People's Contest: The Union and Civil War, 1861–1865.* New York: Harper & Row, 1988.

Thomas, E. M. *The Confederate Nation: 1861–1865.* New York: Harper & Row, 1979.

Volo, D. D., and J. M. Volo. *Daily Life in Civil War America.* Westport, Conn.: Greenwood Press, 1998.

POLITICAL LIFE

|

GOVERNMENT
& POLITICS

|

United States,
1850-1865

Victorian England

China

Latin America

VICTORIAN ENGLAND

Great Britain (the political unit made up of England, Scotland, Wales, and Ireland) is, officially, ruled by a sovereign with the advice of Parliament. Parliament, like the U.S. Congress, has two branches. The upper house is the House of Lords, which is primarily based on heredity. Members of the House of Commons are elected. The British government differs from that of the United States in having no absolute separation of powers between its legislative, executive, and judicial branches. The prime minister and the cabinet are members of Parliament; the House of Lords has ultimate judicial authority and operates (although only rarely) as the highest court of appeal.

England has no written constitution, although the term British Constitution is used to describe the accumulated laws and traditions that determine how the government operates and to define the relationship between individuals and the state. In the early 19th century, the central government was primarily limited to foreign relations, defense, and justice. Its powers and activities grew rapidly during the Victorian period as it began to control domestic affairs and take responsibility for citizens' health and safety.

By 1837 the monarchy had taken its modern form. Formally, the queen selected the prime minister—but in actuality, her choice was determined by Parliament's political leaders. She was always kept informed of government business, but she no longer had any real power except for the moral and symbolic influence she was able to exercise.

The prime minister, usually the leader of the political party with the most seats in the House of Commons, was the effective head of government. He could be a member of either house, although he was increasingly apt to be a commoner rather than a peer. As a member of Parliament, he represented a single constituency; unlike the president of the United States, the prime minister is not elected by the country as a whole.

The prime minister selected a cabinet to advise him on specific issues, provide political leadership in Parliament, and take responsibility for the major administrative departments of government. The number of men in the cabinet varied but was usually about 14; the cabinet included a chancellor of the exchequer (treasury), a foreign secretary, a home secretary, a colonial secretary, and a secretary of war. Members of the cabinet were chosen from both houses of Parliament; the foreign secretary, by tradition, was usually from the House of Lords. The cabinet was bound by a principle of collective responsibility. When they debated in private, each cabinet minister could argue for his own position; but once they made a decision, all had to support it or resign. Even the prime minister could lose an argument in the privacy of a cabinet meeting. He would then faithfully promote the policy that the cabinet determined.

An English peer automatically became a member of the House of Lords when he inherited his title (as duke, marquess, earl, viscount, or baron) and reached the age of 21. The House of Lords also included representatives from the Scots and Irish peerage, the archbishops of York and of Canterbury, and a set number of bishops from the Church of England. The size of the House of Lords varied, because titles were sometimes inherited by minors who could not yet take their seats, and new peers were created from time to time. The range in the Victorian period was between 421 and 577. Many aristocrats attended sessions only on ceremonial occasions; the ordinary business in the House of Lords was carried out by a small group of peers who had strong political interests.

The number of seats in the House of Commons was 658 until 1885, when it was increased to 670. A member is referred to as a Member of Parliament, abbreviated MP (usually with no periods: for example, John Bright, MP). They are elected but—in another crucial difference between British and U.S. government—need not live

Queen Victoria as a young woman in 1839. This image was based on a drawing by R. J. Lane and published in Walter Besant's *Fifty Years Ago* (1888). Courtesy of Paley Library, Temple University.

in the district they represent. In theory, a young man interested in politics would make his ambitions known to landowners and other influential people in a district, and they would invite him to stand (rather than run) for a seat. In practice, the national political parties came to exercise a great deal of control by suggesting which candidates should be adopted to stand for election in which districts.

Until 1858, everyone elected to the House of Commons was required to have a certain amount of property. There was no pay for MPs until the 1880s. Political service was viewed as a duty for men of substance whose private income was such that they would not be influenced by economic or other obligations. Membership widened during the century. Following the removal of religious qualifications, the first Jewish member was seated in 1858; the atheist Charles Bradlaugh was seated in 1888. Socialists and working men were elected during the latter part of the period.

Elections are not as predictable as in the U.S. system. They must be held after five years, but may be called at any time. The prime minister and cabinet usually resign whenever they are defeated in an important vote in the House of Commons. Although this is known as the fall of a government, it is a regular part of the political process and not necessarily a major crisis. Because it means that the prime minister's party no longer controls enough votes to pass legislation, a new election is held. Political parties were changing and unstable during the 19th century; there were several small factions, and it was not unusual for an MP to switch parties. Members of the government—that is, the prime minister and cabinet—generally belonged to the same party, although some coalition governments included men from several factions.

Victorian elections were disorderly. Crowds tossed eggs and vegetables and shouted so candidates could not be heard. Political agents bribed voters with liquor and other treats. Until 1872 there was no secret ballot. A voter simply went to the polling place and announced his choice out loud to a clerk. This made it very difficult for him to vote for anyone except the candidate supported by his landlord or employer.

Parliament itself could also be rowdy. Neither chamber is big enough to hold all the members. In the Commons, they sit not at separate desks looking toward the speaker (as in the U.S. Congress) but elbow-to-elbow on crowded benches. The benches face each other across an aisle—and seem to encourage shouting during a heated debate. Parliamentary sessions began at 4 P.M. and continued until very late at night or into the early morning hours.

During the course of the century, Parliament became increasingly active in regulating economic conditions, public health, education, and other aspects of national life. Therefore the civil service—the paid government employees who run agencies, sit on commissions, collect taxes, enforce regulations, and so forth—became much larger and more professional. In 1837 almost all posts were filled through patronage. A man got a government job—whether as a minor tax clerk or as a colonial governor—not because of his qualifications but through the influence exerted by his family or friends. Although reforms were often proposed, not until 1870 was there a professional civil service with entry through competitive examination. The examination for beginning jobs that would eventually lead to senior posts in domestic or colonial service was constructed so that it favored men from prestigious schools and universities. Examinations that required specific skills (e.g., accounting or chemical engineering) led to more routine jobs. Later in the century a separate women's examination for clerical posts was added.

Most Victorians paid little attention to Parliament because it was remote from their daily lives. Local government was more visible. The basic unit of local government was called the parish, although it no longer necessarily had the same boundaries as a Church of England parish. In the traditional system dating from medieval times, the parish was responsible for policing and mending roads. Each parish was also obliged to look after its own poor, which it did well or badly in a great variety of ways depending on local needs and resources. The New Poor Law of 1834 was intended to reform the welfare system; it will be discussed below under a separate heading.

Most functions of local government were carried out by justices of the peace appointed by the county's Lord Lieutenant. (The other duties of the Lord Lieutenant, who was almost always a peer and the county's largest landholder, were largely ceremonial.) Justices of the peace had to own land and belong to the Church of England. In the countryside, the local squire was almost certain to be a justice. Clergymen could also be appointed. The justice was an unpaid amateur; he did not need to have any training in law or administration. Serving as justice was a gentlemanly obligation—and a remaining vestige of the paternal authority that upper-class men exerted over the lower orders.

Justices of the peace supervised the paid parish officials who managed poor relief and fixed roads. They also served as magistrates: for petty criminal offenses, the local justice heard the case, passed judgment, and pronounced the sentence. In more serious matters, he ordered that the suspect be bound over for trial before a judge.

The old system of local government was largely superseded during the Victorian years. As the interlocking and widespread nature of many social and economic problems became clear, Parliament began to create agencies that oversaw larger areas. Highways, hospitals, sewers, prisons, workplace safety, the inspection of slaughterhouses, and similar matters could not be funded and managed by individual parishes. A succession of local government acts created new administrative units with elected officials. Justices of the peace lost most of their powers in 1889, although they continued to serve as magistrates.

This photograph of Queen Victoria near the end of her reign was captioned "Her Majesty Today" and published in the *English Illustrated Magazine* in 1897.

During the 1870s, women became eligible to serve on school boards and certain other local government agencies. When voting was a right reserved for landowners with a stake in the country, women were almost necessarily excluded. After successive reform bills enfranchised middle-class and then working-class men, however, women's lack of landed property was no longer a reason to keep them from voting. Late-Victorian legislators began to accept the idea that women should have a voice in the matters that seemed to fall within their special sphere of expertise—matters such as education, welfare, and health. By the end of the century, women could vote in most municipal and county elections. National affairs such as defense and foreign policy were still reserved for men. In 1897, various local suffrage organizations joined forces as the National Union of Women's Suffrage Societies with Millicent Garrett Fawcett as president. The dramatic campaign of disruption and civil disobedience led by Emmeline Pankhurst began soon after 1900, although women did not win the parliamentary vote until 1919 (Mitchell, *Daily Life*, 87–91).

To read about government and politics in Chaucer's England, see the entries on Europe in chapter 6 ("Political Life") in volume 2 of this series; for Elizabethan England, see the entry on England in the section "Government" in chapter 6 ("Political Life") in volume 3 of this series; for 18th-century England, see the entry on England in the section "Government" in chapter 6 ("Political Life") in volume 4 of this series.

FOR MORE INFORMATION

Keith-Lucas, B. *English Local Government in the Nineteenth and Twentieth Centuries*. London: Historical Association, 1977.

Mitchell, S. *Daily Life in Victorian England*. Westport, Conn.: Greenwood Press, 1996.

Mitchell, S., ed. *Victorian Britain: An Encyclopedia*. New York: Garland Press, 1998.

POLITICAL LIFE

|

GOVERNMENT
& POLITICS

|

United States,
1850-1865

Victorian England

China

Latin America

CHINA

The 19th century was a turbulent time for China's government. The government faced pressure both internally and externally. Several rebellions weakened the government's hold on power. Foreign trade, missionaries, and war with outside powers lessened China's ability to govern the population and minimized its spheres of influence. The role of government was widely debated. Some favored the traditional form of government, based on Confucian ideals. Others rejected the old ways in favor of new, modern, and for the most part western-influenced forms of government.

During the 19th century, China was ruled by the Qing dynasty. The Qing first came to power in 1644 when the Manchus to the north of China took advantage of a rebellion in China. Peasant rebel leader Li Zicheng led a revolt and overthrew the Ming Court in Beijing. Two days later, a Manchu emperor replaced him on the throne. The Manchus declared the new court the Qing dynasty. The dynasty lasted until 1911, when uprisings resulted in the establishment of a nationalist government.

Governance during the Qing dynasty was typified by the Chinese term *jingshi* (world ordering). *Jingshi* primarily centered on internal affairs within China. The political doctrines of the Qing drew from records found in the treaties of earlier dynasties and were heavily influenced by the teachings of Confucius, a philosopher during the 5th and 6th centuries B.C.E. Confucianism places a high degree of importance on the moral character of human relationships, including the vital function that the family plays as the basic unit of society. Confucianism also encourages people to respect and obey the emperor. The teachings of Confucianism provided the framework for the training of government officials.

The Qing Court delegated authority within the empire by appointing provincial governors and district magistrates. Provincial governors were responsible for establishing bureaucratic efficiency and ensuring that the government could monitor and control all aspects of local society. While an important function of the governors was to gain a strong rapport with the local population, they also repaired perceived deficiencies of local culture, particularly when economic productivity was a concern. The governors also monitored and scrutinized the district magistrates and other subordinates. The key preoccupation of the governors was how to achieve a more effective governance of the Chinese Empire's burgeoning population without increasing government budgets or personnel.

The formal title of the district magistrate was one who knows the people, and he was referred to as the local official. People also referred to the magistrate as their father and mother official and called themselves his children. These names stressed the intimate role that the magistrate played in the local community. The ideal magistrate was thought of as an extended member of the families in the community. When the community suffered, the magistrate also suffered as a member of the family.

The district magistrates had a wide range of duties that varied from locality to locality. The magistrates also compiled and submitted casebooks to the provincial governors. These casebooks described in detail such matters as tax collections, local customs, incidence of crime, and agricultural output. The magistrates were expected to maintain a high standard of conduct and provide an example of civilized behavior to people in the community.

The Qing maintained their stability of power within the empire by balancing the level of attention given to the Chinese, Manchus, Tibetans, and Mongols. While Manchus were given important positions in the bureaucracy, matching positions were created for Chinese officials.

However, the Manchus were assertive in establishing the legitimacy of their ruling position. Chinese men were forced to style their hair like the Manchus, and there was a strict censorship of literary works. Cruel punishments were inflicted on authors who wrote literary works with anti-Manchu sentiments.

During the rule of the Qing, there was a decline in the influence of the emperors. This was exemplified in the increasing influence in the period from 1856 to 1908 of Tz'u Hsi , the empress dowager, who was the Emperor Xiangfeng's favorite consort. She exerted a tremendous amount of power in China. In 1898, Tz'u Hsi ordered the house arrest of the emperor and was the de facto ruler of China until her death in 1908.

The Qing government's level and scope of power was dramatically affected by outside aggression. In 1840, the Chinese underwent a humiliating defeat in the Opium War with Britain. In the resulting treaty, China ceded Hong Kong to the British. The Anglo-French expedition of 1856 to 1860, sometimes called the Second Opium War, ended with the occupation of Beijing and the flight of the Qing Court to Jehol in the Manchurian homeland. The resulting Treaty of Tianjin opened up many port cities to foreign powers, including Shanghai, where the International Concession and the French Concession quickly outgrew the old city.

The Qing dynasty faced an immense amount of pressure from internal rebellions. These rebellions surfaced as a result of a growing population combined with a scarcity of usable agricultural land. Also, the increased presence of missionaries fueled hatred against foreigners, which led to further rebellion in the provinces. The most serious internal rebellion was the Taiping Rebellion. It was led by Hong Xiuquan, whose encounters with Western missionaries led him to believe he was the younger brother of Jesus Christ. The rebellion took tens of millions of lives before being suppressed in 1864. Suppressment of the internal rebellions placed an incredible strain on the imperial treasury, which contributed to the disintegration of the Qing dynasty.

Southern China was an important source of nationalism and political innovation in China, particularly in Guangdong. In the 1890s, a strong challenge to the Qing Court came from the visionary reformer Kang Youwei and his disciple, Liang Qichao, both from Guangdong. The result was the 100 Days Reforms of 1898. Reforms to the government bureaucracy and the examination system for local officials were propagated, and social reforms were instituted. The 100 Days ended with a palace coup, the house arrest of the emperor by the empress dowager, the execution of some reformist activists, and the flight of others, including Kang and Liang.

When the empress dowager died in 1908, the two-year-old Emperor Puyi ascended to the throne. The Qing government was now weak in power and lacked a clear sense of direction. Uprisings flared up around the country because many people were angry about the foreign built and financed railway system. Disaffected Chinese troops and revolutionaries in Wuhan province, who were led by Sun Yat-sen, took control of Wuhan and rode on the back of the large scale Railroad Protection uprisings to victory all over China. Two months later, representatives from 17 provinces throughout China gathered in Nanjing to establish the Provisional Republican Government of China. This nationalist government ended China's 4000-year period of dynastic cycles.

To read about government and politics in China under the Tang dynasty, see the China entries in chapter 6 ("Political Life") in volume 2 of this series.

~Dana Lightstone

FOR MORE INFORMATION

Central Intelligence Agency. *Central Government Organizations of the People's Republic of China*. Washington, D.C.: Central Intelligence Agency, Directorate of Intelligence, 1986.

Shaw, Y., ed. *Changes and Continuities in Chinese Communism*. Boulder: Westview Press, 1988.

POLITICAL LIFE
|
GOVERNMENT
& POLITICS
|
United States,
1850-1865

Victorian England

China

Latin America

LATIN AMERICA

At the beginning of the 19th century, Latin America was ruled by Spanish and Portuguese colonial officials. Then the Napoleonic Wars caused a political earthquake that toppled governments in the Old and New Worlds. A decade of struggle ensued during which Latin America gained its independence. Unfortunately, an era of violence and instability followed as the new nations sorted out who would control their governments. Only after mid-century did most nations institutionalize government, which included regular elections and a division of powers. This process closely paralleled the ones that attended economic development and urban growth. The road to a democratic, pluralistic society was underway after a very rough beginning.

Latin American leaders created their first governments as a reaction to the French invasion of Spain and Portugal. Unfortunately, leaders soon divided into various factions based on conflicting ideas of autonomy and class. In Mexico, for example, Father Miguel Hidalgo led a social revolution that threatened the lives and property of affluent citizens, temporarily alienating them from supporting independence. In Argentina, the residents of Buenos Aires successfully established their independence by fighting off two British invasions, but then they succumbed to divisive political battles. In the case of Brazil, the monarchy fled from Portugal to Rio de Janeiro and converted the latter into the capital of an empire. In 1822, the Portuguese king's son, Pedro, created a unique variant of decolonization when he declared Brazil's independence.

In most regional capitals of the Spanish Empire, prominent residents created provisional legislatures and wrote national constitutions. Meanwhile, colonial officials such as Peruvian viceroy José Fernando Abascal used guile and force to reassert their power. A lengthy, violent struggle ensued as patriotic military leaders tenaciously fought to oust colonial bureaucrats. As the opposing sides battled, great liberators like Simón Bolívar and José de San Martín preferred to rule autocratically rather than consult with local legislatures. They achieved independence, but did so at high a price. Not only were their nations devastated, they had established a tradition of authoritarian rule.

The liberators themselves proved unable to govern. Soon a new group of authoritarians called caudillos overthrew them. Belonging to the landed or commercial elite, these caudillos used alliances and intimidation to control their nations. In Mexico, for example, hacienda owner Antonio López de Santa Anna fought a variety of domestic and foreign enemies. In Argentina, estate owner Juan Manuel de Rosas resisted European intimidation while subduing local gaucho leaders. In Chile, merchant Diego Portales ousted liberals and imposed a conservative political regime to foster mining and trade. Only after mid-century did the landholding and commercial elite succeed in limiting the power of the caudillos through strengthened legislative, administrative, and judicial institutions.

Most Latin Americans were affected by the turmoil of national governments because it increased violence and retarded national development. Nevertheless, because early governments were so weak, their administrations rarely reached the rural areas where more than 90 percent of the people lived. For the majority, the hacienda owner or a native cacique, or chief, controlled their lives. These leaders defined community obligations and resolved most conflicts. Large peasant communities lived on the huge cattle haciendas extending from northern Mexico to the South American pampas. The owners ordered workers to herd, brand, or slaughter animals. The owners settled worker disputes without the intervention of local authorities. Similarly, slave communities inhabited the sugar, tobacco, and coffee plantations of Brazil and Spanish America. Plantation owners exercised almost total control over these people's lives. In the case of women, the landowner or his wife made periodic demands on peasant's wives and daughters, but domestic servants or slaves usually performed the daily chores.

Surprisingly enough, as late as mid-century, autonomous Native American communities survived in the vast regions of northern Mexico, the Amazon basin, and the Patagonia. In these areas, either the elders or the tribal chiefs settled disputes and allocated resources. Nevertheless, with the expansion of railroads and markets, these native areas became profitable for ranching and agriculture. To subdue the Indians and strip them of their land, national armies undertook periodic military campaigns. The new plantation and hacienda owners who acquired native lands then coerced the conquered people into such jobs as cane cutting, mule driving, and cattle herding.

By the end of the 19th century, the growth of production and trade transformed Latin American capitals. An influx of migrants and immigrants swelled such cities as Buenos Aires, Mexico City, and Santiago into cosmopolitan centers. A new political agenda emerged as a commercial class demanded uniform enforcement of property rights and contracts. This class also sought to secularize society by limiting the power of the church. Fed up with caudillos, the commercial middle class created legislatures that became forums for collective decisions and demanded a responsible, educated bureaucracy. The middle class also created local governments, enforcing law and order in an urban space carved out from the jurisdiction of the haciendas and plantations. For the first time, government had a major impact on people's daily lives. It provided security and education while beginning to regulate public services. In Brazil, the values of new economic groups were represented by the military. In 1889, the army decided to create a republican constitutional government by overthrowing the monarchy of Pedro II.

By 1900, urban growth strengthened the middle class, which now provided much of the technical expertise to run business and government. Nevertheless, the elite continued to dominate the selection of political leaders. To wrest power from them, in countries such as Chile and Argentina, the middle class created the Radical Party. In spite of numerous obstacles, in the 20th century, at the height of its power, this party controlled all branches of government. Another emerging challenge to elite-run government was the rise of organized labor. In urban and mining regions, workers demanded improved compensation and political rights. The elite tried to prevent these emerging groups from gaining power. As the middle class and labor sought political power, violent struggles occurred. Latin American became more urban, pluralistic, and democratic than the hacienda and plantation society of an earlier era. Nevertheless, unresolved social issues continued to challenge government and undermined its authority in the 20th century.

~*John L. Rector*

FOR MORE INFORMATION

Kapiszewski, D. *Encyclopedia of Latin American Politics*. Westport, Conn.: Greenwood Press, 2002.

Wiarda, H. J., and H. F. Kline, eds. *Latin American Politics and Development*. 5th ed. Boulder, Colo.: Westview Press, 2000.

ISLAMIC WORLD

Through the 19th century, the political life of the Muslim world was dominated by the empire of the Ottoman Turks, which became the longest ruling dynasty in Islamic history, lasting over 600 years. See the entry on the Ottoman Turks in the section "Government" in chapter 6 ("Political Life") in volume 3 of this series for a description of the empire's governmental structure. The Ottoman Empire toppled at the end of World War I. See the Islamic World entry in the section "Government" in chapter 6 ("Political Life") in volume 6 of this series for a discussion of the structures that succeeded the mighty Turkish Empire.

Law and Crime

POLITICAL LIFE

LAW & CRIME

United States,
1850-1865

United States,
Western Frontier

Victorian England

China

Latin America

Three themes stand out when considering law and crime in the 19th century. First, there is a tension between law and lawlessness. Frontiers and borderlands seemed to exist largely without regulation. As such they were often violent places. The American frontier provides numerous examples. For instance, miners and cowboys were rarely without their guns and knives. Drunken fights frequently turned lethal. Violent force was also sometimes necessary to defend claims on gold mines. Similarly in England, it was much safer to be in the cities than the countryside. In fact, urban crime rates dropped precipitously during the century because of the professionalization of police forces, a decrease in poverty, better city lighting, and the growth in public schools. (Young teenagers now had something to occupy their time.) Cities were still dangerous. For example, middle-class and upper-class families had to be careful. Criminals frequently abducted their children for ransom and to steal their clothing. Nevertheless, cities were safer than outlying areas. These trends did not always hold true, and in fact the opposite appeared to be true in China where cities were more unsafe than the countryside and where violence was more frequent in urban areas. In Latin America, violence and disorder could be found in both urban and rural areas during the early decades of the century when the region fought to free itself from Spain. Disorder gradually declined after mid-century as the new republican governments gained control of their territories and developed modern legal systems.

Second, punishments were violent and harsh. Here, China and Latin America were consistent with the United States and England. Justice was swift, brutal, and often deadly in China as it was on the American frontier. In the United States, the punishment for theft—not to mention murder—was often hanging. Those who were not sentenced to death still bore horrific sentences. For example, one man convicted of stealing gold on the frontier had his head shaved, received 100 lashes, and had his ears cut off. At the turn of the century, punishments in England were equally severe. There were over two hundred capital crimes for which the punishment was hanging. By the end of the century that number had been reduced to four crimes punishable by death: murder, piracy, treason, and arson. Very little distinction was made for the age of defendants. The execution of children for arson and other crimes was not uncommon. Many convicts who were not executed were transported to Australia to serve their sentences. By the time this practice came to an end over 140,000 people had been taken to Australia.

The last organizing theme about law and crime in the 19th century was race. In 19th-century America, particularly in the South, the legal system meted out harsher punishments for African Americans than for whites. Moreover, there was an entire system of laws, called Black Codes, which only applied to slaves. Blacks were violently beaten for petty crime and even for insolence against whites. White slaveholders had near unlimited legal power to beat, maim, and kill their slaves. Blacks had no legal recourse against this because they did not have legal standing in courts of law. They frequently were barred from testifying and could not subpoena whites. The legal system in the United States was racist and decidedly unfair. Similar inequalities existed for blacks and indigenous people in Latin America where slavery continued in some countries until the end of the century and rural peasants of Indian descent enjoyed only limited political and economic rights for much of that period.

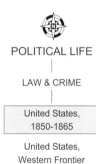

POLITICAL LIFE
|
LAW & CRIME
|
United States,
1850-1865

United States,
Western Frontier

Victorian England

China

Latin America

UNITED STATES, 1850–65

There were two major law and order issues during the Civil War era. The first dealt with the unfair and unjust legal system that pertained to African American slaves. Unlike white employees, slaves were not free to change their condition should it become too burdensome. They could be physically chastised by their masters for many forms of disobedience, for insolence involving a white person, and for petty crimes. Incredibly, masters did not have unlimited legal power over their slaves. A slave accused of a felony could not be purposely mutilated, maimed, or killed as a punishment without the intervention of a court. The jurisdiction of these courts varied from place to place, but generally their procedures were set down in the Black Codes.

Of course, a slave defendant was not entitled to a jury trial. However, a hearing officer was required to determine the merits of the case and to act as a finder of fact. The county would then mete out punishment to slaves found to be guilty of serious crimes. As the hearing officers came from the community of free white slaveholders, questions of guilt or innocence were often moot. Nonetheless, the slave was allowed to make a defense. In such a case, the defendant needed to rely upon his own testimony or the testimony of other slaves. Slaves could not subpoena whites to testify. Both the Black Codes and custom gave great leeway to the officers of the court in determining the nature of any punishment.

As slaves were valuable property, masters looked down on any form of physical punishment that permanently devalued their slaves. Some masters intervened in behalf of their slaves even when their guilt had been firmly established. Hamstringing, various forms of dismemberment, and death, while not complete figments of the abolitionists' imaginations, were uncommon punishments for mere disobedience or petty crime. If only for economic reasons, the master wanted to maintain a chastised but physically capable slave in his employ, not a handicapped cripple. Punishments most often took the form of an informal laying on of the ever-present lash, while a hitching up to the whipping post for a formal flogging was reserved for major offenses. Masters also had the option of selling the unrepentant slave to the far South, into the interior, or to the disease-infested sugar plantations in lieu of punishment. The slaves themselves attest to such goings-on, and in very few narratives are such events absent.

Slave owners rarely punished their bondsmen personally. This was left to the overseer. Much of the physical abuse distributed to slaves came from these often coarse and uncultivated men. Overseers came and went on individual plantations, and "some were too severe on the Negroes . . . brutified by their employment, [and] little better than the Negroes they managed." These white men were aided by slave drivers, who, although black slaves themselves, could apply the lash with pitiless regularity and were used to chase down fugitives. Some blacks, like the slave drivers, were characterized as white folks' servants, devoted to the master and his family and alienated from the general slave community. They were viewed by other slaves with disgust, as it was feared that they might curry favor with the master at the expense of other slaves by betraying them.

Ostensibly, flogging was the most widespread form of cruelty practiced by these persons; yet Americans believed even the most outrageous tales of immense abuse. Corporal punishment in many forms was highly evident throughout white society, even in the North. Schoolmasters caned their disobedient or lazy students; fathers accompanied their progeny on repeated trips to the woodshed with razor strop or belt in hand; prisoners were ruthlessly beaten with sticks and whips by their jailers; and soldiers and sailors were frequently punished by flogging, sometimes to the point of death. Notwithstanding these facts, slaves were certainly exposed to excessive and unwarranted cruelty through no fault of their own.

The second law and crime issue that arose during the Civil War was the major riots both in the North and the South. In the North, European immigrants showed a particularly strong prejudice against the African Americans. This was most obviously manifest during the 1863 New York City draft riots. Beyond a few recruiters and government officials who happened to be in the wrong place at the time, the targets of the mostly Irish rioters were generally blacks. *Harper's* reported that "no class of our foreign population is more jealous of its own liberties than the Irish, and there is also none which more strongly resents every liberty accorded to the Negro race." One black was "seized by the mob, and, after his life had been nearly beaten out, his body was suspended from a tree, a fire kindled under him, and, in the midst of excruciating torments, he expired." There may have been upwards of seventy black victims among the servants and workers of the hotels and restaurants in New York. An observer noted, "These things were done deliberately, and not in the heat of passion . . . and were moved by a political prejudice."

By comparison, Southerners were generally ambivalent in their attitudes toward Negroes, requiring considerable formality from them, but treating them with disdain or paying them no mind at all. In some circumstances slaves were able to earn a small amount of cash by doing extra work, turning their talents to a particularly artful or craftsmanlike project, or receiving the equivalent of tips. One slave, "a money making and saving boy," was said to have accumulated more than $500 in this manner, only to have it stolen by a foraging party of black federal soldiers. Very elderly slaves, unable to work in their old age, were often "pensioned off," being provided with a small sum of cash or being given a shack and a regular issue of food on the plantation. Some states had laws requiring slave owners to make such provisions so that elderly slaves, and those freed under manumission provisions, did not become a burden on society.

A severe food shortage seems to have developed in urban areas of the South in the latter part of March 1863. Initially a group of women in Salisbury, North Carolina, demanded that store owners charge them no more than the fixed price the government would ordinarily pay for foodstuffs and goods. Some of the merchants obliged the ladies by lowering their prices. There were several such episodes in the South at the same time. The most significant took place in the capital city of Richmond, where Mary Jackson promoted a concerted action by the women of that city to influence the price of goods and foodstuffs.

Beginning at the Belvidere Hill Baptist Church, the women, armed with persuaders such as pistols, knives, and hatchets, and led by Mary Jackson, marched on Capital Square in protest. Here the governor of Virginia, John Letcher, spoke to the crowd and expressed his sympathy, but he offered no concrete solution to their problem. As the crowd disgorged from the square, the gathering of women clearly became a mob and began to loot the stores and take the goods of the merchants. Seemingly no attempt was made to buy articles at

Union prisoners at Andersonville Prison, illustration by Thomas Nast, 1865. © Library of Congress.

any price, including prices fixed by the government. A number of merchants simply tried to close their doors, and at least one, a Mr. Knott, tried to appease the women by handing out packages of sewing needles—considered a luxury item at the time.

This episode was widely reported in the antigovernment papers and the Northern press as a bread riot. Although there is no indication that any bread was taken or asked for, some foodstuffs, including bread, meat, and rice, were distributed to the needy by the Young Men's Christian Association. "Boots are not bread, brooms are not bread, men's hats are not bread, and I have never heard of anybody's eating them," retorted a government clerk to the reports.

The riot was not a particularly large affair, and from its beginning at the Belvidere Church to its end in the downtown merchant quarter, it lasted little more than two hours. Nonetheless, President Davis had gone so far as to threaten to have the mob fired upon by the Public Guard, which had mobilized in the streets. The Richmond *Examiner* suggested that future rioters be shot on the spot. The city council initiated a formal investigation of the affair and found the riot to be totally unjustified. Several of the instigators of the protest were arrested. Of these, 12 women were convicted of misdemeanors, and four men and one woman, Mary Jackson, were convicted of felonies (Volo and Volo, 58–59, 70–73).

To read about law and crime in the United States in the 20th century, see the United States entries in the section "Law and Crime" in chapter 6 ("Political Life") in volume 6 of this series.

FOR MORE INFORMATION

Bernstein, I. *The New York City Draft Riots: Their Significance for American Society and Politics in the Age of the Civil War.* New York: Oxford University Press, 1990.

Blassingame, J. W. *The Slave Community: Plantation Life in the Antebellum South.* New York: Oxford University Press, 1972.

Volo, D. D., and J. M. Volo. *Daily Life in Civil War America.* Westport, Conn.: Greenwood Press, 1998.

UNITED STATES, WESTERN FRONTIER

The western frontier was a violent place. With the prevalence of knives and guns carried on miners' persons, it was not unlikely that a fight, often caused by drunkenness, escalated from fists to more lethal weapons. However, early on, there was little actual crime despite literal lawlessness. Perhaps because everyone harbored the hope of finding vast wealth, there appeared to be little need to steal. People safely left their tools on site, and there are numerous accounts of miners leaving sacks of gold dust unattended—and unmolested—in their tents as they were at work all day digging for more.

A pragmatic ad hoc democracy tailored rules to local conditions. Staking claims illustrates this process. Where gold deposits were especially rich, claims might be as small as 10 feet square. In other localities a miner might be required to stand in the

POLITICAL LIFE
|
LAW & CRIME
|
United States,
1850-1865

United States,
Western Frontier

Victorian England

China

Latin America

center of his dig and heave his pick as far as he could to establish the corner bound-aries of his claim. His name having been recorded, the miner would leave his pick and shovel to mark his claim; in one locale if he had not returned by the first of June, when water would have subsided enough to work the claim, any other man could take his place. Near the town of Eldorado, a company could claim as much of the stream as it could drain. Committees elected in each camp or mining district made up the rules, applying solid common sense. Many such rules established by local committees were so sound that they later were incorporated into the California mining codes and water laws.

However, with the influx of thousands of miners from all over the United States and the world came some with checkered pasts. Such fugitives from the law else-where were the subjects of a contemporary ballad:

What was your name in the States?
Was it Johnson or Thompson or Bates?
Did you murder your wife and flee for your life?
O, what was your name in the States?

Crime, when it did occur, was dealt with swiftly and decisively. W. B. Royall outlined legal principles succinctly: "The best of law prevails; the law of honor. A man may set his gold in the street, and no one dare touch it, for death is inevitably the reward of the rogue." There were no jails; moreover, while wanting to enforce justice or at least deter further crime, miners wanted to get back to their claims as soon as possible. J. Goldsborough Bruff remembers one man who stole two bags of gold dust and was sentenced to have his head shaved, his ears cropped, and then to be whipped with a gun-cleaning rod before being banished from town. In other locations lashes were laid on with riatas (or lariats); a quick exodus was encouraged by promising an additional 50 lashes on the bare back each day the miscreant stayed in town. Bayard Taylor justifies the punishment one man received for steal-ing 98 pounds of gold: he received 100 lashes, had his head shaved, and had both ears cut off.

It may conflict with popular ideas of morality but, nevertheless, this extreme course appeared to have produced good results. In fact, in a country without not only bolts and bars, but also any effective system of law and government, this Spartan severity of discipline seemed to be the only security against the most frightful disorder. The result was that, except for some petty acts of larceny, thefts were rare. . . . the risk was so great that such plunder could not be carried on to any extent.

When the crime was murder, capital punishment—by hanging or shooting—was employed. Usually people were executed after a trial by a jury hastily assembled from among the miners. In other instances criminals underwent Judge Lynch's Court—arrest, a voice vote from the citizenry, sometimes a mob, and almost immediate stringing up. One of the most extreme examples of lynch law occurred in Dry Dig-gings. There, five miners who spoke only Spanish or French were caught stealing and were immediately flogged. Two of them were accused of previous theft and murder and—without proof of guilt—were hung. For years afterwards, Dry Diggings was called Hangtown.

Especially as anti-foreign sentiments grew, non-Americans were the victims of harsh punishment that was intended, in part, as a deterrent to crime. Sometimes bandits took on the status of folk hero. Joaquin Murietta was one such character, though there is uncertainty as to whether he was actually only one man or a composite of many. At any rate, Frank Marryat described the grotesque end of "a famous Mexican robber, Joaquin Carillo." With much effort and loss of life, he had finally been caught in 1851 and decapitated:

When I left San Francisco his head was to be seen by the curious preserved in spirits of wine; and however revolting such a spectacle may be, it is a punishment that one would think would deter the reflective from crime. Fancy one's features distorted by the convulsive throes of violent death, staring whitened and ghastly from a glass bottle, turned from with horror by the gaping crowd, and then deposited, for all ages, growing more hideous with each year on the shelves of a surgical museum!

(Jones, 145–47).

To read about law and crime on the colonial frontier of North America, see the entries on the Colonial Frontier and New England in the section "Law, Crime, and Punishment" in chapter 6 ("Political Life") in volume 4 of this series.

FOR MORE INFORMATION

Jones, M. E. *Daily Life on the Nineteenth Century American Frontier*. Westport, Conn.: Greenwood Press, 1998.

Scamehorn, H. L., ed. *The Buckeye Rovers in the Gold Rush*. Athens: Ohio University Press, 1965.

Utley, R. *Billy the Kidd: A Short and Violent Life*. Lincoln: University of Nebraska Press, 1989.

VICTORIAN ENGLAND

In 1800, there were about two hundred types of capital crimes—crimes for which the punishment was execution by hanging. Many reforms in criminal law took place between 1808 and 1838. People convicted of offenses such as shoplifting, theft, housebreaking, forgery, and burglary were no longer sentenced to death. In 1841, 11 capital crimes remained on the statute book, but the only criminals actually executed were those convicted of murder. For other capital offenses, the judge would pronounce the death sentence and then recommend that it be commuted to transportation or imprisonment. By 1861, there were four capital crimes: murder, piracy, treason, and setting fire to an arsenal or dockyard. (Fire was equivalent to terrorism at a time when naval ships were constructed of wood and loaded with gunpowder.)

It is very difficult to measure changes in the crime rate, because standards of reporting differ so much. Historians do, however, generally agree that there was less crime in England during the Victorian era than in earlier times, and that the crime rate diminished even more as the period went on. In addition, crime became less

POLITICAL LIFE

LAW & CRIME

United States,
1850-1865

United States,
Western Frontier

Victorian England

China

Latin America

violent. About 90 percent of the cases serious enough to go to trial were crimes against property. Riots, brutal robberies, and murders became uncommon. In London in the 1890s, with a population of 5 million people, there were only about twenty homicides per year.

The falling rate of criminal behavior had many causes: less poverty, better lighting, educational and other measures that kept children and teens off the streets, professional police forces, the temperance movement, and restrictions on the sale of alcohol. These and other broad changes made society much more orderly. Early in the 19th century, the English lower classes were seen as naturally rowdy. Drunken riots at sporting events were common in the 1840s but newsworthy in the 1880s (because by then they were rare). The public was much less tolerant of fighting and cruelty. There was very little of the casual violence that now makes cities unsafe.

The common crimes included theft, stealing from shops or street sellers' stands, pickpocketing, and burglary. Property was at risk in the country as well as the city, especially as urban policing grew better. People of any substance did not generally leave their houses unattended. Even when the family went to church on Sunday, one or two servants remained at home. Certain elements of Victorian architecture, such as heavy wooden shutters, iron gratings, and high walls topped with broken glass, are a reminder that there never was a golden age of honesty when everyone could be trusted.

Because there was a market for used clothing, one crime that parents feared was the abduction of a well-dressed child. The motive was not to collect ransom (which is terribly risky for the kidnapper); the child would soon be turned loose in its underwear and brought home crying by the police. This was one reason why middle-class and upper-class youngsters were accompanied by a nursemaid even when walking across a square to play with friends, and why women and teenaged girls brought a servant along when they went to do errands. Etiquette manuals advised ladies that when they were paying calls on foot, their clothing must "not be gay or have anything about it to attract attention." Silks, plumes, jewelry, and lace could be worn only when going out in a carriage.

In the countryside, poaching was a widespread crime. Game birds and wild animals, according to the law, could be killed only by landowners. However, hungry rural laborers found it hard to resist trapping rabbits and edible birds. Aristocrats and the gentry employed gamekeepers, whose job was to make sure there was good shooting on the estate during autumn; they looked after the game, protected breeding grounds—and hunted down poachers. Although the brutal mantraps (concealed pits, sometimes with spikes set in the bottom) that had been used earlier were outlawed by Victorian times, the gamekeeper carried a shotgun. Furthermore, the magistrate who tried and sentenced accused poachers was usually the local squire—that is, a major landowner.

Children over age seven were considered to be morally responsible beings. They were sentenced to the same prisons as adults and were executed for capital crimes. As late as 1839, a boy nine years of age was hanged for setting a building on fire. People worried a lot about juvenile crime, because the dislocations of industrialization created a relatively large population of orphaned, homeless, and runaway youngsters. After the middle of the century, reformatory and industrial schools began to provide education and vocational training for young offenders, and magistrates were given more leeway in choosing an appropriate sentence for children under age 14. In the latter part of the century, juvenile crime as well as adult crime diminished.

The system known as common law arises from precedents and decisions made by earlier judges. English law is complex because of its very long history. By 1837, however, many of the important principles had been codified in laws passed by Parliament. Common law covers all criminal cases and most civil disputes. In London, three courts were involved: the Queen's Bench heard criminal cases; Common Pleas decided civil cases over matters such as contracts, ownership of land, and injuries; and Exchequer settled cases involving money owed to the national treasury. (Chancery, which will be discussed below in the section entitled "The Law and Private Life," took up additional civil matters.) Judges from the London courts also went on circuit to visit county towns to preside over assizes (i.e., court sessions in provincial towns), where they tried the cases that had come up since their last visit.

Although boys and men were incarcerated in the same prisons, they exercised separately, as shown in this 1861 illustration from Henry Mayhew's *London Labour and the London Poor.* Courtesy of Paley Library, Temple University.

There were two categories of crime: indictable (which in the United States would be felonies) and summary (misdemeanors). The serious crimes, which led to indictment and trial by jury, included murder, armed robbery, burglary, larceny, fraud, rape, and significant violations of public order. Summary offenses included petty theft, poaching, vagrancy, drunkenness, vandalism, and taking part in minor disorders. Prostitution was not against the law, but prostitutes were often charged with misdemeanors such as annoying passersby or public drunkenness.

Summary (minor) offenses were tried by the local justice of the peace or, in cities, by a police magistrate. He heard the charges, questioned the prisoner and witnesses, made a decision, and passed sentence. There was no jury, and ordinarily no lawyers were involved. The justice, who seldom had any legal training, was the local squire or clergyman or some other man of substance—a man who had enough standing in the community so that people respected him and enough money that he was not likely to take bribes. The justice could sentence guilty prisoners to a few weeks or months in the local house of corrections, impose fines, or require public work such as road mending. Whipping was a common sentence for boys found guilty of vandalism or petty theft and for men who assaulted women or children. By Victorian times, female prisoners could no longer be whipped, but they were otherwise treated in much the same way as males.

When the crimes were serious, the justice would have the accused bound over to be tried at the quarter sessions, held four times a year, when all the justices in a county met together to decide cases. The most severe cases went to the assizes, which took place once or twice a year in various larger towns. Judges came from London and cases were tried in front of a jury.

Trials were perhaps less fair than they later became in the 20th century. People accused of crimes could not take the stand in their own defense until 1898. There was no public defender to give free advice to prisoners who could not afford an attorney; indeed, sometimes the accused was not allowed to have defense counsel at all. On the other hand, judges intervened to ask questions, and juries tended to be lenient. When stealing a horse was a capital crime, for example, a jury might decide to find the accused guilty of stealing only a bridle. (The horse just followed along because the bridle was fastened around its head.)

The use of long-term imprisonment to punish criminals began during the Victorian period. People convicted of minor crimes had generally been sentenced to 30 days or three months in the local house of correction (often called the bridewell). The gaol (pronounced jail) held people awaiting trial. The most famous was Newgate, the gaol for prisoners who would be tried at London's central criminal court (known as Old Bailey). In Newgate, as in most local gaols and bridewells, prisoners did not have separate cells but were crowded together in large rooms where they slept on the floor. There was no segregation of children from adults (although the sexes were kept separate). Newgate did, however, have secure cells for prisoners who had already been tried and were sentenced to death.

Executions took place two or three days after the sentence was handed down. Until 1868, the prisoner was hanged in public. When a crime was particularly notorious (e.g., a woman found guilty of killing her lover, or a multiple murderer), the crowds were enormous. People took their children to see the criminal executed and learn a moral lesson; souvenirs were peddled; and pickpockets made themselves very busy, undeterred by the example that public hangings were supposed to provide. After 1868, executions took place behind prison walls. A black flag was raised to let the waiting crowd know when the criminal was dead.

Criminal transportation was an alternative to hanging; the death penalty was often commuted to a sentence of transportation for 7 years or 14 years. Penal settlements in Australia were established in 1788, when prisoners could no longer be sent to the American colonies. At first the prisoners built roads, cleared land, and made harbors. Women convicts cooked, cleaned, and did laundry for the other prisoners and for guards and government officials. Educated convicts did clerical work and other minor administrative tasks. After Australia began to attract emigrants (and was no longer simply a penal colony), prisoners were assigned to do contract labor for free settlers.

Children as well as adults were sentenced to transportation. In the 1840s there was a separate penal settlement for boys at Point Puer. (*Puer* is Latin for boy.) Young convicts were generally given some schooling and taught a trade. Before transportation came to an end, about 140,000 convicts had been sent to Australia. They could return to England after their sentence expired, but passage back was not provided; they had to pay for it by having money sent to them or earning it as free laborers. Most of them chose to stay in Australia, where work was plentiful and wages were high. The sentence of transportation was abolished in 1857, although some criminals with long sentences continued to be sent to Australia instead of being housed in English prisons. The last convict ship sailed in 1867.

In the 1850s, when sentences of penal servitude replaced transportation for serious crimes, true prisons began to be constructed: massive, secure buildings where convicted criminals could be confined in cells. These were not, in England, called penitentiaries—the Victorian penitentiary was a charity, usually run by women, designed for penitence and reform. Prostitutes, unmarried pregnant women, runaways who had been sleeping on the streets, and other girls or women would enter a penitentiary voluntarily (although often, no doubt, under pressure from a justice of the peace). After spending a year or two in healthy living, prayer, and vocational training, the penitent would be helped to emigrate or to find a suitable job in England.

Some of the improvements in public safety during the 19th century were brought about by the development of efficient police forces. In preindustrial times, all citizens were supposed to take turns of duty as constables: preventing crime, maintaining order, and presenting criminals in court. The system worked only in small communities where everyone knew everyone else. By the 18th century, most towns of any size had paid constables, but there were no laws governing them. The system was inefficient and often corrupt. When there were riots or other serious dangers, the army was brought in to keep order.

The Metropolitan Police Act of 1829 created a full-time paid police force in London. The city was divided into 17 districts. Each district, headed by a superintendent, had four inspectors and 16 sergeants. Under each sergeant were nine constables: eight patrolled beats and the ninth was on reserve in the station house. The police district that was located in Great Scotland Yard also had the commissioner's staff, clerks, and additional reserves. The first mission of the police was to establish social control. Their job was to prevent riots, break up fights, curb public drunkenness, restrict begging, and stop street crime.

When Victoria's reign began, London's police had already demonstrated their effectiveness. Legislation encouraged other towns to establish professional forces. By mid-century there were competent police in cities such as Birmingham and Manchester, but many other areas still had no regular force. In 1856, national standards for organization and training were established.

To become a London Metropolitan Police constable in the 1850s, a man had to be 5 feet 8 inches tall. Because most people were shorter than nowadays (owing to poor nutrition), constables had a meaningful physical presence. Most of them were former soldiers or sailors. They had two weeks of training. Unmarried police constables lived and ate in barracks. They were not well paid, but they could legally earn extra money when hired to watch the crowd at theaters or knock on doors in the morning to wake people who had no clocks. Police in the countryside often spent most of their working life as the sole constable in a village. The county superintendent retained the right to give permission for marriage, because the constable's wife became his backup and assistant. The telegraph was used in both the country and

This drawing from *Police!*, a book by Charles Tempest Clarkson and J. Hall Richadson (1889), illustrates a London constable's garb and tools, including the "bull's eye" lantern at his hip.

337

city for communications between headquarters, police stations, and (eventually) outdoor call boxes, which constables could open with a key.

The Metropolitan Police Detective Department was established in August 1842 with two inspectors and four sergeants. Its headquarters was in Scotland Yard—a name that has remained although the actual location has been moved several times. (In 1878 it was reorganized as the Criminal Investigation Department, or CID, which remains the official title.) From the beginning, detectives not only investigated crimes but also had anticrime duties such as working in disguise to spot pickpockets in a crowd. By the end of the century the CID had 800 members. Their education, training, prestige, and pay were higher than that of other police. Howard Vincent, a barrister who reformed the CID and was its director from 1878 to 1884, developed a uniform criminal record system, produced a manual of criminal law for the police to use, and established the Special Branch (originally the Special Irish Branch), which has the duty of protecting royalty and keeping track of political extremists (Mitchell, 95–101).

To read about law and crime in Chaucer's England, see the entry on Europe in the section "Law" in chapter 6 ("Political Life") in volume 2 of this series; for Elizabethan England, see the entry on England in the section "Justice and Legal Systems" in chapter 6 ("Political Life") in volume 3 of this series; for 18th-century England, see the entry on England in the section "Law, Crime, and Punishment" in chapter 6 ("Political Life") in volume 4 of this series.

FOR MORE INFORMATION

Altick, R. D. *Victorian People and Ideas*. New York: W. W. Norton, 1973.

Howe, R. *The Story of Scotland Yard: A History of the C.I.D. from the Earliest Times to the Present Day*. London: Arthur Barker, 1965.

Mitchell, S. *Daily Life in Victorian England*. Westport, Conn.: Greenwood Press, 1996.

POLITICAL LIFE
|
LAW & CRIME
|
United States,
1850-1865

United States,
Western Frontier

Victorian England

China

Latin America

CHINA

In the 19th century, crime in China was relatively low. The most common crime was theft and this occurred mostly in the large cities. In most cases theft was committed for one to eat or feed one's family. Murders did occur but were relatively few. As far as records show, crime in 19th century China was about two percent of crime in the United States today.

The court system in China began in the 16th century. It was designed as a way of dividing the authoritative positions so as to give those most competent the most important roles in keeping order among the public. A high district official was given power to make decisions, much like a judge, regarding the verdict and the punishment of the convict. This power was only given to the most competent of officials. Such an official was treated with a degree of respect almost equal to that of royalty. Although the Chinese court system developed completely separately from that of

Western nations, there were many aspects in common, particularly the role of the judge and the questioning of suspects and witnesses.

During the 18th and 19th centuries, due to the influence of foreign traders and missionaries, courts in China began to represent those of Western nations more than before. However, certain judicial elements from the period prior to foreign influence still held strong. These included the use of torture to get confessions or information in general and harsh punishments, including lashings. This brought about not only criticism from foreigners, but also from Chinese people involved in radical movements to change some of what they viewed as archaic remnants of China's past. The judicial system became one of many ways that China's society was divided in opinion.

When looking for a confession, the most common form of torture used by the Chinese courts was a beating with a bamboo stick. There were also incidents of innocent witnesses, or even people with no information on the crime, being tortured in search of a confession. In some cases the victim was forced to confess something other than the truth, simply because it was what the court workers wanted to hear, and thus the torture would stop. This demonstrates a high degree of corruption in the courts. Clearly if the judge wanted a particular person convicted, drawing this conclusion, whether or not it was the truth, was not difficult.

Beatings with a bamboo stick cause quite a bit of pain, often enough to make the victim unconscious, but if done properly do not cause any permanent health problems. This method was most often used in criminal cases, but there is evidence that some courts also used this technique in civil cases. There are also records that show that drops of water repeatedly applied to the forehead over a long period of time, more commonly known as Chinese water torture, were also used to get a witness or a criminal to confess.

Once someone was found guilty of a crime, punishments tended to be harsh. Beatings with a bamboo stick or water torture were used as punishment for small crimes. Imprisonment and monetary fines were also common for smaller crimes, such as theft and minor vandalism. Conditions in some prisons were so poor that it was not uncommon for prisoners to die from starvation or diseases connected to the poor hygiene standards of the prisons. When, in 1858, a group of British merchants working in Canton visited a local prison, one man described the cells as "rat infested, dirty, and perhaps the worst living conditions on earth."

Adultery was rarely considered a crime, and thus rarely punishable. However, there were some cases in which the death penalty or other harsh punishments were given for cases of adultery. In all of these cases the person said to be guilty was the wife of a high government official. Murder was usually punishable by death.

The most common method of the death penalty was during a ceremony where the community would come to watch skilled martial artists perform a complex dance that incorporated the chopping off of the guilty person's head. Several times they might approach the victim as if to end his or her life, yet when the blade was as little as one centimeter from the neck of the guilty, they would then back away. The artist then continued with the choreographed performance. One can only imagine the level of fear and agony experienced by the victim. Eventually, the death strike was for real. As blood streaked off of their swords, the dance continued. For the audience this was considered a form of entertainment.

In terms of traditional versus modern beliefs regarding the judicial system, European, American, and Japanese traders, missionaries, and officials began criticizing the Chinese judicial system for elements considered to be brutal. As in many societies, foreign views led many of the natives to reconsider aspects of their own society that they previously took for granted. Others, in rejection of foreign influence, opposed these new views and clung more tightly than ever to the old ways.

Social movements rejecting the old Chinese system of government, education, and other aspects of society, including the judicial system, sprung up throughout China. Many of these movements were connected to universities. The large number of young and impressionable young minds made way for new ideas to grow in this environment. Over the course of the second half of the 19th century, in response to these movements, there does seem to have been a decrease in beatings and public death ceremonies, particularly in the large cities, where foreign influence was particularly influential. However, corruption in the courts does not seem to have decreased, jail conditions did not improve, and crime rates grew as China entered the 20th century.

To read about law and crime in China under the Tang dynasty, see the China entry in the section "Law" in chapter 6 ("Political Life") in volume 2 of this series.

~*Dana Lightstone*

FOR MORE INFORMATION

Ahern, E. M. *Chinese Ritual and Politics*. Cambridge: Cambridge University Press, 1981.
Allee, M. A. *Law and Local Society in Late Imperial China*. Stanford: Stanford University Press, 1994.

POLITICAL LIFE
|
LAW & CRIME
|
United States,
1850-1865

United States,
Western Frontier

Victorian England

China

Latin America

LATIN AMERICA

The development of national legal systems in the newly independent republics of Latin America was heavily influenced by the general lawlessness and political oppression that flowed from the wars of independence. Consisting mainly of the decrees and pronouncements on colonial affairs issued by the Crown over the centuries, Spanish colonial law was based on Roman civil law and on Christian traditions of justice and morality. Colonial law tended to focus on the protection of property, a principle that remained important to the political and social elites who governed Latin America for most of the 19th century and to the growing middle class that developed in the urban centers of the region in the last decades of the century. However, until national governments could gain control of their newly won territories, ongoing warfare and the collapse of colonial authority led to a rise in assaults, thefts, murders, and political violence in much of the region and forced emerging national legal systems to place a new emphasis on the protection of individual rights.

Before 1850, criminal activity in many areas of Latin America was widespread and serious. In the 1830s, thieves and bandits were so common in many parts of Mexico that European visitors were obliged to arm themselves if they wished to travel about the country. Government authority was so weak that criminals robbed and murdered with impunity, terrifying the unprotected populace. Even as late as 1872, when Mexico was emerging from a period of civil war and foreign occupation, Tiburcio Montiel, the governor of one federal district, reported that criminal activity in his jurisdiction was truly alarming. Montiel informed the government that he had 20,813 persons under arrest, 13,034 men and 7,779 women. This unusually high number of arrests was a consequence both of the social and political disorder of recent decades and of the inability of the national government to maintain a stable and functioning court system.

During the 1850s and 1860s, Mexico was plagued by a host of colorful criminal characters. Jesús Arriaga, known popularly as Chucho el Roto (Chucho the Broken One), operated in the area around Mexico City. This famous delinquent was the Mexican Robin Hood, combining his robberies with acts of violence ostensibly directed at those who oppressed the poor. Another famous delinquent was Agustín Lorenzo, known for the rapidity of his crimes and the way he would vanish after he had committed them. Other famous Mexican bandits of the mid-19th century included Ojos de Vidrio, who operated in Nuevo León, and a gang known as the Sinaloenses, because they were mainly active in Sinaloa. Members of this bandit group included Heraclio Bernal, Juan Soldado, and Malverde, whose exploits have made him a sort of patron saint of modern Mexican delinquents.

Nineteenth-century Argentina also had its share of famous bandits with flamboyant nicknames, including El Petizo Orejudo (Big-eared Shorty), La Hormiga Negra (Black Ant), El Pibe Cabeza (Kid Cabeza), Mate Cocido (Weak Tea), and El Loco Prieto (Crazy Blackie). Although many of these figures achieved popular acclaim for their adventures, they were hardened criminals who committed many violent acts against the local population. Argentina also suffered from the criminalization of the gauchos, the cowboys of the pampas, large numbers of whom were driven by economic hardship in the countryside to the cities, where they fell into a life of crime. In such Argentine cities as Tapalqué, Azul, Tandil, Junín, Pergamino, Río Cuarto, Villa Mercedes, and San Rafael, poverty and rapid social change alienated many and caused crime to skyrocket in the mid-19th century. Robbery, homicide, domestic violence, street fights, and conflicts over land were the must common criminal events.

Social conflict in Colombia was caused by unresolved agrarian problems. High land prices, the displacement of small farmers, and the political and economic power of large landholders caused much unrest and violence in the countryside. Another significant cause of Colombian crime was the rise in partisan political violence and electoral fraud, as the Liberal and Conservative Parties fought each other for control of the national government. Such political conflict continued for most of the century. In 1839, conservatives committed acts of violence against the liberal government then in power, while liberals launched attacks against the conservative governments of Rafael Núñez in the 1880s and Miguel Antonio Caro in the 1890s.

Fought mainly in Panama, which was then a province of Colombia, the Thousand Days War, a civil war fought between 1899 and 1902, led to further political instability and to the loss of Panama, which became an independent state under the auspices of the United States, which was itself interested in constructing a canal across the narrow isthmus.

Brazil was a Portuguese colony until 1822, when Pedro, the son of the king of Portugal, proclaimed himself emperor of Brazil, which he and his son ruled until the establishment of a republic in 1889. Crime in 19th-century Brazil was characterized by bitter disputes over the control of land, ownership of which was concentrated in relatively few hands, and the continued existence of slavery, which by its very nature bred violence and injustice. Over its colonial history, Brazil imported huge numbers of slave laborers from Africa to work the country's plantations and mines. Although Emperor Pedro II freed his personal slaves in 1840, and some northern districts ended slavery in the early 1880s, the institution was not finally abolished throughout Brazil until 1888. Because the act freeing Brazilian slaves did not compensate slave owners for the loss of their property, the institution's abrupt abolition caused further unrest and disorder. By the turn of the century, the new Brazilian republic, like most other states of Latin America, was just beginning to achieve the political and economic stability required to combat crime and create a strong and effective legal system.

~Angela María González Echeverry

FOR MORE INFORMATION

Aguirre, C. A., R. Buffington, and C. M. MacLachlan, eds. *Reconstructing Criminality in Latin America*. Wilmington, Del.: Scholarly Resources, 2000.

Aguirre, C. A., and R. D. Salvatore, eds. *The Birth of the Penitentiary in Latin America: Essays on Criminology, Prison Reform, and Social Control, 1830–1940*. Austin: University of Texas Press, 1996.

Rico, J. M. *Crimen y justicia en América Latina*. México: Siglo Veintiuno Editores, 1977.

Salvatore, R. D., A. Carlos, and G. M. Joseph, eds. *Crime and Punishment in Latin America: Law and Society since Late Colonial Times*. Durham, N.C.: Duke University Press, 2001.

POLITICAL LIFE
|
EMPIRE
|
United States,
1850-1865

United States,
Western Frontier

Victorian England

Islamic World

Empire

Why do nations conquer and build empires? "God, Gold, and Glory" is the stock answer. Countries take over other countries to please their gods, to expand their economies, and to gain international fame. Indeed, when looking at the 19th century, one can see these motives at work. Consider the largest empire of the time, the British Empire. By the end of the century, Queen Victoria not only ruled the United Kingdom but also over 75 different territories. True, there was a difference between England's colonial rule in Egypt and India and its influence in St. Kitts and Grenada. However, no other nation had such an empire. It was designed to gather the world's gold, that is those resources that could be turned into profits. England's empire also spread religion and culture. This is especially true if one looks at the Muslim world in the 19th century.

England was not the only colonial power in the Middle East. The Ottoman Empire had conquered and controlled much of the region since the 12th century. Yet, beginning in 1498, Europeans began to extend their economic and political reach into the area, and then in 1750 Britain overtook the French and Dutch as the main colonizing power. The British were able to reap significant economic gain from their colonies. They also imparted Western technology as well as Christianity. As is illustrated especially with this encyclopedia's India entries, the British influences created tensions between the rulers and the ruled.

The United States also had imperial designs, but most of them were concentrated in the West. Initially, and unlike its European peers, the Americans were able to expand without firing a shot. In 1801, President Thomas Jefferson bought a gigantic tract of land from France that stretched from the Mississippi River to the Rocky Mountains. The price was extremely low—$15 million for 828,000 acres. That was approximately four cents an acre! Eventually President Jefferson and later subsequent presidents would send in the military to secure and expand their new empire. The economic opportunities in the West were nearly omnipresent. Miners, merchants, cowboys, farmers, and soldiers all found steady and profitable work.

While the search for gold—both literally and figuratively—was the main motive for American expansion, there was another reason. During the years before the Civil War, many Americans came to see colonization as a way to deal with slavery. The African city of Monrovia was founded as a freedman's colony, a place where African slaves could be repatriated. Behind this colonization plan was the American Colonization Society led by Henry Clay, Andrew Jackson, and Francis Scott Key. The movement was not very popular among white or black Americans, and abolitionists were strongly opposed. William L. Garrison, the unofficial leader of the abolitionists, believed colonizers to be supporters of slavery in disguise. Eventually the movement disappeared because it was unworkable. Even moving half of the American slave population meant that 2.5 million people would have to be transported to Africa. Clearly, this was an imperial failure when compared to the conquest of the West.

UNITED STATES, 1850–65

Many proponents of emancipation looked to gradualism and colonization, rather than immediate emancipation and inclusion, to relieve the supposed incongruities of the races living peacefully together. Gradual emancipation provided that children born as slaves could be freed on attaining maturity, having been given a skill or education in the interim so that they might provide for themselves. Similarly formed legislation had quietly obliterated slavery throughout the New England states by mid-century. Private parties among antislavery proponents favored the removal of free blacks to colonies established far from the Americas. The African city of Monrovia was founded as a freemen's colony in 1821 in this manner. Less dramatic

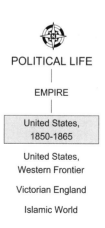

POLITICAL LIFE
|
EMPIRE
|
United States,
1850-1865

United States,
Western Frontier

Victorian England

Islamic World

suggestions were also made to remove freed blacks to the Indian Territories, Florida, the Caribbean Islands, and Central America.

While many Northerners were against slavery, they were also remarkably prejudiced against blacks. They were averse to having them live in their communities and inclined to leave the issue of universal emancipation alone. Radical abolitionists—always a minority among antislavery advocates—were loath to accept the slow pace of gradual emancipation and were becoming increasingly militant in their frustration. This militancy was not universally shared even among antislavery proponents. Abolitionist speakers were threatened with tar and feathers in New England towns as late as 1850, and an antislavery speaker, Elijah P. Lovejoy, was murdered by a mob in the free state of Illinois in 1837. It was widely held that free blacks would come North to compete for scarce jobs in the cities, and an economic downturn in 1857 did not help to relieve this fear.

There was a growing recognition that slavery was a great moral and social evil.

The treatment of blacks in Northern states was often brutish, and they were despised and treated with contempt. In the decades after independence, towns and cities had been flooded by thousands of freed blacks, some of whom had fought in the Revolutionary army; and any plan for a general abolition of slavery had to deal with the touchy problem of free blacks living in a white-dominated, racist society. This led many sympathetic whites to fear for the ultimate welfare and safety of a black population suddenly foisted on an unfriendly America should the radicals attain their goal of universal emancipation.

Even among those who volunteered to fight for the preservation of the Union, there was little sympathy for the abolitionists. Wrote one Federal soldier at the beginning of the war, "I don't blame the South an atom. They have been driven to desperation by such lunatics as [William L.] Garrison and [Wendell] Phillips, and these men ought to be hung for it." Another Federal recruit said, "I want to see those hot-headed abolitionists put in the front rank and shot first."

There was a growing recognition, however, that slavery was a great moral and social evil that must be ended soon. But it was also true that slavery had become uneconomical for the smaller planters. As early as 1816, several Southern states, Virginia, Georgia, Maryland, and Tennessee included, had asked that a site for colonization by freed blacks be procured, and they had jointly petitioned the federal government for financial aid to offset the monetary loss involved in emancipating their slaves. The British government had successfully indemnified its slave owners for their loss when the slave trade was ended in 1808, but a similar arrangement was not possible in antebellum America, either financially or politically.

In 1817 the American Colonization Society was formed to encourage free blacks to return to Africa. The organizational meeting was held in no less a prestigious place than the chambers of the House of Representatives. Among its founders were Henry Clay, Andrew Jackson, and Francis Scott Key. The society drew its initial support from all sections of the country and from both slavery and antislavery advocates. Colonization societies outnumbered abolition societies in America right up to the opening of the war. Within two decades of its founding, more than 140 branches of the American Colonization Society were formed in the Southern states, with the majority of chapters in Virginia, Kentucky, and Tennessee. In the North approximately one hundred societies were formed—radical abolition seemingly stealing some of the colonialists' thunder—the majority established in the states of Ohio, New York, and Pennsylvania. Only in Massachusetts did immediate abolition have a greater following than colonization. Of all the states, only Rhode Island and South Carolina had no colonization societies—both had been major import markets in the days of the Atlantic slave trade. Unquestionably, the intervention of Northern moralists into the evolution of antislavery at this point provided a fateful check to any hope of abolition without considerable turmoil.

A minority of free blacks espoused great interest in their African homeland, yet a larger number were interested not in Africa, but in other areas outside the United States. Canada, Central America, and Haiti were all mentioned as possible sites for black emigration. Several prominent free blacks, such as poet James M. Whitfield, the Rev. Henry H. Garnet, and Dr. Martin R. Delancy, called for an emphasis on black nationalism and militant black unity. It was feared that in the United States blacks could always expect to be crawling in the dust at the feet of their former oppressors.

Colonization was very popular politically. At the time, it was estimated by the proponents of colonization that slavery could be abolished by 1890. During the debates with Stephen Douglas in 1858, Lincoln had expressed both support for colonization and a belief in an inherent inequality among the races. He disclaimed any hopes for "social and political equality of the White and Black races," and disavowed any plan to make "voters or jurors of Negroes, nor of qualifying them to hold office, nor to intermarry with white people." Most important, he pledged his support for colonization of freed slaves, saying, "There is a physical difference between the White and Black races which I believe will forever forbid the two races living together on terms of social and political equality." True to his word, in 1862, one year before the Emancipation Proclamation, the president signed a congressional appropriation of $100,000 for the purpose of encouraging black colonization.

But the abolitionists demanded immediate, unreimbursed emancipation and integration of freed blacks into white society, not gradualism and separation. No price, including war and disunion, was too great to pay in the cause of ending slavery and racial prejudice. The rhetoric of Wendell Phillips, a leading abolitionist in Massachusetts, provided an example to the South, and all of America, of just how far the radicals were willing to go when he suggested "trampling the laws and Constitution of the country" to gain their ends. Such rhetoric was seen as a call for civil disorder, even violence, on a massive level.

The radical abolitionists berated the gradualists and colonialists as being less than completely dedicated to the cause of emancipation. In *Thoughts on African Colonization* (1832), William Lloyd Garrison went so far as to suggest that the gradualists and colonialists were actually covert supporters of slavery, allowing Northern slave owners to "sell their slaves south," thereby recouping their considerable investment in slave property. Garrison argued that colonization would make Americans "abominably hypocritical" by allowing free blacks to remain among them only "as inferior beings, deprived of all the valuable privileges of freemen, separated by the brand of indelible ignominy, and debased to a level with the beasts."

Garrison may have been the most vehement of the radical abolitionists. Although he did not, in any real sense, lead the American antislavery movement, he was possibly the most conspicuous of the radicals. In 1845 he wrote in the highly idealized style typical of the movement: "Be faithful, be vigilant, be untiring in your efforts to break every yoke, and let the oppressed go free. Come what may—*cost what it may*—inscribe on the banner which you unfurl to the breeze, as your religious and political motto—'No Compromise with Slavery! No Union with Slaveholders!'"

Although calls to violence were not characteristic of the abolition movement, the rhetoric of the outspoken radicals was couched in inflammatory and unambiguous terms aimed at ending slavery—"Law or No law, constitution or no constitution." Abolitionists vowed to work with "invincible determination" regardless of the consequences. The radicals publicly disavowed the unsettling concept of slaves shedding the blood of their oppressors, but they recognized that there was "no neutral ground in this matter, and the time is near when they will be compelled to take sides."

In the call for a slave rebellion, the goal of which was "to attack the slave power in its most vulnerable point," the South perceived a very real physical threat. There had been three important black insurrections in the South: the Gabriel revolt in 1800, the Denmark Vesey revolt in 1822, and the Nat Turner revolt in 1831. Only the Turner revolt had led to any deaths among whites, but these had numbered mostly women and children among the sixty or so killed. Coupled with the knowledge of major slave revolts and mass murders in the West Indies, such doings were taken seriously by slave owners. Abolitionists endorsed John Brown's attempt to foment an armed slave rebellion in Virginia by attacking Harper's Ferry in 1858. Against this background the writings and speeches of the radicals proved truly heavy rhetoric.

Young Kate Stone's diary reflected her fears in an encounter with slaves recently freed by Federal forces in April 1863: "Looking out the window, we saw three fiendish looking, black Negroes standing around George Richards, two with their guns leveled and almost touching his breast. He was deathly pale but did not move. We thought he would be killed instantly. But after a few words from George . . . they lowered their guns and rushed into the house . . . to rob and terrorize us" (Volo and Volo, 81–85).

FOR MORE INFORMATION

McPherson, J. M. *Battle Cry of Freedom: The Civil War Era*. New York: Oxford University Press, 1990.

Paludan, P. S. *A People's Contest: The Union and Civil War, 1861–1865*. New York: Harper & Row, 1988.

Thomas, E. M. *The Confederate Nation: 1861–1865*. New York: Harper & Row, 1979.

Volo, D. D., and J. M. Volo. *Daily Life in Civil War America.* Westport, Conn.: Greenwood Press, 1998.

UNITED STATES, WESTERN FRONTIER

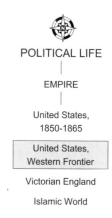

Expansion of the original British colonial settlements on the eastern seaboard began in the middle of the 18th century. The Atlantic seaboard had been inhabited by various frontier types: the fur trader, the fisherman, the hunter, the cattle raiser, the miner, and the pioneer farmer. Each of them utilized—often exploited—the land; all of them, as well as educators, the military, and the clergy, coexisted (sometimes harmoniously, sometimes not) with their predecessors on the land, the Native Americans. With Daniel Boone's opening of the first good wagon route through the Appalachians in 1769, settlers began pouring into the Ohio Valley, ignoring government regulations and dispossessing the Indians who moved like an unwilling vanguard ahead of them. By the end of the 18th century, the flood had reached the Mississippi, the next major geographical barrier after the Appalachians. The United States was no longer a narrow strip along the Atlantic; it now stretched one third of the way across the continent.

Yet, it was President Thomas Jefferson who did more than anyone to open the West for exploration and settlement. In 1801 President Jefferson learned that Spain had secretly ceded Louisiana—most of the land between the Mississippi River and the Rocky Mountains—to France. Acutely conscious of the need for a port at the mouth of the Mississippi if America were to prosper in international trade, Jefferson instructed Robert R. Livingstone, U.S. minister to Paris, to negotiate for such a port or for permanent trading rights in New Orleans; subsequently he sent James Monroe to join Livingstone and provided them with a $2 million appropriation and an option to go as high as $10 million to buy New Orleans.

Although Napoleon had acquired Louisiana with the hope of building a North American empire, he became embroiled in a slave revolt in Haiti led by Toussaint-Louverture. That military action (which some call his Vietnam because so many of his troops were destroyed while fighting guerrilla insurgents), coupled with the threat of war with England, convinced him to abandon his American imperial plans. Thus, instead of discussing the purchase of New Orleans, Napoleon offered to sell all of Louisiana to the United States.

Americans tended to romanticize the expansion of their empire in the West, as this painting by George Caleb Bingham shows. Entitled *Daniel Boone Escorting Settlers through the Cumberland Gap* (1851–52), the painting depicts Boone leading settlers safely through the Appalachian Mountains. Oil on canvas, 31 1/2 × 50 1/4'. Washington University Gallery of Art, St. Louis. Gift of Nathaniel Phillips, 1890.

The agreed-upon price was $15 million, or approximately four cents per acre for about 828,000 square miles, including today's states of Louisiana, Arkansas, Oklahoma, Missouri, Kansas, Colorado, Nebraska, Iowa, Minnesota, North and South Dakota, Wyoming, and part of Montana. Despite Federalist opposition on the grounds that U.S. law made no provision for buying foreign territory, the Senate approved the purchase on October 20, 1803, and in 1804 a territorial government was established. By bold vision and equally bold, though not strictly constitutional, diplomacy, Thomas Jefferson doubled the size of the United States and laid the foundation for it to become a continental nation. He now needed more information on this newly acquired real estate.

Jefferson had long been interested in the trans-Mississippi West. He had proposed three prior explorations: in 1783 he had put the proposition to Revolutionary War hero General George Rogers Clark; three years later he encouraged John Ledyard, a civilian, to walk across Siberia and thence east from the Pacific; and in 1792, as vice president of the American Philosophical Society, he had urged funding for an expedition by André Michaux, a French botanist. For various reasons, none of these proposals succeeded.

For the average American, there were very specific reasons to expand the nation and move into the West. There were those who went west for religious motives: Mormons heading west to practice their religion safe from persecution, and missionaries wanting to convert and civilize Native Americans. Whereas many headed west to establish a permanent new life there, others, like most forty-niners, intended a brief, exploitative sojourn followed by a return to their homes in the East. There were fortune hunters in search of gold or land or railroad subsidies. There were tourists like Prince Maximilian von Wied, who came to hunt game and exotic experiences; and there were immigrants from Europe in search of the American dream. Some brought civilization west. Others, like Simon Kenton, who mistakenly believed the law was after him and fled west to the wilds of Ohio, saw the West as an escape from civilization; they were, literally, outlaws. Washington Irving described them in *Astoria*: "new and mongrel races . . . the amalgamation of the 'debris' . . . of former races, civilized and savage; . . . adventurers and desperadoes of every class and country . . . ejected from the bosom of society into the wilderness." Some Easterners viewed "all emigrants as actually or potentially criminal because of their flight from an orderly municipal life into frontier areas that were remote from centers of control." The Reverend Timothy Dwight, president of Yale, characterized the 18th century West as a vast septic system drawing off the depraved effluvia of New England.

Most, though, simply viewed the West as offering hope for a fresh start, for perennial rebirth, an opportunity to recover manhood, health, and even virtue. In this light, Timothy Flint, writing in 1827, described an agricultural utopia in the West in sharp contrast to the repressive conditions of industrial New England:

Thousands of independent and happy yeomen, . . . who have emigrated from New England to Ohio and Indiana—with their numerous healthy and happy families about them, with the ample abundance which fills their granaries, with their young orchards, whose branches must be propped to sustain the weight of their fruit, . . . would hardly be willing to exchange their free simple empires, their droves of cattle, horses, and domestic animals, and the ability to employ the leisure of half their time as they choose, for the interior of square stone or brick walls, to breathe floccules of cotton, and to contemplate the whirl of innumerable wheels for fourteen hours of six days of every week in the year [in the textile mills]. . . . Farmers and their children are strong, and innocent and moral almost of necessity.

One can conclude, therefore, that neither while the frontier was still in existence (until 1890) nor since has there been a consensus describing or interpreting its meaning or significance. Like a kaleidoscope, the images are constantly reassembling into new patterns. The individual pieces, sometimes colorful, sometimes dull, are suspended in the fluid medium of the larger American culture. The image can, for an infinitesimal instant, be caught in time and space, but external forces—political, social, or economic—can, like the twist of a wrist, create new patterns. Thus, the daily life on the American frontier that followed was a diverse, often contradictory, always changing composite of the lives of individual Americans who, for whatever reason, sought out an ever-moving, ever-changing American frontier (Jones, 8–10, 55–56).

FOR MORE INFORMATION

Jones, M. E. *Daily Life on the Nineteenth Century American Frontier*. Westport, Conn.: Greenwood Press, 1998.

Limerick, P. N. *The Legacy of Conquest: The Unbroken Past of the American West*. New York: W. W. Norton and Co., 1987.

White, R. *"It's Your Misfortune and None of My Own": A New History of the American West*. Norman: University of Oklahoma Press, 1991.

VICTORIAN ENGLAND

The British Empire arose more through commerce than through planned conquest. In 1830, England controlled the seas and accounted for about 45 percent of all world trade. Because it was the first country to industrialize, it had vast quantities of cheap manufactured goods to export. British ships, in return, brought back food and raw materials from countries around the world. Traders, merchants, bankers, investors, and immigrants settled wherever they discovered promising opportunities.

Until about 1870, the empire grew slowly and haphazardly. When there was no established government in place (as in Australia or New Zealand), English explorers claimed territory for the Crown. In other places (as in India), traders initially made agreements with local rulers. New territories were added to protect the borders of existing colonies and ensure the safety of trade routes. Singapore, Hong Kong, and other ports were developed to serve British ships.

Before the Suez Canal opened in 1869, ships reached India and China by sailing around the southern tip of Africa. In 1806, the English paid the Dutch £6 million

POLITICAL LIFE
|
EMPIRE
|
United States,
1850-1865

United States,
Western Frontier

Victorian England

Islamic World

for their settlement at the Cape of Good Hope, because it was an essential resupply point for ships. After the Suez Canal shortened the trip to Southeast Asia, England acquired new colonies in Burma, Borneo, and the South Pacific.

The 1876 Act of Parliament that made Victoria Empress of India crystallized the idea of empire. (The commercial East India Company and then the British government had ruled much of India for a century without calling themselves emperors.) In the 1880s, England joined what has been called the scramble for Africa to keep the continent (and its raw materials and trade routes) from being entirely controlled by France, Belgium, and Germany. Over the space of a few years the African continent was carved up, territory grabbed, governments installed, and troops sent to protect the new colonies from their original inhabitants, who wanted their land back.

(It is important to recognize that borders in Africa were drawn by European conquerors who paid no attention to existing tribal territories. There were not, in the 1880s, central governments for countries named Congo or Kenya or Nigeria. The new states made little sense in terms of Africa's ethnic and cultural divisions—which is one reason why internal conflict continues in countries that became independent in the 1960s with the same boundaries that had been drawn on the map during the 1880s.)

The following colonies, protectorates, and occupied territories were under British rule at the empire's high point in 1900: Aden, Antigua, Ascension, Australia, the Bahamas, Barbados, Basutoland, Bechuanaland, Bermuda, British Guiana, British Honduras, British North Borneo, British Solomon Islands, British Somaliland, Brunei, Burma, Canada, Cape of Good Hope, Cayman-Turks-Caicos Islands, Ceylon, Christmas Island, Cocos-Keeling Islands, Cook Islands, Cyprus, Dominica, the East African Protectorate, Egypt, Falkland Islands, Fiji, Gambia, Gibraltar, Gilbert and Ellice Islands, Gold Coast, Grenada, Hong Kong, India, Jamaica, Labuan, Lagos, Leeward Isles, Malay States, Maldive Islands, Malta, Mauritius, Montserrat, Natal, New Zealand, Newfoundland, Nigeria, Norfolk Island, Northern Rhodesia, Nyasaland, Papua, Pitcairn, St. Kitts and Nevis, St. Helena, St. Lucia, St. Vincent, Sarawak, Seychelles, Sierra Leone, Singapore, Southern Rhodesia, Straits Settlements (Singapore, Penang, Malacca), Sudan, Swaziland, Tonga, Trinidad and Tobago, Tristan da Cunha, Uganda, Virgin Islands, Windward Isles, and Zanzibar.

In addition to ruling these territories, England exercised vast international influence. British investors, engineers, merchants, and businessmen built and ran electric companies, shipping lines, railways, telephone services, banks, and insur-

---

📷 Snapshot

Using Self-Development to Oppose British Imperialism

Our policy is self-development and defensive resistance. But we would extend the policy of self-development to every department of national life; not only Swadeshi and national education, but national defense, national arbitration courts, sanitation, insurance against famine or relief of famine—whatever our hands find to do or urgently needs doing, we must attempt ourselves and no longer look to the alien to do it for us. And we would universalize and extend the policy of defensive resistance until it ran parallel on every line with our self-development. We would not only buy our own goods, but boycott British goods; not only have our own schools, but boycott government institutions; not only organize our league of defense, but have nothing to do with the bureaucratic executive except when we cannot avoid it. At present even in Bengal where boycott is universally accepted, it is confined to the boycott of British goods and is aimed at the British merchant and only indirectly at the British bureaucrat who stands behind and makes possible exploitation by the merchant . . . (Arobindo Ghose)

Political Life | Empire

ance companies around the world. The British consulate was the center of trade for much of South America as well as Russia, China, Persia, and Turkey. London's unquestioned role as the center of world commerce and investment supplied new wealth for mercantile leaders and a steady, prosperous life for the ever-increasing number of middle-class managers and superior clerks.

The Empire may not have had much direct role in English life, but it supplied employment, adventure, and enterprise for ambitious people of all classes. The ease of emigration protected England from the social turmoil that many European countries experienced during the 19th century. A variety of organizations and charities helped artisans, families, working-class men and women, and even homeless children to obtain free or cheap passage to colonies such as Canada and Australia, where jobs and land were plentiful.

The sense of empire (and pride in being an imperial nation) grew during the last decades of the century. Technology linked British possessions around the world. Steamships and the Suez Canal shortened the passage to India to 17 days. Australia could be reached in four weeks. More than half the world's merchant ships carried the British flag. By the century's end, underwater cables and telegraphic landlines sent messages almost anywhere in the empire in a matter of minutes. The mythology of popular imperialism used the colonies, the Union Jack, and pictures of heroic explorers and soldiers for patriotic and commercial purposes.

The term colonies of white settlement designated Australia, Canada, New Zealand, and sometimes South Africa—temperate territories with large numbers of English immigrants who had subdued the original population. Parliament realized that these colonies needed their own representative governments to prevent a repetition of what had happened in the 13 American colonies in 1776. During the second half of the century, various forms of responsible self-government were established, although governors-general appointed by the queen retained their ceremonial roles.

In 1893, New Zealand became the world's first country to grant the vote on equal terms to all adults regardless of sex or race. In the rest of the empire, racial domination was the rule. There was no move toward permitting self-government in countries principally occupied by Africans, Chinese, Indians, or other people of color.

Heroes of the British Empire, such as Lord Roberts, who fought in India, the Second Afghan War, and the Boer War, often used their fame to advertise products like this stomach medicine. Courtesy of the Public Record Office (Kew), Copy 1/169.

The empire's administrators and businessmen developed a way of life devoted to remaining English even though their working years were spent abroad. Few of them came from the aristocracy. (The viceroy or governor might be a peer, but he usually spent most of his time at home and came out to the colony only for state occasions.) Middle-class men—often educated in lesser public schools—occupied positions they could not have achieved in England. At age 18 or 19, without any special training, they passed a foreign service examination or secured a commercial post through family interest and went abroad to the place where they would spend most of their life.

In most colonies a relatively small number of white men ran all the key institutions: the government, the army, the police, the banks, the shipping agencies, and the important business firms. Their subordinates came from the native population, but there was no pretense of equality. In the earlier years of colonization, relationships had been more open. There were, for example, respectable marriages between English men and high-caste Indian women. By the latter half of the 19th century, however, social separation was the rule. The English lived in their own enclave, established a cricket club and an Anglican church, and eagerly entertained English travelers and military officers who passed through.

Careers in the empire meant late marriage. A man went out to his posting and waited to be sure of his prospects. When he had a home leave—often after seven years or more—he went back to England and found a bride or married the woman who had been waiting for him. London department stores featured India Outfits and specialized trousseaus of clothing suited to the climate of other colonies. Chests of household goods and tinned foods packed for transport were also advertised. Private girls' schools offered short courses in domestic science and tropical hygiene that were tailored for intending colonists.

While emigrants to the colonies of white settlement quickly called themselves Canadians or Australians, residents elsewhere thought of England as home. They guarded against letting down their standards, or going native. Victorians were fully dressed by day and changed into something more formal for dinner even in remote tropical outposts. They sent their children back to England at a very young age—magazines advertised seaside boarding homes "suitable for colonial children until old enough for school." And they hoped that by middle age they would have accumulated enough money to buy a comfortable house and enjoy a pleasant retirement in England (Mitchell, *Daily Life,* 282–87).

FOR MORE INFORMATION

Ghose, A. *The Doctrine of Passive Resistance.* Calcutta, India: Arya, 1948.
Mitchell, S. *Daily Life in Victorian England.* Westport, Conn.: Greenwood Press, 1996.
Mitchell, S., ed. *Victorian Britain: An Encyclopedia.* New York: Garland Press, 1998.
Morris, J. *Pax Britannica: The Climax of an Empire.* New York: Harcourt Brace, 1968.

POLITICAL LIFE
|
EMPIRE
|
United States,
1850-1865

United States,
Western Frontier

Victorian England

Islamic World

ISLAMIC WORLD

The term *empire* in the context of the Middle East in the 19th century involves two main elements: first, the final stages of deterioration of the Ottoman Empire, which had control of the majority of the region since the 12th century, and second, the expansion of colonial rule, which dates back to the early 16th century. For over two decades the two powers competed for control of the area, and each was influential in its own way.

Europe's colonial expansion into the Middle East began in 1498, when the Portuguese explorer Vasco de Gama visited the northern coast of Oman. This was the first sign of the colonial empire, which would rule areas of the Middle East well into the 20th century. For many years the Portuguese held control of Oman. However, they viewed Oman as merely a convenient stop-off point for trading ships en route to India and never attempted to penetrate the interior.

Gradually, Portuguese control in the gulf gave way to that of the English East India Company, which had trading links with the area as early as 1616. The English East India Company was privately run and, by this time, was a fairly large establishment with trading posts throughout the Indian Ocean region. However, other trading companies, namely controlled by Dutch, French, and Portuguese, also controlled some of the trade routes in the area. These trading companies were the single most important element in the establishment of colonial rule.

By 1750 Britain attained its goal of overtaking their French and Dutch competitors in the region. By this time the sultans of the Ottoman Empire were basically figureheads, and the political weakness of both Persia and Turkey opened the way to European powers. Persia was particularly weak and unstable at this time and, in the course of just 55 years, was ruled by three different dynasties.

At this time both Britain and Russia had their eyes on Iran. Russia wanted to use Iran to gain access to the Persian Gulf and to India. Britian hoped to keep the Russians away from their precious trade routes to India. In the early 19th century, Iran's leader, Nasser al-Din, was more interested in promoting Iranian culture through art and music than he was in improving his political hold. Russia succeeded in capturing much of Northern Iran. The British gained control of much of the South. At one point Nasser al-Din tried to sell the rights to exploit all of Iran's resources, including mines, banks, and railways, for a mere sum of 40,000 British pounds, followed by payments of 10,000 pounds per year for the next 25 years. However, when the news leaked to the public he was forced to back out of the absurd deal. Nasser al-Din's willingness to exploit the Iranian economy eventually resulted in a revolt, forcing him to give up the throne.

In the early 19th century, the Ottoman Empire struggled to keep its head above water in the midst of some half a dozen wars with Russia and expanding colonial power in the region. In attempts to build a French empire in the Middle East and India, in 1798 Napoleon and his army invaded Egypt. Although the French occupation in Egypt lasted a mere three years, it left a lasting mark: French remains an important language among the Egyptian upper class, and the legal system of Egypt is based on a French model.

In 1801 the British forced the French out of Egypt. This resulted in several years of political unrest. In 1805 Mohammed Ali, an Albanian soldier in the Ottoman army, became the Ottoman sultan's viceroy. Mohammed Ali's goal was to modernize Egypt, and he set about doing this by sending many Egyptians to study in Europe.

In 1818, under orders from the sultan, Mohammed Ali sent an army to retake Arabia from the Bedouin warriors. As it became more and more evident that the sultan relied on Mohammed Ali for military backing, his ambitions grew larger and larger. In the 1830s he successfully conquered Syria. By 1839 he controlled the majority of the Ottoman Empire. The sultan recognized Mohammed Ali as a separate ruler.

Bashir II, Emir of Lebanon from 1788 to 1840, allied himself politically to Mohammed Ali in the invasion of Syria. However, he was forced by Mohammed Ali to impose a high tax on his people, and a revolt broke out. The Turks, with the help of Europeans, routed Mohammed Ali. Bashir II was sent into exile. When his successor, Bashir III, failed to control the politically unstable region and withdrew from office the following year, the age of Lebanese emirs came to an end. In 1842 the Ottomans divided Lebanon into two administrative regions. They appointed two rulers, one Druze (an ethnic group derived from Islam) and one Maronite (an ethnic group that practices Christianity).

Preexisting tensions between the two groups increased. The Christians agitated for a return of the Lebanese emirate. A Druze ruled the southern area, which was dominated by Christians. The population of the south opposed this arrangement. The Ottomans used the tensions as a vehicle for enforcing a divide and rule policy. This model was used by many colonial governments and essentially involves pitting two groups against each other to weaken the society, therefore curbing potential revolts against the government.

Throughout the next couple of decades the Ottoman Empire stagnated. Economic weakness caused it to cede control to some of the foreign powers. Colonial control grew, and the Ottoman Empire became dependent on the will of the colonial powers. In 1860, following a massacre of local Christians in Lebanon, the French sent troops to help the situation. They forced the Druze to agree to set up government posts for Christians. The opening of the Suez Canal by Mohammed Ali's grandson Ismail, in 1869, was one of the main causes of the economic debt that followed. Egypt became economically and politically weak. As a result, in 1882 the British government occupied the country.

To read about the government of the Islamic Ottoman Empire, see the Ottoman Empire entry in the section "Government" in chapter 6 ("Political Life") in volume 3 of this series.

~Dana Lightstone

FOR MORE INFORMATION

Ali, T. Clash of Fundamentalisms: Crusades, Jihads and Modernity. New York: Verso Press, 2002.

Federspiel, H. M. Islam and Development: A Politico-Religious Response. Montreal, Canada: Permika-Montreal, 1997.

War and the Military

The essays in this section should be read together. Each of them provides information on certain aspects of military life and war in the 19th century. Therefore to understand the general overview, one needs to put the pieces together. As in most cases, the whole is indeed greater than the parts. Several themes arise from the these entries. First is the structure of the military in the 19th century. Unlike modern militaries, which do not necessarily reflect the structure of society at large, 19th-century ones sometimes did. Take for example the military in England. Until 1872, if one wanted to be an officer, one had to purchase a commission. This ensured that only the rich were able to hold such ranks. There were exceptions to this rule, as in the case of wartime promotions. But there were no major military engagements during the Victorian era. More familiar to contemporary readers was the basic structure of the military. All major armies were broken into regiments. Similarly there was the traditional pattern of generals, colonels, lieutenants, and various other officers. In England, society looked down upon regular soldiers. They tended to be uneducated and had a reputation for drinking and for violence against civilians.

Soldiers in the United States during the Civil War era did not have that kind of reputation. In fact, as time has worn on, Civil War soldiers have attained perhaps the highest recognition—each year thousands of people reenact Civil War battles. In fact, being a Confederate soldier is more popular now than being a Federal soldier. In any case, whereas the essay on England illuminates the structures of military life, the Civil War entry provides the wartime experiences. So much ink has already been spilled about battles, generals, and soldiers. This piece offers a refreshing view by letting the soldiers speak for themselves through all aspects of the wartime life.

Missing from the entry on the Civil War are the motivations for war. This is covered elsewhere (see the entries on politics and men). However, motivations for war in the West are clearly outlined in the essay about the frontier. At root, the conflict was about land. The Americans wanted Indian land, and the tribes, of course, resisted the expansion. The Americans moved first with treaties. Some were negotiated in good faith, and others were not. In any case, soldiers soon followed the diplomats. The end result was a tragedy and an extermination mentality on the part of the Americans. Not even the actions of humanitarians could repair the damage done on the frontier. As one historian put it in 1881, American relations with Indians in the 19th century constituted a century of dishonor. Similarly, war in Asia had a clear rationale that was to exploit the Chinese people and their economy. The critical year was 1834 when England first attacked China in what became known as the Opium War. This began nearly a century of foreign occupation in China and unequal treaties that enabled other nations to take advantage of China. For Latin America, the century began with decades of war as the various colonies of the region fought for independence from Spain or another colonial power. When the military leaders that rose to power through the successful wars for independence tried to govern, their autocratic tendencies led to uprisings, rebellions, and civil wars within the new states. By the end of the century, various Latin American states fought one another for territory or economic advantage. In the end, to understand the brutal wars and disorders in Asia and Latin America in the 20th century, one first has to understand the wars outlined in these entries.

UNITED STATES, 1850–65

Civil War battlefields were much more extensive than most people would suppose. Even in small engagements, hundreds if not thousands of men might be involved. In large battles a mounted officer, who could freely gallop from place to place, could scarcely travel over the entire field during the course of a day. Dense woods choked with heavy undergrowth or crossed with streams and marshes added to the difficulty of moving large bodies of troops. Commanders were forced to rely almost entirely on the reports of aides or couriers in formulating the military situation on different parts of the field.

With upwards of 100,000 men involved in battle, the individual soldiers saw only what occurred in their own regiment or company and they were limited to a very narrow view of what was going on. Soldiers commonly heard more than they saw and relied on the reports of those coming from the front, which were sometimes incomplete or based on rumor. Nonetheless, this information formed part of the experience of battle for most soldiers. Although we have no way of knowing the experience of those who were killed, the survivors and those wounded who lived long enough to record their feelings have left us a storehouse of journals, diaries, and letters containing the expression of what a Civil War battle was like.

Civil War battles had several distinct parts. The armies roused themselves in the morning and marched out with little foreknowledge that a fateful engagement was about to take place. The opponents sent out scouts to probe in the direction of the enemy, and, ultimately, the armies came into contact and began to skirmish. In each regiment of 10 companies, two were detailed each day to act as skirmishers. These men fanned out before their regiments and engaged the enemy's skirmishers or outposts. Skirmishing between outposts was a constant activity in the war zone, but skirmishers were trained to avoid precipitating an unwanted engagement by pressing too closely. "Skirmishing is not dangerous," observed an imperturbable Federal captain. "Two men mortally and

During the Civil War, Southern raiders often attacked federal supply lines, seizing supplies destined for Union soldiers.

two severely wounded constituted my whole loss in something like three hours fighting out of a company of forty-one muskets." This loss of 10 percent of his force seemed small in contrast to the large losses of a major battle.

Rarely, the opposing commanders decided to make a major fight of a small meeting, or they had a general engagement thrust upon them. A major engagement had many requirements beyond intelligence of the enemy's strength and position. Tactics and strategy were chosen to fit the particular situation, orders dictated, and units informed of their part in the cataclysm. It took time for forces to be marshaled. The column, sometimes miles long, had to be brought up to the battlefield, organized, and sent to strategic positions along the battlefront. Artillery positions and fields of fire had to be found and exploited. The cavalry might be sent to feel out the flanks of the enemy and to determine the possible success of a turning movement. A reserve was organized, and hospitals, signal stations, and supply units were set up. Beginning slowly, the battle began to rage furiously as more and more troops became engaged.

Soldiers often reported a lull in battle, sometimes immediately following a remarkable effort by both sides. Very often a series of small climaxes taken together made it obvious that one side was dominating the field. The opposing sides might now call a truce to care for their wounded and dead, and the losing commander would prepare a rearguard action to cover his retreat. The ability to effectively disengage from the victorious enemy without exposing one's forces to renewed attacks was the true test of a battlefield commander.

A soldier's experiences in battle are both common and unique. More than 10,000 individual engagements made up the Civil War, and no two were exactly the same. Most diaries, letters, and journals of the men who fought describe their experiences in battle. As noted by Col. William. B. Hazen, "The battle . . . the dreadful splendor . . . all my description must fall vastly short." The authors have therefore chosen to simply let the soldiers speak. In what follows no attempt has been made to describe any particular battle. The flow of the narrative imitates the characteristic development of a major engagement. Some sentence restructuring and editing of proper names and units have been done for the sake of continuity. The name of the individual, his rank, and his affiliation are provided with each report. It is hoped that the result will remain true to the spirit of what each man contributed to the written record of the Civil War battle experience.

📷 *Snapshot*	
Soldiers Killed during Civil War in Comparison to Casualties for Other U.S. Wars	
Civil War (1861–65)	617,528
Spanish-American War (1898)	5,462
World War I (1917–19)	112,432
World War II (1941–45)	405,399
Korean Conflict (1951–53)	54,246
Vietnam Conflict	46,079

~(U.S. Bureau of the Census, 1140; Morris and Morris, 274, 326, 351, 475)

Marching to War

We have received orders to cook all our rations, strike our tents very quietly, and be ready to move at any time, which we all think means that we are going to move against the enemy across the river. They, also, have been exhibiting signs of uneasiness for some days past. . . .

I am writing to you now for fear I may not have the opportunity again shortly. I fear not the result, am confident that we, through God, will be victorious.

~*Sgt. Alexander T. Barclay, 4th VA Infantry*

We have been on the march since yesterday, a week. . . . I would take any amount that this trip has the most beautiful scenery I ever beheld since I have been in the army, which is some time.

~*Lt. William B. Taylor, 11th NC Infantry*

We found several patriotic ladies with small feet and big umbrellas waiting to receive us. . . . One of the ladies had an enormous wreath which she was anxious to place on the neck of the General's charger. The horse objected to it seriously.

~*Lt. F. W. Dawson, Staff Officer, ANV*

No one who has not had the experience knows what a soldier undergoes on a march. We start off on a march some beautiful morning in spring. At midday slight clouds are seen floating about; these thicken . . . the rain commences and soon pours down. Poor fellow! He pulls down his hat, buttons up his jacket, pulls up his collar, and tries to protect his gun. In a short while he feels the water running down his arms and legs. . . . We went through equal trials in very dusty marches.

~*Pvt. J. H. Worsham, 21st VA Infantry*

We were about proceeding on our march. . . . [when] the men were allowed to light fires and dry the clothes in which they had shivered all night. At 3 P.M. we received orders to recross the river, and all the drying of clothes had to be done again in the evening.

~*Col. David W. Aiken, 7th SC Infantry*

We soon came to Dumfries Creek which has swollen very much during the night taking away the bridge over the stream. . . . We marched between twenty and thirty miles and when night came my feet were blistered nearly all over so that fifteen minutes after we halted I could hardly walk a step but on taking some salt and water and bathing my feet thoroughly and then applying liquor I managed to get myself in tolerably good marching order for the next day.

~*Pvt. Edwin Weller, 107th NY Volunteers*

Angry was the glare of the sun during those fearful days. . . . Choking, blinding were the clouds of dust that rose from beneath the army's steady tread; parching was that unquenchable thirst which dried the tongue to its very roots. The men fell by tens, twenties, nay by hundreds along the dusty roads. Such days as these prove the true soldier.

~*Capt. John E. Dooley, 1st VA Infantry*

Making Contact

The column, hitherto moving forward with the steadiness of a mighty river, hesitates, halts, steps back, then forward, hesitates again, halts. The colonels talk to the brigadier, the brigadiers talk to the major-general, some officers hurry forward and others hurry to the rear. The infantry stands to one side of the road while the cavalry trots by to the front. . . . Most of the men know . . . they are on the edge of battle. . . . The skirmishers step into the woods and carefully go forward. They load, fire, and reload rapidly while standing six to twelve feet apart, calling to each other, laughing, shouting and cheering. . . . They have at last driven the enemy skirmishers in upon the line of battle, and are waiting. A score of men have fallen here, some killed outright, some slightly, some sorely and some mortally wounded.

~*Pvt. Carlton McCarthy, 2nd Richmond Howitzers*

Soldiers destroying railroad tracks and telegraph poles and burning buildings during *Sherman's March to the Sea.* © Library of Congress.

At first when the boys brought news of the engagement to the company, we were loath to believe them and had it not been for the serious faces of those who gave us the information we would have been tempted to treat it as an attempt at a scare. Quite a number of the members of the company . . . returned with a report confirming the tidings already received. Soon afterwards a number of prisoners, about 300, were marched past where we were resting. As soon as we saw them we crowded up close to the road to get a good look at them. They all seemed to be in the best of spirits, evidently glad to escape the pending battle.

~*Pvt. Joseph A. Lumbard, 147th PA Infantry*

The orders were to be ready at a moment's notice. The lines were forming. Batteries were being placed into position. Dark columns stood motionless. . . . Hospitals were established in the rear, and the musicians and other non-combatants were detailed to bear the stretchers and attend the ambulances. Medical stores were unpacked and countless rolls of bandages placed at hand for use.

~*Ebenezer Hannaford, 6th OH Volunteers*

I now formed my division in the woods. . . . I told the General that the column seemed to be heavily engaged. I thought I had better go in. He replied: "I do not wish to bring on a general engagement today; the rest of the army is not up." . . . Very soon [however] an aide came to me with orders to attack.

~*Maj. Gen. Henry Heth, Division Cmdr. CSA*

A Day of Battle

In general, the terror of battle is not an abiding impression, but comes and goes like throbs of pain; and this is especially the case with veterans who have learned to know when there is a pressing danger and when not; the moment a peril has passed they are as tranquil as if it had never come near.

~*Capt. John W. De Forest, 12th CT*

We soon came to the top of a hill in full view of the field and valley and upon the hill we had the fight. Here men jumped over a fence to the left and formed in battle line. In a short time a line of the enemy came out of the woods in front of us about a mile off; soon another; and yet another. They kept steadily advancing until we could see their officers stepping in front swinging their swords. Suddenly a cloud of smoke arose from their line and almost instantly the balls began to whistle about us and the men next to my right fell. The order rang along the line . . . to load and fire at will, as they call it. I think we fired about five rounds. . . . As soon as the report of our muskets were heard we knew that a very small part of our line was there. The enemy did not return our fire but came rushing down the hill yelling.

~*Sgt. Edwin A. Gearhart, 142nd PA Infantry*

At every step some poor fellow would fall, and as his pitiful cry would come to my ear I almost imagined it the wail of some loved one he had left at home.

~*Capt. John T. James, 11th VA Infantry*

The Colonel was all impatience. "Where the hell is my flag?" He shouted [to the flagbearer], "If I can't get you killed in ten minutes, by God, I'll post you right up among the batteries!"

~*Capt. Abner Small, 16th ME Infantry*

One of our own batteries stationed on a hill in the rear of our line fired two shots which fell short and killed two of our company. I was sent back to inform the Colonel of the fact. . . . I mounted an orderly's horse, a great lumbering beast. As I reached a hill I was obliged to follow the ridge for several hundred yards. The enemy sharpshooters opened fire upon me. . . . I lost my hat, and as it was a new one and cost me seven and a half dollars, I drew my saber and ran the point through the hat and recovered it. I next lost my Navy Colt revolver, but if it had been made of gold, studded with diamonds I would not have stopped for it.

~*Col. Elisha Hunt Rhodes, 2nd RI Volunteers*

There was the thunder of guns, a shrieking, whistling, moaning of shells, before they burst, sometimes like rockets in the air. . . . No results of this conflict could be noted; no shifting of scenes or movement of actors in the great struggle could be observed. It was simply noise, flash, and roar. I had the sensation of a lifetime."

~*William H. Bayly, 13-year-old resident of Gettysburg*

The appearance of the landscape northward from this point was singular and doleful. Hundreds of noncombatants, and many who should have been in the ranks, with many whose bloody clothing showed that their fighting for that day had ended, were drifting rearward confusedly, yet with curious deliberation. Over the space of a mile square the fields, long since stripped of their rail fences, were dotted with wagons, ambulances, pack mules, army followers and stray soldiers, none of them running. . . .

   Defeated and retreating soldiers do not fly at full speed for any considerable distance. After a run of a hundred yards, or less, even though the bullets are still whizzing around them, they drop into a walk. . . . Thence forward they tramp steadily rearward, not in the least wild with fright, but discreetly.

~*Capt. John W. De Forest, 12th CT*

It was a moment of contending emotions of pride, hope, and sadness as our gallant boys stood face to face with those heights, ready to charge upon them. At double-quick and in splendid style they crossed the plain. Our line was perfect. The men could not have made a better appearance had they been on drill.

Just in the rear of the division three batteries of Parrott guns were playing into the works of the enemy, while from the heights above, all the opposing batteries poured a terrible and destructive fire upon the advancing lines. Having gained the rifle pits at the base of the hills, they pushed forward to capture the heights. . . .

There were the hills, enough to fatigue any man to climb them without a load and with no one to oppose. But the boys pushed nobly, steadily on, the enemy steadily retreating . . . our men were falling in every direction . . . but with shouts and cheers . . . with bayonettes fixed, mounted the heights, the enemy retreating in confusion.

~*George T. Stevens, Surgeon, 77th NY Volunteers*

The works commenced were only piles of rails and logs not capable of resisting shells, so we got tools and commenced ditching. By 10 A.M. we had pretty good works. . . . Soon after two lines of battle burst out of the woods in front of us, and started up, on the charge. . . . They came up within 50 paces of the works, before being repulsed. . . .

We have been kept close by sharpshooters, having nothing to protect us but our works. The enemy is on the edge of the woods, three or four hundred yards off while we are in an open field. We could not get out after water until dark. . . . The fire was kept up some time wounding several others, but killing no more. We have been enfiladed all day and have lost many killed and wounded—at night strengthened our works—worked all night.

~*Pvt. John S. Jackman, 1st KY Infantry*

Wounded in Battle

Some of the wounded from the battlefield began to arrive where I was staying. They reported hard fighting, many wounded and killed, and were afraid our troops would be defeated and perhaps routed. The first wounded soldier whom I met had his thumbs tied up. This I thought dreadful, and told him so. . . . Soon two officers carrying their arms in slings made their appearance, and I more fully began to realize that something terrible had taken place. Now the wounded began to come in greater numbers. Some limping, some with their heads and arms in bandages, some crawling, others carried on stretchers or brought in ambulances. Suffering, cast down and dejected, it was truly a pitiable gathering.

~*Tillie Pierce, 15-year-old resident of Gettysburg*

At a distance of about one hundred and fifty yards the enemy were lying down, and rose up in masses and fired one volley. I and one other member of the Brigade fell wounded . . . the bullet cut across my bowels and made a long and ugly wound . . . I was feeling no pain, but felt somewhat dazed. . . .

The grape shot and shell were pouring thick and fast in our rear, a great number falling short of their intended mark, and it made me hopeful that it would soon put an end to my existence. I turned my head to the enemy, thinking that I might be so fortunate as to get shot dead. . . .

As there was no sign of discharge [from the wound] . . . I thought [after a time] that possibly I was not mortally wounded. Then fear was uppermost and I crawled about 50 feet to a well rotted stump, thinking it would protect me from shot. I was not much more than settled behind it when the idea struck me that a grape [from artillery canister] could go through, so I dragged myself to a good sized tree about one hundred feet off and stayed there some time in a reclining position, with head and shoulder resting against the tree. All the while the battle was roaring across the creek.

~Pvt. William A. Fletcher, 5th TX Infantry

[A] man lay near me, dying from a terrible wound through the abdomen, his fair face growing whiter with every laboring breath and his light blue eyes fixed vacantly on the glaring sky . . . I glanced at him pitifully from time to time as he patiently and silently drew towards his end. Such individual cases of suffering are far more moving than a broad spectacle of slaughter.

~Capt. John W. De Forest, 12th CT

A terrific explosion occurred . . . I found myself lying off from my former position and gasping for breath. Around me were brains, blood, and skull bones. The two men who lay to my left had been blown off just above the ears, and that shell had exploded almost directly over me. It had broken several ribs and bruised my left lung cutting my jacket into shreds. My Colonel asked me if I was badly hurt to which I replied I thought I was and called for that which a wounded soldier first wants, a drink of water.

~Sgt. David E. Johnston, 7th VA Infantry

We were in this wheat field and the grain stood almost breast high. The enemy had their slight protection, but we were in the open, without a thing better than a wheat straw to catch a Minnie bullet that weighed an ounce. Of course our men began to tumble. They lay where they fell, or, if able started for the rear. Near to me I saw a man go down, shot through the neck. I made a movement to get his gun, but at that moment I was struck in the shoulder. It did not hurt and the blow simply caused me to step back. I found that I could not work my arm, but . . . it was not serious enough to justify my leaving the fighting line. So I remained, and some time after felt a blow on my left leg, and it gave way, so that I knew the leg was broken. . . . While lying here entirely helpless, and hearing those vicious bullets singing over my head, I suffered from fear.

~Lt. Charles A. Fuller, 61st NY Infantry

The road where we lay was covered with our dead and wounded. A battery of the enemy came thundering along it, and when the officer commanding it saw our dead and wounded on the road, he halted his battery to avoid running over them and his men carefully lifted the dead to one side and carried the wounded to the cellar of a house, supplied them with water, and said they would return and care for them when they had caught the rest of us.

~Sgt. Edward R. Bowen, 114th PA Infantry

I do not know how long it was before I became conscious but the battle was raging furiously; two dead men who were not there when I fell were lying close to me, one across my feet. . . . Two stretcher-bearers came and carried me back about fifty yards to a small stream that ran parallel to our battle line. Here was a depression in the ground some three or four feet below the general level where the wounded would be protected from the musket fire. . . .

When I reached the stream the banks were already lined with many dead and wounded. Some had been carried there, others had dragged themselves to the place to die. Many were needlessly bleeding to death. Many died who would have lived if only the simplest treatment had been in the hands of the men themselves.

My mind was clear . . . I knew I could not get to the rear without help, so made no further attempt. Fortunately my canteen had been filled; my thirst had become great and I had some water to wash the blood from my face.

During this time the battle on our front continued with unlessening fury. . . . Looking back I saw a scattered line of the enemy coming toward us on the double quick. . . . They had to cross around or over the wounded and were cautioned by their officers to be careful not to disturb them more than was necessary. They passed over us carefully, without any unkind actions or words.

~Pvt. Rice C. Bull, 123rd NY Volunteers

I felt a burning, stinging sensation in my thigh, and as if all the blood in my body was rushing to one spot. Finding I was falling on my face, I gave myself a sudden twist which brought me into a sitting position facing the enemy, with my broken leg doubled up over the other. Taking it up tenderly, I put it in its natural position; then tied my handkerchief above the wound, took the bayonet off my gun and made a tourniquet with it. I then took my knapsack off and put it under my head for a pillow. Having made myself comfortable . . . every moment I expected would be my last.

~Pvt. David R. Howard, 1st MD Battalion

Climax

At sunrise our Division advanced against the enemy's works. . . . We lay about forty yards apart. . . . To expose one's person was sure death. . . . Both armies were like hornets. We dug holes with our bayonets to protect ourselves and more than one poor fellow was shot before his little dugout would protect him. We lay there expecting every minute to be gobbled up. The shells passed over us both ways. Some of them fell short of going where they were started for and burst over our heads. We made ourselves in as small bulk as possible. This was a very dangerous position, but we took our chances and trusted to providence. . . . Time goes slowly.

At 7 P.M. everything became as quiet as the grave, we felt it was the calm before the storm. We fixed ourselves as well as possible to be ready for what was coming, and at 8 P.M. it came. The enemy charged our works. . . . These were long fierce charges—they came right up to the works but they could not effect a lodgement . . . We could hear their officers shouting, "Forward, forward!" On they came to be mowed down by the thousand, but we never thought of getting driven out.

At daylight all was quiet. The enemy advanced a white flag, asking permission to bury their dead, which was granted. We had an armistice of two hours. The quietness was really oppressive. It positively made us lonesome for the continual racket which we had endured for so long, both day and night. We sat on the works and let our legs dangle over the front and watched the enemy carry off their dead comrades in silence. . . . When the two hours was up we got back into our holes, and they did the same.

~Pvt. Daniel Chisholm, 116th PA Infantry

The Aftermath

With us for a time all was quiet. There was nothing to disturb us but the occasional cries and groans of the wounded; not a word of complaint was heard. . . . Nearly all knew we were not only wounded but were now prisoners. . . .

Union soldiers in trenches before Petersburg, 1864. © Library of Congress.

The enemy's surgeons went among our wounded looking for those that required amputation. . . . The arms and legs were thrown on the ground, only a few feet from the wounded who lay nearby. As each amputation was completed the wounded man was carried to an old house and laid on the floor. They said they could do nothing at that time for those others less critically wounded. . . . The condition of most of these was deplorable.

~Pvt. Rice C. Bull, 123rd NY Volunteers

Our men had 60 rounds of cartridges each when they went into an action and had used it nearly all when the enemy ran. Our regiment went into the fight with about 650 men and, as we lost about 100 in killed and wounded, you may know that we had pretty hot work. . . . I don't know the total loss in our brigade but should think about 450 killed and wounded. The enemy loss is pretty heavy but I don't believe they lost more than us as they were well protected by their breast works.

~*Lt. George Washington Whitman, 13th NY Militia*

Some of them lay dead within twenty feet of our works—the dead look horrible all swelled up and black in the face. . . . After there was nothing left but stains of blood, broken and twisted guns, old hats, canteens, every one of them reminders of the death and carnage that reigned a few short hours before.

~*Pvt. Daniel Chisholm, 116th PA Infantry*

The ground here is very hard, full of rocks and stones, the digging very laborious work, and the dead are many. As the time is short, they got but very shallow graves. In fact, most of them were buried in trenches dug not over 18 inches deep, and as near where they fell as was possible so as not to have to carry them far. I saw 60 buried in one trench and not one was carried more than 25 feet.

~*Sgt. George A. Bowen, 12th NJ Infantry*

The Pickets on both sides have agreed not to fire on each other, and are getting very friendly. They trade Tobacco for Coffee, and also exchange newspapers, etc. . . . .

This is a beautiful Sabbath day. Quiet. The regiment has marching orders and we lay around in the sun wondering where to go next. At dusk we quietly packed up and fell back without noise or confusion and struck out through the darkness leaving the battlefield behind. This has been a hot place for us as our thinned ranks show.

~*Pvt. Daniel Chisholm, 116th PA Infantry*

Confederate winter quarters in Manassas, Virginia, 1862. © Library of Congress.

[A]n enemy officer came and took a list of all prisoners, having each one sign a parole not to enter active service again until properly exchanged. . . . On returning home, after the battle, I found that my family was notified that I had been badly wounded, it was thought mortally, and was left on the battlefield. Great was their joy when two weeks later, after they had abandoned hope of my being alive, they received a letter from me sent from the hospital.

~*Pvt. Rice C. Bull, 123rd NY Volunteers*

Tell my father I died with my face to the enemy.

~*Col. Isaac E. Avery, 6th NC Infantry*

My Dear Papa,
When our great victory was just over, the exultation was so great that one didn't think of our fearful losses, but now I can't help feeling a great weight at my heart.

~*Capt. Henry L. Abbott, 20th ME Infantry*

(All quotations are from Volo and Volo, 173–87).

To read about war and military affairs in the United States in the 20th century, see the United States entries in the section "War" in chapter 6 ("Political Life") in volume 6 of this series.

FOR MORE INFORMATION

American Memory. <http://memory.loc.gov/ammem/amhome.html/>, accessed July 24, 2003.

Morris, J. B., and R. B. Morris. *Encyclopedia of American History*. 7th ed. New York: HarperCollins, 1993.

Paludan, P. S. *A People's Contest: The Union and Civil War, 1861–1865*. New York: Harper & Row, 1988.

Thomas, E. M. *The Confederate Nation: 1861–1865*. New York: Harper & Row, 1979.

U.S. Bureau of the Census. *Historical Statistics of the United States: Colonial Times to 1970*. Washington, D.C.: GPO, 1975.

Volo, D. D., and J. M. Volo. *Daily Life in Civil War America*. Westport, Conn.: Greenwood Press, 1998.

UNITED STATES, WESTERN FRONTIER

In the 19th century, the military was an omnipresent force on the western frontier. Like later generations of soldiers' comments, life in the army was rather dull with moments of intense action. Charles King's account of a reconnaissance patrol on July 3, 1876, captures the emotions and frustrations of the Fifth Cavalry. As the sun rises the men are grooming their horses: "the tap of the curry comb and the impatient pawing of hooves . . . music in the clear, crisp bracing air." As the men are inhaling morning coffee, word comes that Indians have been seen in the valley. The men "jump into boots and spurs . . . rattle the bits between the teeth of our excited horses," and move out at a "spanking gait" behind the scout, Buffalo Bill. Though this is the first chase of the campaign, "there is hardly a trace of nervousness" even among the newest troops. As they deploy, left hands firmly grasping the "already foaming reins," right hands on their carbines, "excitement is subdued but intense." For most of the day the scouts see Indian signs, but the troop sees no Indians. Although once or twice the scouts get close enough to exchange shots, the day is one of frustration. After hours in the saddle the men catch sight of their foe, "miles ahead, and streaking . . . for the Powder River country as fast as their ponies can carry them." Though the company commander will not abuse his horses in a wild goose chase, "we have galloped 30 miles in a big circle before catching sight of our chase, and our horses are panting and wearied. . . . We head for home, reach camp, disgusted and empty-handed, about four P.M. Two 'heavy weights' . . . horses drop dead under them, and the first pursuit of the Fifth is over."

The rising and falling action of the day becomes a metaphor for much of the Indian wars and of the national debates on how to end them. Yet the outcome was inevitable. King concludes his narrative of campaigning with Crook with the observation that though "our engagements were indecisive at the time (and Indian fights that fall short of annihilation on either side generally are)," the campaign was ultimately successful: Sitting Bull driven to refuge "across the line" in Canada, his subordinates "broken up into dejected bands that, one after another, were beaten or starved into submission," and, the following year, "the grand ranges of the Black

Hills and Big Horn, the boundless prairies of Nebraska and Wyoming were as clear of hostile warriors as, two years before, they were of settlers."

Robert M. Utley argues that until the middle of the 19th century the changes of Indian culture had been "evolutionary and mostly within the bounds of traditional culture. Henceforth they would be revolutionary and finally destructive of traditional culture." Step by step, eastern woodlands Indians had been pushed onto the prairies and plains, adapting to their new environments as did the whites who pushed them. Cattlemen ranged up from the South; homesteaders, from the East; and miners, from the West, bringing with them new technologies. Some of these, like the breech-loading rifle, the Indians quickly adopted; but others, like the telephone (or whispering spirit) left them awestruck, literally shaken from hearing a comrade's voice from a house an eighth of a mile away and convinced that an army that had such inexplicable objects surely had powerful medicine.

The four great transcontinental railroads and all their branch lines wrought even greater change—so great that General William Tecumseh Sherman observed in his final report as general of the army that although the actions of the army and the influx of settlers had been powerful forces for change, "the *railroad* which used to follow in the rear now goes forward with the picket line in the great battle for civilization with barbarism, and has become the *greater* cause." Jacob Cox, secretary of the interior, concurred:

Instead of a slowly advancing tide of migration, making gradual inroads upon the circumference of the great interior wilderness, the very center of the desert has been pierced. Every station upon the railway has become a nucleus for a civilized settlement, and a base from which lines of exploration for both mineral and agricultural wealth are pushed in every direction.

The significance of the white flood was not lost on the Apache leader Cochise, who reflected, "Nobody wants peace more than I do. I have killed 10 white men for every Indian I have lost, but still the white men are no fewer; and my tribe is growing smaller and smaller. It will disappear from the face of the earth if we do not have a good peace soon." The reservation system sought to "remove Indians from the path of on-rushing whites" and thus save them from destruction. To this end, a whole new set of treaties was signed during the last third of the 19th century.

The legal basis for such treaties was Chief Justice John Marshall's decision in *Cherokee*

Harper's Weekly published this picture of Fort Larned, Kansas, on June 8, 1867. The military presence on the frontier was very important to the westward expansion of the United States. Kansas State Historical Society, Topeka, Kansas.

Nation v. Georgia, 1831, which concluded that even though the Cherokees were a "distinct political society" capable of self-government, they were not truly a foreign nation; rather, the Indians were "domestic dependent nations" who "occupied territory to which the United States asserted a title independent of the Indians' will, which would take effect when the Indians give up possession." Many of the treaties subsequently signed had included in perpetuity clauses guaranteeing protection and possession of new lands west of the edge of settlement, in the words of an old trade treaty, "for as long as the grass shall grow and the rivers run." Yet the Five Civilized Tribes who had been sent to Indian Territory witnessed the Oklahoma land rush; the Santee Sioux, after the 1862 Minnesota uprising, lost their reservation—as did the Winnebagos, who, ironically, had remained peacefully uninvolved; and after the discovery of gold in the Black Hills, the Great Sioux Reservation underwent drastic shrinkage.

At least one recent scholar has suggested that the purpose of treaty making was to "benefit the national interest without staining the nation's honor." A Georgia governor explained it less euphemistically: "Treaties were expedients by which ignorant, intractable, and savage people were induced without bloodshed to yield up what civilized people had the right to possess by virtue of that command of the Creator . . .—be fruitful, multiply, and replenish the earth, and subdue it." If the earth was to be subdued, so too must be the Indians, who logically and instinctively recognized this fact. Thus, despite their recognition of the inevitable, there were many impediments to treaties involving land cession west of the Mississippi.

In some instances a treaty was not signed, or even approved of, by the whole tribe. From Jefferson's time onward, government officials had erred in selecting the leader with whom to deal; their external and arbitrary elevation of an individual to prominence—if not to power—caused schisms in tribal unity. And true tribal leaders, such as Red Cloud of the Oglala Sioux, constantly walked a tightrope between their white overseers and their own people. In many instances a rift developed between peace chiefs who were somewhat more pragmatic, willing to compromise in the face of the inevitable, and young warriors who were more idealistic and wanted freedom, not accommodation. Among the Kiowas during 1867, the peace chief Kicking Bird gained supporters while Satanta remained adamantly insolent to whites. And at the Medicine Lodge Creek treaty council, Black Kettle and about 50 lodges came in early, while the remaining 200 lodges camped 30 miles away before eventually joining the talks.

Frequently the Indians did not fully understand the implications of a treaty. Albert Barnitz observed that only with great difficulty were the Cheyennes persuaded to "touch the pen," or sign the Medicine Lodge treaty. In his journal entry of October 28, 1867, he tends to empathize with them: " *[T]hey have no idea that* they are giving up or that they have ever given up the country which they claim as their own, the country north of the Arkansas." Barnitz is well aware of the likely results of the white duplicity: "The treaty all amounts to nothing, and we will certainly have another war sooner or later . . . in consequence of misunderstanding of the terms of present and previous treaties." He does, however, record lighter moments of mutual experimental acculturation: Ten Bears practicing on an army bugle, and Senator Henderson trying on buffalo robes.

The implications of lack of understanding were often quite serious. In Washington for a meeting with President Grant, Red Cloud was angry when he recalled that "in 1868 men came out and brought papers. We could not read them and they did not tell us truly what was in them. . . . When I reached Washington the Great Father explained to me what the treaty was, and showed me that the interpreters had deceived me." Newspapers reported the meeting. The *New York Times* editorialized: "The attempt to cajole and bamboozle [the Indians] as if they were deficient in intelligence, ought to be abandoned, no less than the policy of hunting them down like wild beasts." The *New York Herald* concurred: "Palaver has very little effect on the Indian character. . . . [F]aithlessness on our part in the matter of treaties, and gross swindling of the Indians . . . are at the bottom of all this Indian trouble."

Sometimes whites bargained in bad faith, speaking with "forked tongues." While peace commissioners negotiating for permission to open the Bozeman Trail promised that travelers would be confined to the roadway and would not be allowed "to molest or disturb the game in the country through which they passed," Colonel Carrington revealed that his orders were to build a chain of forts to protect the trail. The Indians were furious. Red Cloud did not mince words: "Great Father sends us presents and wants new road. But white chief goes with soldiers to steal road before Indian says yes or no!" Some historians feel this led directly to the Fetterman massacre and thus to General Sherman's vow of "vindictive earnestness against the Sioux, even to their extermination, men, women, and children."

Sometimes the problem was one of translation. General Nelson A. Miles recalls one instance in which a translator ad-libbed a promo for a local trader, telling the Arapahos that the "Great Father hoped they would gather large quantities of buffalo robes and furs . . . , bring them all to Bent's fort, and sell them cheap." Miles wonders what the Indians thought of this "absurd message." Another instance was more tragic. When the army was trying to convince Crazy Horse to lead Oglala scouts against the Nez Percé, he finally agreed, saying "he would fight until not a Nez Percé was left." The bungling translator said he would fight "until not a white man was left." Crazy Horse was, naturally, arrested; he was killed in an escape attempt.

Some Indians simply did not want to be corralled. Sitting Bull told General Miles that "God Almighty made him an Indian, and did not make him an agency Indian either, and he did not intend to be one." Daklugie, telling of the choice he and other Apaches must make between a degraded life on the San Carlos reservation and life off the reservation hunted by troops of the United States and Mexico, remembered, "All of us knew that we were doomed, but some preferred death to slavery and imprisonment." Others, like Chief Joseph of the Nez Percé, didn't want to abandon sacred land or land where their ancestors were buried.

Finally, many, being aware of past broken promises, simply did not feel they could trust the treaty negotiators. For example, in 1865 the Poncas, a small peaceful tribe, had been guaranteed a 96,000-acre reservation along the Missouri River north of the Niobrara. Only three years later, through the Fort Laramie treaty, the "United

States—without consulting the Poncas—ceded the entire Ponca reservation to the Sioux, the Poncas' traditional enemies."

Even an army general was not immune. Little Chief of the Northern Cheyennes surrendered to General Miles because he trusted him. "You have not lied yet, and I am going to surrender to you"; he believed Miles's promises that they could stay on the Yellowstone. Similarly, when Chief Joseph surrendered to Miles in northern Montana in October 1877, Miles promised they could return to Idaho in the spring. He was overruled by General Sherman, who declared the Nez Percé prisoners of war and ordered them to Fort Leavenworth, where many died. One wonders what these Indians thought of Miles. One wonders what Miles thought as his efforts of humanely bringing in Indians was undermined.

It seems certain that Indians would conclude that they could not trust the promises of the government or its agents. Perhaps of equal significance, such a fiasco reveals the deep divisions among those making Indian policy—a division between the hardliners and those who believed it was possible to subdue by kindness. It is important to note that this dichotomy was not synonymous with the division between the military and civilians, for there were hard line civilians and humane officers.

Colonel Richard I. Dodge believed Indians did not fight fair.

General George Armstrong Custer was among the hardliners, though he did not usually go so far as to demonize the Indian. He even once said that if he were an Indian, he would want to be free and not live on reservations. However, he rejected the noble savage "as described in Cooper's interesting novels" as untrue. Speaking from firsthand experience of war with the Plains Indian, he describes him as a "savage in every sense of the word; not worse, perhaps, than his white brother would be similarly born and bred, but one whose ferocious nature far exceeds that of any wild beast." He argued that the delegation Indians who visited Washington and the Indians whom peace commissioners met in council were of one persona, "perhaps his most serviceable," but not a complete picture. Custer believed that many Indian agents either could not or would not enforce the peace, and he verges on the bitterly sarcastic when he notes that Indians are receiving from traders the very same new weapons the army has only recently received. Ultimately, he argues, "no teaching, argument, reasoning, or coaxing" will induce the Indian to change his mode of life unless it is "preceded and followed closely by a superior physical force. In other words, the Indian is capable of recognizing no controlling influence—[not eastern philanthropists, not Christian missionaries, not well-meaning teachers]—but that of stern arbitrary power."

Colonel Richard I. Dodge believed Indians did not fight fair—referring to their surprise attacks on wagon trains and their refusal to stand and fight; and he once wrote that the "noblest of virtues to the Indian are comprehended in the English words—theft, pillage, rapine, and murder." However, he blamed government policy for keeping "alive a warlike spirit by encouraging acts of aggression," specifically by having allowed hide hunters to deplete the buffalo herds, thereby leaving the Indians starving on reservations. Moreover, he condemned the ready access to alcohol as a catalyst to violence. He could not condone the Indians' violence, but he could understand its causes.

General William Tecumseh Sherman felt punishment under the law was the best deterrent to hostilities and depredations. "We can never stop the wild Indians from murdering and stealing until we punish them." Taking a shot at Indian agents, he observed that if a white man committed such acts he would go to prison, whereas "if an Indian commits these crimes, we give him better fare and more blankets. . . . Under this policy, the civilization of the wild red man will progress slowly."

Albert Barnitz believed peace councils to be shams. The "presents will be distributed, and the new guns . . . and in the Spring we will repeat the pleasant little farce of a Big Indian War, and a hand-full of men to carry it on. . . . The Indians," he wrote to his wife, Jennie, in August 1867, "must be thoroughly whipped before they will respect us, or keep any peace, and they haven't been whipped yet very much to speak of."

Many army officers respected their enemies and understood their motivations, even as they argued for tough policies. Some civilians were far less sympathetic. When Senator Doolittle spoke in Denver in 1865 on Indian policy, he asked what he thought was a rhetorical question—Should the Indians be placed on reservations and taught to support themselves, or should they be exterminated? "There suddenly arose such a shout," he recalled, "as is never heard unless upon some battlefield—a shout loud enough to raise the roof of the Opera House—'Exterminate them! Exterminate them!'" And Frances Roe, reflecting in 1888 on the end of an era, remarked, "We have seen the passing of the buffalo and other game, and the Indian seems to be passing also. But I confess that I have no regret for the Indians—there are still too many of them!"

Most army officers did not develop such an "ideology of hostility" toward the Indians; rather, aware of the "fraud, corruption, and injustice" they had suffered, officers were, as a class, ambivalent toward their foes. On the one hand, they felt "fear, distrust, loathing, contempt, and condescension"; on the other, "curiosity, admiration, sympathy, and even friendship." The eastern humanitarians, for the most part, were less ambivalent, many pointing to the Sand Creek Massacre (which was not the work of the regular army) as a chief illustration of why the military could not be trusted to civilize the Indians. Most of them were equally certain about what they wanted the Indian to become: a peaceful, Christian farmer, demonstrating the Puritan work ethic, living within the law on his own plot of land, and aspiring to U.S. citizenship. This goal, they believed, could best be accomplished by civilians—missionaries, teachers, and government officials of good moral character (Jones, 112–14, 234–41).

To read about war and military affairs on the colonial frontier of North America, see the entries on the Colonial Frontier and New England in the section "Warfare" in chapter 6 ("Political Life") in volume 4 of this series.

FOR MORE INFORMATION

Jones, M. E. *Daily Life on the Nineteenth Century American Frontier*. Westport, Conn.: Greenwood Press, 1998.

Nabokov, P., ed. *Native American Testimony: An Anthology of Indian and White Relations: First Encounter to Dispossession.* New York: Harper & Row, 1979.

Schubert, F. N. *Black Valor: Buffalo Soldiers and the Medal of Honor, 1870–1898.* Wilmington, Del.: SR Books, 1997.

Utley, R. M. *Frontier Regulars: The United States Army and the Indian: 1866–1891.* Bloomington: Indiana University Press, 1973.

VICTORIAN ENGLAND

Until the system of purchase was ended in 1872, a man who wanted to enter the army as an officer usually had to buy his commission. He (or his family) deposited the purchase money with an agent, who then searched for an appropriate regiment that had an opening. A commission would be for sale if the officer who held it was promoted or wanted to sell out (which simply meant to leave the army; no disgrace was involved). Meanwhile, the young man also found contacts who could recommend him to the regiment's other officers. To buy a commission, then, a man needed enough money to pay the asking price and the proper social status to fit in.

The purchase system was defended because it helped ensure that officers would come from a class high enough to be respected by soldiers who made up the rank and file. The price of a commission varied according to the regiment's prestige. The most desirable were guard regiments, also known as household troops because they protected the monarch. Because the guards were usually stationed in London, men who were waiting to inherit a peerage and younger sons of the aristocracy paid £1,200 or more to be a lieutenant in the Life Guards or Horse Guards, which were cavalry regiments. The Scots Guards, Grenadier Guards, and Coldstream Guards (infantry units) were only slightly less prestigious.

Guard officers had elegant uniforms and light duties that were mostly ceremonial. Especially during the London season, they could spend their evenings at grand balls and other social events. When the guard officer was a younger son, most people suspected he was looking for a wealthy bride and would sell out once he found her.

The cavalry was especially glamorous, because aristocratic men traditionally fought on horseback. Cavalry officers were known for their dash and daring—and for their wealth. An officer in a high-prestige regiment not only had to buy his commission but also needed a private income or an allowance from his father. His military pay was not nearly enough to cover the cost of good horses, fine wine, and a busy social life.

Commissions in other regiments—which usually rotated between overseas duty and short stays in a garrison or barracks somewhere in England—were cheaper. They ran from about £400 (in the infantry) up to £800 for a cavalry posting. Promotions were also bought: when there was an opening available, an officer purchased the next higher rank and sold the one he was leaving. To buy a promotion, a man sometimes exchanged into another regiment. Many regiments, however, had strong traditional loyalties and did not welcome officers who bought in from elsewhere.

There were exceptions to the purchase system. In wartime, when commanders were needed, officers were promoted on merit. Because there were no major conflicts throughout most of the Victorian period, a serious and ambitious career officer might choose a regiment stationed in some dangerous and unhealthy part of the empire. In that way he would earn more rapid (and cheaper) promotions.

Artillery and engineer commissions were not for sale. They went to career officers with special training from the Royal Military Academy at Woolwich. The Indian Army was also a separate matter. Its officers were British (usually from Scotland or England), and most of its soldiers were recruited in India from peoples with a warrior tradition: Sikhs, Gurkhas, Dogras, and Mahrattas. A certain proportion of non-Indian soldiers and sergeants were assigned to each regiment for the sake of control. A middle-class man with the right contacts could get a commission in the Indian Army without paying for it. Most of the officers were professionals who lived on their military pay—and their social prestige was correspondingly low.

The army was organized by regiments. A regiment, commanded by a colonel, had anywhere from 8 to 20 or more companies (depending on the date and the field of operations). Each company had (in theory) 100 men, although the actual number varied between 60 and 120, and was commanded by a captain who was assisted by two to four junior officers. These were usually lieutenants, although there might be a young ensign—a boy 16 or 17 years old who would be commissioned as a lieutenant when he was mature enough. The headquarters company, which supported the colonel and the regiment as a whole, had additional officers for administrative, medical, and other services.

After the purchase system ended, most lieutenants came into the army directly from one of the public schools—but they still needed influence to obtain the best assignments. The social gap between officers and enlisted men remained enormous. Promotion from the ranks into the officer corps was extremely rare, although a few long-service sergeants were allowed to finish their careers as commissioned riding masters or quartermasters to boost their pensions. The gentleman ranker who enlisted to escape romantic or financial woes was far more common in popular fiction than in actuality.

A photo of British Admiral Milne and his wife taken between 1855 and 1865. © Library of Congress.

The common soldier's lot was hard. Until 1847, a man enlisted for life (or until medically discharged). Various other schemes were then tried while the army tried to balance its need for experienced regiments overseas with its hope that shorter enlistments would bring better recruits. In the middle of the century the basic period of enlistment was 21 years. By 1870 it was 12 years, with the option of serving six years on active duty and six in the reserve. Another means of developing long-service professionals was the enlistment of boy-soldiers. They were signed on at age 15 and fulfilled three years of apprenticeship (usually as drummers, buglers, armorers, tailors, or cooks) before formally joining the regiment at age 18.

The basic pay for a private was one shilling per day, but deductions were made for food, washing, hair cutting, and some items of uniform. Even with lodging supplied, a soldier's earnings were less than a farm laborer's except for one thing: he had secure year-round employment. Soldiers were recruited from rural areas where agricultural work was in short supply, from the impoverished Irish, and through semivoluntary enlistments: young men brought before a magistrate for minor offenses such as fighting who were given a choice between gaol and the army, and other men who found it useful to disappear into the ranks to escape debts or disgrace.

Most people looked down on soldiers. It was widely assumed that they were drunks, criminals, or men too unskilled for any other work. In the 1850s, less than half of all enlisted men could sign their name. At home or abroad, soldiers slept in barracks and had little privacy or free time. They were kept busy with drill and chores to limit the opportunity for drinking and fighting. Discipline was harsh. Flogging was the punishment even for minor offenses until 1881. Regiments were away from home for years on end, often in unhealthy tropical climates. Mothers mourned when their sons took the shilling or went for a soldier.

On the other hand, there were cadres of long-service professional soldiers for whom the army was a family tradition and a way of life. Rankers could increase their pay by earning good-conduct badges and marksmanship medals, by taking up extra duty as officers' servants, or by learning skills such as telegraphy or surveying.

A limited number of enlisted men were allowed to marry on the strength, which entitled them to a room in married quarters. The number varied between three percent and seven percent. Their wives had a recognized status and earned money by doing the regiment's laundry and sewing. Marriage off the roll, when a man did not have permission, was not punished; but the wife had no quarters or allowance, and her transportation was not provided when the regiment moved.

All noncommissioned officers at the rank of sergeant or higher could be married. Until the army medical corps was formed in the 1870s, sergeants' wives did most of the nursing. Schooling was provided for the children of noncommissioned officers and soldiers who married on the strength. Sergeants' daughters often became pupil teachers, married noncommissioned officers, and continued to serve as army schoolmistresses. Children educated by the army, in turn, became the most professional of its recruits. Census records from the end of the century show that a large proportion of noncommissioned officers had been born at military stations somewhere in the empire.

At any given moment, about half the army was at home and the other half abroad. In 1897, there were 52 infantry battalions in India, 23 in Ireland, 7 in Malta, 6 in South Africa, 3 at Gibraltar, 3 in Egypt, 2 at Mauritius, and 1 each in Canada, the West Indies, Singapore, Bermuda, Ceylon, and Hong Kong. Engineers were everywhere, doing surveying and stringing telegraph wires. Officers had extraregimental assignments training local military forces, providing medical services for foreign rulers, accompanying explorers and diplomats, and drifting around the world gathering intelligence.

Commissions in the navy were obtained through contacts and influence, although naval officers did not buy them outright. The navy was more apt to be a real career and often a family trade; because ships could be away from England for years at a time, the naval service did not have much appeal for men who wanted to spend a few seasons doing something glamorous before they settled down.

Navy life began very young. After his family secured an appointment, a boy joined a training ship when he was 12 or 13 years old. He then served at sea as a midshipman, doing whatever the officers told him to do. After six years, if he passed an examination, he could be commissioned when an opening was available. Because the senior officers who appointed new lieutenants tended to favor their own sons and nephews, naval officers came from a limited number of families.

Promotion was strictly by seniority. There was, however, no system of retirement; even very old captains tended to hang on to their command. The half pay system functioned as a sort of reserve. The size of the navy was periodically reduced—at the end of the Napoleonic wars, after the Crimean War, and at other times when policies shifted. Because the most senior men did not have to retire, younger captains (who had commanded a ship when a larger naval force was needed) were relieved of their duties and put on half pay. They could be called back to active service if an older captain died or if the number of ships was once more increased.

As in the army, the gap between officers and men was seldom crossed. Early in the period, seamen were hired for a single voyage and discharged when it was over. (Impressment—involuntary enlistment of sailors in a port or even from a ship at sea—was technically still available, but it was not actually used in Victorian times.) Unlike the army's common soldiers, the navy's ordinary seamen were almost all English (rather than Irish); going to sea was a customary way of life for boys and men from coastal towns.

The terms of naval service were reformed during the 1850s. Seamen were enlisted for 10 years; if they served for 20 years they became eligible for a pension. As in the army, the pay, food, punishment, and general living conditions were terrible. Sailors on merchant ships, however, were treated just as badly and they did not have the security or pension that naval service provided. As a consequence, the navy could depend on enlisting a reasonably competent class of seamen.

Naval technology was utterly transformed between the beginning and the end of the Victorian period. The point of transition is visible in an *Illustrated London News* picture of ships leaving for the Baltic in 1855. Most of the fleet were great wooden two-deckers and three-deckers crowded with sail, but two iron-hulled steamships were also present. The Crimean War of 1854–56 signaled the end for wooden warships: the entire Turkish fleet went up in flames after Russian incendiary shells began a chain of explosions. By the end of the century, England's main line of defense lay in sleek steel-hulled battleships and cruisers. In addition to their speed and firepower, the new ships required fewer crew (no sails to set) and had a great deal more interior space.

The new technology brought a new midrange of engineers and petty officers into the navy and raised the professional standards for training commissioned officers. At the end of the century, cadets still entered the service at age 12 (after an examination and an interview) but spent two years at Osborne (which served as the navy's secondary school) and two additional years at the Royal Naval College at Dartmouth. At age 16, cadets who had changed their mind could leave the navy, and those whose performance was unsatisfactory were dismissed. Those who remained served three years at sea as midshipmen, had three additional years of specialized training (some of it at sea), and were commissioned as lieutenants when they reached age 22 (Mitchell, 277–82).

To read about war and military affairs in Chaucer's England, see the entry on Europe in the section "Warfare" in chapter 6 ("Political Life") in volume 2 of this series; for 18th-century England, see the entry on England in the section "Warfare" in chapter 6 ("Political Life") in volume 4 of this series; for 20th-century Europe, see the Europe entry in the section "War" in chapter 6 ("Political Life") in volume 6 of this series.

FOR MORE INFORMATION

Cook, C., and B. Keith. *British Historical Facts, 1830–1900*. New York: St. Martin's Press, 1975.
Mitchell, S. *Daily Life in Victorian England*. Westport, Conn.: Greenwood Press, 1996.
Spiers, E. *The Army and Society, 1815–1914*. New York: Longman, 1980.

CHINA

POLITICAL LIFE

WAR & MILITARY

United States,
1850-1865

United States,
Western Frontier

Victorian England

China

Latin America

In 1834, the beginning of the Opium War marked the start of a major turn of events in the course of Chinese history. This and subsequent victories led the British, followed by other Western nations and Japan to impose a series of unequal treaties on China. Over the course of the 19th century, Western powers came to control areas of China known as leaseholds and spheres of influence, opium was legalized, missionaries were allowed to proselytize in China, and takes were kept low on exports and imports. These events marked the transition between an indigenous Chinese culture and a culture heavily influenced by outside ideologies.

There are three main factors that led to the outbreak of the Opium War. First, since the arrival of the first Portuguese traders three centuries earlier, China had successfully dealt with foreign traders on their own terms. All foreign traders were, for the most part, limited to the port of Guangzhou, and any communication had to go through the Chinese Merchant Guild. The British East India Company, a monopoly licensed by the British government, grew resentful of these restrictions. The British philosophy of free trade called for governments not to interfere in trade interactions and led to a heightened resentment.

The second factor was the imbalance of trade between China and Great Britain. By the middle of the 18th century most British people drank tea. Most of this tea was exported from China. The fact that the British could not find products to import to China in exchange for the tea caused silver to drain from the British reserves. At this time European powers considered silver bullion reserves to be the main element of a nation's wealth and power. This trade imbalance also led to an increase in wealth in China.

The British made several failed attempts to remedy this situation, before discovering that opium from India was the answer to solving the problem of the trade imbalance. The East India Company had a monopoly on opium in the Bengal region of India. Farmers in the area were forced to grow poppy, the plant from which opium is derived.

The East India Company derived a trade triangle, which prevented them from being directly involved in the illegal trading of opium, yet achieved the result of trading opium for tea. Private British traders bought opium from the company on credit, sold it to Chinese smugglers, and then paid the East India Company's representatives in Guangzhou. Tea was then purchased with the money. By the 1820s China began to feel the results of silver draining out of the country, as the result of the opium trade.

In addition to economic hardships, an increasing number of Chinese people of all classes became addicted to opium. While China attempted to stamp out the import of opium, smugglers continued to prosper from the lucrative business, and local officials were often bribed with large sums of money to ignore the problem.

In March of 1839 the Chinese government sent an official named Lin Zexu to Guangzhou with an assignment to put an end to the opium trade. Lin Zexu had already been very successful at weeding out opium in Fujian, his own province of jurisdiction. Upon his arrival in Guangzhou he demonstrated that, unlike many officials at the time, he could not be bribed to ignore his mission of putting an end to the opium trade. Within a few months, he had taken such a strong action against the Chinese Merchant Guild and the Western traders that he successfully seized around twenty thousand chests of opium, which the British stored in Guangzhou.

This was one of many incidents enabling Britain to gain support for military action against China. Had opium been the sole issue of debate between the Chinese and the British, the war would most likely never have broken out. However, to the British, Lin Zexu's uncompromising stance seemed arrogant and unreasonable. Lin Zexu called for foreigners caught in the process of opium trade to be turned over to Chinese officials for punishment. The British viewed this as a matter of principle and they were not willing to give in to the punishment. The lack of treaty relations meant that there was no established procedure for the administration of justice in incidents between foreigners and Chinese. The British were not willing to turn suspects over to the Chinese legal system, which they considered barbaric and inhumane. When Lin Zexu countered by expelling all British from China and breaking off all trade between the two countries, major hostilities broke out. In 1840 a British military force assembled and was ready to fight the Opium War.

Because the Chinese were not prepared to fight the British forces, it was only a matter of weeks before the Chinese were defeated and forced to surrender. The treaty that resulted ceded Hong Kong to the British, called for indemnities of 6 million yuan, and put an end to trade. However the emperor did not recognize the treaty. As a result, in 1841 British forces invaded the coast, taking Fujian and eastern Zhejiang. In April of 1842, they moved into Chang Jiang, and with guns pointed at Nanjing, the Qing emperor signed the humiliating Treaty of Nanjing.

The Qing dynasty was also under pressure from internal rebellions. The most serious of these rebellions was that of the Taiping, in 1850. This was, for the most part, the result of the Opium War. As one of the effects of the Opium War was to divert trade from Canton to Shanghai, the loss of employment and economic distress in Canton fueled this rebellion. This rebellion began in the Guangxi province in the South and eventually made its way as far north as Beijing. The leader of the Taiping rebellion was Hong Xiuquan. His encounters with Christian missionaries led him to proclaim himself the younger brother of Jesus Christ. The movement's ideology was heavily Christian-based. They forbade opium, tobacco, and gambling, encouraged agricultural reform, and opposed slavery, prostitution, and foot binding. In 1864, after the deaths of millions of people, the Taipings were defeated by a coalition of Qing and Western forces. The Europeans preferred a weak Qing government to a potentially stronger united China under a Taiping government.

To read about war and military affairs in China under the Tang dynasty, see the China entry in the section "Warfare" in chapter 6 ("Political Life") in volume 2 of this series.

~Dana Lightstone

FOR MORE INFORMATION

Collins, M. *Foreign Mud: An Account of the Opium Imbroglio at Canton in the 1830's and the Anglo-Chinese War That Followed*. New York: New Directions, 2002.

Hernon, I. *The Savage Empire: Forgotten Wars of the 19th Century*. Gloucestershire, U.K.: Sutton Publishing, 2000.

Tend, S., and J. K. Fairbank. *China's Response to the West*. Cambridge: Harvard University Press, 1954.

LATIN AMERICA

POLITICAL LIFE

WAR & MILITARY

United States, 1850-1865

United States, Western Frontier

Victorian England

China

Latin America

The 19th century in Latin America was a time of great upheaval as nations fought bloody wars for independence and for control over territory and populations. Autonomy introduced a new age for local leaders; independence heroes, caudillos, and military strongmen emerged as former colonial authorities abandoned the region.

The independence wars dominated the region for the first quarter of the century. In 1810, strong independence movements began in Mexico and Venezuela and quickly spread; by 1825, mainland Spanish American territories had gained their autonomy. Many Caribbean islands followed suit, except for Cuba and Puerto Rico, which remained Spanish colonies until the end of the century.

The concept of independence gained hold well before the military pushes began. Many of those who led the movements were influenced by European Enlightenment philosophers; they were particularly aware of events in France after 1789, as well as of the experiences of the United States, including the formulation of a national constitution and the development of a federal government.

Histories of the independence period in Latin America often highlight the role of particular individuals, like Simón Bolívar, who believed that declaring independence meant nothing as long as Spanish colonial powers remained on American soil. Thus, in an effort to rid the continent of colonial influence, Bolívar and other proponents of independence launched massive cross-continental operations. The army of José Francisco de San Martín, for example, marched from Argentina to Chile and Peru, and Bolívar and his troops toiled throughout northern South America.

The many years of struggle caused massive human and economic devastation; most countries took several decades to return to their prewar economic statures. Furthermore, as countries attempted to recuperate, they faced continued threats of foreign invasion. Mexico, for example, endured attacks by Spanish forces in the late 1820s and early 1830s; French forces occupied parts of the country in 1838 and again from 1862 to 1866. War with the United States (1846–48) ultimately forced Mexico to relinquish its northern territories of California, Arizona, and New Mexico. South American countries confronted similar challenges. In the 1830s and 1840s, French forces, on two separate occasions, blockaded Buenos Aires, Argentina. In the 1880s, Spain seized an island off the shores of Peru and attacked Valparaíso, Chile.

Because few Latin American nations emerged into independence with clearly defined frontiers, border ambiguities led to severe frictions and even armed conflict between neighboring governments, as each sought control over territory, populations, and resources. In the Cisplatine War of 1825, for example, Argentina and Brazil fought for possession of Uruguay. However, because neither country overpowered the other, both ultimately conceded Uruguay's independence. Forty years later, Uruguay joined forces with Argentina and Brazil in a war against Paraguay for control of the La Plata River basin. This conflict, known as the War of the Triple Alliance (1865–70), was particularly devastating for Paraguay. The war virtually eradicated the country's male population, and the five-year occupation that followed the war saw foreign forces dismantle many of Paraguay's progressive institutions. Another dispute erupted into war between 1879 and 1883, when Chile, Peru, and Bolivia fought for possession of the Atacama Desert (and its rich nitrate deposits) in what came to be known as the War of the Pacific.

In the aftermath of the independence wars, caudillos emerged to fill the power vacuum left by the retreat of colonial governments. Caudillos were local warlords or military strongmen who established strict order over extensive regions. They operated with impunity and taxed, spent, and punished as they wished. In the words of one caudillo, "I neither want nor like ministers who think. I want only ministers who can write, because the only one who can think am I, and the only one who does think am I" (Burns, 118). Many caudillos were responsible for important modernization campaigns in which they laid miles of railroad tracks, roads, and telegraph wires. Famous 19th-century caudillos include Rafael Carrera (Guatemala), Juan Manuel de Rosas (Argentina), Antonio López de Santa Anna (Mexico), and Ramón Castilla (Peru).

During the 19th century, militaries also emerged as political forces in Latin America. This trend was particularly true after the 1860s and 1870s, when governments began contracting European officers to professionalize local military institutions. These foreign visitors heavily influenced military academies like Guatemala's Escuela Politécnica, where Spanish, French, Polish, and British officers imported manuals, curricula, and procedures. They also introduced reforms in national military doctrines, instituted routine maneuvers, and encouraged arms and equipment purchases.

By the early 1900s, Latin American officers and soldiers wore uniforms, bore arms, and drilled in styles reminiscent of their European mentors.

Many officers became convinced that their armed forces could correct national defects, but their involvement in politics often had detrimental effects. Economies slowed as militaries absorbed massive proportions of national budgets. For example, in Mexico between 1821 and 1845, the military budget exceeded the total national income on 14 different occasions (Burns, 119). Militaries also stunted democratic growth because, like caudillos, they used force as the basis of their rule, tolerating no dissent or opposition.

Despite the stern hands of caudillos and soldiers, the century saw frequent uprisings. In the Caste War of Mexico's Yucatán peninsula (1847–55), the indigenous Maya population rebelled against the expanding sugar and henequen plantations, which stole their land, forced their labor, and threatened traditional lifestyles. Like these Maya, peasants throughout the region rose in violent protest, often against government imposition of new taxes and laws.

Another important source of rebellion was slavery. Indeed, it can be argued that one slave revolt in Saint Domingue (Haiti) spurred the entire region's independence. In January 1804, after more than a decade of war against French colonials, black and mulatto generals proclaimed the new state of Haiti, the first independent republic in Latin America.

> *Many Latin American officers became convinced that militaries could correct national defects.*

Freedom did not come so early for slaves in other countries. Mexico, Central America, and some South American countries emancipated slaves in the 1820s; elsewhere, slavery ended in the 1850s. Several countries—including Puerto Rico, Cuba, and Brazil—halted the slave trade in mid-century but did not emancipate slaves until much later. In Brazil, more than one million new slaves arrived before the end of the trade in the early 1850s and, because final abolition did not occur until 1888, violence increased as slaves killed slave owners, burned crops, and fled plantations.

In conclusion, the 19th century was a time of great instability. The wars of independence, along with frequent local wars and rebellions, caused much unrest. One of the few constants throughout this period was the strongman rule of first the caudillos and, later, the militaries. In fact, it was during this period that militaries laid the groundwork for their even more prominent role in 20th-century Latin American politics.

For the affect of the Latin American wars of independence on trade and regional economies, see the Latin America entry in the section "Trade" in chapter 3 ("Economic Life") in this volume.

~*Molly Todd*

FOR MORE INFORMATION

Burns, E. B. *Latin America: A Concise Interpretive History.* 5th ed. Englewood Cliffs, N.J.: Prentice Hall, 1990.

James, C. L. R. *The Black Jacobins: Toussaint L'Ouverture and the San Domingo Revolution.* New York: Random House, 1963.

Loveman, B. *For La Patria: Politics and the Armed Forces in Latin America.* Wilmington, Del.: Scholarly Resources, 1999.

Loveman, B., and T. M. Davies, eds. *The Politics of Antipolitics: The Military in Latin America.* Rev. ed. Wilmington, Del.: Scholarly Resources, 1997.

Lynch, J. *The Spanish American Revolutions, 1808–1826.* Rev. ed. New York: W. W. Norton and Co., 1988.

Nelson, R. *The Caste War of Yucatán.* Rev. ed. Stanford, Calif.: Stanford University Press, 2001.

Rugeley, T. *Yucatán's Maya Peasantry and the Origins of The Caste War.* Austin: University of Texas Press, 1996.

ISLAMIC WORLD

At the turn of the 20th century, the Muslim world was irrevocably transformed by World War I, which destroyed the long-standing Ottoman Empire, a state that had seemed so powerful throughout the 19th century. See the Islamic World entry in the section "War" in chapter 6 ("Political Life") in volume 6 of this series for a discussion of 20th-century warfare that grew out of the destruction that ended 19th-century society.

POLITICAL LIFE
|
REFORM MOVEMENTS
|
United States,
1850-1865

United States,
Western Frontier

Victorian England

Islamic World

Reform Movements

Within the continuities of any historical era are the seeds of change. Most change does not come randomly or haphazardly or coincidentally. Rather people fashion their own futures, and reform movements are central to this. In the 19th century, there were hundreds of reform movements in the United States, in England, and in other parts of the world. There are few commonalities among all these movements. In fact, many of them are quite idiosyncratic. The antebellum dietary reform movement in the United States was quite unique. People like Sylvester Graham sought to create perfect foods like Graham's cracker that would in turn create social harmony through gastrointestinal regularity. And yet, many reform movements in the 19th century were politically charged. This was certainly true of the Young Turks who formed a nationalist political movement in Turkey and eventually gained full power over the government.

Perhaps the most transformative reform movement in 19th-century United States was abolitionism. Abolitionism was a political as well as a social movement that sought to liberate black slaves and empower them politically. Moreover, to succeed, abolitionists needed to attain political power. The movement to end slavery existed in the 18th century but took on new urgency in the decades preceding the Civil War. Among its leaders were William L. Garrison and Frederick Douglass, both of whom were directly involved in other reform movements such as the pacifist and women's movements. Abolitionism had a tremendous effect, and by 1865 slavery had been eliminated, albeit at a horrific cost. Other reform movements in America began in the 19th century but had their greatest influence in the 20th. Such was the case with temperance. Reformers identified the problems that alcohol created. Prohibition was, however, decades away.

Like the United States, England also had social and political reform movements. At the center was the movement to improve or at least change the lives of the poor. In 1834, Parliament passed the Poor Law Amendment, which reorganized the ways in which the poor received aid. Nearly all people who needed public assistance were to enter the workhouse where they labored for their room and board. Workhouses had horrible reputations. Administrators made poor people's lives quite difficult, to make them not want aid. Families were split up. Labor was hard, and hours were long. The ultimate goal was to shame the poor out of relief and ideally into a more productive life. In the end, England was unsuccessful in eliminating poverty. In fact, none of the 19th-century reform movements achieved all their goals. Rather, the actions of reformers led to new historical situations and future movements for change.

UNITED STATES, 1850–65

POLITICAL LIFE

REFORM MOVEMENTS

United States,
1850-1865

United States,
Western Frontier

Victorian England

Islamic World

The majority of reform movements initiated prior to the Civil War were essentially benevolent. Philanthropic reforms focused almost solely on the visibly degraded elements of society, whose condition proved an embarrassment to the nation. These included paupers, drunkards, orphans, illiterates, Indians, slaves, prostitutes, and prisoners. Reform activities were popular primarily with the middle and upper classes and were characterized by a laudable "urge to remedy visible social ills, alleviate suffering and discourage behavior that was considered immoral." Although reform movements were common to urban areas generally, the home of reform was Boston. Many social reformers agreed that "Boston rules Massachusetts, Massachusetts rules New England, and New England rules the nation."

Above all, the most important reform movement was abolitionism. Those who identified themselves as abolitionists generally eschewed allegiance to a particular religious group, but a good number were intimately involved in their religions, particularly the newly formed sect of Unitarianism. However, those belonging to the Congregational, Presbyterian, and Quaker denominations predominated in the movement. The Methodists and Baptists were quite split over the issue, and very few Catholics rose to prominence in the largely Protestant antislavery circles. The Quaker sect was probably the most unified in its position against slavery. Yet the crusade for the immediate social and political equality of blacks was championed with a religious fervor by many men and women.

Lewis Tappan, a New York merchant, abandoned his Calvinist roots to become the treasurer of the American Unitarian Association. He was a supporter of the American Board of Commissioners for Foreign Missions and the American Bible

Society. In 1833 he established the American Antislavery Society in New York but split with the Massachusetts-based abolitionists over ancillary issues raised by Garrison. Thereafter, he worked increasingly for the Negro through the American Missionary Association and through support of the Underground Railroad.

Theodore Tilton joined the *New York Observer*, a Presbyterian weekly, in 1853. However, he found the paper's editorial attitude toward abolition lukewarm and moved on to become the editor of the *Independent*, a Congregational journal with more radical views on emancipation. Tilton turned the *Independent* into a first-class journal. He attracted writers such as E. B. Browning, John Greenleaf Whittier, and William L. Garrison, and he regularly printed the sermons of Henry Ward Beecher, the prominent pastor of the Plymouth Church in Brooklyn, New York. Tilton and Beecher joined forces in 1861 and used the paper to fight aggressively for emancipation and a more vigorous prosecution of the war. Tilton's promising career was ruined in a failed lawsuit against the preacher in which an affair between his wife and Beecher was made public.

The majority of social reformers were motivated by a genuine sense of moral obligation.

Sidney H. Gay was the editor of the *New York Tribune* from 1857 to 1865. As a young man Gay had become convinced that slavery in any form was absolutely and morally wrong. He became a member of Garrison's group of abolitionists and edited the *American Antislavery Standard* in New York from 1843 to 1857.

Many different types of people were drawn into abolitionism and other reform movements. Some community leaders opted for positions in these highly visible secular organizations solely to improve their social standing. Some obviously enjoyed the work because it satisfied their own aspirations and salved their feelings of frustration. Others crossed the lines between reform movements, working on one social ill and then another. William Lloyd Garrison, for example, began as a temperance advocate in 1828, founded the American Antislavery Society in 1833, and took up the causes of feminism and radical pacifism in the 1840s.

Much of the resistance to reform was based in a natural social inertia, but some of it was caused by the inability of the activists to articulate the scope and righteousness of their agenda to the public. The activists proved most controversial in their insistence on immediate and total reform and in their unwillingness to compromise. This was particularly true of the radical abolitionists. Moreover, reformers demanded that the government supplement intellectual persuasion with legal coercion in many areas. Nonetheless, the majority of social reformers were motivated by a genuine sense of moral obligation and national pride.

The growing popularity of the temperance movement can serve as an example in this regard. From colonial times, a moderate use of strong drink was considered acceptable by all but the most radical portions of the population. The colonial population, magistrates, and clergy, in the absence of potable water, had consumed alcohol in prodigious quantities. Nonetheless, alcohol quickly became a target of 19th-century social reformers. When Secretary of War Jefferson Davis criticized the use of a statue of the Goddess of Liberty to adorn the top of the United States Capitol in 1850, one of the proffered recommendations for a substitute was a statue of the Goddess of Temperance. While the proposal was dismissed by the officials in Washington, the temperance crusaders, undaunted by the rebuff, put their movement into high gear. The failed campaign nonetheless produced a good deal of positive propaganda. Newspapers ran stories of drunken street brawls and bitter domestic scenes brought on by alcoholic consumption. Illustrations portrayed the general doom of the drunkard in its many guises in the shadow of the unfinished Capitol.

Immigrant families, following European custom, often used alcohol as a cultural prerogative, giving beer, light wines, and rum to children to strengthen the blood and prevent disease. Nonetheless, the dangers of immoderate drinking were real, and alcoholism could end in disaster. Many men actually drank away their wages, leaving their wives and children destitute. For the alcoholic, suicide became a cliché. Strong drink was often cited as the cause for eternal damnation and earthly licentiousness, as well as spouse abuse and rape.

In fact, the temperance movement was very closely allied with women's issues and may have mirrored a rising tide of women's discontent with their place in the social order. Women took up the temperance struggle by forming prayer groups and railing against saloons with their bottles, mirrors, and portraits of reclining nudes. A melodramatic scene printed on the cover of *Harper's Weekly* in 1858 showed a young wife and children, the alcoholic head of the family missing, turned out of their tenement into the cold. Whether the mother was widowed or abandoned—there was no suggestion of waywardness or immoral propensities in her appearance—the picture emphasized, once again, the message of a close connection between women's issues and social activism on many fronts.

Alcohol was viewed as both the cause and the balm of the economic despair found among the poor in the urban slums. As the root cause of their problems, regular appearances in the local tavern with "jolly companions" were considered the "ultimate attainment of the confirmed drunkard." Conversely, temperance was equated with love, purity, truth, fidelity, marital stability, economic prosperity, social position, and religious salvation.

The temperance movement was set back for a time by the defection of activists to the abolitionist cause and the exigencies of living in a war-torn nation. Yet the temperance reformers increased the stakes of their game and insisted on total abstinence from alcohol in any quantity or strength and supplemented their demands with calls for its legal prohibition. Temperance forces succeeded in passing prohibition legislation in a half dozen Northern states, but many of these laws were subsequently found to be unconstitutional. Not until the 20th century did temperance legislation find solid ground in an amendment to the federal Constitution. This shift from moderate and sometimes symbolic goals to conclusive ones, carved into the legal fabric of the nation, was typical of many of the reform movements of the 19th century.

One of the earliest reform organizations was the Society for the Prevention of Pauperism. In a country supposedly blessed with economic abundance, it was difficult to understand the causes and conditions that led to poverty among a large segment of the population. Americans in Colonial times had adopted a calm and complacent cure for poverty. Disinclined to design large programs to relieve poverty and reluctant to lay blame upon the poor for their condition, the colonials quickly and without tedious investigation simply provided support for the destitute. This support often took the form of financial aid, food, firewood, or clothing brought to the homes of the needy. If the recipients were disabled or suffering from extreme age, the support was funneled through the households of relatives or friends.

Traditional American culture, still in vogue in the South, exhibited a broader acceptance of the poor than was found in industrialized and urbanized areas in the North. Eighteenth-century Americans, in sharp contrast to 19th-century reformers, viewed a well-ordered society as hierarchical, with each social level enjoying its own special privileges and obligations. Unfortunately this conception made the poor a permanent fixture of the social order. If the poor were "always with us," asserted the Founding Fathers, using a biblical reference to justify the continued presence of the unfortunate in a supposedly enlightened social order, then "let God be praised" for the opportunity to help them.

Southern attitudes in the 19th century continued to reflect much the same perspective. The black slave was visibly marked by God to show his natural place in the social order. The place of the laborer or the artisan in Southern society was part of the natural order, not a demeaning or disparaging imposition from which one sought to escape. Moreover, the leadership of society was equally well established in the leading families of the South as a natural consequence of God's will. Of course, the needy were much less conspicuous and more sparsely concentrated in the largely rural areas of the South in the 19th century, much as they had been in Colonial America, and the task of providing for their support under trying circumstances was thereby made less onerous.

Beginning in the 1820s, poverty came to be seen as unnatural in a bountiful America. Moreover, an implicit faith in the perfection of America left many among the socially conscious with the notion that poverty was capable of eradication if the systematic roadblocks and reluctance to change in the old order were removed.

Nonetheless, if colonials had made little effort to eliminate poverty, at least they did not punish and seek to isolate the poor. Colonial complacency quickly gave way in the 19th century to a heightened suspicion of the poor themselves. "Surely the poor were partly to blame for their own misery, having succumbed to the vice of idleness or intemperance. Yet . . . they were not inherently depraved but rather were the victims of the numerous temptations set before them by society." As religious thought became increasingly secular, God's will and the ravages of original sin no longer seemed satisfactory explanations for the condition of the poor.

Reform advocates railed against towns that licensed grog shops and saloons. They defamed politicians who allowed gambling halls and dens of iniquity to flourish. Moreover, they castigated the poor themselves. New York's Society for the Prevention of Pauperism found that most of the poor of the city required support because they were so "depraved and vicious." The poor were increasingly viewed as human raw material "to be acted upon, to be improved, manipulated, elevated, and reformed."

Of course, none of the reformers thought to ask the poor what they felt were the primary causes of their condition. The poor may have listed unfair labor practices, ethnic or religious bias, and unscrupulous landlords as causes of their plight; but they were generally quiet on the subject. The reform movement of the 19th century was characterized as one of activism of the haves for the have nots rather than a demand for reform from those who were oppressed. This form of personal protest would not become popular until late in the century.

Activists formed a sort of reform elite that not only had the conceit to decide what areas of society needed reformation but also attempted to differentiate between the worthy poor, whose lot was due to misfortune, and the corrupted and unworthy idlers. Widows with small children were almost universally viewed as worthy of public assistance. An investigatory committee in 1827 unhesitatingly reported that the vice found in large eastern cities was attributable in large part to the actions of the poor themselves. The reformers concluded that eliminating the stain of poverty from the fabric of American society would require the isolation of the poor from their sources of temptation and the instruction, by force if necessary, of the destitute in the habits of industry and labor. This grandiose plan resulted in the institution of a series of almshouses. The poor, regardless of the particular circumstances of their plight, would receive aid only while confined within the almshouse. Once inside, they would be taught order, discipline, and responsibility.

A group of New England philanthropists was assured in 1843 that the almshouse was "a place where the tempted are removed from the means of their sin, and where the indolent, while he is usefully and industriously employed . . . is prepared for a better career." Notwithstanding these assurances, the almshouses failed to relieve the problem of prolonged poverty or its symptoms. The truly depraved and corrupted among the poor avoided such institutions. Almshouses became filled to overcrowding with the helpless, the decrepit, the abandoned, and the very young. The emphasis on rehabilitation and personal reformation, initially a primary goal of the antipoverty reformers, quickly became irrelevant as the most heart-rending members of the poor community were hidden behind brick walls. A committee in New York reported in 1857 that the general conditions found in such institutions had degenerated into a cruel and punitive system of custodial care.

> *The poor would receive aid only while confined within the almshouse.*

Social conservatives, North and South, particularly deplored the development of free public schools that admitted children from many class, ethnic, and family backgrounds and inculcated in them a set of novel values that stressed social equality. The development of the public schools was paralleled by the institution of a Catholic school system in the immigrant-filled cities of the North. Such notions were seen as a threat to traditional fundamental values and represented a clear danger to the status quo, to be avoided at all costs.

The dimensions of the schemes put forth by the reformers of the 19th century were exceeded only by the depth of their failure. The poor remained in their crime-ridden environment, alcohol flowed freely until the 20th century, and the freed slaves remained on the bottom rung of social and economic life. Yet, despite the incongruity between the utopian ideals of the reformers and the consequences of reality, mindless social tinkering and disgraceful forms of public altruism persisted and proliferated until well after the Civil War. Only the uncompromising conviction of the reform activists of the correctness of their self-proclaimed solutions to America's social ills, and their unrelenting hounding of public officials, could have kept such failed social experiments in existence (Volo and Volo, 40–46, 85–86).

To read about reform in the United States in the 20th century, see the United States entries in the section "Reform" in chapter 6 ("Political Life") in volume 6 of this series.

FOR MORE INFORMATION

American Memory. <http://memory.loc.gov/ammem/amhome.html/>, accessed July 24, 2003.

Burns, K. *The Civil War*. PBS Video, 1990. Film.

McPherson, J. M. *Battle Cry of Freedom: The Civil War Era*. New York: Oxford University Press, 1990.

Volo, D. D., and J. M. Volo. *Daily Life in Civil War America*. Westport, Conn.: Greenwood Press, 1998.

POLITICAL LIFE

|

REFORM MOVEMENTS

|

United States,
1850-1865

United States,
Western Frontier

Victorian England

Islamic World

UNITED STATES, WESTERN FRONTIER

Humanitarian reform movements in the West often focused on American Indians. Most army officers did not develop such an "ideology of hostility" toward the Indians; rather, aware of the "fraud, corruption, and injustice" they had suffered, officers were, as a class, ambivalent toward their foes. On the one hand, they felt "fear, distrust, loathing, contempt, and condescension"; on the other, "curiosity, admiration, sympathy, and even friendship." The eastern humanitarians, for the most part, were less ambivalent, many pointing to the Sand Creek Massacre (which was not the work of the regular army) as a chief illustration of why the military could not be trusted to civilize and to help the Indians. Most of them were equally certain about what they wanted the Indian to become: a peaceful, Christian farmer, demonstrating the Puritan work ethic, living within the law on his own plot of land, and aspiring to U.S. citizenship. This goal, they believed, could best be accomplished by civilians—missionaries, teachers, and government officials of good moral character.

Such reformers who hoped to subdue the Indian by kindness initially found encouragement during the Grant administration. In 1873 the secretary of the interior set forth a comprehensive peace policy in which government and churches would cooperate to bring the benefits of civilization to Indians on reservations. By the end of the 1870s a set of priorities had emerged, supported by secretaries of the interior, commissioners of Indian affairs, and Christian reformers. These included the following:

to put Indians to work as farmers or herders, thereby weaning them from their "savage life" and making them self-supporting;

to educate young people of both sexes in order to "introduce to the growing generation civilized ideas, wants and aspirations";

to allot parcels of land to individual Indians, not to the tribe, in order to foster individual pride of ownership rather than tribal loyalty;

to dispose of surplus reservation lands remaining after individual titles had been obtained, with the money from sales to be used to provide for Indians' expenses; and

to treat Indians like all other inhabitants of the United States under the laws of the land.

The Christian reformers were firmly convinced that Indians were capable of civilization and that it was the injustice or inefficiency of government that had impeded the process. However, they lacked any appreciation of Indian culture and approached their mission with "an ethnocentrism of frightening intensity."

Ironically, many army officers—Nelson A. Miles, George Crook, even George Armstrong Custer—had a better understanding of Indian culture than did these reformers. General Miles, for one, counseled patience: "Accustomed as they were from childhood to wild excitement of the chase, or of conflict. . . . taught that to kill was noble and labor degrading, these Indians could not suddenly change their natures and become peaceful agriculturists." Preferring to avoid war and to bring hostiles into reservations without another campaign, Crook went so far as to argue for decent treatment of those he had known as adversaries. Addressing the West Point graduates of 1884, he concluded:

With all his faults, and he has many, the American Indian is not so black as he has been painted. He is cruel in war, treacherous at times, and not over cleanly. But so were our forefathers. His nature, however, is responsive to treatment . . . based on justice, truth, honesty and common sense. It is not impossible that the American Indian would make a better citizen than many who neglect the duties and abuse the privileges of that proud title.

This debate between hardliners and peace advocates culminated in a debate as to whether the Department of the Interior or the War Department should be in charge of the Indians' acculturation. Most thinking people felt that it mattered less which manifested control than that the vacillations and contradictions in policy cease. The editor of the *Army and Navy Journal*, having analyzed the effects of ambivalence, concluded, "We go to [the Indians] Janus-faced. One of our hands holds the rifle and the other the peace-pipe, and we blaze away with both instruments at the same time. The chief consequence is a great *smoke*—and there it ends" (Jones, 241–42).

FOR MORE INFORMATION

Jones, M. E. *Daily Life on the Nineteenth Century American Frontier.* Westport, Conn.: Greenwood Press, 1998.

Multicultural American West. <http://www.wsu.edu:8080/~amerstu/mw/>, accessed July 24, 2003.

Prucha, F. P. *The Great Father: The United States Government and the American Indians.* Abr. ed. Lincoln: University of Nebraska Press, 1986.

VICTORIAN ENGLAND

Societies need some way to look after people who cannot take care of themselves and have no family to do it. The system used in England before 1834 dated from

POLITICAL LIFE
|
REFORM MOVEMENTS
|
United States,
1850-1865

United States,
Western Frontier

Victorian England

Islamic World

the time of Queen Elizabeth I. Each parish had to provide for its own poor by means of taxes, or poor rates, paid by residents who owned or rented property over a certain value. Not only was the system inefficient, but also it varied widely from place to place depending on the capability of local officials and the amount of money they could collect. Because parishes did not want to spend their funds on people who were not, strictly speaking, their own responsibility, poor people who had been born in some other parish were often simply told to move on.

> *People could not leave the workhouse during the day.*

The Poor Law Amendment Act of 1834, commonly called the New Poor Law, entirely reorganized the administration of welfare. The 15,000 or so individual parishes were combined into 643 unions. Each union was to build a workhouse. Under the New Poor Law, "outdoor relief" in the form of money and food for people who stayed in their own homes was available only for the elderly and disabled. It was meant to provide a supplement that would help their families look after them. All other persons who needed public assistance were to enter the workhouse, where they would do suitable labor in return for their food and housing.

Despite its horrible reputation, the New Poor Law workhouse was in some ways better than the earlier system. A single parish, before 1834, might put all the people who could not care for themselves in one place: orphans, unemployed adults, the elderly, the sick, the disabled, and the mentally incapacitated were all mixed together and for the most part left to tend each other. In a union workhouse, where there were far more people, the various groups could be given separate lodging and appropriate treatment.

The other core principle of the New Poor Law was, however, the concept of less eligibility. Administrators (known as poor law guardians) were ordered to be sure that people in the workhouse had a less eligible standard of living than the poorest working people outside. The idea was to make the workhouse so unpleasant that people would take any job at all rather than ask for relief. People were put into separate wards by age and sex. Families were split up and elderly couples divided from each other. In the earliest years, parents did not have the right even to see their children. People could not leave the workhouse during the day and come back at night; those who claimed public assistance went into the house and stayed there until they had some way to support themselves outside. Most workhouses required everyone to wear coarse clothes of some distinctive and uniform color. Smoking and drinking were forbidden. Outsiders could visit only during limited hours and in the presence of a matron or master. The New Poor Law union workhouse was often the first large public institution to be built in a town; it loomed on the outskirts as a massive, high-walled, and forbidding presence.

The inmates, under supervision, did the labor of running the workhouse. Women cooked, cleaned, and sewed. People who did nursing and certain unpleasant jobs such as burying the dead were paid with a ration of tobacco or alcohol. Finding enough work for able-bodied men was a problem. Most workhouses assigned them to boring and laborious tasks such as breaking up stones to make gravel for road mending. Elderly people were set to picking oakum, which involved teasing apart matted ropes so the hemp could be used by the navy for caulking ships.

This labor did not train people for employment: it was simply a deterrent, designed to make people think twice about claiming relief. Yet it was soon evident that Parliament was wrong in assuming there were a lot of loafers who had to be discouraged from going on public assistance. Only about one-fourth of the pauper population, it turned out, consisted of able-bodied adults. The separate wards of the workhouse began to develop into separate institutions. By the end of the century there were public hospitals for the chronically ill; asylums for the mentally handicapped; schools for blind, deaf, and disabled children; homes for the elderly; and other appropriate public institutions for people incapable of self-support.

Orphanages and children's homes were among these new institutions. They took in both children whose parents were dead and children whose parents could not support them. Boys were taught a trade such as carpentry or shoemaking; girls were prepared for domestic service. There were also training ships to supply naval recruits. Indeed, pauper children received more schooling than many outside the workhouse system. Overseers of the poor felt they needed an extra boost to become self-supporting adults. They were not sent out on their own until they were 15 or 16 years old, although children outside the workhouse often worked full-time starting at the age of 12.

In fact, despite the official tenet of less eligible, most workhouse administrators did not allow the paupers in their charge to be as overworked and malnourished as the poorest laborers. They wanted able-bodied people to obtain jobs and stop living on the public dole, which meant they had to be healthy enough to work. Before going into the workhouse, people were supposed to exhaust their own resources, which included selling everything they owned. This rule was not enforced, especially when breadwinners were ill; they were allowed to keep the tools and clothing they would need to go back to work when they recovered. Local authorities also discovered that providing outdoor relief briefly in cases of temporary unemployment was much less expensive than housing whole families in the workhouse.

But although the New Poor Law never worked as uniformly as intended, the stigma attached to going into the workhouse was deliberate. It was designed not only to discourage loafers but also to encourage prudence. To avoid the workhouse, women would marry before having children. Poor families would avoid having more children than they could support. People would save money to provide a cushion in case they became ill. Grown children would make sacrifices to look after their elderly parents.

The workhouse was especially hated for dividing couples who had been married for many years. (Most people thought it was a good idea to separate younger residents by sex so women would not be victimized by men. Even in the case of married couples, the reasoning went, if they could not support the children they already had, why should they be allowed to produce more?) Another source of loathing was the fear of dissection: by law, medical schools could be given the body of anyone who died in the workhouse unless it was promptly claimed by relatives who could provide a burial. Most of all, perhaps, people feared the workhouse because of its disgrace.

Some historians believe that the New Poor Law did help diminish pauperism—people who had any other recourse at all avoided the workhouse at whatever cost. In addition, there was an expanding market for unskilled labor in the mid-19th century, and several organizations helped able-bodied poor people emigrate to Australia and North America. The workhouse was a terrible idea, however, for dealing with people who were temporarily unemployed because of illness, layoffs, or family problems. And the lingering stigma of the workhouse created a sense of humiliation among people who needed to ask for help.

Two other aspects of the workhouse system need to be mentioned. Its infirmary served as a public hospital or nursing home for people with long-term illnesses. There were hospitals run by charities and medical schools that treated poor people at little or no cost, but most of them only admitted patients who were likely to be cured. Very few hospitals took patients in the last stages of tuberculosis, which was the most frequent cause of death during the period. The workhouse infirmary was a hospital for the poor and a hospice for people who had no family available to do the nursing.

The workhouse also had (often in a separate building) a casual ward, which gave food and lodging for one night (or, in some cases, three nights) to people with no money and no fixed place of residence: tramps, poor people walking to another part of the country to seek work, seasonal labor, seamen who had spent their pay and were heading back to port for another ship, or navvies moving from gang to gang. The casual ward also served as an occasional shelter for the urban homeless who did not want to claim relief because they preferred to live on the streets. They would take a night's lodging once in a while when they wanted to escape bad weather and get a morning meal (Mitchell, *Daily Life*, 91–95).

FOR MORE INFORMATION

Best, G. *Mid-Victorian Britain, 1851–1875*. London: Weidenfeld and Nicolson, 1971.

Crowther, M. A. *The Workhouse System, 1834–1929: The History of an English Social Institution*. London: Batsford Academic and Educational, 1981.

Mitchell, S. *Daily Life in Victorian England*. Westport, Conn.: Greenwood Press, 1996.

Mitchell, S., ed. *Victorian Britain: An Encyclopedia*. New York: Garland Press, 1998.

POLITICAL LIFE
|
REFORM MOVEMENTS
|
United States,
1850-1865

United States,
Western Frontier

Victorian England

Islamic World

ISLAMIC WORLD

During the 19th century the Middle East underwent major political reform. Simultaneously, several movements struggled to undermine the existing political order; in particular, to overthrow Colonial rule. One of the most important ways that Muslims have tried to meet European challenges is through nationalism.

One of the earliest of these movements, which had perhaps the greatest impact on Islamic and world history, was Turkish nationalism. Although the Europeans called the country Turkey, during the 19th century neither the rulers, nor the subjects of the Ottoman Empire identified themselves as Turks. The reason for this is that the Ottoman Empire was a Muslim state. It was created by a Turkish dynasty, and many Turks supported the Ottoman rule. The language spoken by most people in this area was a form of Turkish that was heavily influenced by Persian. The surrounding areas also heavily influenced the administration and culture. Most people in Turkey considered themselves either Ottomans or Muslims.

Beginning around the late 1860s, upper-class, liberal reformers attempted to build a new Ottoman nationality that would unify all the different communities in the empire. However, the nationalism that they chose was heavily Muslim. Members of the Turkish Christian community generally opposed these ideas and attempted to define themselves within a separate Christian Turkish identity.

The loss of virtually all of the empire's European provinces by the end of the 1870s changed the nature of the Ottoman state, and thus the nature of the Turkish reform movement. For the first time in several centuries an Ottoman sultan found himself ruling an empire that was overwhelmingly Eastern and Islamic. Around this time the Ottoman government made a conscious decision to stress the realm's Islamic identity.

As a result, the identity of reformers changed. Sultan Abdul Hamid forbade the involvement of many of the old reformers who were formally aligned with the Ottoman establishment. However, Abdul Hamid's efforts to strengthen the empire and his own rule paved the way for a new generation of liberal nationalist reformers. He built schools and encouraged modern education, including technical education and Western philosophy. As a result, many of the students became infiltrated with modern ideas and thus became opponents of the sultan's regime, particularly his strategy of absolutism.

There were many nationalist movements at this time, but arguably the best organized and most widely known is the Young Turks movement. Members of this organization were generally from lower or lower-middle-class backgrounds. Unlike earlier reformers, they were not interested in maintaining Ottoman culture, including the Turko-Persian language. They were mostly from an ethnic Turkish background and defined Ottomans as Turks, not Arabs. This was the main element in their creation of a Turkish identity, separate from the Ottoman state.

Dissatisfaction surfaced not only in Turkey, but also throughout the entire region. In Macedonia, the most valuable remaining part of the empire, nationalities were extremely mixed, and a viable solution to nationalist pressure was particularly difficult. Revolt movements, some Muslim, some Christian, filled the area. It became clear that if there were no Ottoman regeneration soon, the disorder in Macedonia would result in the downfall of the entire Ottoman Empire.

In 1905, Europe forced the Ottoman government to reform the administration of Macedonia and to make the government less autonomous. After this the Young Turks made connections with dissatisfied groups and some government officials in Macedonia's chief city, Salonika. They were successful in gaining support because many people in Macedonia were dissatisfied with the weakness of the sultan's government and fearful of the loss of more important territory.

A few years later the Committee of Union and Progress staged a revolt in Macedonia. The army, instead of suppressing the revolt, joined in the cause. The committee was then able to overthrow the government and installed a new government.

However, the establishment of a new type of government met several obstacles. First, the surrounding territories attacked the revolution, out of fear that the new government might also attempt to move in on their territory. Second, the government faced a lot of internal opposition. Most people wanted a more decentralized government in which they could have more say.

Finally, the structure of the new Ottoman government itself was extremely disorganized. There was no clear leadership. The Committee of Union and Progress gave the greatest support to the new government. However, this organization was not the government. Kamil Pasha, the grand vizir, was not a Young Turk nor did he want anything to do with this organization. He viewed their leadership role in the revolution as merely accidental.

The Young Turks were in a dangerous position, where they would either seize control or be completely pushed aside. Using their strong influence and representation in Parliament, they were able to push Kamil Pasha out of office. This inspired a conservative uprising in the capital. In the aftermath of the uprising the Committee of Union and Progress and the army emerged as leading forces in the new government.

While the new government was a parliamentary democracy, modeled after the governments of England and France, it was far from liberal in ideology. Many of the authorities of the various regions of the empire were the same people who were in office in the time of Abdul Hamid. As in the past, they used force in reaction to any sort of political agitation or unrest.

Because there was so much internal dissatisfaction, the region was extremely chaotic for the next few years. This caused the Europeans to attack. The Italians seized Libya, then Bulgaria. Serbia and Greece attacked Turkey. Albania declared independence. When all was said and done, the empire lost all of its European provinces with the exception of Thrace.

The Young Turks emerged stronger than ever and soon gained control of the government. At this time it became evident that without the European provinces, mainly ethnic Turks inhabited the empire. The nationalism put forth by the Young Turks, who were ethnic Turks within a larger Muslim identity, was accepted now more than ever before.

To read about reform in the Islamic World in the 20th century, see the Islamic World entry in the section "Reform" in chapter 6 ("Political Life") in volume 6 of this series.

~Dana Lightstone

FOR MORE INFORMATION

Gocek, F. M., ed. *Social Constructions of Nationalism in the Middle East*. Albany: State University of New York Press, 2002.

Hanioglu, M. S. *Preparation for a Revolution: The Young Turks*. Oxford: Oxford University Press, 2001.

Karsh, E. *Empires of the Sand: The Struggle for Mastery in the Middle East, 1789–1923*. Cambridge, Mass.: Harvard University Press, 1999.

POLITICAL LIFE: WEB SITES

http://www.stvincent.ac.uk/Resources/WMidPol/1880/index.html
http://www.crimelibrary.com/jack/jackmain.htm
http://www.orange.k12.oh.us/teachers/ohs/tshreve/apwebpage/readings/juvcrime19cbr.html
http://www.royalty.nu/Asia/China/TzuHsi.html
http://www.wponline.org/vil/Books/SH_CA/chapter_4.htm
http://www.yale.edu/lawweb/avalon/19th.htm
http://www.fredericksburg.com/CivilWar
http://sunsite.utk.edu/civil-war/warweb.html

7

RECREATIONAL LIFE

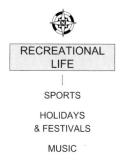

RECREATIONAL
LIFE
|
SPORTS

HOLIDAYS
& FESTIVALS

MUSIC

LEISURE TIME

Several activities define recreational life. They range from music to organized sports to leisure time games to the celebration of holidays and festivals. As in all centuries, recreation was a central part of daily life in the 19th century. And yet, the Victorian Age made its unique historical contributions. Indeed, the English had a particularly important influence on a lot of recreation, particularly music, games, and leisure time play. Play is serious business. All mammals play, but humans have cultivated recreation into a high art. After family and work, most of our energies and time are devoted to recreational activities, and as any modern sports enthusiast knows, we play with as much passion as we work. What are recreational activities? There are several characteristics that all play shares: First of all, it is voluntary—one can't be forced to play. As such, it is in fact the very essence of freedom, and even slaves and prisoners treat themselves to games or music or dance for the sheer voluntary quality of the activities. Second, recreation is also outside of real life, limited in time, duration, and space. Thus, playtime by contrast almost defines work time; recess at school not only offers a break from study, it marks the serious times when one is to learn. Third, recreation has its own rules that are more rigorous and predictable than anything we can find in our more complex real lives. At the end of the game—and there is a definitive end—there is a winner and loser, and the rules are clear. Of course, cheating is always a possibility (archaeologists have even found loaded dice in Anglo-Saxon settlements), but even unsportsmanlike conduct is recognizable. It may be that we love games precisely for the clarity of the rules. Finally, recreational life builds a group identity among the players, and this is true even of individual sports like archery or bicycling, for archers see themselves as linked with others who share the pastime.

While recreational activities in the 19th century, such as games and sports, share these general characteristics with recreational activities from all centuries, the particular forms of recreation that they chose shed light on who they were and what they valued. In play, they prepared themselves for the rest of their lives. For examples, games on the American western frontier, such as sharpshooting, honed skills for war, while Indian, American, and English folk music stimulated creativity and honored the past. Violent sports from dogfights to boxing allowed participants to face violence in life, and team sports like football and baseball prepared them to work together in an economy of separation of skills. Importantly, the holidays that they celebrated point to their cherished values. In India for example, despite the British colonial occupation, traditional holidays such as Diwali or Deepavali celebrations (which generally last five days) went on as normal, thus providing a link to the precolonial past and providing a clear statement about the limits of the colonial government. Nineteenth-century recreational activities also illuminate the class relationships in places such as England, India, and the United States. In England, for example, the kinds of music one sang and played often depended on one's social class. It was not just a matter of the fact that the upper classes had access to better instruments. Working-class musicians had cheaper instruments, but they also performed music about their lives, their hardships, their dreams, and their realities. As the section on economic life in this encyclopedia suggests, these aspects of life differed by class. Similarly, sports in the United States changed dramatically, becoming professional and corporate. In so doing, professional athletes began the process of separating themselves materially from amateurs. Finally, all aspects of recreational life in India had a caste dimension. Games, holidays, music, and leisure time activities varied greatly by the social group into which one was born. As in other aspects of daily life, accident of birth had a significant role. Thus by studying the recreational life of 19th century people, we can more fully understand the societies in which they belonged.

FOR MORE INFORMATION

Bethel, E. R. *The Roots of African-American Identity: Memory and History in Free Antebellum Communities.* New York: St. Martin's Press, 1997.

Ehrlich, C. *The Music Profession in Britain Since the Eighteenth Century: A Social History.* New York: Oxford University Press, 1985.

Huizinga, J. *Homo Ludens: A Study of the Play Element in Culture.* Boston: Beacon Press, 1964.

Pal, P., ed. 2000, *Reflections on the Arts in India.* Mumbai, India: Marg Publications, 2000.

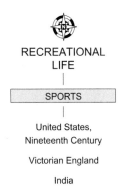

RECREATIONAL
LIFE

SPORTS

United States,
Nineteenth Century

Victorian England

India

Sports

As far as we can tell, humans have always loved sports. Even today, or perhaps even more so today, people spend much of their daily lives thinking, talking, watching, and participating in athletic competition. Almost all cultures have had some sort of spectacle. The Greeks had the Olympics. The Romans had their circuses and blood sports. The Maya had their ball courts. And in the history of sports, the 19th century is an important 100 years. Organized sports, particularly in America and England, underwent a transformation ultimately leading to professionalization. Some aspects of sports did not change. Playing games has always been one way in which social groups have learned to divide themselves.

In America, during the 19th century, sports in essence grew up. At the turn of the century, public games had more of a colonial feel and were heavily influenced by folk traditions. Fishing, sharpshooting, and rail splitting were the popular games. In cities, sports such as billiards had many devotees, but largely from the working class. In fact, in America as in other countries, what sports one liked or practiced had a lot to do with class. Middle- and upper-class Americans did not want to be seen participating in what they saw as lower-class rabble. Track, boating, and football were for the elite. Moreover, as athletic clubs developed especially after the Civil War, rules were laid down. By the end of the century, American football was nearly in its modern form. Baseball too had modernized. Based on the English game rounder, baseball had developed its own rules, struggled to become respectable (e.g., umpires originally wore top hats and tails), and formed leagues. By the turn of the century, baseball was America's sport, and it reflected American social values. The middle- and upper-class sponsors of baseball frowned on the working-class demand for cold beer at the games. Moreover and significantly, baseball, like nearly all American sports, was segregated between blacks and whites.

Compare these two themes of American sports—professionalization and social discrimination—with the essays on England and India, and one will find commonalities. In England, many famous sports adopted formalized rules and a clear organization. Take football (known as soccer in the United States). From 1840 to 1860, men from public schools set up a uniform code so that they could play against each other without disagreement about the rules. The first professional teams were gathered in the 1860s and the Football Association was established in 1863. Players of rugby (a form of football), tennis, and cricket experienced similar trends.

English organized sports did include working-class players, but the associations and even the teams often had a decidedly upper-class composition. In fact, it was a common practice to organize one's rich friends and hire a few working-class teammates who were known for their athletic skill. Such class distinctions were evident in America and other places such as India.

Traditional Indian games had a caste flavor. For example, competitive fishing was for the members of the mullah, or fisher caste. Similarly, hunting cheetah or rhinoceros was a sport for the elite. When England conquered India, the elite tended to adopt English games. Tennis was reserved almost exclusively for the rich. Cricket was initially an elite sport, but its popularity soon grew well beyond that social group. Eventually cricket became a sort of national sport for India, and Indian nationalists in the struggle for independence used it as a source of pride. To this day, cricket as well as soccer competition between England and its former colonies represent much more than a mere game. They represent a chance for the formerly subjugated to defeat the colonial power.

UNITED STATES, 19TH CENTURY

In 19th-century America, sports varied considerably along geographic, class, and racial lines. Thus what sporting activities one participated in often depended on

RECREATIONAL
LIFE

|
SPORTS
|
United States,
Nineteenth Century

Victorian England

India

who one was and where one was. In this, social games in America in the 1800s resembled those of the past. Yet, sports changed greatly during the century. By 1900, commercialized sports as well as modern forms of popular games like baseball and football had arrived.

On the frontier of the United States, sports clung largely to folk traditions. Organized events and associations were not common. In many ways, sports on the frontier had a certain colonial flavor. Spectacle remained largely an eastern U.S. phenomenon. Rather, in the West, games came from daily life and labor. Since fishing and hunting were matters of survival, contests such as shooting and angling were quite popular. Rewards for besting one's neighbor included a turkey, a side of beef, or a jug of whiskey. Other games were quasi-athletic, such as rail splitting and wrestling. These folk games remained popular in rural areas well into the 20th century.

In the 1870s, professional hunters traveled West to kill buffalo. Often the buffalo meat went unused and was left to rot. © Library of Congress.

In the growing urban industrial areas of the United States, sports took on a different structure that relied heavily on class and race. The importance of class can be seen in an experience of John Quincy Adams, the sixth president of the United States and son of the second president, former revolutionary John Adams. On May 25, 1825, John Quincy Adams bought a used billiard table for $50 and brought it into the White House, spending many nights playing pool with friends. Adams's desire to play billiards turned into a national controversy. Congress was outraged. One newspaper editor explained why: "When we find the fathers and matrons of our country engaged in persuading young men from practices which lead to destruction, we greatly fear that the too frequent answer will be, 'Why, the President plays billiard!'" Billiards was a lower-class game, not fit for the upper class. In fact, many games from bowling to cards to darts that could be played in a saloon flaunted Victorian social norms of hard work, religious duty, and self-control. From the view of the upper and middle classes, playing working-class games was in essence joining the unproductive rabble.

Working-class sports often centered on the saloon. Billiards was quite popular as was boxing, cockfights, and racing. Fights often drew the largest crowds. Few accounts survive of the men who engaged in rough-and-tumble fighting, the pervasive form that involved kicking, biting, hair-pulling, gouging (tearing the opponent's eye out of its socket), and balloching (emasculation). There are some legends about Southern planters who pitted their slaves against those of neighboring plantations. One such legend involves Tom Molyneux, a Virginia slave, who fought his way to freedom at the turn of the century by defeating another slave.

Middle- and upper-class sports, which are better documented, had some relationship with those of the working class. However, they generally were not as bloody and usually were more commercial. Also, the sports of the rich were better organized. In cities along the East Coast and in the Midwest, sporting clubs began to spring up in the 1850s. Initially there were cricket clubs, racquet clubs, and athletic (i.e., track and field) clubs. Slowly even these clubs developed a class distinction as yacht clubs required the money of older, more elite families. Nonetheless, these urban sporting clubs brought public spectacle to cities. For example, in the 1870s, the New York Athletic Club built the first cinder track in the United States and sponsored national amateur track-and-field events and later it sponsored national boxing, wrestling, and swimming events.

While rich fathers attended genteel sports events, their sons at college attended and participated in their own aristocratic games. Aside from rowing, or crew, the intercollegiate sport that became quite popular in the late 19th century was football. Originally a folk game, football took on a new importance on the campuses of Harvard, Princeton, Yale, and other elite schools. Although still in a nascent stage not far from rugby and soccer, football was popular. In 1876, students from Columbia, Harvard, Princeton, and Yale founded the Intercollegiate Football Association and adopted rules governing the game. Initially, touchdowns counted for one point and kicked goals for four. Later other numerical values were added such as the safety (two points), field goal (five points), and a goal following a touchdown (2 points). Other rules and strategies that modern fans of the game would recognize were the work of Walter C. Camp, a legendary Yale football player and coach, whose Yale teams amassed an amazing collective record of 324 victories, 17 losses, and 18 ties.

Despite the growth in football's popularity, the dominant national sport was baseball, a sport whose social rules demonstrated the class and racial antagonisms of the 19th century. Like football, baseball's traditions go back to a simple English folk game called rounders. Contrary to the myth, General Abner Doubleday had absolutely nothing to do with the invention of the game. In fact, the game was well established before Doubleday took an active interest in it. In 1845, Alexander Cartwright, a New York bookseller, organized the Knickerbocker Base Ball Club. The popularity of the club's games encouraged others to form their own teams. The matches themselves faintly resembled the modern game. For example, the umpire was not placed behind home plate but rather sat at a table along the third base line and was dressed in tails and a black top hat. In 1858, about 50 clubs formed the National Association of Base Ball Players, an organization that dramatically increased the game's visibility. It was not always popular as charges of gambling and fixed games (known as hippodroming) frequently followed the games and teams.

In 1876, baseball began to take on its modern appearance when a few men led by William A. Hulbert, president of the Chicago baseball club, founded the National League of Professional Base Ball Clubs. Charter teams came from Boston, Chicago, Cincinnati, Louisville, Hartford, St. Louis, Philadelphia, and New York. The National League was dominated by owners and not players. In fact, the league was largely a cartel that controlled the movement and salaries of players. Upset at the system that denied them the lion's share of the profits from commercial baseball, many players broke out of the National League in 1889 by forming the ill-fated Players League, which lasted only a season. The National League's dictatorial rules and methods chaffed some others the wrong way and led to the expulsion of the Cincinnati club for selling beer at its games. Cincinnati's baseball club then organized the American Association of Base Ball Clubs, known now as the American

League but known then as the Beer Ball League as four of the six clubs were closely associated with breweries.

One of professional baseball's features in the 19th century was that it banned virtually all black players. There were a few examples of teams that had one or two African Americans but most clubs upheld a lily-white standard. It was not until 1945 when Jackie Robinson signed with the Montreal Royals, a minor-league affiliate of the Brooklyn Dodgers, that the racial barriers in professional baseball began to change.

Black players formed their own leagues, as well as their own athletic associations, and had their own stars like Moses Walker, a phenomenal baseball player. Integration was exceedingly difficult to maintain. Initially, for instance, the League of American Wheelmen accepted black bicyclists. But in the 1890s, Southern whites threatened to leave the league if it did not exclude African Americans. Bowing to Southern white pressure, the wheelmen's association adopted a whites-only membership policy. Still, America's best biker, Marshall W. "Major" Taylor, a black from Indianapolis, broke record after record in national events. White conspiracies to exclude Taylor failed as promoters and bicycle manufacturers found it profitable to market the "fastest bicycle rider in the world."

In 19th-century America, as sports evolved, they took on both geographic, class, and racial characteristics. Sports also began to be a national and commercially viable industry. Baseball's development surely illustrates this, as do others sports like boxing. In fact, if America had one national sports hero in the 19th century it would be John L. Sullivan, the "Boston Strong Boy," whose career made the sport of boxing a national obsession. In the 1880s, he toured the United States offering the gigantic sum of $1,000 to anyone who could go four rounds with him. Sullivan carefully avoided all black boxers, particularly Peter Jackson, who could have knocked him out. In 1889, in a nationally covered bout, Sullivan met his match in Jake Kilrain. Their bare-knuckle contest went 75 rounds before the referee awarded the match to Sullivan. By the end of the next century, the sport would be even more commercialized, even more of a spectacle. But athletes like Sullivan would be a thing of the past as sporting life became integrated.

To read about sports in the United States in the 20th century, see the United States entries in the section "Sports" in chapter 7 ("Recreational Life") in volume 6 of this series.

~Andrew E. Kersten

FOR MORE INFORMATION

Betts, J. R. *America's Sporting Heritage*. Reading, Mass.: Addison-Wesley, 1974.
Black Baseball Players. <http://www.blackbaseball.com>, accessed July 24, 2003.
Peterson, R. *Only the Ball Was White*. Englewood Cliffs, N.J.: Prentice-Hall, 1970.
Rader, B. G. *American Sports: From the Age of Folk Games to the Age of Spectators*. Englewood Cliffs, N.J.: Prentice-Hall, 1983.

VICTORIAN ENGLAND

Sports were a crucial aspect of English daily life. Participation in organized games began early in life as parents believed that athletics helped their children grow. Sports at English public schools and universities developed the manly code of character: team spirit, loyalty, and a stiff upper lip unmoved by triumph, defeat, or pain. Men who took part in matches between Oxford and Cambridge earned a blue (the equivalent of a letter in U.S. school sports). Originally a ribbon, it was dark blue at Oxford and light blue at Cambridge. The Oxford-Cambridge boat race, a competition between eight-man crews, took place in late March or early April. The Henley Regatta, during the first week in July, was first held in 1839. In addition to being a major outdoor event of the London social season, Henley was an occasion for serious competition between club, school, and university crews.

Most of the sports that have been central to 20th-century international competition were codified and professionalized in England during the 1800s. The game that the rest of the world calls football (known as soccer in the United States) was standardized between 1840 and 1860. Men from various public schools created a set of uniform rules in 1848 so they could play against each other (or play on the same college or army team) without constant disagreements. Local soccer clubs not connected with any school were formed, and before long some of them had paid players.

The first fully professional teams developed in the 1860s. The Football Association, founded in 1863, initially regulated competition for both amateurs and professionals. As the workweek grew shorter and railways made it easier for large crowds to attend games, the professional clubs built their own grounds and charged admission. With the formation of the Football League in 1885, the structure of soccer as a professional spectator sport attained virtually its modern form.

Rugby football grew out of a disagreement over the Football Association's rules. Men from some public schools (including Rugby) where the ball could be handled as well as kicked refused to accept the newly codified form of the game. They also did not like it when working-class professionals were allowed to join the gentlemanly amateur clubs where grown-up schoolboys continued to play games. Thus although rugby is far more violent than soccer, it remained throughout most of the 19th century essentially an amateur sport for aristocrats and the gentry.

Cricket was played in public schools, at universities, and by village and country-house teams formed when young men home for the summer recruited local boys to join them for games. (Cricket requires 11 players on each side.) County clubs emerged in the 1860s. They were made up of gentlemen and players; that is, they combined local amateurs with a few working-class men hired for their athletic skill. The pay was originally intended simply to make up for the wages a man lost when he stayed away from work for a match that could last several days.

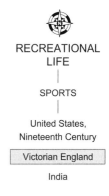

RECREATIONAL
LIFE
|
SPORTS
|
United States,
Nineteenth Century
Victorian England
India

This picture from the book *Outdoor Games and Recreations for Boys* shows popular sports for Victorian men in the 1890s.

Cricket is played on a roughly oval ground that can vary in size. The game's most important field, Lord's (in London), is 180 yards long and 140 yards wide. (Nineteenth-century matches also took place on military parade grounds, village greens, local pastures, and other open spaces.) Two wickets are placed 22 yards apart along the centerline of the oval. Each wicket is made of three stakes (or stumps) 28″ high that are stuck into the ground with two wooden sticks (called bails) balanced in grooves along the top. One team of 11 players is spread out around the field, while one batsman from the other team takes up a position in front of each wicket. The ball is bowled alternately a certain number of times (it varies with the level of play) from a position behind one wicket toward the batsman who defends the other wicket.

The object for the bowler (i.e., pitcher) is to dislodge the bail from its position on top of the wicket. When he does so, the batter is out. The batter's object is (1) to protect the wicket, and (2) to hit the ball hard enough so he can score a run by reaching the other wicket before the ball is fielded and thrown back into play. (When one batter hits the ball, both must run; they change positions at the wickets.) As many as six runs can be scored on one hit. There are many subtleties in fielding and scoring; in essence, one inning lasts until 10 batsmen have been put out, and the game is won by the side with the highest total number of runs.

The county championship in cricket (which is still being held) was regularized in 1873, and test matches between England and Australia (which serve as cricket's world championship) began in the 1880s. Some school matches—especially the one between Eton and Harrow—were also crucial dates in the athletic year. Cricket takes a long time to play; matches may be spread over several days. Except at the highest levels of professional competition, spectators are as much engaged by the summer sunshine, the conversation, and the refreshment tent as they are by the action.

Tennis, once an indoor game for royalty, was revived by the Victorians as a family pastime for people with large enough lawns. The net was higher than it is now, and the racquets more like those used for badminton. Both serves and volleys were done in a gentle underhand. As the game grew popular, people with no lawns banded together and built suburban tennis clubs. Good players came to appreciate the smoother, standardized club courts. The All-England Lawn Tennis and Croquet Club, founded in 1869, became the governing body of tennis and began organizing championship tournaments at its grounds in Wimbledon in 1877.

England's Amateur Athletic Association was founded in 1880 to organize university and club championships in athletics (usually called track and field in the United States). Athletic contests were strongly promoted by public schools and the military; because many events required little space and no equipment, they were also popular at factory outings and country fairs. Some elementary schools had an annual sports day with footraces and jumping contests.

In addition to sponsoring meets, the Amateur Athletic Association standardized events, kept records, and helped organize the first modern Olympic competition in 1896. Records from that event show the difference made by training, equipment, and improved general health during the past hundred years. The 100-meter dash that opened the 1896 Olympics was won in a time of 12.5 seconds. The marathon was completed in 2 hours 58 minutes, and the winning high jump was 5′ 11 1/4″. In the 1990s, a good marathon time was 2 hours 12 minutes, and high-school boys could do a 7′ high jump and a 10.8-second 100-meter dash.

Horse racing, unlike most sports, was already well established before the 19th century began, but official regulation was consolidated when the Jockey Club became the governing body for British racing in the 1860s. Races were held more often because horses could be moved by rail instead of having to be walked from course to course. In the 1870s, racecourses were enclosed and stands were built.

Special bank holiday fares toward the end of the century brought enormous crowds to racetracks. Like certain other traditional pastimes, racing was patronized chiefly by aristocrats and working men; few among the middle classes and very few respectable women went to the races. The four-day meeting at Ascot in June, however, was a central feature of the social season, attended by upper-class women and men wearing their most elegant summer clothes.

This illustration from the May 1899 edition of *Pall Mall Magazine* shows women enjoying bicycling. Courtesy of Paley Library, Temple University.

The Derby, a race for three-year-old horses, is run at Epsom Downs in Surrey in late May or early June. Derby Day was an unofficial public holiday in the 19th century. Even Parliament suspended business. There was as much activity outside the racecourse as on it; many people came primarily for the sideshows, food, and general excitement. The Grand National Steeplechase (a race for hunters, with a variety of hurdles, ditches, and other jumps) was first run at Aintree near Liverpool in 1839.

Racetrack and offtrack betting were commercialized during the Victorian period. (Individuals have presumably always made private bets with friends.) When professional bookmakers opened city offices, many people who had seldom gone to the track started making regular bets and followed the racing papers. Telegraph connections enabled major bookmakers to post results almost instantly. Like racing itself, betting on the races was not a respectable thing for women or middle-class men to do.

Boxing also united men of the aristocracy and lower classes while excluding almost everyone else. The brutal bare-knuckle sport—which gave spectators a chance to place bets on a battle that lasted until one fighter could not stand up—was modernized with rules endorsed by the Marquess of Queensberry in 1867. Boxers were required to wear padded gloves; matches ended if one fighter could not rise unaided after a count of 10. The Amateur Boxing Association was founded in 1880. Weight classes were set up toward the end of the century; the first heavyweight championship fight, in 1892, matched James L. Corbett and John L. Sullivan (Mitchell, *Daily Life*, 217–21).

To read about sports in Chaucer's England, see the entry on Europe in the section "Sports and Games" in chapter 7 ("Recreational Life") in volume 2 of this series; for Elizabethan England, see the entry on England in the section "Games and Sports" in chapter 7 ("Recreational Life") in volume 3 of this series; for 18th-century England, see the entry on England in the section "Games" in chapter 7 ("Recreational Life") in volume 4 of this series.

FOR MORE INFORMATION

Harris, H. A. *Sport in Britain: Its Origins and Development.* London: Paul, 1975.
Mitchell, S. *Daily Life in Victorian England.* Westport, Conn.: Greenwood Press, 1996.
Mitchell, S., ed. *Victorian Britain: An Encyclopedia.* New York: Garland Press, 1998.

RECREATIONAL
LIFE
|
SPORTS
|
United States,
Nineteenth Century

Victorian England

India

INDIA

There are several traditional Indian sporting activities, such as hunting and fishing, but it is the British who introduced competitive sports in India. Cricket is the only of these sports to become widely popular among Indians. Polo was popular among the English in India and some members of the elite Indian class. Horseback riding was also introduced, but as for competition, it was only common among a small, elite sector of society. Tennis was also reserved for the most elite members of Indian society. Soccer did not become popular until recently.

Hunting was mainly an activity reserved for the elite, in particular the royal families. The royal families had a responsibility to protect the people from wild beasts. If it was reported that a cheetah, a rhinoceros, or some other creature was attacking livestock or chickens, it was the responsibility of the royal family to hunt down the animal. Even as children the young regional princes and princesses rode on elephants and hunted with large rifles. Often the slain beasts were stuffed and displayed in the royal palace.

Fishing, on the other hand, was a sport mainly reserved for members of the low mullah, or fisher caste. Members of this community are born into this profession. Fishing was considered an unclean profession or activity.

In areas where there was a community of English people, there was often a gymkhana club. The word gymkhana is derived from the Hindi *gendhana*, which means ball house. In these clubs English people and elite Indians played tennis, squash, badminton, table tennis, and billiards. Horses could sometimes also be hired for riding, and some gymkhana clubs, particularly those in the hills where the climate is cooler, also had outdoor skating rinks.

The British introduced cricket in the early colonial period. It is played with a wicket, similar to a baseball bat, only flat instead of rounded. A ball is pitched, similar to in baseball, only the pitcher intentionally makes the ball bounce before reaching the batter. The wicket is then swung low to the ground to hit the ball. The person who has just hit the ball runs.

The first recorded cricket match, which took place in the western state of Gujarat, was played in 1721. The participants were mostly English men stationed in India, and a few Indians, newly introduced to the game also joined in.

Because Calcutta was the seat of British power in the early colonial period, this was the first area where cricket clubs were formed. The Calcutta cricket club is the second oldest in the world, following the M.C.C. of London. However, it was mostly the English who played on these teams, and the matches that they participated in did little to attract local people to the games. Calcutta cricket was English cricket.

As the British consolidated their power throughout India and became increasingly present in Bombay, cricket spread to the west coast of India. By the early 19th century cricket had caught on among many Indian people in Bombay, particularly those of the Parsi religious community. There is no explanation as to why the game was more attractive in this region and among this community. There is evidence that it was through an English schoolteacher who taught cricket to his young students that the game first became popular among the residents of Bombay.

In 1848 a group of Parsis formed the Oriental Cricket Club. Some of the great plans that this organization had included coaching its team members by professionals from England and overseas tours. However the club was dissolved only two years later.

Soon after this a few other teams sprang up around Bombay. These were also formed by members of the Parsi faith. By the late 1850s these teams competed and held their own against British teams in India. Their enthusiasm for the game spread to other communities in Bombay, as well as throughout India. It became clear that cricket was quickly becoming a national pastime.

As early as 1877 there was talk of some of the teams touring England and Australia to compete. A visit to England materialized in 1886. The playing results were poor. The Indian team won only 1 game in 28. They lost 19 games and drew the rest. Two years later, when they visited England again, the results were far better. The Indian team won 8 of their 31 games, lost 11, and drew the rest.

These matches were a major transitional point, when enthusiasm for cricket grew more than ever before. Members of other religious groups became involved in cricket, and, in the midst of the early stages of the struggle for independence from England, cricket became a source of great nationalist pride.

~Dana Lightstone

FOR MORE INFORMATION

Bose, M. *A Maidan View: The Magic of Indian Cricket*. London: Allen and Unwin, 1986.
Docker, E. W. *History of Indian Cricket*. Delhi, India: Macmillan Co. of India, 1976.

LATIN AMERICA

People readily adopt each other's sports in the course of globalization, and this was true in Latin America during the 19th century. As the political influence of Europeans and North Americans slowly receded from Latin America in the 19th century, it paved the way for Latin Americans to make their own impact on European sports. See the Latin America entry in the section "Sports" in chapter 7 ("Recreational Life") in volume 6 of this series for the results of this fruitful and fun cultural exchange.

Holidays and Festivals

Daily life can certainly be monotonous. Working every day digging for gold or cleaning chimneys or taking charge of a household (while rewarding personally or materially) can leave one craving something more. Regardless of their religious or political importance, holidays and festivals have the effect of changing the pace of daily life, and as a result people look forward to them. That said, it is important to note that like other aspects of daily life, holidays and festivals were shaped by race, class, and ethnicity.

In the 19th century the old holidays were still cherished. In America, Christmas was universally popular. It gave soldiers on the western frontier something to look forward to, and in England, it was a day (as Charles Dickens significantly pointed out) for family and a day without work. Similarly in India, traditional holidays and festivals maintained their importance. Despite the introduction of a colonial power and its culture, Diwali or Deepavali celebrations (which generally last five days) went on as normal.

Although many people clung to their holiday traditions, they also bore witness to the creation of dozens of new holidays during the century. In the United States, new holidays were closely linked to the most powerful historical event of the 19th century, the Civil War. After the war there were competing remembrances. In fact there were two general Memorial Days, one in the North and one in the South. Eventually, there was only one Memorial Day and it reflected the conservative mood of the times. No African Americans were allowed to partake in the celebrations. A similar social fight broke out between the radical labor festival (May Day) and the conservative one (Labor Day). Again the conservatives won, as Labor Day became the official worker holiday in America. In England and India, holidays changed too, but not as profoundly as in America. For instance, in England, holidays were expanded. By the end of the century, there were several more days off from work than there had been in 1800. In Latin America, festivals and celebrations were often multicultural, a combination of the African, European, and indigenous traditions that comprised the society of the region. Latin American holidays were also often multipurpose, mixing religion, national celebrations, and life cycle rituals.

When reading and comparing these entries, pay specific attention to the ways holidays and festivals both unite and separate people. In particular, look for race, class, ethnicity, and geography as categories for analysis.

UNITED STATES, 1865–1900

While Americans still cherished and celebrated their two main public holidays, the Fourth of July and Washington's Birthday, they added nearly two dozen more during the 19th century, particularly in the period after the Civil War. These holidays did not illustrate any consensus or general social harmony. Rather, they raised con-

406

tentious and at times divisive political, racial, class, and ethnic issues. American holidays in the 19th century, however, did have some common themes. Nearly all stressed middle-class values and patriotism.

Ultimately Memorial Day became a celebration to unite much of the nation. However, at first, there were two dueling holidays, one in the North and one in the South. White Southerners used Memorial Day to commemorate fallen Confederate soldiers. The origins of the holiday tell us as much about stoic Southern masculinity as about their construction of femininity. In 1862, as the story goes, Confederate soldier Charles J. Williams of Columbus, Georgia, died of disease. Out of feminine duty, his wife and young daughter buried him at home and every day brought flowers to his grave. Although the story about Williams is apocryphal, it nevertheless started the tradition of Southerners visiting Confederate graves. Although the holiday quickly spread throughout the South, former Confederates and their families never settled on one universal day. In fact there were at least eight Memorial Days celebrated from April 26 to June 13.

Like the Southern holiday, the Northern Memorial Day had key parts played by women and children, particularly orphans. And like the South's, the North's holiday began at church with sermons and service and then traveled to the cemetery for decorations, rhetoric, taps, and 21-gun salutes. Northerners felt that their holiday was the national one and fought to end Confederate celebrations by uniting America under one Memorial Day to be celebrated in late May. Eventually, through the work of the Grand Army of the Republic, an association of Union Civil War veterans, the federal government recognized Memorial Day in 1876. Southern participation in the holiday was secured after both Southern and Northern whites began to exclude African Americans from the commemoration.

Like Memorial Day, Emancipation Day had a lot to do with the nature of race relations in late 19th-century America. Initially, the holiday, which celebrated the freeing of the slaves and the struggle for full citizenship, was integrated. Blacks and whites who had supported the end of slavery joined together on various days in various states to laud the actions of Abraham Lincoln and the Republican Party. Typically, at these gatherings, middle-class values were also touted. In 1890, for example, at the Richmond Emancipation Day, John Mitchell, Jr., editor of the *Richmond Planet*, told the gathered crowd to "educate your children, buy property, be religious . . . [and] cultivate in [your children] a spirit to work." The politicians, ministers, entrepreneurs, and various professionals who led similar processions gave messages like Mitchell's. By 1890, Emancipation Day was largely a black holiday as whites turned to Memorial Day to remember the Civil War. Within the black community, there was not a consensus however. Although January 1 was designated as the universal holiday date, celebrations continued on different days from January 1 to June 19, or Juneteenth, the day that African Americans in Texas learned of their emancipation.

Social divisions were evident in another set of holidays created in the 19th century. Labor Day and May Day were (and still are) competing working-class celebrations. May Day is the older of the two. In 1867, Chicago labor unions sponsored the first May Day to lobby for an eight-hour working day. By the 1880s, May Day was connected to other labor demands as well as socialist politics. More conservative labor unionists, particularly in the American Federation of Labor, who opposed socialism invented another worker holiday, Labor Day, which is celebrated in September. Labor Day was more of a contained celebration in which tradesmen showed off their crafts and ideas on floats. Holiday celebrations were generally segregated by race (if not exclusionary) and stressed patriotism and, by the end of the century, commercialism as unions rented out their floats to businesses for advertisements. In 1894, the federal government made Labor Day a legal holiday. May Day, which is still associated with more radical politics, became an unofficial holiday, eventually more popular outside the United States than inside it.

In addition to holidays that were at the nexus of class, race, and politics, there were also new ethnic holidays. Most immigrant groups celebrated at least one national holiday. Poles in America had several that commemorated their failed constitutions, uprisings against the Russians, and leaders such as Tadeusz Kosciuszko, the Polish George Washington. Irish Americans honored St. Patrick and other official and unofficial saints and martyrs. Filipinos gathered to honor the 1896 execution of José Rizal by the Spanish, and the Czechs celebrated Jan Hus, the 15th-century Reformation leader who promoted the Bohemian language and opposed the Germanization of Bohemia. American Jews celebrated many holidays from Passover to Chanukah to Lag b'Omer, which commemorated a Jewish revolt against the Romans. Two characteristics seem to unite the various immigration holidays: the active role of children in the celebrations and middle-class values. An example of the latter can be drawn from the Mexican American fiesta honoring St. Augustine. Traditionally, the holiday had two parts, a solemn two days of church services and three weeks of raucous partying. But in the 19th century, middle-class Mexican Americans began to criticize festive vice. By the end of the century, Mexican American leaders had replaced the partying with another holiday celebrating Mexican independence. This event became a model of orderly patriotism and middle-class virtue.

The growth of ethnic holidays occurred at the same time as an increase in American patriotic holidays. At the end of the 19th century, reformers who sought to Americanize immigrants and instruct the young in good civic ideals invented several new celebrations such as Constitution Day, Columbus Day, and Lincoln's Birthday. Although immigrants tended to ignore these commemorations, schoolteachers did not. In fact, the most popular patriotic holiday of the era, Flag Day, was originally designed for students. Teachers found these public days a perfect time to instruct their pupils in proper civic virtue.

As the creation of Flag Day demonstrates, American holidays in the 19th century were not lighthearted affairs. Rather, serious political and social issues lay at their roots. Whether Americans gathered to remember the Civil War, commemorate Emancipation, or celebrate workers, the holiday itself was a contentious and sometimes divisive event whose end result was not to unify the nation but to express a certain political sensibility. In this, 19th-century Americans were not that much different from 21st-century Americans.

To read about holidays and festivals in the United States in the 20th century, see the United States entries in the section "Leisure" in chapter 7 ("Recreational Life") in volume 6 of this series.

~Andrew E. Kersten

FOR MORE INFORMATION

Bethel, E. R. *The Roots of African-American Identity: Memory and History in Free Antebellum Communities*. New York: St. Martin's Press, 1997.

Litwicki, E. M. *America's Public Holidays, 1865–1920*. Washington, D.C.: Smithsonian Institution Press, 2000.

Newman, S. P. *Parades and the Politics of the Street: Festive Culture in the Early American Republic*. Philadelphia: University of Pennsylvania Press, 1997.

Ryan, M. P. *Civil Wars: Democracy and Public Life in the American City during the Nineteenth Century*. Berkeley: University of California Press, 1997.

UNITED STATES, WESTERN FRONTIER

Holidays and festivals were an important aspect of frontier daily life. Despite the fact that the trip to the Pacific and back was arduous and often dangerous, the Corps of Discovery maintained morale by celebrating—sometimes spontaneously, sometimes on special holidays. At a place they named Independence Creek, they celebrated in 1804 the first Fourth of July west of the Mississippi. At sunrise and at sunset they fired the swivel gun mounted aboard the keelboat. Though the day was somewhat marred when Joseph Field was bitten by a rattlesnake, Captain Meriwether Lewis treated him with a poultice of Peruvian bark, which drew out the poison. That evening an extra gill of whiskey was issued to all hands. (The usual daily ration was one gill. Lewis had bought all the whiskey that could be carried without sacrificing other important supplies, but it was not enough to last the trip, even when watered down.) The last of it was poured to celebrate July 4, 1805, a sad moment indeed, though while they were descending the Columbia one of the party, J. Collins, improvised and presented them with "verry good *beer* made of the Pa-shi-to-quar-mash [camass] bread" that had repeatedly gotten wet and had thus gone moldy. In the interim the captains occasionally issued an extra ration to maintain morale. For example, on the evening of Reed's court martial, August 18, which was also Lewis's birthday, "the evening was closed with an extra gill of whiskey and a Dance untill 11 o Clock."

Lewis and Clark were conscious of the need for entertainment. On April 26, 1805, when they reached the junction of the Yellowstone River, Lewis wrote, "much pleased at having arrived at this long wished for spot, . . . in order to add in some measure to the general pleasure . . . [of] our little community, we ordered a dram to be issued to each person; this soon produced the fiddle, and they spent the evening with much hilarity, singing & dancing, and seemed as perfectly to forget their past toils as they appeared regardless of those to come." On Christmas Day 1804, the cannon was fired three times as the flag was raised and everyone was served a ration of rum. Some men went out to hunt while others spent the day dancing. Though they were now at Fort Mandan, "the Savages did not Trouble us as we had requested them not to come as it was a Great medician [medicine] day with us," wrote Sergeant Ordway.

The second Christmas, at Fort Clatsop, was far more bleak. At sunrise the soldiers woke the captains with a rifle volley and song. Then they exchanged presents. Clark received a pair of moccasins that one private had made and a woven basket from another; Sacajawea gave him two dozen white weasel tails; and Lewis gave him a vest, underdrawers, and socks. The captains, though keeping some tobacco for future trade with the Indians, distributed half of it among the men who smoked; the non-smokers each got a handkerchief. Aside from that, the day, like most of their stay on the Pacific, was miserable. Clark wrote, "We would have Spent this day the nativity of Christ in feasting, had we any thing either to raise our Sperits or even gratify our appetites, our Diner concisted of pore Elk, So much Spoiled that we eate it thro' mear necessity, Some Spoiled pounded fish and a few roots."

Although the Corps of Discovery celebrated Christmas 1804 alone, they shared that winter's New Year's celebrations with the Mandans. They visited one of the villages where they entertained their hosts with Private Cruzatte's fiddle playing. One soldier danced on his hands, but the central attraction was York, Clark's servant, who especially fascinated the Indians. They were astonished that so "large a man should be so active"; moreover, they were suspicious of his color, and some of them tried to rub off the black.

Several days later the Mandans invited the garrison to join them for the buffalo dance. Held in the communal earthen lodge, the dance began to the music of rattles and drums. The old men, dressed in their best, ceremoniously arrived and seated themselves in a circle. Soon the young men, accompanied by their wives, filed in and took their seats in an outer circle behind the elders. Following a smoking ceremony the young men, one by one, offered their young wives, who presented themselves naked to the old men. As Clark then described the ceremony, "the Girl then takes the Old man (who verry often can Screcely [scarcely] walk) and leads him to a Convenient place for the business, after which they return to the lodge." The purpose of the ceremony, Clark notes, "is to cause the buffalow to Come near So that They may kill them." Because the buffalo migrated great distances during the winter in search of grass, the Mandan held the buffalo dance to attract them. Moreover, the Mandan believed "that power—in this case, the hunting abilities of the old men—could be transferred from one man to another through sexual relations with the same woman." The Americans, thought by the Mandans to have "great good luck and big medicine," benefited. They too were offered young women, and many participated in the ceremony with extraordinary zeal. Four days later the Mandan had a good buffalo hunt.

Although their relations with the Mandans were the most prolonged, Lewis and Clark also recorded social activities with other tribes along their route. While among the Nez Percé, they enjoyed watching and occasionally participating in horse races; "several of [these Nez Percé horses, wrote Clark] would be thought swift horses in the atlantic states." This was high praise from a Virginian. In addition, Clark records the men whiling away the time before they could cross the Bitterroot Mountains by holding "foot races . . . [between] the men of our party" and the Indians, "after which our party devided and played at prisoners base untill night." After dark there was fiddle music and dancing.

Breaking the monotony for miners were days set apart for celebration and meditation. Many companies had written into their articles of incorporation mandatory stops for Sunday. This was not, however, a day of true rest. "The men were generally busy mending wagons, harness yokes, shoeing the animals etc. and the women washed clothes, boiled a big mess of beans, to be warmed over for several meals, or perhaps mended clothes. . . . If we had devotional services the minister-pro-tem stood in the center of the corral while we kept on with our work."

In contrast, the Fourth of July was marked almost universally by patriotic celebration. Most companies, heavily armed, used the Fourth as an excuse to fire their guns. The Buckeye Rovers fired a gun for every state in the Union and one for California and the gold diggings. In the excitement, one of the Rovers shot off his thumb. Many companies reached the Rockies around the Fourth. One made punch and cooled it with a lump of snow from a snowbank. Another made ice cream and flavored it with wild peppermint. Another company, after a 13-gun salute at sunrise, slept in. This luxury was followed by a formal ceremony: a prayer, a reading of the Declaration of Independence, an oration, and music including "Hail Columbia" and "The Star Spangled Banner." Dinner included "ham, beans, boiled and baked, biscuits, john cake, apple pie, sweet cake, rice pudding, pickle vinegar, pepper sauce and mustard, coffee, sugar and milk." After the dinner, the toasting began. "The boys had raked and scraped together all the brandy they could, and they toasted, hurrayed, and drank till reason was out and brandy was in." Later the boys danced by moonlight. Many suffered hangovers on July 5 (Jones, 65–66, 130).

To read about holidays and festivals on the colonial frontier of North America, see the entries on the colonial frontier and New England in the section "Holidays" in chapter 7 ("Recreational Life") in volume 4 of this series.

FOR MORE INFORMATION

Ambrose, S. E. *Undaunted Courage: Meriwether Lewis, Thomas Jefferson, and the Opening of the American West.* New York: Simon & Schuster, 1996.

Holiday, J. S. *The World Rushed In: The California Gold Rush Experience.* New York: Simon & Schuster, 1981.

Jones, M. E. *Daily Life on the Nineteenth Century American Frontier.* Westport, Conn.: Greenwood Press, 1998.

VICTORIAN ENGLAND

As in America, holidays and festivals were a changing aspect of daily life in the 19th century. Preindustrial workers lived by the rhythms of an agricultural year.

Some traditional rural customs vanished during the 19th century, but others were transformed: their disruptive pagan elements became more modest. Whereas the older May Day rituals built up to dancing in the fields and a night of sexual liberty, the Victorians tamed the holiday and made it into a children's festival, with young girls in white dresses decorating a maypole in front of the church. Guy Fawkes bonfires (on November 5) and Christmas mumming (in which elaborately disguised men and boys performed plays featuring sword fights or mock battles) also survived, but in less rowdy forms than previously existed.

Many formerly popular country sports came to an end because Victorian reformers perceived their cruelty. Badger baiting (setting terriers on a penned badger), bull-baiting, and cockfighting were outlawed. A form of football (known in America as soccer) once played on Shrove Tuesday pitted one whole village against another with few rules and no tactics: the game was a mob shoving bout that often led to a riot. Squires and clergymen turned their energy to arranging village sports competitions with organized teams and rules that would keep things from getting out of hand.

In Lancashire and other northern areas, traditional "wakes" involved feasting and games on a summertime saint's day. Whitsun (the seventh Sunday after Easter) was often a two-day festival. By 1800, although some parish fetes survived, the wakes became a short summer holiday. Mills closed down; machines were cleaned and repaired while mill hands went off in groups to the seashore. Working-class Londoners enjoyed a late summer excursion by taking the whole family into Kent and camping out in the fields while everyone earned money by picking hops.

The local public house (pub) was the center of most workingmen's recreation. During the 19th century, the cramped drinking space in an individual householder's front room was increasingly replaced by grand new premises. In addition to the public bar (which served as living room and meeting room for men from the neighborhood), there might be a separate room for billiards and darts, a reading room with newspapers, and a parlor where women and children could get refreshments.

In 1841, the only holidays for banking and government workers were Christmas Day and Good Friday. Later, the Bank Holiday Act of 1871 added the day after Christmas, Easter Monday, the last Monday in May, and the first Monday in August. Other employers soon followed suit. The two summer Mondays—not linked to any religious or patriotic celebration—made for long weekends of outdoor fun. Clubs and Sunday schools hired wagonettes for group excursions; families made quick railway trips to the seashore. Mothering Sunday (the fourth Sunday in Lent) had by custom been a day when young servants were given extra time to go home for a visit. Boarding schools picked up the idea and scheduled a spring break for that week, although Mothering Sunday did not become commercialized as Mother's Day until the 20th century.

The most significant holiday change was the Victorian transformation of Christmas. Since the 17th century, Christmas had been a simple religious holiday for most respectable people, although old traditions such as the Yule log and mummers' plays survived in some places. Families who exchanged gifts at any time during the winter season did it on New Year's Day.

Prince Albert brought the German custom of decorated Christmas trees to the family celebrations at Windsor. Christmas cards grew popular after the penny post was established in 1840. By the 1860s, the middle-class English Christmas had taken shape. From late November, luxury goods filled shop windows and booksellers displayed piles of Christmas books and holiday annuals, which were a kind of gift book with poems, stories, and handsome illustrations. Grocers heaped their shelves with fruits, nuts, and sweets. Soon geese and turkeys hung in the chilly air outside the butcher shops. Working people saved for their holiday meal by putting a few pence every week into a Christmas club at a pub or local market; if they had no oven, the goose would be cooked at the baker's shop.

The Christmas pudding had to be made several days in advance. Mrs. Beeton's recipe calls for raisins, currants, mixed peel, breadcrumbs, suet, eggs, and brandy. A silver threepenny piece and some other charms were hidden in the pudding. Every member of the family took a turn at stirring the batter. Then it was pressed into a buttered mold, tied into a piece of cloth, boiled for six hours, and hung up in the kitchen to age.

Christmas Eve was a time for carols and family gatherings. After the children went to bed, their presents would be arranged by the tree and their stockings would be filled with nuts, an orange, chocolates, and a small gift or two. On Christmas Day, after the children had their stockings, many families went to church and did some act of charity—taking food to a poor family or distributing gifts in a children's hospital.

This front cover illustration from the *Illustrated London News* for Christmas 1876 demonstrates growing English nationalist pride. Note the flags on the top of the tree. Courtesy of The Library Company of Philadelphia.

The traditional Christmas dinner was roast goose with potatoes, applesauce, and other side dishes. (Turkey was more expensive.) At each person's place was an English Christmas cracker—a cardboard tube covered in crepe paper or tissue paper tied at the ends. When the ends were pulled, the cracker opened with a pop and spilled out candies, small favors, and a paper hat. As a climax to the meal, brandy was poured over the pudding and lighted; the flaming pudding was carried to the table. After it was served (with sweet custard or hard sauce), the hidden charms engaged everyone's attention. Who would get the ring and marry during the year? Who would find the silver piece and become rich, or the button and remain a bachelor?

The day after Christmas was known as Boxing Day because coins or boxes of cast-off clothing were traditionally distributed to the poor. In Victorian times, it became a servants' holiday. Domestic servants who lived nearby went home for a visit; their employers ate leftovers and recovered from Christmas dinner. Other families organized a treat or party; in some large houses there was a servants' ball. City dwellers gave tips to the lamplighter and postman and delivery boys; in the country, landowners sent game to their tenants and sponsored a treat for the parish Sunday school.

Another new Christmas tradition involved a family visit to the pantomimes that began their annual run on Boxing Day. In its Victorian form, the pantomime was a musical revue with elaborate production numbers. Its plot was loosely based on a fairy tale or other familiar story such as "Dick Whittington" or "Aladdin." The principal boy was played by an attractive actress (in tights and a tunic that showed off her legs), and the role of dame (the stepmother or wicked witch) was always played by a man, usually a well-known comedian. By the century's end, the pantomime had become a principal source of income for theaters and a magical family outing enjoyed by people of virtually every social class (Mitchell, *Daily Life,* 209–13).

To read about holidays and festivals in Chaucer's England, see the Europe entry in the section "Festivals and Holidays" in chapter 8 ("Religious Life") in volume 2 of this series; for 18th-century England, see the entry on England in the section "Holidays" in chapter 7 ("Recreational Life") in volume 4 of this series.

FOR MORE INFORMATION

Miall, A., and P. Miall. *The Victorian Christmas Book*. New York: Pantheon Books, 1978.
Mitchell, S. *Daily Life in Victorian England.* Westport, Conn.: Greenwood Press, 1996.
Mitchell, S., ed. *Victorian Britain: An Encyclopedia*. New York: Garland Press, 1998.

RECREATIONAL
LIFE
|
HOLIDAYS
& FESTIVALS
|
United States,
1865-1900

United States,
Western Frontier

Victorian England

India

Latin America

INDIA

In India there are several different religious groups, and each has its own set of holidays. Hinduism, which is the religion of the majority of India's population, varies greatly from region to region. As a result there are several regional holidays practiced by Hindus from various communities, often in honor of a particular local deity. Most of the holidays follow the Indian lunar calendar, which is a highly complicated system based on astrology. Prior to independence there were no national holidays, although postindependence India celebrates many such holidays.

The most widely celebrated Hindu holiday is Diwali, also known in some regions as Deepavali. This is celebrated on the 15th day of the month of Kartika, which falls in October or November of each year. The festival is traditionally dedicated to the god Krishna, although various regions also celebrate other gods at this time. For example, in Mumbai the goddess Lakshmi is celebrated, while in Calcutta the goddess Kali plays a major role in the festivities.

The festival lasts for five days. On the first day houses are cleaned and doorsteps are decorated with intricate chalk designs. The second day is dedicated to Krishna's victory over Narakasura, a legendary tyrant. In some areas of India, particularly in the far south, it is common for people to take an oil bath on the morning of the second day, and then to put on brand new clothing. The third day is devoted to the worship of Lakshmi, the goddess of fortune. Day four is in remembrance of the mythical visit of the friendly demon Bali. On the fifth day men generally visit their sisters and a ceremony takes place in which the sister puts *tika*, or crimson powder, on the forehead of her brother.

Each night oil lamps are hung throughout the streets to show Rama the way home from his period of exile. This story comes from the *Ramayana*, which tells the story of Rama's mythical retreat into the woods, and his journey back to his kingdom.

During the British period Diwali gradually became a gift-giving holiday, similar to Christmas in countries with a large Christian population. Giving and receiving of sweets is common during Diwali, and more recently among many communities a large plethora of material objects are received and exchanged on this holiday.

Another major Hindu holiday is Dussehra, celebrated in Asvina (September/October). This is a 10-day holiday celebrating Durga's victory over the buffalo-headed demon Mahishasura. In some areas it begins with the burning of images of the demon king Ravana and his accomplices. This symbolizes the triumph of good over evil. In some areas it has a different name. In Calcutta the festival is known as Durga Puja. In parts of southern India, and in Gujarat it is known as Navaratri, and takes place over only nine days. In Delhi it is known as Ram Lila (Life of Rama), and is celebrated with large processions and reenactments of the Ramayana.

Another Hindu holiday is Sri Ramanavami, which celebrates the birth of Rama. Sri Ramanavami falls in the lunar month of Chaitra, which falls in March or April. In the week leading up to this holiday the *Ramayana* is widely read.

Rath Yatra, which falls in Asadha (June/July), celebrates Krishna's journey to visit his aunt. On this day representations of Krishna and his two siblings are paraded through the streets on chariots.

Raksha Bandhani, which is in Sravana (July/August), is when girls make amulets to tie around the wrists of their brothers and male cousins to protect them in the coming year. The boys reciprocate with gifts.

Shavan Purnima, in the month of Bhadra (August/September) is a day of fasting for high-caste Hindus. On this day Brahmin men replace the sacred thread that they always wear over their left shoulder with a new thread.

Pongal is a Tamil festival celebrated for the most part only in the southern Indian state of Tamil Nadu. It marks the end of the harvest season. It is observed on the first day of the Tamil month of Thai, which is in the middle of January. On the first day *pongal* (a mixture of rice, sugar, lentils, and milk) is made to symbolize prosperity in the next harvest season. On the third day the cattle are washed and decorated with colored paint, and then fed the pongal. In the state of Andra Pradesh a similar festival known as Makar Sankranti is celebrated at this time. Onam, the most important festival of Kerala, is celebrated after the autumn harvest is gathered. The festival commemorates the early visit of the ousted legendary King Mahabali, whose reign witnessed great prosperity. Onam is celebrated with, among other things, feasting, gifts, and snake-boat racing.

Holi, which is mainly celebrated in northern India, takes place in the month of Phalguna (February/March). On this day, in celebration of the end of winter people throw colored water and powder at one another.

Shivaratri, a few weeks after Holi, is the day of Hindu fasting dedicated to Shiva, who, according to myth, danced on this day when the world was first created. Chanting of mantras, or religious hymns, follows processions.

Muslim holidays follow the Islamic calendar, which falls about 11 days earlier each year. One major Muslim holiday is Milad-un Nabi, which commemorates the birth of Mohammed. This holiday takes place in May or June, and is celebrated in areas with a large Muslim population.

Id-ul-Fitr celebrates the end of the Muslim month of fasting, known as Ramadan. This generally falls between December and January. Id-ul-Zuhara commemorates Abraham's attempt to sacrifice his son Isaac in the Old Testament. It generally falls in February or March.

The biggest Jain holiday in India is Mahavir Jayanti, which falls in March or April. It celebrates the birth of Mahavira, who was the founder of Jainism. An important Sikh holiday is Nanak Jayanti, which takes place in November or December, and marks the birthday of Guru Nanak, the founder of the Sikh religion. Christmas and Easter are celebrated in areas with a large Christian population.

Buddha Jayanti takes place in May or June and celebrates the Buddha's birth, his enlightenment, and his achievement of nirvana. Processions of monks carrying sacred scriptures pass through the streets in heavily Buddhist areas. Drukpa Teshi, in August or September, celebrates the first teaching of the Buddha. Celebrations are similar to those of Buddha Jayanti.

To read about holidays and festivals in ancient India, see the India entry in the section "Holidays, Festivals, and Spectacles" in chapter 7 ("Recreational Life") in volume 1 of this series.

~*Dana Lightstone*

FOR MORE INFORMATION

Hall, D., and J. Viesti. *Celebrate in South Asia.* New York: Lothrop, Lee and Shepard Books, 1996.

Thomas, P. *Festivals and Holidays of India.* Bombay, India: D. B. Taraporevala and Sons, 1971.

RECREATIONAL
LIFE
|
HOLIDAYS
& FESTIVALS
|
United States,
1865–1900

United States,
Western Frontier

Victorian England

India

Latin America

LATIN AMERICA

Festivals and celebrations were a motley mix in 19th-century Latin America. They were often multicultural, a combination of African, European, and indigenous traditions. They were also often multipurpose, mixing religion, patriotism, and life cycle rituals.

One of the most famous festivals of Latin America, Carnival, illustrates well this mix of traditions. Celebrated in most Spanish American countries, Brazil, and much of the Caribbean, it was a pre-Lenten event (from the Latin *carne vale*, or "farewell to flesh") that also incorporated African and indigenous traditions.

In Recife, Brazil, *carnaval* included the *maracatú* procession. During colonial times, slaves elected their own royalty and ambassadors to serve as intermediaries between masters and slaves. New rulers were crowned in lavish ceremonies that included a lively *maracatú* procession into town. Figurines of African animals led the parade, with the king, queen, and court following, stopping to dance before churches en route. Although these kingdoms disappeared following their abolition in 1888, the *maracatú* continued as part of Recife's *carnaval* tradition, along with the indigenous *caboclinho* dances, whose choreography symbolized the Indians' attempts to avoid domination by white *conquistadors.*

Carnival in Trinidad and Tobago illustrated similar syncretism. Festivities began with a torchlight procession in blackface, patterned after the procession of slaves on their way to fight fires in sugarcane fields. This procession was called *canboulay*, from *cannes brulées*, or "burned cane," and included music and masked dancing. After emancipation, as Carnival evolved into a rather raucous event, governments attempted to crack down on it; only after the 1881 Canboulay Riots injured dozens of police did officials succeed in restricting festivities.

Latin Americans also commemorated many strictly religious occasions, including Christmas and Easter. For Easter, many areas celebrated throughout *Semana Santa*, or Holy Week, holding masses and decorating altars. Effigies of Judas were burned or hanged in public squares throughout Latin America. In a Haitian custom, dozens of Judas effigies fled on Good Friday, upon the announcement of Christ's death. Early Saturday morning, whole towns began the hunt; brandishing an assortment of weapons, the townspeople hunted down and destroyed the Judases so that by noon, the countryside was strewn with remnants of the effigies.

All over Latin America, elaborate *Semana Santa* processions took place. In Popayán, Colombia, a remarkable candlelight procession occurred every year, even throughout the lengthy independence struggles and other wars. Warring parties often called truces to allow the famed parade to proceed. People from Antigua, Guatemala, paraded life-sized figures of Christ through town. The costumed Christ-bearers and guards carefully passed over ornate carpets of dyed sand, sawdust, flowers, and pine needles that depicted scenes from nature and the Bible. In many Central American towns, *Semana Santa* festivities coincided with the corn planting season; in addition to events with biblical symbolism, visitors could also witness Maya fertility rites for rain and bountiful crops.

All Saints' Day (November 1) and All Souls' Day (November 2) were also recognized in many areas of Latin America. In Mexico, where the holiday came to be known as El Día de los Muertos (Day of the Dead), families visited the graves of their loved ones, bringing flowers, candles, and other decorations, along with food and drink. In their homes, many Mexicans set up *ofrendas*, elaborate altars to their dearly departed, with candles, photographs, and favorite foods.

Other festivities occurred on national and local patron saint days. For example, on December 12, Mexicans honored their national patron saint, Nuestra Señora de Guadalupe (the Virgin Mary of Guadalupe), with pilgrimages to the revered Church of Guadalupe on Tepeyac Hill. According to legend, on this date in 1531, the Virgin Mary appeared before an Indian convert, Juan Diego; as Diego tried to convince the bishop of the apparition, an image of Mary miraculously materialized on his blanket. On May 11, Brazilians also honored Mary, known there as Our Lady of Aparecida.

Not all patron saint celebrations were of strictly Catholic tradition. The people of Puno, Peru, for example, honored Manco Capac and Mama Ocllo, the legendary founders of the Inca dynasty, who were sent by their father, the Sun, to inhabit the Island of Titicaca. Every November 5, celebrations included a reenactment of the arrival of these first rulers to the island; the reenactment included a fleet of balsas, or lake-reed skiffs, floated upon the water, followed by a royal barge carrying the deities.

Many celebrations were not religious in origin but marked important dates in each nation's development. In the first part of the century, for example, as countries gained independence from European colonial powers, the new republican governments initiated commemorations of their country's independence day. Celebrations included patriotic speeches and parades, dedication of parks and monuments, and religious ceremonies.

As the years passed, other independence-related festivities appeared. Venezuelans, for example, turned independence hero Simón Bolívar's birthday (July 24) into a national holiday. Mexicans honored one of the nation's earliest and most beloved presidents, Benito Juárez, on his birthday (March 21) as well as on the anniversary of his death, when flags flew at half-mast. In their Cinco de Mayo (May 5) celebrations, Mexicans commemorated their 1862 victory in Puebla against French invaders, a triumph that demonstrated their firm desire for independence and self-determination.

There were also many crop- and harvest-related celebrations. The Quiché Indians of Guatemala marked the beginning of the principal corn-planting season (March–April) with a series of ceremonies to bless the corn seed and the soil of their fields. In November, Haitians celebrated their annual yam harvest feast, known as Manger-yam. At this festivity, which included songs and dances, locals could not partake in the feast until the yams had first been ceremoniously washed and portions offered to local deities.

Throughout the 19th century, Latin Americans celebrated many occasions: historical events, religious days, and life cycle rituals (harvest time, weddings, births, and funerals). Events frequently combined traditions and beliefs from Africa, Europe, and the Americas. Throughout the course of the century, many celebrations became more commercialized, mixing not only devotion and diversion, but also pleasure and business.

~Molly Todd

FOR MORE INFORMATION

Garciagodoy, J. *Digging the Days of the Dead: A Reading of Mexico's Días de Muertos.* Niwot: University Press of Colorado, 1998.

Milne, J. *Fiesta Time in Latin America.* Los Angeles: Ward Ritchie Press, 1965.

Sichel, M. *South America.* London: B. T. Batsford, 1986.

Thompson, S. E., and B. W. Carlson. *Holidays, Festivals, and Celebrations of the World Dictionary.* Detroit: Omnigraphics, 1994.

CHINA

In the ancient world, the Chinese excelled in bringing diverse and talented performers to palaces and city squares to celebrate the many festivals that marked their annual calendar. Even today, Chinese acrobats, dancers, and musicians tour the world bringing their age-old skills to modern audiences. See the China entry in the section "Entertainment" in chapter 7 ("Recreational Life") in volume 2 of this series for a description of the range of Chinese entertainment that continued into the 19th century.

Music

RECREATIONAL
LIFE
|
MUSIC
|
United States
Victorian England
India
Latin America

In her entry about Victorian England, Sally Mitchell argues that music was more important to daily life than it is now. Although hard to believe, it may well be true. At an early age schoolchildren were taught to sing. And singing was an important part of their lives not only in church but also among their associations, including labor unions and social groups. Like in so many aspects of daily life, class made a difference with music. Working-class women and men sang and danced to folk music and played with small pianos and fiddles. The upper classes had more money to spend on professional instruments and professional singers.

Folk music was similarly important in the United States. Although there were no overly successful classical composers during the 19th century, folk composers like Stephen Collins Foster, who wrote "Oh! Susanna," made a permanent impression upon the culture. Moreover, American folk music was quite inventive. During the 19th century, American composers reinvented the singing scale to accommodate new melodies. The traditional do, re, mi, fa, sol, la, si (or ti) gave way to fa-sol-la-fa-sol-la-mi, thus ushering in a new era in singing. American musicians also popularized what was called Ethiopian music. White Americans flocked to see other whites in blackface makeup sing Negro music, particularly spirituals. These acts with their over- and undertones of racism were an indication of the interest in the exotic aspects of music and culture.

This penchant for the exotic was a part of a larger cultural movement in the 19th century known as Romanticism. The British were also interested in music that they thought was a little unusual to them. Hence it's not surprising that they loved Indian folk music. The origins of Indian music are ancient. What drew the British to it was not only the styles, harmonies, rhythms, and melodies, but the instruments. Indian musicians frequently used the vina, a guitarlike instrument with 24 frets and 7 strings and the *chitracina,* which is fretless and has 21 strings. Finally, one aspect of Indian music that drew Western attention to it was its spirituality. Professional musicians in India had religious connections. Their music was an extension of prayer and ritual. And yet, as with the British and the Americans, music was also a way to tell stories and entertain.

As Latin America recovered from the independence wars of the early 19th century, the arts, and especially music, suffered. Latin American music in the 19th century was heavily influenced by European trends, primarily the classical tradition, which resonated especially with the middle and upper classes. National styles and themes in music did not become popular until the end of the century. Still, musical development in Latin America was not dissimilar from trends elsewhere. Perhaps music is one of the commonalities of daily life that bind all people.

RECREATIONAL
LIFE
|
MUSIC
|
United States

Victorian England

India

Latin America

UNITED STATES

During the 19th century, American music did not share the same place on the world stage as European music. In fact, at most, it was considered a weak, ugly cousin. Europeans dominated the Western world's music scene not only in terms of creativity but also in terms of performance. There were some exceptions, of course. One cannot study 19th-century music without acknowledging the influence of the American James Lyon. In the late 18th and early 19th centuries, one finds American symphonies playing Lyon, but always in conjunction with other more famous composers like Handel. Indeed, one might speculate that those attending concerts in the United States listened patiently to Lyon while waiting to hear the main feature, a work by someone like Handel. Europeans also held most professional music jobs, not only on the Continent and in England, but also in the United States. That fact alone speaks volumes about the state of American music in the Victorian era. As the great music historian Gilbert Chase put it, Americans wrote and played "with more zeal than skill" (Chase, 112). It would not be until the 1950s that American music would take over the world. In the meantime, there were significant developments, even in the 19th century, particularly in the areas of folk music and performance.

Although the genteel traditions in music such as opera gathered a small following in the United States, native-born composers floundered as their works paled in comparison to the European classics. To those who revered highbrow music, this was nearly unbearable. The distinguished 19th-century American educator John Hubbard criticized American composers in 1808:

Almost every pedant, after learning his eight notes, has commenced [a career as an] author. With a genius, sterile as the deserts of Arabia, he has attempted to rival the great masters of music. On the leaden wings of dullness, he has attempted to soar into those regions of science, never penetrated but by real genius. From such distempered imagination, no regular productions can be expected. The unhappy writers, after torturing every note in the octave, have fallen into oblivion, and have generally outlived their insignificant works. (Chase, 123)

Clearly, American musical genius did not lie with what became known as classical music. Rather, folk music seemed to capture the American experience, character, and interests.

American folk music, which dealt with religious and nonreligious themes, was not merely popular. It was also profitable. The way to make money was to publish arrangements. During the antebellum period, the biggest music business mogul was Lowell Mason, who published sacred American folk music. His *Carmina Sacra* sold 500,000 copies between 1841 and 1858. *The Hallelujah*, another Mason collection, sold 150,000 copies, earning Mason the unbelievably fantastic sum of $100,000. Antebellum religious movements fueled the sheet music and music anthology industry. And there was plenty of room for Mason's rivals, who also profited handsomely. One of the ways publishers distinguished themselves was by introducing musical innovations. For example, in 1801, two American singing-school masters, William Smith and William Little, simplified the singing scale. Traditionally, the scale was represented by the symbols do, re, mi, fa, sol, la, si (or ti). Smith and Little removed the first three symbols and reinvented the scale as follows: fa-sol-la-fa-sol-la-mi. Their simplified folk music tune book, *The Easy Instructor*, quickly became a hit, precisely because it was simple. The Fasola method was adopted by music teachers, particularly in rural areas that lacked many students and instruments.

American folk music was also popular in terms of performance. In the 19th century, Americans flocked to listen to music that they thought was either exotic or romantic. Of particular interest were African American spirituals. Visiting Europeans first brought national and international attention to Negro music. They were struck not only by the beauty but by the religious symbolism of the songs. African American spirituals were a unique blend of African and European ideas, melodies, and harmonies. Moreover, the songs fit into the religious revivals of the age. Anyone listening to or singing a spiritual was moved by the words and swayed by the rhythms. As Northerner and architect Frederick Law Olmstead wrote after visiting a black church service in New Orleans in the 1830s, "I was once surprised to find my own muscles all stretched, as if ready for a struggle—my face glowing, and my feet stamping—having been infected unconsciously . . . with instinctive bodily sympathy with the excitement of the crowd" (Chase, 220). So popular was black music that several groups took it on the road. Among the most famous and most successful monetarily were the Fisk (University) Jubilee Singers who toured the United States and made tens of thousands of dollars.

Black music and culture had a powerful affect on 19th-century Americans and led to the strange invention of minstrel parody of black life and music known as the Ethiopian business. The exact origins of this minstrel show are unclear. It seems that it was first popularized by Thomas Dartmouth Rice, also known as Daddy or Jim Crow Rice. In 1827, Rice performed in Albany, New York, dressed in a blue swallow-tailed coat and wearing burnt cork on his face to make it appear as if he were an African American. His show centered on the character of an old black man, ill with arthritis, who spoke in broken English and sang "a genuine Negro song" (Chase, 234). The racist (and before the Civil War, pro-Confederate) characterizations were a hit with white American audiences. Eventually the Jim Crow minstrel shows launched the careers of many famous artists, including Stephen Collins Foster, popularizer of the Ethiopian business of black minstrelsy and a terrific songwriter. Among Foster's credits include "Oh! Susanna." Foster was a transformative figure in American music whose influence reached far beyond the 19th century and affected instruments from the hurdy-gurdy to the electronic synthesizer and artists like Ray Charles.

Foster's career typifies 19th-century American music. Although influential and notable, it was not widely appreciated or revered at the time. It struggled to find critical acclaim in an era dominated by European music, composers, and performers. And it would have to wait until the world accepted it.

To read about music in the United States in the 20th century, see the United States entries in the section "Music" in chapter 7 ("Recreational Life") in volume 6 of this series.

~*Andrew E. Kersten*

FOR MORE INFORMATION

Chase, G. *America's Music: From the Pilgrims to the Present.* Urbana: University of Illinois Press, 1987.

Emerson, K. *Doo-dah!: Stephen Foster and the Rise of American Popular Culture.* New York: Simon & Schuster, 1997.

Levine, L. W. *Black Culture and Black Consciousness: Afro-American Folk Thought from Slavery to Freedom.* New York: Oxford University Press, 1977.

RECREATIONAL
LIFE
|
MUSIC
|
United States

Victorian England

India

Latin America

VICTORIAN ENGLAND

Making as well as hearing music was more a part of Victorian daily life than of modern-day life. Schoolchildren of all classes were trained to sing. Traditional folk songs and country dances flourished in rural areas. Hymns were important to most religious services; many churches had several different choirs as well as hearty congregational singing.

Playing the piano was an essential accomplishment for young ladies—and many middle-class and upper-class women who were forced to practice for an hour a day throughout childhood developed an abiding pleasure in playing. Inexpensive upright pianos were available for middle-class homes. There was a healthy commercial trade in sheet music, and magazines printed reviews to let readers know what music was available and how difficult it was to play. Music was a part of most social gatherings. Wealthy people hired professionals or issued special invitations to talented amateurs; middle-class and working-class people brought sheet music along when they went to a party. Workers who could not afford a cottage piano invited someone with a fiddle.

Organized musical groups were sponsored by employers, trade unions, churches, and Nonconformist chapels. Most towns had at least one brass band; in some places every factory had one. Bands held competitions at which they played dance tunes, military marches, and special arrangements of flashy orchestral pieces. Oratorio societies also flourished. Choral singing was especially popular among the working class. There were vast festivals at which dozens of choirs competed. Finally, as a triumphant conclusion, thousands of singers would join in a performance of Handel's "Hallelujah Chorus."

Most social dancing early in this period was in the form of folk dances, reels, and other figures through which couples moved while barely touching hands. The waltz, introduced at the beginning of the 19th century, was somewhat disreputable because the partners held each other. Its reputation soared, however, when Queen Victoria and Prince Albert—who were not yet married—danced a waltz together at her coronation ball.

In the upper classes, young children of both sexes took dancing lessons. After the boys went to school, girls continued their instruction. Either a teacher came to the house once or twice a week, or a servant walked the girls to a dancing class attended by others in the same social circle. Dancing was not only an essential skill but also a way to acquire graceful movements and an upright posture.

Adult women and men danced at private balls and at dancing parties in middle-class houses: the furniture was pushed back, the carpet rolled up, and a professional pianist or an accommodating friend was engaged to provide the music. Semiprivate balls were sponsored by hunt clubs, military regiments, and organizations whose members paid subscriptions to support a monthly or quarterly dance. Promenade concerts at pavilions in seaside towns provided summer visitors a respectable opportunity to dance. The tea dance, introduced in 1845, was an afternoon event with a small band of strings and piano. Working people danced to fiddle music in barns and in the open air, as well as at taverns.

This illustration from the July 17, 1886, edition of *The Girl's Own Paper* shows young middle-class women practicing on a piano and a violin, two expensive instruments.

When the gentry and upper classes had house parties, they often engaged in private theatricals, charades (acting out a word), and *tableaux vivants* in which people dressed up to represent a painting or a famous historical moment. The fun was in the preparation, the dressing up, and the joke of having (for example) a young man with a luxuriant moustache put on a gown and veil to portray a seductive woman (Mitchell, 225–26).

To read about music in Chaucer's England, see the entry on Europe in the section "Music and Dance" in chapter 7 ("Recreational Life") in volume 2 of this series; for Elizabethan England, see the entry on England in the section "The Arts" in chapter 7 ("Recreational Life") in volume 3 of this series; for 18th-century England, see the entry on England in the section "Arts and Hobbies" in chapter 7 ("Recreational Life") in volume 4 of this series.

FOR MORE INFORMATION

Altick, R. D. *Victorian People and Ideas*. New York: W. W. Norton, 1973.

Ehrlich, C. *The Music Profession in Britain Since the Eighteenth Century: A Social History*. New York: Oxford University Press, 1985.

Mitchell, S. *Daily Life in Victorian England*. Westport, Conn.: Greenwood Press, 1996.

RECREATIONAL
LIFE

MUSIC

United States

Victorian England

India

Latin America

INDIA

Various forms of Indian music were popular during the colonial period. Colonial influence also caused an increased interest in various classical forms of Indian music. In addition, there are many types of folk music, which are popular in certain areas of India.

Classical Indian music traces its roots back to the Vedic period (the first few hundred years of the common era), when religious poems chanted by priests were first collected in an anthology called the Rig-Veda. Over the millennia classical music was shaped by many influences, and the legacy today is two main schools: Carnatic, which is the classical musical style of southern India, and Hindustani, which is the classical musical style of northern India. The two styles have common origins and share several characteristics. The two styles use the raga, which is the melodic pattern of the music, and the tala, which is the rhythmic meter characterized by the number of beats.

Both styles are performed by small ensembles of anywhere from two to six musicians. Hindustani music is more influenced by Persian music (a result of Moghul rule), while Carnatic music is more theory based. There is no set pitch in either style. One of the most recognizable differences between the two forms is that Carnatic music makes a much greater use of voice, while Hindustani music has a more purely instrumental base.

A typical southern Indian concert includes a singer or a main melody instrument, a secondary melody instrument, a stringed instrument, and one or two percussion instruments. One of the main instruments used by Carnatic musicians is the vina, which has 24 frets and seven strings. It is held by the left hand pressing between the frets or pulling on the strings to produce ornamentations. A less commonly used string instrument is the *chitracina,* which is fretless, has 21 strings and is played like a slide guitar. The guitar, the mandolin, and the violin are also used in Carnatic music. These instruments were adopted from the West during the 19th century. The *nagaswaram,* which is a double-reed flute, and the *venu,* a side-blown flute, are the most commonly used wind instruments in Carnatic music. The mridangam, a double-sided hand drum is the most popular Carnatic percussion instrument. The most commonly used drone in Carnatic music is the tambura, which is plucked throughout the concert.

Hindustani music generally includes the same main elements of Carnatic music, minus the vocalist. The main Hindustani instruments include the sitar and the tabla, which are both well known to Western audiences. Other popular instruments include the *surbahar,* which is a larger and shorter-necked version of the sitar. Two commonly used wind instruments are the *bansuri,* a side-blown bamboo flute, and the *shehnai,* which resembles an oboe. The hand-pumped keyboard harmonium is used as a secondary melody instrument for vocal music.

The most popular Carnatic vocal piece is called a *kriti,* or devotional song. These songs were created less than 200 years ago. The most common forms of Hindustani music are the *kyyal* and the *thumri;* the latter is a classical style based on devotional literature.

Many professional musicians in India see their work as connected to religion. There is a distinct tradition of respect for one's guru, or teacher. The instruments themselves are also seen as things that must be treated with respect, and there are various prayers and rituals connected to praising one's guru and one's instrument. Often a guru's death anniversary is honored by the guru's student each year with a large celebration. The student's students also honor their guru's guru, thus becoming part of a tradition of the particular guru.

During the 19th century almost all instrumentalists were male. Both male and female vocalists were common. Quite often parents trained their own children, and even other children in their family, thus creating a family musical tradition. Professional musicians were almost entirely Brahmins.

During the colonial period the British took an interest in Indian arts, including music. This led to an increased interest in the arts among urban upper-class Indians. Appreciation of the arts became less a form of religious devotion, and more a sign of class and Western ideals.

Classical music is enjoyed by a relatively small section of society. Most people are more familiar with their own local folk forms, which vary greatly from region to region. Folk music is popular during festivities and important village ceremonies. In many areas folk music is an important element of everyday life. For example, in many regions work songs are commonly sung during physical labor. These songs are usually sung a capella, although there are also certain types of folk instruments, such as basic flutes or drums that are used in festivals.

Other types of performers, such as traveling storytellers, magicians, and snake charmers sometimes also use song to entertain their audiences. Some storytellers wander from village to village to perform songs based on the Hindu epics. This is a popular form of entertainment in some parts of India.

One of the more obscure types of performers is the *Hijas*, or hermaphrodites who dress as women and sing at weddings and other celebrations. *Hijas* also appear at births so that they can take the baby if it is also a hermaphrodite. They are considered inauspicious, and as a result are very unwelcomed. Typically, the *hija* starts to sing and refuses to leave until receiving pay for the performance.

Sufi music, which is mainly a Muslim tradition, was also popular during this period. Sufi music was generally popular in the northern plains, and in the area that is now Pakistan. This form of music uses instruments that are similar to those used in classical Hindustani music, and a very particular form of chanting. Many of the songs are devotional, while others deal with other subjects, such as romance. Like classical Carnatic and Hindustani music the Sufi tradition is often passed down from father to son and shares the tradition of an important guru-student relationship.

To read about music in ancient India, see the India entry in the section "Dance, Music, and Theater" in chapter 7 ("Recreational Life") in volume 1 of this series.

~Dana Lightstone

FOR MORE INFORMATION

Audio Recordings
Khan, N. F. A. *Mustt Mustt*. Real World Music, 1993, compact disc.
Shankar, R. *Chants of India*. Arourag, 1996, compact disc.

Books

Matatkar, S., ed. *Aspects of Indian Music: A Collection of Essays*. New Delhi, India: Sangeet Natak Akademi, 1987.

LATIN AMERICA

As Latin American societies restructured themselves in the decades following the independence wars of the early 19th century, many of the arts languished. Although literature was widely popular, music lagged behind. Much of the music Latin Americans enjoyed in the 19th century was highly influenced by European trends, primarily the classical tradition, which tended to express middle- and upper-class values and aesthetics. It was not until later in the century that national styles and themes appeared and gained in popularity.

At the turn of the century, chapel masters dominated much of the region's music making. For decades, composers focused their attentions on creating music for church services and spent little time exploring outside themes. Over the years, composers broadened their subject matter and sought wider audiences; eventually, such masters as the Brazilians José Mauricio Nunes García and Francisco Manuel de Silva, and the Argentine José Antonio Picasarri, established schools as well as philharmonic societies and ensembles (Bethell, 18).

Both inside and outside of church, Latin American music was highly influenced by European trends. Minuets, mazurkas, polkas, and waltzes arrived in the Americas in the first half of the century, and piano and song recitals, light musical theater, and symphonic poems were in vogue. Perhaps the most popular musical form was opera. Italian and French operas were especially fashionable in South America. Beginning in the 1820s, Buenos Aires, Argentina, regularly hosted international opera troupes; by 1850, the city mounted two dozen shows each year. Throughout the course of the century, at least 12 theaters opened in the city, including the Teatro Colón, which quickly ranked Buenos Aires among the world's opera capitals (Bethell, 19). In the 1830s, a French visitor to Peru wrote that "[s]cores from our operas are sung in the salons . . . A little while longer, and people will not go to mass unless they can hear good music there" (Keen and Wasserman, 232).

During the colonial period, Spain had prohibited the writing and dissemination of certain literary subjects in its American territories—in particular those subjects that addressed indigenous themes (Bethell, 10). Thus, it was not until well after Latin American nations gained their independence that local composers began experimenting with more national themes. By the 1870s, an era of musical nationalism had timidly begun. More composers and musicians expressed themes specific to their countries and incorporated local traditional and popular music forms into their works. Operas were a particularly common way of illustrating these themes. Mexican composer Aniceto Ortega adopted a romantic perspective on the Aztecs in his opera *Guatimotzín* (1871). Argentine composer Arturo Berutti borrowed the folk melodies of the country's gauchos (cowboys) and Andean Indians, presenting them in such works as *Pampa* (1897) and *Yupanki* (1899). Another Argentine, Hargreaves, became

RECREATIONAL LIFE

|

MUSIC

|

United States

Victorian England

India

Latin America

well known for his stylization of rural music forms, such as the *cielito, gato, setilo,* and *décima,* which he rendered in *Aires nacionales* (1880). Works of the period often meshed local and European styles, creating hybrid forms such as the Paraguayan polka or tropical waltzes.

By the end of the century, symphony and chamber orchestras existed in many major Latin American cities. Those same cities also usually boasted respectable conservatories and music education centers. Many Latin American composers and performers obtained international recognition, including Venezuelan pianist, composer, and singer Teresa Carreño; Cuban violinist José White; and Mexican soprano Angela Peralta. The famed Italian composer Giuseppe Verdi, after seeing José de Alencar's *Il Guarany* (Brazil, 1870), stated that it was the work of a "truly musical genius" (Bethell, 312).

Although European classical styles dominated middle- and upper-class Latin America, the region also was home to innumerable local and popular musical forms. In the circum-Caribbean region, these styles were highly influenced by the rhythms and instruments introduced by African slaves. Often, African and Hispanic traditions intermingled, giving rise to new local styles, such as Afro-Cubanism and various Brazilian rhythms. Popular music also often adopted the instruments of local indigenous populations, such as the Andean pan flute. Other popular styles included the Argentine *milonga*, the forerunner of tango; the Brazilian *modinha* and *chôro;* Cuban *contradanza* and *guajiro* folk music; and the music of Argentine gauchos, including *payadores, gatos, vidalitas,* and *tristes.*

In conclusion, for much of the 19th century, Latin American music tended to be highly Europeanized and classical in style. Later in the century, composers from the region began experimenting with styles and themes of truly local flair. This trend continued to expand through the end of the century, launching many artists into international fame.

~Molly Todd

FOR MORE INFORMATION

Bethell, L., ed. *A Cultural History of Latin America: Literature, Music and the Visual Arts in the Nineteenth and Twentieth Centuries.* Cambridge: Cambridge University Press, 1998.

Keen, B., and M. Wasserman. *A Short History of Latin America.* Boston: Houghton Mifflin, 1984.

ISLAMIC WORLD

In music, architecture, and art, the empire of the Ottoman Turks continued the traditions established early in Islamic history and created a vibrant artistic culture that dominated the Muslim world throughout the 19th century. See the Islamic World entry in the section "The Arts" in chapter 7 ("Recreational Life") in volume 3 of this series for a discussion of this artistic tradition, which included music.

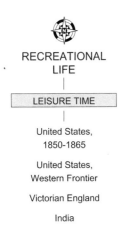

RECREATIONAL
LIFE
|
LEISURE TIME
|
United States,
1850-1865

United States,
Western Frontier

Victorian England

India

Leisure Time

In addition to aspects of daily life such as music, there is another commonality among all people: we all get bored. The one complaint often expressed by Civil War–era soldiers was that camp life was monotonous. Similarly on the frontier, things could be quite quiet. Even before one arrived in the West, days could pass exceedingly slowly. Onboard ships traveling to California, passengers and sailors counted the dull minutes, hours, and days until they could disembark. Some cultures such as the English discouraged idleness. For example, girls were told that their hands should never be still. They were expected to pass their leisure time with some kind of productive activity. Yet, even without such proscriptions, people tended to fill their downtime with some game or pastime. It seems to be a part of the human condition.

When work is over, when meals are hours away, and when children do not need direct attention, people play games and engage their hobbies. Games themselves have always existed, but historians only recently have begun to take them seriously. Some games have a larger impact than others. Clearly Indian games have had a major impact upon Westerners. There are two in particular that became popular outside of India: Parcheesi and Snakes and Ladders (which is known in the West as Chutes and Ladders). Western games took root in India too. Cricket and football (soccer) became common in all regions in India during the 19th century. In America, English games never became popular ways to spend leisure time. Rather baseball was the sport. But there were other ways to kill time. Civil War soldiers passed the dull moments with snowball fights, greased pig chases, singing, and gambling. In fact, gambling was common to many American locales. On the Western frontier, miners and cowboys took gambling quite seriously, which was one of the reasons why violence was so prevalent.

Finally, it is important to note that leisure activities have a class aspect. Middle-class families engaged in pastimes that were different from those of working-class families. The upper classes had the finances to purchase such items as the zoetrope and the phantascope, which were image viewing devices. Similarly, only upper-class English women could afford to have collections of valuables such as spoons or china. And yet despite the class distinctions, all people filled their quiet hours with rewarding activities, daily activities that gave meaning and happiness to lives filled with hard work and sometimes tragedy.

UNITED STATES, 1850–65

The single complaint most often expressed by Civil War soldiers was that of being bored. Camp life was "one everlasting monotone, yesterday, today, and tomorrow." Pickets, or sentries, went on duty at the front for two days of every six. A federal officer noted that guard duty was the very last duty that soldiers learned to perform

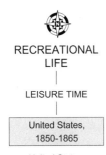

RECREATIONAL
LIFE
|
LEISURE TIME
|
United States,
1850-1865

United States,
Western Frontier

Victorian England

India

"accurately and thoroughly," as they were required to shoot any man, including comrades, found running the guard. Burial and fatigue details took up much of a soldier's remaining time not devoted to drill. If there was anything that the troops needed to excel in, it was tactical evolution. An officer noted with remarkable pride, "We had been drilled in battalion and drilled in brigade till we went like a machine." Yet the soldiers repudiated such regimental pride and complained, "The first thing in the morning is drill, then drill again. Between drills . . . we sometimes stop . . . and have a roll call." If things went wrong during drill, especially if an officer blundered, the general quickly moved to "the scene of confusion with a face of anguish." By the time the camp was established, firewood was gathered, cooking was finished, and weapons were cleaned, the soldier had little free daylight time for entertainment.

A federal officer observed, "I had no amusement beyond occasional old newspapers and rare walks to the position of some neighboring battery or regiment." Nonetheless, individuals and groups did find some time for entertaining activities. Letter and journal writing, reading, whittling, drawing, and painting were common entertainments. Games such as checkers, chess, dice, and dominoes were popular with small groups, as were card games such as poker, cribbage, euchre, and old sledge. Game boards were often drawn on the inside of the ever-present gum blanket, and stones, bones, and corncobs served as game pieces. Gambling was strictly forbidden by military law, but the prohibition was almost impossible to enforce. Soldiers were reluctant to have dice and cards found among any personal effects that might be sent home upon their death and often disposed of them before going into battle. A popular, but probably specious, story that made the rounds of the camps was that of an inveterate card player who received a ball to his chest that passed through all the cards of a deck he was carrying save one, the ace of spades, which saved his life.

Large group activities included snowball fights, chasing greased pigs, or climbing poles, and playing football and baseball. Singing was a very popular activity. Generally speaking, the soldiers were interested in sentimental rather than patriotic tunes. Ballads such as "Just Before the Battle, Mother" and "Somebody's Darling" were very popular. The men sang about their sweethearts in "Aura Lea," "Lorena," and "The Yellow Rose of Texas." A Rebel favorite was "All Quiet along the Potomac," and "Tenting Tonight on the Old Camp Ground" was a Northern favorite. "Dixie," "John Brown's Body," "The Bonnie Blue Flag," and "The Battle Cry of Freedom" were sung less often by the toil-weary troops than by the patriotic populace.

In sharp contrast with the romantic image of groups of soldiers huddled in comradeship around the campfire, many men separated themselves from the group each night and settled at small solitary fires at the edge of the camp. After a full day of marching between 20 and 30 miles, the men's feet were often blistered nearly all over so that they could hardly take a step further. Edwin Weller, with the 107th New York Volunteers, found that "on taking some salt and water and bathing my feet thoroughly and then applying liquor I managed to get myself in tolerably good marching order for the next day." Other men simply fell to the ground to rest, too tired to invest the further effort of pitching a tent, and happy to go to their blankets to sleep supperless and unsheltered. "The march done, the fevered feet bare to the evening breeze, the aching limbs outstretched, the head laid on the blanket roll which had been such a burden through the day, the pipe in the mouth, nature revived a little and found that life retained some of its sweetness." One Federal noted of day-to-day soldiering, "It is a healthy, monotonous, stupid life, and makes one long to go somewhere, even at the risk of being shot."

On the home front, Americans had access to a number of leisure activities. Many seemed to have enjoyed a variety of optical phenomena in their drawing rooms and parlors. Some photographs were stereographs, two simultaneously recorded images set side by side, giving a three-dimensional view when seen through a viewer designed for the purpose, known as a stereoscope or stereopticon. Such devices go back to 1838, and stereographs of period places, buildings, monuments, and naval vessels predominate. Very few stereotypes of battle dead survive, and no stereotypes of the poor or of the squalid condition of the nation's slums are known to exist. Photographers understood that to sell their pictures they would have to appeal to well-heeled customers who did not wish to be reminded of the nation's failures.

Propelled by a fascination with photography, optical novelties were very much in vogue. The magic lantern had been around for over 200 years, used by showmen and hucksters to beguile audiences with mystical images. It consisted of a metal box into which an oil lamp was placed; a polished metal reflector that focused the light on a painted slide; and a hole with a lens through which the light was projected. These lanterns were notably improved as a result of photographic discoveries, and their use became widespread. Lanterns were used by lecturers to enhance their presentations, and they became very popular as a parlor toy to show comic pictures. A number of hand-colored glass slides of the war have recently been restored.

Another optical curiosity was the zoetrope. This consisted of a revolving drum with equally spaced slits around the sides. The interior of the drum contained a series of sequential pictures. The pictures were taken by a series of still cameras activated by trip wires. Walking men and running horses were prominent subjects of the zoetrope. When the drum was rotated, the pictures gave the impression that they were moving. Because it could be viewed by many people at one time, the zoetrope enjoyed popularity as a parlor amusement.

A similar device was the phantascope. This simple contrivance was comprised of a cardboard disc with a series of slits equally spaced around the center and a handle that acted as a pivot around which the phantascope was rotated. The reverse side contained a series of pictures set between the slits. When the operator held the device in front of a mirror and rotated the disc, the pictures appeared to be moving.

There were many things to do in the parlor. The decade beginning in 1860 spawned an abundance of cultural institutions in the North and West. War involvement and subsequent poverty retarded a similar movement in the South for almost 20 years. The interest in art, music, literature, and nature that permeated the parlor surged forth, creating museums, symphonies, libraries, and parks. These, in turn, engendered a plethora of ancillary institutions such as literary societies, study groups, and reading clubs.

These organizations were gender specific. Male organizations attracted businessmen and professionals. In addition to the obvious activities such organizations would conduct, they created a venue that was ripe for the founding of additional social projects. The distaff version of these clubs provided activities for middle- and upper-class women beyond domestic and church endeavors. The clubs furnished an arena for women to pursue their intellectual development. Study clubs met twice monthly for 10 months a year to discuss such topics as literature, history, and art. Meetings commonly were held in members' homes and consisted of conversation, presentation of papers, and subsequent discussions.

Many civilians, particularly the women who were doomed to sit out the war while their husbands and lovers fought, found reading one of the few sources of entertainment available to them. Like their loved ones in the army camps, many women read in groups and met regularly to do so. Books were frequently read aloud, making it possible to share the books and newspapers that were "all too scarce in the print-starved Confederacy." Even in the North, where books were widely available, oral presentation by an articulate reader often enhanced the literature and allowed the majority of the women to do other chores such as sewing and embroidery while they listened. Reading aloud became an activity with many of the characteristics of theater. Books provided women with an almost pure escape from the realities of war, suffering, and death. More important, oral presentation discouraged continual war gossip among the women, and the camaraderie of the group helped to alleviate depression and gloom among those who were without loved ones, displaced from their homes, and anxious about their own futures.

PLAIT FOR NEEDLE-BOOK COVER.

Ladies magazines like *Peterson's Magazine* regularly published craft projects intended for women.

To some extent, literary society or study club meetings took the place of the public lectures that had enjoyed tremendous popularity from about 1840 forward. The war had interrupted many lecture series, which were curtailed, and in some cases suspended. Lectures had been particularly popular among ambitious young men, many of whom joined their cause on the battle line. Northerners demanded that the remaining lecturers make their concern matters related to the conflict. Topics sought by lecture audiences included denunciations of the South, glorification of Union causes, and narrations detailing the reforms that would follow the Northern victory. Popular speakers included Senator Charles Sumner, Major General Cassius Clay, Theodore Tilton, and Wendell Phillips.

Games have always been popular in America. One popular game was solitaire, played on a circular board containing 33 holes. Marbles or pegs were placed in all but the center hole. A peg was moved forward, backward, or sideways but not diagonally, over an adjacent peg, which was then removed from the board. The game ended when the remaining pegs could not make a move. The object of the game was to have only a single peg remaining, preferably in the center hole.

Board games were just coming into their own in America. Most board game publishers were located in the Northeast, particularly in Boston and New York. "The Mansion of Happiness, an Instructive Moral and Entertaining Amusement" is generally acknowledged as the first board game published in the United States. This 1843 game closely resembled the formerly imported "The Game of Goose," but had a distinctly moral message. Players landing on squares marked "gratitude" or "honesty" advanced more rapidly toward their goal. "The Game of Goose" was a board game distinguished by an elaborate spiral containing 63 squares. Players rolled the dice and advanced along the board, incurring a variety of changes in fortune involving penalties and bonuses. The game dated from the 18th century and served as inspiration for a host of imitators.

American board makers copied other games as well. "The Game of Pope and Pagan, or the Siege of the Stronghold of Satan by the Christian Army" and "Mohamet and Saladin, or the Battle for Palestine" were both based on the centuries-old game fox and geese. Other published games took the form of card games and included "Dr. Busby," "Yankee Trader," "Uncle Tom's Cabin," "Heroes," "Master Redbury and His Pupils," and "Trades." The last of these consisted of lithographed cards; some depicted such tradesmen as shoemakers, farriers, and tax gatherers, and others showed the symbols of each trade. The object of the game was to collect tricks that matched the tradesman with his symbol. It is thought that this game served as the inspiration for the very popular English game "Happy Families."

Other popular games included cribbage, checkers, tangrams, and lotto—a forerunner of bingo—which was played with cards featuring three horizontal and nine vertical rows. Five numbers from 1 to 90 appeared on the cards; the remaining spaces were blank. Children's versions of the game were developed to teach spelling, multiplication, botany, and history (Volo and Volo, 145–47, 218–20).

To read about leisure time in the United States in the 20th century, see the United States entries in the section "Leisure" in chapter 7 ("Recreational Life") in volume 6 of this series.

FOR MORE INFORMATION

McPherson, J. M. *Battle Cry of Freedom: The Civil War Era.* New York: Oxford University Press, 1990.

Stanchak, J. E., ed. *Leslie's Illustrated Civil War.* 1894. Reprint. Jackson: University Press of Mississippi, 1992.

Volo, D. D., and J. M. Volo. *Daily Life in Civil War America.* Westport, Conn.: Greenwood Press, 1998.

RECREATIONAL
LIFE
|
LEISURE TIME
|
United States,
1850-1865

United States,
Western Frontier

Victorian England

India

UNITED STATES, WESTERN FRONTIER

Leisure activities were a central part of daily life on the frontier. For example, migrants bound for the western frontier had to pass the time somehow. Many simply enjoyed observing nature. There are journal entries about dolphins, porpoises, butterflies, whales, cape pigeons, squids, turtles, sharks, and albatrosses. Chores consumed some time, including catching rainwater in barrels and taking turns at the washtub, though Prentice Mulford described the lazy man's method—tying a shirt to a line and trailing it behind the ship. (Those utilizing this method, however, had to learn how to use a needle to mend their clothes.) Some—out of necessity or boredom—took on sailors' jobs standing night watch, reefing sails, helping to cut and gather wood, and getting fresh water while on shore. Often, as the ship's crew grew "more & more helpless every day with lame hands [and] lame arms," passengers had to pitch in "or we shall never reach our . . . destination." Most passengers, however, felt such work was not their responsibility.

Before sailing, Frank Buck bought 58 books and a B.(ack) G.(ammon) board and a dozen packs of cards. "We have 24 rifles, powder and shot, harpoons, fishing tackle, and a sail boat . . . to amuse ourselves on our long voyage," he wrote. He also planned to study Spanish—"to exchange my French for Spanish and learn that on the voyage."

Music was also an important diversion, with passengers taking the initiative in arranging programs. Some recalled waltzing on the cabin roof; others, the pleasure of exchanging musical numbers with the few ships they passed. Occasionally there were opportunities to visit other emigrants; passengers from the *Olivia* and the *Boston*, for example, visited the *Robert Bowne* while in harbor in the Straits of Magellan.

Once again aboard ship, many passengers spent time studying; subjects mentioned in journals include French, Spanish, and astronomy. Lectures were presented on phrenology, astronomy, and medical issues such as the evil effects of mercury and bloodletting. Especially as the voyages wore on, seemingly interminably, the audiences became less receptive and the critiques more brutal.

Ellis noted that "some of the passengers are exercising their ingenuity at the invention and construction of machines for washing gold. Several plans have been exhibited, many of which will no doubt answer the purpose." But he realized that although they were becoming seasoned travelers, they were novices at mining: "it is impossible for us [to decide which inventions will work] until we arrive at the scene of our labours." Others discovered that the wood found ashore at Port Famine in the Straits of Magellan was easy to work; they passed the time making "small boxes, letter stamps, and other toys which serve as a memento of the voyage." Even amid tedium, many passengers recognized the momentous nature of the voyage and the adventure that would follow.

All was not serious, however. Passengers sat around in the evening "cracking nuts & jokes." Others "played a rub at whist." Once into the Pacific, life became more relaxed. Passengers resumed their old habits of lounging around the decks in shirtsleeves and slippers, writing, reading, learning to make different kinds of knots, smoking, telling stories, and, inevitably, talking about what great things they were going to do when they got to San Francisco.

Sundays were usually spent singing sacred music accompanied by musical instruments. Often such hymn sings were followed by a promenade on deck. On board the *Robert Bowne* a passenger read the Episcopal service and lectured on the subject "Is God a Being?" Nationalism was high; thus, the Fourth of July, "one of the greatest days in America," was celebrated aboard most ships. (Many had hoped to be in San Francisco to celebrate.) Aboard the *North Bend* many shaved for the first time since leaving Boston. The steward killed the last pig and "made us an excellent pie for our 4th of July dinner." Aboard the *Robert Bowne* the "73rd anniversary of American Independence [was not] forgotten by Americans amidst the perils of the sea." At daybreak the holiday was greeted by passengers firing off guns and pistols. At 11:00 A.M. everyone assembled on deck to participate in a formal program including prayer,

"Hail Columbia" sung by a passenger, the reading of the Declaration of Independence, an oration, 13 toasts, and the benediction, all followed by "Yankee Doodle" on the bugle played by another passenger.

Despite attempts at entertainment, life grew more tense as passengers' anticipation of arrival in San Francisco increased, only to be frustrated by Pacific calms or winds that blew ships far to the west. Aboard the *California* the problem was compounded. When it arrived at Panama, 700 ticket holders who had crossed the isthmus vied for its 250 berths. The result, wrote Captain Cleveland Forbes, was a "ship filled to cramnation . . . & everyone looking out for himself with peculiar aptness."

Forbes, a competent and upright man, was appalled at the passengers' behavior. Though there were many decent people, both in cabin and steerage, "we have also many of the scum of creation, Black legs, gamblers, thieves, rummers & Drunkards, and if we make the trip without difficulty & great loss to the ship by their pilfering and waste, I will be much surprised." Although Forbes hoped for the best, his worst fears were realized. Many were loudly discontented with the ship's crowded conditions, but not one of them was willing to be left behind. Many trashed the ship, which was completing its maiden voyage. Forbes, again, was appalled:

It is heart rendering to see them abuse the furnature [*sic*]. Handsome cushions & Mattresses are brought on deck [in part to provide resting spots anywhere but in the crowded decks below] and laid on the wet & coal dust and are spat upon & trodden upon by those one might expect the worse conduct from, but all seem to be bound to California with the idea that low conduct & uncouth deportment is necessary to make them appear of importance.

Conventions of society began to break down as everyone looked out for himself. Not even ministers were immune. Forbes described one of these "Rev. Devines" at mealtime: "While saying grace [he] was hauling a dish of green peas towards his plate and in conclusion emptied the whole on his plate," looking for more and devouring his meal as if his life depended on it. Such behavior abated a bit as the weather turned worse. Forbes observed: "Many of the Passengers are sea sick which makes them more quiet."

Passengers' behavior was so bad, on the whole, after Panama, that Forbes swore that he would not command the ship again for $10,000. Nor did passengers who had endured the trip around South America want to repeat it. Charles Ellis wrote, in no uncertain terms, "One thing is certain, if ever I am permitted to visit America again . . . I shall take some different rout than crossing the Atlantic & Pacific." What he could not yet know was that the long confinement, lack of exercise, poor diet, and exposure often meant that emigrants to California coming via the Cape arrived in poor condition for the arduous work of mining. Those coming overland or by mixed land-sea routes—if they survived—generally acquired a resilient toughness during the journey.

Once on the frontier, the new Westerners began to travel to their final destination. Although the trek was long and difficult, emigrants took opportunities to break the tedium. Because so many were on the trail at once, people could visit over evening campfires with those from other companies. This, too, lessened provinciality as people from Vermont sang with those from New Jersey and people from Ohio swapped stories with those from Washington City.

Mrs. Margaret Catherine Haun, one of a party from Clinton, Iowa, described how, during the day, "we womenfolk" visited from wagon to wagon, making "congenial friends" with whom to walk "ever westward," telling of loved ones left back in "the States," sharing dreams for the future, and even "whispering a little friendly gossip of emigrant life." In the evening "tatting, knitting, crocheting, exchanging receipts for cooking beans or dried apples or swopping food for the sake of variety kept us in practice of feminine occupations and diversions." She noted that although most went early to bed, an hour or so around the campfire was relaxing. "The menfolk lolling and guessing, or maybe betting, how many miles we had covered during the day. We listened to readings, story-telling, music and songs and the day often ended in laughter and merrymaking."

Arriving at settlements and forts such as Salt Lake City and forts Kearney and Laramie broke the monotony and provided opportunities to reprovision and to post letters for home. Like tourists ever since, the emigrants' first views of natural landmarks such as Chimney Rock or Scotts Bluff or the Rockies themselves left them in awe. And, like tourists since, passing gold-seekers left their names, slogans, and graffiti carved and daubed in tar on Independence Rock. Arriving at such landmarks also gave travelers a sense of progress. In addition, other types of people they met helped to break the monotony. They met wagons loaded with furs going east; these too gave them opportunities to send mail home. Some met—and were horrified by— "Frenchmen married to squaws." There were soldiers moving to new postings in Oregon, and deserters from Fort Laramie seduced by the news of gold.

For cowboys, boredom, broken by work, dominated life in the bunkhouses. Cowboys who were literate (and many were, having received good educations) read everything from novels and farm journals to labels on tomato cans or the wallpaper itself. Poker was popular, even though on some ranches card playing and gambling of every description were strictly forbidden; dominoes were also popular. Music helped while away the evenings; many cowboys played banjos, mouth organs, fiddles, Jew's harps, or guitars. Sometimes cowboys held kangaroo courts, the accused being ineptly defended from trivial or trumped-up charges, and the punishment being outrageously humiliating, such as being tossed in a horse trough.

> *Those who could not afford candles by which to read would build a small brush fire.*

Life—and death—in the mines was often brutal, always hard. But on occasions miners did find relaxation and entertainment. Winter was a slack time in the mines because of snow and rain. Some miners thus went into nearby towns or even to San Francisco; others waited out the time in their mountain cabins. Those who stayed entertained themselves or simply relaxed from the backbreaking labor. They slept in, played cards, washed their clothes, read, and speculated on their next year's success. Miners were hungry for news from the East, so old copies of newspapers were read assiduously, even when they were months old. Those who could not afford candles (at $4 a pound) by which to read would build a small brush fire, and as one miner kept the fire going, his partner would read aloud. Though Bayard Taylor claimed never to have seen miners read, other diarists made repeated references to books. And despite the primitive life many led, most readers preferred good books to trash. John Banks recalled reading "several romances," only one of which, *Trapper's Bride*, was good.

> *The saloon was built of wood while surrounding businesses were still made of canvas.*

For many who came overland, books had been one of the first items jettisoned because of their weight. Many of the novels Banks saw on the trail or in California "were written by depraved minds." But on the shelves of his cabin he had "quite a number" of good things to read: mostly medical books and magazines, *Knickerbocker's*, and *Blackwoods*, and the *Edinburgh Review*, an old copy of a biography of great men, Lyell's *Geology*, two books of philosophy, and "an English work entitled *Dialogues of Devils*," which "comes far short of *Paradise Lost*." Prentice Mulford remembered that as early as 1854 or 1855 the "boys" at Hawkin's Bar pooled their money and sent down to San Francisco for books to establish a library including geology books and a full set of American encyclopedias, "heavy and nutritious mental food rising into the lighter desserts of poetry and novels." He described one miner who read as he ate; he "devoured beef and lard, bacon and beans and encyclopedias, Humboldt's 'Cosmos' and dried apples, novels and physical nourishment at . . . the same time."

However, not all miners were readers, nor were books everywhere available. Consequently, many miners enjoyed other activities in the mining towns. High on the list were drinking and gambling. Lacking any other home or social circle, they frequented tavern tents where, according to J. D. Stevenson, "cards are the only books to be found." Though miners might be cautious at first, as more liquor was consumed and stakes raised, many left to sleep on the ground and awoke "with aching heads and empty purses." However, whether in the mining camps or in Sacramento or San Francisco, the saloon was often the best house in town, offering miners what might have been their only aesthetic experience. The saloon was built of wood while surrounding businesses were still made of canvas; often the decor included gilt-framed mirrors and paintings; musicians frequently added to the ambience with instruments including the piano, flute, violin, cello, and trumpet; and in Sacramento "Ethiopian melodists . . . nightly call upon 'Susanna!' and entreat to be carried back to Old Virginny." One miner recalled that nearly everyone drank, and that of 100 people passing his cabin, "twenty or thirty go reeling." Much behavior seemed predicated on a single goal: to make money. Another miner, somewhat shocked, wrote of a doctor who "keeps a trading post, sells whiskey, etc. through the week, drinks brandy freely and preaches on Sunday. Who cares? Not the Devil!"

Since mining itself was so often a matter of luck, it is not surprising that games of chance were popular. The most commonly played game was monte, though dealers were also adept at euchre, faro, grab, and vingt-et-un. Professional gamblers followed miners to every new strike.

Their diggings are in the pockets of the miners and not in the pockets of the [river] bars. . . . They offer the simple and foolish as good a chance to lose the results of months of labor and privation in an hour as is done in the more showy and magnificent halls in the city. . . . Generally a few days spent in one place is sufficient to drain the font of the gambling miner's stream, and when all have "come down with the dust" who will pay tribute to folly, the gambler rolls up his blanket, shoulders his pile, and climbs to another bar.

In San Francisco and Sacramento, "from good authority we are told that there are several Methodist ministers . . . now dealing monte . . . for the purpose of gain." Repeatedly, the gold rush allowed people to redefine themselves.

Moreover, the saloons and gambling houses allowed miners to enjoy the presence of women, who were decidedly scarce in California. About the attractions of one gambling house, one miner wrote that in addition to a "splendidly" stocked bar and a band of musicians, "abandoned women visit these places openly. I saw one the other evening sitting quietly at the monte table, dressed in white pants, blue coat, and cloth cap, curls dangling over her cheeks, cigar in her mouth and a glass of punch at her side. She handled a pile of doubloons with her blue kid gloved hands, and bet most boldly." William Perkins reflected on all such activities: "The want of respectable female society, rational amusements, and books, has aided greatly to demoralization of many whose natural character would have kept them aloof from temptation had there been any other means but the gambling houses and drinking saloons, to have assisted them in whiling away the hours not devoted to labor."

Though less frequently noted, there was other recreation. One man mentioned going pistol shooting in the cemetery. Another forked out $2 to spend an evening in a leaking tent to watch a circus, apparently consisting mostly of juggling and acrobatics. Several mentioned attending a bull and bear fight, in which the two animals were tethered just within reach of each other and gored, gouged, scratched, and bit each other. In areas where there were large numbers of Mexican miners, bullfights were held. Dancing was popular. In the camps, men often had to dance with men, one wearing a handkerchief to designate himself as the woman. In the towns, surprisingly elaborate balls were organized. William Perkins described one in Sonora for which 50 invitations were issued:

The music was a piano, a violincello, a harp, a violin, and a couple of guitars; the dances, all those fashionable in the old world. . . . There was also plenty of singing in French and spanish; and the supper was something really wonderful for the mountains. Ices, creams, blancmange, pastry, cold ham and fowls, pheasant pies, quail pasties. . . . And then the wines! . . . Cargoes of the richest wines produced in France and the Mediterranean were sent to San Francisco in the first excitement of the gold fever. . . . For some months we had been purchasing exquisite champagnes, clarets, Burgundies, sherries, even Lachrymachristi. . . . At the supper, two dozen of claret, three dozen of champagne, and one dozen of Burgundy were consumed; a very moderate quantity. . . . It was broad daylight when the "women folks" were taken home, and we addressed ourselves to our daily duties, very well satisfied with our first Ball in California, and quite proved that our half savage life had not made us forget the steps of the Mazurka and Polka.

Dame Shirley, with her rather tart tongue, told of the hazards of such a ball. Though on the evening of the ball at Indian Bar everyone behaved well, men nonetheless expectorated; as a result, "there was some danger of being swept away in a flood of tobacco juice." However, since the floor was uneven the juice collected in puddles, which dancers could usually avoid, "merely running the risk of falling prostrate upon the wet boards in the midst of a gallopade" (Jones, 106–8, 128–30, 177–78).

To read about leisure time on the colonial frontier of North America, see the entries on Colonial Frontier and New England in the sections "Games and Arts" and "Hobbies" in chapter 7 ("Recreational Life") in volume 4 of this series.

FOR MORE INFORMATION

Ambrose, S. E. *Undaunted Courage: Meriwether Lewis, Thomas Jefferson, and the Opening of the American West.* New York: Simon & Schuster, 1996.

Jones, M. E. *Daily Life on the Nineteenth Century American Frontier.* Westport, Conn.: Greenwood Press, 1998.

Scamehorn, H. L., ed. *The Buckeye Rovers in the Gold Rush.* Athens: Ohio University Press, 1965.

RECREATIONAL
LIFE

LEISURE TIME

United States,
1850-1865

United States,
Western Frontier

Victorian England

India

VICTORIAN ENGLAND

Girls were told that their hands should never be idle. When not doing something else, women felt they should be busy at some kind of needlework. Those who had servants to sew and mend the family clothing occupied their time with embroidery, tatting, crochet, fancy knitting, and other needle crafts. Many contemporary hobbyists treasure the storehouse of stitches, patterns, and ideas found in Victorian needlework manuals and women's magazines.

Two styles of embroidery were especially popular: Berlin work and white-on-white embroidery. Berlin work made use of bright strands of wool for counted-thread designs. Although it resembles the work now called needlepoint or petit point, high-quality Berlin work involved a wide variety of stitches in addition to cross-stitch and filling stitch. Most Berlin work was purely decorative. Scenic pictures were framed to hang on the wall or used as fire screens. Bellpulls, eyeglass cases, dresser tidies, cushions, protective shoe cases, watch fobs, and similar items were made for Christmas gifts.

White-on-white embroidery, which could be combined with cutwork and sometimes with fine beading, was used to decorate baby clothing and household linens. Many women who could afford to have a dressmaker nevertheless made (and embroidered) their own underclothing and their babies' best dresses. William Morris and his daughter May Morris revived interest in traditional English crewel. For the devout, church needlework was a satisfying occupation. Published instruction manuals helped women of the congregation produce kneelers, vestments, banners, frontals, and altar linen.

Knitting was largely practical: stockings, mittens, caps, shawls, and soft jackets for babies or invalids. (The jersey, or sweater, was a garment worn primarily by sailors, fishers, and some other working people.) Virtually every girl learned to knit, and most women had a knitting project to pick up when the light was poor or the conversation too interesting to pay attention to anything more demanding. Tatting and crochet were used to make fancy edgings for household linens, petticoats, and other garments. Elaborate crochet patterns for lace collars, table covers, bedspreads, and other projects were printed both in *Englishwoman's Domestic Magazine* and in working-class women's papers.

Many other crafts and hobbies were recommended to adults and young people as useful and worthwhile means of filling leisure time. Shellwork, beadwork, upholstery, drawing and painting, calligraphy and manuscript illumination, woodcarving, mosaic work, painting on glass and china, and making wax flowers are only a few examples. People also made decorations for mantles and dressing tables, stenciled walls and furniture, painted silk for fans and screens, tinted photographs, and did leatherwork.

Family magazines read by the working class and the middle class were full of "parlour pastimes" for evenings at home: chess, backgammon, songs for family singing, hints for acting charades, optical illusions, scientific tricks, demonstrations to do with simple equipment, puzzles, and word games. The most popular Victorian card game was whist, which was an early form of bridge.

Photography was a popular new hobby at the century's end. Early cameras required a lot of equipment. Many of the first amateur photographers were upper-class women who had ample money, time, and darkroom space. People had their photograph taken only on important occasions. Cheap box cameras, introduced in 1888, were an instant sensation. They made photography possible for working people and even for children.

Collecting was done by people of all classes. Victorian collections found in antique stores today include albums of stamps, autographs, picture postcards, favorite quotations (neatly copied and dated), and souvenirs of special occasions. Working-class girls filled scrapbooks with designs made from the colored advertising cards that merchants handed out for free.

Natural history was also very popular. Amateur naturalists combined hobby and science; they collected fossils, seaweeds, mosses, ferns, fungi, butterflies, and other insects—and they did the basic descriptive and classification work on many species. Bird watchers began keeping local records. Once microscopes became widely

available, specimen clubs spent Saturday afternoons making excursions and examining the samples they brought back. Rustic hobbies gave city and suburban people a reason to make trips into the country and a way to bring nature home. Even a

---

 Snapshot

English Doublets, 1879

Invented by Lewis Carroll, author of *Alice's Adventures in Wonderland,* this game was first described in the magazine *Vanity Fair* in 1879.

Directions: Change one word into the other, altering only one letter at a time. All the steps between must be actual words, as:

Drive PIG into STY:

PIG
pit
sit
sat
say
STY

The following may also be done:

Raise FOUR to FIVE
Dip PEN into INK
Make WHEAT into BREAD
Touch CHIN with NOSE
Change TEARS into SMILE
Get COAL from MINE
Make FLOUR into BREAD
Make EEL into PIE
Evolve MAN from APE
Prove PITY to be GOOD
Cover EYE with LID

~[Mitchell, 231]

small room could have an aquarium or terrarium. Those with more space had greenhouses, ferneries, exotic houseplants, and caged birds.

Girls pressed flowers for both scientific and sentimental reasons. They made small bouquets as party favors. Popular handbooks explained the language of flowers—the meaning of each bloom or combination in a bouquet. The meanings, however, varied in different books, just as the interpretation of dreams varied between the dream books that were also popular.

Household pets became common only after 1800. Before that, watchdogs and other working dogs lived outside; pet animals were an upper-class indulgence. By the Victorian period, however, the English were already notorious for their sentimental love of dogs. Some historians believe that newly urbanized people yearned for the animals that had shared their lives in the country, whereas others credit the growth in surplus money in allowing people the ability to feed their pets and the leisure to walk and play with them. During the second half of the century, the Kennel Club established standards for the different breeds and began holding dog shows. Exhibitors at some shows included coal miners and other working-class men who bred dogs as a hobby.

Somewhat later, exotic cats such as Siamese and Persians became popular. (Most households also kept a working cat to patrol for mice. One is clearly visible in the publicity photograph of a scientific and sanitary professional cooking school that advertised in women's magazines.) Other popular pets included rabbits, guinea pigs, squirrels, dormice, white mice, doves, and exotic birds (Mitchell, 230–33).

To read about leisure time in Chaucer's England, see the entries on Europe in chapter 7 ("Recreational Life") in volume 2 of this series; for Elizabethan England, see the entries on England in the sections "Games" and "Sports and Outdoor Pursuits") in chapter 7 ("Recreational Life") in volume 3 of this series; for 18th-century England, see the entries on England in the sections "Games and Arts" and "Hobbies" in chapter 7 ("Recreational Life") in volume 4 of this series.

FOR MORE INFORMATION

Altick, R. D. *Victorian People and Ideas*. New York: W. W. Norton, 1973.
Harrison, J. F. C. *The Early Victorians, 1832–1851*. London: Weidenfeld and Nicolson, 1971.
———. *Late Victorian Britain, 1875–1901*. London: Fontana Press, 1990.
Mitchell, S. *Daily Life in Victorian England*. Westport, Conn.: Greenwood Press, 1996.

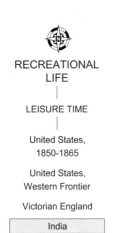

RECREATIONAL
LIFE
|
LEISURE TIME
|
United States,
1850-1865

United States,
Western Frontier

Victorian England

India

INDIA

Leisure activities varied greatly in 19th-century India. Many board games were popular at this time. There is a long tradition of board games in India. Chess is thought to have originated in India in the 6th century c.e. During the 19th century chess was very popular in both urban and rural areas.

Parcheesi also originated in India around the same time as chess. Snakes and Ladders, which was the inspiration for Chutes and Ladders, is also native to India. Both were popular during this time period.

Carrom was another popular game that originated in India. It involves a wooden board about two feet long on each side. In each corner is a small hole. At the start of a game nine black coins, nine white coins, and a pink coin called the queen are placed in the center of the board. The object is to make the coins go into the holes, by flicking them with two fingers. Two teams of two players each compete, with partners sitting across from each other.

Another traditional game that was popular in the 19th century is called Kho-kho. In this game, which is similar to tag, the defending team sends in players in batches of three. A member of the opposing team chases these players along an oblong field toward the goal at the end. Other members of the opposing team crouch in squares drawn along a centerline, and if they manage to touch one of the people being chased, the person who has been touched is out. Both boys and girls played this game.

Kabaddi (known as *hu-tu-tu* in parts of southern India) is also similar to tag. There are two teams of 12 players each. The playing field is divided in two. One side sends a raider into the opponent's half. The raider must touch as many of the opposing team's members as possible and return to the home side. However, this must be done in one breath, chanting the name of the game the entire way. If the raider runs out of breath before returning to the home side, or steps outside the boundary, he or she is out.

Cricket also became popular during this time. Introduced by the British, the game became popular throughout India and is still enormously popular. It is played with a wicket, similar to a baseball bat, only flat instead of rounded. A ball is pitched, similar to in baseball, only the pitcher intentionally makes the ball bounce before reaching the batter. The wicket is then swung low to the ground to hit the ball. The person who has just hit the ball runs. All ages participated in pickup games in the streets or fields.

Other spectator activities included plays, musical concerts, puppet shows, and dance. Street theater, often with religious context, was a popular form of entertainment in the villages. A troupe of actors traveled from village to village and charged a small fee to everyone who came to watch the show. In some instances when a member of the cast portrayed a god or goddess, members of the audience viewed the actor as the actual god. Paradoxically, showmanship was considered a job worthy of little respect.

In bigger cities there were more permanent theaters. During the 19th century in Calcutta the British form of drama became popular among the upper class. Plays by Rabindanath Tagore were sometimes performed, and on some occasions English plays, mainly by Shakespeare, were also performed.

Musical concerts were another popular form of entertainment. Most music also had a religious context, although other pieces were simply love songs. The shows were often several hours long, and some even went all night, particularly musical depictions of Hindu epics such as the *Ramayana*.

In the western state of Rajasthan, there is a long tradition of puppet shows. Elaborate marionettes are made and used to perform dramas, also often with a religious context. Traditionally the puppeteers stand behind the puppets, so that they are completely visible. Yet, when watching the show the audience tends to focus only on the puppets.

There are several forms of traditional dance in India. Most have religious significance. There are also hundreds of folk traditions of dance, of which most also have religious significance. Watching dance was a popular activity in both urban and rural areas during the 19th century.

Visiting the local temple was also a common activity in India. At night, after partaking in religious rituals at the temple, families or individuals would often congregate around the temple, or inside the temple at the steps surrounding a large tank of water, which is often present in temples, particularly in southern India. This was seen as a social time when people chatted with friends, and children played.

Both Hindus and Muslims generally look down on consumption of alcohol. However, throughout India local brews were fairly common. Some of these included arak, which is made from fermented rice, and toddy, which is made from fermented coconut and palmyra palm juice, and was found mainly in the south. Because of the social stigma of drinking, those who did partake in drinking sometimes had a tendency to drink too much and too often. Among those who consumed alcohol in 19th-century India there is evidence of a high rate of alcoholism.

Tobacco, either in the form of *bidis*, or little cigarettes rolled up in a dried leaf, or taken from a *huka*, or water pipe, was also common. Very few women smoked, but a large percentage of men smoked, often in groups while sitting around together at a tea stall, or at the village meeting place.

Cannabis, and sometimes even opium were somewhat popular in some parts of India, mainly by religious people, as it was viewed as a means of reaching a higher level of spiritual enlightenment. Drinks made from *bang*, or the dried leaves of the cannabis plant, were commonly used during religious ceremonies. Sadhus, or religious ascetics, often smoked hashish from a chillum, or a type of pipe usually made out of clay.

~Dana Lightstone

FOR MORE INFORMATION

Banjeree, U. K., ed. *Bengali Theatre: 200 Years*. New Delhi, India: Publications Division, Ministry of Information & Broadcasting, Govt. of India, 1999.

Londhe, V., M. Agneswaran, and K. Rele, eds. *Handbook of Indian Classical Dance Terminology*. Bombay, India: Nalanda Dance Research Centre, 1992.

Pal, P., ed. *2000, Reflections on the Arts in India*. Mumbai, India: Marg Publications, 2000.

RECREATIONAL LIFE: WEB SITES

http://www.enoreo.on.ca/socialstudies/pioneer-virtual/games/html
http://www.victorianstation.com/leisureoverview.htm
http://www.indianchild.com/festivals_in_india.htm

http://memory.loc.gov/ammem/collections/finder.html
http://www.croquetamerica.com/overview.asp
http://www.pdmusic.org/1800s.html
http://www.contemplator.com/folk.html
http://www.victorianbazaar.com/hobbies.html
http://www.videoccasions-nw.com/history/jw19th.html

8

RELIGIOUS LIFE

RELIGIOUS LIFE
|
MORALITY

RELIGION

The human world is made up of more than the material and social environments that surround us. Throughout history, people have left records of their recognition of, and longing for, something larger than themselves. This desire to transcend daily life forms the basis for people's religious faith. Religions have two intertwined components—belief and rituals—the second derives from and preserves the former. Thus, through careful enactment of rituals, the faithful believe they can rise above the mundane realities of day-to-day life, and historians find that the study of religious practices offers a window into people's spiritual beliefs.

Religious beliefs have served to help people make sense of the natural world— from its beauties to its disasters. For example, an ancient Egyptian pharaoh (Akhenaton) and a medieval Christian saint (Francis) both wrote magnificent poetry praising the blessings of this world. In addition, the Buddha and the Hebrew Scriptures' Book of Job both talk about the deep suffering of this life. Similarly, the Qur'an (Koran) provides Muslims with Allah's messages to men and women. In these ways, religion has always helped people make sense of the world and provides some security that the world around them is at least somewhat rational and serves a larger purpose.

At the same time, religious rituals serve the needs of society. The faithful reinforce their social ties by worshiping together, and sociologists of religion argue that religion is the symbolic worship of society itself. Sacred songs, dances, and feasts have always served to bind communities closer together, and in these ways the religious and secular lives of the people mingle. This intimate relationship between religious beliefs, rituals, and societies makes the study of religious life a fruitful one. The complex nature of societies also yields complexities in religious beliefs and practices. In this volume alone, over one dozen religions are mentioned, explained, and analyzed. Throughout history, we can follow the reforms and indeed revolutions in religious ideas that have profoundly shaped our past. Moreover, some religious men and women have led movements that brought them into sharp conflict with followers of other faiths. For example, in the United States, certain Protestants launched attacks on Catholics. Even before that Christianity and Islam had squared off in the Middle East as well as in Europe. Thus, religious belief and practice served both to bring people together and to divide societies.

Through the study of religious life, we can learn about how people viewed the natural and supernatural, how rituals organized people's daily lives, and how beliefs brought out the best (and the worst) in people. At the same time, we can glimpse the deep longing in the human soul that has generated some of people's noblest thought.

FOR MORE INFORMATION

Altick, R. D. *Victorian People and Ideas*. New York: W. W. Norton, 1973.

Dawood, N. J., trans. *The Koran*. Baltimore: Penguin Books, 1966.

Raboteau, A. J. *Slave Religion: The "Invisible Institution" in the Antebellum South*. New York: Oxford University Press, 1978.

Robinson, N. *Islam: A Concise Introduction*. Washington, D.C.: Georgetown University Press, 1999.

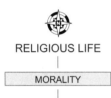

RELIGIOUS LIFE
|
MORALITY
|
United States, 1850-1865

Victorian England

China

Islamic World

Morality

Morality is the general notion of what is right and what is wrong. At first blush, this seems simple enough. All people have a code of ethics by which they live. However, understanding how morality actually works and how it has changed over time is a complicated task. As one will glean from the entries in this section, ethics often depend on who one is, where one is, and what one is doing. For instance, in 19th-century China, there was no one particular morality. One's beliefs depended on religion, whether Confucian or Christian, and on politics, whether traditionalist or modernist. Moreover, the hard-and-fast rules that make one thing right and one thing wrong are in fact difficult to discern. When reading the entries below, pay close attention to the ways in which morality changes to meet the needs of a specific time. Also, note that different cultures have different moral standards. Moreover, when these cultures meet, there are frequent ethical clashes.

Given these truisms about morality, when we think of the 19th century, we tend to think about the phrase Victorian morality. That has come to imply prudery, hypocrisy, sexual repression, and social control. Although English moral standards did include aspects of these attributes, there were other more influential ethical notions. One was that people were to be self-reliant and not look to others for aid or assistance. Corollaries to this idea were the notions that economic and personal rewards derived from hard work, frugality, and self-denial. Thus work itself had moral virtue. Working the right way meant living the right way. In other words, a moral approach to work produced independence and respectability, two of the highest virtues in English society.

The English as well as other Europeans brought these moral standards and others to the parts of the world that they colonized. As the entries on the Muslim world and China indicate, Chinese and Muslim morality often clashed with European precepts. Drawing the distinctions and contradictions between European, Chinese, and Muslim moralities can be overdone. Muslims shared a belief system in which one God created the world, and honoring that God was an important aspect of ethical behavior. Similarly, living the right life for both Muslims and Europeans meant getting married and having children. Likewise, the Confucian emphasis on family is akin to the Christian ideal. But other Muslim and Chinese moral codes ran counter to European ones. In particular, Europeans and Muslims fought over the proper structure of family and the proper place of women. When Europeans colonized the Middle East they sought to end the practice of polygamy and improve the status of women through education. They also fought over cultural pluralism. At least in their colonies, Europeans tolerated a certain amount of religious diversity. Muslims often held quite negative views of those that they considered *infidels*. These cultural contests over morality fed into the nationalist movements opposed to European colonization and led to wider cultural battles in the 20th century.

Finally, aside from the moral conflicts between societies, pay special attention to the moral conflicts within individuals. One of the central ethical dictums in the United States is the prohibition on murder. Killing is wrong. Or is it? Perhaps better explained: killing is wrong under most circumstances. Read the entry on the Civil War carefully and notice how traditionally moral codes of honor and duty get transformed in war. By saying this, we do not imply that the Civil War soldiers were immoral. Rather, one must recognize that morality itself is malleable and changes to suit the immediate needs of a particular time and a particular place.

UNITED STATES, 1850–65

Normally killing others is wrong, except during war. War creates a peculiar morality that transforms ethical codes from valuing life into codes valuing honor and duty. It is strange that federal volunteers most often associated their service with duty, while honor seems to have motivated Confederate volunteers. Although the two are not mutually exclusive, there is some truth in viewing the South as a society with a profound sense of honor, whereas the North was driven by a communal conscience analogous to a compact made with God. Americans of the early 19th century were strongly influenced by such sentiments. The consciousness of duty resonated particularly well with the parallel development of social reform in the North. To shirk duty was to violate the collective conscience and to offend morality by omission. Duty was viewed as a personal responsibility rather than a collective obligation. "We all of us have a duty to perform in this life," wrote one volunteer. It was not enough to support the war from a distance when duty required that a man place his life on the line. Many Confederates also cited obligations to duty, but they were much more likely to speak of honor.

Honor was primarily a masculine concept that dealt with one's public image and reputation. There is ample evidence of a link among the romantic themes of adventure, glory, and honor that appeared in the popular literature of the period and the letters and diaries of the Southern volunteers. Nonetheless, Southerners also viewed honor in a contemporary light, and the continued popularity of dueling

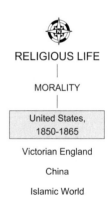

RELIGIOUS LIFE

|

MORALITY

|

United States,
1850-1865

Victorian England

China

Islamic World

attests to the vitality of the sentiment in the Southern psyche. Confederate soldiers often wrote of being dishonored in the eyes of their "revolutionary ancestors" should they fail to defend the cause. Nonetheless, the appeals to duty and honor were most often found among the letters and journals of the more literate upper classes.

Among less popular motivations such as adventure, excitement, patriotism, and ideology, Civil War soldiers were also affected by a need to prove their masculinity. Southerners tended to be more boastful in this regard than the Yankees. "They were amiable, gentle, and unselfish in disposition, yet were fearless and daring in spirit, and devoted . . . to those bodily exercises that make the strong and vigorous man," noted one observer. Northerners tended to be more circumspect, worrying whether they would pass the test of manhood posed by battle. The psychological importance of passing this test should not be minimized. Particularly among the young volunteers, the experience of battle, "seeing the elephant" in 19th-century terms, was seen as a rite of passage.

A young woman wrote, "It seems very patriotic and grand . . . [to die] for one's country. . . . A lot of us girls went down to the train and took flowers to the soldiers as they were passing through and they cut buttons from their coats and gave [them] to us as souvenirs." Young men quickly repudiated the romance, adventure, and glory of war once they had "seen the elephant," but a young man's performance on the battlefield quite literally separated the men from the boys.

Perhaps the many references to sentiment were a reaction to the pressures brought upon the men by the communities and social groups to which they belonged. As volunteers generally served in companies and regiments raised from the eligible men in a local neighborhood, it may have been socially impossible for them to do otherwise. A contemporary commentator noted, "The associations of . . . boyhood and early manhood were with these people . . . [their] dearest and most intimate friends and companions. . . . These men found gratification in a military organization composed of those of their own class."

If the recruits' own motivations for volunteering, as set down in their personal letters and diaries, are not accepted at face value, it is difficult to rationalize how so many individuals could have been willing to die for a cause or how such massive volunteer armies could have been raised. Nonetheless, it remains an extraordinary fact that during the first year of the war all those who enlisted and fought on one side or the other chose to do so (Volo and Volo, 101–3).

To read about morality in the United States in the 20th century, see the United States entries in the section "Morality" in chapter 8 ("Religious Life") in volume 6 of this series.

FOR MORE INFORMATION

Mitchell, R. *Civil War Soldiers: Ideology and Experience*. New York: Simon & Schuster, 1985.
Volo, D. D., and J. M. Volo. *Daily Life in Civil War America*. Westport, Conn.: Greenwood Press, 1998.
Zwick, E. *Glory*. 1989. Film.

VICTORIAN ENGLAND

The phrase *Victorian morality* is often used with contempt. It has come to imply prudery, hypocrisy, sexual repression, and rigid social control. This entry explores certain widespread Victorian moral ideals to understand their value—and their failings. Remember, however, that widespread does not mean universal. All stereotypes simplify the real world, and most people's values are too complex to express in easy maxims.

Formerly, biographies of great men worthy of emulation had concentrated on political, military, and religious leaders. Writer Samuel Smiles, by contrast, drew examples in *Self-Help* from the lives of inventors, businessmen, and industrialists. He gave special praise to the self-taught worker-engineers whose mechanical devices revolutionized transportation and factory production. People who emphasized self-help were skeptical about genius or natural ability; success, they believed, came instead from practical experience and perseverance. Necessity, difficulty, and even poverty were welcomed as spurs to achievement.

Self-help provided a powerful counterweight to the rankings of social class. Humble origins could be seen as an asset rather than as something to conceal. A businessman or industrialist who reached the top even though he began to work as a child and had to study late into the night after laboring all day was more admirable than the successful man who began with greater advantages. The sense of pride in rising from rude beginnings was (in English society) fairly new; it helped make Dinah Mulock Craik's 1856 novel *John Halifax, Gentleman* (a very readable rags-to-riches story) one of the century's bestselling books.

Self-help in action led to a massive adult education movement with study groups run by workers themselves, as well as workingmens' colleges where university graduates taught classes. However, some advocates of self-help distrusted formal learning and praised only the useful knowledge gained through experience. In any event, success required moral discipline and ethical behavior as well as hard work; there was no admiration for people who got ahead by cutting corners or deluding others.

The values associated with evangelical religion helped promote the growth of business and the advance of middle-class men. Although hard work, frugality, and self-denial were apt to bring economic rewards, most evangelicals believed it was wrong for a man to devote his life to work simply because he wanted to get rich. Hard work was seen as a moral good in itself; if wealth followed, it was a fitting recognition of the man's virtue.

The moral virtue of work extended beyond the world of paid employment. Working-class and middle-class people bolstered their sense of worth by feeling contempt for the idle rich. The leisured life became less common among the gentry and aristocracy. Women at home felt guilty if they were idle. Some families thought that reading books was a kind of laziness; even studying should be postponed until evening when the day's work was done. The feeling that every person should be usefully employed did a great deal to promote charity, philanthropy, social welfare work, and public service by women and men whose income came from other sources.

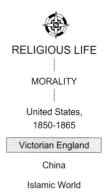

RELIGIOUS LIFE
|
MORALITY
|
United States,
1850-1865

Victorian England

China

Islamic World

Respectability was another Victorian watchword. It was used as a primary social distinction, often more important than the class line. Especially among the poor and the lower middle class, being respectable was a way to maintain self-respect and public reputation.

Respectable has no absolute definition. For some nonconformists, dancing, playing cards, and going to the theater were not respectable. Young people who valued their reputation for respectability did not eat on the street, wear flashy clothing, speak in loud voices, or in any way call attention to themselves. A respectable family had tidy clothes, a clean house, and good manners; its members were chaste, sober, and honest. A well-to-do man who was clearly not respectable—who did not pay his debts, or who openly kept a mistress—would not be invited into the homes of most men in his class.

Respectability was closely associated with the concept of independence, which required people to look after themselves and bear troubles without complaint. Because uncomplaining independence was considered a virtue, people felt shamed if they had to ask for charity or accept poor relief.

Independence required working at a job that provided an adequate income. Self-denial and thrift were needed to stay out of debt. Respectable people in the lower middle class and skilled working class had a horror of purchasing anything on credit or using the pawnshop to raise money, even in an emergency. Working-class children were advised to avoid the tally-man (who sold clothing and household goods on the installment plan) and to save money by using clothing clubs, friendly societies, and the post-office savings bank. An 1876 domestic economy book for elementary-school girls exhorted: "If you can't pay for it, do without. People who buy for cash get better prices than those who need credit." If someone is sick and out of work, the book said, a good woman will have friends to depend on; she will not beg, but she will accept help without losing her self-respect because she has given help to others when she can.

The importance of self-sufficiency was perhaps strongest in the lower middle class. A common maxim was "keep yourself to yourself." There was a strong inhibition against telling anyone about personal problems or family difficulties. Neighbors kept their distance; people seldom invited anyone except relatives into their houses. It was important never to go outside without being properly dressed. In the lower middle class, men as well as women had very little social life. They seldom went into a pub, although not necessarily because of temperance; they might drink bottled beer with meals. Free time on Saturday afternoon was spent taking children to the park. There was a strong emphasis on bringing up children well and protecting them from corrupting influences. Mothers did more child care than in other classes; the only servant was usually a girl-of-all-work for the cleaning and heavy chores.

Independence and thrift were also important to the rest of the middle class. There was some suspicion, however, of people who accumulated wealth for their children to inherit. Unearned money might tempt them into idleness. The goal, rather, was to live comfortably and to educate sons so they would also be able to earn a good living. Most middle-class men who could afford it bought life insurance to protect their widows, but there was a growing sense by the end of the period that it was better to train a daughter so she could support herself if necessary. Careful fathers earlier in the century had made burdensome sacrifices to accumulate investments that would provide a moderate income for daughters who did not marry.

Earnest and serious were other terms of approval. Levity, frivolity, and vanity were frowned upon. Earnestness did not exclude pleasure, but it did suggest that people needed recreation for health and restoration, not as self-indulgence. Hygiene was cast in moral terms. Diseases were said to be caused by drink or overindulgence; they could be prevented through moderation, baths, exercise, and making sure the garbage was collected and the house and street were kept clean.

Most of the lesser virtues associated with respectability circled back, once again, to characteristics that promoted business efficiency and economic success: punctuality, early rising, orderliness, concern for little things, self-denial, self-control, initiative, constructive use of leisure, prudent marriage. These traits were widely promoted in lectures, books, sermons, magazines, and workingmen's self-help societies. A handbook for clerks published in 1878 advised them to cultivate patience, courtesy, and deference; to be quiet and unassuming in their clothing; and to take care that their speech was clear and correct. Thus, in the ideology of the period, both working-class and middle-class men could move up in the world and become independent and respectable citizens (Mitchell, 259–65).

FOR MORE INFORMATION

Altick, R. D. *Victorian People and Ideas*. New York: W. W. Norton, 1973.
Harrison, J. F. C. *The Early Victorians, 1832–1851*. London: Weidenfeld and Nicolson, 1971.
———. *Late Victorian Britain, 1875–1901*. London: Fontana Press, 1990.
Mitchell, S. *Daily Life in Victorian England*. Westport, Conn.: Greenwood Press, 1996.

CHINA

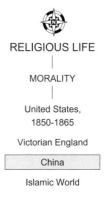

Morality is one of the main elements defining any society. It is highly varied between societies, and as a result, when two very different cultures come into contact, morality often comes into focus and highlights the differences between various cultures. During the 19th century, as trade relations with Europe increased, China came into contact with foreign countries more than ever before, and as a result, conflicting concepts of morality came into focus. At this time two very different concepts of morality competed: the old, based on Confucian ideals, and a new, modern idea of morality, which was heavily influenced by foreign concepts and ideologies. Those who rejected the new believed that only because of traditional Confucian morality had China survived and maintained its culture despite the fall of the state to foreign conquerors. The differing views are made evident by various political movements that took place during this time.

Confucius (551–479 B.C.E.) is the father of this philosophy. However, the main ideals of Confucian philosophy, such as ancestor worship, social hierarchy, and the importance of family existed as a major part of the Chinese belief system long before Confucius. Confucius reinforced these ideals, which continued, long after his death, to be even further engrained into the beliefs of many Chinese people. The Han dynasty (206 B.C.E.–24 C.E.) established Confucianism as the state religion and it remained so until the fall of the Qing dynasty in 1911. Since the eighth century the Analects, which is considered the most important of the Confucian texts, has been an important part of the school curriculum throughout China.

Confucianism is more than a political philosophy; it is a complete way of life. In short, the main concepts of Confucianism are (1) family is the basic unit of society, and (2) social hierarchy is important and upholds the social order of society. This means that women are expected to defer to men, children to parents, younger brothers to older brothers, and everyone is expected to defer to the emperor. Confucianism also rejects a code of law, because having such a code implies an inability to work things out by negotiation.

Those favoring the new ideas believed that the only way for China to progress in the modern world was to reject certain elements of traditional Confucian culture and to replace it with something new. Those who held this view saw modernization as requiring liberation from the past. An antitraditionalist movement began, which rejected the Confucian ideals. During the 19th century the antitraditionalist movement was relatively small in number, and for the most part their platform was relatively moderate. They attacked certain aspects of Confucianism, often in the name of a purified and revitalized Confucian belief system. It was not until the early 20th century that an open assault on Confucianism began.

The leaders of the antitraditionalist movement looked very much to the West. Positivism was their main inspiration, John Dewey and Bertrand Russell their main idols. They strived towards scientific and technological development. They viewed materialism and consumerism as the way of the future.

Mostly members of the younger generation, the antitraditionalists were for the most part Western educated. They were not necessarily schooled in the West, but rather in missionary schools, as that form of Western-style education was by now somewhat well established in China. Many of the leaders of the non-traditionalist political movements were college professors, often easily able to sway intellectual young minds to follow the professors' own somewhat radical views.

The Taiping Rebellion, which followed China's defeat in the Opium War, is perhaps the clearest example of two conflicting sets of moral values. The leader of this rebellion, Hong Xiuquan (1813–64) was from a peasant family belonging to the Hakka minority group and living near Guangzhou. On one of his many trips to Guangzhou to take the provincial civil service examination, which he had repeatedly failed, he heard a Christian missionary speak, and took with him some of the offered religious texts. The following year he once again failed the examination, and as a result, he suffered a nervous breakdown. During this time he had several visions. In one vision an old man appeared to him and said that men should be worshiping Hong, but instead were serving demons. In another, a different man instructed Hong in the slaying of demons. In yet another Confucius was scolded for his bad philosophy and evil morals, and repented his ways. Hong concluded that Shangdi (a deity of ancient Chinese tradition) and Jesus Christ, who he believed to be his own older brother, had commissioned him to eliminate demon worship. He quickly gained a large following. Perhaps most persuasive to many was the fact that he was able to convince his own family of the rightness of his cause.

Hong continued his study of Christianity by reading translations of sermons and by studying with Reverend Issachar J. Roberts, an American Southern Baptist missionary. Hong, joined by members of his family, led idol-breaking missions throughout the region. These missions aroused both local feelings of dissatisfaction with the government and with traditional ideals, as well as the displeasure of the local authorities.

Fed up with harassment from government officials, Hong and his followers staged a revolt. In 1851 they succeeded in overthrowing the Manchu regime. Hong assumed the title of Heavenly King. They named the dynasty *Taiping,* or "great deed." The Taiping dynasty rejected the Confucian belief system and advocated monotheism, which until then was a nonexistent concept in China.

In 1860 the Manchus, with the help of British and French military forces, defeated the Taiping dynasty and reclaimed power. Again the debate of traditional versus new came into sharp focus. Many viewed the Manchu restoration in the Western regions as a reclaiming of the old, traditional ways of China. Others saw this as a time when great modernization was possible. The conservative Confucians placed hope in the fact that old institutions had stood the test of time. Many Chinese people at this time believed that even though it was necessary to adopt Western guns and ships, and other forms of technology, old moral standards must be upheld to preserve the character of the nation

~*Dana Lightstone*

FOR MORE INFORMATION

Boardman, E. P. *Christian Influence upon the Ideology of the Taiping Rebellion, 1851–64.* Madison: University of Wisconsin Press, 1952.

Clarke, P., and J. S. Gregory, eds. *Western Reports on the Taiping: A Selection of Documents.* Honolulu: University Press of Hawaii, 1982.

ISLAMIC WORLD

During the 19th century, morality for many Muslims meant a combination of observation of the Muslim faith and colonial views of morality. Together, these views often formed an uneasy combination. *Morality,* because of its nature and the fact that it essentially defines what is right and what is wrong, perhaps highlights the differences between the European colonists and the native inhabitants of the colonies more than any other topic.

At the core of the Muslim belief system is the idea that Allah, or God, put all creatures on earth, and it is the responsibility of all creatures to submit to Allah. Humans are the only creatures who can choose not to submit. By following the five pillars of Islam a person can assure a safe passage into the afterworld. The five pillars

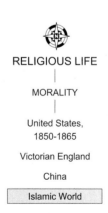

RELIGIOUS LIFE
|
MORALITY
|
United States,
1850-1865

Victorian England

China

Islamic World

are as follows; *shahadah*, or profession of the faith, *salat*, or compliancy in prayer, *zakat*, or alms-giving, *sawm*, fasting during the month of *Ramadan*, and *hajj*, which means that each Muslim should make at least one pilgrimage to Mecca in the course of his or her life.

While observance of the five pillars was an important part of morality among religious Muslims, there were also many ideals that were generally held to be important among most Muslims, including those did not regularly observe the religion itself. Family was considered very important. Single adults were often frowned upon and had little role in society. Childless couples were also looked down upon, in part because they were not passing on the faith to offspring. In certain Muslim-dominant areas at this time, particularly parts of Africa and the Middle East, and among certain ethnic groups in India and Indonesia, polygamy was completely accepted and not frowned upon. Among the majority of Muslims at this time infidelity for men was not considered immoral.

Some of the main aspects that the British colonizers criticized and sought to reform included polygamy, infidelity, and certain attitudes towards women. In Iran and Egypt a debate on polygamy arose, leading many members of the indigenous elite class to rethink their actions. In India, a debate on the role of women arose, including an attack on purdah, or the idea of keeping women inside of the home. This was aimed not only at Muslims, but also at Hindus who had adopted this custom during the course of hundreds of years of Muslim rule. Similar debates on the status of women also erupted in parts of the Middle East. In many areas the English also attacked the fact that many Muslims did not receive a formal education outside of the study of the Qur'an.

Many Muslims had never before questioned the role of women in society, or other aspects of their culture that Europeans sought to reform. The idea of a woman staying inside, or wearing clothing that covered her entire body and almost all of her face, seemed barbaric to many Europeans. To many Muslims at this time, the roles of women in European society, their clothing, and their lifestyles, seemed equally distasteful, shameful, degrading, and sacrilegious. Many Muslim women pitied European women, because of the distasteful manner in which they had to act to get the attention of men, and to be successful in society. Further, many Muslims thought that because of the lifestyle of most Europeans, they would never be redeemed by Allah.

While the views of outsiders regarding morality caused many indigenous people to reject aspects of their own culture and adopt the cultural views of the colonizers, others among them rejected these outside views. There was a trend in which members of the elite class clung to aspects of their own culture even more tightly than before. Movements sprang up that supported aspects of the indigenous culture that had not been looked down upon prior to the arrival of the Europeans. The idea behind this was that the colonizers were being closed-minded in not accepting views other than their own, and were culturally insensitive. Just because something is sanctioned by one culture or religion and not another does not make it more or less correct. Those who recognized this concept of cultural relativism rejected foreign views. Others, in an effort to fit in with those in power, and to gain power and prestige within the colonial society, bought into the colonizers' ideas of right and wrong and adapted accordingly.

The view that European influence should be rejected spread, and by the second half of the 19th century in much of the colonized Muslim-dominant world, popular belief was that there was something direly, morally wrong with Europe. Colonialism and imperialism were obvious evils: that is, their exploitation of resources and people in politically and industrially weaker nations. Many Muslims who visited these nations observed that while they exploited the people of other nations, each of them was, at home, a democracy with a liberal and tolerant outlook. Along with this concept arose nationalist movements, and it is such movements that brought down the colonial world. Ironically, many of these countries, in the wake of independence, borrowed a similar, exploitative model of government within their own countries.

In the wake of nationalist movements throughout the area, several new philosophies within Islam arose. Earlier, European influence had changed education in many areas, and more science was being taught in the schools. In Delhi, in the 18th century, Shah Waliy Allah created a curriculum that placed religion first and rejected modern scholarly disciplines such as science. In other parts of North India in the late 19th century there was a trend of schools and seminaries based on this philosophy, the two most prominent being the Deoband seminary and Aligarh Muslim University. It makes sense that in the heat of nationalist sentiment, over a century later, Shah Waliy Allah's ideas became popular.

In other areas of the Muslim world similar schools began to open up. In Muslim-dominant states such as Egypt, Afghanistan, and Libya, these movements represented an attack on colonialism. In India these movements were not only a way to counteract colonialism, but also represented a desire to cling to Islam in the wake of growing Hindu/Muslim tensions.

~Dana Lightstone

FOR MORE INFORMATION

Ahmed, A., ed. *Knowledge-Morality Nexus*. Lahore, Pakistan: Concept Media Books, 1995.
Weigel, G. *Idealism without Illusions*. Washington, D.C.: Ethics and Public Policy Center, 1994.

Religion

Religion is a fundamental aspect of daily life. The need to believe in something higher is common to all people, everywhere. The entries that follow explore several religions in a handful of regions. Take special note of the cross-cultural similarities and differences. For example, you might explore how often religions have prophets or sacred texts, how they are structured in terms of theology, or how they are rooted in architecture and politics. Also, be sure to recognize the vast differences in beliefs

RELIGIOUS LIFE
|
RELIGION
|
United States,
1850-1865

Victorian England

China

India

Islamic World

Latin America

and practices. Although religion itself is a common aspect of daily life, it is highly complex and multifaceted, especially in the 19th century.

Despite the diversity, 19th-century religions shaped daily life in similar ways. All provided codes for living a good and proper life. For Muslims, an understanding of morality began with the teachings of Muhammad as they were recorded in the Qur'an. In the United States during the 19th century, many Americans based their religious beliefs and practices on the Bible, and in Latin America most people continued to follow the traditions and practices of the Catholic Church. In fact, both Islam and Christianity share some basic features including the idea of sacred scriptures and monotheism. In stark contrast to this was 19th-century Hinduism, which was only one of the many religions of India. Hindus did not believe in only one god. In fact, by the 19th century, the Hindu pantheon consisted of over 300 million deities. And yet, Hinduism, like Islam and Christianity and even other religions such as China's Confucianism and Daoism, provided a means to structure and direct one's life in an ever-increasingly complicated and morally ambiguous world.

In addition to shaping one's intellectual and spiritual life, religions impacted one's daily and weekly activities. In Victorian England for example, Sunday was the main day for worship. Morning services were held before noon with a second service in the afternoon or early evening. There were sermons at both services, but communion only in the morning. This schedule gave a basic rhythm to the week. Similarly, religious practice provided a daily structure in the Muslim world. The second pillar of faith is *salat*, or prayer. Muslims are required to pray five times each day.

Religion also affected daily life in at least one other way. Notice how religion and politics were related. In the United States, religious movements had significant roles in the recasting of American politics and economics. In the 19th century, the United States became a much more religiously diverse nation. Judaism, Catholicism, as well as several new Protestant sects became influential social and political forces. Many religious groups such as the Quakers and Baptists became connected to antislavery activities. The introduction of religious arguments into the slavery question shaped not only people's view of America's *peculiar institution* but also influenced how a great many Americans perceived the Civil War. Religion entered into politics in other world regions and in different ways too. In the Middle East as well as in India, support for certain religions such as Islam and Hinduism became one way to oppose colonization. In Latin America, the struggle to reduce the political power and social influence, particularly over education, of the Catholic Church was one of the central political themes of the century. Thus, as in other centuries, religion was not only a structure of daily life but also a tool that people used to change their environment.

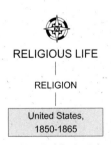

RELIGIOUS LIFE
|
RELIGION
|
United States,
1850-1865

Victorian England

China

India

Islamic World

Latin America

UNITED STATES, 1850–65

The United States had been predominantly Protestant and Christian from its inception. Although the population was mainly Episcopal (Anglican or Church of England) in colonial times, the American Revolution had shed many of the country's links with the established Church in England. The Founding Fathers had almost all been Protestants, but this Protestantism had been essentially related to Puritanism as represented by the Congregational churches. In the colonial period Scotch-Irish immigrants had added an element of Presbyterianism, and later the Baptist Church became popular. Both of these were largely within the same religious tradition. Protestantism remained the dominant mode of religious affiliation into the 19th century, with the Episcopal Church remaining strong in the South. The predominantly Lutheran Germans and Scandinavians were the first to introduce a new element to the religious mix. Nonetheless, their churches were essentially Protestant, and they were assimilated with little fuss into the American social fabric.

At the time the nation was founded, Jews made up such a small proportion of the population that their presence was mathematically insignificant. However, in 1845 a European economic depression caused many Jews to immigrate to North America. German Jews made up the largest portion of this wave of immigration, with the majority clustering in the urban centers of America. For example, the Lower East Side of Manhattan—famous for its tenement houses, neighborhood groceries, and clothing stores—became an enclave of Judaism. Between 1850 and 1860, the number of Jews in America tripled, to 150,000—a significant number, but still less than one-half of one percent of a population of 32 million Americans.

The German Jews brought with them to America the idea of Reform Judaism. In their synagogues, they introduced innovations in ritual, used both German and English, and allowed men and women to be seated together. Nonetheless, most still observed the traditional dietary laws in their homes. Apparently, Jews experienced little overt anti-Semitism. This may have been due to their isolation and their small

number. A significant number of Jewish individuals played important roles as government officials and army officers in the Civil War.

However, it was the Christian religious revival at the beginning of the century that most affected American society. Evangelism, with its strong emotional appeal, was particularly influential among 19th-century Americans. By the 1830s the Methodist and the Baptist churches had become the two largest denominations in the country. Methodism, in particular, offered a new view of theology. The tenets of Methodism were more comforting and humanitarian than the stern predestination and selective salvation of the Puritans. The older denominations, which stressed the total depravity of man, seemed to be at odds with the democratic spirit of America. By mid-century most American

 Snapshot

William Miller and Millennialism, 1840s

Following the American Revolution, at the dawn of the 19th century, a religious revival engulfed the United States. One of the most significant figures of that revival was William Miller, who believed that the end of the world was imminent. Miller's apocalyptic vision was based on his reading of the Bible, particularly the Book of Revelations, and a very complicated mathematical formula. By his reasoning, he was able to place a date on the Second Coming of Jesus Christ, March 1843. When Christ did not appear, Miller revisited his calculations and put the date off one year to 1844. Following the second Great Disappointment in Miller's movement, the Millerites disbanded. Millennial movements continued after Miller, but they tended not to affix firm dates to their belief in the coming of the end of the world.

~[See PBS Frontline, <http://www.pbs.org/wgbh/pages/frontline/shows/apocalypse/explanation/amprophesy.html>.]

Protestants had come to believe in their free will to choose a path to salvation by placing themselves in a position to receive God's grace if they were worthy of it. This belief was to have a profound effect on the way soldiers faced death in battle as they strove to be worthy of God's protection by exhibiting courage and steadiness under fire.

The newer religions stressed repentance, individual awakening, and conversion, and reflected the same trends in secular society. Unitarians and Disciples of Christ broke away from established churches, while Mormons and Adventists sprang from the soil of America itself. Mormons were so feared and hated in America that they were driven to isolation in the West in the prewar years.

Only the Quaker sect, one of the oldest in America, seems to have had a unanimous position on the questions of the war—renouncing violence and supporting abolition. Both the Baptists and the Methodists split along sectional lines in the 1840s over doctrinal and organizational controversies exacerbated by the issue of slavery. The other church sects equally lacked a strong spirit of fellowship. There was an increased tension in religious circles between social activism and private religious expression. Some of the community's leaders opted for positions in secular organizations rather than religious ones in an attempt to effect social change. Ordinary people, however, remained more interested in matters of spirituality.

Americans feared the power of the Catholic Church.

Added to this confusion were the new immigrants, particularly the Irish, who were predominantly Roman Catholic. In the 1830s the Roman Catholic Church was possibly the only religion in America not divided over doctrine. The church was intolerant of criticism, unapologetically authoritarian, resolute, and unalterable in its structure. It was the oldest religion in the Western world, and it demanded the unquestioned obedience of its members to the will of the Pope. It was the Catholic Church that grew fastest because of the mass immigration of the 1840s and 1850s.

The Catholics were prospering. They established an educational system that still exists, as well as colleges and seminaries that provided some of the best higher education available in the country at the time. A European touring the United States in 1831 said of the Catholic colleges in Maryland: "These colleges are full of Protestants. There is perhaps no young man in Maryland who has received a good education who has not been brought up by Catholics."

A Protestant crusade to stem the growing influence of the Catholics in America began in the 1820s and grew in proportion to the increase in Catholic immigration. This movement, truly reactionary and discriminatory, was rooted in a traditional abhorrence of the Roman church and was aimed at the recent Catholic American immigrant. Americans feared the power of the Catholic Church. Even in the South, where concern over immigration and papal absolutism was marginal, due in large part to a significant minority population of French and Spanish ancestry, the authoritarian structure of the Catholic Church was viewed as incompatible with American principles and capable of marshaling Catholic immigrants against traditional American institutions.

Black churches were also quite active during the Civil War era. Even in the absence of physical abuse or brutality, the institution of slavery did great harm to slaves. Southern blacks countered by drawing great strength from a number of traditional and cultural sources. In the years before the abolition of the slave trade, new arrivals from Africa exhibited a heavy dependence on their own tribal religions. In Louisiana and the West Indies many African religious practices came to be fused into a widespread religion known as Voodoo, "which penetrated into every level of Black society." Slaves bought charms and amulets to control their masters, obtain money, ensure love or good health, or bring harm and even death to enemies and nonbelievers. The New Orleans *Delta* reported in 1854 that the participants "strip themselves naked and then commence a strange, wild sort of Indian dance." Wild orgies, the drinking of blood, necromancy, and human sacrifice were all attributed to Voodoo by white observers.

White society deemed such activities pagan, innately evil, and inconsistent with its own dedication to Christianity. Many African religious practices were rooted in a communication with the natural world and the joyful expression of an overt sexuality that shocked the more prudish Protestants. By extension, whites came to be intolerant of all forms of African culture that they did not understand. Slave owners, even benevolent ones, effectively stripped the black of his tribal religious culture. Slaves were expected to exhibit moral behavior reflecting the mores of the God-fearing Christians whom they served. The responsibility for Christianizing the slaves, baptizing their infants, and nurturing in them a fear of the Lord was seriously regarded by whites. Many slaves were therefore forced to attend conventional religious instruction for the good of their souls.

White Southerners used their religion to validate the concept of race-based slavery, but their religion made the masters neither more humane to their slaves nor more likely to emancipate them. Some of the most brutal masters were avid churchgoers. A Southern woman wrote in her journal with regard to slave owning, "The purest and holiest men have owned them, and I see nothing in the scriptures which forbids it." White ministers often preached to the blacks in a manner calculated to make the slave satisfied with his lot as an expression of the will of God. It was not unusual for the white clergy to own one or two slaves as servants. Sometimes slaves were provided by the congregation as part of the *living* or endowment given to the minister. Some churches, especially the Methodists and Baptists of the South, thought the social issues surrounding slavery scarcely worth consideration when contrasted to the saving of the heathen soul. Since many of the white man's churches upheld slavery, many blacks became suspicious of organized religions with white origins.

There were churches established exclusively for slaves by their owners, but the presiding white ministers, who were in the forefront of defending slavery from the pulpit as the natural and correct place for the black race, were generally disliked. Most free Negroes in New Orleans attended the Catholic Church, where they enjoyed an almost equal standing with the white congregation. Separate black congregations grew in number among many sects because the white congregations of their denomination did not welcome black freemen. A growing army of black ministers was thereby able to found parishes among the freemen and slaves of the South. The African Methodist Episcopal (A.M.E.) Churches had the most prominent black ministers of the period. In New Orleans there was a Methodist Church congregation supported by more than 600 slaves; and the black Baptist Church had 500 members.

White authorities feared any large meeting of blacks and broke up these religious services on a regular basis for the most trivial of reasons.

There were two very different types of religious services common to black churches. In the upper-class churches, populated by large numbers of freemen, there was a great dedication to religious form and ceremony. The services were less passionate and affected a greater intellectual appeal and attention to social problems than in the lower-class churches. The communicants of the lower-class churches were primarily composed of slaves and poor blacks that held a strong belief in the power of God in their everyday lives. They emphasized revelations, visions, dreams, and outward expressions of redemption. Worship was often accompanied by shouts, cries, dancing, and other forms of joyful noise. Nonetheless, in each form, some of the African music, folk heritage, and dance survived. Over time, blacks were able to blend many of their African beliefs with the biblical teachings of Christianity. Both types of worship, although generally dividing the black community along class lines, served to uphold the structure of black life in a nation that cared little for blacks except as chattel and laborers. The church proved to be one of the more durable black institutions.

As the Civil War wore on, all religious Americans became more and more reflective. The Christian Commission and its western affiliate were late in forming, and there is some dispute over the role they played in the war. Both sprang from an association of the YMCA, the American Bible Society, and the American Tract Society, and they were somewhat more evangelical in their agenda than the Sanitary Commission. Most historians agree that the Christian Commissions provided quality reading materials for the troops and established a moral standard for the soldiers of the federal army. However, their agenda was essentially religious in nature. Although there was some friction between the various organizing groups, no less than $500 million was raised by the Christian Commissions for religious and philanthropic purposes.

Most regiments had resident chaplains. One Confederate general, Leonidas Polk, was a consecrated bishop of the Episcopal Church. Religious tracts and Bibles were circulated throughout the army camps. Nonetheless, federal captain J. W. De Forest observed that "the men are not as *good* as they were once; they drink harder and swear more and gamble deeper." The same officer noted, however, "The swearing mania was irrepressible. In the excitement of the charge it seemed as if every extremity of language was excusable, providing it would help toward victory." Bible societies, moral reform organizations, and social uplift associations of all kinds sent missionaries and representatives into the field in an attempt to improve the physical and moral environment of the troops.

Public demonstrations of piety and religious worship, organized by ministers, priests, lay preachers, and the men themselves, were common events in camp and were well attended by the troops. General Jackson's fanatical Presbyterian evangelical devotion came to be almost stereotypical of Confederate religious sentiment. Nonetheless, when two dozen general officers of the Confederate army were seen at the same church service in 1864, it was suggested that "less piety and more drilling of commands would suit the times better" (Volo and Volo, 38–40, 73–74, 169).

To read about religion in the United States in the 20th century, see the United States entries in the section "Religion" in chapter 8 ("Religious Life") in volume 6, of this series.

FOR MORE INFORMATION

Genovese, E. D. *Roll, Jordan, Roll: The World the Slaves Made.* New York: Pantheon Books, 1976.

McPherson, J. M. *Battle Cry of Freedom: The Civil War Era.* New York: Oxford University Press, 1990.

Raboteau, A. J. *Slave Religion: The "Invisible Institution" in the Antebellum South.* New York: Oxford University Press, 1978.

Volo, D. D., and J. M. Volo. *Daily Life in Civil War America.* Westport, Conn.: Greenwood Press, 1998.

VICTORIAN ENGLAND

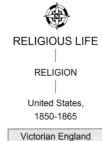

RELIGION

United States,
1850-1865

Victorian England

China

India

Islamic World

Latin America

The Church of England or Anglican Church remained the predominant religion of England in the 19th century. In this church, the parish clergyman's post was known as a *living*. The right to appoint a clergyman to the living depended on how the parish was organized; it might belong to a bishop, a cathedral chapter, a college, or an individual landowner. Thus contacts and influence were important. Leading clergymen were usually relatives (or schoolmates) of aristocrats or substantial squires. Fellows at Oxford and Cambridge might wait many years for a vacancy in a parish controlled by their college so they could resign their fellowship and get married. Livings might also be bought when the person with a right to appoint the clergyman needed money.

A clergyman's income depended on parish resources, and it could be quite substantial or barely adequate. He was called either *rector* or *vicar*, depending on how the parish was funded. There was no difference in status or authority between the two titles. A *curate*, however, was a clergyman without his own living. Sometimes he was a *perpetual curate* who had full charge of a parish that had no resident priest (this was the case for the Reverend Patrick Brontë, father of Charlotte, Emily, and Anne). Other curates (particularly young ones) were hired by a clergyman to help do the work in a large parish. Because their pay was fairly low, young curates were generally single—and traditionally a source of great interest to unmarried women in the parish. Like college fellows, a curate might endure many long years of waiting for a living that would enable him to support a wife.

Other parish officials included the churchwarden, the parish clerk, the sexton, the verger, and the pew-opener. The post of churchwarden was honorary and unpaid. He was elected by the congregation and usually came from its upper social classes. The parish clerk kept records and might read the scriptures and lead responses during the service. He had to be literate, but because the salary was insignificant, the post was often held by a schoolmaster or a small-tradesman. The sexton and verger came from the laboring classes: the sexton rang the bells and dug graves, and the verger looked after the inside of the church. The pew-opener was usually an elderly woman who collected tips by escorting important parishioners and wedding guests to their seats.

Church attendance was highest in rural villages with a resident squire and a traditional way of life. The clergyman conducted Sunday services, oversaw the village school, and performed marriages, baptisms, and funerals. In a small village or a slum parish, the clergyman might well be the only person with a university education. Residents turned to him for information of all sorts. He was often a magistrate. If the income provided by the living was narrow, he might take a local gentleman's son as pupil or have a few boarders in his house to prepare them for entry to public schools.

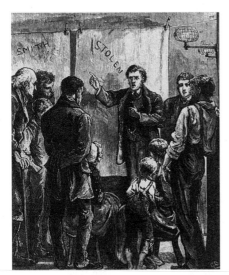

This illustration from an 1883 edition of *The Quiver: An Illustrated Magazine for Sunday and General Reading* shows an evangelical preacher conducting services in a common lodging house.

A parish clergyman was expected to be married. His wife was on calling terms with the gentry and middle-class women of the parish, and she enlisted their help in visiting poor and working-class parishioners. In urban parishes, district visiting was increasingly organized as the century went on; women had a roster of assigned days and duties. A visitor came into the cottage or lodging, asked questions, offered advice, read a prayer or passage from the Bible, and (if the parishioner was literate) left behind a printed tract or a moral story for the children. Elderly people may actually have enjoyed the company, but for most people the visit was tolerable only because it offered access to social welfare services. The clergyman's wife or the district visitors arranged for wine or nourishing food when someone was ill, supplied blankets in winter, provided clothing for newborns and for girls about to go out to service. They could line up votes to get parishioners admitted to hospitals, orphan homes, almshouses, and other privately-run charitable institutions that were far more acceptable than the workhouse.

Sunday morning services in the parish church were usually held at 10 A.M. A second service was held in mid-afternoon in villages or early evening in town. There were sermons at both services, but communion only in the morning. Marriages, funerals, and christenings usually took place before the morning service; only after mid-century were they performed on weekdays. The families of the squire and clergyman sat at the front of the church. Sometimes they had high-sided box pews with doors that were furnished with comfortable cushions and a charcoal brazier for cold days. Other substantial families paid rental fees to have their own pews toward the front of the church. Free seats for poor people were at the back.

At the beginning of the century, many clergymen had been fairly lax—showing up to read a sermon once or twice on Sunday, but devoting most of their time to country sports, scientific or literary hobbies, and other gentlemanly pleasures. Later, evangelicalism invigorated the clergy and the Oxford movement gave them a sense of calling. Aside from paying more attention to their religious duties, energetic parish clergymen hired architects to restore their churches, added daily morning and evening prayers, installed organs, encouraged the choir to become more professional, and set up new charitable and social organizations such as Mothers' Unions, clubs for boys and girls, penny savings banks, and altar guilds. An annual church fête and a Sunday school treat kept volunteers busy for weeks in advance.

Most children were christened at about one month of age, with three godparents (two of the same sex as the child). Even parents who did not go to church had their babies christened—the government began officially registering births only in 1837, and people were used to having parish records to prove when and where they were born. Confirmation, at age fourteen or fifteen, was less common. Adolescents who were serious about religion attended classes, after which the bishop of the diocese formally received them as members of the church. Girls wore white dresses and boys wore black suits for the ceremony (Mitchell, 247–50).

To read about religion in Chaucer's England, see the entries on Europe in the section "Religion" in chapter 8 ("Religious Life") in volume 2 of this series; for Elizabethan England, see the entries on England in the section "Religion" in chapter 8 ("Religious Life") in volume 3 of this series; for 18th-century England, see the entries on England in the section "Religion" in chapter 8 ("Religious Life") in volume 4 of this series.

FOR MORE INFORMATION

Altick, R. D. *Victorian People and Ideas*. New York: W. W. Norton, 1973.
Mitchell, S. *Daily Life in Victorian England*. Westport, Conn.: Greenwood Press, 1996.
Wand, J. W. C. *Anglicanism in History and Today*. London: Weidenfeld and Nicolson, 1961.

CHINA

In the 19th century most Chinese people practiced religion. However, since the cultural revolution attempted to remove traditional elements of Chinese society in the late 1960s, the percentage of Chinese practicing religion has dwindled to a mere 5–10 percent. Among the minority groups, which include Muslims, Tibetan Buddhists, Catholics, and Jews, religious practice remains high.

Chinese religion is the product of four major ideologies: Daoism, Confucianism, Buddhism, and ancient animist beliefs. These systems were inextricably intertwined in 19th-century popular Chinese belief. The founders of Daoism, Confucianism and Buddhism have all been deified. They are worshiped in Chinese homes along with the family's own ancestors, and a pantheon of gods and spirits that consists of representatives from all four traditions mentioned above.

Daoism is the only major religion to originate in China. According to myth, Lao-tzu founded Daoism during the 7th century B.C.E. Little is known about him, and there is some doubt as to whether he existed at all. The name Lao-tzu means *Old Master*, and it is widely believed that he was the keeper of government archives in an area of Western China. It is also believed by many that Lao-tzu was a consultant of Confucius.

According to tradition, late in his life Lao-tzu rode a water buffalo towards what is now Tibet, so that he could spend his last years alone in peace. As he left a

RELIGIOUS LIFE
|
RELIGION
|
United States,
1850-1865

Victorian England

China

India

Islamic World

Latin America

gatekeeper asked for a record of his beliefs. He left the *Tao Te Ching* (*The Way and Its Power*), which is the major Daoist text.

Zhuangzi (399–295 B.C.E.) is considered the most influential Daoist writer after Lao-tzu. His most well-renowned work is a collection of short stories called *The Book of Zhuangzi*. In 143 B.C.E. a man named Zhang Daoling transformed the ideas of these two Daoist philosophers into an actual religion.

The concept of Dao is at the center of the philosophy of Daoism. Dao cannot be perceived because it exceeds the capacity of the human senses. Roughly defined, it is the way of the universe, and the way in which humans should order their lives so as to be in sync with the natural order.

Confucianism is more of a philosophy than a religion, yet it has become an important aspect of Chinese religious belief. Confucius was born around 551 B.C.E. in the area that is now Shandong province in Eastern China. Although little is known of his life he seems to have aspired to a high post in government. However, the highest he held was a minor political commissioner in his home state. In his old age he retired to devote himself to his writings.

The principle idea behind the philosophy of Confucius involves the moral character of human relationships. Women obey and defer to men, younger brothers to elder brothers, and sons to fathers. Everyone respects and obeys the Emperor.

Confucianism rejects a code of law, because such a code implies an inability to work things out by negotiation. However, this method of keeping order proved ineffective in China. The result was oppression of those lacking power in the social structure, as the legal system was arbitrary, and as a result very corrupt.

The family is considered the basic unit of society. This idea was enforced by Confucius but not created by him. Confucius also reinforced the practice of ancestor worship.

It was not until after his death that Confucius' beliefs became important societal ideals. Mencius (372–289 B.C.E.), with the publication of his book *The Book of Mencius*, helped raise awareness of Confucius' philosophy. Later, during the Han dynasty Confucianism became the state religion, and the teachings became the basic discipline for training government officials. This practice remained until the end of the Qing dynasty in 1911. The main Confucian text, *The Analects*, have been important in Chinese education since the 8th century.

Prince Siddhartha Gautama (563–483 B.C.E.) of North India is the founder of Buddhism. At the age of 36 he left the palace walls for the first time in his privileged life. For the first time he saw suffering, sickness, and cruelty, and immediately left the comforts of the palace and set out to find the answer to how to release oneself from suffering in the world. The prince studied with many Hindu *gurus*, or religious teachers. He found that the self-denial involved in Hinduism (mainly fasting) only made his body and mind weak and did not bring him any closer to enlightenment. One night, sitting beneath a banyan tree, he went into a deep meditation and emerged having achieved enlightenment. His title Buddha means *the enlightened one*.

Buddha spent the next four decades of his life spreading his philosophy. The main aspect of Buddhist philosophy is the notion that all life is suffering. Everyone is subject to the traumas of birth, sickness, death, and separation from what they love.

The cause of suffering is desire for personal fulfillment. Contentment can only be achieved when such desires are overcome. To overcome such desires one must follow the *eightfold path*.

According to the Buddha's teachings, to practice the religion it is necessary to renounce material possessions and remove oneself from the work force. As these are difficult criteria for most people to follow, the religion never gained a large following in India. It was reserved for the monasteries, which acted almost as universities, where monks went to study and practice Buddhism. Lay people sometimes provided financial support but did not practice the religion itself.

Buddhism gradually split into two schools: Theravada and Mahayana, enabling the religion to gain a large following in China, and other areas of Asia. Theravada means *little vehicle*. Mahayana means *big vehicle*. It is called by this name because of its ability to reach more people than Theravada. This is due to the fact that it allows not only monks to practice, but laymen as well. This is the form of Buddhism that is more commonly practiced in China.

To read about religion in China under the Tang Dynasty, see the China entries in the section "Religion" in chapter 8 ("Religious Life") in volume 2 of this series.

~Dana Lightstone

FOR MORE INFORMATION

Confucius. *The Analects*. Translated by Arthur Waley. New York: Alfred A. Knopf, 2000.
LaFleur, W. R. *Buddhism: A Cultural Perspective*. Englewood Cliffs, N.J.: Prentice-Hall, 1988.
Lao-tzu. *Tao Te Ching*. Translated by Stephen Mitchell. New York: HarperCollins, 2000.

INDIA

India's major religion, Hinduism, is practiced by approximately 80 percent of the population. Prior to the foundation of the primarily Muslim nation of Pakistan, at the time of independence, nearly 30 percent of India's population was Muslim. Today this religion makes up only about 12 percent of India's population, while Pakistan and Bangladesh have primarily Muslim populations. Other minority religions such as Christianity, Judaism, Jainism, Buddhism, Sikhism, and Zorostrianism are also represented in India.

Hinduism is difficult to define. Some argue that it is more an association of religions, with many vastly different subgroups. Hinduism has no founder, no central authority, and no hierarchy. There is no single scripture like the Bible or the Qur'an. Rather, the sacred texts of Hinduism (the *Mahabharta*, the *Ramayana*, and the *Bhagavad Gita*) come in many forms, each one representing regional differences in the oral tradition of these stories. Hindus do not believe in proselytizing, and there is no way to convert to Hinduism. According to Hindu belief, to be a Hindu one must be born a Hindu and into a caste.

While beliefs and practices vary widely from region to region, there are several unifying factors. These include common beliefs in reincarnation, karma (conduct or

RELIGIOUS LIFE

RELIGION

United States,
1850-1865

Victorian England

China

India

Islamic World

Latin America

action) and dharma (behavior connected to one's position in society). Hindus believe that one is reborn, and the quality of each rebirth is dependent on one's karma in the previous life. By fulfilling one's duties in life, one can increase his or her chances of being born into better circumstances, which may mean being born into a higher caste, or for a woman, being born male in the next life. By gaining sufficient knowledge one might escape the cycle of death and rebirth, and achieve *moksha,* or liberation. Women are considered incapable of achieving *moksha.* Women can only hope to be reincarnated as male, and then strive for liberation.

The Hindu pantheon consists of as many as 300 million deities. Different regions worship different deities, but there are certain deities who are worshiped by most Hindus. Brahma is a formless, eternal god, considered the source of all existence. Vishnu is the preserver or sustainer and is associated with *right action.* Shiva is the destroyer, but without whom creation could not occur. These are perhaps the three most important and widely worshiped deities of Hinduism.

Islam was introduced into India by invading armies in the 9th through 17th centuries. Islam came to South India through Arab traders. Islam is monotheistic. In Islam the purpose of humans is submission to the divine will. God's word is relayed by prophets, the most recent of whom was Muhammad. Devout Muslims pray in a mosque or at home five times a day. To show reverence they bow in the direction of Mecca.

Missionaries first introduced Christianity in India in the 4th century. During the colonial period, Portuguese, Dutch, Danish, French, and British involvement in India led many missionaries to the country, and during this time the Christian population greatly expanded. Today there are over 18 million Christians in India, around three-quarters of whom are South Indian.

Guru Nanak introduced Sikhism in the Punjab (in the Northwest of India and Southeast of Pakistan) in the 15th century. The religion was created at a time of social unrest and was an attempt to fuse the best of Islam and Hinduism. Sikhs believe in one god and reject the worship of idols. Like Hindus and Buddhists, they accept the concept of karma, and rebirth. A fundamental belief of Sikhism is the concept of *Khalsa,* which is belief in a chosen race of soldier-saints who follow a strict code of moral conduct. There are five emblems that are to be worn by all Sikh men: a comb, a certain type of drawers, a saber, a steel bracelet, and hair that has not been cut. It is considered sacrilegious for any Sikh, male or female, to cut his or her hair.

Buddhists make up a very small percentage of India's population. The religion began with the Buddha, around 500 B.C.E. Buddha taught that life is based on Four Noble Truths: suffering, which is caused by craving for worldly things; one can find release from suffering by eliminating craving; the way to eliminate craving is by following the eightfold path, which is a set of morals by which to live.

A contemporary of the Buddha founded Jainism. Jainism is based on a philosophy of Ahimsa, or nonviolence. Strict Jains take this to the point that they wear masks over their mouths so as not to even breath in any insects, as killing them is a form of violence.

Zoroastrianism began in Persia and was known to the ancient Greeks. It played a strong role in influencing the evolution of Judaism and Christianity. The philosophy is based on a dualistic nature whereby good and evil are locked in continuous battle, with good always triumphing. During the British period many Parsis moved into commerce and industry. They adopted many British customs, and continue to be prominent in society.

Prior to the arrival of the British, Hindus and Muslims existed relatively harmoniously. In many cases the religions were fluid, meaning that people often considered themselves to belong to one faith but also adopted some customs of another. However, the British attempted to divide the local population among religious lines, therefore making the Indian population fragmented, weaker, and easier to rule. This led members of both religions to cling more tightly to their own identity, and led to an increase of tension between the two groups.

By the eve of independence on January 26, 1947, tensions were such that one united independent India did not seem feasible. Therefore, the idea emerged of two independent nations: India, which would have a mainly Hindu population, and Pakistan, a nation of primarily Muslims. There was much dispute over this plan, and deservedly so. The borders were vague, and Kashmir remains disputed territory. As Hindus fled to India, and Muslims to Pakistan, several million people of both faiths were abused, raped, and killed. This exodus was one of the largest in the history of the world. In the past fifty-five years since independence several wars and other violent disputes were fought in this region.

To read about religion in ancient India, see the India entry in the section "Religion" in chapter 8 ("Religious Life") in volume 1 of this series; for India in the 20th century, see the India entry in the section "Religion" in chapter 8 ("Religious Life") in volume 6 of this series.

~Dana Lightstone

FOR MORE INFORMATION

Dawood, N. J., trans. *The Koran*. Baltimore: Penguin Books, 1966.

Garg, G. R., ed. *Encyclopedia of the Hindu World*. New Delhi, India: Concept Publishers, 1992.

Goldman, R. P., trans. *The Valmiki Ramayana*. Honolulu: The East-West Center, 1995.

Singh, K., ed. *Current Thoughts on Sihkism*. Chandigarh, India: Institute of Sikh Studies, 1996.

ISLAMIC WORLD

The prophet Muhammad founded Islam as a religion in Arabia in the 7th century. The Arabic word *Islam* means *to surrender* and believers undertake to surrender to the will of Allah, which is the word that Muslims use for God. The will of Allah is revealed in the Qur'an, which in Arabic means *reading* or *recitations*. God supposedly

gave the words of the scriptures to Muhammad. God then encouraged Muhammad to act as a messenger to all of humanity.

Muslims believe in only one God and believe that this God is unique and has no equal power. Everything in the universe is believed to be created by Allah, and the role of every living thing on earth is to submit to Allah entirely. Of the living things on earth humans are the only ones with a choice: they can choose to submit or to disobey. The weakness of humans is their sense of independence that leads to a tendency to disobey. The role of the prophets, of which the most recent was Muhammad, is to call humanity back to the will of God. Over time, because of pride, humanity begins to again stray from this will, and God will send in another prophet.

Following Muhammad's death a succession dispute split the movement into two sects, the Sunnis and the Shiʿites. The Sunnis are generally more religious, although there are many exceptions to this rule. They look for meaning within the views of members of the community. The Shiʿites on the other hand believe that only *imams*, who are religious leaders, are able to reveal the hidden and complex meanings of the Qur'an. The orthodox view is that there have been 12 imams, the last of whom was Muhammad.

All Muslims are expected to observe the five pillars of Islam. The first of these is *shahadah*, or profession of faith. This means that to become a Muslim one must state the Islamic creed: "There is no God but God, and Muhammad is the messenger of God." Shiʿite Muslims add to the end of this "and Ali is the representative of God."

The second pillar is *salat*, or prayer. Muslims are required to pray five times each day, although Shiʿites only pray three times a day, because at two of these prayer sessions they recite one prayer directly after another. Before praying Muslims are expected to perform certain ablutions. In Shiʿite mosques this is usually done in a pool of water, while in Sunni mosques this is most often done in a fountain. The prayers are performed while facing the direction of the Kaaba, the ancient shrine at the center of the Grand Mosque in Mecca.

The next of the five pillars is *zakat*, or alms giving. Muslims are required to give a percentage of their annual income to help the poor. *Sawam*, or fasting, is to be done every day from sunrise to sunset during the month of Ramadan. The very old, very young, the ill, and those in the process of rigorous journeys are exempt from fasting. This celebrates Muhammad's first revelation in 610 c.e. The last of the five pillars is *hajj*, which means pilgrimage. At least once in a lifetime each Muslim is required to make the pilgrimage to Mecca. This should be performed during a specific few days in the first and second weeks of the Muslim month of Zu-I-Hejjeh. Visiting Mecca at any other time of the year is known as a *little pilgrimage*.

Among the many duties incumbent on Muslims, the best known, and the least understood is that of jihad. This word is most often translated into English as *holy war*. However, it literally means *striving in the way of the faith*, and has been the subject of much debate among Muslim scholars for the past several decades. It is often viewed in a spiritual sense, as opposed to having a violent context.

Muslims are also expected to follow fairly strict dietary regulations forbidding the consumption of animals with cloven feet (such as pigs), the consumption of alcohol, or the consumption of animals that died of natural causes instead of being slaughtered in the proper way. Under Islamic law, as is also the case with Jewish dietary law, animals for food must be killed in the least painful and cleanest way possible. This involves cutting a particular vein in the animal's throat with one smooth stroke.

Mosques are basically the same worldwide. Outside of the mosque is usually a large courtyard where men can wash before going to pray. Minarets are placed at the cardinal points and it is from here that the chants are projected throughout the town, calling the faithful to prayer. There is at least one *iwan*, or large covered hall that is dedicated to communal prayer. The iwan facing Mecca is the focal point of prayer. A small alcove in the wall indicates this. This is called a mihrab. Next to the mihrab is a pulpit from which the imam leads the service each Friday. This pulpit is called a *minbar*. Some minbars are sunk into the ground, so that the person closest to Mecca, the imam, is lowered to demonstrate his humility before Allah. The floor is generally covered with carpets, on which the men kneel down and bow to God, facing Mecca. This is where men pray five times a day if they are able to make it to the mosque. If they live too far from the mosque they can pray in their own home or another space. In most mosques in the 19th century women were not admitted.

Mosques serve not only a religious function in society, but are often also a place to socialize. Classes in the Qur'an are taught in the courtyard. Groups of children and adults meet at the mosque to socialize. A trip to the mosque is a common family outing. It is even common for people to use a mosque as an escape from the heat, and to find a shady corner to sit and read or nap.

In the 19th century Islam played an interesting role in society. This was a time when various nationalisms competed in the struggle to overthrow colonial rule. While some nationalists neglected religion in favor of other national identities, others clung more tightly than ever to Islam, as a way of reclaiming their identity in the midst of foreign political and cultural domination.

To read about religion and family life in the medieval Islamic World, see the Islamic World entries in the section "Religion" in chapter 8 ("Religious Life") in volume 2 of this series; for the Islamic World in the 20th century, see the Islamic World entry in the section "Religion" in chapter 8 ("Religious Life") in volume 6 of this series.

~Dana Lightstone

FOR MORE INFORMATION

Engineer, A. *Rational Approach to Islam*. New Delhi, India: Gyan Publishing House, 2001.
Morris, N. *Islam*. Columbus, Ohio: Peter Bedrick, 2001.
Robinson, N. *Islam: A Concise Introduction*. Washington, D.C.: Georgetown University Press, 1999.

LATIN AMERICA

In discussing Latin American religious life in the 19th century, it is impossible to separate the institutional life of the Roman Catholic Church in Latin America and the religious life of the people of Latin America.

RELIGIOUS LIFE
|
RELIGION
|
United States,
1850-1865

Victorian England

China

India

Islamic World

Latin America

The church in Latin America was greatly affected by the independence movement. The drive for independence was partly caused by the Spanish government, which, first, expelled the Jesuits from the empire in 1767, sending many sons of the Latin American elites into exile, and second, extended the Act of Consolidation to the empire in 1804, thus undermining the financial structure of the colonial elites and the church. The independence movement divided and weakened the church. The bishops who had been appointed by the crown under the system of the *patronato real* mostly remained loyal to Spain and many abandoned their dioceses during the wars of independence. The lower clergy, who had been severely hurt by the Act of Consolidation, sided with independence and actively participated in independence movements throughout Latin America. In Mexico, Fathers Miguel Hidalgo and José Maria Morelos organized the early independence movement, while many priests in other parts of Latin America participated in independence movements and served in constitutional conventions and as legislators. Other clergymen were important in promoting the independence cause among the masses, by presenting it as a holy war and calling on the people to support the movement.

> *The lower clergy actively participated in independence movements.*

In the first three decades of independence, the postcolonial church remained weak. In places where the bishops had fled or died, it was impossible to replace them immediately. The Spanish crown placed great pressure on the pope not to recognize the new countries. At the same time, the new republics demanded the right to control church appointments, as the Spanish crown had done under the *patronato real*, but Rome refused to make such a concession. The result was that most dioceses were without bishops for many years and the number of priests declined, as did the ability of those who remained to administer the sacraments.

After the middle of the century, the church faced new, hostile political and intellectual currents throughout Latin America. Liberalism, which professed a belief in progress, the essential goodness and improvability of human beings, free and open economic markets, and the autonomy of individuals, became the dominant political philosophy in many Latin American countries. The new liberal political leadership attacked the economic base of the church in the name of economic development and utilitarianism, a philosophy that placed a high value on the useful and practical. In addition, the new intellectual current of positivism, which stressed the importance of positive knowledge derived from the observation and study of nature, presented its scientific methods as an alternative to religion and attracted large numbers of the elites. In states under liberal leadership such as Mexico, Guatemala, and Ecuador, the church suffered severe persecution, and it was deprived of its lands and its control of education in most countries.

Religious life suffered as the number of local vocations to the priesthood declined throughout the 19th century. Also, the number of religious declined as liberal governments began seizing convent properties and abolishing or expelling religious orders. To compensate for the loss, the Latin American church began to rely on foreign clergy to help meet its needs. In the last decades of the century, the Latin American church began to experience a period of reform as its ties to Rome grew. Concerned by the decline of church influence in society, the new bishops improved the standards of priestly education. Pope Pius IX (r. 1846–78), who as a young priest had traveled to South America in the late 1820s, took great interest in developments in Latin America and in 1859 opened the Latin American College in Rome, which became a major center for educating future Latin American bishops. As a result, the Latin American church was Romanized and integrated more closely with the universal church than it had ever been in the colonial period.

In Brazil, the colonial church had been much weaker than its Spanish American counterpart. In 1759, the Jesuits were expelled from Brazil. The Brazilian independence movement was led by the crown prince of Portugal, who became Emperor Pedro I (r. 1822–31). After independence, the church remained weak and closely tied to the imperial crown, which retained the *padroado real*. While the Brazilian church was not disestablished until after the fall of the monarchy in 1889, it too experienced the attack of liberalism and positivism. Emperor Pedro II (r. 1831–89) was indifferent toward religion and would not tolerate the attempts of the bishops to condemn the Freemasons, members of a fraternal organization that practiced secret rituals.

Popular religious practices expressed the teachings and beliefs of the church. While most people were baptized Catholic, attendance at mass and the reception of the sacraments declined throughout the century. Participation in the sacraments varied with gender, class, and ethnicity. Women were more likely than men to fulfill their religious obligations. The elites tended to lapse in the faith and become influenced by liberalism, positivism, and freemasonry. The mestizo population was the most active in the sacramental life of the church. The Indian people, who received the sacraments irregularly, retained great respect for the clergy and were very attentive in their personal devotions. While only a minority knew the catechism by heart and lived it, most people could recite the Ten Commandments, the Nicene Creed, and the basic prayers.

Throughout the century, popular piety remained strong among the masses of mestizos and Indians. The devotion to the saints and the Virgin Mary, pilgrimages, and personal religious vows remained common methods by which people expressed their faith, regardless of whether they were fully active Catholics or only attended church occasionally. The strength of their piety was publicly demonstrated by their mass presence in the great pilgrimages to the shrines of Our Lady of Guadalupe in Mexico, the Virgin of Lujan in Argentina, and the Lord of Miracles in Peru. Popular piety was also expressed through membership in the lay brotherhoods. The *confradías* in many Latin American countries and the *irmandades* in Brazil were organized by different socioeconomic or ethnic groups and were a source of corporate identity. They organized communal religious festivities that honored the Virgin Mary or their patron saint. They also played an important role as mutual aid societies that provided assistance to members in times of crisis.

The weak presence of the church in 19th-century Latin America forced the toleration of non-Catholic religious systems. One form of such a religious system blended African and Catholic religious practices. It was common among peoples who had been only superficially evangelized, such as the African populations of Brazil and the Caribbean. Among its main examples is *Candomnblé* in Brazil—a form of Spiritism, or the belief in communication with spirits, that combined prayers and rituals borrowed from Catholicism with African religious beliefs. Another form was Messianism, which had its most prominent examples at Canudos and Joaseiro in Brazil. These movements were organized around messianic leaders, whose followers looked to them for deliverance from social catastrophe brought on by local economic decline. The last form of non-Catholic religious expression was the appearance of Protestant sects. The first Protestants forced their entry into Latin America in the economic agreements signed with Great Britain and the United States in the course of the 19th century; these groups usually did not engage in evangelization. They were followed in the late-19th century by the Bible societies and by groups of Evangelicals who began to make inroads among the new immigrant populations in the cities where the Catholic Church was slow to organize its presence.

~*Paul Brasil*

FOR MORE INFORMATION

Dussel, E., ed. *The Church in Latin America, 1492–1992.* Maryknoll, N.Y.: Orbis Books, 1992.

Goodpasture, H. M., ed. *Cross and Sword: An Eyewitness History of Christianity in Latin America.* Maryknoll, N.Y.: Orbis Books, 1989.

Lynch, J. "The Catholic Church in Latin America, 1830–1930." In *The Cambridge History of Latin America,* ed. Leslie Bethell, 527–95. Vol. 4. Cambridge: Cambridge University Press, 1986.

Martínez de Codes, R. M. *La Iglesia Católica en la América Independiente. Siglo XIX.* Madrid: Editorial Mapfre, 1992.

Mecham, J. L. *Church and State in Latin America: A History of Political Ecclesiastical Relations.* Rev. ed. Chapel Hill: University of North Carolina Press, 1966.

RELIGIOUS LIFE: WEB SITES

http://www.nhc.rtp.nc.us/tserve/nineteen.htm
http://www.iad.org/books/intro.html#allah
http://people.cryst.bbk.ac.uk/~ubcg09q/dmr/intro.htm
http://adaniel.tripod.com/religions.htm
http://www.chinaknowledge.de/
http://www.gliah.uh.edu/historyonline/usdeath1.cfm
http://www.webbangladesh.com/islam/introduction.htm

PRIMARY SOURCES

CHILD LABOR IN VICTORIAN ENGLAND, 1843

Modern readers are continually shocked by the prevalence of child labor in the 19th century. During the century, however, reformers sought to eliminate the use of child workers. In the following document, British officials summarize their 1843 investigation into the practice of child labor. Their findings helped the movement end the use of child labor.

1. That instances occur in which Children begin to work as early as three or four years of age; not infrequently at five, and between five and six; while, in general, regular employment commences between seven and eight; the great majority of the Children having begun to work before they are nine years old, although in some few occupations no Children are employed until they are ten and even twelve years old and upwards.

2. That in all cases the persons that employ mere Infants and the very youngest Children are the parents themselves, who put their Children to work at some processes of manufacture under their own eyes, in their own houses; but Children begin to work together in numbers, in larger or smaller manufactories, at all ages, from five years old and upwards. . . .

4. That in a very large proportion of these Trades and Manufactures female Children are employed equally with boys, and at the same tender ages: in some indeed the number of girls exceeds that of boys; and in a few cases the work, as far as it is performed by those under adult age, is carried on almost entirely by girls and young women. . . .

19. That in some few instances the regular hours of work do not exceed ten, exclusive of the time allowed for meals; sometimes they are eleven, but more commonly twelve; and in great numbers of instances the employment is continued for fifteen, sixteen, and even eighteen hours consecutively. . . .

31. That in all these occupations, in all the districts, some of the Children are robust, active, and healthy, although in general even these are undersized; but that, from the early ages at which the great majority commence work, from their long hours of work, and from the insufficiency of their food and clothing, their "bodily health" is seriously and generally injured; they are for the most part stunted in growth, their aspect being pale, delicate, and sickly, and they present altogether the appearance of a race which has suffered general physical deterioration.

From the *Second Report of the Commissioners on the Employment of Children* as quoted in Sally Mitchell, *Daily Life in Victorian England* (Westport, Conn.: Greenwood Press, 1996), 43–44.

A BRITISH VIEW OF INDIAN SOCIAL CUSTOMS, 1840

As a British official who spent much time in India, Mountstuart Elphinstone became an active participant in shaping a new administrative system in the territories. His goal did not involve a renunciation of local tradition; instead he worked to maintain Indian social customs, which he wrote about in the excerpt below.

The food of the common people, both in the country and in towns, is unleavened bread with boiled vegetables, clarified butter or oil, and spices. Smoking tobacco is almost the only luxury. Some few smoke intoxicating drugs; and the lowest casts only, and even they rarely, get drunk with spirits. Drunkenness is confined to damp countries, such as Bengal, the Concans, and some parts of the south of India. It increases in our territories where spirits are taxed; but is so little of a natural propensity that the absolute prohibition of spirits, which exists in most native states, is sufficient to keep it down. Opium, which is used to great excess in the west of Hindostan, is peculiar to the rajputs and does not affect the lower classes. All but the poorest people chew betel (a pungent aromatic leaf), with the hard nut of the areca, mixed with a sort of lime made from shells, and with various spices, according to the person's means. Some kinds of fruit are cheap and common . . .

Though they have chess, a game played with tables and dice as backgammon is, and cards (which are circular, in many suits, and painted with Hindu gods, etc., instead of kings, queens, and knaves), yet the great indoor amusement is to listen to singing interspersed with slow movements which can scarcely be called dancing. The attitudes are not ungraceful, and the songs are pleasing; but it is, after all, a languid and monotonous entertainment; and it is astonishing to see the delight that all ranks take in it; the lower orders, in particular, often standing for whole nights to enjoy this unvaried amusement. These exhibitions are now often illuminated, when in rooms, by English chandeliers; but the true Hindu way of lighting them up is by torches held by men, who feed the flame with oil from a sort of bottle constructed for the purpose. For ordinary household purposes they use lamps of earthenware or metal. . . .

Great attention is paid to ceremony. A person of distinction is met a mile or two before he enters the city; and a visitor is received (according to his rank) at the outer gate of the house, at the door of a room, or by merely rising from the seat. Friends embrace if they have not met for some time. Bramins are saluted by joining the palms, and raising them twice or thrice to the forehead: with others, the salute with one hand is used, so well known by the Mahometan name of salaam. . . . Visitors are seated with strict attention to their rank, which on public occasions it often takes much previous negotiation to settle. Hindus of rank are remarkable for their politeness to inferiors, generally addressing them by some civil or familiar term, and scarcely ever being provoked to abusive or harsh language. The lower classes are courteous in their general manners among themselves, but by no means so scrupulous in their language when irritated. All visits end by the master of the house presenting betel leaf with areca nut, etc., to the guest; it is accompanied by attar of roses or some other perfume put on the handkerchief, and rosewater sprinkled over the person; and this is the sign for taking leave. . . .

Among the most striking of the religious exhibitions is that of the capture of Lanka, in honor of Rama, which is necessarily performed out of doors. Lanka is represented by a spacious castle with towers and battlements, which are assailed by an army dressed like Rama and his followers, with Hanuman and his monkey allies. The combat ends in the destruction of Lanka, amidst a blaze of fireworks which would excite admiration in any part of the world, and in a triumphal procession sometimes conducted in a style of grandeur which might become a more important occasion. . . .

The regular dress of all Hindus is probably that which has been mentioned as used in Bengal, and which is worn by all strict Bramins. It consists of two long pieces of white cotton cloth, one of which is wrapped round the middle and tucked up between the legs, while part hangs down a good deal below the knees; the other is worn over the shoulders, and occasionally stretched over the head, which has no other covering. The head and beard are shaved, but a long tuft of hair is left on the crown. Mustachios are also worn, except perhaps by strict Bramins. Except in Bengal, all Hindus who do not affect strictness now wear the lower piece of cloth smaller and tighter, and over it a white cotton or chintz or silk tunic, a colored muslin sash round the middle, and a scarf of the same material over the shoulders, with a turban; some wear loose drawers like the Mahometans. . . .

It is well known that Indian widows sometimes sacrifice themselves on the funeral pile of their husbands, and that such victims are called suttees. The practice is ascribed by our missionaries to the degraded condition to which a woman who outlives her husband is condemned. If the motive were one of so general an influence, the practice would scarcely be so rare. It is more probably that the hopes of immediately entering on the enjoyment of heaven and of entitling the husband to the same felicity, as well as the glory attending such a voluntary sacrifice, are sufficient to excite the few enthusiastic spirits who go through this awful trial. . . .

The sight of a widow burning is a most painful one; but it is hard to say whether the spectator is most affected by pity or admiration. The more than human serenity of the victim, and the respect which she receives from those around her, are heightened by her gentle demeanor and her care to omit nothing in distributing her last presents, and paying the usual mark; of courtesy to the bystanders; while the cruel death that awaits her is doubly felt from her own apparent insensibility to its terrors.

From Mountstuart Elphinstone, "Indian Customs and Manners, 1840," <http://www. fordham.edu/halsall/india/1840elphinstone.html>

THE STORY OF AN ENGLISH CROSSING-SWEEPER, 1849

In Victorian England, children took all sorts of jobs to support themselves and their families. In this account, a boy tells about his life and work as a crossing-sweeper. It was published in Henry Mayhew's 1849 expose *London Labour and the London Poor*, which examined the conditions of England's poorest workers.

I'm twelve years old, please, sir, and my name is Margaret R—, and I sweep a crossing in New Oxford-street, by Dunn's passage, just facing Moses and Sons', sir; by the Catholic school, sir. Mother's been dead these two year, sir, and father's a working cutler, sir; and I lives with him, but he don't get much to do, and so I'm obligated to help him, doing what I can, sir. Since mother's been dead, I've had to mind my little brother and sister, so that I haven't been to school; but when I goes a crossing-sweeping I takes them along with me, and they sits on the steps close by, sir. If it's wet I has to stop at home and take care of them, for father depends upon me for looking after them. Sister's three and a-half year old, and brother's five year, so he's just beginning to help me, sir. I hope he'll get something better than a crossing when he grows up.

I generally takes about sixpence, or sevenpence, or eightpence on the crossing, from about nine o'clock in the morning till four in the evening, when I come home. I don't stop out at nights because father won't let me, and I'm got to be home to see to baby.

From Henry Mayhew, *London Labour and the London Poor* (1849); as quoted in Sally Mitchell, *Daily Life in Victorian England* (Westport, Conn.: Greenwood Press, 1996), 46–47.

RULES FOR GOOD SERVANTS, 1901

Class distinction was an important element of Victorian English society. In this excerpt from a self-help guidebook for workers published in 1901, the rules for interclass relations are outlined. Note the stress on formality, deference, and respect for the upper class.

Always move quietly about the house, and do not let your voice be heard by the family unless necessary.

When meeting any ladies or gentlemen about the house, stand back or move aside for them to pass.

Should you be required to walk with a lady or gentleman, in order to carry a parcel, or otherwise, always keep a few paces behind.

Do not smile at droll stories told in your presence, or seem in any way to notice, or enter into, the family conversation, or the talk at table, or with visitors; and do not offer any information unless asked, and then you must give it in as few words as possible. But if it is quite necessary to give some information unasked at table or before visitors, give it quietly to your master or mistress.

From the Ladies' Sanitary Association, *Rules for the Manners of Servants in Good Families* (1901); as quoted in Sally Mitchell, *Daily Life in Victorian England* (Westport, Conn.: Greenwood Press, 1996), 51.

AN INDIAN WEIGHS THE ADVANTAGES AND DISADVANTAGES OF BRITISH RULE, 1871

Dadabhai Naoroji spent much of his life in the political arena of England. He advocated heavily for the peoples of his native India and emphasized the impact of England on the Indian economy. His writing below weighs the advantages and disadvantages of European involvement.

THE BENEFITS OF BRITISH RULE FOR INDIA:

In the Cause of Humanity: Abolition of *suttee* and infanticide. Destruction of *Decoits, Thugs, Pindarees,* and other such pests of Indian society. Allowing remarriage of Hindu widows, and charitable aid in time of famine. Glorious work all this, of which any nation may well be proud, and such as has not fallen to the lot of any people in the history of mankind.

In the Cause of Civilization: Education, both male and female. Though yet only partial, an inestimable blessing as far as it has gone, and leading gradually to the destruction of superstition, and many moral and social evils. Resuscitation of India's own noble literature, modified and refined by the enlightenment of the West.

Politically: Peace and order. Freedom of speech and liberty of the press. Higher political knowledge and aspirations. Improvement of government in the native states. Security of life and property. Freedom from oppression caused by the caprice or greed of despotic rulers, and from devastation by war. Equal justice between man and man (sometimes vitiated by partiality to Europeans). Services of highly educated administrators, who have achieved the above-mentioned results.

Materially: Loans for railways and irrigation. Development of a few valuable products, such as indigo, tea, coffee, silk, etc. Increase of exports. Telegraphs.

Generally: A slowly growing desire of late to treat India equitably, and as a country held in trust. Good intentions. No nation on the face of the earth has ever had the opportunity of achieving such a glorious work as this. I hope in the credit side of the account I have done no injustice, and if I have omitted any item which anyone may think of importance, I shall have the greatest pleasure in inserting it. I appreciate, and so do my countrymen, what England has done for India, and I know that it is only in British hands that her regeneration can be accomplished. Now for the debit side.

THE DETRIMENTS OF BRITISH RULE:

In the Cause of Humanity: Nothing. Everything, therefore, is in your favor under this heading.

In the Cause of Civilization: As I have said already, there has been a failure to do as much as might have been done, but I put nothing to the debit. Much has been done, though.

Politically: Repeated breach of pledges to give the natives a fair and reasonable share in the higher administration of their own country, which has much shaken confidence in the good faith of the British word. Political aspirations and the legitimate claim to have a reasonable voice in the legislation and the imposition and disbursement of taxes, met to a very slight degree, thus treating the natives of India not as British subjects, in who representation is a birthright. Consequent of the above, an utter disregard of the feelings and views of the natives. The great moral evil of the drain of wisdom and practical administration, leaving none to guide the rising generation.

Financially: All attention is engrossed in devising new modes of taxation, without any adequate effort to increase the means of the people to pay; and the consequent vexation and oppressiveness of the taxes imposed, imperial and local. Inequitable financial relations between England and India, i.e. the political debt of 100,000,000 clapped on India's shoulders, and all home charges also, though the British Exchequer contributes nearly 3,000,000 to the expense of the colonies.

Materially: The political drain, up to this time, from India to England, of above 500,000,000, at the lowest computation, in principal alone, which with interest would be some thousands of millions. The further continuation of this drain at the rate, at present, of above 12,000,000 per annum, with a tendency to increase. The consequent continuous impoverishment and exhaustion of the country, except so far as it has been very partially relieved and replenished by the railway and irrigation loans, and the windfall of the consequences of the American war, since 1850. Even with this relief, the material condition of India is such that the great mass of the poor have hardly tuppence a day and a few rags, or a scanty subsistence. The famines that were in their power to prevent, if they had done their duty, as a good and intelligent government. The policy adopted during the last fifteen years of building railways, irrigation works, etc., is hopeful, has already resulted in much good to your credit, and if persevered in, gratitude and contentment will follow. An increase of exports without adequate compensation; loss of manufacturing industry and skill. Here I end the debit side.

SUMMARY:

To sum up the whole, the British rule has been: morally, a great blessing; politically, peace and order on one hand, blunders on the other; materially, impoverishment, relieved as far as the railway and other loans go. The natives call the British system "Sakar ki Churi," the knife of sugar. That is to say, there is no oppression, it is all smooth and sweet, but it is the knife, notwithstanding. I mention this that you should know these feelings. Our great misfortune is that you do not know our wants. When you will know our real wishes, I have not the least doubt that you would do justice. The genius and spirit of the British people is fair play and justice.

From Dadabhai Naoroji, *The Benefits of British Rule, 1871*, in Modern History Sourcebook at http://www.fordham.edu.

AN ENGLISH SERVANT'S DIARY, SATURDAY, JULY 14, 1860

All in a day's work. This excerpt from a servant's diary, dated July 14, 1860, indicates the kind of work that she (and others like her) did every day. Note how physical and repetitive her labors were. Also, notice how she worked for others and not for herself.

Opened the shutters & lighted the kitchen fire. Shook my sooty things in the dusthole & emptied the soot there. Swept & dusted the rooms & the hall. Laid the hearth & got breakfast up. Clean'd 2 pairs of boots. Made the beds & emptied the slops. Clean'd & wash'd the breakfast things up. Clean'd the plate; clean'd the knives & got dinner up. Clean'd away. Clean'd the kitchen up; unpack'd a hamper. Took two chickens to Mrs. Brewer's & brought the message back. Made a tart & pick'd & gutted two ducks & roasted them. Clean'd the steps & flags on my knees. Blackleaded the scraper in front of the house; clean'd the street flags too on my knees. Wash'd up in the scullery. Clean'd the pantry on my knees & scour'd the tables. Scrubbed the flags around the house & clean'd the window sills. Got tea at 9 for the master & Mrs. Warwick in my dirt, but Ann carried it up. Clean'd the privy & passage & scullery floor on my knees. Washed the dog & clean'd the sinks down. Put the supper ready for Ann to take up, for I was too dirty & tired to go upstairs. Wash'd in a bath & to bed.

From *The Diaries of Hannah Cullwick, Victorian Maidservant*, edited by Liz Stanley (1984); as quoted in Sally Mitchell, *Daily Life in Victorian England* (Westport, Conn.: Greenwood Press, 1996), 51–52.

WIDOW'S MOURNING WEAR IN VICTORIAN ENGLAND, 1888

The Victorian Era continues to be known for its code of ethics, applicable to most situations. In this example of proscriptive literature from a self-help book published in 1888, the proper attire for widows is addressed. Also note what other information about widow behavior is provided. Women were to mourn their husbands for at least two years!

The regulation period for a widow's mourning is two years. Of this period crape should be worn for one year and nine months—for the first twelve months the dress should be entirely covered with crape, and for the remaining three months trimmed with crape; during the last three months black without crape should be worn. After two years, half-mourning is prescribed.

The widow's cap should be worn for a year and a day. Lawn cuffs and collars should be worn during the crape period.

Widowers should wear mourning for the same period as widows, but they usually enter society much sooner. A widow is not expected to enter into society under twelve months, and during that time she should neither accept invitations nor issue them.

From *Manners and Rules of Good Society* (1888); as quoted in Sally Mitchell, *Daily Life in Victorian England* (Westport, Conn.: Greenwood Press, 1996), 163.

THE REVISED CODE OF 1862: STANDARDS OF ACHIEVEMENT

Those familiar with the recent movement to create educational standards will find the next document of particular interest. The 1862 Revised Code for Standards of Achievement lists the curricular guidelines for Victorian era English students. The standards centered literally on the three Rs.

Standard I
Reading: Narrative in monosyllables.
Writing: Form on blackboard or slate, from dictation, letters, capital, and small manuscript.
Arithmetic: Form on blackboard or slate, from dictation, figures up to 20; name at sight figures up to 20; add and subtract figures up to 10, orally, from examples on blackboard.

Standard II
Reading: One of the narratives next in order after monosyllables in an elementary reading book used in the school.
Writing: Copy in manuscript character a line of print.
Arithmetic: A sum in simple addition or subtraction, and the multiplication table.

Standard III

Reading: A short paragraph from an elementary reading book used in the school.

Writing: A sentence from the same paragraph, slowly read once, and then dictated in single words.

Arithmetic: A sum in any simple rule as far as short division (inclusive).

Standard IV

Reading: A short paragraph from a more advanced reading book used in the school.

Writing: A sentence slowly dictated once by a few words at a time from the same book, but not from the paragraph read.

Arithmetic: A sum in compound rules (money).

Standard V

Reading: A few lines of poetry from a reading book used in the first class of the school.

Writing: A sentence slowly dictated once, by a few words at a time, from a reading book used in the first class of the school.

Arithmetic: A sum in compound rules (common weights and measures).

Standard VI

Reading: A short ordinary paragraph in a newspaper, or other modern narrative.

Writing: Another short ordinary paragraph in a newspaper, or other modern narrative, slowly dictated once by a few words at a time.

Arithmetic: A sum in practice bills of parcels.

From *Parliamentary Papers, 1862*; as quoted in Sally Mitchell, *Daily Life in Victorian England* (Westport, Conn.: Greenwood Press, 1996), 168–69.

CULTURAL CONFLICTS IN 19TH-CENTURY PERSIA

European imperialism in Persia included various areas of conflict, such as the tobacco industry, important in an area dominated by smokers. Sayyid Jamal ad-Din wrote the following letter to a religious leader. While his influence is unclear, the leader soon after convinced the public to quit smoking as a sign of discontent.

Religious leader of the people, Ray of the Imams Light, pillar of the edifice of Religion, Tongue attuned to the exposition of the Unhidden Law, Your Reverence . . . Hasan Shirazi—may God protect by your means the fold of Islam, and avert the plots of the vile unbelievers!— . . .

O most mighty Religious Guide! Verily the Shah's purpose wavers, his character is impure, his perceptions are failing and his heart is corrupt. He is incapable of governing the land, or managing the affairs of this people, and has entrusted the reins of government in all things great and small to the hands of a wicked freethinker, a tyrant and usurper, who reviles the Prophets openly, and heeds not God's Law, who counts for nothing the religious authorities, curses the doctors of the Law, rejects the pious, condemns honorable Sayyids and treats preachers as one would treat the vilest of mankind. Moreover since his return from Europe he has taken the bit between his teeth, drinks wine openly, associates with unbelievers and displays enmity toward the virtuous. Such is his private conduct; but in addition to this he has sold to the foes of our Faith the greater part of the Persian lands and the profits derived from them, for example, the mines, the roads leading to them, the roads connecting them with the frontiers of the country, the inns about to be built by the side of these extensive means of travel which will spread out through all parts of the kingdom, and the gardens and fields surrounding them. Also the river Karun and the guesthouses which will arise on its banks up to its very source, and the gardens and meadows which adjoin it, and the highway from Ahwaz to Teheran, with the buildings, inns, gardens, and fields surrounding it. Also tobacco, with the chief centers of its cultivation, the lands on which it is grown, and the warehouses, carriers, and sellers, wherever these are found. He has similarly disposed of the grapes used for making wine, and the shops, factories, and winepresses pertaining to this trade throughout the whole of Persia; and so likewise soap, candles, and sugar, and the factories connected with their manufacture. Lastly there is the Bank: what must you understand about the Bank? It means the complete handing over of the reins of government to the enemy of Islam, the enslaving of the people to that enemy, the surrendering of them and of all dominion and authority into the hands of the foreign foe. . . .

And you, O Proof, if you will not arise to help this people, and will not unite them in purpose, and pluck them forth, by the power of the Holy Law from the hands of this sinner, verily the realms of Islam will soon be under the control of foreigners, who will rule . . . as they please and do what they will. . . .

I further assure Your Eminence, speaking as one who knows and seeks, that the Ottoman Government will rejoice in your undertaking of this effort and will aid you in it, for it is well aware that the intervention of Europeans in the Persian domains and their ascendancy there will assuredly prove injurious to its own dominions. Moreover all the ministers and lords of Persia will rejoice in a word in this sense uttered by you, seeing that all of them naturally detest these innovations and are constitutionally opposed to these agreements, which your actions will give them the opportunity to annul, that perhaps they may restrain this evil of covetousness which has been sanctioned and approved. . . . All is from you, by you and in you, and you are responsible for all before God and men. . . .

As for my own story and what that ungrateful tyrant did to me . . . the wretch (the shah) commanded me to be dragged, when I was in sanctuary in the shrine of Shah 'Abdu'l-'Azim and grievously ill, through the snow to the capital with such circumstances of disrespect, humiliation, and disgrace as cannot be imagined for wickedness (and all this after I had been plundered and despoiled). Verily we belong to God and verily unto him do we return!

Thereafter his miserable lackeys placed me, despite my illness, on a pack-saddle, loading me with chains, and this in the winter season, amid the snow-drifts and bitter, icy blasts, and a company of horsemen conveyed me to Khaniqin, guarded by an escort. And he had previously written to the . . . Turkish governor, requesting him to remove me to Basra, knowing well that, if he left me alone, I should come to you, . . . and inform you of his doings and of the state of the people, and explain to you what had befallen the lands of Islam through the evil deeds of this infidel, and would invoke your help, O Proof, for the True Faith, and convince you to come to the assistance of the Muslims. For he knew for a certainty that, should I succeed in meeting you, it would not be possible for him to continue in his office, involving as it does the ruin of the country, the destruction of the people, and the encouragement of unbelief. . . . Moreover his conduct was made more blameworthy and mean in that, in order to avert a general revolt and quiet the popular agitation, he accused the party whom zeal for religion and patriotism had impelled to defend the sanctuary of Islam and the rights of the people of belonging to the Babi sect. . . . What is this weakness? What this cowardice? How is it possible that a low-born vagabond and contemptible fool should be able to sell the Muslims and their lands for a vile price and a paltry sum, scorn the *ulama*, treat with disrespect the descendants of the Prophet, and slander in such a fashion Sayyids of the House of 'Ali? Is there no hand able to pluck up this evil root and so to appease the wrathful indignation of the Muslims, and avenge the descendants of the Chief of God's Apostles (upon whom and whose household be blessings and salutations)? . . .

From Sayyid Jamal ad-Din, *Letter to Hasan Shirazi*, in *The Human Record, Sources of Global History, Fourth Edition, Volume II: Since 1500*, edited by Alfred J. Andrea and James H. Overfield (New York: Houghton Mifflin Company, 2001). Originally appeared in Edward G. Brown, *The Persian Revolution of 1905*. London: Frank Cass, 1966.

PUPIL TEACHERS: QUALIFICATION OF VICTORIAN ENGLISH CANDIDATES, 1847

In today's world most teachers need to have advanced degrees, but this was not so in Victorian England. Here are the qualifications for student teachers in 1847. Despite any questions that we might have about their credentials, these student teachers were nonetheless engaged in an important process to become certified instructors.

They must be at least thirteen years of age, and must not be subject to any bodily infirmity likely to impair their usefulness as pupil teachers.

Candidates will also be required,—

1. To read with fluency, ease, and expression.
2. To write in a neat hand, with correct spelling and punctuation, a simple prose narrative slowly read to them.

3. To write from dictation sums in the first four rules of arithmetic, simple and compound; to work them correctly, and to know the tables of weights and measures.

4. To point out the parts of speech in a simple sentence.

5. To have an elementary knowledge of geography.

6. *In schools connected with the Church of England*, they will be required to repeat the Catechism, and to show that they understand its meaning, and are acquainted with the outline of Scripture history. The parochial clergyman will assist in this part of the examination. *In other schools* the state of the religious knowledge will be certified by the managers.

7. To teach a junior class to the satisfaction of the Inspector.

8. Girls should also be able to sew neatly and to knit.

From *Parliamentary Papers, 1847*; as quoted in Sally Mitchell, *Daily Life in Victorian England* (Westport, Conn.: Greenwood Press, 1996), 172.

PUBLIC SCHOOL BOYS IN VICTORIAN ENGLAND, 1857

The following passage is taken from *Tom Brown's Schooldays*, a novel by Thomas Hughes. The story was based on Hughes's real experiences at Rugby School at the dawn of the Victorian age. As one can tell from the selection, some education issues appear to be timeless: class size, mean teachers, and mischievous students.

The lower-fourth form, in which Tom found himself at the beginning of the next half-year, was the largest form in the lower school, and numbered upwards of forty boys. Young gentlemen of all ages from nine to fifteen were to be found there, who expended such part of their energies as was devoted to Latin and Greek upon a book of Livy, the "Bucolics" of Virgil, and the "Hecuba" of Euripides, which were ground out in small daily portions. The driving of this unlucky lower-fourth must have been grievous work to the unfortunate master, for it was the most unhappily constituted of any in the school. Here stuck the great stupid boys, who, for the life of them, could never master the accidence. . . . There were no less than three unhappy fellows in tail coats, with incipient down on their chins, whom the Doctor and the master of the form were always endeavouring to hoist into the upper school, but whose parsing and construing resisted the most well-meant shoves. Then came the mass of the form, boys of eleven and twelve, the most mischievous and reckless age of British youth. . . . The remainder of the form consisted of young prodigies of nine and ten, who were going up the school at the rate of a form a half-year, all boys' hands and wits being against them in their progress.

From Thomas Hughes, *Tom Brown's Schooldays* (1857, chapter 8); as quoted in Sally Mitchell, *Daily Life in Victorian England* (Westport, Conn.: Greenwood Press, 1996), 175.

NORTH LONDON COLLEGIATE SCHOOL: SOCIAL STANDARDS, 1850s

Beginning in the 1850s, middle-class parents and reformers in England realized that the education that girls received needed quick improvement. As a result, new schools were established such as the North London Collegiate School. In this remembrance, a young girl describes happy memories of this school. She felt more comfortable there in part because she was with pupils of her own class standing.

One advantage of the school I felt immediately. Ever since my father's death we had been hard up. . . . I didn't mind going without a summer trip to Cornwall or the sea-side, not having fires enough in the winter, never having a new dress (only "passed-ons" from cousins), and dreading every order for a new text-book. But I did bitterly mind that the girls in my private school should notice my poverty. For instance, one day the news had gone round that Mary Thomas had got a new dress, and I was elated, until one keen-eyed girl discovered that it was only an old one turned.

Now at North London I sensed at once a different atmosphere. No one asked where you lived, how much pocket-money you had, or what your father was—he might be a bishop or a rat-catcher. Girls would openly grumble at having to buy a new text-book. The only notice taken of another girl's dress that I ever heard made a funny contrast to what I had experienced in the private school. I was told after I had left school that I had been a constant wonder for the length of time that one dress had lasted me, and that this had called forth admiration, not contempt.

From M. V. Hughes, *A London Girl of the 1880s* (1946); as quoted in Sally Mitchell, *Daily Life in Victorian England* (Westport, Conn.: Greenwood Press, 1996), 182.

KARL MARX VIEWS THE AMERICAN CIVIL WAR, 1861

Karl Marx is known first and foremost as an influential social and political thinker who helped to spark a worldwide movement to eliminate capitalism and empower the working classes. Marx was also a social critic and an astute contemporary observer. Here he describes the American Civil War and provides some interesting analysis of the Southern Confederacy. His account was published in *Die Presse* on November 7, 1861.

One sees, therefore, that the war of the Southern Confederacy is in the true sense of the word a war of conquest or the extension and perpetuation of slavery. The greater part of the border states and Territories are still in the possession of the

Union, whose side they have taken first through the ballot-box and then with arms. The Confederacy, however, counts them for the "South" and seeks to conquer them from the Union. In the border states which the Confederacy has occupied for the time being, it holds the relatively free highlands in check by martial law. Within the actual slave states themselves it supplants the hitherto existing democracy by the unrestricted oligarchy of three hundred thousand slaveholders.

With the relinquishment of its plans of conquest the Southern Confederacy would relinquish its capacity to live and the purpose of secession. Secession, indeed, only took place because within the Union the transformation of the border states and Territories into slave states seemed no longer attainable. On the other hand, with a peaceful cession of the contested territory to the Southern Confederacy the North would surrender to the slave republic more than three-quarters of the entire territory of the United States. The North would lose the Gulf of Mexico altogether, the Atlantic Ocean from Pensacola Bay to Delaware Bay, and would even cut itself off from the Pacific Ocean. Missouri, Kansas, New Mexico, Arkansas, and Texas would draw California after them. Incapable of wresting the mouth of the Mississippi from the hands of the strong, hostile, slave republic in the South, the great agricultural states in the basin between the Rocky Mountains and the Alleghenies, in the valleys of the Mississippi, the Missouri, and the Ohio, would be compelled by their economic interests to secede from the North and enter the Southern Confederacy. These northwestern states, in their turn, would draw after them all the Northern states lying further east, with perhaps the exception of the states of New England, into the same vortex of session.

Thus there would in fact take place, not a dissolution of the Union, but a *reorganization* of it, a *reorganization on the basis of slavery*, under the recognized control of the slaveholding oligarchy. The plan of such a reorganization has been openly proclaimed by the principal speakers of the South at the Congress of Montgomery and explains the paragraph of the new Constitution which leaves it open to every state of the old Union to join the new Confederacy. The slave system would infect the whole Union. In the Northern states, where Negro slavery is in practice unworkable, the white working class would gradually be forced down to the level of helotry. This would accord with the loudly proclaimed principle that only certain races are capable of freedom, and as the actual labor is the lot of the Negro in the South, so in the North it is the lot of the German and the Irishman, or their direct descendants.

The present struggle between the South and the North is, therefore, nothing but a struggle between two social systems, between the system of slavery and the system of free labor. The struggle has broken out because the two systems can no longer live peacefully side by side on the North American continent. It can only be ended by the victory of one system or the other.

If the border states, on the disputed areas of which the two systems have hitherto contended for mastery, are a thorn in the flesh of the South, there can, on the other hand, be no mistake that, in the course of the war up to now, they have constituted the chief weakness of the North. One section of the slaveholders in these districts simulated loyalty to the North at the bidding of the conspirators in the South;

another section found that in fact its was in accordance with their real interests and traditional ideas to go with the Union. Both sections have uniformly crippled the North. Anxiety to keep the "loyal" slaveholders of the border states in good humor; fear of throwing them into the arms of secession; in a word, tender regard for the interests, prejudices, and sensibilities of these ambiguous allies, has smitten the Union government with incurable weakness since the beginning of the war, driven it to half measures, forced it to dissemble away the principle of the war and to spare the foe's most vulnerable spot, the root of the evil—*slavery itself*.

When, only recently, Lincoln pusillanimously revoked Frémont's Missouri proclamation on the emancipation of Negroes belonging to the rebels, this occurred merely out of regard for the loud protest of the "loyal" slaveholders of Kentucky. However, a turning point has already been reached. With Kentucky, the last border state has been pushed into the series of battlefields between the South and the North. With real war for the border states in the border states themselves, the question of winning or losing them is withdrawn from the sphere of diplomatic and parliamentary discussions. One section of slaveholders will throw away the mask of loyalty; the other will content itself with the prospect of compensation such as Great Britain gave the West Indian planters. Events themselves drive to the promulgation of the decisive slogan—emancipation of the slaves.

That even the most hardened Democrats and diplomats of the North feel themselves drawn to this point, is shown by some publications of very recent date. In an open letter, General Cass, Secretary of State under Buchanan and hitherto one of the most ardent allies of the South, declares emancipation of the slaves the *coniditio sine qua non* of the Union's salvation. In his last review for October, Dr. Brownson, the spokesman of the Catholic party of the North, on his own admission the most energetic adversary of the emancipation movement from 1836 to 1860, publishes an article *for* Abolition.

"If we have opposed Abolition heretofore," he says among other things, "because we would preserve the Union, we must *a fortiori* now oppose slavery whenever, in our judgment, its continuance becomes incompatible with the maintenance of the Union, or of the nation as a free republican state," Finally, the *World*, a New York organ of the diplomats of the Washington Cabinet, concludes one of its latest blustering articles against the Abolitionists with the words:

On the day when it shall be decided that either slavery or the Union must go down, on that day sentence of death is passed on slavery. If the North cannot triumph *without* emancipation, it will triumph *with* emancipation.

From Karl Marx, "Civil War in the United States," in Karl Marx and Frederick Engels, *The Civil War in the United States* (New York: International Publishers, 1969), 79–83.

ON THE OREGON TRAIL, 1857

The Oregon Trail was blazed in the early 1840s by men like John C. Frémont and Kit Carson, who sought their fortunes in the American West. Within the decade, thousands of people were following their footsteps. The trip was dangerous, and many did not make it. In the following document, Helen Carpenter describes her perilous journey.

Although there is not much to cook, the difficulty and inconvenience in doing it amounts to a great deal—so by the time one has squatted around the fire and cooked bread and bacon, and made several dozen trips to and from the wagon—washed the dishes . . . and gotten things ready for an early breakfast, some of the others already have their night caps on—at any rate it is time to go to bed. In respect to women's work, the days are all very much the same—except when we stop . . . then there is washing to be done and light bread to make and all kinds of odd jobs. Some women have very little help about the camp, being obliged to get the wood and water . . . make camp fires, unpack at night and pack up in the morning—and if they are Missourians they have the milking to do if they are fortunate to have cows. I am luck in having a Yankee for a husband, so am well waited on . . .

When the sun was just peeping over the top of the mountain, there was suddenly heard a shot and blood curdling yell, and immediately the Indians we saw yesterday were seen riding at full speed directly toward the horses . . . father put his gun to his shoulder as though to shoot. . . . The Indians kept . . . circling . . . and halooning . . . bullets came whizzing through the camp. None can know the horror of it, who have not been similarly situated . . . [the Indians] did not come directly toward us, but all the time in a circular way, from one side of the road to the other, each time they passed, getting a little nearer, and occasionally firing a shot . . . Father and Reel could stand it no longer, they must let those Indians see how far their Sharps rifles would carry. Without aiming to hit them, they made the earth fly. . . .

It is now 18 days since we have seen a train . . . [we] found the body of a nude woman on the bank of the slough. . . . A piece of hair rope was around her neck . . . From appearances it was thought she had been tortured by being drawn back and forth through the slough, by this rope around her neck. The body was given the best burial that was possible, under the circumstances. . . .

From Helen Carpenter, "On the Oregon Trail," in Erik Bruun and Jay Crosby, *Our Nation's Archive: The History of the United States in Documents* (New York: Black Dog, 1999), 319–20.

ADVICE FOR WESTERN TREKKERS, 1859

To assist travelers moving out to the western frontier, Randolph Marcy, a captain in the U.S. Army, published *The Prairie Traveler: A Handbook for Overland Expeditions* (1859). In this excerpt, Marcy lists the needed supplies for the trip. Take note of his descriptions of American Indians and their keen abilities.

Supplies for a march should be put up in the most secure, compact, and portable manner.

Bacon should be packed in strong sacks of a hundred pounds to each; or, in very hot climates, put in boxes and surrounded with bran, which in a great measure prevents the fat from melting away.

Flour should be packed in stout double canvas sacks well sewed, a hundred pounds in each sack.

Butter may be preserved, and skimming off the scum as it rises to the top until it is quite clear like oil. It is then placed in tin canisters and soldered up. This mode of preserving butter has been adopted in the hot climate of southern Texas, and it is found to keep sweet for a great length of time, and its flavor is but little impaired by the process.

Sugar may be well secured in India-rubber or gutta-purcha sacks, or so placed in the wagon as not to risk getting wet.

Desiccated or dried vegetables are almost equal to the fresh, and are put up in such a compact and portable form as easily to be transported over the plains. They have been exclusively used in the Crimean war, and by our own army in Utah, and have been very generally approved. They are prepared by cutting the fresh vegetables into thin slices and subjecting them to very powerful press, which removes the juice and leaves the solid cake, which after having been thoroughly dried in an oven, becomes almost hard as a rock. A small piece of this, about half the size of a man's hand, when boiled, swells up so as to fill a vegetable disk, and is sufficient for four men. It is believed that the antiscorbutic properties of vegetables are not impaired by desiccation, and they will keep for years if not exposed to dampness. Canned vegetables are very good for campaigning, but are not so portable as when put up in the other form. . . .

When the deer are lying down in the smooth prairie, unless the grass is tall, it is difficult to get near them, as they are generally looking around, and become alarmed at the least noise.

The Indians are in the habit of using a small instrument which imitates the bleat of the young fawn, with which they lure the doe within range of their rifles. The young fawn gives out no scent upon its track until it is sufficiently grown to make good running, and instinct teaches the mother that this wise provision of nature to preserve the helpless little quadruped from the ravages of wolves, panthers, and other carnivorous beasts, will be defeated if she remains with it, as her tracks can not be concealed. She therefore hides her fawn in the grass, where it is almost impossible to see it, even when very near it, goes off to some neighboring thicket within call, and makes her bed alone. The Indian pot-hunter, who is but little scrupulous as to the means he employs in accomplishing his ends, sounds the bleat along near the places where he thinks the game is lying, and the unsuspicious doe, who imagines that her offspring is in distress, rushes with headlong impetuosity toward the sound, and often goes within a few yards of the hunter to receive her death-wound. . . .

I once undertook to experiment with the instrument myself, and made my first essay in attempting to call up an antelope which I discovered in the distance. I succeeded admirably in luring the way victim within shooting range, had raised upon my knees, and was just in the act of pulling trigger, when a rustling in the grass to my left drew my attention in that direction, where, much to my surprise, I beheld a huge panther within about twenty yards, bounding with gigantic strides directly toward me. I turned my rifle, and in an instant, much to my relief and gratification, its contents were lodged in the heart of the beast.

From Randolph Marcy, "A Handbook for Overland Expeditions," in Erik Bruun and Jay Crosby, *Our Nation's Archive: The History of the United States in Documents* (New York: Black Dog, 1999), 320–21.

CONSTITUTION OF THE CONFEDERATE STATES OF AMERICA, 1861

The Constitution of the Confederate States of America was hastily assembled. In structure, this constitution, like the government it established, mirrored that of the United States. There were two significant differences, however. In the Confederacy, slavery was completely legal (if not encouraged). Additionally, the states had the majority of the political power. These two features were central to the Confederacy's political structure but also created serious liabilities during the Civil War.

We the people of the Confederate States, each state acting in its sovereign and independent character, in order to from a permanent government, establish justice, insure domestic tranquility, and secure the blessings of liberty to ourselves and our posterity—invoking the favor and guidance of Almighty God—do ordain and establish this Constitution for the Confederate States of America.

Article I. Section 1. All legislative powers herein delegated shall be vested in Congress of the Confederate States, which shall consist of a Senate and House of Representatives.

Section 2. (1) The House of Representatives shall be . . . chosen every second year by the people of the several States; and the electors of each State shall be citizens of the Confederate States, and have the qualifications requisite for electors of the most numerous branches of the State Legislature; but no person of foreign birth, not a citizen of the Confederate States, shall be allowed to vote for any officer, civil, or political, State or Federal. . . .

(2) Representatives and direct taxes shall be apportioned among the several States which may be included within this Confederacy, according to their respective numbers, which shall be determined by adding to the whole number of free persons, including those bound to service for a term of years, and excluding Indians not taxed, three-fifths of all slaves. The actual enumeration shall be made within three years after the first meeting of the Congress of the Confederate States, and within every subsequent term of ten years, in such manner as they shall by law direct. The number of Representatives shall not exceed one for every fifty thousand, but each

State shall have at least one Representative; and until such enumeration shall be made the State of South Carolina shall be entitled to choose six; the State of Georgia ten; the State of Alabama nine; the State of Florida two; the State of Mississippi seven; the State of Louisiana six; and the State of Texas six. . . .

Section 9. (1) The importation of Negroes of the African race, from any foreign country, other than the slaveholding States or Territories of the United States of America, is hereby forbidden; and Congress is required to pass such laws as shall effectually prevent the same.

(2) Congress shall have the power to prohibit them any State not a member of, or Territory belonging to, this Confederacy. . . .

Article IV. Section 2. (1) The citizens of each State shall be entitled to the privileges and immunities of citizens of several States, and shall have the right to transit and sojourn in any State of this Confederacy, with their slaves and other property; and the right of property in said slaves shall not be thereby impaired. . . .

(3) No slave or other person held to service or labor in any State or Territory of the Confederate States, under the laws thereof, escaping or [un]lawfully carried into another, shall, in consequence of any law or regulation therein, be discharged from such service or labor; but shall be delivered up on claim of the party to whom such slaves belongs, or to whom such service or labor may be due . . .

Section 3. (3) The Confederate States may acquire new territory; and Congress shall have power to legislate and provide governments for the inhabitants of all territory belonging to the Confederate States, lying without the limits of the several States, and may permit them, at such times, and in such manner as it may by law provide, to form States to be admitted into the Confederacy. In all such territory, the institution of Negro slavery, as it now exists in the Confederate States, shall be recognized and protected by Congress and by the territorial government; and the inhabitants of the several Confederate States and Territories shall have the right to take to such territory any slaves lawfully held by them in any of the States or Territories of the Confederate States. . . .

Article V. Section 1. (1) Upon the demand of any three States, legally assembled in their several Conventions, the Congress shall summon a Convention of all the States, to take into consideration such amendments to the Constitution as the said States shall concur in suggesting at the time when the said demand is made; and should any of the proposed amendments to the Constitution be agreed on by the said Convention—voting by States—and the same be ratified by the Legislatures of two-thirds thereof—as the one or the other mode of ratification may be proposed by the general convention—they shall thenceforward form a part of this Constitution. But no State shall, without its consent, be deprived of its equal representation in the Senate. . . .

Article VII. 1. The ratification of the conventions of five States shall be sufficient for the establishment of this Constitution between the States so ratifying the same.

2. When five States shall have ratified this Constitution in the manner before specified, the Congress, under the provisional Constitution, shall prescribe the time for holding the election of President and Vice-President, and for the meeting of the electoral college, and for counting the votes and inaugurating the President. They

shall also prescribe the time for holding the first election of members of Congress under this Constitution, and the time for assembling the same. Until the assembling of such Congress, the Congress under the provisional Constitution shall continue to exercise the legislative powers granted them; not extending beyond the time limited by the Constitution of the Provisional Government.

Adopted unanimously by the Congress of the Confederate States of South Carolina, Georgia, Florida, Alabama, Mississippi, Louisiana, and Texas, sitting in convention as the capitol, in the city of Montgomery, Alabama, on the Eleventh day of March, in the year Eighteen Hundred and Sixty-One.

From "Constitution of the Confederate States of America, 1861," in Erik Bruun and Jay Crosby, *Our Nation's Archive: The History of the United States in Documents* (New York: Black Dog, 1999), 342–43.

A SLAVE DESCRIBES A SLAVE AUCTION IN THE ANTEBELLUM SOUTH, 1841

One of the most pernicious aspects of the slave system was the slave market, where slaves were bought and sold and where families were destroyed and lives irreversibly altered. In this passage, a slave describes the cruelty and inhumanity of the slave system, particularly the slave market. When reading the section, be mindful of how such a firsthand account might have affected the political climate of the years preceding the Civil War.

In the first place we were required to wash thoroughly, and those with beards to shave. We were then furnished with a new suit each, cheap, but clean. The men had hat, coat, shirt, pants, and shoes; the women frocks of calico, and handkerchief to bind about their heads. We were now conducted into a large room in the front part of the building to which the yard was attached, in order to be properly trained, before the admission of customers. The men were arranged on one side of the room, the women at the other. The tallest was placed at the head of the row, then the next tallest, and so on in the order of their respective heights. Emily was at the foot of the line of women. Freeman [Theophilus Freeman, owner of the slave pen] charged us to remember our places; exhorted us to appear smart and lively—sometimes threatening, and again, holding out various inducements. During the day he exercised us in the art of "looking smart," and of moving to our places with exact precision.

After being fed, in the afternoon, we were again paraded and made to dance. Bob, a colored boy, who had some time belonged to Freeman, played on the violin. Standing near him, I made hold to inquire if he could play the "Virginia Reel." He answered he could not, and asked me if I could play. Replying in the affirmative, he handed me the violin. I struck up a tune, and finished it. Freeman ordered me to

492

continue playing, and seemed well pleased, telling Bob that I far excelled him—a remark that seemed to grieve my musical companion very much.

Next day many customers called to examine Freeman's "new lot." The latter gentleman was very loquacious, dwelling at much length upon our several good points and qualities. He would make us hold up our heads, walk briskly back and forth, while customers would feel of our hands and arms and bodies, turn us about, ask us what we could do, make us open our mouths and show our teeth, precisely as a jockey examines a horse which he is about to barter for purchase. Sometimes a man or woman was taken back to the small house in the yard, stripped, and inspected more minutely. Scars upon a slave's back were considered evidence of a rebellious or unruly spirit, and hurt his sale.

An old gentleman, who said he wanted a coachman, appeared to take a fancy to me. From his conversation with Burch [Freeman's business associate], I learned he was a resident in the city. I very much desired that he would buy me, because I conceived it would not be difficult to make my escape from New Orleans on some northern vessel. Freeman asked him fifteen hundred dollars for me. The old gentleman insisted it was too much as times were very hard. Freeman, however, declared that I was sound of health, of a good constitution, and intelligent. He made it a point to enlarge upon my musical attainments. The old gentleman argued quite adroitly that there was nothing extraordinary about the Negro, and finally, to my regret, went out, saying he would call again. During the day, however, a number of sales were made. David and Caroline were purchased together by a Natchez planter. They left us, grinning broadly, and in a most happy state of mind, caused by the fact of their not being separated. Sethe was sold to a planter of Baton Rouge, her eyes flashing with anger as she was led away.

The same man also purchased Randall. The little fellow was made to jump, and run across the floor, and perform many other feats, exhibiting his activity and condition. All the time the trade was going on, Eliza was crying aloud, and wringing her hands. She besought the man not to buy him, unless he also bought herself and Emily. She promised, in that case, to be the most faithful slave that ever lived. The man answered that he could not afford it, and then Eliza burst into a paroxysm of grief, weeping plaintively. Freeman turned around to her, savagely, with his whip in his uplifted hand, ordering her to stop her noise, or he would flog her. He would not have such work—such sniveling; and unless she ceased that minute, he would take her to the yard and give her a hundred lashes. Yes, he would take the nonsense out of her pretty quick—if he didn't, might he be d—d. Eliza shrunk before him, and tried to wipe away her tears, but it was all in vain. All the frowns and threats of Freeman, could not wholly silence the afflicted mother. She kept on begging and beseeching them, most piteously, not to separate the three. Over and over again she told them how she loved her boy. A great many times she repeated her former promises—how very faithful and obedient she would be; how hard she would labor day and night, to the last moment of her life, if he would only buy them all together. But it was of no avail; the man could not afford it. The bargain was agreed upon, and Randall must go alone. Then Eliza ran to him; embraced him passionately; kissed him again and again; told him to remember her—all the while her tears falling in the boy's face like rain.

Freeman damned her, calling her a blubbering, bawling wench, and ordered her to go to her place, and behave herself, and be somebody. He swore he wouldn't stand such stuff but a little longer. He would soon give her something to cry about, if she was not mighty careful, and *that* she might depend upon.

The planter from Baton Rouge, with his new purchase, was ready to depart,

"Don't cry, mama. I will be a good boy. Don't cry," said Randall, looking back, as they passed out of the door.

What has become of the lad, God knows. It was a mournful scene indeed. I would have cried myself if I had dared.

From "A Slave Auction Described by a Slave, 1841," in Herbert Aptheker, *A Documentary History of the Negro People in the United States, Volume I: From Colonial Times Through the Civil War* (New York: Citadel Press, 1951), 206–9.

VIEWS OF A 19TH-CENTURY MUSLIM ON RELIGION, WOMEN, SLAVES, AND WAR

In opposition to a number of rulers who became Muslim for primarily non-religious reasons, groups of dedicated Muslims called for a series of jihads, or holy wars. A leader of the first jihad, Usman dan Fodio, also wrote extensively on religion, women, and war. Excerpts from his writings are provided below.

ROYAL RELIGION

It is well known that in our time Islam in these countries mentioned above is widespread among people other than the sultans. As for the sultans, they are undoubtedly unbelievers, even though they may profess the religion of Islam, because they practice polytheistic rituals and turn people away from the path of God and raise the flag of worldly kingdom above the banner of Islam. All this is unbelief according to the consensus of opinion.

The government of a country is the government of its king without question. If the king is a Muslim, his land is Muslim; if he is an Unbeliever, his land is a land of Unbelievers. In these circumstances it is obligatory for anyone to leave it for another country. There is no dispute that the sultans of these countries venerate certain places, certain trees, and certain rocks and offer sacrifice to them. This constitutes unbelief according to the consensus of opinion. . . .

THE TREATMENT OF WOMEN AND SLAVES

Most of our educated men leave their wives, their daughters, and the slaves morally abandoned, like beasts, without teaching them what God prescribes should be taught them, and without instructing them in the articles of the Law which concern them. Thus, they leave them ignorant of the rules regarding ablutions, prayer, fasting, business dealings, and other duties which they have to fulfill, and which God commands that they should be taught.

Men treat these beings like household implements which become broken after long use and which are then thrown out on the dung-heap. This is an abominable crime! Alas! How can they thus shut up their wives, their daughters, and their slaves in the darkness of ignorance, while daily they impart knowledge to their students? In truth, they act out of egoism, and if they devote themselves to their pupils, that is nothing but hypocrisy and vain ostentation on their part.

Their conduct is blameworthy, for to instruct one's wives, daughters, and captives is a positive duty, while to impart knowledge to students is only a work over and above what is expected, and there is no doubt but that the one takes precedence over the other.

Muslim women—Do not listen to the speech of those who are misguided and who sow the seed of error in the heart of another; they deceive you when they stress obedience to God and to his Messenger (May God show him bounty and grant him salvation), and when they say that the woman finds her happiness in obedience to her husband.

They seek only their own satisfaction, and that is why they impose upon you tasks which the Law of God and that of his Prophet have never especially assigned to you. Such are—the preparation of food-stuffs, the washing of clothes, and other duties which they like to impose upon you, while they neglect to teach you what God and the Prophet have prescribed for you.

Yes, the woman owes submission to her husband, publicly as well as in intimacy, even if he is one of the humble people of the world, and to disobey him is a crime, at least so long as he does not command what God condemns; in that case she must refuse, since it is wrong of a human creature to disobey the Creator.

THE CALL TO HOLY WAR

That to make war upon the heathen king who does not say "There is no God but Allah" on account of the custom of his town, and who makes no profession of Islam, is obligatory by assent, and that to take the government from him is obligatory by assent.

And that to make war upon the king who is an apostate, and who has abandoned the religion of Islam for the religion of heathendom is obligatory by assent, and that to take the government from him is obligatory by assent; And that to make war against the king who is an apostate—who has not abandoned the religion of Islam as far as the profession of it is concerned, but who mingles the observances of Islam with the observances of heathendom, like the kings of Hausaland for the most part—is also obligatory by assent, and that to take the government from him is obligatory by assent.

And to make war upon backsliding Muslims who do not own allegiance to any of the Emirs of the Faithful, is obligatory by assent, if they be summoned to give allegiance and they refuse, until they enter into allegiance; . . .

And that residence in enemy territory is unlawful by assent; . . .

And to enslave the freeborn among the Muslims is unlawful by assent, whether they reside in the territory of Islam, or in enemy territory;

And to make war upon the oppressors is obligatory by assent, and that wrongfully to devour their property is unlawful by assent, for "Use is made of their armor against them, and afterwards it is returned to them"; and their enslavement is unlawful by assent; . . .

From Usman dan Fodio, *The Human Record, Sources of Global History, Fourth Edition, Volume II: Since 1500*, edited by Alfred J. Andrea and James H. Overfield (New York: Houghton Mifflin Company, 2001).

CUMULATIVE INDEX

Boldface numbers refer to volume numbers. A key appears on all verso pages.

4:50; punishment, 4:386–88, 487; religious practices, 4:486–88; science, 4:170–71; sedition, 4:388; starvation, 4:243; tea, 4:257; technology, 4:171–72; theater, 4:433; theft, 4:387–88; water supply, 4:171–72; weather, 4:171; wheat, 4:106–7; windmills, 4:172; women, 4:48–52, 433; women's clothing, 4:302–3; worship, 4:486–87

Australian Aboriginals: ancient history of, 1:14–15; apprenticeships, 1:61; archers, 1:418; art, 1:240–41; bark painting, 1:241; beds, 1:281; body painting, 1:315; camps, housing, 1:281; canoes, 1:165–66; ceremonial clothing, 1:315; children, 1:61–62; clans, 1:261, 281; clothing, 1:314–15; colors, 1:314, 315; cooking methods, 1:260; costumes, 1:315; cycad palm seeds, 1:261; dance, 1:432–34; death, burial, and the afterlife, 1:432–33; diet, 1:260, 261; dreamtime, 1:15, 192, 229, 240–41, 432–33, 469; eating habits, 1:260–61; education, 1:28–29, 191–93; eels, 1:419; engravings, 1:240–41; family life, 1:28–29; fireplaces, 1:281; fish, 1:261, 418; fishing, 1:418; food, 1:166, 260–62; food preservation, 1:260; games, 1:418–19; government, 1:339, 356–58; grains, 1:260; hairstyles, 1:315; headbands, 1:314; headdresses, 1:315; health and medicine, 1:229, 469; holidays and festivals, 1:281–82; housing, 1:281–82; hunting, 1:418–19; incest, 1:28; jewelry, 1:315; language and writing, 1:180–82, 192; marriage, 1:28; meat, 1:261, 418; message stick, 1:181; mosquitoes, 1:281; multilingualism, 1:180–81; music, 1:432–34; musical instruments, 1:432–33; nonverbal communication, 1:181; observation and experimentation, 1:229; oral tradition, 1:192; paintings and drawings, 1:240–41, 432–33; pirates, 1:154; plant foods, 1:261; polygamy, 1:28; pottery, 1:260; priests and religious ritual, 1:469; professions, 1:192; religious art, 1:241; religious beliefs, 1:261, 468–70; religious purification, 1:282; revenge, 1:390; rites of passage, 1:469; rivers, 1:165–66; rock art, 1:240–41; rural life and agriculture, 1:260; sand art, 1:240–41; schools, 1:191–92; science, 1:228–30; 17th & 18th Centuries, 4:19; shields, 1:400; smallpox, 1:21; smoke signals, 1:181; songs and storytelling, 1:166, 181, 192, 240, 432–33; sports, 1:418–19; theater, 1:432–34; toys, 1:62, 192; trade, 1:151–53; travel and transportation, 1:152, 165–67; wall decorations, 1:281; warfare, 1:389–91; weapons, 1:400–401; women, 1:191–92, 229, 356, 418–19, 432–33; x-ray art, 1:241; yams, 1:261

Australian prison labor: agriculture, 4:50; alcoholic beverages, 4:257–58; civil rights, 4:387; clothing, 4:286; cohabitation, 4:32–33; description of first criminals transported, 4:499–501; food, 4:242; historical overview, 4:21–22; marriage, 4:32–33; punishment, 4:387–88; women's clothing, 4:302–3

Austria as part of Holy Roman Empire, 3:283, 287

Austria-Hungary (1910–20), 6:1–2

Austronesian language, 2:175

Authoritarianism in Latin America, 5:325

Automation: United States (1920–39), 6:360; United States (1960–90), 6:131. *See also* Assembly lines

Automobiles: effect of, 6:348; India (19th Century), 5:301; Japanese brands, 6:362, 363; Latin America (20th Century), 6:314; United States (1920–39), 6:114–15, 356–58; United States (1960–90), 6:361

Autopsies, 1:292

Autumnal equinox, 4:439

Auxila, 1:385–86

Avant-garde movement: film, 6:514; Soviet Union, 6:551

Ave Maria, 3:77, 132

Averroës, 2:165

Aves sin nido (Matto de Turner), 5:197

Avicenna (Ibn Sina), 2:156–57, 179, 192

Awilum, 1:329–30

Axes. *See* Tools; Weapons

Ayllus, 3:53, 107, 282, 377

Aymoray, 3:391

Ayres, Lew, 6:525

Ayuntamiento, 3:287

Ayurveda, 1:302; 5:210–11

Ayurvedic medicine, 6:286, 287

Azcatpotzalco, 3:104

AZT, 6:283–84

Aztec: almanacs, 3:140; art, 3:353–56; astronomy, 3:185, 189; barter, 3:122; baths, 3:234; beans, 3:248; blood offerings, 3:297, 298, 388; calendars, 3:123, 140, 151–52; capes, 3:233; chastity, 3:69; childbirth, 3:47–48, 83–84; child labor, 3:48–49, 85–86; children, 3:83–87; city life, 3:122–24; cloaks, 3:233; clothing, 3:232–34; cocoa, 3:122; codices, 3:217; commoners, 3:280–81; copper, 3:122; cosmetics, 3:234; cotton, 3:232; creation stories, 3:139; death, burial, and the afterlife, 3:51, 401–2; deities, 3:5, 373–76; drugs, 3:281; early history, 3:2–6; education, 3:47–48, 84–85, 182–86; fasting, 3:388; feathers, 3:341, 355–56; fishing, 3:48; food, 3:248; games, 3:326–28; genealogy, 3:217; government, 3:296–99; hierarchy, 3:280–81; human sacrifices, 3:387–89, 423–24; language, 3:168–69, 218; life cycles, 3:47–52; literature, 3:216–19; maize, 3:104, 248; marriage, 3:32, 49–51; money, 3:122; mythology, 3:5, 123, 140, 184; names, 3:47; nobility, 3:280–81; numbers, 3:85, 140, 151; omens, 3:218, 354; painting, 3:218–19, 341, 354–55; peyote, 3:281; physicians, 3:424–25; pictographs, 3:168; poetry, 3:354; prayers, 3:47, 68; priests and religious rituals, 3:84, 387–89; punishment of children, 3:49, 86, 184, 187; pyramids, 3:103, 297; religious beliefs, 3:373–76; religious purification, 3:31, 67; rural life, 3:102–4; sacred story: beginnings and endings, 3:139, 399–402; sandals, 3:233; sculpture, 3:355; servants, 3:401; sexuality, 3:69, 260; shields, 3:233; skirts, 3:232; slaves, 3:281; sports, 3:326–28; squash, 3:248; taxes, 3:103; temples, 3:50, 67, 184, 367, 387–88; textiles, 3:424; time, 3:139–41; tobacco, 3:185; warriors, 3:51, 124, 171, 185, 223, 232, 233, 281; women, 3:67–71, 424–25; writing, 3:157, 168

Ba, 1:512

Ba-bird, 1:467

Babi Yar, 6:6

Baby and Child Care (Spock), 6:69

Baby Boomers (Light), 6:41

Babylon, 1:1, 3, 101–2, 121

Bacalar, 3:231

Bacchai, 1:201

Backe, Alexander D., 5:152

Backgammon: England (15th & 16th Centuries), 3:318; Europe (Middle Ages), 2:372

Bacon: Civil War soldiers, 5:224; England (Victorian era), 5:219, 237; United States (Civil War era), 5:224; United States (Western Frontier), 5:230, 232

Bacon, Nathaniel, 4:390–91

Bacon, Roger, 2:158, 161

Bacon's Rebellion, 4:390–91

Badminton, 6:509

Baghdad as part of Ottoman Empire, 3:20

Baghdad (Middle Ages), 2:117–19; as commercial center, 2:142; as educational center, 2:148; fortification, 2:108, 117

Baghdad (19th Century), 5:146

Bagpipes: England (15th & 16th Centuries), 3:343; Europe (Middle Ages), 2:387; Italy (15th & 16th Centuries), 3:340

Bahadur Shah II, 5:14

Baker, George, 6:571

Bakers: England (Victorian era), 5:110; Europe (Middle Ages), 2:97

Bakker, Jim and Tammy, 6:584, 587

Baklava, 3:245

Baktashi, 3:369

Bakufu, 4:96, 144–46, 357–59

Baku-han, 4:357–58

Baldwin, Charles, 5:29

Baldwin, James, 6:152, 216, 223

Bali, 5:414

Balias, 3:80

Balkan languages, 3:165

Balkan Wars of 1912-1913, 6:2

Ball, Lucille, 6:247–48

Ballads, Spanish, 3:345

Ballet, 1:429. *See also* Dance

Ball games: Europe (Middle Ages), 2:370; Japan (17th & 18th Centuries), 4:424; Maya, 3:215–16, 314–16, 325, 397–98; Rome (ancient), 1:414, 415

Ball gowns. *See* Gowns

Balls: England (17th & 18th Centuries), 4:451–52; England (Victorian era), 5:422

Balowoka, 4:135

Bamboo shoots, 2:205

Banana, Yoshimoto, 6:238

Bananas: China (Tang Dynasty), 2:205; England (Victorian era), 5:239; India (ancient), 1:85; India (19th Century), 5:244; Islamic World (Middle Ages), 2:207; Latin America (19th Century), 5:97, 133–34; Polynesia, 2:212

Banditos, 3:309

Bandits: Latin America (19th Century), 5:341; Rome (ancient), 1:163; United States (Western Frontier), 5:333

Bands in Victorian era, 5:422

Bandy ball, 3:316

Bang, 5:253

Bangalore, India and computer industry, 6:254

Bangles, 5:286

Banishment. *See* Exile

Bank of England, 5:139

Bankruptcy and Great Depression, 6:165

Banks, John: on food, 5:232, 233; on gold mining, 5:297, 298; on morality, 5:59; novels read by, 5:188–89, 436; on rattlesnakes, 5:204; on suicide, 5:205

Banks, Joseph, 2:210

Banks and banking: China (Tang Dynasty), 2:101–3; England (17th & 18th Centuries), 4:139–40; England (Victorian era), 5:111, 114, 350; Great Depression, 6:165; Islamic World (Middle Ages), 2:143–44; Japan (20th Century), 6:453

Banneker, Benjamin, 5:151

Banns, 2:42; 4:41

Banquets: China (Tang Dynasty), **2:**60, 83; Greece (ancient), **1:**253; India (20th Century), **6:**316; Islamic World (Middle Ages), **2:**85; Mesopotamia, **1:**343; Rome (ancient), **1:**256–57, 430; Soviet Union, **6:**318; Vikings, **2:**397–98

Bansuri, **5:**424

Baptism: Catholicism (Spain, Italy, England), **3:**380–81; Christianity (England, Spain, Italy), **3:**31, 396; England (15th & 16th Centuries), **3:**32, 74; Europe (Middle Ages), **2:**79, 410; Italy (15th & 16th Centuries), **3:**37–38, 79; Kongo (17th & 18th Centuries), **4:**485; Latin America (19th Century), **5:**471; Latin America (20th Century), **6:**43; Protestantism (England), **3:**365, 382; Soviet Union, **6:**598; Spain (15th & 16th Centuries), **3:**34, 76–77

Baptists: England (17th & 18th Centuries), **4:**491–92; Soviet Union, **6:**597; United States (Civil War era), **5:**456, 457, 458, 459; United States (1920–39), **6:**569, 570. *See also* Southern Baptist Convention

Baraka, **4:**467

Barbarians. *See* Foreigners, treatment of

Barbary Coast, **3:**18

Barbers: Europe (Middle Ages), **2:**182; Mesopotamia, **1:**360; Spain (15th & 16th Centuries), **3:**192

Barbettes, **2:**239, 259

Barbour, Emma Sargent, **5:**163, 164, 165

Barca, Calderón de la, **3:**212

Barcelona, **3:**287

Bardi family, **3:**8

Barges, **2:**139. *See also* Shipping; Ships and vessels

Barkesdale, William, **5:**314–15

Barkova, Anna, **6:**233

Bark painting, **1:**241

Barley: Byzantium, **2:**208; China (Tang Dynasty), **2:**204; England (15th & 16th Centuries), **3:**92, 241; Europe (15th & 16th Centuries), **3:**236; Vikings, **2:**126, 203

Barley break game, **3:**58, 317

Barnard, Christiaan, **6:**277

Barnett, Margaret, **6:**303

Barnitz, Albert, **5:**367, 370

Baronets, **5:**113

Barons and baronesses, **3:**271

Baroque art, **4:**453

Barracks. *See* Camps, military

Barranda, Joaquín, **5:**179

Barreda, Gabino, **5:**179

Barros Arana, Diego, **5:**19

Barrow, Bonnie and Clyde, **6:**416

Bars. *See* Taverns

Barter: Africa (17th & 18th Centuries), **4:**135; Aztec, **3:**122; Latin America (19th Century), **5:**246; 17th & 18th Centuries, **4:**132–33

Barth, Alan, **6:**527

Barton, Bruce, **6:**572

Baseball: Japan (20th Century), **6:**508; players' strike (1981), **6:**506; United States (Civil War era), **5:**429; United States (19th Century), **5:**397, 399–400; United States (1920–39), **6:**500–501; United States (1960–90), **6:**503, 504–5

Basements and cellars, **5:**262

Bashir II (Lebanon), **5:**354

Bashir III (Lebanon), **5:**354

Basilica churches, **2:**447

Basketball: Africa (20th Century), **6:**510; Europe (20th Century), **6:**499; invention of, **6:**499, 502; United States (1920–39), **6:**502; United States (1960–90), **6:**504

Basmati rice, **5:**243

Basque language, **3:**161

Bas-reliefs, **1:**230–31

Bassa dansa, **3:**347

Bastet, **1:**476

Batab, **3:**296, 311

Batabob, **3:**295

Bates, Daisy, **6:**443

Bathhouses: Byzantium, **2:**403–4; Islamic World (Middle Ages), **2:**232; Rome (ancient), **1:**100, 414

Bathing: Europe (Middle Ages), **2:**181; Greece (ancient), **1:**278; India (ancient), **1:**301, 336, 449; India (19th Century), **5:**265; India (20th Century), **6:**589–90; Rome (ancient), **1:**85; United States (1920–39), **6:**272; Vikings, **2:**261. *See also* Bathing rooms

Bathing rooms: India (ancient), **1:**301; Mesopotamia, **1:**271; Rome (ancient), **1:**414

Bathrooms: India (19th Century), **5:**265; India (20th Century), **6:**344. *See also* Bathing rooms; Latrines; Toilet facilities

Baths: Aztec, **3:**234; England (17th & 18th Centuries), **4:**226; Japan (17th & 18th Centuries), **4:**229

Batista, Fulgencio, **6:**480

Batman (film), **6:**529

Battering rams: Byzantium, **2:**361; Mesopotamia, **1:**372

Battle casualties: Greece (ancient), **1:**295, 378, 379, 381–82; Japan (20th Century), **6:**493; Korean War, **6:**370, 470; Latin America (20th Century), **6:**44, 479; Mesopotamia, **1:**287, 370, 372, 373; Rome (ancient), **1:**369; Soviet Union in World War II, **6:**488, 489; Vietnam conflict, **6:**370, 470; World War I, **6:**63, 261–62, 267–68, 349

Battle of. *See* specific battle

Batu Khan, **2:**220

Bauer, Brian, **3:**403

Bayezit I, **3:**10

Bayezit II, **3:**12, 19, 292

Bayle, Pierre, **4:**475

Bayonets, **6:**354–55

Bay Psalm Book, The, **4:**214

Bazalgette, Joseph, **5:**141

Bazin, André, **6:**514

Beans: Aztec, **3:**248; Civil War soldiers, **5:**222; Inca, **3:**2; Japan (17th & 18th Centuries), **4:**248; Latin America (19th Century), **5:**246; Maya, **3:**101, 246; United States (Civil War era), **5:**222; United States (Western Frontier), **5:**228, 230

Bear: Europe (Middle Ages), **2:**378; Inuit, **6:**321

Bear baiting: England (15th & 16th Centuries), **3:**330; Europe (Middle Ages), **2:**371; Middle Ages, **2:**369

Beards: Europe (Middle Ages), **2:**257, 260; Greece (ancient), **1:**325; Mesopotamia, **1:**317; Vikings, **2:**260

Beardsley, Aubrey, **5:**10

Beat generation, **6:**225, 542

Beatings. *See* Corporal punishment; Domestic violence; Punishment

Beatles, **6:**543, 545, 553

Beat to Quarters (Forester), **4:**218

Beavers, **5:**48–49, 119, 122, 228

Becker, Nubia, **6:**77

Bede, venerable, **2:**169

Bedouin. See Nomads

Bedrooms: England (15th & 16th Centuries), **3:**254; England (Victorian era), **5:**262–63, 264; Europe (Middle Ages), **2:**131; India (19th Century), **5:**265; Italy (15th & 16th Centuries), **3:**258; Middle Ages, **2:**301; Rome (ancient), **1:**280

Beds: Australian Aboriginals, **1:**281; China (Tang Dynasty), **2:**272; Civil War military, **5:**256; England (Victorian era), **5:**264; Europe (Middle Ages), **2:**267, 268–69; Islamic World (Middle Ages), **2:**273; Italy (15th & 16th Centuries), **3:**258–59; Japanese (Middle Ages), **2:**267; Mesopotamia, **1:**273; Middle Ages, **2:**267; North American colonial frontier, **4:**274; Vikings, **2:**228, 267, 270

Bedu masks, **4:**446

Beecher, Henry Ward, **5:**382

Beedle, Irwin P., **5:**187

Beef. *See* Meat

Beer: Africa (20th Century), **6:**331; England (15th & 16th Centuries), **3:**238–39; England (17th & 18th Centuries), **4:**262; England (Victorian era), **5:**239, 241; Europe (Middle Ages), **2:**214; Greece (ancient), **1:**266; Japan (20th Century), **6:**330; Latin America (19th Century), **5:**245; Mesopotamia, **1:**263, 286; Middle Ages, **2:**213; New England, colonial, **4:**265; North American colonial frontier, **4:**259–60; Nubia, **1:**259; Rome (ancient), **1:**269; United States (1920–39), **6:**307; United States (Western Frontier), **5:**409

Bees: Maya, **3:**247; Mesopotamia, **1:**78; Rome (ancient), **1:**85. *See also* Honey

Beetle. *See* Scarab beetle

Beeton, Isabella, **5:**237

Beeton, Samuel, **5:**191

Beggars: China (Tang Dynasty), **2:**325; England (15th & 16th Centuries), **3:**272; India (20th Century), **6:**58; Latin America (19th Century), **5:**97; Spain (15th & 16th Centuries), **3:**275

Beggar's Opera, The (Gay), **4:**450

Belgium: asylum offered to Jews, **6:**563; food in 15th & 16th Centuries, **3:**235; Holy Roman Empire, part of, **3:**283, 287

Belize: language, **3:**166; sculptures, **3:**351

Belknap, Keturah Penton, **5:**278

Bell, John, **5:**312–13, 316

Bello, Andrés, **5:**19

Bells: Europe (Middle Ages), **2:**387; Middle Ages, **2:**407

Belts: Europe (Middle Ages), **2:**238; Latin America (19th Century), **5:**289; Mongols, **2:**245, 246; Native Americans (colonial frontier of North America), **4:**304; United States (Civil War era), **5:**273; Vikings, **2:**240, 241

Bembo, Pietro, **3:**213

Benedictine monks (Middle Ages), **2:**435, 436

Benedict of Nursia, **2:**435, 436

Benjamin, Judah P., **5:**317

Benjamin, Walter, **6:**597–98

Benjamin, the Jew of Granada (Maturin), **5:**183

Bentineck, William, **5:**67

Benton, Thomas Hart, **5:**6

Beowulf, **2:**169

Berdan's Sharpshooters, **5:**291

Berenguer, Ramón, **3:**287

Berggolts, Olga, **6:**234

Bergsson, Niculas, **2:**162

Beria, Lavrenty, **6:**425

Bering land bridge, **3:**2

Berke Khan, **2:**429

Canzoniere (Petrarch), **3:**213

Capac Raymi, **3:**52, 88, 142, 391

Cape Horn, account of sea voyage (1615), **4:**519–21

Capes: Aztec, **3:**233; Maya, **3:**231; Spain (15th & 16th Centuries), **3:**228

Capital punishment. *See* Death penalty

Capone, Al, **6:**326

Capping, **2:**84

Capra, Frank, **6:**521

Caps: England (Victorian era), **5:**285; nightcaps, **5:**282; United States (Civil War era), **5:**276

Captain Blood (Sabatini), **4:**218

Captains: British Royal Navy, **4:**365, 383; merchant vessels (17th & 18th Centuries), **4:**362

Captives: Native Americans (colonial frontier of North America), **4:**389–90, 418, 434–35; Native Americans (colonial New England), **4:**411. *See also* Prisoners of war

Captives as slaves: ancient world, **1:**108; China (Tang Dynasty), **2:**316; Mesopotamia, **1:**109, 373; Middle Ages, **2:**310; Polynesia, **2:**290, 300, 366; Rome (ancient), **1:**114; Vikings, **2:**314

Captivity narratives of North American colonial frontier, **4:**205–6

Caracol, **3:**120

Caradeuc de la Chalotais, Louis-René, **4:**191

Carapulcra, **5:**245

Caravans: China (Tang Dynasty), **2:**138–39; India (ancient), **1:**148; Mesopotamia, **1:**78, 141, 156, 157, 158; Spain (15th & 16th Centuries), **3:**112. *See also* Trade

Cárdenas, Lázaro, **6:**172, 371, 385

Cardinals, **3:**364

Cards: development and spread of, **2:**369; England (15th & 16th Centuries), **3:**315, 317–18; England (17th & 18th Centuries), **4:**421; Europe (Middle Ages), **2:**372; Italy (15th & 16th Centuries), **3:**315, 323; Japan (17th & 18th Centuries), **4:**424; life at sea (17th & 18th Centuries), **4:**428; New England, colonial, **4:**426; Spain (15th & 16th Centuries), **3:**315, 321; United States (Civil War era), **5:**429; United States (Western Frontier), **5:**433

Cargo. *See* Shipping

Carillo, Joaquin, **5:**333

Carlisle Indian School, **5:**161, 170

Carlyle, Thomas, **5:**10

Carmichael, Stokely, **6:**152, 448–49

Carnatic music, **5:**424, 425

Carnival: Italy (15th & 16th Centuries), **3:**63, 135, 322, 347; Latin America (19th Century), **5:**416–17; Spain (15th & 16th Centuries), **3:**135

Caro, Miguel Antonio, **5:**341

"Carolingian miniature," **2:**169

Carolingians, **2:**2, 32, 148. *See also* Europe (Middle Ages)

Carols, **2:**388

Carpenter, Helen, **5:**487–88

Carpenter, Scott, **6:**187

Carpentry: England (Victorian era), **5:**110; Europe (Middle Ages), **2:**267; Islamic World (Middle Ages), **2:**273; Mesopotamia, **1:**120

Carpet. *See* Floors and floor coverings

Carpini, Friar Giovanni Di Plano, **2:**245, 265, 342

Carrara, **3:**99

Carrera, Rafael, **5:**378

Carriage dress, **5:**284

Carroll v. U.S. (1925), **6:**416

Carrom, **5:**441

Carson, Kit, **5:**46, 87

Carson, Rachel, **6:**17–18, 224

Carter, Richard, **5:**206

Carthage, **1:**10

Cartier, Jacques, **4:**9

Cartography: Greece (ancient), **1:**227; Mesopotamia, **1:**221

Cartoons, animated, **6:**521

Cartwright, Alexander, **5:**399

Carvel-built hulls, **4:**324

Carvings: Africa (17th & 18th Centuries), **4:**445, 446; Rome (ancient), **1:**106; Vikings, **2:**100–101. *See also* Stone carvings

Castanets, **3:**346

Caste systems: India (ancient), **1:**117, 329, 337–39; India (19th Century), **5:**26–27, 42, 52, 118; India (20th Century), **6:**57, 126, 135–37, 140, 155, 316, 343; Islamic World (19th Century), **5:**26; Latin America (19th Century), **5:**17

Caste War (Latin America), **5:**379

Castiglione, Baldasar, **3:**213, 413–14

Castile: historical overview, **3:**1, 10; language and writing, **3:**161; music, **3:**345; taxes, **3:**275; universities, **3:**175–76; wheat, **3:**95. *See also* Spain *entries*

Castilian language, **3:**161–62, 218

Castillo, Bernal Diaz del, **3:**421–22

Castillo, Ramón, **5:**378

Castles: Edo (17th & 18th Centuries), **4:**337; Europe (Middle Ages), **2:**224–25; Japan (17th & 18th Centuries), **4:**408; Middle Ages, **2:**223, 301; Windsor Castle, **5:**141

Castramentation, **5:**255

Castration, **1:**62, 64, 286. *See also* Eunuchs

Castro, Fidel, **6:**8, 371, 480

Catalán language, **3:**161–62

Cataloguing and classifying: Greece (ancient), **1:**226; Mesopotamia, **1:**219–20

Cataluña: houses, **3:**256; language, **3:**161

Catapults, **2:**361

Catechism: England (15th & 16th Centuries), **3:**172; Italy (15th & 16th Centuries), **3:**38; Latin America (19th Century), **5:**471

Catfish, **5:**228

Cathedral schools: Europe (Middle Ages), **2:**148–50; Vikings, **2:**152, 153

Catherine of Siena, **3:**55

Catholic Church: Australia, colonial, **4:**487; celibacy, **2:**31, 33; diplomatic recognition of Vatican by U.S., **6:**586; dissent in Europe (Middle Ages), **2:**411; dissent in United States (1960–90), **6:**586; education funding and, **6:**200; England (17th & 18th Centuries), **4:**471–72, 491; film industry and, **6:**520; Japan (20th Century), **6:**600; Jews and, **6:**141–42; Latin America (19th Century), **5:**19, 469–72; Latin America (20th Century), **6:**43, 591–93; legal jurisdiction (Middle Ages), **2:**328–29, 434; Middle Ages, **2:**2, 4, 160, 410, 433–36; Native Americans (colonial frontier of North America), **4:**470–71; New France, **4:**470–71; seven sacraments of, **2:**411; social activism in Latin America (1960–90), **6:**592–93; Soviet Union, **6:**597; split from Greek Orthodox, **2:**407, 409, 425–26; United States (Civil War era), **5:**309, 458, 459; United States (1920–39), **6:**36, 569; United States (1960–90), **6:**579;

Vatican II and ecumenical changes, **6:**577, 581, 592. *See also* Catholicism *entries*

Catholicism (France), **4:**355

Catholicism (Spain, Italy, England): angels, **3:**363; baptism, **3:**380–81; Bible, **3:**379; bishops, **3:**364; cardinals, **3:**364; confession, **3:**380, 382; confirmation, **3:**380–81; Crucifixion, **3:**362; deities, **3:**362–64; devils, **3:**363; English separation from, **3:**15; Franciscans, **3:**364; holy orders, **3:**380, 382; Jesus Christ in, **3:**362; last rites, **3:**380, 382; Latin, **3:**379; marriage, **3:**31; mass, **3:**379; matrimony, **3:**380–81; Messiah, **3:**362; Ottoman Empire, **3:**166; *Pater Noster*, **3:**132, 364; Pentecost, **3:**363; priests and religious rituals, **3:**364, 380–82; Protestantism, opposition in Spain, **3:**344; religious beliefs, **3:**361, 362–64; Resurrection, **3:**362–63; sacraments, **3:**20, 380–82; sacrifices, **3:**363; saints, **3:**363; sins and sinners, **3:**363; Trinity, **3:**363. *See also* Popes

Catholic Worker, **6:**574

Catlin, George, **5:**103

Cat-o-nine-tails, **4:**400

Cato the Elder, **1:**115, 299

Cats in Victorian England, **5:**440

Cattle: Africa (17th & 18th Centuries), **4:**105; Australia, colonial, **4:**242; Byzantium, **2:**209; India (ancient), **1:**85; India (19th Century), **5:**252; Latin America (19th Century), **5:**133; Latin America (20th Century), **6:**314; Mesopotamia, **1:**77; Nubia, **1:**259; Rome (ancient), **1:**85. *See also* Livestock

Cattle drives, **5:**106–7

Cattle stations in Latin America, **5:**267

Catullus, **1:**70–71, 203

Caudillos, **5:**325, 326, 377, 378, 379

Caute, David, **6:**527

Cavagliere, **3:**276

Cavalry: Africa (17th & 18th Centuries), **4:**403; England (Victorian era), **5:**371; United States (Civil War era), **5:**357

Cave dwellings of China, **2:**229

Caves as housing (colonial New England), **4:**280

Caviar, **2:**209

Caxton, William, **3:**209

Celebration. *See* Holidays, festivals, and spectacles

Cellars, **5:**262

Celler, Emmanuel, **6:**71

Cemeteries, **5:**29. *See also* Tombs; Tombstones

Cempoala, **3:**22

Cenote of Sacrifice, **3:**47

Censor, Roman, **1:**337

Censorship: China (19th Century), **5:**323; Europe (20th Century), **6:**218; film industry, **6:**518, 520, 531, 532–33; India (20th Century), **6:**531; Japan (20th Century), **6:**237; McCarthyism, **6:**377; music, **6:**552–53; Soviet Union, **6:**233, 234–35, 256, 532–33, 536, 552–53; United States (1940–59), **6:**38; World War II films, **6:**525

Census data: for Soviet Union, **6:**23; for United States, **6:**13

Centaurs, **1:**335

Centuries, **1:**351

Centurions, **1:**384

Cephalus, **1:**521

Cerberus, **1:**520

Cereal crops. *See* Grains

Cerén, **3:**250, 262

Cervantes Saavedra, Miguel de, **3:**206, 210–12, 410–11

C-Group Nubians, **1:**13, 312, 387

Centuries), **3:**241; United States (Western Frontier), **5:**234

Deus ex machina, **1:**427

Devi, Phoolan, **6:**79–80

Devil in Catholicism, **3:**363

DeVoto, Bernard, **5:**46–48, 231

Devshirme, **2:**318; **3:**349

Dewey, John, **5:**177, 452; **6:**199, 200, 204

Dharma, **1:**206, 352–53, 466; **5:**466

Dhotis, **5:**286

Dial-a-prayer, **6:**573

Dialects: Europe (Middle Ages), **2:**168; Greece (ancient), **1:**176, 334; India (ancient), **1:**431; Italy (15th & 16th Centuries), **3:**163; Japan (17th & 18th Centuries), **1:**212; Rome (ancient), **1:**189; Spain (15th & 16th Centuries), **3:**161–62; Sumerian, **1:**194. *See also* Language

Diamonds in Latin America, **5:**132

Diapers: life at sea (17th & 18th Centuries), **4:**79; United States (1960–90), **6:**361

Diarrhea, **5:**199, 204

Díaz, Porfirio, **5:**159, 179

Dice: England (15th & 16th Centuries), **3:**318; Europe (Middle Ages), **2:**367, 369, 372; India (ancient), **1:**449; Italy (15th & 16th Centuries), **3:**323; Mesopotamia, **1:**406; Rome (ancient), **1:**415–16; Spain (15th & 16th Centuries), **3:**315, 321; United States (Civil War era), **5:**429; Vikings, **2:**375

Dickens, Charles: Christmas, writings on, **5:**406; Lao She, influence on, **5:**195; magazines, stories published in, **5:**189–90; popularity in U.S., **5:**181, 184–85; white collar workers, writings on, **5:**83, 110

Dickstein, Morris, **6:**222

Dictators of ancient Rome, **1:**351

Diderot, Denis, **4:**210

Diet: Africa (17th & 18th Centuries), **4:**240–42, 430; Australia, colonial, **4:**49, 51, 242–43; Australian Aboriginals, **1:**260, 261; Aztec, **3:**248; Byzantium, **2:**190, 197, 208–10; changes after European conquest of Americas, **3:**221–22, 236; China (19th Century), **5:**248; China (Tang Dynasty), **2:**128, 187, 197, 204–6, 455; Civil War soldiers, **5:**219–27; as cure (Middle Ages), **2:**179; England (15th & 16th Centuries), **3:**238–39; England (1914–18), **6:**303; England (17th & 18th Centuries), **4:**140, 245–48; England (Victorian era), **5:**218, 237–42; Europe (Middle Ages), **2:**124, 197, 198–201, 277; France (1914–18), **6:**303; Germany (1914–18), **6:**303, 304; Greece (ancient), **1:**256; Inca, **3:**105, 106; India (19th Century), **5:**219, 242–44; India (20th Century), **6:**315–17; Inuit, **6:**320–21; Islamic World (Middle Ages), **2:**282; Islamic World (19th Century), **5:**247, 468–69; Italy (15th & 16th Centuries), **3:**242; Japan (17th & 18th Centuries), **4:**114, 146, 229, 248–50; Japan (20th Century), **6:**319–20; Latin America (19th Century), **5:**219, 244–47; Latin America (20th Century), **6:**314–15; Maya, **3:**246–47; Mesopotamia, **1:**246, 263; Native Americans (colonial New England), **4:**250–51; Native Americans (New England, colonial), **4:**61–62; New England, colonial, **4:**117–18, 250–53; 19th Century, **5:**218–48;

North American colonial frontier, **4:**244–45; Nubia, **1:**259; Ottoman, **3:**244–45; Polynesia, **2:**210–12; Rome (ancient), **1:**256; seamen, **4:**253–55; 17th & 18th Centuries, **4:**238–55; United States (1920–39), **6:**306–9; United States (Western Frontier), **5:**218, 227–37; Vikings, **2:**202–3. *See also* Food; *specific types of food and drink*

Diet (Japan governmental body), **6:**399–400

Diet plans, **6:**280, 302, 310

Digest of Roman Law, **1:**365

Dillinger, John, **6:**416

Dining rooms in Victorian England, **5:**263

Dinner: England (15th & 16th Centuries), **3:**237; England (17th & 18th Centuries), **4:**247; England (Victorian era), **5:**219, 238, 240–42; Europe (Middle Ages), **2:**201; Latin America (20th Century), **6:**315; life at sea (17th & 18th Centuries), **4:**254; New England, colonial, **4:**252; North American colonial frontier, **4:**244; Ottoman Empire, **3:**244; 17th & 18th Centuries, **4:**239; United States (Western Frontier), **5:**234. *See also* Meals

Dinner parties. *See* Banquets

Diocletian, **1:**389

Dionysius, **1:**480, 492

Dioscorides, **2:**181, 188

Diphtheria: England (Victorian era), **5:**209; Spain (15th & 16th Centuries), **3:**194

Diplomats (Mesopotamia), **1:**139, 155, 343

"Dirty wars" (Latin America 20th Century): deaths in, **6:**8, 33, 44; historical overview of, **6:**480–81; Honduras, **6:**370; women's role in protests, **6:**61, 77

Disciples of Christ, **5:**458

Disco, **6:**547

Discovery, **6:**189

Discovery and Conquest of Mexico, The (Castillo), **3:**421–22

Discrimination: Africa (20th Century), **6:**193; Catholic Church condemnation of, **6:**577; China (Tang Dynasty), **2:**324; England (17th & 18th Centuries), **4:**492–93; India (20th Century), **6:**110, 140, 154–56; Inuit, **6:**161; Japan (20th Century), **6:**140, 159–61; Jews (17th & 18th Centuries), **4:**483; Latin America (20th Century), **6:**134; Title IX of Education Amendments of 1972, **6:**618–19; 20th Century, **6:**139–61; United States (1920–39), **6:**145–49, 516; United States (1940–59), **6:**16, 150–51, 375–76; United States (1960–90), **6:**110, 129, 151–54. *See also* Anti-Semitism; Civil rights movement

Diseases: Africa (17th & 18th Centuries), **4:**220–21; Africa (20th Century), **6:**293–95; China (Tang Dynasty), **2:**185–86; England (17th & 18th Centuries), **4:**224; England (Victorian era), **5:**451; Europe (Middle Ages), **2:**181; 15th & 16th Centuries, **3:**188–90, 194, 196, 199; Greece (ancient), **1:**294–98; India (ancient), **1:**301–2; Inuit, **6:**295–96; Japan (20th Century), **6:**291; Mesopotamia, **1:**284–88; Native Americans (colonial New England), **4:**88, 231; 19th Century working-class people, **5:**217; North American colonial frontier, **4:**223; Paris (Middle Ages), **2:**114–15; Puritans, religious doctrine, **4:**233; Rome (ancient), **1:**298–301; Soviet Union, **6:**288; Spain (15th & 16th Centuries), **3:**194; United States (Civil War era), **5:**137; United States (1960–90), **6:**278; Vikings, **2:**164. *See also specific diseases*

Disney, Walt, **6:**98, 521

Disneyland, **6:**98–99

Dispensaries, **4:**225

Disraeli, Benjamin, **5:**10

Dissection: Greece (ancient), **1:**296; Mesopotamia, **1:**287; Rome (ancient), **1:**301

Dissenters, **4:**471–73, 491–92

Distilleries in colonial New England, **4:**265–66

Ditches, **4:**333

Divination: Inca, **3:**392–93; Japan (17th & 18th Centuries), **4:**423

Divine Comedy (Dante), **2:**461; **3:**396

Divine right of kings, **3:**284

Divine River judgments in Mesopotamia, **1:**359, 362, 526

Diviners: Greece (ancient), **1:**379; Mesopotamia, **1:**370, 527; Rome (ancient), **1:**495, 496. *See also* Entrails, reading of

Divorce: ancient world, **1:**39–40; Byzantium, **2:**63; Catholic Church views on (1960–90), **6:**577; China (Tang Dynasty), **2:**41, 46–47; England (17th & 18th Centuries), **4:**37–38; Europe (Middle Ages), **2:**41, 42; Greece (ancient), **1:**45, 47, 68; India (19th Century), **5:**41; Islamic World (Middle Ages), **2:**40, 49; Islamic World (19th Century), **5:**38; Japan (17th & 18th Centuries), **4:**40; Jesus Christ on, **3:**381; Maya, **3:**46; Mesopotamia, **1:**39, 41, 42; New England, colonial, **4:**42; Polynesia, **2:**68; Rome (ancient), **1:**37, 50; 17th & 18th Centuries, **4:**29; Spain (15th & 16th Centuries), **3:**35, 59; 20th Century, **6:**33; United States (1920–39), **6:**35–36; United States (1940–59), **6:**38; United States (1960–90), **6:**42; United States (Western Frontier), **5:**60; Vikings, **2:**44–45, 57

Diwali, **5:**396, 406, 414–15

Dix, Dorothea, **5:**199

Dixie Primer for Little Folks, **5:**160, 167

Dixie Speller, **5:**160, 167

Dixon, James, **4:**487

Dixon, Thomas, **6:**140, 146

Dobiwallas, **5:**52

Doblado, Leucadio, **3:**227

Dockers (China), **5:**94, 115

Doctorow, E.L., **6:**379

Doctors. *See* Healers and healing; Physicians

Doctors' Plot (Soviet Union), **6:**158

Doctor Zhivago (Pasternak), **6:**614–16

Dodge, Richard I., **5:**280, 369

Doenitz, Karl, **6:**412

Doges: Italy (15th & 16th Centuries), **3:**276; Venice, **3:**277

Dogfighting: 15th & 16th Centuries, **3:**313; Middle Ages, **2:**369

Dogs: England (Victorian era), **5:**440; Mesopotamia, **1:**78, 93; Paris (Middle Ages), **2:**114; Polynesia, **2:**212; United States (Western Frontier), **5:**229; Vikings, **2:**462. *See also* Hunting dogs

Dog shooting, **4:**424

Dog tents, **5:**254, 258

Dokia Makrembolitissa, **2:**63

Dolabra, **1:**386

Dom Casmurro (Machado de Assis), **5:**197

Domestic life: ancient world, **1:**19–72; defined, **1:**19; **2:**29; **6:**31; 15th & 16th Centuries, **3:**29–88; Middle Ages, **2:**29–92; 19th Century, **5:**25–79; 17th & 18th Centuries, **4:**27–100; 20th Century, **6:**31–108. *See also* Children; Family life; Marriage; Sexuality

Domestic Revolutions (Mintz & Kellogg), **6:**39

Domestic violence: Africa (17th & 18th Centuries), **4:**47; China (Tang Dynasty), **2:**333; Europe (Middle Ages), **2:**43; Islamic World (Middle Ages), **2:**48; Latin America (20th Century),

Feuds

Heating: England (15th & 16th Centuries), 3:254; gas utilities, 6:336. *See also* Fireplaces

Heaven: Aztec, 3:139, 399; Christian belief in, 2:461; Christianity and, 3:394, 396; Inca, 3:404; Spain (15th & 16th Centuries), 3:344

Hebrew language, 3:161, 210

Hectic fever, 5:208

Hector, 1:377, 378–79

Hegira: first Hegira of Muhammed's followers, 2:36; of Mohammed, 2:12, 419

Height of people: England (Victorian era), 5:237; Europe (Middle Ages), 2:183; 19th Century, 5:218; United States (Civil War era), 5:42–44

Heimdall, 2:413

Heirs. *See* Estates and inheritances

"Hekanakt's Instructions to His Household," 1:539–41

Hel, 2:412, 462

Helados, 5:245

Helgason, Star Oddi, 2:162

Heliostats, 2:286

Hell: Buddhist belief in, 2:467; Christian belief in, 2:458, 460–61; 3:365, 394, 396; Inca, 3:404

Hellenistic era, 1:226, 237–38

Hello Girls in World War I, 6:65

Hell's Angels, 6:546

Helmets: Byzantium, 2:361; Europe (Middle Ages), 2:349; Greece (ancient), 1:396; Islamic World (Middle Ages), 2:357; Mesopotamia, 1:392; Polynesia, 2:365; Rome (ancient), 1:399; United States (Western Frontier), 5:280; Vikings, 2:352, 353; World War I, 6:355

Helva, 3:245

Hemingway, Ernest, 6:222–23

Hemlock, 1:364

Hemp, 2:253

Hendrik, Hans, 6:240

Hendrix, Jimi, 6:544

Henequen, 5:133–34

Henley Regatta, 5:113, 401

Henna, 1:325

Henry, Alexander, 5:125

Henry, Joseph, 5:152

Henry II (king of France), 2:368

Henry IV (king of England), 3:12–13

Henry IV (king of France), 4:355, 356, 474

Henry V (king of England), 3:13

Henry VI (king of England), 3:13–14

Henry VII (king of England), 3:14–15, 251

Henry VIII (king of England), 3:14–15, 17, 251, 366, 409

Henry V (Shakespeare), 3:11

Henry of Navarre, 4:355

Hensley, Willie, 6:604

Henty, G.A., 5:191

Hepatoscopy. *See* Entrails, reading of

Hephaestus, 1:470, 480–81

Hera, 1:479, 480

Heraldry, 2:33

Heralds, 1:360

Herbal medicine: India (ancient), 1:301–2; Mesopotamia, 1:285; North American colonial frontier, 4:222–23; Rome (ancient), 1:300; Vikings, 2:184–85

Herberg, Will, 6:573, 577

Herbs and spices: China (Tang Dynasty), 2:138; Europe (Middle Ages), 2:200, 201; Greece (ancient), 1:255; India (19th Century), 5:243; Italy (15th & 16th Centuries), 3:242; Maya, 3:247; Mesopotamia, 1:247–48; New England, colonial, 4:252; North American colonial frontier, 4:245; 17th & 18th Centuries, 4:238–39; Spain (15th & 16th Centuries), 3:240; United States (1920–39), 6:307; Vikings, 2:203

Hercules, 1:428

Herms, 1:481

Hernández, Francisco, 3:194

Hernández, José, 5:196

Hernias, 3:195

Herod, 3:135

Herodotus: Babylon, construction of, 1:101; on Battle of Marathon, 1:379; on clothing, 1:309; on Democedes of Crotona, 1:295; on education, 1:187, 188; on eunuchs, 2:69; on the Persians, 1:335; on war, 1:494; on women's role, 1:32, 488

Heroes: Europe (Middle Ages), 2:169; Greece (ancient), 1:377, 461–62; Polynesia, 2:176, 177–78; Vikings, 2:172

Hero Twins: Aztec, 3:361; Maya, 3:205, 215–16, 316, 325, 371, 386, 397–98, 416–19

Herpes, 6:282. *See also* Venereal diseases

Herrera, Fernando de, 3:161

Herring, 2:203

Herschel, William and Caroline, 4:175

Herzog, Werner, 6:515

Hesiod: on agriculture, 1:82; food and drinks of, 1:268; on Greek Mythology, 1:460–61, 478, 479; on marriage, 1:44; on slavery, 1:112

Hestia, 1:20, 481, 482

Hetairai, 1:63, 67, 267

Hetzmek, 3:32, 44, 74, 82

Hidalgo: Castile, 3:269, 274; Spain (15th & 16th Centuries), 3:269, 273, 275

Hidalgo, Miguel, 5:325, 470

Hides, 5:19. *See also* Leather

Hierarchy. *See* Social structure

Hiereus, 1:493

Hieroglyphics: Mesopotamia, 1:172; Nubia, 1:180

Higher Education Act of 1965, 6:382

High schools: United States (Civil War era), 5:167. *See also* Education; Schools

High tea, 5:241

Hijab, 2:244

Hijas, 5:425

Hiking, 3:335

Hildgard of Bingen, 2:51, 54, 477–78

Hillard's Fifth Reader, 5:166

Himmler, Heinrich, 6:413

Hindenberg, Paul von, 6:5

Hindi language, 5:78

Hinduism: alcoholic beverages and, 5:252; development of religion, 1:13; 6:588; differences from Buddhism, 2:417; India (19th Century), 5:14, 414, 456, 465; India (20th Century), 6:588–91; major bodies of Hinduism, 6:588; male role in, 6:57–58; marriage (20th Century), 6:46; Muslim vs. Hindu feud in India, 6:9, 10; polytheism, 5:456; vegetarianism of, 6:316

Hindustani music, 5:424, 425

Hine, Thomas, 6:339, 341

Hinin, 4:378–79

Hipparete, 1:47

Hippocras, 2:215

Hippocrates, 1:46, 294, 295; 2:188; 3:193

Hippocratic Oath, 1:57, 295

Hippocratic school, 1:295–97

Hippodamus of Miletus, 1:97

Hird, 2:305

Hirdskra, 2:305

Hiroshi, Noma, 6:237

Hisabetsu Burakumin, 6:159–60

Historical and Critical Dictionary (Bayle), 4:475

Historical overview: Africa, 6:25–26; Africa (17th & 18th Centuries), 4:14–16; ancient world, 1:1–17; Australia, colonial, 4:19–22; Australian Aboriginal history, 1:14–15; Byzantium, 2:17–20; China (19th Century), 5:11–14; China (Tang dynasty), 2:7–12; England (17th & 18th Centuries), 4:2–4; England (Victorian era), 5:8–11; Europe, 2:1–5; 15th century: Europe and Ottoman Empire, 3:7–14; France (17th & 18th Centuries), 4:5–6; Greek, ancient, 1:6–8; India (ancient), 1:11–13; India (19th Century), 5:14–16; Islamic World (Middle Ages), 2:12–17; Islamic World (19th Century), 5:16–17; Japan (17th & 18th Centuries), 4:17–19; Latin America (19th Century), 5:17–20; life at sea (17th & 18th Centuries), 4:7–9; Mesoamerica and South America through the 15th century, 3:2–6; Mesopotamia, 1:1–3; Middle Ages, 2:1–28; Mongols, 2:20–23; New England, colonial, 4:13–14; North American colonial frontier, 4:9–13; Nubia, 1:13–14; Polynesia, 2:23–25; Roman, ancient, 1:8–10; 17th & 18th Centuries, 4:1–26; 16th century: Europe, Ottoman Empire, and the Americas, 3:15–24; 20th Century, 6:1–30; United States Civil War, 5:1–4; United States (Western Frontier), 5:4–8; Vikings, 2:5–7. *See also* Chronology

Historical Record (Chinese), 2:163

History of Rome (Livy), 1:205, 553–55

History of the Indians of Connecticut (DeForest), 5:188

Histoyre du Mechique, 3:217

Hitler, Adolf: anti-Semitism of, 6:6, 145; on Evian Conference and asylum offered to Jews, 6:562; suicide of, 6:413

Hivernants, 5:124

HIV positive. *See* AIDS

HMOs. *See* Health maintenance organizations

Hobbes, Thomas, 1:327; 2:287; 3:267; 4:343; 5:305; 6:369

Hockey: England (15th & 16th Centuries), 3:316; invention of, 6:499; Japan (17th & 18th Centuries), 4:424

Hoess, Rudolf, 6:406, 408, 412

Hogs. *See* Pigs

Holiday, Billie, 6:148, 538

Holidays, festivals, and spectacles: Africa (17th & 18th Centuries), 4:430–32; ancient world, 1:434–50; Australia, colonial, 4:432–34; Australian Aboriginals, 1:281–82; Byzantium, 2:210, 404; China (19th Century), 5:418; China (Tang dynasty), 2:449–50, 454–57; England (15th & 16th Centuries), 3:130–31; England (17th & 18th Centuries), 4:436–37; England (Victorian era), 5:411–14; Europe (Middle Ages), 2:148, 151, 449, 450–52; Greece (ancient), 1:212, 412, 425, 427, 438–41; India (ancient), 1:190, 448–50; India (19th Century), 5:414–16; India (20th Century), 6:316; Islamic World (Middle Ages), 2:450, 457–58; Italy (15th & 16th Centuries), 3:134–35; Japan (17th & 18th Centuries), 4:437–40; Latin America (19th Century), 5:246, 416–18; life at sea (17th & 18th Centuries), 4:442–43; Mesopotamia,

United States (Western Frontier), **5**:254, 259–61; Vikings, **2**:222, 226–29

Housing and Urban Development Act of 1965, **6**:382

Housing cost: Greece (ancient), **1**:276; Latin America (19th Century), **5**:268

Housing materials: Australian Aboriginals, **1**:281; China (Tang Dynasty), **2**:230–31; Europe (Middle Ages), **2**:222, 223–24; Greece (ancient), **1**:277; India (19th Century), **5**:264, 265, 266; India (20th Century), **6**:334, 343; Inuit, **6**:335, 346–47; Islamic World (Middle Ages), **2**:222, 232; Japan (20th Century), **6**:346; Mesopotamia, **1**:270; Middle Ages, **2**:222; Polynesia, **2**:222–23, 233–35; Rome (ancient), **1**:279; United States (Western Frontier), **5**:254, 260; Vikings, **2**:222, 226. See also specific type of material (e.g., concrete, bricks)

Housing projects, federally subsidized, **6**:342–43

Houston, Jeanne Wakatsuki, **6**:525

Howard, Catherine, **3**:15

Hreppar, **2**:295

Hrotswitha of Gandersheim, **2**:396, 397

Hsia Dynasty, **5**:11

HUAC. See House Un-American Activities Committee

Huacas, **3**:203, 377, 390, 391

Huanacauri, **3**:52–53, 88

Huánuco, **3**:126

Huari people: agriculture, **3**:91, 106; history of, **3**:5

Huascar, **3**:22

Huaso, **5**:289

Huastecan language, **3**:167

Huayna Capac, **3**:7, 22–23, 126

Hubal, **2**:418

Hubbard, John, **5**:420

Hubble space telescope, **6**:189

Hudson River, **4**:317

Hudson's Bay Company, **5**:123

Huey tecuilhuitl, **3**:69

Hughes, Langston, **6**:223

Hughes, Thomas, **5**:484

Huguenots: France (17th & 18th Centuries), **4**:474; North American colonial frontier, **4**:373, 470

Huipil, **3**:231; **5**:288

Huipilli, **3**:50

Huitzilpochtli, **3**:5, 109, 123, 284, 297–98

Hukkas, **5**:53

Hula dances, **2**:394

Hulbert, William A., **5**:399

Hülegü, **2**:22, 38, 429

Hulls, **4**:323–24

Humanism, development of, **3**:8, 116, 163

Human rights: Islamic World (20th Century), **6**:592; Latin America Catholic Church and (20th Century), **6**:592; standards of, **6**:7. See also Morality

Human sacrifices: Aztec, **3**:387–89, 423–24; Inca, **3**:390–93; Maya, **3**:385–86; Mesopotamia, **1**:486; Polynesia, **2**:364, 365, 366

Human waste disposal: Changan in Tang dynasty, **2**:116; England (Victorian era), **5**:141, 264; Europe (Middle Ages), **2**:123; Greece (ancient), **1**:298; India (19th Century), **5**:265; Islamic World (Middle Ages), **2**:232; London (15th & 16th Centuries), **3**:108; London (Middle Ages), **2**:111; Mesopotamia,

1:92, 272; Middle Ages, **2**:95, 108; Paris (Middle Ages), **2**:114; Rome (ancient), **1**:100, 280; Spain (15th & 16th Centuries), **3**:256; United States (1960–90), **6**:361. See also Waste disposal

Humor and satire: Aucassin and Nicolett, **2**:485–88; Japan (17th & 18th Centuries), **4**:213. See also Jokes

Humors of the body: Galenic science, **4**:227; India (ancient), **1**:301–2; India (20th Century), **6**:286; Rome (ancient), **1**:298–300

Hunab, **3**:371

Hun Ahau, **3**:215, 397

Hunahpu, **3**:215, 371, 397, 417–19

Hundred Years' War, **2**:4, 346–47; **3**:12

Hungary: houses, **3**:261; Magyars, **2**:2; as part of Holy Roman Empire, **3**:18, 283, 287; as part of Ottoman Empire, **3**:20; Shtokavian spoken in, **3**:165; war against Ottoman Empire, **3**:12

Hung Chao, **2**:11

Hunger in America (TV documentary), **6**:313

Hung Hsiu-Ch'üan, **5**:13

Hungress Days Congress, **6**:436

Huni, **1**:514–15

Huns, Chinese wars with, **2**:354

Hunter, Jim "Catfish," **6**:506

Hunthausen, Raymond G., **6**:586

Hunting: Africa (17th & 18th Centuries), **4**:47, 105, 240–41; ancient world, **1**:404–19; Australian Aboriginals, **1**:418–19; China (Tang Dynasty), **2**:315, 381–82; England (15th & 16th Centuries), **3**:330; England (17th & 18th Centuries), **4**:420; Europe (Middle Ages), **2**:198, 379–80; Greece (ancient), **1**:410–14; India (19th Century), **5**:397, 404; Islamic World (Middle Ages), **2**:382–84; Italy (15th & 16th Centuries), **3**:338; Master of Game (Edward, Duke of York), **2**:483–85; Maya, **3**:99, 247; Mesopotamia, **1**:392, 405–8; Middle Ages, **2**:368, 377–86; Mongols, **2**:363, 377, 384–86; North American colonial frontier, **4**:137–39; Nubia, **1**:259, 416–18; Rome (ancient), **1**:414–16, 445–46; United States (19th Century), **5**:398; United States (1920–39), **6**:500; United States (Western Frontier), **5**:47, 229, 230–31; Vikings, **2**:202, 374, 380–81. See also Fishing; Trappers and trapping

Hunting dogs: Europe (Middle Ages), **2**:379–80; Middle Ages, **2**:378

Hunyadi, John, **3**:12

Hurinsaya, **3**:282

Hurons (17th & 18th Centuries): social structure, **4**:372; tattoos, **4**:448

Husayn, **2**:457–58

Husband's role. See Family life; Marriage

Hu Shi, **5**:195

Hutchins, Robert, **6**:200–201

Hutchinson, Anne, **4**:396

Hyde, Henry, **6**:74

Hyde Amendment, **6**:74

Hydraulic mining, **5**:299

Hydraulic (water) organ, **1**:430

Hydrogen bomb. See Nuclear weapons

Hydropathy, **5**:211

Hygiene: England (17th & 18th Centuries), **4**:225; England (Victorian era), **5**:451; Greece (ancient), **1**:278; India (ancient), **1**:259; India (20th Century), **6**:589; Japan (17th & 18th Centuries), **4**:229; Mesopotamia, **1**:248; 17th & 18th Centuries, **4**:219; United States (1920–39), **6**:272; Vikings, **2**:260–61

Hyksos, **1**:395

Hymns: England (Victorian era), **5**:422; Greece (ancient), **1**:424, 438; India (ancient), **1**:206; Mesopotamia, **1**:194–95

Hyslop, John, **3**:125

IBM, **6**:119, 252

Ibn Abd al-Wahhab, **6**:423

Ibn 'Asakir, **2**:157

Ibn Fadlan, **2**:137–38, 260–61, 463, 478–79

Ibn Hanbal, Ahmad, **6**:423

Ibn Miskawayh, **2**:138

Ibn Sa'udi, **6**:451

Ibn Sina (Avicenna), **2**:166–67, 179, 192

Ibn Taymiya, Ahmad B., **6**:450–51

Ibrahim b. Ya'qub al-Turtushi, **2**:57

Icarus, **1**:448

Ice cream, **5**:245

Iceland: historical overview, **2**:7; poor persons (Middle Ages), **2**:295. See also Vikings

Ice skating, **4**:420

Ichikawa Kon, **6**:535

I Ching (Book of Changes), **2**:164; **4**:423

Icons, **2**:426, 433, 441; Ethiopia (17th & 18th Centuries), **4**:447

Ideograms, **1**:172

Idlers on merchant vessels (17th & 18th Centuries), **4**:363

Idli, **5**:243

Idolatry and Protestantism, **3**:382

"Idol singers" (Japan), **6**:556

Id-ul-Fitr, **5**:416

Ie, **4**:379; **6**:48–49

Ieharu, **4**:18

Ienobu, **4**:17

Ife Kingdom, **4**:14

Igbo (17th & 18th Centuries), **4**:369

Iglu, **6**:346

Ihiyotl, **3**:51, 401

Ihram, **2**:423–24

Ikki, **4**:394–95

Île de la Cité (Paris), **2**:112, 113

Iliad (Homer): Achilles, **1**:369, 378; depicting Greek Mythology, **1**:478, 479, 481; description of, **1**:200; educational role, **1**:188; excerpt from, **1**:547–50; on racial prejudice, **1**:335

Il-khan Ghazan, **2**:22

Il-khanid dynasty, **2**:38

Ilkum, **1**:371

Illapa, **3**:376–77, 391–92

Illegitimate children: England (17th & 18th Centuries), **4**:93–94; Europe (Middle Ages), **2**:292; Latin America (20th Century), **6**:43, 45; North American colonial frontier, **4**:35

Illnesses. See Diseases; specific disease

Illness of Central America, The (Mendieta), **5**:158

Ill People, An (Arguedas), **5**:158

Illustrated London News, **5**:192

Illustrious August (Xuanzong): dance performance by and for, **2**:390, 392; economic policies of, **2**:253, 306; elderly, treatment of, **2**:91; harem of, **2**:316; officials of, **2**:71; reign of, **2**:10; sports as favorite of, **2**:376

I Love Lucy (TV show), **6**:247–48, 566

Imams, **2**:457; **3**:42; **5**:468

Imhotep, **1**:476

Immigration: British colonies, **4**:12; Chinese quota to U.S., **6**:526; Jewish quota to U.S., **6**:143; Jews from Soviet Union to Israel, **6**:159; Latin America (19th Century), **5**:19–20, 98, 117, 267, 326; Latin America (20th Century), **6**:44; New England, colonial,

4:13–14; United States (Civil War era),
5:135, 137–38, 309, 383; United States
(1929–59), 6:127; United States (1960–90),
6:382; United States (Western Frontier), 5:6
Immigration Act of 1965, 6:382
I'm OK, You're OK (Harris), 6:280
Imperatore, 3:276
Imperial College of the Holy Cross of Tlatelolco,
3:218
Imperial Council (Ottoman Empire), 3:293
Imperialism of Islamic World, 5:455
Imperial Treasury (Ottoman Empire), 3:293
Impotence. *See* Sexuality
Impressment of seamen, 4:399
Inanna, 1:471, 473
Inca: adobe, 3:263–64; alpacas, 3:2, 105, 107;
architecture, 3:357; art, 3:3, 357–58;
astronomy, 3:141, 142; calendars, 3:141–42,
152–53, 204–5; childbirth, 3:52, 87; child
labor, 3:52; children, 3:87–88; city life,
3:124–27; clothing, 3:234–35; coca, 3:105,
248–49, 390; cooking methods, 3:249, 391;
corn, 3:2, 248–49; cotton, 3:105; creation
story, 3:126, 282, 402–4; dance, 3:358;
death, burial, and the afterlife, 3:54, 404;
deities and doctrines, 3:376–78; divination,
3:392–93; drums, 3:357; ducks, 3:249; early
history, 3:2–6; Early Horizon Period, 3:3;
Early Intermediate Period, 3:3; education,
3:186–87; feathers, 3:235; fish, 3:249; flutes,
3:357–58; food, 3:248–50, 390; footraces,
3:328; furniture, 3:263–66; games, 3:328;
gold coins, 3:234–35; government, 3:7, 299–
301; guitars, 3:357; hair, 3:52, 87, 235; harps,
3:357; health and healing, 3:202–5, 392–93;
hierarchy, 3:281–83; houses, 3:263–66;
human sacrifices, 3:390–93; Initial Period,
3:3; irrigation, 3:106; jewelry, 3:234–35;
kings, 3:282; laborers, 3:282; language and
writing, 3:169; Late Horizon Period, 3:7; Late
Intermediate Period, 3:7; life cycles, 3:52–54;
literature, 3:219–20; llamas, 3:2, 105, 107,
144, 249, 391–93; loincloths, 3:53, 88; map
of empire, 3:17; marriage, 3:32, 53–54;
martial games, 3:328; masks, 3:238; masonry,
3:264–65; meat, 3:249; Middle Horizon
Period, 3:3, 392; Moche culture, 3:3–5, 357;
music, 3:357; mythology, 3:109, 126, 219–20,
402–4; names, 3:52, 87; omens, 3:393;
piercings, 3:53, 88; pigs, 3:249; polygamy,
3:52, 142–43; population, 3:124, 125;
potatoes, 3:2, 105, 204, 248; prayers, 3:219;
Preceramic Period, 3:2; priests and religious
rituals, 3:88, 389–93; puberty rituals, 3:33,
52–53, 87–88, 391; religious beliefs, 3:376–
78; roads, 3:105; rural life, 3:104–8; sacred
stories, 3:402–4; servants, 3:71, 144; sorcery,
3:392–93; sports, 3:328; squash, 3:2, 249;
stone carvings, 3:251, 357; surgery, 3:203;
teachers, 3:72, 187; temples, 3:125, 263, 264,
376, 377, 390; time, 3:141–44; tobacco,
3:249, 250; torture, 3:311; tunics, 3:143,
234–35; vegetables, 3:105; warriors, 3:53, 74,
88, 328; women's roles, 3:71–72; wool, 3:105,
143, 234
Incantations. *See* Prayers
Incest: Australian Aboriginals, 1:28; ban on, Europe
(Middle Ages), 2:33; Mesopotamia, 1:65
In Defense of Eunuchs (Theophylaktos), 2:76–77
Indentured servants: Latin America (19th Century),
5:246; New England, colonial, 4:148–49,
163, 381, 426; North American colonial
frontier, 4:155, 156

Independence movements and wars: Africa (20th
Century), 6:25–26; India (19th Century),
5:467; 6:9; Latin America (19th Century),
5:17, 19, 132, 245, 324–25, 355–56, 377
India (ancient): animal games, 1:450; archers,
1:449; astrology, 1:216; astronomy, 1:216;
bathing, 1:301, 336, 449; bathing rooms,
1:301; bullfighting, 1:450; calendar and time,
1:216–17; caravans, 1:148; castes, 1:117,
329, 337–39; cattle, 1:85; chariot races,
1:449; children, 1:38; clans, 1:465; costumes,
1:431; craftsmen, 1:86; dance, 1:431–32;
daughters, 1:38; deities, 1:464, 484; dialects,
1:431; dice, 1:449; diseases, 1:301–2;
drinking water, 1:258; eclipses, 1:216;
elephants, 1:353; fasting, 1:449; food, 1:257–
58; gambling, 1:449; gift exchanging, 1:449;
gladiators, 1:449; gold coins, 1:137;
government, 1:352–54; grains, 1:258; guilds,
1:137, 148; healers, 1:301; healing plants and
herbs, 1:301–2; health and medicine, 1:301–
2; history of, 1:11–13; holidays, festivals, and
spectacles, 1:190, 448–50; honey, 1:258;
humors of the body, 1:301–2; hygiene, 1:259;
hymns, 1:206; intercalary month, 1:216;
kings, 1:352–54; language and writing,
1:179–80; literature, 1:206–7; lunar calendar,
1:216; maps, 1:12; marriage, 1:38;
mathematics, 1:216; meat, 1:258;
menstruating women, 1:38; milk and dairy
products, 1:258; money, 1:131, 137–38;
music, 1:431–32; musical instruments, 1:432;
Muslim conquest of, 2:15; 6:8–9; mythology,
1:206; nonviolence, 1:258, 353; oligarchy,
1:353; philosophy, 1:206–7; plays, 1:431;
poetry, 1:207; pollution, 1:338; professions,
1:339; religious beliefs, 1:38, 258, 464–66;
religious beliefs about medical problems,
1:301–2; religious purification, 1:258, 301,
449; rural life and agriculture, 1:85–86, 257–
58; sacrifices, 1:449; Sanskrit, 1:179–80, 206,
207, 258, 431; scriptures, 1:206; self-
immolation, 1:38; Shiva, 1:449; slaves,
1:117; social structure, 1:329, 337–39;
spiritualism, 1:206; sports, 1:449; taxes,
1:138; theater, 1:431–32; trade, 1:148–49;
tragedic plays, 1:431; tribes, 1:465; usury,
1:137; vedas, 1:180, 206, 338; vegetarianism,
1:258; wine, 1:258; women, 1:37–39; yoga,
1:206, 465; zero, 1:216
India (19th Century): Afghan invasion, 5:14;
alcoholic beverages, 5:54, 442; apartments,
5:265–66; arranged marriages, 5:39;
automobiles, 5:301; bananas, 5:244; bangles,
5:286; bathing, 5:265; bathrooms, 5:265;
bedrooms, 5:265; board games, 5:440; bread,
5:243; bride-price, 5:39; British rule, 5:477–
79; 6:9; bungalows, 5:265; cannabis, 5:442;
carrom, 5:441; caste systems, 5:26–27, 52,
118; chess, 5:440; child labor, 5:26, 76–77;
children, 5:40, 76–78; chutney, 5:243;
classical music, 5:424; clay huts, 5:264;
clothing, 5:218, 285–87; coconut milk,
5:252; coffee, 5:248–49; colonialism, 5:14;
concerts, 5:441; cookbooks, 5:243; cooking,
5:244; cooking methods, 5:243–44, 265;
cotton, 5:14, 302–3; cotton gin, 5:302–3;
cows, 5:252; cricket, 5:78, 404–5, 441; curry,
5:219; dance, 5:442; death, burial, and the
afterlife, 5:40; deities, 5:456; desserts, 5:244;
disease, 5:253; divorce, 5:41; dowries, 5:39;
dowry, 5:39, 53; drink, 5:251–53; drugs,
5:211; drunkenness, 5:252–53; eating
utensils, 5:244; education, 5:67; epilepsy,

5:211; factories, 5:77, 301; family life, 5:39–
41; feminism, 5:26; fireplaces, 5:266; fishing,
5:397; floors and floor coverings, 5:266; folk
music, 5:395; food, 5:218, 219, 242–44; fruit,
5:244; games, 5:78; gymkhana, 5:404;
hashish, 5:442; health and medicine, 5:210–
12; herbs and spices, 5:243; historical
overview, 5:14–16; holidays and festivals,
5:414–16; hopscotch, 5:78; housing, 5:254,
264–66; hunting, 5:397; hydropathy, 5:211;
independence, 5:467; infant mortality, 5:77;
inoculation, 5:211; insanity, 5:211; irrigation,
5:14; jewelry, 5:286; kabaddi, 5:441;
Kashmir, dispute over, 5:467; kho-kho,
5:441; languages, 5:78; leisure time, 5:440–
44; leprosy, 5:211; lime soda, 5:253;
literature, 5:195; maps, 5:15; marriage, 5:27,
53, 286; meals, 5:53; meat, 5:243; men,
5:52–54; middle class, 5:39; milk and dairy
products, 5:252; music, 5:424–26; musical
instruments, 5:424; nuts, 5:53–54, 244;
occupations, 5:52–53; opium, 5:54; origins,
5:14; Pakistan, separation from, 5:467;
parcheesi, 5:428; ploughs, 5:302; plumbing,
5:265; polytheism, 5:456; puppets, 5:441–42;
quinine, 5:253; raga, 5:424; railroads, 5:291,
302; reform movements, 5:66; religion,
5:465–67; remarriage, 5:40; rice, 5:243;
roofing, 5:264; rural life and agriculture,
5:291; sandals, 5:287; skirts, 5:286; soccer,
5:428; social customs, British view of, 5:474–
76; social structure, 5:254, 285–86; sports,
5:404–5; steamships, 5:291; street food,
5:243; sugar, 5:252; tea, 5:14, 248–49;
technology, 5:301–4; telegraphs, 5:301;
tennis, 5:397; textiles, 5:302; theater, 5:441;
threshing, 5:302; tobacco, 5:53; toilets,
5:265; tonic water, 5:253; transportation,
5:14; upper class, 5:39; vacation homes,
5:266; vegetables, 5:243; veranda, 5:265;
veterinarians, 5:212; weaving, 5:302; women,
5:66–68, 244; working class, 5:39; yogurt,
5:211, 253
Indian Institutes of Technology, 6:254
Indian Mutiny of 1857, 5:10, 14, 16
Indian National Congress, 5:16
Indians, American. *See* Native Americans *entries*
Indians, Latin America, 5:17, 19, 326. *See also*
Maya
India (20th Century): AIDS, 6:287; animism,
6:588; apartments, 6:344–45; arranged
marriages, 6:32, 46, 136, 590; assassinations,
6:10, 47, 79; banquets, 6:316; bathing,
6:589–90; bathrooms, 6:344; beggars, 6:58;
bread, 6:316; caste system, 6:57, 126, 135–
37, 140, 155, 316, 343; censorship, 6:531;
charity, 6:317; childbirth, 6:590; child labor,
6:88, 104, 105; children, 6:46–47, 88, 103–5;
coffee, 6:301, 316; communication, 6:253–
55; computers, 6:254; Constitution, 6:136–
37, 389; cooking methods, 6:316–17;
corruption, 6:389; cremation, 6:588;
daughters, 6:45, 58, 103–4; death, burial, and
the afterlife, 6:58, 79, 588, 590;
discrimination, 6:110, 140, 154–56; dowry,
6:45, 78–79, 104; drink, 6:316; drinking
water, 6:287, 344; economic life, 6:9, 388;
education, 6:104, 105; education of women,
6:78; elections, 6:389, 390; electricity, 6:300;
family life, 6:45–48; fasting, 6:316; feminism,
6:79; film, 6:512, 530–31; food, 6:301, 315–
17; gardening, 6:344; government, 6:388–90;
health and medicine, 6:285–88; historical
overview, 6:8–10; holidays and festivals,

Indigo

1: Ancient World	4: 17th and 18th C.
2: Medieval World	5: 19th C.
3: 15th and 16th C.	6: Modern World

6:316; hospitals, 6:287; housing, 6:300, 334, 343–45; humors of the body, 6:286; hygiene, 6:589; independence, 6:371; infant mortality, 6:45–46; language, 6:388–89; literature, 6:228–30; malaria, 6:287; marriage, 6:32, 33, 46, 78, 104, 156, 590; meat, 6:316; men, 6:57–59; menstruation, 6:104; mosques, 6:343; mythology, 6:79, 228; old age, 6:47, 58; patriarchy, 6:57–59, 78; patrilineages, 6:46–47; political life, 6:10, 78; poultry, 6:316; poverty, 6:388; railroads, 6:255, 389; rape, 6:79; religious beliefs, 6:568, 588–91; religious purification, 6:316; religious rituals, 6:46–47, 58, 104, 316; rice, 6:301, 315–16; riots, 6:389; rural life and agriculture, 6:334; schools, 6:344; shrines, 6:345; slums, 6:344; social structure, 6:135–37; sons, 6:45, 47, 58, 103–4; sports, 6:509; tea, 6:301, 316; technology, 6:254–55; temples, 6:343, 589; urban life, 6:334, 344–45; vegetarianism, 6:316; wells, 6:344; wheat, 6:301, 316; widows, 6:79, 156; women, 6:78–80, 156, 611–12

Indigo, 5:132
Indra, 1:352
Industrial Revolution in England, 5:8
Industry: Africa (17th & 18th Centuries), 4:120–21; China (19th Century), 5:115, 156; England (17th & 18th Centuries), 4:2, 123–26, 124; England (Victorian era), 5:92–93, 109, 300; Great Depression, 6:164; India (19th Century), 5:77, 291, 301; Japan (17th & 18th Centuries), 4:126–28; Latin America (20th Century), 6:170–71; life at sea (17th & 18th Centuries), 4:130 32; New England, colonial, 4:13, 128–30; North American colonial frontier, 4:121–23; 17th & 18th Centuries, 4:118–32; United States (Civil War era), 5:2–3; United States (20th Century), 6:110, 114–16
Indus Valley civilization. See India (ancient)
Infant care: England (Victorian era), 5:239–40; Europe (Middle Ages), 2:80; Middle Ages, 2:78. See also Child care; Wet nurses
Infanticide: Egypt (ancient), 1:56; Greek and Roman, 1:57, 58; 6:141; Japan (17th & 18th Centuries), 4:74–75; Mesopotamia, 2:64; Polynesia, 2:68; Vikings, 2:81–82
Infant mortality: England (15th & 16th Centuries), 3:33, 75; Europe (Middle Ages), 2:79; Greece (ancient), 1:46, 59, 295; India (19th Century), 5:77; India (20th Century), 6:45–46; Islamic World (Middle Ages), 2:85, 318; Latin America (20th Century), 6:314; Mesopotamia, 1:52; Spain (15th & 16th Centuries), 3:77; 20th Century, 6:88; United States (Civil War era), 5:29; United States (1920–39), 6:67; Vikings, 2:34, 81
Infections. See Diseases
Infertility. See Childless couples
Infidels in Islamic World (19th Century), 5:447
Infirmaries, 5:390. See also Hospitals
Inflation: England (15th & 16th Centuries), 3:93, 111, 271; United States (1920–39), 6:436; United States (Western Frontier), 5:61
Influenza: England (15th & 16th Centuries), 3:189; England (Victorian era), 5:209; Europe (20th Century), 6:62–63; Spain (15th & 16th

Centuries), 3:194; United States (1920–39), 6:272
Inheritance. See Estates and inheritances
In-line skates, 6:505
Inns: Greece (ancient), 1:162; Rome (ancient), 1:164
Inoculation. See Vaccination
Inquisition, 2:326, 411. See also Spanish Inquisition
Insanity. See Mental illness and treatment
Insecticides, 6:260, 275
Insects: China (Tang Dynasty), 2:205, 206; United States (Western Frontier), 5:105, 254. See also specific insects
Insider trading (Japan), 6:400–401
Institutes of the Christian Religion (Calvin), 3:366
Insulae, 1:280
Insurance: England (Victorian era), 5:350–51; long-term care insurance (Japan), 6:292. See also Health insurance
Integration. See Civil rights movement; School desegregation
Intellectual life: ancient world, 1:169–241; China (Tang Dynasty), 2:11; 15th & 16th Centuries, 3:155–220; France (17th & 18th Centuries), 4:56–58; Middle Ages, 2:4, 145–94; 19th Century, 5:149–216; 17th & 18th Centuries, 4:167–236; 20th Century, 6:181–298. See also Art; Literature
Intercalary month: India (ancient), 1:216; Mesopotamia, 1:209; Rome (ancient), 1:214
Intercourse. See Sexuality
Internal Security Act of 1950, 6:376
International Workers of the World, preamble, 6:619–20
Internet, 3:155; Japan (20th Century), 6:259
Interstate Highway Act of 1956, 6:362
Inti, 3:53, 376–77, 391–92
Intifada, 6:483
Inti Raymi, 3:391
Inuit: breast feeding, 6:321, 322; cancer, 6:322; childbirth, 6:296; children, 6:50–51, 107; Christianity, 6:603; colonial rule, 6:402; cooking methods, 6:367; discrimination, 6:161; diseases, 6:295–96; education, 6:196, 214–15; environment, 6:296, 321–22; family life, 6:33, 50–51; food, 6:302, 320–22; fur trade, 6:347; government, 6:401–4; health and medicine, 6:261, 295–96, 295–98; historical overview, 6:26–27; housing, 6:51, 346–48; hunting, 6:321; kinship, 6:402; language, 6:214–15; life expectancy, 6:296; literature, 6:239–41; mercury and, 6:302; missionaries, 6:603; music, 6:557–58; names, 6:50; newspapers, 6:240; Nunavut land claims agreement (1993), 6:620–22; old age, 6:51; patrilineages, 6:50; poetry, 6:239; pollution, 6:296, 321–22; religion, 6:603–4; shaman, 6:295; social activism, 6:604; technology, 6:349, 367–68; tuberculosis, 6:296; writing, 6:239–40
Inuit Circumpolar Conference, 6:403
Inuktitut language, 6:214–15, 239, 240–41, 403
Inupiat Ilitqusiat, 6:604
Inventions: England (17th & 18th Centuries), 4:176–77. See also Science; Technology
Investiture Controversy, 2:328
Invisible Man (Ellison), 6:441
Invitation to an Inquest: A New Look at the Rosenberg and Sobell Case (Schneir), 6:380
Ionian Rationalism, 1:225
Ionians, 1:225, 333; vs. Dorians, 1:333. See also Greece (ancient)
Ionic architecture, 1:504–5
Iormungand, 2:412

Iowa cattle drives, 5:106
Iqbal, Muhammad, 6:229
Iran, 3:20; European colonialism in, 5:353; government, 6:390–91; language, 6:390; revolution, 6:11; war with Iraq, 6:11; women's roles, 5:37
Iran hostage crisis, 6:392
Iraq, 3:20, 164; European control, free from, 6:483; invasion of Kuwait, 6:478; war with Iran, 6:11. See also Islamic World (Middle Ages)
Ireland, 3:235, 340; Dublin, founded by Vikings, 2:99; towns founded by Vikings, 2:99
Iron: China (Tang Dynasty), 2:275, 280; England (17th & 18th Centuries), 4:176; England (Victorian era), 5:300; Europe (Middle Ages), 2:124, 275, 276; Islamic World (Middle Ages), 2:275; Italy (15th & 16th Centuries), 3:99; Maya, 3:351; New England, colonial, 4:129; Vikings, 2:100, 126
Iron Age, 1:122, 371. See also Mesopotamia
Irons, electric, 6:335
Ironworkers (Japan), 4:409
Iroquois: confederation of tribes, 4:348; New France, 4:10; religious beliefs, 4:469; social structure, 4:372; tribal government, 4:349; villages, 4:332
Irrigation: Byzantium, 2:130, 284; China (Tang Dynasty), 2:127, 197; Inca, 3:106; India (19th Century), 5:14, 302; Islamic World (Middle Ages), 2:282–83; Maya, 3:102; Mesopotamia, 1:75, 78, 79; Nubia, 1:87
Irving, Washington, 5:348
Isaac, Jorge, 5:196
Isabel de Valois, 3:211
Isabella, 3:10, 176, 287, 288, 345
Isadore of Seville, 2:169
Isherwood, Christopher, 6:219
Ishmael, 2:418, 424
Ishtar, 1:471, 488, 510
Isidore of Seville, 2:180–81
Isidoros of Miletus, 2:285, 447
Isis, 1:289, 430, 475, 476, 477
Isla Cerritos, 3:7
Islam: Africa (20th Century), 6:433, 601, 602; alcoholic beverages and, 3:237, 245; 5:252; charity, 6:595; Christianity, relationship with, 6:11; death, burial, and the afterlife, 3:43; ethical behavior as part of, 2:409; fasting, 6:595; founding of, 2:12, 417–25; 5:16, 467–68; 6:10; guilds, 3:119; Hindu vs. Muslim feud in India, 6:9, 10; India, Muslim conquest of, 6:8–9; India (19th Century), 5:466; Jews, relationship with, 2:421; 6:11; life cycles, 3:30–31; Mongols and, 2:429; monotheism, 3:361; Ottoman Empire, 3:65; pork and food restrictions, 2:207–8; 3:241, 245; 6:316; prayers, 5:454, 456, 468, 469; 6:595; prophets and prophecy, 6:594; rituals, exclusion from, 3:30–31; Soviet Union, 6:23, 597; views on women, religion, slaves, and war, 5:494–96; women's dress, 5:287. See also Five Pillars of Islam; Hajj; Muhammad; Qur'an (Koran); Sharia; Shi'ites
Islamic World (Middle Ages): abandonment of spouse, 2:49–50; age of marriage, 2:85–86; alcoholic beverages, 2:283; archers, 2:358; astronomy, 2:147, 166; banks and banking, 2:143–44; banquets, 2:85; bathhouses, 2:232; beds, 2:273; board games, 2:401; bride-price, 2:47, 62; bubonic plague, 2:85; camels, 2:129, 142; carpentry, 2:273; chairs, 2:267, 273; chess, 2:369; childbirth, 2:423; children, 2:84–86; circumcision, 2:85; civil wars, 2:357; clothing, 2:243–45; coffee, 2:219;

532

concubines, 2:48; cooking methods, 2:207, 232; cotton, 2:283; couches, 2:273; cremation, 2:468; death, burial, and the afterlife, 2:467–68; defeat by Charles Martel, 2:2; divorce, 2:40, 49; dowry, 2:47; drink, 2:219; drinking water, 2:213, 219; drugs, 2:166, 192; eating utensils, 2:273; education, 2:85, 147, 155–57; entertainment, 2:401–2; eunuchs, 2:30, 70, 72–74; fairs, 2:143; festivals and holidays, 2:450, 457–58; figs and dates, 2:207; fish, 2:207; food, 2:206–8, 273, 282; fortifications, 2:358; fruit juices, 2:219; fruits, 2:207, 282; furnishings, 2:273–74; games, 2:401; geometry, 2:166; glass, 2:283; grains, 2:206; harems, 2:72, 232–33; health and medicine, 2:147, 156, 166, 178–79, 188; helmets, 2:357; historical overview, 2:12–17; hospitals, 2:166; housing, 2:231–33; housing materials, 2:222, 232; hunting, 2:382–84; infant mortality, 2:85, 318; iron, 2:275; irrigation, 2:282–83; kinship, 2:35–37; language and literature, 2:174–75; law, 2:325–26, 338–40; libraries, 2:165; logic, 2:165, 166; map of, 2:13; marketplaces, 2:104–5; marriage, 2:39, 47–50; mathematics, 2:147, 165, 166; merchants, 2:321; military service, 2:73; milk and dairy products, 2:207; money, 2:132; moneychangers, 2:104–5; mosques, 2:104, 445–46; music, 2:166; musical instruments, 2:283; nomads, 2:128, 143, 231; olives and olive trees, 2:206; ovens, 2:232; philosophy, 2:165, 166; pillows, 2:273; plague, 2:85; poetry, 2:402; polo, 2:402; polygamy, 2:40, 48; punishment, 2:326; races, 2:402; raptors, 2:383; reading and writing, 2:155–56; religious beliefs, 2:299, 417–25; religious buildings, 2:445–46; rice, 2:206; roads, 2:142; rural life and agriculture, 2:93, 128–29, 282; schools, 2:156, 165; science, 2:165–67, 188; sherbets, 2:192; sieges, 2:358; slaves, 2:310, 317–18; smallpox, 2:166; social structure, 2:35, 297–99; surgery, 2:166, 179; tea, 2:219; teachers, 2:156–57; technology, 2:282–83; toys, 2:85; trade, 2:132, 142–44; universities, 2:156; urban life, 2:95, 103–5; vegetables, 2:207, 282; veils, 2:236, 244; warfare and weapons, 2:282, 355–59; weights and measures, 2:105; wheat, 2:206; women, 2:30, 60–62, 157, 232, 244; women's quarters, 2:61, 232–33; wrestling, 2:402; writing, 2:156. *See also* Crusades (Middle Ages)
Islamic World (19th Century): Albanian independence, 5:392; alcoholic beverages, 5:468; British power in, 5:16–17, 353; caste systems, 5:26; children, 5:38; clothing, 5:454; colonialism, 5:16–17; divorce, 5:38; education, 5:181; empire, 5:352–54; European colonialism in, 5:352–53; family life, 5:37–38, 454; fasting, 5:454; food, 5:247; government and politics, 5:327; harems, 5:37; historical overview, 5:16–17; housing, 5:37; imperialism, 5:455; infidels, 5:447; liberalism, 5:391; literature, 5:198; Macedonian revolt, 5:391–92; marriage, 5:27, 447; modernization, 5:17; monotheism, 5:456; morality, 5:453–55; mosques, 5:469; music, 5:427; nationalism, 5:390–91; poetry, 6:231; polygamy, 5:37, 447; Portuguese power in, 5:16, 353; reading, 5:38; reform movements, 5:390–94; religion, 5:38, 467–69; servants, 5:37; tobacco use, 5:481–83; Turkish nationalism, 5:390–91; urban and rural environments, 5:146–48; war and the

military, 5:380; women, 5:37, 66, 447, 454; Young Turks, 5:390–91
Islamic World (17th & 18th Centuries): Africa, 4:134, 183–85, 347, 371, 431, 464, 466–67, 483–85; monotheism, 4:464–65
Islamic World (20th Century): colonial rule of, 6:230; courts and judges, 6:423–24; death penalty, 6:424; family life, 6:52; food, 6:322–23; fundamentalism, 6:450; government, 6:390–92; historical overview, 6:10–11; housing, 6:348; human rights, 6:592; law and crime, 6:404, 422–24; literature, 6:230–33; morality, 6:568; poetry, 6:231; reform, 6:450–52; religious beliefs, 6:568, 594–96; sharia system, 6:422–24; theater, 6:231; toys, 6:87; urban life, 6:179; warfare, 6:482–84; women, 6:60, 87; World War I, effect on, 6:482; World War II, effect on, 6:482
Ismail, 5:354
Israel: formation of, 6:7, 483; Soviet Jews emigrating to, 6:23
Israeli-Palestinian conflict, 6:11, 483; literature about, 6:232; Six-Day War, 6:581; Yom Kippur War, 6:364
Istanbul, 3:118, 292, 348
Italian, The (Radcliffe), 5:183
Italian language: development of, 3:157; education and, 3:177; England (15th & 16th Centuries), spoken in, 3:173; Middle Ages, 2:168
Italy (15th & 16th Centuries): adultery, 3:63; apothecaries, 3:197; art, 3:346–48; artisans, 3:277; baptism, 3:37–38, 79; beds, 3:258–59; blood sports, 3:338; bread, 3:242; capital punishment, 3:308–9; cards, 3:315, 323; catechism, 3:38; Charles I as ruler of, 3:287; chastity, 3:62; cheese, 3:243; chess, 3:323; childbirth, 3:78–79; child care, 3:79–81; child labor, 3:38, 81; children, 3:78–82; city life, 3:115–17; city states, 3:8; clothing, 3:228–30; common law, 3:306; cooking methods, 3:243; counts and countesses, 3:276; courts and judges, 3:132, 163, 290, 302, 307–8; courtyards, 3:257; dance, 3:347–48; death, burial, and the afterlife, 3:40–41; dialects, 3:163; division between Spain and France, 3:16; doges, 3:276; doors, 3:257; dowry, 3:39–40, 62, 117; drinking water, 3:117; dukes and duchesses, 3:276; education, 3:81, 177–80; emperor, 3:276; fishing, 3:335, 338; food, 3:242–43; footwear, 3:228–29; fruit, 3:243; furniture, 3:258–59; galleys, 3:309; gambling, 3:323–24; games, 3:63, 321–24; gardening, 3:337; genealogy, 3:179, 276; government, 3:289–91; grand dukes, 3:276; guilds, 3:41; gypsies, 3:346–47; health, 3:195–99; herbs and spices, 3:242; hierarchy, 3:275–78; holidays and festivals, 3:134–35; hours, calculation of, 3:132–33; houses, 3:257–59; hunting, 3:338; iron, 3:99; jousting, 3:315, 322–23; justice and legal systems, 3:302, 306–9; kings, 3:276; knights, 3:276; landowners, 3:275; language and writing, 3:162–64; law enforcement, 3:307, 308; life cycles, 3:37–41; literacy, 3:116, 164; literature, 3:212–14; malaria, 3:196; map of Renaissance Italy, 3:9; marble, 3:99; marquis and marchinesses, 3:276; marriage, 3:39–40, 61, 347; martial games, 3:315, 321–22; masonry, 3:99; names, 3:37, 79; olive trees and olive oil, 3:243; outdoor pursuits, 3:335–39; painting, 3:212; pasta, 3:242; patricians, 3:115, 277; peasants, 3:97–98, 134, 163, 242, 259, 285, 290; physicians, 3:115; poor

persons, 3:98–99; population, 3:98; pork, 3:236, 243; prayers, 3:41, 132; priests and religious rituals, 3:277–78; princes, 3:276; processions and parades, 3:135, 278; public officials, 3:277–78; rural life, 3:97–99; servants, 3:115–17; sexuality, 3:39, 61, 62; shipping, 3:8; sports, 3:63, 321–24; surgery, 3:195; swimming, 3:335; taxes, 3:97, 289, 291; teachers, 3:115, 177; textiles, 3:99; theater, 3:336; time, 3:131–36; tournaments, 3:315, 321–22; trades and crafts, 3:116; tunics, 3:347; tutors, 3:81, 177; typhus, 3:196; universities, 3:178; vegetables, 3:242; villas, 3:251; wheat, 3:242; widows, 3:40; wills, 3:40–41; wine, 3:243; witchcraft, 3:198; women's roles, 3:61–64; wool, 3:8. *See also* Catholicism (Spain, Italy, England)
Italy (Middle Ages), historical overview, 2:2
Italy (20th Century). *See* Europe (20th Century)
Itami Juzo, 6:535
Iturbide, Agustín de, 5:117
Itza Maya, 3:5
Itzamna, 3:370–71
Iugera of land, 1:84
Ius, 1:366
Ius commune, 3:306
Ivory: Mesopotamia, 1:273; Nubia, 1:312
Ixchel, 3:372, 385
Ixtab, 3:372, 385
Izculli, 3:85
Iznik tile, 3:348
Iztaccihuatl, 3:69, 186
Izvestiya, 6:256

Jackets: England (Victorian era), 5:281; United States (Civil War era), 5:273–74
Jackson, Andrew, 5:181, 343, 344
Jackson, Irene Dobbs, 6:445
Jackson, Kenneth, 6:362
Jackson, Mary, 5:330
Jackson, Peter, 5:400
Jackson, Robert, 6:410
Jackson, Shirley, 6:222
Jackson, Thomas, 5:295, 460
Jacobites, 3:164
Jacquerie, 2:311
Jade, 3:351
Jails: China (19th Century), 5:340; China (Tang Dynasty), 2:334; England (17th & 18th Centuries), 4:393; England (Victorian era), 5:336
Jainism: development of, 6:8, 588; founding of, 1:11, 465; India (19th Century), 5:14, 416, 466; India's caste system and, 1:338; money lending and, 1:137; vegetarianism, 1:258
Jalal al-Din Rumi, 3:368
Jamal al-Din Savi, 3:368
James I (king of England), 3:110
James II (king of England), 4:350
James, G.P.R., 5:191
James, William, 6:564
Jamestown settlement, 4:10
Jam ʿiyyat-i Ulama-i Islam, 6:451
Jane Fonda's Workout Book, 6:507
Janissaries, 3:164, 369
Japanese-American internment during World War II, 6:16–17, 150, 525
Japan (17th & 18th Centuries): abortion, 4:96; acupuncture, 4:229–30; adoption by merchants, 4:75; advertising, 4:457; agriculture, 4:17, 113–15, 177; armor, military, 4:409; art, 4:455–57; autumnal equinox, 4:439; ball games, 4:424; baths,

King Kong (film), **6:**520

King Lear (Shakespeare), **5:**187

King Philip (Wampanoag chief), **4:**411–12

Kings: Africa (17th & 18th Centuries), **4:**430–31; divine right of kings, **3:**284; England (17th & 18th Centuries), **4:**352; Europe (Middle Ages), **2:**303, 329; France (17th & 18th Centuries), **4:**355–56; Inca, **3:**282; India, **6:**388; India (ancient), **1:**352–54; Italy (15th & 16th Centuries), **3:**276; Kongo, **4:**348; Luba, **4:**348; Lunda, **4:**348; Maya, **3:**278, 294; Mesopotamia, **1:**340–44, 370, 372; Naples, **3:**276; Sparta, **1:**349; Vikings, **2:**304–5. *See also* Pharaohs; Royalty

Kinich Ahau, **3:**361, 371

Kinoshita Keisuke, **6:**534–35

Kinsey, Alfred, **6:**37

Kinsey reports, **6:**37

Kinship: Africa (17th & 18th Centuries), **4:**368–69; Europe (Middle Ages), **2:**32–33; Inuit, **6:**402; Islamic World (Middle Ages), **2:**35–37; Japan (20th Century), **6:**401; Middle Ages, **2:**30–39; Mongols, **2:**37–39; Vikings, **2:**34–35. *See also* Family life

Kip, Leonard, **5:**91

Kipling, Rudyard, **5:**191

Kipp, James, **5:**126

Kippers, **5:**241

Kirakos of Ganjak, **2:**265

Kirisute-gomen, **4:**396

Kirman. *See* Mongols

Kirtles: England (15th & 16th Centuries), **3:**222, 224, 225; Europe (15th & 16th Centuries), **3:**223

Kissinger, Henry, **6:**476, 477

Kitab Allah, **2:**155, 418

"Kitchen debate" (Nixon vs. Khrushchev), **6:**339–40

Kitchens: England (Victorian era), **5:**262, 263; India (19th Century), **5:**265; Japan (17th & 18th Centuries), **4:**278

Kite flying, **6:**509

Knapsacks (Civil War), **5:**294

Knickerbockers, **5:**282

Knights: England (15th & 16th Centuries), **3:**271; England (Victorian era), **5:**113; historical overview, **2:**4; Italy (15th & 16th Centuries), **3:**276; in military operations, **2:**282, 291, 346; as part of aristocracy, **2:**302, 303; in religious orders, **2:**169

Knights of Saint John, **3:**276

Knights Templars, **2:**4, 443

Knitting, **5:**438–39

Knives: United States (Western Frontier), **5:**331. *See also* Eating utensils; Weapons

Knot makers at sea, **4:**460

Koinê, **1:**176

Kola nuts, **4:**240

Kolkhozniki, **6:**174–75

Komeito, **6:**600

Kongo (17th & 18th Centuries): Christianity, **4:**468; Halloween, **4:**431; healers and healing, **4:**221; kings, **4:**348; marriage, **4:**31; slave trade, **4:**16. *See also* Africa (17th & 18th Centuries)

Koran. *See* Qur'an

Korean War, **6:**370, 470

Korkut, **3:**292

Korolev, Sergei, **6:**190

Korzenik, Joseph, **6:**144

Kosher food, Jesus on, **3:**362. *See also* Jews

Kosode, **4:**294–95, 301, 310–11

Kosovo, Battle of, **3:**12

Kosterina, Nina, **6:**81

Kotex, **6:**274

Koubou, Abe, **6:**238

Koubikoularioi, **2:**74–75

Koufax, Sandy, **6:**503

Koumiss: China (Tang Dynasty), **2:**217; Mongols, **2:**220

Kouyou, Ozaki, **6:**236

Kreisler, Fritz, **6:**461

Krishna, **1:**207; **5:**414, 415

Kriti, **5:**424

Krupp, Alfred, **6:**413

Kshatriya, **1:**338

K'u, **3:**370–71

Kublai Khan, **2:**22

Kukla, **3:**350

Ku Klux Klan (KKK), **6:**54, 140, 145–48

Kukulcan, **3:**371

Kulaks, **6:**174

Kulich, **6:**598

K'ung Fu-tzu, **4:**477–78

Kuns, **3:**137–38

Kurdistan as part of Ottoman Empire, **3:**20

Kurosawa Akira, **6:**534

Kurtas, **5:**287

Kusatao, Nakamura, **6:**238

Kush, **1:**13

Kushner, Tony, **6:**379

Kusugak, Avaaluk, **6:**241

Kutulun, **2:**66

Kuwait, U.S. liberation of, **6:**478

Kuznetsov, Andrei, **6:**532

Kyogen, **4:**444

Kyoho reforms, **4:**17–18

Kyoto (17th & 18th Centuries), **4:**337

Kyyal, **5:**424

Labeling of food, **6:**311

Labor Day, **5:**406, 407

Labor movement: China (19th Century), **5:**96. *See also* Labor unions

Labor unions: anti-discrimination and, **6:**151; Europe (World I era), **6:**112–13; United States (1920–39), **6:**439–40; United States (1960–90), **6:**40, 111, 131–33

Labradores, **3:**94

Lacandon Maya, **3:**370

Lacquer, **4:**127–28

Ladu, **5:**244

Lafayette, Madame, **4:**209

Lake Mohonk Conference, **5:**169

Lakes. *See specific lakes by name*

Lakshni, **5:**414

La Malinche, **3:**168–69

La Mancha, **3:**256, 410

Lamashtu, **1:**51

Lamb, **5:**246. *See also* Sheep and goats

Lamentation over the Destruction of Ur, **1:**372

Lamentation-priests (Mesopotamia), **1:**487

Lampman, Robert, **6:**119

Lamps: Byzantium, **2:**107; China (Tang Dynasty), **2:**272; Greece (ancient), **1:**278; North American colonial frontier, **4:**174; Spain (15th & 16th Centuries), **3:**256; Vikings, **2:**202, 228

Lances. *See* Weapons

Landa, Diego de, **3:**199, 231, 278–79, 325, 398, 419–21

Landowners: England (15th & 16th Centuries), **3:**286; Europe (Middle Ages), **2:**52, 123, 303, 312–13; Italy (15th & 16th Centuries), **3:**275; Latin America (20th Century), **6:**134, 313; Mesopotamia, **1:**330, 371; Middle Ages, **2:**122, 310; New England, colonial, **4:**147; Polynesia, **2:**300; Soviet Union, **6:**397; Spain (15th & 16th Centuries), **3:**95

Land reform programs in Latin America, **6:**171–72, 592

Landucci, Luca, **3:**411–13

Lang, Andrew, **5:**193

Language: Africa (17th & 18th Centuries), **4:**202–4; Africa (20th Century), **6:**178, 212; ancient world, **1:**170–82; Australian Aboriginals, **1:**180–82, 192; Aztec, **3:**168; Castile, **3:**161; China (Tang Dynasty), **2:**173–74; England (15th & 16th Centuries), **3:**158–59, 172; England (17th & 18th Centuries), **4:**206–7; Europe (Middle Ages), **2:**148–49, 167, 168–70; Greece (ancient), **1:**176–77; Inca, **3:**169; India (ancient), **1:**179–80; India (19th & 20th Century), **6:**229; India (19th Century), **5:**78; India (20th Century), **6:**388–89; Indian films, dubbing required, **6:**530; Inuit, **6:**214–15; Islamic World (Middle Ages), **2:**174–75; Italy (15th & 16th Centuries), **3:**162–64; Japan (17th & 18th Centuries), **4:**211–12; Latin America (20th Century), **6:**101–2, 133; Maya, **3:**166–67; Mesopotamia, **1:**343; Middle Ages, **2:**146, 167–78; Native Americans (colonial frontier of North America), **4:**204–5; North American colonial frontier, **4:**204–5; Ottoman Empire, **3:**164–66; Polynesia, **2:**167, 175–78; Rome (ancient), **1:**179; 17th & 18th Centuries, **4:**200–218; Spain (15th & 16th Centuries), **3:**161–62; United States (1920–39), **6:**198; Vikings, **2:**167, 170–73

La Noche Triste, **3:**21

Lantern Festival, **2:**455

Lanterns, **2:**272

Lao She, **5:**182, 195

Lao-Tzu, **2:**415, 416; **5:**463–64

Laptops, **6:**253

Larceny: England (Victorian era), **5:**335; United States (Western Frontier), **5:**332. *See also* Theft

Lardner, Ring, Jr., **6:**526–27

Larpenteur, Charles, **5:**48

Lashes in British Royal Navy, **4:**400

Las Madres and the disappeared, **6:**61, 77

Lassies, **5:**253

Last Judgment (Michelangelo), **3:**40

Last rites: Catholicism (Spain, Italy, England), **3:**31, 380, 382; Europe (Middle Ages), **2:**459, 460

Last Supper, **3:**379

Latham, Jean, **6:**224

Latimer, Hugh, **3:**409–10

Latin: Aztec and, **3:**218; Catholic Church masses discontinuing use of, **6:**582, 591; Catholicism (Spain, Italy, England), **3:**379; England (15th & 16th Centuries), **3:**32–33, 159, 172–73; Europe (15th & 16th Centuries), **3:**157, 170–71; Europe (Middle Ages), **2:**147, 150, 156, 167, 168, 169; introduced into Americas by Spanish, **3:**157–58; Italy (15th & 16th Centuries), **3:**79, 162–63, 179; Middle Ages, **2:**146; Ottoman Empire, **3:**165; Rome (ancient), **1:**179, 189; Spain (15th & 16th Centuries), **3:**175, 177; Vikings, **2:**171

Latin America (15th & 16th Centuries): Archaic Age, **3:**2; ball games, **3:**314–16, 397–98; early civilizations, **3:**3; justice and legal systems,

3:309–12; maize, 3:221, 237; missionaries, 3:23; painting, 3:340; people coming into via Bering land bridge, 3:2; slaves, 3:23; Toltec Empire, 3:5, 280. *See also* Aztec; Inca; Maya

Latin America (19th Century): alpacas, 5:288; apartments, 5:254; architecture, 5:266; artisans, 5:117; assault, 5:340–41; authoritarianism, 5:325; bananas, 5:97, 133–34; bandits, 5:341; baptism, 5:471; beans, 5:246; beef, 5:97, 133, 245; beer, 5:245; beggars, 5:97; belts, 5:289; boots, 5:289; bureaucracy, 5:97, 326; buttons, 5:289; cacao, 5:132; caste systems, 5:17; catechism, 5:471; cattle, 5:133; cattle stations, 5:267; charity boards, 5:245; child care, 5:97; children, 5:79–80; chiles, 5:245; chocolate, 5:245; cholera, 5:213; cleaning, 5:97; clocks, 5:289; clothing, 5:287–90; coca, 5:246; coffee, 5:19, 97, 132–33, 245, 246, 325; colonialism, 5:340; construction, 5:97; cooking methods, 5:97; copper, 5:19, 132; corn, 5:133, 245, 247; cotton, 5:133, 246; crimes, 5:340–42; desserts, 5:245; diamonds, 5:132; diseases, 5:213; drink, 5:245; drinking water, 5:245; education, 5:69–70, 178–80; electric insulation, 5:133; eugenics, 5:158; evolution, 5:158; family life, 5:41; feathers, 5:289; feminism, 5:55, 70; festivals, 5:416; fish, 5:245; folk music, 5:427; food, 5:219, 244–47; footwear, 5:289; fowl, 5:245; freemasonry, 5:19, 471; fruit, 5:246; goats, 5:246; gold, 5:132; government and politics, 5:324–27; haciendas, 5:17, 267, 325, 326; hats, 5:289; health and medicine, 5:213–16; hides, 5:19; historical overview, 5:17–20; holidays and festivals, 5:246, 416–18; honey, 5:245; honor, 5:68–69; hospitals, 5:214; housing, 5:254, 266–68; ice cream, 5:245; immigration, 5:19–20, 98, 117, 267, 326; indentured servants, 5:246; independence, 5:17, 19, 324–25, 355–56, 377; independence wars, 5:132; indigo, 5:132; jewelry, 5:288, 289; lamb, 5:246; legal systems, 5:340; liberalism, 5:19, 267–68, 470, 471; literacy, 5:178; literature, 5:196–98; llamas, 5:288; maps, 5:18; mass, 5:471; meat, 5:97, 133, 245; medical academies, 5:214; men, 5:54; merchants, 5:117; messianism, 5:472; middle class, 5:99, 117, 326; migrant labor, 5:97–98, 133–34; military forces, 5:378–79; mining, 5:17; minuets, 5:426; murder, 5:340; music, 5:426–27; mutton, 5:133; navigation, 5:17; necklaces, 5:289; nitrates, 5:97, 133–34; noodles, 5:245; opera, 5:426; opium, 5:246; orchestras, 5:427; organized labor, 5:326; pan flutes, 5:427; peasants, 5:69, 96–98, 117; peppers, 5:245; piercings, 5:289; plantations, 5:17, 118, 146, 267, 326, 379; polkas, 5:426; population, 5:17, 267; pork, 5:245; positivism, 5:158, 179, 471; potatoes, 5:245; prayers, 5:471, 472; priests, 5:19, 97, 117, 470–71; protests, 5:247; puddings, 5:244, 245; railroads, 5:19, 247, 378; rebozos, 5:288; religion, 5:469–72; religious rituals, 5:19, 97, 117, 471, 472; rice, 5:245, 246; riots, 5:247; roads, 5:378; robbery, 5:341; royalty, 5:117; rubber, 5:133; rum, 5:245; rural life and agriculture, 5:96–97, 246–47; sacraments, 5:471; saints, 5:471; salads, 5:245; sarapes, 5:288–89; science, 5:158–60; servants, 5:246, 326; shame, 5:68–69; shawls, 5:288; shirts, 5:288; shrines, 5:471; silk, 5:288; silver, 5:19, 132; skirts, 5:288, 289; slums, 5:267; social mobility, 5:116; social structure,

5:116–18; spiritism, 5:472; sports, 5:405; spurs, 5:289; steam engines, 5:159; steamships, 5:19, 159; suburbs, 5:267; sugar, 5:19, 97, 132–34, 246, 325; tango, 5:427; tattoos, 5:289; tea, 5:245; telegraphs, 5:159, 378; tenements, 5:267, 268; theater, 5:426; theft, 5:340; tin, 5:97, 132; tires, 5:133; tobacco, 5:19, 132, 325; trade, 5:132–35, 288, 326; transportation, 5:17, 97; trousers, 5:288, 289; tuberculosis, 5:213; United States power in, 5:20; urban life, 5:146, 266–67; utilitarianism, 5:470; vaccination, 5:214; vegetables, 5:246; violence, 5:340; wages, 5:246; waltzes, 5:426; war and the military, 5:377–80; wheat, 5:97–98, 133, 245; whiskey, 5:246; wine, 5:245; women, 5:68–70, 97; wood, 5:132; wool, 5:288; work, 5:96–98; working class, 5:117. *See also* Slaves in Latin America (19th Century)

Latin America (20th Century): assassinations, 6:592; automobiles, 6:314; baptism, 6:43; battle casualties, 6:44, 479; cattle, 6:314; child labor, 6:8, 88, 102–3; children, 6:43, 56, 88, 101–3; cocoa, 6:314; coffee, 6:314; coups d'état, 6:387, 480; crimes, 6:420–21; discrimination, 6:134; domestic violence, 6:57; economic life, 6:387; education, 6:88, 101–2; electricity, 6:300; family life, 6:43–45; famine and starvation, 6:313, 315; fathers' role, 6:56; feminism, 6:76; food, 6:313–15; gangs, 6:420; godparents, 6:44; government, 6:384–88; grains, 6:314; historical overview, 6:7–8; housing, 6:300, 348; illegitimate children, 6:43, 45; immigration, 6:44; industry, 6:170–71; infant mortality, 6:314; landowners, 6:134, 313; land reform programs, 6:171–72, 592; language, 6:101–2, 133; law, 6:420–22; malnutrition, 6:314; marriage, 6:43; meat, 6:314; men, 6:43, 44, 55–57; mining, 6:56, 103, 134; Nazi escape to, 6:413; poor persons, 6:172, 388, 421; population, 6:171; populism, 6:385; priests, 6:591–92; religious belief, 6:133, 591–94; rural life and agriculture, 6:101, 102, 135, 170–72, 314; servants, 6:103; single-parent households, 6:33, 44; slums, 6:8, 171; social activism, 6:592–93; social structure, 6:110, 133–35; spiritism, 6:593; sugar, 6:314; unemployment, 6:172, 420; United States relations, 6:466; urban life, 6:162, 170–72; voting rights, 6:56; wages, 6:103; warfare, 6:8, 171, 479–82; women, 6:45, 60, 75–78; women, work of, 6:43, 56–57, 76; work, 6:44, 56, 125

Latin American College (Rome), 5:471
Latrines: ancient Athens, 1:102; Greece (ancient), 1:278; India (19th Century), 5:266; Islamic World (Middle Ages), 2:232; Mesopotamia, 1:92, 271; Rome (ancient), 1:280, 444; World War I, 6:464
Lattimore, Owen, 6:376
Laudes, 3:347
Laundry: England (17th & 18th Centuries), 4:275; Europe (Middle Ages), 2:239; Vikings, 2:228
Lavatories. *See* Latrines; Toilet facilities
La Venta, 3:3
Law: Africa (20th Century), 6:431–34; ancient world, 1:358–68; Australia, colonial, 4:386–89; Byzantium, 2:325, 340–41; China (Tang Dynasty), 2:11, 154, 326, 332–38; England (Middle Ages), 2:4; England (17th & 18th Centuries), 4:384–85, 391–94; Europe (Middle Ages), 2:32, 151, 327–29; Greece (ancient), 1:363–65; Islamic World (Middle

Ages), 2:325–26, 338–40; Islamic World (20th Century), 6:422–24; Japan (17th & 18th Centuries), 4:394; Japan (20th Century), 6:429–31; Latin America (20th Century), 6:420–22; life at sea (17th & 18th Centuries), 4:398–401; Massachusetts Bay Colony, 4:384; Mesopotamia, 1:359–62; Middle Ages, 2:325–44; Mongols, 2:326, 341–44; New England, colonial, 4:396–98, 426; North American colonial frontier, 4:389–91; Rome (ancient), 1:365–68; Soviet Union, 6:424–29; 20th Century, 6:404–34; United States (1920–39), 6:414–17; United States (1960–90), 6:417–20; Vikings, 2:305, 326, 329–32
Law enforcement: ancient Athens, 1:103, 363; China (Tang Dynasty), 2:334; England (15th & 16th Centuries), 3:302; England (17th & 18th Centuries), 4:392; England (Victorian era), 5:337–38; Italy (15th & 16th Centuries), 3:307, 308; Japan (17th & 18th Centuries), 4:395; Japan (20th Century), 6:493; Rome (ancient), 1:366; 17th & 18th Centuries, 4:385; Soviet Union, 6:424–25; Spain (15th & 16th Centuries), 3:113, 303–4
Lawn tennis. *See* Tennis
Law of Common Education (Argentina), 5:180
Lawrence of Arabia (film), 6:482
Laws of Eshnunna, 1:40
Laws of Hammurabi, 1:545–47; adultery, 1:65; artisan payment, 1:119; description of, 1:358, 361–62; dispute mediation, 1:1–2; family life, 1:21; governments, 1:342; health and medicine, 1:284, 287; incest, 1:65; judicial standards, 1:360; marriage, 1:42; military service, 1:371; social structure, 1:329
Lawson, James, 6:442, 574
Lawsuits (Japan), 6:401
Lawyers. *See* Attorneys
Lazarillo de Tormes, 3:210
Lazzaroni group, 5:152
Leach's Complete Spelling Book, 5:164
Leaseholders, 3:272
Leather: Europe (Middle Ages), 2:238, 239, 276; Greece (ancient), 1:310, 312; Japan, 6:160; Mesopotamia, 1:31, 77, 122, 303; Middle Ages, 2:247; Mongols, 2:51, 66, 245, 362; Nubia, 1:312–13; United States (Western Frontier), 5:123
Lebanon: European control, free from, 6:483; Ottoman power in, 5:354. *See also* Islamic World *entries*
Lebed, Alexander, 6:490
Lécluse, Henri de, 6:463
Lectures (United States [Western Frontier]), 5:433
Ledyard, John, 5:348
Lee, Robert E., 5:296, 317
Leeches. *See* Bloodletting
Le Fanu, Sheridan, 5:191
Legacies. *See* Estates and inheritances; Wills
Lega Italica, 3:8
Legal systems. *See* Courts and judges; Law
Legates, 1:383–84
Leggings of Native Americans, 4:288–89, 304
Legislature: New England, colonial, 4:361; Rome (ancient), 1:351. *See also specific name of legislative body (e.g., Diet, Parliament)*
Legumes. *See* Vegetables
Leidang, 2:351
Leif Erikson, 2:7, 162
Leisure time. *See* Entertainment
Lemba cult, 4:221
LeMond, Greg, 6:499
Lemuria, 1:442

Japan (17th & 18th Centuries), **4**:322; Japan (20th Century), **6**:259; seamen, **4**:217
Mailer, Norman, **6**:220–21
Mair, **5**:37, 39
Maize: Australia, colonial, **4**:106–7; Aztec, **3**:104, 221, 237, 248; Inca, **3**:2, 221, 237, 248–49; Latin America (19th Century), **5**:133, 245, 246, 247; Maya, **3**:100–102, 221, 237, 246; United States (Western Frontier), **5**:230; Vikings, **2**:126
Makar Sankranti, **5**:415
Makeup. *See* Cosmetics
Makioka Sisters, The (Jun'ichirou), **6**:237
Malaeska, the Indian Wife of the White Hunter (Stephens), **5**:187
Malaria: England (15th & 16th Centuries), **3**:189; Europe (15th & 16th Centuries), **3**:166; India (19th Century), **5**:253; India (20th Century), **6**:287; Italy (15th & 16th Centuries), **3**:196; New England, colonial, **4**:88; United States (1940–59), **6**:275
Malatesta family, **3**:8
Malcolm X, **6**:152, 448, 595
Male prostitution, **1**:67–68
Malaria, **1**:295
Maliki, **3**:65
Malil, **3**:262
Malintzin, **3**:168
Mallorca, **3**:161
Malls, shopping, **6**:169–70
Malnutrition: England (17th & 18th Centuries), **4**:225; Latin America (20th Century), **6**:314; seamen, **4**:234; United States (1920–39), **6**:307; United States (1960–90), **6**:313
Malpractice. *See* Medical malpractice
Malta Knights of Saint John, **3**:276
Mama-Cocha, **3**:376
Mamaconas, **3**:72, 187, 390
Māui, **2**:177–78, 469
Mama Ocllo, **5**:417
Mama-Quilla, **3**:376
Mamluks, **2**:317–18, 319
Manahuatzin, **3**:399
Manchu Dynasty, **5**:453
Manco Capac, **3**:109, 126, 282, 402–4; **5**:417
Manco Inca, **3**:23
Mandal Commission Report (India), **6**:156
Mandamiento, **5**:134
Mandarins, **2**:296, 454
Mandel, Yelena, **6**:159
Mandela, Nelson, **6**:433
Mandelshtam, Osip, **6**:233
Mande (17th & 18th Centuries), **4**:153–54
Mandeville, Bernard, **4**:143–44
Mandulis, **1**:468
Manhattan Project, **6**:184, 185, 469
Manic depression, **6**:281
Manioc: Inca, **3**:105; Maya, **3**:246
Mannes, Marya, **6**:97, 565
Man Nobody Knows, The (Barton), **6**:572
Manorialism, **2**:290, 291, 311
Manors and manor houses: England (15th & 16th Centuries), **3**:253; Europe (Middle Ages), **2**:123–24, 290, 291; Middle Ages, **2**:301; Spain (15th & 16th Centuries), **3**:95
Manslaughter, **3**:302. *See also* Homicide
Mansour, **2**:117, 118

Mantas: Aztec, **3**:233; Maya, **3**:231
Mantillas, **3**:223, 227
Mantle, Mickey, **6**:503
Mantua: Countess of, **3**:229; Duke of, **3**:339
Manturcalla, **3**:391–92
Manuductio Ad Ministerium (Mather), **4**:214
Manufacturing industry: England (17th & 18th Centuries), **4**:123–24; Europe (Middle Ages), **2**:276; North American colonial frontier, **4**:121–22
Manumission, **1**:115
Manus marriage in Roman Empire, **1**:48–49, 50
Manu Smriti, **1**:338
Manzikert defeat of Byzantium (1071), **2**:356
Mappa mundi, **1**:220–21
Maps: Africa (18th Century), **4**:15; Australia (1606–1818), **4**:20; Aztec Empire, **3**:12; Byzantine Empire, **2**:18; China (19th Century), **5**:12; China (Tang Dynasty) divided into three kingdoms (Wei, Shu, and Wu), **2**:9; China under Tang dynasty, **2**:8; Crusades, **2**:14, 16; England and Wales (16th Century), **3**:4; England (1789), **4**:3; England (Victorian era), **5**:9; Europe and Mediterranean (Middle Ages), **2**:3; France (1789), **4**:3; Greece (ancient), **1**:7, 225; Inca Empire, **3**:17; India (ancient), **1**:12; India (19th Century), **5**:15; Islamic World (Middle Ages), **2**:13; Japan (1550–1853), **4**:18; Latin America (19th Century), **5**:18; Maya, **3**:13; Mesopotamia, **1**:2, 155, 220; Mongol conquests, **2**:21; Oceania (Middle Ages), **2**:24; oceanic trading routes (17th Century), **4**:8; Ottoman Empire, **3**:19; Paris (Middle Ages), **2**:113; Proclamation Line of 1763, **4**:11; Renaissance Italy, **3**:9; Rome (ancient), **1**:9; Spain (16th Century), **3**:7; United States (19th Century), **5**:5; United States (Western Frontier), **5**:5; Vikings in the North, **2**:6. *See also* Cartography
Maqlû, **1**:525
Maquahuitl, **3**:233
Marable, Manning, **6**:153
Marabouts (17th & 18th Centuries), **4**:347, 467
Maracatú, **5**:416
Marathon, Battle of, **1**:379
Marble, **3**:99
Marcheses, **3**:276
March on Washington, 1963, **6**:447
Marcian (Byzantine emperor), **2**:426
Marconi, Guglielmo, **6**:241, 243
Marco Polo: on Mongols drinking koumiss, **2**:221; trading journey to Mongols, **2**:22, 94, 133, 140, 363; *Travels of Marco Polo*, **2**:481–83
Marcus, Greil, **6**:540–41
Marcy, Randolph, **5**:488–90
Marduk, **1**:456, 471, 472, 474
Mare Mount settlement, **4**:441
Margaret (queen of England), **3**:13
Mari, **1**:140
María (Isaac), **5**:196
Marianismo, **6**:55, 75, 77
Marine Corps, **6**:64
Marines (British Royal Navy), **4**:365
Maris, Roger, **6**:503
Marjoram, **4**:223
Marketplaces: Byzantium, **2**:106; China (Tang Dynasty), **2**:101–3; Europe (Middle Ages), **2**:98, 133; Greece (ancient), **1**:97; Islamic World (Middle Ages), **2**:104–5; Mesopotamia, **1**:91
Marling, Karal Ann, **6**:340
Marlowe, Christopher, **3**:206, 208, 209, 342
Mármol, José, **5**:197

Marquess of Queensberry, **5**:403
Marquis and marchinesses: England (15th & 16th Centuries), **3**:271; Italy (15th & 16th Centuries), **3**:276; Spain (15th & 16th Centuries), **3**:274
Marriage: Africa (17th & 18th Centuries), **4**:30–32, 46–47; ancient world, **1**:39–50; Australia, colonial, **4**:32–33; Australian Aboriginals, **1**:28; Aztec, **3**:32, 49–51; Catholicism (Spain, Italy, England), **3**:31, 380–81; China (19th Century), **5**:447; China (Tang Dynasty), **2**:45–47; England (15th & 16th Centuries), **3**:33; England (17th & 18th Centuries), **4**:35–38, 55; England (Victorian era), **5**:27, 34, 64–65, 110, 352, 373, 462; Europe (Middle Ages), **2**:41–43, 434; Greece (ancient), **1**:44–47; Hindu, **6**:590; Inca, **3**:32, 53–54; India (ancient), **1**:38; India (19th Century), **5**:27, 39, 53, 286; India (20th Century), **6**:32, 33, 46, 78, 104, 156, 590; Islamic World (Middle Ages), **2**:39, 47–50; Islamic World (19th Century), **5**:27, 37, 447; Italy (15th & 16th Centuries), **3**:39–40, 61, 347; Japan (17th & 18th Centuries), **4**:38–40; Japan (20th Century), **6**:49; Latin America (20th Century), **6**:43; love and (17th & 18th Centuries), **4**:28; Maya, **3**:45–46; Mesopotamia, **1**:21, 22, 40–43; Middle Ages, **2**:30, 39–50; Native Americans (colonial frontier of North America), **4**:34; New England, colonial, **4**:40–43, 62; New South Wales, **4**:32; North American colonial frontier, **4**:33–35; Ottoman Empire, **3**:42–43, 65; Protestantism (England), **3**:31; Rome (ancient), **1**:36, 47–50, 69, 385; seamen, **4**:43–45; 17th & 18th Centuries, **4**:27–45; slavery, **5**:27; slaves in colonial America, **4**:42; Spain (15th & 16th Centuries), **3**:35, 59; United States (1920–39), **6**:35; United States (1960–90), **6**:39; United States (Western Frontier), **5**:27; Vikings, **2**:43–45. *See also* Annulment of marriage; Brother-sister marriage; Dowry
Marriage contracts: China (Tang Dynasty), **2**:45; Europe (Middle Ages), **2**:41; Middle Ages, **2**:40
Marriage of slaves: Mesopotamia, **1**:110, 489; New Orleans, **5**:28
Mars, **1**:483
Marsden, Samuel, **4**:486–87
Marshall, John, **5**:366
Marshall, Thurgood, **6**:442
Marshall Plan, **6**:469
Martens, **5**:122
Martial arts in Japan, **4**:410
Martial games: England (15th & 16th Centuries), **3**:331; Inca, **3**:328; Italy (15th & 16th Centuries), **3**:315, 321–22; Spain (15th & 16th Centuries), **3**:315, 320
Martial sports in Europe (Middle Ages), **2**:370
Martine, Arthur, **5**:274
Martineau, Harriet, **5**:63
Martín Fiero (Hernández), **5**:196
Martín Rivas (Blest Gana), **5**:197
Martyrs, Muslim, **2**:457
Marx, Karl, **3**:207, 360; **5**:485–87
Marxism, **6**:137
Mary (queen of Netherlands), **4**:2
Mary I (queen of England), **3**:15, 409
Marye, Etienne-Jules, **6**:512
Maryland: government (17th & 18th Centuries), **4**:350–51; slavery in, **5**:86, 121
Mashkan-shapir, **1**:91
Masia, **3**:256

New England, colonial, 4:62; 19th Century,
5:41–54; North American colonial frontier,
4:53; 17th & 18th Centuries, 4:45–65;
Soviet Union, 6:82; support of family
(colonial frontier of North America), 4:35;
20th Century, 6:52–60; United States (Civil
War era), 5:42–46, 448; United States (20th
Century), 6:34, 53–55; United States
(Western Frontier), 5:46–50

Menarche, 6:273

Men-at-arms in Middle Ages, 2:346–47

Mencius, 5:464

Mendieta, Salvador, 5:158

Menelaus, 1:520

Menes. *See* Narmer

Menestras, 5:246

Mengele, Joseph, 6:405, 410

Men of Tomorrow, 6:54

Men's clothing: Australia, colonial, 4:285–87;
China (Tang Dynasty), 2:242–43; England
(17th & 18th Centuries), 4:290–92; England
(Victorian era), 5:269, 281–82; Europe
(Middle Ages), 2:237–38, 239; France (17th
& 18th Centuries), 4:292–94; Greece
(ancient), 1:310–12; India (19th Century),
5:286; Japan (17th & 18th Centuries),
4:294–96; Latin America (19th Century),
5:288–89; Middle Ages, 2:236; Mongols,
2:245; Native Americans (colonial frontier of
North America), 4:287–89; Native
Americans (colonial New England), 4:296–
97; New England, colonial, 4:296–98; North
American colonial frontier, 4:287–90; Nubia,
1:312–13; Polynesia, 2:255, 394; Puritans,
4:297, 298; seamen, 4:298–300; 17th & 18th
Centuries, 4:284–300; United States (Civil
War era), 5:274–76; United States (Western
Frontier), 5:277–78; Vikings, 2:240. *See also*
Suits; Uniforms; *specific items (e.g., shirts,
trousers, underwear)*

Men's liberation movement in United States, 6:55

Menstruation: Aristotle on, 1:297; *Causes and Cures*
(Hildgard of Bingen), 2:477–78; India
(ancient), 1:38; India (20th Century), 6:104;
Mesopotamia, 1:64; Muslims, 2:423;
Polynesia, 2:67; United States (1920–39),
6:273–74

Mental illness and treatment: Greece (ancient),
1:297; India (19th Century), 5:211;
Mesopotamia, 1:286; United States (1940–
59), 6:276; United States (1960–90), 6:130–
31, 280–81

Menteshe, 3:292

Mercenaries (ancient Greece), 1:380–81

Mercenarii, 1:129

Merchants: Africa (17th & 18th Centuries), 4:331;
Aztec, 3:122, 281; China (Tang Dynasty),
2:229, 321, 324; England (Victorian era),
5:111; European class in 15th & 16th
Centuries, 3:269; Europe (Middle Ages),
2:226, 290, 322; 15th & 16th Centuries,
3:89; Islamic World (Middle Ages), 2:321;
Japan (17th & 18th Centuries), 4:75, 145–
46; Latin America (19th Century), 5:117;
Maya, 3:200, 278, 372; Ottoman Empire,
3:118–19; Spain (15th & 16th Centuries),
3:114, 274; Vikings, 2:240, 294. *See also*
Trade

Merchant vessels (17th & 18th Centuries):
clothing, 4:299; food, 4:253; government,
4:362–63; idlers, 4:363; punishment, 4:385,
399; seamen, 4:363; second mates, 4:363;
shipmasters, 4:362. *See also* Life at sea

Mercury: Inuit, 6:302; United States (1960–90),
6:312

Meredith, James, 6:447, 449

Mergers, 6:132

Meritocracy (China), 2:296, 306

Meroitic Empire, 1:14. *See also* Nubia

Merovingian dynasty, 2:2

Merry Mount, 4:441

Mesoamerica. *See* Aztec; Inca; Latin America
entries; Maya

Mesopotamia: abandonment by spouse, 1:42–43;
abandonment of children, 1:52, 64; abortion,
1:52; accounting, 1:171–72, 174, 184, 196–
97; adoption, 1:42, 53; adoption of slaves,
1:53, 110; adultery, 1:42; algebra, 1:219;
amulets, 1:51, 318, 524, 528, 529, 530;
animals, 1:272; appeals, 1:359, 360;
appearance, 1:317–19; apprenticeships, 1:54;
architecture, 1:271; art, 1:230–32; astrology,
1:219, 526, 528–29; astronomy, 1:209, 219,
221, 528–29; banquets, 1:343; barbers, 1:360;
bas-reliefs, 1:230–31; bathing rooms, 1:271;
battering rams, 1:372; battle casualties,
1:287, 370, 372, 373; beards, 1:317; beds,
1:273; beer, 1:263, 286; bees, 1:78; birds,
1:220, 527; board games, 1:406; boat
building, 1:157; bows and arrows, 1:393–94;
boxing, 1:405; brain surgery, 1:286; branding
of slaves, 1:489; bread, 1:246; bricks, 1:270;
bride-price, 1:40–41; bronze, 1:232, 272, 318;
calendar and time, 1:208–9, 528; camels,
1:78, 156; canoes, 1:158; captives as slaves,
1:109, 373; caravans, 1:78, 141, 156, 157,
158; carpentry, 1:120; cartography, 1:221;
castration, 1:62, 64, 286; cataloguing and
classifying, 1:219–20, 220; cattle, 1:77;
chairs, 1:272; chariots, 1:391, 392; cheese,
1:246, 263; childbirth, 1:51–52, 285, 287;
childless couples, 1:42; children, 1:21–23,
51–55; clans, 1:119; clay tablets, 1:173–75,
183–84; clothing, 1:303–5; colors, 1:232,
234, 271, 303–4; concubines, 1:65, 110;
construction industry, 1:121; contraception,
1:64, 66; contracts, 1:142; cooking methods,
1:247–48; 2:246–47; corpses, care of, 1:506;
correspondence, 1:196; cosmetics, 1:317–19,
318; counterfeit money, 1:132; courts and
judges, 1:359–60; craftsmen, 1:119–22, 330;
creation stories, 1:453–54, 507; crowns,
1:318; cuneiform, 1:1, 172–74, 218–19;
curses, 1:525; dance, 1:420–22; daughters,
1:22, 52; death, burial, and the afterlife,
1:456, 507–11; death penalty, 1:361; debt
slavery, 1:109, 133; decimal system, 1:218;
deities, 1:119, 455–56, 471–74, 486–87;
deportation, 1:330, 371; dice, 1:406; diet,
1:246, 263; diplomats and ambassadors,
1:139, 155, 343; diseases, 1:284–88;
dissection, 1:287; diviners, 1:370, 527;
divorce, 1:39, 41, 42; dogs, 1:78, 93;
donkeys, 1:77–78, 156, 158; doors, 1:271;
dowry, 1:40–41, 110; dreams and dream
interpretation, 1:455; drink, 1:263; drinking
water, 1:92; drugs, 1:220, 283, 285–86; dyes,
1:121, 303; eating habits, 1:247; economic
life, 1:74; education, 1:54, 183–86; eldercare,
1:53, 110; engineering, 1:392; entrails,
reading of, 1:527; envelopes, 1:174; epics,
1:194–96; equinoxes, 1:209, 219; estates and

inheritances, 1:53–54, 110; ethnicity, 1:330;
eunuchs, 1:65; exorcists, 1:283, 284, 285,
527, 528; eye doctors, 1:283; family life,
1:21–23; famine and starvation, 1:287, 501;
fasting, 1:341, 509, 528; fathers' role, 1:21–
22; fertility plays and festivals, 1:437;
fireplaces, 1:271; fish, 1:247; floods, 1:76;
floorplans, 1:271; floors and floor coverings,
1:121, 273; food, 1:246–49; footwear, 1:304;
foreigners, treatment of, 1:330, 344;
fortifications, 1:369–70; fowl, 1:247–48; fruit,
1:246–47; furnishings and goods, 1:272, 273;
games, 1:405–8; geometry, 1:219; ghosts,
1:509–10, 529; glass, 1:121; gold coins,
1:131, 132; gold jewelry, 1:317, 318;
government, 1:339, 340–44; grains, 1:246;
guilds, 1:119; hairstyles, 1:317–19; harems,
1:286, 347; headdresses, 1:317; health and
medicine, 1:283–88; helmets, military, 1:392;
heralds, 1:360; herbs and spices, 1:247–48;
hieroglyphics, 1:172; historical overview,
1:1–3; history of, 1:1–3; holidays, festivals,
and spectacles, 1:435–37; homosexuality,
1:64; honey, 1:247; horses, 1:78, 140; hours,
calculation of, 1:209; housing, 1:270–73;
human sacrifices, 1:486; human waste
disposal, 1:92, 272; hunting, 1:392, 405–8;
hygiene, 1:248; hymns, 1:194–95; ideograms,
1:172; incest, 1:65; infant mortality, 1:52;
intercalary month, 1:209; irrigation, 1:75, 78,
79; ivory, 1:273; javelins, 1:394; jewelry,
1:317–19; kings, 1:340–44, 370, 372;
lamentation-priests, 1:487; landowners,
1:330, 371; language and writing, 1:1, 171–
75, 183, 184, 196, 197, 343; latrines, 1:92,
271; law, 1:359–62; leather, 1:122, 303;
lesbianism, 1:65; lexical lists, 1:220; life
expectancy, 1:287; lighting, 1:271; linen,
1:303; literature, 1:184, 193–97; locusts,
1:76, 287; looting of conquered nations,
1:317, 370–71, 372–73; lunar calendar,
1:208–9; lunar festivals, 1:436; luxury items,
trade in, 1:140; magic and superstition,
1:283, 284, 524, 525–31; map of, 1:2;
marketplaces, 1:91; marriage, 1:21, 22, 40–
43; marriage of slaves, 1:110, 489;
mathematics, 1:218–19; meat, 1:246–47;
medical fees, 1:283–84; medical malpractice,
1:287; medical texts, 1:285–86; menstruating
women, 1:64; mental illness, 1:286; metal
artwork, 1:232; metalworkers, 1:122;
midwives, 1:52, 283; military draft, 1:371;
milk and dairy products, 1:246, 263; money,
1:76, 130, 131–33; mourning rights, 1:508–9;
mud huts, 1:271; music, 1:347, 420–22, 487;
musical instruments, 1:421; mustaches, 1:317;
mythology, 1:194–96, 436, 453–54, 455, 509;
names, 1:22, 52, 119, 453; natural disasters,
1:287; new year's celebration, 1:435–37;
nomads, 1:79–80; numbers, 1:173, 218;
obelisks, 1:231; old age, 1:287; omens, 1:272,
285, 436, 526–28; onions, 1:246; oracles,
1:530; ovens, 1:247; paint, 1:232; paintings
and drawings, 1:231, 232; palaces, 1:90, 92,
342; parents, care of, 1:53, 110; paternity
issues, 1:54; perfume, 1:319; perjury, 1:359;
physicians, 1:283–84; pictographs, 1:1, 172,
174; picture carvers, 1:231; plague, 1:287;
plays, 1:435, 436; poetry, 1:196; polo, 1:406;
polygamy, 1:42; pornography, 1:63; pottery,
1:120; prayers, 1:194, 486–87, 525, 530;
pregnancy, 1:285, 287; prescriptions, 1:286;
priests and religious ritual, 1:65, 407, 437,
454, 484, 485–89, 526–27; prisoners of war,

health and medicine, **4**:222–23; jewelry, **4**:449; languages, **4**:204–5; leggings, **4**:288–89, 304; marriage, **4**:34; masks, **4**:222; men's clothing, **4**:287–89; men's roles, **4**:53; military strategy, **4**:404–5; moccasins, **4**:288, 304–5; New France settlement, **4**:10; polygamy, **4**:34; Protestantism and, **4**:471; punishment, **4**:385; Quakers and, **4**:490; raids, **4**:389; ransom, **4**:389–90; recreational life, **4**:417–18; religious beliefs, **4**:469; shirts, **4**:288; skirts, **4**:304; as slaves, **4**:390; social structure, **4**:372; tattoos, **4**:448–49; tools, **4**:122; trails, **4**:318; tribes and confederations, **4**:349–50; trousers, **4**:288; villages, **4**:332; visions quests, **4**:68; wampum, **4**:138; warfare, **4**:404–6; weapons, **4**:404; women's clothing, **4**:304–5; women's roles, **4**:52–54

Native Americans (colonial New England): cannibalism, **4**:488–89; child labor, **4**:76; councils, **4**:360; dances, **4**:440; death, **4**:88; diseases, **4**:88, 231; education, **4**:195–96; food, **4**:61–62, 250–51; games, **4**:68; government, **4**:359–60; hairstyles, **4**:297; health and medicine, **4**:231–32; holidays and festivals, **4**:440; land, confiscation, **4**:410–12; marriage, **4**:41; Massachusetts Bay Colony relations, **4**:13; men, work of, **4**:62; men's clothing, **4**:296–97; murder of Indian boy, governor's account, **4**:515–16; nature as religion, **4**:479, 488; population, **4**:379, 412; powwows, **4**:440; priests, **4**:489; prisoners of war, **4**:412; raids, **4**:411–12; religious beliefs, **4**:479; religious rituals, **4**:440, 488–89; rural life and agriculture, **4**:62; sachem, **4**:360; sale of land to settlers, **4**:147; shamans, **4**:489; slaves, **4**:412; social status, **4**:367; soup, **4**:250; sports, **4**:425; sweat baths, **4**:231–32; tobacco, **4**:440; trade, **4**:147; tribes, **4**:359, 411; warfare, **4**:410–12; wigwams, **4**:279; women, work of, **4**:61; women's clothing, **4**:312

Native Americans (Western Frontier), **5**:122–25, 168–71, 355, 365–70, 386–87
Nativist Party, **5**:137, 309
Natron, **1**:513
Nattmal, **2**:163
Natural disasters: China (Tang Dynasty), **2**:315; Maya, **3**:262; Mesopotamia, **1**:287. *See also specific type (e.g., Floods)*
Natural gas, **5**:135, 141–42
Natural history, **5**:439–40
Naturalism, **6**:217
Nature of Things, The (Bede), **2**:169
Nause Mikio, **6**:534
Naval battle entertainments in ancient Rome, **1**:447
Naval officers: British Royal Navy, **4**:199–200, 363–65, 382–83, 407; merchant vessels (17th & 18th Centuries), **4**:362–63
Naval warfare (17th & 18th Centuries): battle tactics, **4**:413–15; England against France, **4**:6, 7–9; narratives, **4**:217–18
Navaratri, **5**:415
Navarra, **3**:161
Navigational methods: Latin America (19th Century), **5**:17; oceans (17th & 18th Centuries), **4**:179–80; Vikings, **2**:162, 280
Navigators (17th & 18th Centuries), **4**:198–99

Navy: ancient world, **1**:391; Byzantium, **2**:361; England's defeat of Spanish Armada, **3**:16; England (17th & 18th Centuries), **4**:44, 64–65; England (Victorian era), **5**:373–75; Fatimid (Middle Ages), **2**:359; Germany (1910–20), **6**:1; Greece (ancient), **1**:397–98, 519; Japan, **6**:493; Ottoman Empire, **3**:21; Rome (ancient), **1**:399–400; Vikings, **2**:351; wages (17th & 18th Centuries), **4**:164–65; World War I, **6**:4, 64. *See also* British Royal Navy (17th & 18th Centuries); Life at sea
Navy Board of British Admiralty, **4**:364
Navy Nurse Corps, **6**:62
Nazis: propaganda films, **6**:514; rise to power, **6**:6; war crimes and trials, **6**:405–13. *See also* Holocaust
Neapolitan dialect, **3**:163
Neave, Airey, **6**:411–12
Nebrija, Antonio de, **3**:161
Nebuchadnezzar, **1**:101–2, 121
Necklaces. *See* Jewelry
Neckties, **5**:275
Nectanebo II, **1**:151
Needlework: England (Victorian era), **5**:92, 438; Europe (Middle Ages), **2**:54, 149; United States (Civil War era), **5**:58
Neem trees, **6**:286
Nefertiti, **1**:467
"Negro cloth," **5**:277
Nehru, Jawaharlal, **6**:9, 10, 47, 137, 254, 388–89
Nehru, Motilal, **6**:47, 79
Nemontemi, **3**:140
Neoclassical art, **4**:453, 454
Neo-Confucianism, **4**:59, 377–78, 422, 456, 478; **6**:567
Neorealists, **6**:514
Nephthys, **1**:475, 476
Nergal, **1**:473, 510
Nerge, **2**:384–85
Nero: assassination of, **1**:496; buildings and arches developed under, **1**:106; music, **1**:431; Olympic game participation, **1**:411; palace of, **1**:107; as Seneca's pupil, **1**:204; theater, **1**:448
Nestorians, **2**:191–92, 429; **3**:164
Netanyahu, Benjamin, **6**:483
Netherlands: epidemics in 15th & 16th Centuries, **3**:190; part of Holy Roman Empire, **3**:283, 287. *See also* Dutch Republic; Europe *entries*
Netherworld. *See* Death, burial, and the afterlife
Neti, **1**:473
Netzahualcoyotl, **3**:141, 310
Nevada divorce laws (1920–39), **6**:36
New Age doctrine, **6**:585
New Ague, **3**:189
New Amsterdam, **4**:339–40
New Balance running shoes, **6**:503
New Bedford, Massachusetts whaling industry, **4**:131
New Christian Right, **6**:587
New Cultural Movement (China), **5**:182, 194
New Deal: agricultural programs, **6**:436–37; alphabet agencies, **6**:371; electricity, **6**:437–38; government reform, **6**:370, 372–73; historical overview, **6**:14–15; preparation for World War II, **6**:374–75; success of, **6**:435
New England, colonial: adultery, **4**:98; agriculture, **4**:13, 102–3, 116–18; alcoholic beverages, **4**:265–66; apprentices, **4**:77–78; art, **4**:457–59; banns, **4**:41; beer, **4**:265; blacks, **4**:380, 398, 442; bowling, **4**:426; branding, **4**:397; bundling, **4**:98; Calvinism, **4**:216; cards, **4**:426; caves as housing, **4**:280; child labor, **4**:76–78; children, **4**:76–78, 426–27; church

attendance, **4**:496; cider, **4**:265; clergy, **4**:481; college, **4**:380; cooking methods, **4**:250–52; courts and judges, **4**:397–98; courtship, **4**:42; crimes, **4**:396–98, 426–27; crops, **4**:116–18; dance, **4**:458; death and burial, **4**:88–89; death penalty, **4**:396–97; dinner, **4**:252; diseases, **4**:88; distilleries, **4**:265–66; divorce, **4**:42; dresses, **4**:313; drink, **4**:265–67; drinking water, **4**:265; eating utensils, **4**:252; education, **4**:182, 195–98, 380; election of black governor, **4**:442; elementary schools, **4**:196–97; fast days, **4**:440–41; fish, **4**:131–32, 251; food, **4**:117–18, 250–53; fornication, **4**:397; free blacks, **4**:162–63; fruit, **4**:251; furniture, **4**:281; gambling, **4**:426; games, **4**:425–27; government, **4**:345, 359–62; gowns, **4**:313; grain mills, **4**:128; grains, **4**:117, 251; grammar schools, **4**:197; health and medicine, **4**:231–33; herbs and spices, **4**:252; historical overview, **4**:13–14; holidays and festivals, **4**:440–42; horse racing, **4**:426; housing, **4**:279–82; immigration, **4**:13–14; indentured servants, **4**:148–49, 163, 381, 426; industry, **4**:13, 128–30; iron, **4**:129; law, **4**:396–98, 426; laws concerning clothing, **4**:313; life expectancy, **4**:232; literature, **4**:214–16; livestock, **4**:117; love, **4**:62; magistrates, **4**:397–98; malaria, **4**:88; marriage, **4**:40–43, 62; marriage contracts, **4**:41; material life, **4**:237–38; meals, **4**:252; meat, **4**:251; medical care, **4**:232–33; meetinghouses, **4**:482; men, **4**:61–63; men's clothing, **4**:296–98; milk and dairy products, **4**:251; murder of Indian boy, governor's account, **4**:515–16; music, **4**:459; mutilation as punishment, **4**:397; names of colonies and areas, **4**:350; paintings and drawings, **4**:458–59; physicians, **4**:232; poetry, **4**:215; portraiture, **4**:459; professions, **4**:161 63; publication of banns, **4**:41; punishment, **4**:385; rape, **4**:98–99; recreational life, **4**:417–18; religion, **4**:77, 161–62, 178–79, 464–65, 479–81, 495–98; religion and government, **4**:344, 361; religious art, **4**:458–59; religious education, **4**:195–96; representation, **4**:361; royal colonies, **4**:350; rum, **4**:265–66; runaway servants, **4**:398; sawmills, **4**:128; science, **4**:169, 178–79; seafood, **4**:251; seamen's wives, **4**:43; seaports, **4**:339; sermons, **4**:216; servants, **4**:117, 148–49, 153, 281, 380–81, 397–98, 426; settlements, **4**:360–61; sex crimes, **4**:98–99; sexuality, **4**:92, 97–99; shipbuilding, **4**:129; shuffleboard, **4**:426; slave quarters, **4**:281; slaves, **4**:13–14, 63, 78, 117, 130, 163, 232, 252, 398, 442, 471; slave trade, **4**:148, 380; smallpox, **4**:88; social structure, **4**:379–81; sports, **4**:425; tea, **4**:256; technology, **4**:169, 178–79; tennis, **4**:425; textiles, **4**:129; theater, **4**:458; tombstones, **4**:89; trade, **4**:147–49; treatises, **4**:216; vegetables, **4**:117, 251–52; voting rights, **4**:496; warfare, **4**:14, 410–13; wealth, social status, **4**:367; wedding ceremonies, **4**:42; whaling industry, **4**:129–30, 131; whippings, **4**:396; widows, **4**:88–89; wigs, **4**:297–98; witchcraft, **4**:397; women, **4**:61–63; women, work of, **4**:62–63, 116, 162; women's clothing, **4**:312–14; work, **4**:116; work hours, **4**:117. *See also* British colonies in North America
New English Canaan (Morton), **4**:441
New Era of the 1920s, **6**:12

New France (17th & 18th Centuries): church and clergy, 4:489; drunkenness and impurity, 4:503–4; exploration and colonization, 4:9–10; fur trade, 4:137; government, 4:351; guns, 4:405; military service, 4:405; religious beliefs, 4:470–71; social structure, 4:372; warfare, 4:405

New Guinea. See Polynesia

New Holland, 4:19

New Jersey government (17th & 18th Centuries), 4:350

New Orleans (Civil War era): cemeteries in, 5:28; churches in, 5:459; newspapers, 5:315, 459; slave marriages in, 5:28; slavery in, 5:84–85

New Poor Law (England), 5:35, 321, 381, 388–90

Newport, Rhode Island seaports, 4:339

New School for Social Research, 6:203

News of the World (newspaper), 5:192

New South Wales Corps, 4:50

Newspapers: England (17th & 18th Centuries), 4:208; England (Victorian era), 5:192; Inuit, 6:240; Japan (20th Century), 6:259; New Orleans (Civil War era), 5:315, 459; Soviet Union, 6:233, 256–57; United States (1960–90), 6:226–27, 312

Newsreels, 6:525

Newton, Isaac, 4:474–75

"New woman" (Victorian England), 5:55, 65

New year's celebration: China (Tang Dynasty), 2:454–55; England (15th & 16th Centuries), 3:130; Greece (ancient), 1:213; Italy (15th & 16th Centuries), 3:133–34; Japan (17th & 18th Centuries), 4:438; Mesopotamia, 1:435–37; Spain (15th & 16th Centuries), 3:133–34

New York Athletic Club, 5:399

New York City (Civil War era): buildings, 5:139; draft riots, 5:100, 329; immigration, 5:135; population, 5:136–37

New York City (post-colonial War era): horse-drawn vehicles, 6:348–49; women, 6:75

New York government (17th & 18th Centuries), 4:350

New York Opera Association, 6:547

New York Tribune, 5:86

New Zealand. See Polynesia

NFL Europe, 6:499

Niagara Falls, 4:317

Nibelungenlied, 2:169

Nicaragua: government in 20th Century, 6:387; revolution, 6:480. See also Latin America entries

Niceas, 1:112

Nicene Creed, 2:410, 426

Niebuhr, Reinhold, 6:564, 566

Nightcaps, 5:282

Nightingale, Florence, 5:10, 63

Nightshirts. See Sleepwear

Night soil. See Human waste disposal

Nika riots against Justinian, 2:120

Nike, 6:504

Nile River, 1:3, 75, 80, 86, 159

Nimrud, 1:3, 159

Nineteenth Amendment, 6:66, 70

Nine to Five, 6:131

Ninety-Five Theses, 3:19, 365

Ninevah, 1:3, 159

Ninkhursaga, 1:472

Ninlil, 1:472

Ninurta, 1:472

Nippon Telephone and Telegraph (NTT), 6:259

Nirvana, 2:417

Nissan, 6:362, 363

Nitrates, 5:97, 133–34

Nivelle, Georges, 6:4

Nixon, Richard: African American relations, 6:154; on crime, 6:417; election of 1968, 6:153, 417; election of 1972, 6:476, 477; gas crisis and, 6:363–64; human rights under, 6:129; "kitchen debate" with Khrushchev, 6:339–40; McCarthyism and, 6:376; on Oppenheimer, 6:185; on Vietnam War, 6:561; Vietnam War, ending of, 6:477–78

Njord, 2:413

Nobel Prizes: American winners, 6:191; Japanese winners, 6:192; Soviet Union winners, 6:190

Nobility: Aztec, 3:280–81; England (15th & 16th Centuries), 3:270–71; England (17th & 18th Centuries), 4:374; France (17th & 18th Centuries), 4:142, 356; Maya, 3:278; Spain (15th & 16th Centuries), 3:273–74; Venice, 3:277. See also Aristocracy

Nöker, 2:37–38

Nomads: China (Tang Dynasty), 2:229; Islamic World (Middle Ages), 2:128, 143, 231; Mesopotamia, 1:79–80; Mongols as, 2:20

Nomarchs, 1:347, 362

Nomen, 1:27

Noncognitive ethicists, 6:564

Nonconformists, 4:472

Nonverbal communication (Australian Aboriginals), 1:181

Nonviolence: India (ancient), 1:258, 353. See also Civil rights movement

Noodles (Latin America), 5:245

No Ordinary Time: Franklin and Eleanor Roosevelt. The Home Front in World War II (Goodwin), 6:374

Norfolk Island, Australia: marriage, 4:32–33; punishment, 4:387–88

Norimono, 4:321

Normandy, 2:7

Norse-Icelandic culture. See Vikings

North American colonial frontier: accidents, children, 4:223; adoption ceremonies, Native American, 4:418, 429, 434–35; agriculture, 4:53, 108–10, 173, 373–74; alcoholic beverages, 4:258–60; animal husbandry, 4:109; apprentices, 4:155–56; art, 4:448–50; astronomy, 4:173; beds, 4:274; beer, 4:259–60; blacks, 4:373–74; books, 4:205–6; breast feeding, 4:69; brick houses, 4:273; calendars, 4:173–74; candles, 4:174; canoes, 4:317; captives, 4:205–6, 429, 434–35; captivity narratives, 4:205–6; childbirth, 4:69; child labor, 4:69, 155–56; child mortality, 4:223; children, 4:67–69; cider, 4:260; city life, 4:331–33; clearing of land, 4:109; clothing, 4:122–23; colonists, settlement, 4:372–73; colonization, 4:10–13; consent to marriage, 4:35; cooking methods, 4:244; crimes, 4:389–91; crops, 4:108–9; death, 4:82–83; diseases, 4:223; ditches, 4:333; doors, 4:273; dowry, 4:34–35; drink, 4:258–60; education, 4:155–56, 182, 186–88; estates and inheritances, 4:82–83; ethnicity, 4:372–73; fertilizers, 4:109; fireplaces, 4:273–74; food, 4:244–45; forts, 4:332–33; fruit, 4:244; furniture, 4:274; fur trade, 4:137–39, 259; gardening, 4:244–45; garrison houses, 4:332–33; government, 4:349–52; governors, 4:350–51; guns, 4:405; hay, 4:109–10; health and medicine, 4:222–24; herbal medicine, 4:222–23; herbs and spices, 4:245; hogs, 4:109–10; holidays and festivals, 4:434–36; horse-drawn vehicles, 4:318; housing, 4:272–73; husband's duty to support of family, 4:35; illegitimacy, 4:35; indentured servants, 4:155; indentures, 4:156; Indian trails, 4:318; industry, 4:121–

23; lamps, 4:174; languages, 4:204–5; law, 4:389–91; lean-to houses, 4:273; life expectancy, 4:223; literacy, 4:186–87, 205; literature, 4:205–6; livestock, 4:109–10; log cabins, 4:273; manufacturing industry, 4:121–22; marjoram, 4:223; marriage, 4:33–35; material life, 4:237–38; meals, 4:244; meat, 4:244–45; men, 4:53; men's clothing, 4:287–90, 289; military officers, 4:406; military service, 4:401, 405; militias, 4:390–91, 405–6; missionaries, 4:489–90; names of colonies and areas, 4:350; old age, 4:82; pork, 4:244–45; portages, 4:317; premarital sex, 4:34; preservation of foods, 4:244; professions, 4:53, 155–56; proprietary colonies, 4:350–51; punishment, 4:389–91; ransom, 4:389–90; real estate deeds, 4:54; rebellions, 4:390–91; recreational life, 4:418; religion, 4:373, 464–65, 469–71, 488–90; river transport, 4:316–17; royal colonies, 4:350–51; science, 4:172–73; sewing, 4:122; slaves, 4:471; soapmaking, 4:123; social structure, 4:372–74; spinsters, 4:54; taverns, 4:260; technology, 4:172–74; textiles, 4:122–23; tobacco, 4:109; tools, 4:121–22; toys, 4:69; trade, 4:137–39; transportation, 4:316–18; travel and transportation, 4:315–16; vegetables, 4:244; warfare, 4:404–6; water routes, 4:316–18; weapons, 4:404–5, 405–6; weaving, 4:122; "whiskey blanc," 4:259; widows, 4:82–83; wills, 4:82; women, 4:52–54, 122, 186–87; women's clothing, 4:304–5; work, 4:53

North Carolina: cotton, 5:121; tobacco, 5:120–21

Northumberland, Duke of, 3:15

North West Company, 5:123

Norton, Andre, 6:224

Norway. See Vikings

Norwich, 3:190

No theater tradition, 4:456

Notre-Dame Cathedral (Paris), 2:443

Nouveau roman, 6:218

Novels: England (17th & 18th Centuries), 4:207–8; England (Victorian era), 5:189–91; Europe (20th Century), 6:218; France (17th & 18th Centuries), 4:209–10; Inuit, 6:240–41; Islamic World (20th Century), 6:231–32; United States (Civil War era), 5:182–83; United States (1940–59), 6:220

Novosti, 6:257

NOW. See National Organization for Women

Nubia: appearance, 1:326; archers, 1:387, 417; art, 1:240; beer, 1:259; body painting, 1:312; bows and arrows, 1:387–88; cattle, 1:259; clothing, 1:312–14; crowns, 1:313; culinary ability, 1:259; death, burial, and the afterlife, 1:466–67; diet, 1:259; eating habits, 1:259; fish, 1:259; fishing, 1:416; floods, 1:87; food, 1:259–60; fowl, 1:259; fruit, 1:259; games, 1:416–18; gold jewelry, 1:240, 312; government, 1:354–56; grains, 1:259; hats, 1:313; headbands, 1:312; headdresses, 1:313; hieroglyphics, 1:180; history of, 1:13–14; hunting, 1:259, 416–18; irrigation, 1:87; ivory, 1:312; jewelry, 1:312, 313; language and writing, 1:180; leather, 1:312–13; linen, 1:312; luxury items, trade in, 1:149; map of Egypt (ancient) and Nubia, 1:5; meat, 1:259; men's clothing, 1:312–13; milk and dairy products, 1:259; oil, 1:259; religious beliefs, 1:466–68; rural life and agriculture, 1:86–88; sanctuaries, 1:467; sandals, 1:313; sheep and goats, 1:87; soul, 1:259; sports, 1:416–18; temple art, 1:240; trade, 1:139, 149–51; tribes, 1:354; warfare and weapons, 1:149–51,

356, 387–89; wild animals, hunting of, 1:259, 405, 416; wine, 1:87, 259; women's clothing, 1:312–13

Nuclear energy: Japan, 6:192; United States (1960–90), 6:364–65

Nuclear family, defined, 1:21

Nuclear threat, 6:40, 183. *See also* Cold War

Nuclear weapons: invention of, 6:183, 184; United States (1939–45), 6:468–69, 493

Nudity: 15th & 16th Centuries, 3:223; Greek art, 1:237–38. *See also* Sexuality

Nullification crisis (United States), 5:313–14, 316

Numbers: Arabic numerals, 2:165; Aztec, 3:85, 140, 151; England (15th & 16th Centuries), 3:160; Maya, 3:136–37, 200–202; Mesopotamia, 1:173, 218; Roman numerals, 2:165

Numina, 1:454–55

Nun, 1:475

Nunavut Territory: creation and government of, 6:403; land claims agreement (1993), 6:620–22

Nuncheon, 2:201

Núñez, Rafael, 5:341

Nuns: Buddhism, 2:432; Civil War hospitals, 5:201; convents (Byzantium), 2:64; Europe (Middle Ages), 2:53–54, 258, 434–35; Latin America (20th Century), 6:591–92; Middle Ages, 2:51

Nur al-Din, 2:359

Nuremberg Trials, 6:404, 410–12

Nurses: England (Victorian era), 5:110; Soviet Union, 6:290; World War I, 6:61–62

Nursing homes, 6:383

Nut (Egyptian goddess), 1:475, 476

Nutrition: development of field of, 6:302–3; United States (1920–39), 6:307–8; United States (1960–90), 6:310–11, 312

Nuts: Africa (17th & 18th Centuries), 4:240; Byzantium, 2:209; China (Tang Dynasty), 2:204, 206; Greece (ancient), 1:255; India (19th Century), 5:53–54, 244; Vikings, 2:203

Nuzi: women's role, 1:30–31. *See also* Mesopotamia

Nyamakala, 4:154

Nye, David E., 6:358–59

Oath of the Horatii, The (David), 4:454

Oaxaca, Valley of, 3:3

Oaxacan Civilization, 3:3

Obelisks (Mesopotamia), 1:231

Observation and experimentation: Australian Aboriginals, 1:229; China (Tang Dynasty), 2:164; Europe in Middle ages, 2:161; Holocaust victims, 6:409, 410; Islamic World (Middle Ages), 2:167

Obstetrics. *See* Childbirth

Oca, 3:105

Occupations. *See* Professions and occupations

Oceanic exploration and travel: England (17th & 18th Centuries), 4:7–9; map (17th Century), 4:8; 17th & 18th Centuries, 4:1–2, 7, 315

Ocelotl, 3:233

Ochpaniztli, 3:69, 186

O'Connor, Flannery, 6:221

O'Connor, Sandra Day, 6:74

Ocopa, 5:245

Octavian, 1:10. *See also* Augustus Caesar

Odin, 2:399, 412, 413–14

Odoric of Pordenone, Friar, 2:266

Odyssey: on death, burial, and the afterlife, 1:520; educational role of, 1:188; on magic, 1:533; on money, 1:134; on slavery, 1:111, 112; stories of, 1:200, 481; on travel and transportation, 1:161; on women, 1:33–34

Oedipus the King (Sophocles), 1:200

Office of Economic Opportunity, 6:381

Officers. *See* Military officers; Naval officers

Office work, 6:117

Ogden, Peter Skene, 5:47, 49

Oghul Qaimish, 2:65, 246

Ögödei, 2:221, 246, 343, 363, 428

OGPU (Unified State Political Administration), 6:426

Oil: Japan (17th & 18th Centuries), 4:249; lighting in Spain (15th & 16th Centuries), 3:256; Nubia, 1:259. *See also* Olive trees and olive oil

Okitsuga, Tanuma, 4:18

Olaf Sigurdson (Viking king), 2:7

Olaf Skotkonung (Viking king), 2:137, 415

Olaf Tryggvason (Viking king), 2:137, 279, 374, 397, 415

Old age: China (Tang Dynasty), 2:87, 90–92; England (17th & 18th Centuries), 4:84; Europe (Middle Ages), 2:87, 88–89, 183; Greece (ancient), 1:297; India (20th Century), 6:47, 58; Inuit, 6:51; Japan (17th & 18th Centuries), 4:86, 359; Japan (20th Century), 6:292; life at sea (17th & 18th Centuries), 4:89–92; medical care (United States 1960–90), 6:382–83; Mesopotamia, 1:287; Middle Ages, 2:86–92; New England, colonial, 4:88–89; North American colonial frontier, 4:82–83; Rome (ancient), 1:297; 17th & 18th Centuries, 4:80–92; Vikings, 2:87, 89–90

Old Bailey, 5:336

Old English, 3:159

Old Jules (Sandoz), 5:31–32

Oligarchy in India, 1:353

Oliphant, Margaret, 5:191

Oliver Twist (Dickens), 5:181, 185, 190

Olive trees and olive oil: Byzantium, 2:130, 208, 284; Greece (ancient), 1:83, 144, 255, 440; Islamic World (Middle Ages), 2:206; Italy (15th & 16th Centuries), 3:243; Rome (ancient), 1:85, 99, 256

Ollamaliztli, 3:315–16, 326

Ollo podrida, 3:241

Olluca, 5:246

Olmec Civilization, 3:3

Olmstead, Frederick Law, 5:421

Olmstead v. U.S. (1927), 6:416

Olympic Games: Africa (20th Century), 6:510; England (Victorian era), 5:402–3; Europe (20th Century), 6:499; Greece (ancient), 1:6, 63, 66, 211, 381, 411–13, 479; reinitiated in 1896, 6:498; South Africa ban, 6:511; 20th Century, 6:498; United States (1960–90), 6:506–7

Omecihuatl, 3:373

Omens: ancient world, 1:524–25; Aztec, 3:218, 354; China (Tang Dynasty), 2:164; Greece (ancient), 1:379; Inca, 3:393; Mesopotamia, 1:272, 285, 436, 526–28; Polynesia, 2:364, 365. *See also* Diviners; Entrails, reading of

Ometecuhtli, 3:373

Ometeotl, 3:341, 354, 373–74

Omeyocan, 3:139, 373

Onam, 5:415

"On Being Brought from Africa to America" (Wheatley), 4:215

One Day in the Life of Ivan Denisovich (Solzhenitsyn), 6:234

One Flew over the Cuckoo's Nest (film), 6:281, 528

One Hundred Days of Reform of 1898 (China), 5:324

Ongghot, 2:428

Only Yesterday (Lewis), 6:12

Onsen, 4:229

On the Origin of Species by Means of Natural Selection (Darwin), 5:154

Opera: Latin America (19th Century), 5:426; New York Opera Association, 6:547

Opium: China (19th Century), 5:131, 375–76; England (Victorian era), 5:207; India (19th Century), 5:54, 442; Latin America (19th Century), 5:246

Opium War: causes of, 5:375; Chinese defeat in, 5:323; effects of, 5:130; foreign influence resulting from, 5:176; historical overview, 5:13; start of, 5:132, 355; Taiping Rebellion resulting from, 5:452

Oppenheimer, J. Robert, 6:184, 185–86

Oracle of Pachacamac, 3:392

Oracles: ancient world, 1:485; Greece (ancient), 1:493–94; Mesopotamia, 1:530

Oral tradition: Australian Aboriginals, 1:192; Europe (Middle Ages), 2:169; Middle Ages, 2:145–46, 167; Polynesia, 2:23, 25, 176; Vikings, 2:172

Oratory (ancient Rome), 1:191, 203, 205

Orchestras: Latin America (19th Century), 5:427; United States (1920–39), 6:245

Ordeal by Slander (Lattimore), 6:376

Ordeals to determine innocence/guilt: Europe (Middle Ages), 2:327; Vikings, 2:330

Order of Santo Stefano, 3:276

Ordinary seamen on merchant vessels (17th & 18th Centuries), 4:363

Oregon Trail, 5:6, 487–88

Oresme, Nicole, 2:161

Oresteia, 1:200–201

Orfeo, 3:213

Organically grown food, 6:312

Organized crime (Soviet Union), 6:430

Organized labor: Latin America (19th Century), 5:326. *See also* Labor unions

Organ transplants, 6:277

Orhan, 3:180

Oriental Acquaintance (DeForest), 5:188

Origen, 2:70, 76

Orisha, 4:466

Orlando furioso (Ariosto), 3:206, 213

Orlando innamorato (Boiardo), 3:206, 213

Orphanages (England), 5:35, 389

Orphics, 1:520

Ortaoyuno, 3:350

Ortega, Aniceto, 5:426

Ortenberg, David, 6:158

Orthodox Church. *See* Greek Orthodox Church; Russian Orthodox Church

Osaka (17th & 18th Centuries), 4:144–45, 337

Osamu, Dazai, 6:237

Oshogatsu, 4:438

Osiris: death of, 1:289; description of, 1:476; family of, 1:475; as god of the dead, 1:476, 507, 512; Set's feud with, 1:471

Osman, 3:10

Ostia, 1:147–48

Ostraka, 1:178–79, 188

Ostrogothic kingdom, 2:2

Other America, The (Harrington), 6:120, 129, 380

Otogi-zoshi, 4:213

Otomies, 3:5

Otranto, 3:12

Southern Christian Leadership Conference (SCLC), **6:**444

Southern Cross, **3:**204

Southern Maya, **3:**167

South Pacific (musical and movie), **6:**223

Soviet-Afghanistan War, **6:**11, 82, 490–91

Soviet Union: anti-Semitism, **6:**144, 156–59; art, **6:**233, 234–35; atheism, **6:**596; attorneys, **6:**395; banquets, **6:**318; baptism, **6:**598; battle casualties in World War II, **6:**488, 489; censorship, **6:**233, 234–35, 256, 532–33, 536, 552–53; children, **6:**596; cholera, **6:**288; churches, **6:**597; civil war, **6:**173; classical music, **6:**551–52; collectivism, **6:**174–75, 318; communication, **6:**255–58; communism, **6:**371, 392–99; Communist seizure of power (1917), **6:**622–24; Constitution, **6:**397–99, 596, 624–25; cooking methods, **6:**318; corruption, **6:**290; courts, **6:**393–95; death penalty, **6:**425, 428; demise of, **6:**21, 470; desertion from military service, **6:**487; diseases, **6:**288; drink, **6:**318; education, **6:**195, 196, 208–10; elections, **6:**397, 399; epidemics, **6:**288; espionage, **6:**427; ethnic composition of, **6:**22–23; famine and starvation, **6:**173, 317; feldshers, **6:**289–90; film, **6:**512, 515, 532–33; food, **6:**139, 317–19; formalism, **6:**551; gangs, **6:**554; government, **6:**392–99; gun control, **6:**425; health and medicine, **6:**288–90; historical overview, **6:**21–24; Iran, invasion of, **6:**391; juvenile delinquency, **6:**554; KGB, **6:**485–86; landowners, **6:**397; law and crime, **6:**404, 424–29; law enforcement, **6:**424–25; life expectancy, **6:**288; literacy, **6:**209; literature, **6:**216, 219–20, 233–36, 551; men, **6:**82; military draft, **6:**484, 491; military service, **6:**484–87; militia, **6:**424–25; music, **6:**536, 550–54; newspapers, **6:**233, 256–57; nurses, **6:**290; organized crime, **6:**430; painting, **6:**234–35; party structure, **6:**395–96; physicians, **6:**288–89; poetry, **6:**233, 234–35; prisons and prisoners, **6:**430; public officials, **6:**398; punishment, **6:**395, 396; radio, **6:**257; rationing, **6:**318–19; Red Army, **6:**486; religion, **6:**596–98; restaurants, **6:**318; rock and roll, **6:**553–54; rural life and agriculture, **6:**172–75, 317–18; science, **6:**183, 190–91; secret police, **6:**424–25; social structure, **6:**22, 137–39; space exploration, **6:**187, 190, 349; teachers, **6:**210; television, **6:**257–58; theater, **6:**235–36; tombstones, **6:**598; typhus, **6:**288; universities, **6:**209; urban experience, **6:**172–76; war, **6:**80–81, 484–92; weapons, **6:**488–89; white-collar crime, **6:**430; women, **6:**60, 80–83; women, work of, **6:**60, 82, 288–89, 395. *See also* Stalin, Joseph

Soy sauce, **4:**264

Space exploration: Japan, **6:**192; products resulting from, **6:**300; Soviet Union, **6:**187, 190, 349; United States (1960–90), **6:**186–89, 349

Space shuttle, **6:**188–89

Space station, **6:**190

Spain (15th & 16th Centuries), **3:**161; annulment of marriage, **3:**35, 36, 59; apothecaries, **3:**192–93; apprentices, **3:**77–78; arithmetic, **3:**35; art, **3:**344–46; ballads, **3:**345; baptism, **3:**34, 76–77; barbers, **3:**192; beggars, **3:**275;

bloodletting, **3:**193–95; bodices, **3:**227; book burning, **3:**210; breakfast, **3:**240; breast feeding, **3:**60; brothels, **3:**321; bubonic plague, **3:**194; bullfighting, **3:**329, 332–33; candles, **3:**256; capes, **3:**228; capital punishment, **3:**304; cards, **3:**315, 321; castanets, **3:**346; charity, **3:**60; chess, **3:**321; chickens, **3:**96; childbirth, **3:**34, 76; child care, **3:**60, 77; child labor, **3:**34–35; children, **3:**76–78; chocolate, **3:**241; city life, **3:**112–15; clothing, **3:**77, 226–28; collars, **3:**227–28; commoners, **3:**274–75; communal property, **3:**95; confirmation, **3:**34; Council of War, **3:**211; counts and countesses, **3:**274; courts and judges, **3:**132, 305; dance, **3:**346; death, burial, and the afterlife, **3:**36; dental care and problems, **3:**195; desserts, **3:**241; dialects, **3:**161–62; dice, **3:**315, 321; diphtheria, **3:**194; disease, **3:**36, 194; divorce, **3:**35, 59; doublets, **3:**228; dowry, **3:**60; drinking water, **3:**95; dropsy, **3:**194; ducks, **3:**96; duels, **3:**306; dukes and duchesses, **3:**274; dysentery, **3:**194; edema, **3:**194; education, **3:**35, 77, 174–77; emigration, **3:**35; farthingales, **3:**227–28; fevers, **3:**194; food, **3:**240–41; fruit, **3:**95, 112; furniture, **3:**255–56; galleys, **3:**305; games, **3:**320–21; gazpacho, **3:**241; gold coins, **3:**114; government, **3:**194, 287–89; guilds, **3:**114–15, 274; guitars, **3:**321, 345–46; habeas corpus, **3:**305; hair, **3:**192; health, **3:**192–95; herbs and spices, **3:**240; hierarchy, **3:**273–75; holidays and festivals, **3:**134–35; hours, calculation of, **3:**132–33; houses, **3:**255–56; human waste disposal, **3:**256; infant mortality, **3:**77; influenza, **3:**194; javelins, **3:**315, 320; jewelry, **3:**114; jousting, **3:**315, 320; justice and legal systems, **3:**303–6; lamps, **3:**256; landowners, **3:**95; language and writing, **3:**35, 161–62; law enforcement, **3:**113, 303–4; life cycles, **3:**34–37; lighting, **3:**256; literature, **3:**210–12; livestock, **3:**112; manor property, **3:**95; map in 16th Century, **3:**7; marquis and marchionesses, **3:**274; marriage, **3:**35, 59; martial games, **3:**315, 320; meat, **3:**240–41; merchants, **3:**114, 274; municipal charters, **3:**287; municipal councils, **3:**287; music, **3:**345; names, **3:**34, 76–77; nobility, **3:**273–74; outdoor pursuits, **3:**332–35; painting, **3:**340, 344; pantaloons, **3:**228; peasants, **3:**34, 36, 77, 94–97, 176, 241, 256, 273, 275; physicians, **3:**192–93; pigs, **3:**112; poetry, **3:**345; pork, **3:**241; prayers, **3:**77, 132, 275; private revenge, **3:**305–6; processions and parades, **3:**38, 59, 63, 78, 135, 304; property, **3:**95; reading, **3:**35, 60; religious festivals, **3:**78; revenge, **3:**305–6; roads, **3:**112; rodents and vermin, **3:**194; rural life, **3:**94–97; sauces, **3:**240–41; sculpture, **3:**344; sexuality, **3:**59; sheep and goats, **3:**96, 112; silver, **3:**114; slaves, **3:**275; smallpox, **3:**194; sports, **3:**320–21; surgery, **3:**192–93; syphilis, **3:**194; tapestries, **3:**255; taxes, **3:**95, 176, 212, 269, 274, 275, 288; theater, **3:**314, 330, 333–35; time, **3:**131–36; torture, **3:**20, 305; tournaments, **3:**315, 320; trades and crafts, **3:**112–14; tunics, **3:**304; tutors, **3:**174, 177; typhus, **3:**194; unification, **3:**8–10; universities, **3:**175–76; vegetables, **3:**95, 96, 112, 241; viscounts and viscountesses, **3:**274; wheat, **3:**95, 112; widows, **3:**60; wills, **3:**60; windows, **3:**36, 59, 255; wine, **3:**95–96, 241; women's roles, **3:**59–61. *See also* Catholicism (Spain, Italy, England)

Spain (Middle Ages). *See* Europe (Middle Ages)

Spain (17th & 18th Centuries): France, wars against, **4:**356; maritime trade, **4:**151; oceanic exploration, **4:**7; seaports in New World, **4:**339

Spain (20th Century): film, **6:**514; literature, **6:**217, 219. *See also* Europe (20th Century)

Spanish-American War, **5:**20

Spanish Armada, **3:**15, 169, 210

Spanish Inquisition, **3:**19, 193, 198, 210

Spanish language: development of, **3:**157; England (15th & 16th Centuries), spoken in, **3:**173; Middle Ages, **2:**168

Sparta: abandonment of children, **1:**58; burial of dead soldiers, **1:**379; capital punishment of criminals, **1:**364; currency of, **1:**134–35; Dorian origin of, **1:**333; foreigners, treatment of, **1:**335; historical overview, **1:**6–7, 8; kingship of, **1:**349; literacy, **1:**178; matricentral homes, **1:**59; Olympic games, **1:**413; population of, **1:**333; procreation, importance of, **1:**66; professions, **1:**188; sexuality, **1:**66. *See also* Greece (ancient); Peloponnesian War

Spartacus, **1:**116–17

Spears. *See* Weapons

Spectacles. *See* Holidays, festivals, and spectacles

Speer, Albert, **6:**412

Speller (Webster), **5:**160, 164

Spelling, **3:**160. *See also* Literacy

Spencer, Herbert, **6:**564

Spenser, Edmund, **3:**206, 209

Sperry, Elmer, **6:**183, 184

Sphinx, **1:**234

Spices. *See* Herbs and spices

Spies. *See* Espionage

Spillane, Mickey, **6:**573

Spinsters, **4:**54

Spiritism: Latin America (19th Century), **5:**472; Latin America (20th Century), **6:**593

Spirits: Africa (17th & 18th Centuries), **4:**221, 484; festivals (17th & 18th Centuries), **4:**429; Japan (17th & 18th Centuries), **4:**422–24; Native Americans (colonial frontier of North America), **4:**67–68

Spiritual Exercises, **3:**210

Spiritualism in India, **1:**206

Spock, Benjamin, **6:**69, 88, 97, 204; Vietnam protests, **6:**473

Spoils of war. *See* Looting of conquered nations; Prisoners of war

Spoken language. *See* Language

Sports: Africa (precolonial), **6:**509; Africa (20th Century), **6:**509–11; ancient world, **1:**404–19; Australian Aboriginals, **1:**418–19; Aztec, **3:**326–28; blood sports, **3:**329, 338; Byzantium, **2:**402; Cambridge, **5:**401; China (Tang Dynasty), **2:**375–77; England (15th & 16th Centuries), **3:**58, 316–20; England (17th & 18th Centuries), **4:**418–19, 420–21; England (Victorian era), **5:**401–4; Europe (Middle Ages), **2:**370–73; Europe (20th Century), **6:**497–500; Greece (ancient), **1:**410–14; Inca, **3:**328; India (ancient), **1:**449; India (19th Century), **5:**404–5; India (20th Century), **6:**509; Italy (15th & 16th Centuries), **3:**63, 321–24; Japan (20th Century), **6:**508–9; Latin America (19th Century), **5:**405; Maya, **3:**324–26; Mesopotamia, **1:**405–8; Middle Ages, **2:**368–77; 19th Century, **5:**396–405; Nubia, **1:**416–18; Oxford, **5:**401; Rome (ancient), **1:**414–16, 446–47; 17th & 18th Centuries, **4:**418–19; Spain (15th & 16th Centuries), **3:**320–

21; 20th Century, **6:**496–511; United States (19th Century), **5:**397–400; United States (1920–39), **6:**500–503; United States (1960–90), **6:**503–8; Vikings, **2:**373–75. *See also* Physical fitness; Races; *specific types (e.g., Golf, Running, Tennis)*
Sports Illustrated (magazine), **6:**497
Spousal abuse. *See* Domestic violence
Spring holidays: England (17th & 18th Centuries), **4:**436–37; Japan (17th & 18th Centuries), **4:**438
Springsteen, Bruce, **6:**546, 548
Spurs, **5:**289
Sputnik, **6:**190
Spy, The (Cooper), **5:**186
Spying. *See* Espionage
Squash: Aztec, **3:**248; Inca, **3:**2, 249; introduction to Europe from Americas, **3:**236; Maya, **3:**246. *See also* Vegetables
Squires, **5:**113
Sri Ramanavami, **5:**415
Sruti, **1:**206
Stadiums in ancient Greece, **1:**412
Stagedoor Canteen (film), **6:**524
Stage Door Canteens in World War II, **6:**524
Stairs: England (Victorian era), **5:**263; Mesopotamia, **1:**271
Stalin, Joseph: agricultural practices, **6:**317; anti-Semitism of, **6:**157–58; arts, control of, **6:**233–34; collectivism program of, **6:**174; on Communist seizure of power (1917), **6:**622–24; educational programs, **6:**210; film industry and, **6:**533; government reform, **6:**371, 396–97; relocation of people under, **6:**22; scientific community and, **6:**190–91; secret police (NKVD), **6:**393, 426, 427–28; on Soviet soldiers, **6:**487–88
Stalingrad, Battle of, **6:**489
Stampedes, **5:**108
Standing Bear, Luther, **5:**170–71
Stanton, Edwin M., **5:**200
Stanton, Elizabeth Cady, **6:**70
Star festival (Japan), **4:**439
Starvation. *See* Famine and starvation
State University of New York at Stonybrook, **6:**201, 202
Statues: Africa (17th & 18th Centuries), **4:**446–47; Inca, **3:**391; Protestantism (England), **3:**382; Rome (ancient), **1:**239. *See also* Sculpture; Temple statues
Steam engines: England (Victorian era), **5:**300; Latin America (19th Century), **5:**159
Steamships: England (Victorian era), **5:**10, 351; India (19th Century), **5:**291, 301–2; Latin America (19th Century), **5:**19, 134, 159; United States (Western Frontier), **5:**6
Steele, Danielle, **6:**227
Steinbeck, John, **6:**222–23, 525
Steinem, Gloria, **6:**72
Stephens, Alexander, **5:**317
Stephens, Ann, **5:**187
Stephenson, David C., **6:**147–48
Sterling, Dorothy, **6:**224
Steroid use by athletes, **6:**507
Stevens, Wallace, **6:**225
Stevenson, Adlai, **6:**69, 377–78
Stevenson, J.D., **5:**233
Stevenson, Robert Louis, **4:**218
Stewart, Elinore, **5:**104, 206
Stimson, Henry L., **6:**410
Stirrups: Byzantium, **2:**285; invention and spread of use, **2:**282, 302, 345, 358
Stoa, **1:**97
Stock-car racing, **6:**505

Stockings, **4:**291, 307
Stolypin, Peter, **6:**173
Stone, Kate, **5:**346
Stone, Sarah, **5:**276
Stone carvings: Inca, **3:**251, 357; Mesopotamia, **1:**231
Stonehenge, **3:**155
Stonework. *See* Stone carvings
Stoneworkers in Mesopotamia, **1:**231
Stoolball, **3:**316
Storage: Europe (Middle Ages), **2:**269; Middle Ages, **2:**267; Vikings, **2:**270–71
Storytelling: Africa (17th & 18th Centuries), **4:**202–4; Australian Aboriginals, **1:**166, 181, 192, 240; Mesopotamia, **1:**193, 196. *See also* Mythology
Stowe, Harriet Beecher, **5:**57, 182, 186–87
Strabo, **2:**139
Strappado, **3:**308
Stratford-upon-Avon, **3:**208, 273
Street food (India), **5:**243
Street lights, **5:**135, 141–42
Streicher, Julius, **6:**412, 413
Streptomycin, **6:**274
Strikes. *See* Labor unions
Stuarts, **4:**2
Stubbes, Phillip, **3:**332, 343
Student accommodations: Europe (Middle Ages), **2:**150; Islamic World (Middle Ages), **2:**157
Student Nonviolent Coordinating Committee (SNCC), **6:**448–49
Students. *See* Education; Universities
Stylus or *stylos:* Greece (ancient), **1:**188; Mesopotamia, **1:**173–75; Rome (ancient), **1:**190
Sublette, William, **5:**126
Submarines (World War I), **6:**5, 303
Subsistence Department, **5:**222
Substitution during Civil War, **5:**99, 101
Suburbs: Latin America (19th Century), **5:**267; United States (1940–59), **6:**339; United States (1960–90), **6:**40
Subways (England), **5:**10
Sudra, **1:**338
Suetonius, **1:**100
Suez Canal, **5:**10, 349–50, 351, 354
Suffrage: England (Victorian era), **5:**306–7; United States (1920–39), **6:**66. *See also* Voting rights
Sufi music, **5:**425
Sufism: Africa (17th & 18th Centuries), **4:**485; Ottoman Empire, **3:**348–49; religious beliefs, **3:**367–69
Sugar: Byzantium, **2:**198, 209; England (1914–18), **6:**303; Europe (Middle Ages), **2:**200; India (19th Century), **5:**252; Latin America (19th Century), **5:**19, 97, 132–34, 246, 325; Latin America (20th Century), **6:**314; United States (Civil War era), **5:**2, 120–21, 220, 222, 249; United States (1920–39), **6:**306, 307; United States (Western Frontier), **5:**230, 251
Suger, Abbot, **2:**443
Suicide: Holocaust ghettos, **6:**271; Japan (20th Century), **6:**59, 60, 106, 211, 237; Jonestown, Guyana, suicides of People's Temple members, **6:**585; Rome (ancient), **1:**444, 522; United States (Western Frontier), **5:**205
Sui dynasty, **2:**7, 139
Suiheisha, **6:**161
Suits: England (Victorian era), **5:**269, 281; United States (Civil War era), **5:**275–77; United States (Western Frontier), **5:**278
Suleyman I, **3:**20
Suleyman Khan, **3:**292

Sulla, **1:**534
Sullivan, Ed, **6:**540, 541, 543
Sullivan, Gerald, **6:**477
Sullivan, John L., **5:**400, 403
Sullivan, Kathryn, **6:**74
Sultans of Ottoman Empire, **3:**292
Sulzbach, Herbert, **6:**459, 462
Sumerian civilization. *See* Mesopotamia
SUME (rock band), **6:**558
Summa Theologiae (Aquinas), **2:**160
Sumner, Senator Charles, **5:**3, 57, 431
Sumo wrestling: China (Tang Dynasty), **2:**369; Japan (17th & 18th Centuries), **4:**424; Japan (20th Century), **6:**508
Sumptuary laws: China (Tang Dynasty), **2:**295, 302; Europe (Middle Ages), **2:**236, 302; **3:**223; Italy (15th & 16th Centuries), **3:**229
Sun: astronomy, **3:**201; calendar based on, **3:**189, 204–5; healing based on, **3:**193; Hero Twins and, **3:**215; Maya, **3:**136, 199, 361
Sunday: England (17th & 18th Centuries), **4:**436; England (Victorian era), **5:**92; movie attendance (United States 1920–39), **6:**517; religious observance (United States 1920–39), **6:**570; Soviet Union, **6:**598
Sunday, Billy, **6:**571
Sundials: Byzantium, **2:**286; England (15th & 16th Centuries), **3:**129; Greece (ancient), **1:**211
Sundiata, **4:**203
Sun King (Louis XIV of France), **4:**356
Sunna, **3:**367; **6:**422
Sunnis: Islamic World (19th Century), **5:**468; Malcolm X as member, **6:**597; Ottoman Empire, **3:**182; Soviet Union, **6:**597; split with Shi`ites, **2:**298; **6:**390; Sufism (Ottoman Empire), **3:**367
Sunstroke, **5:**203
Sun Temples, **1:**503
Sun-Tzu, **2:**344, 354
Sun Yat-sen, **5:**324
Super Bowl, **6:**504, 506
Superheterodyne, **6:**244
Superstition. *See* Magic and superstition
Supper: England (15th & 16th Centuries), **3:**129, 237; England (17th & 18th Centuries), **4:**247; England (Victorian era), **5:**241, 242; Europe (Middle Ages), **2:**201; New England, colonial, **4:**252; North American colonial frontier, **4:**244. *See also* Meals
Suprema, **3:**288
Supreme Court: Japan (20th Century), **6:**430–31; right to rule on the constitutionality of laws, **6:**400
Surbahar, **5:**424
Surgeons aboard ship, **4:**233–34
Surgery: Byzantium, **2:**189; England (15th & 16th Centuries), **3:**190–91; England (17th & 18th Centuries), **4:**224; Inca, **3:**203; Islamic World (Middle Ages), **2:**166, 179; Italy (15th & 16th Centuries), **3:**195; Mesopotamia, **1:**286; Rome (ancient), **1:**301; Spain (15th & 16th Centuries), **3:**192–93
Surgical instruments (Mesopotamia), **1:**286
Surpu, **1:**525
Surrealism, **6:**217–18
Surtees, Robert Smith, **5:**191
Surveyors in Victorian England, **5:**93
Suyus, **3:**300
Sven Estridsson (king of Denmark), **2:**398
Sven Forkbeard (Viking king), **2:**137
Swaddling, **4:**305–6
Swaggart, Jimmy, **6:**584, 587

United States (1850–65)

housing, 5:120, 255–59; illiteracy, 5:44–45; immigration, 5:135, 137–38, 309, 383; infant mortality, 5:29; integration, 5:168; jackets, 5:273–74; jury trial, 5:328; knapsacks, 5:294; leisure time, 5:428–32; linen, 5:271; literacy, 5:182; literature, 5:182–88; lotto, 5:431; magic lanterns, 5:430; meat, 5:220, 222, 223, 224; men, 5:42–46, 448; middle class, 5:28; military draft, 5:99–101; militias, 5:71–72; milk and dairy products, 5:249; morality, 5:447–48; music, 5:420–22; muskets, 5:292–93; needlework, 5:58; nightshirts, 5:276; novels, 5:182–83; nullification, 5:313–14, 316; occupations, 5:45; painting, 5:429; patriotism, 5:448; peas, 5:223; philanthropy, 5:381, 385; photography, 5:430; pistols, 5:292; plantations, 5:84, 86, 118–20, 137; pocket watches, 5:2–3; population of cities, 5:135–37; pork, 5:219, 222, 224; potatoes, 5:222; poverty, 5:137, 139, 383–85; Prohibition, 5:380; prostitutes, 5:58; public schools, 5:385; punishment, 5:328–29; quilts, 5:58; railroads, 5:219, 290, 294–96; rations, 5:223–24; reading, 5:429, 431; reform movements, 5:381–86; religion, 5:456–61; ribbons, 5:273; rice, 5:2, 220, 222, 223; riding habits, 5:274; roads, 5:219, 294; rural life and agriculture, 5:2, 3, 86; salt, 5:226–27; sashes, 5:273; secession, 5:313–18; sharpshooting, 5:293; shirts, 5:273, 275; silk, 5:271, 275; singing, 5:429; skirts, 5:271, 273; social clubs, 5:431; social structure, 5:99–102; soldiers, 5:42–44, 356, 357; solitaire, 5:431; substitution, 5:99, 101; sugar, 5:2, 120–21, 220, 222, 249; suits, 5:275–77; tangrams, 5:431; tariffs, 5:380; teachers, 5:167; technology, 5:291–96; temperance movement, 5:382–83; tents, 5:254, 255, 257–59; tobacco, 5:2, 118, 120–21, 220; trade, 5:119–22; trousers, 5:275; uniforms, 5:290, 291–92; universities, 5:44, 167; urban life, 5:135–39; vegetables, 5:222, 223; vests, 5:273–74, 275; voodoo, 5:459; waistbands, 5:273; waistcoats, 5:275; war and the military, 5:356–65; wedding dresses, 5:274; wheelwrights, 5:121; whittling, 5:429; women, 5:56–59; wool, 5:271, 276; work, 5:83–87; work hours, 5:28, 83, 86; writing, 5:429. *See also* Civil War (United States); Slaves in United States (Civil War era)

United States (1850–65). *See* United States (Civil War era)

United States (19th Century): baseball, 5:397, 399–400; bicycling, 5:400; billiards, 5:397, 398; boating, 5:397; boxing, 5:398, 399, 400; cockfighting, 5:398; cricket, 5:398; fishing, 5:397, 398; folk music, 5:395, 421; football, 5:397, 399; fundamentalism, 6:571; gunpowder, 5:153; holidays and festivals, 5:406–9; hunting, 5:398; maps, 5:5; racing, 5:398; rail splitting, 5:397; rowing, 5:399; science, 5:151–53; sharpshooting, 5:397; sports, 5:397–400; swimming, 5:399; track, 5:397, 398–99; wages, 5:3; wrestling, 5:399

United States (1920–39): alcoholic beverages, 6:307; automation, 6:360; automobiles, 6:114–15, 356–58; baseball, 6:500–501; basketball, 6:502; bathing, 6:272; beer,

6:307; bread, 6:306; children, 6:502; civil rights movement, 6:140; coffee, 6:307; communication, 6:242–46; cooking methods, 6:336; courtship, 6:33–34; dating, 6:34–35; death penalty, 6:415; discrimination, 6:145–49, 516; diseases and epidemics, 6:272, 307; divorce, 6:35–36; drink, 6:307, 324–28; education, 6:195, 196–99; electricity, 6:333, 335–37, 356, 358–59; family life, 6:33–36; film, 6:515–23; food, 6:301, 306–9; football, 6:501; fruits, 6:307; fundamentalism, 6:571; gas utilities, 6:336; golf, 6:500, 502; government, 6:372–73; grains, 6:307; health and medicine, 6:67, 272–74; herbs and spices, 6:307; historical overview, 6:12–14; housing, 6:128, 335–38; hunting, 6:500; hygiene, 6:272; immigration, 6:127; infant mortality, 6:67; inflation, 6:436; labor unions, 6:439–40; language, 6:198; law and crime, 6:414–17; lighting, 6:333, 336–37, 359–60; lynching, 6:140, 148–49; malnutrition, 6:307; marriage, 6:35; meat, 6:306, 307; menstruation, 6:273–74; milk and dairy products, 6:307; minimum wage, 6:440; morality, 6:563–66; music, 6:245–46, 537–39; nutrition, 6:307–8; office work, 6:117; pigs, 6:436–37; poor persons, 6:128; pork, 6:307; potatoes, 6:306; prayers, 6:572; radio, 6:242–46, 500, 501; railroads, 6:307; record industry, 6:537–39; reform, 6:435–41; refrigeration, 6:336; religion, 6:569–72; rural life and agriculture, 6:128, 273, 307; science, 6:183–85; sexuality, 6:34–35, 273, 512, 517–18; social structure, 6:126–28; sports, 6:500–503; suffrage, 6:66; sugar, 6:306, 307; symphony orchestras, 6:245; taxes, 6:126; teachers, 6:197; technology, 6:116, 273, 356–61; toys, 6:335; unemployment, 6:127; urban life, 6:163–66, 273; vegetables, 6:307; voting rights, 6:494; wages, 6:116; white-collar workers, 6:116–17; women, 6:66–67, 117, 511–12, 517; work, 6:114–18; work hours, 6:359

United States (1940–59): abortion, 6:37; adult education, 6:203; anti-Semitism, 6:7, 16; art, 6:15; birthrate, 6:96, 118; censorship, 6:38; children, 6:88, 96–99, 375; civil rights movement, 6:140, 441–45; Cold War, 6:376–77; communication, 6:246–49; computers, 6:119; contraception, 6:37, 38; credit cards, 6:118; crimes, 6:97; death penalty, 6:379–80; discrimination, 6:16, 150–51, 375–76; diseases, 6:275, 276; divorce, 6:38; drug culture, 6:224; drugs, 6:260, 274–76; education, 6:18, 88, 199–205; electricity, 6:118, 334; entertainment, 6:97–99; environment, 6:17; espionage, 6:376, 378–80; family life, 6:37–39; film, 6:247, 523–28; furniture and furnishings, 6:340; government, 6:373–80; health and medicine, 6:274–76; historical overview, 6:14–18; homosexuality, 6:38; housing, 6:119–20, 128, 166–69, 334, 338–42; immigration, 6:127; libraries, 6:224; life expectancy, 6:70, 260, 275, 276; literature, 6:216, 220–26; mental health treatment, 6:276; morality, 6:563–66; music, 6:536, 539–42; poetry, 6:222, 224–25; poor persons, 6:128; population, 6:118; radio, 6:246–47; reform, 6:441–46; refrigeration, 6:309, 334, 336; religion, 6:572–75; religious education, 6:200; riots, 6:16; rural life and agriculture, 6:119–20, 128, 334; school desegregation, 6:443–44; science, 6:185–90; sex discrimination, 6:67, 69; sexuality, 6:37–

38; social structure, 6:126–28; suburbs, 6:339; taxes, 6:126; teachers, 6:199; technology, 6:68, 119, 333–34; television, 6:88, 97–99, 247; theater, 6:223; toys, 6:98; unemployment, 6:127; urban life, 6:166–69; voluntarism, 6:17; war, 6:469–79; weapons, 6:119; women, 6:17, 38, 67–70, 341, 375; work, 6:118–21, 375. *See also* World War II

United States (1960–90): abortion, 6:73–74, 612–14; AIDS, 6:282–84; alcoholic beverages, 6:328–29; alcoholism, 6:323, 328; anti-intellectualism, 6:216, 227–28; anti-Semitism, 6:445; artificial sweeteners, 6:312; attention deficit disorder (ADD), 6:281–82; attention deficit hyperactive disorder (ADHD), 6:281–82; automation, 6:131; automobiles, 6:361; baseball, 6:503, 504–5; basketball, 6:504; bicycles, 6:504; birthrate, 6:39, 40, 42; bottled water, 6:329; boxing, 6:497, 504, 505; breast feeding, 6:312; cable television, 6:249; cancer, 6:285; child care, 6:42, 99–100; children, 6:99–101; civil rights movement, 6:20, 140, 446–50; classical music, 6:547, 549–50; communication, 6:242, 249–53; community colleges, 6:204, 205–6; computers, 6:250–51; contraception, 6:39; crimes, 6:417; depression, mental, 6:281; diapers, 6:361; diet plans, 6:280, 302, 310; discrimination, 6:110, 129, 151–54; diseases, 6:19, 278, 280, 282; divorce, 6:42; drink, 6:328–30; drunk driving, 6:323, 329; eating disorders, 6:280; economic life, 6:40; education, 6:205–8, 381, 382; environment, 6:19, 361; fallout shelters, 6:40; family life, 6:39–43; feminism, 6:73–75; film, 6:528–30; food, 6:302, 309–13; food stamps, 6:313; football, 6:504; footwear, 6:503; fundamentalism, 6:581; gas prices and shortage, 6:363–64, 478; golf, 6:504; government, 6:380–84; gun control, 6:418; health and medicine, 6:18, 19, 276–85; health clubs, 6:505, 507; health insurance, 6:278, 284–85; health maintenance organizations (HMOs), 6:278, 285; historical overview, 6:18–21; housing, 6:40, 152, 342–43, 382; human waste disposal, 6:361; immigration, 6:382; Kuwait, liberation of, 6:478; labeling of food, 6:311; labor unions, 6:40, 111, 131–33; law and crime, 6:417–20; life expectancy, 6:382; literature, 6:226–28; magazines, 6:227; malnutrition, 6:313; marriage, 6:39; men's liberation movement, 6:55; mental health treatment, 6:130–31, 280–81; mergers, 6:132; morality, 6:563–66; music, 6:536, 542–50; newspapers, 6:226–27, 312; nuclear energy, 6:364–65; nursing homes, 6:383; nutrition, 6:310–11, 312; organically grown food, 6:312; organ transplants, 6:277; physical fitness, 6:505, 507; physicians, 6:278, 284–85; poor persons, 6:128–29, 380–84; population, 6:19; postmodernism, 6:21; priests, 6:582; professional sports, 6:506; recipes, 6:312; reform, 6:446–50; religion, 6:208, 575–88; restaurants, 6:312; rock and roll, 6:536, 542–50; running, 6:503, 504, 507; school desegregation, 6:446, 447; school prayer, 6:578, 587; science, 6:185–90; secondhand smoke, 6:279; secular humanism, 6:582; sex discrimination, 6:71, 74–75; sexual harassment, 6:55; sexuality, 6:542, 549; shopping centers, 6:169–70; single-parent households, 6:33, 42; slums, 6:342–43; smoking, 6:278–79; soft drinks, 6:323, 329;

ABOUT THE CONTRIBUTORS

General Editor

Joyce E. Salisbury is Frankenthal Professor of History at University of Wisconsin–Green Bay. She has a doctorate in medieval history from Rutgers University. Professor Salisbury is an award-winning teacher: she was named CASE (Council for Advancement and Support of Education) Professor of the Year for Wisconsin in 1991 and has brought her concern for pedagogy to this encyclopedia. Professor Salisbury has written or edited more than 10 books, including the award-winning *Perpetua's Passion: Death and Memory of a Young Roman Woman*, *The Beast Within: Animals in the Middle Ages*, and *The West in the World*, a textbook on western civilization.

Volume Editor

Andrew E. Kersten received his B.A. in History at the University of Wisconsin–Madison and his M.A. and Ph.D. at University of Cincinnati. Since 1997, he has taught in the History Department at the University of Wisconsin–Green Bay. Kersten has been published in the *Queen City Heritage*, *The Michigan Historical Review*, and *The Missouri Historical Review* and has contributed to several anthologies and encyclopedias, and is the author of *Race, Jobs, and the War: The FEPC in the Midwest, 1941–1946* (2000) and the co-editor of *Politics and Progress: The State and American Society since 1865* (2001). Currently, he is writing a history of the American Federation of Labor during World War II.

Additional Contributors

Paul Brasil, Western Oregon University
Eduardo Alfonso Caro, Arizona State University
Gregory S. Crider, Wingate University
David William Foster, Arizona State University
Angela María González Echeverry, Arizona State University
Dana Lightstone, University of Wisconsin–Madison
Ramona Ortiz, Arizona State University
John L. Rector, Western Oregon University

About the Contributors

Paula Rentmeester, University of Wisconsin–Green Bay
Molly Todd, University of Wisconsin–Madison

We also acknowledge the following authors of Greenwood Publishing's "Daily Life Through History" series, whose books contributed much to entries in the current volume:

Mary Ellen Jones, *Daily Life on the 19th-Century American Frontier*.
Sally Mitchell, *Daily Life in Victorian England*.
Dorothy Denneen Volo and James M. Volo, *Daily Life in the American Civil War*.